# Puerto Rico and Baseball

— 60 BIOGRAPHIES —

EDITED BY BILL NOWLIN AND EDWIN FERNÁNDEZ

ASSOCIATE EDITORS: LEN LEVIN AND CARL RIECHERS

Society for American Baseball Research, Inc.
Phoenix, AZ

Puerto Rico and Baseball: 60 Biographies
Edited by Bill Nowlin and Edwin Fernández
Associate editors: Len Levin and Carl Riechers

Copyright © 2017 Society for American Baseball Research, Inc.
All rights reserved. Reproduction in whole or in part without permission is prohibited.

ISBN 978-1-943816-53-8
(Ebook ISBN 978-1-943816-52-1)

Cover and book design: Gilly Rosenthol

Photo credits:

National Baseball Hall of Fame: 7, 13, 19, 24, 47, 53, 60, 79, 89, 121, 134, 140, 147, 161, 176, 211, 215, 220, 223, 231, 238, 268, 277, 281, 289, 294, 297, 301, 308, 321, 334, 340, 347, and 373.

Jorge Colón-Delgado Collection: 4, 16, 33, 56, 67, 69, 82, 85, 94, 106, 107, 125, 129, 130, 164, 272, 296, 322, 325, 355, 360, 368, 369, 376, 383, 388, and 393.

El Mundo Digital Project at the University of Puerto Rico: 27, 40, 44, 62, 150, 168, 179, 185, 187, 206, 217, 233, 245, 251, 265, 278, and 337.

Boston Red Sox: 110, 198, 201, 317, and 328.

Pittsburgh Pirates: 74, 228, and 229.

Chicago White Sox/Ron Vesely: 113 and 116.

Mark Souder: 406 and 408.

Acheltron: 158.

Baltimore Orioles: 192.

Haydee Navarro: 254.

Society for American Baseball Research
Cronkite School at ASU
555 N. Central Ave. #416
Phoenix, AZ 85004
Phone: (602) 496-1460
Web: www.sabr.org
Facebook: Society for American Baseball Research
Twitter: @SABR

# CONTENTS

1. Introduction ......................................... 1
   *Edwin Fernández*

## THE PLAYERS

2. Roberto Alomar .................................... 3
   *Chris Jones*

3. Sandy Alomar, Sr. ................................ 12
   *Irv Goldfarb*

4. Sandy Alomar, Jr. ................................ 18
   *Joe Wancho*

5. Luis Arroyo ........................................ 23
   *Rory Costello*

6. Benny Ayala ....................................... 32
   *Rory Costello*

7. Carlos Baerga .................................... 38
   *Joe Wancho*

8. Juan Beníquez .................................... 43
   *Jonathan Arnold*

9. Carlos Bernier ................................... 46
   *Charles F. Faber*

10. Hiram Bithorn ................................... 52
    *Jane Allen-Quevedo*

11. Bobby Bonilla ................................... 59
    *Mark Souder*

12. Iván Calderón .................................. 66
    *Dan Potter*

13. John Candelaria ................................ 72
    *Steve West*

14. Orlando Cepeda ................................. 78
    *Mark Armour*

15. Pedro "Perucho" Cepeda ........................ 84
    *Edwin Fernández*

16. Roberto Clemente ............................... 87
    *Stew Thornley*

17. Francisco "Pancho" Coimbre .................. 104
    *Joseph Gerard*

18. Alex Cora ...................................... 109
    *Scott Cummings*

19. Joey Cora ...................................... 112
    *Alan Cohen*

20. José "Cheo" Cruz (Dilan) Sr. ................ 119
    *Jane Schupmann Hewitt*

21. José Luis Cruz ................................ 124
    *Thomas Brown*

22. Iván DeJesús, Sr. ............................. 128
    *Richard Cuicchi*

23. Carlos Delgado ................................ 133
    *Paul Hofmann*

24. Eduardo Figueroa .............................. 139
    *Rory Costello*

25. Rubén Gómez ................................... 146
    *Thomas Van Hyning*

26. Juan González ................................. 157
    *Edwin Fernandez*

27. José Hernández ................................ 163
    *Marlene Vogelsang*

28. Roberto Hernández ............................. 166
    *Alan Cohen with Matt Merullo*

29. Willie Hernández .............................. 173
    *Gary Gillette*

30. Sixto Lezcano ................................. 183
    *Brian Wood*

31. Javy López ..................................... 191
    *Kyle Eaton*

32. Mike Lowell ................................... 197
    *Bill Nowlin*

33. Cándido Maldonado ............................ 205
    *Tom Hawthorn*

34. Félix Mantilla ............................................. 209
   *Rick Schabowski*

35. Luis "Canena" Márquez ........................ 214
   *Amy Essington*

36. Edgar Martínez ...................................... 219
   *Emily Hawks*

37. Orlando Merced .................................... 227
   *Justin Cabrera*

38. Félix Millán ............................................ 230
   *Jane Allen-Quevedo*

39. Bengie Molina ....................................... 236
   *John Vorperian*

40. Willie Montañez .................................... 244
   *Chuck Johnson*

41. Roger Moret .......................................... 249
   *Seamus Kearney*

42. Jaime Navarro ....................................... 253
   *Gregory H. Wolf*

43. Julio Navarro ......................................... 261
   *Rory Costello*

44. Luis Olmo .............................................. 267
   *Rory Costello*

45. José A. Pagán ........................................ 276
   *Bill Johnson*

46. Juan Pizarro .......................................... 280
   *Rory Costello*

47. Jorge Posada ......................................... 288
   *Scott Dominiak*

48. Vic Power .............................................. 293
   *Joe Wancho*

49. Jim Rivera ............................................. 300
   *Richard Smiley*

50. Iván Rodríguez ...................................... 306
   *Steve West*

51. Rey Sánchez .......................................... 316
   *Bill Nowlin*

52. Benito Santiago .................................... 320
   *Thomas Brown*

53. José G. "Pantalones" Santiago .............. 324
   *Edwin Fernández*

54. José R. Santiago ................................... 327
   *Edwin Fernández and Bill Nowlin*

55. Rubén Sierra ......................................... 333
   *Adam J. Ulrey*

56. Danny Tartabull .................................... 339
   *Charles F. Faber*

57. Dickie Thon .......................................... 345
   *Bob LeMoine*

58. José Valentín ........................................ 353
   *Steven Schmitt*

59. Javier Vázquez ...................................... 359
   *Norm King*

60. José Vidro ............................................. 365
   *Mark S. Sternman*

61. Bernie Williams .................................... 372
   *Rob Edelman*

# BALLPARKS

62. Parque Sixto Escobar ........................... 381
   *Rory Costello*

63. Estadio Hiram Bithorn ......................... 391
   *Charles F. Faber*

# MAJOR LEAGUE BASEBALL IN PUERTO RICO

64. Major League Baseball in Puerto Rico ....... 396
   *Mark Souder*

65. Contributors ......................................... 419

# INTRODUCTION

## By Edwin Fernández

**THE AUTHORS AND EDITORS OF** this book have worked very hard to present relevant and interesting details of the lives of these baseball players from Puerto Rico, players who passed up many life's pleasures to achieve excellence in this game that stirs crowds in America and, more recently, in other continents of the globe.

It is also important to learn how baseball came to this Caribbean island and the impact it had on its citizens, many of whom became fans of the sport. Let's take a brief look at those beginnings:

Baseball in Puerto Rico began to be played, in a somewhat organized manner, by the end of the nineteenth century. It has been nearly 121 years since Amos Iglesias, known as the father of Puerto Rican baseball, organized the first game in Puerto Rico between Cuban and Puerto Rican players. From these beginnings, Puerto Rican players have reached a point where many stand out. In the first two decades of the twentieth century, local players competed against those from the island, and from the major leagues, the Caribbean, and the Negro Leagues of the United States. Players such as Pedro Miguel Caratini, Marcelino "El Brujo" Blondet, Millito Navarro, Pancho Coimbre, and Perucho Cepeda, among others, were the pioneers of an avalanche of Puerto Rican professional players that would flood baseball diamonds in the Caribbean and the United States. About 40 Puerto Rican players played in the Negro Leagues. Many of them could not display their skills in the big leagues because of the color line that existed in those leagues until 1947, when Jackie Robinson broke the barrier. Only Hiram Bithorn (1942) and Luis Rodríguez-Olmo (1943) managed to play in the major leagues before that, because of their lighter skin color. The next would be a player of color, Luis "Canena" Márquez, who made his debut on April 18, 1951, with the Boston Braves.

As of the end of 2016, there have been 323 players born in Puerto Rico or descended from Puerto Rican natives who have played in the major leagues. But there are thousands of Puerto Rican professional players who have played in the Caribbean and other professional leagues, including the minor leagues in the United States.

Baseball in Puerto Rico has become the favorite pastime of children and adults. Their love and devotion for their players leads them to follow their performance both on and away from the island. For

"Baseball in Our Insular Possessions — Porto Rico, Philippines, Hawaii," A. G. Spalding Collection, New York Public Library.

the children, players are the role models they dream of emulating when they grow up.

This book, *Puerto Rico and Baseball: 60 Biographies*, also intends to preserve the history of many of these players. It would be impossible to include them all in this volume, but here we find a select sample of the large number of players who have represented their communities and their home island with pride in professional baseball.

Puerto Rico's first professional baseball league was established in 1938. Until 1941 it was affiliated with the National Semi-Pro Baseball Congress in the United States. The league runs for about three months in Puerto Rico during the winter. Tom Van Hyning said in his book, *Puerto Rico's Winter League*, it "is the major leagues' launching pad," enabling many players to jump into Organized Baseball in the United States.

Here are 60 biographies. No story is identical. They all have their peculiarities, but in all of them you will find elements that show the work, the sacrifice, and the struggle through which the great majority have passed to become the professional players they were.

Since the beginning of the twentieth century, Puerto Rico has been a good place in which to play baseball of the best quality. In this book, you will find a summary of the games that major-league teams have played on the Island (both exhibition and some regular-season major-league games). Those games, besides serving as a stage for Puerto Rican players to be able to measure themselves against the good teams of the north, remain as a historic element of baseball in Puerto Rico.

This book is filled with data of great interest to baseball lovers. In reading it you will get to know Perucho, who was compared with Ty Cobb and called the Babe Ruth of Puerto Rico; why Pancho Coimbre was considered one of the best hitters; the story of the great Roberto Clemente; who was "el Divino Loco," the first pitcher to win a major-league game on the Pacific Coast; who was "El Jíbaro"; and even the great achievements of the man who was possibly the most complete catcher who ever stepped on a diamond. I invite you to join us in this journey of stories of Puerto Rican players who achieved their dream of playing as professionals in the sport that has been their passion since they were just kids, baseball.

Enjoy *Puerto Rico and Baseball: 60 Biographies*.

## SOURCES

Colón-Delgado, Jorge. *75 Años de Béisbol Boricua* (San Juan, Puerto Rico: Advanced Graphic Printing, 2013).

Van Hyning, Thomas E. *Puerto Rico's Winter League: A History of Major League Baseball's Launching Pad* (Jefferson, North Carolina: McFarland, 1995).

# ROBERTO ALOMAR

## By Chris Jones

**THE SON OF A LONGTIME MAJOR** leaguer and the younger brother of another, Roberto Alomar was immersed in the world of baseball from an early age.

Roberto's father, Sandy Alomar, spent 15 years as a major-league infielder, and Roberto and his brother, also Sandy, spent most summers in major-league locker rooms. It was during these times that the brothers learned the intricacies of the game from the best players in the world—Nolan Ryan taught 4-year-old Roberto how to pitch while Ryan was a teammate of Sandy, Sr.'s on the Angels.[1] Perhaps just as important, they also learned how to handle themselves like major-league ballplayers. The offseason brought with it the Puerto Rican Winter League (in which his father and three of his uncles all starred) and the annual Caribbean World Series.[2] Roberto frequently made the trek to games with his father, sometimes completing his homework in the dugout.[3]

Roberto Alomar was born on February 5, 1968, in Ponce, on Puerto Rico's south coast, to Santos (Sandy) and Maria (Velasquez) Alomar. He had an older brother, Santos Jr. (Sandy), and a sister, Sandia. They grew up in Salinas, 20 miles from Ponce. Roberto's baseball ability and instincts were evident even as a boy. When he was 6 a scout reportedly saw him playing pepper and inquired of his father (presumably tongue in cheek) if he could sign him.[4] By the age of 7, Roberto was selected as an all-star for the Salinas little league, but was declared ineligible when it was discovered that he was too young to play in the league.[5] The time for Roberto to sign his first professional contract came soon enough. When he was 16 he signed with Caguas in the Puerto Rican Winter League, where he was managed by Felipe Alou.[6] Alou later said that Roberto "was the best I had ever seen. He was a natural and definitely had the instincts that you just don't teach."[7]

On February 16, 1985, shortly after he turned 17, Roberto signed with the San Diego Padres—the same club for which his father was a coach and with which Sandy Jr. had signed two years earlier. While other teams (most notably Toronto) had expressed interest in the middle infielder and made higher offers than the approximately $50,000 Roberto received, Sandy Sr. had given his word to family friend and Padres scout Luis Rosa that Roberto would sign with the Padres.[8]

Unlike many newly signed minor leaguers, Roberto did not have to adjust to living on his own for the first time. He was assigned to the same team, Class-A Charleston in the South Atlantic League, for which his father was a coach and to which Sandy Jr. was also assigned. His mother also made the trip and the family lived together and provided a stable foundation as Roberto's professional career began to flourish.[9] Roberto hit .293 and stole 36 bases for Charleston, and his manager Jim Skaalen recalled that "He was tearing up the league against older college players."[10]

Skaalen moved up along with Roberto the next season to Reno in the Class-A California League.[11] His brother and father, however, did not. Sandy Jr. was ticketed for Double-A Wichita (Texas League) and Sandy Sr. was promoted to coach with the Padres. Roberto later recounted the challenges of his time in Reno: "In the minor leagues everything is different. I was making $700 a month. I had to pay for rent, utilities, food, clubhouse dues. All I had in the house I rented was a mattress on the floor, not even a table. I had no car and had to walk everywhere."[12]

Skaalen, though, saw him maturing on and off the field: "He seemed more relaxed away from his dad and brother. He got stronger and seemed to be enjoying every day. He was far ahead of the rest of the talent at that level, and I began to see the good, solid major-league player he was going to become."[13]

Whatever the challenges off the field, Alomar's play certainly did not suffer. He led the league after 90 games with a .346 average and 123 hits, earning him a promotion to Double-A Wichita (and a reunion with Sandy Jr.).[14] Sharing a one-bedroom apartment with his brother, Roberto continued his torrid pace and finished the season hitting .319 with 12 home runs and 43 stolen bases.[15]

Roberto's minor-league success provided real hope going into the spring of 1988 that he could break camp with the Padres. His performance did nothing to dampen that enthusiasm, as he hit .360 and put together a 10-game hitting streak.[16] Padres manager Larry Bowa noted that "this kid is a finished product. All he has to do is go out there and play. He has all the tools; just turn him loose."[17] The Padres, though, had been burned each of the prior two seasons when they tried to promote second basemen (Bip Roberts and Joey Cora) from Double A to the big leagues, and Bowa was directed to give Roberto the bad news that his season would begin at Triple-A Las Vegas, not San Diego.[18] The 20-year-old Roberto took the news hard, tearfully retreating to the training room, where he was consoled by his father along with several teammates.

For his part, Bowa had no explanation for the sentence he was ordered to deliver: "I told him he did everything I asked," said Bowa. "I just told him to keep his head up, that it's a long season. The chances of Robbie coming to the big leagues in 1988 are pretty good."[19] They were pretty good indeed, as Roberto made quick work of the Pacific Coast League and was leading the league with 14 runs batted in when he was called up to San Diego 2½ weeks into the season.[20]

On April 22, 1988, Roberto stepped into the batter's box as a major leaguer for the first time. On the mound was none other than Nolan Ryan—the same Nolan Ryan who had helped teach him to pitch as a toddler. Unfazed, he beat out an infield single in his first major league at-bat.[21] Roberto finished the season with 145 hits, a .266 batting average, and 24 stolen bases, finishing fifth in the National League Rookie of the Year voting. He was even stronger the next season, his first full year in the big leagues, batting .295 with 42 stolen bases in 158 games.

Continuing his ascent onto the national radar, Roberto was selected for his first All-Star Game in 1990. What made the honor even more special was that Sandy Jr. (who had been traded to Cleveland), was also selected. The two became the first pair of brothers to be selected for an All-Star Game since Jim and Gaylord Perry in 1970.[22] Sandy Sr. reflected on the accomplishments of his two sons: "People have to realize I'm very proud of my kids for the way they act as persons. And they have talent and know how to display that talent."[23]

While it appeared that Roberto had established himself as a core piece of the Padres' future, the Padres had other ideas. After the 1990 season the Padres and Blue Jays struck a blockbuster deal that sent Alomar and outfielder Joe Carter to Toronto in exchange for Fred McGriff and Gold Glove shortstop Tony Fernandez.[24] Along with Alomar and Carter, Blue Jays general manager Pat Gillick had also added center fielder Devon White days earlier as Toronto worked to position itself in the competitive American League East.[25] Padres' general manager Joe McIlvaine said, "We just felt it was something we wanted to give a shot to. It was kind of a gutsy trade on both ends."[26] Roberto was shocked: "I didn't expect it; I didn't understand it," he later recalled.[27]

Surprised or not, Roberto joined a collection of talented players in Toronto and paid immediate dividends north of the border, putting together an early six-game hitting streak as the Blue Jays streaked to the top of the American League East.[28] In May, however, Roberto once again ran into the task of facing Nolan Ryan — now pitching for the Texas Rangers. With two outs in the top of the ninth, the 44-year-old Ryan was one out away from his seventh no-hitter when Roberto strode to the plate. As the *Fort Worth Star Telegram* put it 25 years later, "[T]he kid he'd once coached stood between Ryan and history."[29] Ryan had the last laugh; he struck out Alomar on a 2-and-2 fastball to end the game.[30]

Later in the season, Roberto was once again elected to the All-Star Game, this time as an American League teammate of Sandy Jr. The long ovation he received from the Toronto crowd served as confirmation of how the city had taken to him: "When I was introduced they gave me such a long, loud ovation, I never expected it," Roberto said.[31]

As the season wore on, Alomar kept hitting and the Blue Jays kept winning, clinching the American League East. In his first postseason, Alomar's .474 batting average could not keep Toronto from being eliminated in five games by the Minnesota Twins. Alomar won his first Gold Glove, and it was clear that the Blue Jays were set to contend in the years to come. The offseason brought with it new riches as well: a three-year, $14 million contract that was the highest at the time on three fronts — for a second baseman, for a player 24 or younger, and for a player with four years or less in the major leagues.[32] The average annual value of $4,666,667 made Alomar the ninth-highest paid player in the game.[33]

Bolstered by the acquisition of Dave Winfield in the offseason and David Cone in August, the Blue Jays again clinched the American League East in 1992. At midseason Alomar returned to San Diego for the first time since being traded and participated in the All-Star Game — once again with Sandy Jr. as a teammate.[34]

Alomar was named the most valuable player in the ALCS, with the most memorable moment being his game-tying two run home run off A's closer Dennis Eckersley in the ninth inning of Game Four. He relished the opportunity to be part of the first Blue Jays team to reach the World Series: "I wasn't here when they didn't win in the past. ... I just want to be here in the present when we win the big one, so we won't have to hear anymore about the past."[35] Alomar continued his clutch hitting and superb defense in the World Series, and helped the Blue Jays defeat Atlanta for their first championship. Alomar's contributions led Dave Winfield to comment that "You're one of the best players I've ever seen."[36] Manager Cito Gaston agreed: "I could talk about Robbie for an hour," he said.[37]

After a slow start in 1993, the Blue Jays took off yet again and Alomar had career highs in numerous categories, including 55 stolen bases and 17 home runs. In the ALCS against the Chicago White Sox, he stole four bases as the Blue Jays won, four games to two. In the World Series, against the Philadelphia Phillies, Alomar hit .480 and drove in six runs as the Blue Jays, on Joe Carter's game-winning home run in Game Six, won the World Series for the second year in a row.[38]

With two World Series titles in his back pocket, it was hard to imagine things ever going wrong for Alomar in Toronto. But go wrong they did. After a strike-shortened 1994 season, the Blue Jays began to take a step back in 1995 and look toward the future. This included trading veteran David Cone in July — a move that Alomar protested by sitting out the next game.[39] Alomar was also removed from a game in early July when a fan, Tricia Miller, walked into the Skydome hotel where he lived and told employees that she planned to kill him.[40] Alomar said, "I wasn't shaken by it. I never knew that person. I never really knew what was happening. Cito told me in the dugout. They took me out of the game, but they had caught her by then, so I don't know why."[41]

By the end of the season, with rumors swirling about his future, Alomar was unhappy with what he felt was unfair treatment by the Toronto front office and local media:

"I never said that I want to be traded. … They made it sound like I said, 'Trade me now, I want out of here.' And the fans believed what they read in the papers. When I stood out on the field in Toronto and heard them booing me, I knew they didn't understand or know what the truth was. I hadn't said anything like what the writers wrote. But I could do nothing about it, and I learned how the media is."[42]

With no offer from the Blue Jays, Alomar was ready to hit free agency: "If [the Blue Jays] had offered me something before the All-Star break, then maybe I would've thought about it and gone for it. Now you're in the last week of the season. … Now maybe it's time for me to try the market."[43]

At 27 years old and already a six-time All-Star, Alomar inked a three-year, $18 million contract with the Baltimore Orioles in December 1995.[44] He was thrilled to team up with fellow All-Star Cal Ripken Jr.: "I never expected to play alongside one of the legends of baseball. … It's going to be like a dream come true for me."[45]

Alomar carried his winter-ball success (he led the league in hitting) over to Baltimore, going on a tear to begin the season, hitting .410 in the beginning part of June.[46] Former teammate Tony Gwynn heaped praise on the player Alomar had become, saying, "He has the ability to hit a home run, or work the count and hit a double down the opposite line and do whatever he wants to do. He's probably the best all-around player in the game."[47] Alomar went on to make his seventh consecutive All-Star Game, collect his sixth consecutive Gold Glove and set numerous career highs as the Orioles clinched the American League wild-card playoff spot.[48]

Perhaps the most memorable moment of the season, however, occurred during a late-September game in Toronto. After being called out on strikes in the top of the first, Alomar argued with home-plate umpire John Hirschbeck on his way back to the dugout. When Hirschbeck threw him out of the game, Alomar returned to the field. During the course of the argument, Alomar took offense to being called a derogatory name, and spit in Hirschbeck's face.[49]

Alomar apologized and donated $50,000 toward research into Lou Gehrig's disease, which Hirschbeck's son had.[50] This did nothing to prevent his being relentlessly booed for the remainder of the season and the playoffs, or from receiving a five-game suspension to be served at the start of the 1997 season.[51]

Alomar delivered a game-tying two-out single in the deciding Game Four of the Division Series against Cleveland, and then hit the game-winning home run in the 12th inning.[52] Brother and Indians catcher Sandy Alomar Jr. said, "He's my brother and with all the things that happened with this incident, I felt kind of sorry for him."[53] Roberto was ready to turn the page on the incident: "I've been going through a tough time. … Human beings make mistakes. I apologized to the umpire, his family, and all of baseball. It's time to move on."[54] The Orioles did move on to the ALCS, but were eliminated in five games by the New York Yankees on their way to the World Series title.

The fact that Alomar was even allowed to play in the playoffs did not sit well with many, including major-league umpires. When it was announced that his suspension would be delayed until the next season, the umpires voted to not work the playoffs unless the suspension was changed to apply to the first round.[55] The boycott was abandoned, however, when an agreement was worked out in a Philadelphia federal court.[56]

After he served his five-game suspension to start the 1997 season, Alomar helped the Orioles to 98 wins and the American League East crown. He also took the first step toward putting the spitting incident behind him, publicly shaking hands with Hirschbeck near first base in April before the first Orioles game Hirschbeck called since the incident.[57] Several nagging injuries pestered Alomar throughout the season, including a nagging groin injury in late July that made him miss close to a month of playing time. Alomar said the injury "made me grow up.

I now knew what it was like to be hurt and what you had to do to come back."[58] After defeating the Mariners in the Division Series, the Orioles came up short of the World Series yet again, this time losing to Sandy and the Cleveland Indians in six games.

The Orioles were nowhere near contention in 1998. The season was not without its highlights though, as Roberto collected three hits (one of them a home run) and the All-Star Game MVP award in Denver, making the Alomar brothers back-to-back winners of the award since Sandy had won the year before. As his three-year contract with the Orioles came to a close, Roberto once again found himself on the free-agent market.

It did not take long for Roberto to find a new home. He signed a four-year contract with the Indians, reuniting with Sandy.[59] "It means a lot to be beside my brother, not only to me but to my family," Roberto said.[60] Indians general manager John Hart stated the obvious: "We are elated to have the Alomar brothers in the Indians family."[61] In addition to Sandy, the move to Cleveland also allowed Roberto to team with shortstop Omar Vizquel, who along with Roberto had also won six Gold Gloves. "It would be worth the price of a ticket just to watch Omar and Robbie turn a double play," said Hart.[62]

Free from the injuries that plagued him in 1998, Alomar made an immediate impact on the Indians. "Robbie is one of the few players in the game that can make everybody around him better," Indians manager Mike Hargrove said.[63] The Indians had compiled an enviable offense that exploded out of the gates, and Alomar ended the year with what proved to be a career high 24 home runs. He finished third in the MVP voting (the highest he would ever finish). His hot hitting continued in the playoffs; he went 5-for-8 while the Indians surged to a 2-0 series lead over the Red Sox in the ALDS.[64] The Tribe would not win again, however, and fell in five games.[65]

Although things did not turn out as hoped in October, a late-season meeting helped Alomar to finally turn the page on the spitting incident, which had continued to follow him through the jeers of fans around the country. On September 5, during a rain delay at Camden Yards, John Hirschbeck and family came knocking on the visitor's clubhouse door, asking for Roberto. Hirschbeck's 13-year-old son was a fan, and wanted to meet Roberto. The moment together allowed both families to heal. "I don't see why he should be booed," Hirschbeck said afterward. "If he and I can forgive and forget, why not everyone else?"[66]

The next two seasons also ended in disappointment for the Indians. In 2000 they missed the playoffs altogether despite winning 90 games. They charged back to the playoffs in 2001, but fell in five games in the ALDS to the Seattle Mariners. Alomar won Gold Gloves and was an All-Star in both seasons, and stole a combined 69 bases. He still looked to be in his prime with one year left on his contract. But another change of scenery was in store.

On December 11, 2001, the Indians traded Alomar, pitcher Mike Bacsik, and first baseman Danny Peoples to the New York Mets in exchange for outfielders Matt Lawton and Alex Escobar, relief pitcher Jerrod Riggan, and two players to be named later.[67]

While the move was designed to clear payroll and acquire younger talent, Indians general manager Mark Shapiro knew that the deal would not sit well with all fans. "I think I'll need a flak jacket when I get off the plane [from the winter meetings], probably," he said.[68] Alomar said he was "kind of disappointed … I was real happy in Cleveland and thought I did a great job."[69] Mets General Manager Steve Phillips was elated: "We sit up in that room and all we do is dream all day about different scenarios," he said, adding that "I have to admit that I thought this was a long shot."[70]

But what had seemed like a dream scenario for Phillips at the Winter Meetings would soon turn into a nightmare. The Mets came nowhere near meeting expectations, finishing in last place in the National League East, 26½ games out of first place. Alomar also began to show the first sign of decline, hitting .266 and snapping his 12-year streak of appearances in the All-Star Game. The 2003 season began much the same way, with Alomar hitting .262 on July 1 when the Mets shipped him to the White Sox for three prospects.[71]

All told, Alomar played only 222 games for the Mets, and for his part understood that he did not perform at the high level that the Mets, and he himself, had expected. "Sometimes, you put too much pressure on yourself in New York, and maybe I did that," he said.[72] Along with providing a change of scenery, joining the White Sox allowed him to reunite again with Sandy.[73] But Roberto hit only .253 down the stretch and the White Sox finished in second place in the American League Central, missing the playoffs.

A free agent once again, Alomar signed a one-year deal in the offseason with the Arizona Diamondbacks in the hopes of rejuvenating his career. "If I can get in good shape, I think I can play the way I used to play," he said.[74] Despite missing 56 games with a broken right hand suffered when he was hit by a pitch in late April, he did indeed experience a resurgence of sorts in his limited time on the field with Arizona, carrying a .309 batting average into early August.[75] With the Diamondbacks hopelessly out of contention, Alomar was once again an attractive commodity for teams looking to add a veteran presence for the stretch run. So it was that the White Sox acquired him for the second consecutive season. Alomar struggled mightily in sporadic action, though, batting only .180 in 65 plate appearances as the White Sox once again missed the playoffs.

After multiple seasons of declining performance, Alomar made one last run at extending his career, this time with Tampa Bay, signing a one-year, $600,000 contract in January.[76] When he committed multiple errors in one inning of a spring training game, however, he decided it was time to walk away. "I played a lot of games and I said I would never embarrass myself on the field," he said, adding, "I had a long career, but I can't play at the level I want to play, so it's time to retire. I just can't go anymore. My back, legs and eyes aren't the same."[77] Alomar concluded his 17-year career with a .300 batting average, 2,724 hits, 210 home runs, and 474 stolen bases to go along with 12 All-Star Game selections and 10 Gold Glove awards.

There was no question that Cooperstown would be the final stop of Alomar's career. With some Hall voters still holding the Hirschbeck incident against him, though, he came up eight votes short of admission in his first year of eligibility, in 2010. "I feel disappointed, but next year hopefully I make it in," he said, adding that "at least I was close."[78] Some sportswriters were not as gracious in their assessment of the snub. The *Chicago Tribune*'s Phil Rogers wrote, "If anybody didn't vote for Robbie because of the spitting incident, then shame on them."[79]

Whatever the concerns some Hall voters had in Alomar's first year of eligibility, resistance to his election was all but nonexistent the next year. He was named on 90 percent of the ballots, far over the 75 percent needed for induction into the Hall of Fame.[80] Even Alomar was surprised by the drastic increase in support from the previous year. "I didn't expect to get that many votes," he said.[81]

Alomar, who went into the Hall wearing a Blue Jays cap, opened his induction speech in Spanish and spoke fondly of his father's and brother's impact on his life and career.[82] Sandy Jr. recounted the brothers' year-long wager as teammates/roommates for

Class-A Charleston: "We said whoever had the best game, would get the bed. I slept on the couch the whole year."[83] He added, "We didn't win a championship together but we won this together. And this is a big one. In my heart, you are a Hall of Famer."[84]

Statistics aside, it is the way Alomar's former teammates describe him that truly tells the story of the player that he was. Toronto teammate Pat Hentgen, asked how he described Alomar to present-day players, said, "I tell them Robbie was a career .300 hitter, a clutch hitter, a guy who could hit for power, a great baserunner and basestealer … and (pause) his best asset of all was his glove."[85] The Orioles' B.J. Surhoff perhaps best summed up Alomar's baseball career: "Robbie could beat you with the bunt, with the extra base, with the homer. He could beat you with a stolen base. He could beat you by going from first to third, a baserunning move. He could beat you by making plays in the field. Robbie's a baseball player. And a damn good one at that."[86]

Alomar continued to be involved in baseball after his retirement. In January of 2016, he and his wife, Kim, launched Foundation 12, a Canadian charitable organization serving youth baseball players.[87]

## NOTES

1. "25 Years Later, Nolan Ryan Remembers His Seventh No-Hitter," *Fort Worth Star-Telegram*, April 30, 2016, star-telegram.com/sports/mlb/texas-rangers/article74925477.html.
2. Norman L. Macht, *Roberto Alomar* (Childs, Maryland: Mitchell Lane Publishers, Inc., 1999), 9-11.
3. Macht, 3.
4. Macht, 10.
5. "Like Father Like Son?: Padres Think Roberto Alomar Is a Bit More Than a Chip Off the Old Block," *Los Angeles Times*, April 22, 1988, articles.latimes.com/1988-04-22/sports/sp-2096_1_roberto-alomar.
6. Macht, 15.
7. Ibid.
8. Macht, 16.
9. Ibid.
10. Macht, 17.
11. Macht, 18.
12. Macht, 18.
13. Macht, 19.
14. Macht, 19.
15. Macht, 21.
16. "Padre Notebook: Few Except Feeney Appear Satisfied as Roberto Alomar Is Sent Down," *Los Angeles Times*, March 26, 1988, articles.latimes.com/1988-03-26/sports/sp-354_1_roberto-alomar.
17. Macht, 23.
18. "Padre Notebook."
19. Ibid.
20. "Like Father Like Son?"
21. Macht, 25-26.
22. "Alomars an All-Star Family: Padres: Roberto Alomar, Along With Teammate Tony Gywnn, Is Named an NL Reserve. Brother Sandy Had Already Been Selected as The Starting AL Catcher for Tuesday's Game," *Los Angeles Times*, July 6, 1990, articles.latimes.com/1990-07-06/sports/sp-113_1_sandy-alomar-jr.
23. Ibid.
24. "Blue Jays Land Carter, Alomar From Padres San Diego Gets Fernandez and McGriff in Deal," *Baltimore Sun*, December 5, 1990, articles.baltimoresun.com/1990-12-06/sports/1990340005_1_blue-jays-fred-mcgriff-tony-fernandez.
25. Ibid.
26. Ibid.
27. Macht, 31.
28. "Padres Winning December Deal Looks Like Tie With Blue Jays in April," *Baltimore Sun*, April 21, 1991, articles.baltimoresun.com/1991-04-21/sports/1991111135_1_blue-jays-roberto-alomar-deal.
29. "25 Years Later."
30. Ibid.
31. Macht, 33.
32. "BASEBALL; Cadaret and 8 Others Settle Contract," *New York Times*, February 8, 1992, nytimes.com/1992/02/08/sports/baseball-cadaret-and-8-others-settle-contracts.html.
33. Ibid.
34. Macht, 35.
35. "Blue Jays Eck Out a 7-6 Victory in 11: AL Game 4: Alomar's Two-Run Homer Off Eckersley Ties It in Ninth as A's Blow 6-1 Lead," *Los Angeles Times*, October 12, 1992, articles.latimes.com/1992-10-12/sports/sp-138_1_blue-jays.
36. Macht, 37.
37. "Alomar's MVP Play Points to New Star," *Baltimore Sun*, October 15, 1992, articles.baltimoresun.com/1992-10-15/sports/1992289072_1_alomar-blue-jays-toronto.

38. Macht, 42.
39. Macht, 43-44.
40. "Orioles' Multitalented Alomar Is Second to None," *Washington Post*, March 31, 1996, washingtonpost.com/archive/sports/1996/03/31/orioles-multitalented-alomar-is-second-to-none/b8cd697d-9630-464e-bcd9-84d6ba8db8cf/?utm_term=.9d34bd1c1107.
41. Ibid.
42. Macht, 44.
43. "Jays' Alomar in No Rush to Decide '96 Destination He, Molitor Express Interest in Joining Ripken," *Baltimore Sun*, September 27, 1995, articles.baltimoresun.com/1995-09-27/sports/1995270116_1_alomar-blue-jays-second-baseman.
44. "O's Wave Money Wand Building Winner: Signing Six-Time All-Star Roberto Alomar Adds Exclamation Mark to New General Manager's Swift Revamping of Orioles," *Baltimore Sun*, December 22, 1995, articles.baltimoresun.com/1995-12-22/news/1995356066_1_gillick-orioles-roberto-alomar. New manager Davey Johnson was informed of the signing in the dentist's chair when he answered a call from General Manager Pat Gillick who said, "Well, you've got yourself an All-Star second baseman." Johnson claimed to not feel any pain for the remainder of the day. "Alomar finds O's 2nd to none Six-time All-Star signs, three-year, $18 million deal," *Baltimore Sun*, December 22, 1995, articles.baltimoresun.com/1995-12-22/sports/1995356093_1_roberto-alomar-cone-orioles.
45. Macht, 47.
46. Macht, 46, 51-52.
47. "Alomar Hitting His Prime at Plate," *Los Angeles Times*, May 28, 1996, articles.latimes.com/1996-05-28/sports/sp-9201_1_alomar-hitting.
48. Macht, 51-52.
49. Macht, 52-53.
50. Macht, 54.
51. Ibid.
52. "Alomar Shows Some Spit and Polish," *Los Angeles Times*, October 6, 1996, articles.latimes.com/1996-10-06/sports/sp-51279_1_sandy-alomar.
53. Ibid.
54. Ibid.
55. "Umpires Vote to Boycott Over Alomar," *New York Times*, October 1, 1996, nytimes.com/1996/10/01/sports/umpires-vote-to-boycott-over-alomar.html.
56. "Umpires Abandon Boycott," *Los Angeles Times*, October 2, 1996, articles.latimes.com/1996-10-02/sports/sp-49681_1_umpires-working-game.
57. Macht, 57.
58. Macht, 59.
59. Macht, 62.
60. "Cleveland Lures Roberto Alomar," CBS News, November 23, 1998, cbsnews.com/news/cleveland-lures-roberto-alomar/.
61. Ibid.
62. Ibid.
63. "Alomar: Villain Turned Hero in Cleveland," *Los Angeles Times*, June 27, 1999, articles.latimes.com/1999/jun/27/sports/sp-50609.
64. "Baines Goes Deep as Indians Move One Game From Sweep," *Baltimore Sun*, October 8, 1999, articles.baltimoresun.com/1999-10-08/sports/9910080129_1_roberto-alomar-baines-cleveland.
65. "Red Sox Ace Out Indians," *Los Angeles Times*, October 12, 1999, articles.latimes.com/1999/oct/12/sports/sp-22770/2.
66. "Score One for Friendship," *Baltimore Sun*, October 27, 1999, articles.baltimoresun.com/1999-10-27/news/9910270108_1_roberto-alomar-john-hirschbeck-holy-water/3.
67. "Indians Trade Alomar to Mets," *Southeast Missourian* (Cape Girardeau, Missouri), December 12, 2001, semissourian.com/story/54375.html.
68. "Indians Trade Alomar to Mets," CBC Sports, December 11, 2001, cbc.ca/sports/baseball/indians-trade-alomar-to-mets-1.257404.
69. Ibid.
70. "Indians trade Alomar to Mets," *Southeast Missourian*, December 12, 2001, www.semissourian.com/story/54375.html.
71. "Mets Trade Roberto Alomar to White Sox," *New York Times*, July 1, 2003, nytimes.com/2003/07/01/sports/baseball/mets-trade-roberto-alomar-to-white-sox.html.
72. Ibid.
73. Sandy signed with Chicago prior to the 2003 season.
74. "Alomar Jr. Joins Diamondbacks, CBC Sports, January 7, 2004, cbc.ca/sports/baseball/alomar-jr-joins-diamondbacks-1.516620.
75. "Diamondbacks Trade Alomar to White Sox," *Orlando Sentinel*, August 6, 2004, articles.orlandosentinel.com/2004-08-06/sports/0408060185_1_dominican-republic-clemens-white-sox.
76. "Notebook: Roberto Alomar: "It's Time to Retire," *Seattle Times*, March 20, 2005, seattletimes.com/sports/notebook-roberto-alomar-its-time-to-retire/.
77. Ibid.
78. "Hall Passes: Alomar 8 Short," *Baltimore Sun*, January 7, 2010, articles.baltimoresun.com/2010-01-07/sports/1001060140_1_hall-s-veterans-committee-john-hirschbeck-roberto-alomar.
79. Ibid.
80. "Alomar, Blyleven Elected to Hall of Fame," *Baltimore Sun*, January 5, 2011, articles.baltimoresun.com/2011-01-05/sports/bs-sp-hallofame-01-20110105_1_sandy-alomar-sr-pitcher-bert-blyleven-induction.
81. Ibid.

82 "Alomar, Blyleven and Gillick Enter Baseball Hall of Fame," *USA Today*, July 24, 2011, usatoday30.usatoday.com/sports/baseball/hallfame/2011-07-24-hall-of-fame-alomar-blyleven_n.htm.

83 Ibid.

84 Ibid.

85 "Robbie Was Best of the Best," *Toronto Sun*, July 16, 2011, torontosun.com/2011/07/16/robbie-was-best-of-the-best.

86 "Alomar Falls Just Short in First Bid for Hall of Fame," *Baltimore Sun*, January 7, 2010, articles.baltimoresun.com/2010-01-07/sports/bal-sp.alomar07jan07_1_roberto-alomar-greatest-second-basemen-ballot/2.

87 See Foundation 12 website: alomarsports.com/foundation-12/.

# SANDY ALOMAR, SR.

## By Irv Goldfarb

**A** SPEEDY, TALENTED, AND VERSAtile infielder, Sandy Alomar, Sr. spent half a century in professional baseball as a player, coach, and manager. That time included 11 full seasons plus parts of four others in the majors from 1964 through 1978. Alomar made the American League All-Star team in 1970 and was a member of the New York Yankees when they reached the World Series in 1976. His biggest contribution to professional baseball, however, might have been his two very talented sons. Sandy Alomar, Jr. played in 20 big-league seasons and was a six-time All-Star. Roberto Alomar was inducted into the Hall of Fame in 2011.

Santos Alomar Conde was born in Salinas, Puerto Rico on October 19, 1943. His parents were Demetrio Alomar Palmieri, a sugar-mill machine operator, and Rosa Conde Santiago. There were eight children overall in the family.[1] Small in stature at 5-feet-9 and 140 to 155 pounds, Sandy was the only one of the family's four ballplaying brothers to make it to the major leagues. Antonio (Tony) and Rafael got as high as Triple A; Demetrio played Class-C and D ball. All played in the Puerto Rican Winter League (PRWL).

The Alomar baseball heritage was also visible on the maternal side. Rosa's cousin, Ceferino "Cefo" Conde, pitched 14 seasons in the PRWL, from 1938-39 through 1952-53. Infielder Ramón "Wito" Conde, Cefo's son, played pro ball from the early 1950s through 1970—including 14 games with the Chicago White Sox in 1962.

Santos starred for both Luis Muñoz Rivera High School in his hometown and for the local American Legion team. He signed as an amateur free agent with the Milwaukee Braves before the 1960 season, receiving a bonus of about $12,000. The scout was Luis Olmo, the second Puerto Rican to play in the majors. Olmo had seen Alomar ever since he was a youth in Little League and Pony ball.[2] Sandy was just 16 when he signed at the same time with brother Demetrio, who was then 21. He was supposed to report to Eau Claire, Wisconsin in the Class-C Northern League after the school year ended.[3] As it developed, though, he did not play in the U.S. in 1960. He was on the restricted list (perhaps because of his age).[4]

Still only 17 in 1961, Alomar began his ride on the minor-league whirlwind still familiar to young players. To his delight, when he landed in the Midwest League, he found himself teamed with Demetrio in the Davenport, Iowa infield. He later admitted that this fortuitous situation helped make his transition to American baseball more comfortable.[5] He made stops in (among other places) Austin, Boise—where he hit a lofty .329 in 1962—and Denver. Alomar began his PRWL career in the winter of 1961-62 with the Arecibo Lobos. He spent six seasons with the Wolves, followed by six with the Ponce Leones.

Alomar was called up from Milwaukee's Triple-A Denver club in September 1964. He made his major league debut on September 15, a little over a month shy of his 21st birthday. He started at shortstop in the first game of a doubleheader at County Stadium and batted eighth, singling in a run in his first at-bat off St. Louis left-hander Ray Sadecki. A popup and groundout followed, before a pinch-hitter replaced him leading off the eighth. Besides batting 1-for-3, Alomar also made an error in the 11-6 loss. He started at short again in the second game, but had the misfortune of facing ace Bob Gibson, who struck Alomar out twice.

In 53 at-bats over 19 games in his first big-league stint, Alomar hit .245 with a double and 6 RBIs. He played the bulk of the following year for the Atlanta Crackers, which had become the Braves' AAA team that season. He did appear in 67 more games for the big club, however, batting .241 with 8 RBIs while playing second base as well as shortstop. He also stole 12 bases.

The Braves' major league franchise made its heralded move to Atlanta to start the 1966 season, but Alomar's opportunities to make an impression were growing fewer. Spending most of that season in Richmond (the Braves' new AAA home), Sandy—now playing mainly second base—got only 44 at-bats with the major league club, collecting merely a double and three singles for an .091 average. In 117 total games for the Braves over parts of three seasons, Alomar hit just .210 with four extra base hits, 16 runs batted in, and only 13 steals. He had made nine errors in the infield. Alomar's days with the team that brought him to the United States were quickly coming to an end.

Before the 1967 season, the Braves sent Sandy to Houston as the player to be named later in a deal that had brought future Hall of Famer Eddie Mathews to the Astros. A month later, however, Houston moved him along to New York for utilityman Derrell Griffith. The Mets, entering only their sixth season as a major league franchise, were looking for a versatile infielder—shortstop Bud Harrelson was not yet ready and veteran second baseman Chuck Hiller was considered a weak glove man. "It was a case of trading a good bat for a good glove and speed," explained Mets GM Bing Devine.[6]

Looking for a way to expand his value at the plate, Alomar came to camp determined to become a switch-hitter, something he had tried in his rookie season with the Braves with limited success. Unfortunately, the results didn't change. He spent most of the year with the Mets' International League team in Jacksonville, playing all four infield positions and the outfield but hitting only .209. When the Mets did recall him, Sandy got just 22 at-bats without a hit (this 0-for-22 streak stood for a time as a Met record for hitless futility.) And before the season was over, he was gone.

On August 15, Alomar was once again a player named later. He was shipped to the White Sox to complete an earlier deal that had also sent third-base great Ken Boyer to Chicago. It was at this point that Alomar became disillusioned. "It was a nightmare," he told a reporter in an interview three years later when asked about the season in which he was on the roster of four different major league teams. "Like a piece of garbage…They treat me like I was something they could throw away when they want to…They brainwash me. They tell me I cannot hit, that I good glove man…they say I am too little to not wear down. They make me believe these things myself…almost." However, he had a backer in the White Sox organization: coach Grover Resinger, who knew him from his days with the Braves and from the minor leagues.[7]

When he had been sent back to the minors in June 1967, Alomar admitted he had thought of quitting and going back to Puerto Rico. "And then I look at my four mouths to feed and one on the way…and I think that for one last chance Sandy will go to the minors."[8] Santos, Jr. had been born during the 1966 season while his dad was playing in Atlanta; Roberto was the "one on the way." The first Alomar child was a daughter named Sandia. Sandy and María Angelita Velázquez had gotten married on December 23, 1963.[9]

In the Second City, however, Alomar's prospects began to brighten. He appeared in only 12 games

during the remainder of the 1967 season, but in 1968, Sox manager Eddie Stanky finally made Sandy a regular. Under the tutelage of scout and hitting instructor Deacon Jones, Alomar upped his average to .253, at one point in the season reaching .274. Infield mate Luis Aparicio was impressed: "That fellow has improved 150%," remarked the future Hall of Famer.[10]

That winter, Ponce won the first of back-to-back PRWL championships. Rocky Bridges, then a coach for the California Angels, managed the 1968-69 squad. Unfortunately, Alomar had a slow start to the '69 big-league season. He was traded again, to the Angels on May 14, in a package for infielder Bobby Knoop. Though Knoop was coming off three consecutive Gold Glove awards, the Angels thought Alomar could do everything except make the pivot as well as or better than Knoop.[11]

Angels' manager Bill Rigney thought he saw in Alomar a chance to kick-start his lineup from the top. "We've never had a leadoff hitter," said Rigney. "If we're going to do it with singles, we might as well do it with speed, too." Rocky Bridges was also excited: "Sandy can run," he remarked. "He'll create excitement. The fans will be looking for him to go every time he's on first."[12]

It was in Anaheim that Sandy Alomar finally settled down. Installed as the everyday second baseman, Alomar had almost 600 plate appearances in 1969, hitting a passable .250 with 30 RBIs, though he stole only 18 bases. With Ponce that winter, the Leones repeated as PRWL champs. The skipper was Alomar's double-play partner with the Angels, Jim Fregosi, in his first job as manager.

If Angel fans were truly looking for Alomar to run every time he got on first, they felt much more confident in 1970. Playing the full 162-game schedule for the first time, Alomar hit .251 in 672 at-bats, driving in 36 runs and swiping 35 bases. He also walked 49 times with only 65 strikeouts, helping make him the leadoff hitter the Angels had been hoping for.

Alomar's season was impressive enough for him to be named as an AL reserve in the All-Star Game after Rod Carew was injured. He took great pride in having his hard work recognized.[13] At Cincinnati's Riverfront Stadium, he went hitless in his one at-bat, flying out against Claude Osteen in the top of the 12th in what's remembered as the "Pete Rose/Ray Fosse" game.

Alomar's professional peak was the 1970-71 winter season. He hit a league-leading .343 in 251 at-bats for Ponce and was named the PRWL's Most Valuable Player. The Leones finished in fourth among the league's six teams that season, however, and were knocked out in the semifinals.

The next season with the Angels proved to be Alomar's most successful in the majors. Now 27 years old, he collected close to 700 at-bats for the second year in a row and hit a new high, batting .260. He also set personal career bests with 179 hits, 42 RBIs, and 39 stolen bases. In addition, he set a major-league record by coming to the plate 739 times without being hit by a pitch (Alomar was struck by a pitched ball only three times in 15 seasons).

Overall, Alomar enjoyed the most productive stretch of his career in Southern California—in a period covering four full seasons and parts of two others, Sandy appeared in close to 800 games, hitting .248 with 162 RBIs; he stole 139 bases in 186 attempts. At 30 years old, the veteran infielder felt he had finally made his mark. Alomar played in a remarkable 648 consecutive games in one stretch from 1969 through September 1973, until he suffered a broken leg when Jerry Hairston Sr. slammed into him while breaking up a double play. This streak—which earned Alomar the nickname "The Iron Pony"—is still 19th-longest in big-league history.

Alomar sat out the 1973-74 winter season in Puerto Rico while he recovered from his broken leg. Meanwhile, in December 1973, the Angels acquired second baseman Denny Doyle from the Philadelphia Phillies. Doyle won the starting job in California that spring, and in July 1974, after playing in just 54 games as a reserve, Alomar was on the move again. His contract was sold to the New York Yankees, who had parted ways with their second baseman since 1967, Horace Clarke, that May.

The change of scenery helped—Alomar batted .269 in 76 games while playing second base in the

Bronx. When he came back for the 1974-75 season in Puerto Rico, he was a member of the Santurce Cangrejeros. He played in five seasons for the Crabbers.

The whole Yankee team got off to a slow start in the 1975 season. Sandy was hitting a meager .205 and even floundering in the field. He began to question himself. "When I'm in my room by myself, that's when I think about the way I am going," he mused. "I think, 'Why do you do this when you could have done that? Why do you miss that pitch…why do you miss that ball?'…There are times when I ask myself whether I can hit or not.

"Sometimes I go to a restaurant and I order and I don't feel like eating…I know, myself, that I'm a better hitter than what I'm doing now. A baseball player—you have to accept the ups and the downs."[14]

Still, the Yankees, meandering to an 83-win, third-place finish in the AL East, kept Alomar in the lineup almost every day. He ended the season hitting .239 in 151 games with 28 steals. His .975 fielding percentage led all major leaguers at the keystone base.

In the Yankees' pennant-winning year of 1976, Alomar, now a utilityman with the emergence of young second baseman Willie Randolph, did everything on the field except pitch and catch. He appeared in 67 games and mirrored his previous season, hitting .239.

More importantly, for the first time in his major league career, Alomar found himself in the post-season, as the Yankees won the AL East and then their first pennant since 1964. In the AL Championship Series against Kansas City, Sandy went 0-for-1 in his single plate appearance, flying out as a pinch-hitter to end New York's 7-4 defeat in Game Four. He was also called on to pinch-run, but was caught stealing second base to end the sixth, in what ultimately turned out to be a Yankee win when Chris Chambliss homered in the bottom of the ninth to win the series. Alomar did not appear in the World Series in that or any other year.

His value as a utility player made him attractive to other teams, however, and the Texas Rangers traded for him in February 1977, in a deal that sent infielder Brian Doyle to the Bronx. Over parts of the next two seasons, Alomar continued in his role as utilityman, hitting .265, mostly as a DH. In 1978, his U.S. career came to a close; he got only 29 at-bats and collected only six hits. He was released by the Rangers at the end of the year.

The final numbers in the majors for Santos Alomar, Sr. are not imposing. Over a 15-year major-league career and over 4,700 at-bats, he hit just .245 with 13 homers, 282 RBIs, and 227 stolen bases (he was caught 80 times). His on-base percentage was a lowly .290, but his fielding percentage was a solid .976.

Alomar did not play in Puerto Rico in the winter of 1978-79 after the Rangers released him. However, he appeared for Santurce in 25 games in 1979-80. He closed out his playing career the following winter with six appearances as player-manager for Ponce. Overall, Alomar hit .270 in over 1,000 games in the PRWL during 18 seasons (the exact number of total games is not certain because the figure is missing for 1963-64). He hit 25 homers and stole 168 bases, leading the league in steals an unequaled six times.

But Sandy Alomar's contribution to the game he loved would not end with his retirement. Back in Puerto Rico, he bought a gas station in Salinas, while his two sons learned the game their father had made his livelihood. While Sandy Jr. and Roberto honed their baseball skills, Sandy, Sr. continued working in baseball, coaching the Puerto Rican national team from 1979-1984. In the 1980s, he coached and managed with Santurce and again with Ponce.

Roberto, who grew to 6 feet, and Sandy, Jr., at 6-feet-5, were both much bigger than their father. When asked about the physical differences in 1997, Sandy, Jr. remarked that his mother was relatively tall at 5-feet-7, while his uncles were all tall as well. "My father is the only midget," he concluded.[15]

Luis Rosa, a San Diego Padres scout working throughout Latin America, came to see both Alomar offspring. He also approached their father about a position in the organization. The Padres' director of minor league scouting was looking for an infield instructor and Alomar had played for San Diego

*L to R: Sandy Alomar, Sandy Alomar Sr., and Roberto Alomar.*

manager Dick Williams when they were both with the Angels. Thus, the Padres hired him, but made it clear that it was not to encourage his talented sons to sign with their team.[16] Eventually, however, they both did.

Their father claims he never pressured either of them to pursue a baseball career. Though Roberto always wanted to be a big-leaguer, Santos, Jr. stopped playing ball for a couple of his teenage years to ride dirt bikes. "My dad gave me a speech," said Sandy, Jr. years later. "He said that riding bikes was a hobby and not a job…you spend money in that. You don't get money."[17]

The senior Alomar tried not to give his sons too much baseball advice either, but Sandy, Jr. believed that being the son of a major leaguer had its advantages and disadvantages. "You have a name that helps you," he said. "But some people do expect you to be the same as your father. That's not right. We're different people."[18]

As his progeny made their way through pro ball, their father's coaching odyssey continued: He served as a coach for the Padres' affiliate in Charleston, South Carolina in its inaugural season—both of his sons were on the team. Sandy Sr. then became a major-league coach for the Padres from 1986 through 1990, so he was on hand when his sons reached The Show in 1988.

Sandy Sr. then joined the Chicago Cubs organization, working as a roving minor-league instructor during the 1990s. He also managed their Williamsport team in the NY-Penn League for part of the 1994 season, as well as their Gulf Coast Rookie League team in 1995 and 1996.

Alomar joined the Cubs' major league staff in 2000 and remained there for three seasons, as bullpen coach and (in 2002) as first-base coach. He then moved to the Colorado Rockies' third-base coaching box for two seasons. Alomar remained connected to the Puerto Rican baseball scene too. He served as general manager of the San Juan Senadores in 1999-

2000. He also managed the national team in regional tournaments in 2003.

Alomar returned to the Mets in 2005, serving as first-base coach for two seasons, third-base coach for two more, and then finally becoming bench coach. He actually managed a game on May 9, 2009, after Jerry Manuel was suspended for an altercation with umpire Bill Welke. When the Mets beat Pittsburgh 10-1 and the Phillies lost to the Braves, the Mets moved into first place in the NL East under Alomar's one-game stewardship.

That season, however, was his last in a big-league uniform, though he managed again in the Gulf Coast Rookie League for the Mets in 2010.

In 2015 Sandy Alomar turned 72. The website Champions of Faith notes that Alomar is a lifelong Catholic and that he calls his wife María "the spiritual leader of the family".[19] They have six grandchildren to date.

In stature, Sandy Alomar Sr. was not a giant. But on the diamond, though he had his share of struggles in the game, his pride and perseverance made him a useful asset. His defensive versatility helped, as did an obvious passion to play as well as he was capable in every game. As Grover Resinger put it in 1970, Alomar had value "defensively, offensively and inspirationally."[20]

In 2014, Alomar himself expressed it this way as he passed on lessons from his decades of wisdom at the Vauxhall Academy of Baseball in Canada. "Size really doesn't matter if you have faith in yourself and you know you can do it. If you sacrifice, and you put the effort in, you will become what you feel it is you should become."[21]

He repeated a different dictum later that year at another baseball camp in Canada. "When you have pride, you have a will. When you have a will, you have respect. When you have respect, you create discipline. Discipline gives you knowledge. Knowledge gives you awareness. And awareness gives you anticipation."[22]

*Thanks to Rory Costello for his input.*

## SOURCES

In addition to the sources in the Notes, the author also consulted Ancestry.com, Myheritage.com, the *Chicago Tribune*, *New York Times*, and *Chicago Daily Defender*, as well as José A. Crescion Benítez, *El Béisbol Profesional Boricua* (San Juan, Puerto Rico: Aurora Comunicación Integral, Inc., 1997).

## NOTES

1  The names of six siblings are available: Luz María, Víctor Manuel, Guillermina, Antonio, Rafael, and Demetrio.

2  Thomas E. Van Hyning, *Puerto Rico's Winter League* (Jefferson, North Carolina: McFarland & Co., 1995), 130-131.

3  "2 Brothers Sign Eau Claire Pacts," *Milwaukee Sentinel*, January 29, 1960: Part 2, 5.

4  *Sporting News Baseball Register*, 1965.

5  Marc Appleman, "Like Father, Like Sons," *Los Angeles Times*, March 5, 1985.

6  Joseph M. Sheehan, "Mets Get Alomar, Infielder, and Send Griffith to Astros," *New York Times*, March 25, 1967.

7  John Wiebusch, "Alomar: Castoff Role a Nightmare," *Los Angeles Times*, June 19, 1970.

8  Wiebusch, "Alomar: Castoff Role a Nightmare."

9  Bob Elliott, "Alomar Fulfilled Island's Dream," *Toronto Sun*, January 12, 2011. *Sporting News Baseball Register*, 1965.

10  "Sports Ledger," *Chicago Defender*, September 3, 1968.

11  Wiebusch, "Alomar: Castoff Role a Nightmare."

12  Ross Newhan, "Angels Acquire Alomar, Priddy in Knoop Trade," *Los Angeles Times*, May 15, 1970: Sports-1.

13  Dick Miller, "Alomar's an Angry Angel, Raps His Rep as 'Unknown'," *The Sporting News*, April 10, 1971: 31.

14  Steve Jacobson, "Alomar Finds Solace of a Sort in Music," *Newsday*, July 24, 1975.

15  George Vecsey, "The Alomars Meet Again in October," *New York Times*, October 8, 1997.

16  Appleman, "Like Father, Like Sons."

17  Ibid.

18  Ibid.

19  www.championsoffaith.com/athletes/athlete_new.asp?athleteID=18

20  Wiebusch, "Alomar: Castoff Role a Nightmare."

21  "Baseball Patriarch Imparts Wisdom," *Vauxhall* (Alberta, Canada) *Advance*, March 7, 2014.

22  Mark Malone, "Alomar Shares Experience at Blue Jays Camp," *Chatham* (Ontario, Canada) *Daily News*, June 25, 2014.

# SANDY ALOMAR, JR.

## By Joseph Wancho

**J**ACOBS FIELD IN CLEVELAND WAS the site for major-league Baseball's 68th All-Star Game on July 8, 1997. A sold-out crowd of 44,916 turned out for the midsummer classic as it returned to the shores of Lake Erie for the first time since 1981. The host Indians ended the first half of the season on a positive note, sweeping Kansas City in a three-game set. They held a 3½-game lead over second-place Chicago at the break.

One of the reasons for the Tribe's success was the unlikely power coming from the bat of Sandy Alomar Jr. The veteran backstop started the season in fine fashion, as he slugged a home run in five consecutive games from April 4-8. His 11 home runs at the break matched his season total of the season before and were just three short of his career-high 14 homers in 1994. "I'm in a zone," said Alomar. "Everything looks like a beach ball."[1]

But it was more than the long ball that Alomar was contributing to the team's fortunes. He owned the second-longest hitting streak in franchise history, 30 games (from May 25 through July 6). The streak, in which Alomar batted .429, was second only to Nap Lajoie's 31-game streak in 1906. "It's been a remarkable run for him," said the Twins' Paul Molitor. "To be able to have the mind-set to call a game (as catcher) and still be able to do that. ..."[2]

For the All-Stars on July 8, pitching was the name of the game. The teams battled to a 1-1 tie through the top of the seventh inning. Each team scored its tally on a home run. Edgar Martínez, who was the first designated hitter elected to the All-Star Game, socked a 2-and-2 offering from Greg Maddux into the left-field plaza in the bottom of the second frame. In the top of the seventh, Braves catcher Javy López led off with a solo shot off the Royals' Jose Rosado.

Jim Thome led off the bottom of the seventh inning by grounding out. Bernie Williams walked and with two outs took second base on a wild pitch by the Giants' Shawn Estes. Alomar, who had replaced Iván Rodríguez in the bottom of the sixth inning, stepped to the plate. "When Sandy went to the plate, Paul O'Neill turned to me and said, 'If all things were fair, Sandy would hit a homer and win the ballgame,'" said Indians manager Mike Hargrove, one of manager Joe Torre's coaches for the game.[3] Sandy sent a 2-and-2 pitch from Estes on a line into the left-field bleachers. "I felt like I was flying," said Alomar. "I've never run the bases so fast on a home run."[4]

The 3-1 AL advantage stood up, as the junior circuit snapped a three-game losing streak. The NL was held to three hits. Alomar became the first Indian to homer in the All-Star Game since Rocky Colavito in 1959. Alomar was voted the game's MVP, the first Indian to be so honored and the first player ever to win the award in his home ballpark. "This is a dream I don't want to wake up from," said Alomar. "You probably only get one chance to play an All-Star Game in your home stadium."[5]

"It was another of those storybook things," said Torre. "I had one last fall [the 1996 World Series], and now this. I was happy for Sandy to win it in his own park."[6]

Santos (Velazquez) Alomar was born on June 18, 1966, in Salinas, Puerto Rico. He was the middle child (older sister Sandia, younger brother Roberto) born to Santos and Maria Alomar. Sandy Sr. suited up for six different teams over a 15-year career in the major leagues. He had a career batting average of .245. He was mainly a second baseman, although he also saw time at shortstop. After his playing days, Alomar coached 15 years on the big-league level. In addition to his time in the major leagues, Sandy Sr. also managed the Puerto Rican National Team.

The elder Alomar did not push his sons into baseball. "The only influence is from them seeing me play," he said.[7] The life of a ballplayer means a lot of travel and time away from the family. Sandy Sr. credited his wife, Maria, with raising their three children, saying, "She deserves more credit than me. I was a ballplayer and couldn't be around that much. She stayed home and raised those kids. That's why they're the kind of people they are."[8]

Roberto Alomar took to baseball right away. He had the natural ability to play the game and at age 7 he made Sandy's little league team for 9-to-12-year-olds. But for Sandy, he had other interests to keep him busy. "Sandy left the game at age 12 and got into dirt-bike riding and karate," said his father. "He was doing dangerous things, more or less. He said the only way he could find excitement in baseball was to become a catcher."[9]

Young Sandy took to catching and was signed as an amateur free agent on October 21, 1983, by the San Diego Padres. After graduating from Luis Munoz Rivera High School in Salinas, Alomar began his journey to the major leagues. It was a long climb indeed. At first, the going was rough for the young catcher, who hit a combined .221 through his first three years in the minor leagues. But like most talented players, Alomar put in the work and by 1987 he blossomed into a coveted prospect in the Padres chain. It became a family affair of sorts, as Roberto joined his older brother on multiple minor-league squads. Sandy Sr. joined San Diego manager Steve Boros' coaching staff in 1986.

In 1988 Alomar was named co-Minor League Player of the Year by *The Sporting News* (with Gary Sheffield of Denver). Alomar, who was the catcher for the Las Vegas Stars of the Pacific Coast League, batted .297 and had career highs in home runs (16) and RBIs (71). "I didn't expect to hit like that," said Alomar. "As the season started, I struggled a little bit, but then I started swinging harder and pulling the ball more and hitting more home runs."[10]

It was reported that 22 of the other 25 major-league clubs were interested in acquiring Alomar. The Padres already had their catcher of the future in Benito Santiago. The time looked right to possibly trade their star prospect and get plenty in return. While Santiago was the National League Rookie

of the Year in 1987, Roberto was promoted to the Padres in 1988 and became their starting second baseman. Sandy was frustrated, feeling there was nothing more he could do on the minor-league level. Rumors persisted that he would be traded, or that Santiago might be moved. One rumor had Alomar headed to Atlanta for All-Star Dale Murphy. "Every organization in the league would love to have a Sandy Alomar," said Atlanta general manager Bobby Cox.[11]

But no deal was ever made and Alomar returned to Las Vegas in 1989. He started the season poorly, batting .242 up to June 5, and then he became a man possessed, batting .351 the rest of the way. For the season, Alomar batted .306, with 13 home runs and 101 RBIs. He showed value behind the plate as well, fielding his position at a .984 clip, and throwing out 34 percent of would-be basestealers (25 of 74). He was once again honored by *The Sporting News* and *Baseball America* as the Minor League Player of the

Year. "It means a lot to me," said Alomar of the award. "The way I felt, I was so frustrated. I figured there was no way I'd win it again."[12]

When the Cleveland Indians front office offered slugging outfielder Joe Carter a multiyear deal at the end of the 1989 season, Carter said, "No thanks." He could be a free agent at the end of the 1990 season, and was looking forward to leaving Cleveland, and getting a fresh start—not to mention snagging a boatload of cash. Alomar, who was getting frustrated with his situation in San Diego, was just hoping for a chance to play in the big leagues. After all, he had accomplished all he could in the minors, and it really did not matter to him whose uniform he was wearing. On December 6, 1989, at the annual winter meetings, Cleveland GM Hank Peters and San Diego GM Jack McKeon hammered out a deal that sent Carter to the Padres and Alomar, infielder Carlos Baerga, and outfielder Chris James to Cleveland.

Alomar was penciled in as the starting catcher as soon as the ink was dry on the trade. He did not disappoint. Cleveland manager John McNamara praised his young backstop in all facets of his game. "To me, he's very, very impressive at blocking balls," said McNamara. "He does it even when there's no need, when nobody is on base. Sandy's been taught well. He's absorbed the teaching, put it to good use.

"Sandy is hitting for a better average than I expected at this stage of his career. He's adjusted very well to major-league pitching. I never had any doubt about his catching, but you just never know about his hitting."[13]

McNamara was not the only person to notice the outstanding play of his prized rookie. All of baseball took notice when Alomar was voted the starting catcher for the American League in the All-Star Game. He was the first rookie catcher ever to start in an All-Star Game. The game would be extra-special, as Roberto, then with San Diego, was also named an All-Star and Sandy Sr. would also join his sons as a coach for the NL at Wrigley Field for the midsummer classic.

Sandy's season was capped off with his being the unanimous choice for the AL Rookie of the Year.

"This award means more to me than the All-Star Game," said Alomar. "You have a lot of chances to be in the All-Star Game, but you've only got one chance to win this award. I was supposed to be Rookie of the Year, and that made it tough. I was traded for Joe Carter, and that made it tough. But the manager and the rest of the guys on the team really helped me."[14] Alomar was the fourth Indian to win the award. He was also awarded a Gold Glove for excellence in fielding his position. He was the first Indian to be so recognized since Rick Manning in 1976.

Alomar was instantly a fan favorite among Indians fans. However, the injuries began to pile up beginning in 1991, his second season. Though Alomar was selected to start the All-Star Game in both 1991 and 1992, he was dealing with myriad setbacks that included back surgery, injuries to his right rotator cuff, his right hip flexor, his right knee (two, caused by sliding), and the webbing between the fingers on his right hand (also twice). The 132 games Alomar played in his rookie year were the most of his career.

The Indians moved across downtown to their new ballpark, Jacobs Field, for the 1994 season. Alomar, despite missing time on the disabled list with the torn webbing on his right hand, was putting together a wonderful season, batting .288 with 14 home runs and 43 RBIs, when the players' strike on August 11 led to the remainder of the season being canceled.

Perhaps because Alomar suffered so many injuries, Cleveland signed Tony Peña before the 1994 season. For the next three seasons, the veteran provided solid leadership and was a reliable substitute for Alomar. It was a great free-agent signing for the Indians, as Alomar was recuperating from knee surgery and did not return to the active roster until June 29, 1995. Still, he batted .300 in 54 starts at catcher that season. The Indians, who sported one of the most potent lineups in baseball, moved Alomar to the bottom of their lineup. "I think Sandy can still hit 10 to 15 homers this year," said manager Mike Hargrove. "He has that kind of power. The thing that is really impressive is the way he's accepted hitting ninth. The number 9 hitter is usually the weakest hitter in the lineup, but that's not the case with this team."[15]

The Indians returned to the postseason for the first time in 41 years, winning their division by 30 games. They marched through the American League playoffs before losing to Atlanta in the World Series.

The Indians won the AL Central from 1995 to 1999. In 1997 they advanced to the World Series again, only to lose to Florida in seven games. Alomar's power surge in 1997 continued in the postseason, as he hit two home runs in the ALDS, one in the ALCS, and two in the World Series.

In 1999 Alomar was reunited with brother Roberto, who signed a free-agent contract with Cleveland. Together with Omar Vizquel, they formed one of the better middle-infield defenses in the big leagues. But Sandy missed most of the season after surgery on his left knee (he started 35 games), and in 2000 he split time with Einar Diaz at catcher. That season he batted .289 and drove in 42 runs.

But the end of an era was near as Alomar and the Indians were unable to negotiate a contract after the 2000 season. Alomar, ever the classy player, took the "life goes on" route and signed with the Chicago White Sox. He split time with Mark Johnson at catcher.

But the White Sox were just as interested in Alomar's ability to teach their young receivers and work with their green pitching staff. He was traded to Colorado in 2002, but returned to the South Side for the 2003 and 2004 seasons. "I got kind of teary-eyed when he got traded," said pitcher Mark Buerhle. "I'm still learning (from him). I'm out there thinking, 'I'm going to throw this pitch,' and he puts something else down. I'm not going to shake him off because he's been around the league a long time."[16]

The White Sox made it clear that they wanted Alomar to work with Miguel Olivo, a catching prospect for whom the front office had high hopes. In 2003 Sandy was reunited again with Roberto, who by this time in his career was serving as a utility player for Chicago.

Alomar spent the remaining years as a backup catcher with Texas (2005), the Los Angeles Dodgers and the White Sox (2006), and the New York Mets (2007). He retired with a .273 batting average in a 20-year career. He hit 112 home runs and 249 doubles, and drove in 588 runs. He threw out just over 30 percent of baserunners, and fielded at a .991 clip at catcher for his career.

Alomar stayed with the Mets as a catching instructor in 2008 and 2009. Manny Acta was hired to replace Eric Wedge as Cleveland's manager in 2010. Acta offered Alomar a job as his first-base coach. "I jumped at it," said Alomar. "For me, it was coming home. No place in baseball means as much to me as Cleveland."[17]

Acta was fired near the end of the 2012 season. Alomar was named interim manager, and looked to be the favorite until Terry Francona's name was thrown into the mix of candidates. "I knew they'd hire him if he wanted the job," said Alomar. "I don't blame them. I understand. He's won two World Series. He's a heck of a guy."[18]

As of 2016, Alomar was Francona's first-base coach. Francona, who played for the Indians in 1988, was a teammate of Alomar's in winter ball with Ponce in the Puerto Rico League. When the Indians acquired Alomar in 1989, Francona gushed at the young man's ability. "He's the best catcher I've ever played with," said Francona. "He's better than Gary Carter when Carter was good. Sandy might not drive in 100 runs like Carter did in his prime, but overall he's a better ballplayer. He's the best defensive catcher I've ever seen. His arm is almost incredible."[19]

When Francona insisted that Sandy Alomar be a part of his staff, he knew exactly what he was getting. Even way back when.

## NOTES

1. Bill Livingston, "Sweet Sandy! AL Triumphs on Alomar Blast," *Cleveland Plain Dealer*, July 9, 1997: 1A.
2. Mel Antonen, "Sandy Alomar's Streak Hits 30," *USA Today*, July 7, 1997: 1C.
3. Paul Hoynes, "Sandy Steals the Show; Alomar's Home Run Lifts AL," *Cleveland Plain Dealer*, July 9, 1997: 1D.
4. Ibid.
5. Ibid.
6. "Sweet Sandy."
7. Chuck Johnson, "Alomar Sons Deepen Roots in Baseball," *USA Today*, July 13, 1990: 2C.

8 Ibid.

9 Ibid.

10 "Big League Awards in the Minors," *The Sporting News*, December 5, 1988: 46.

11 Barry Bloom, "Alomar Hopes That His 'First' Won't Last," *The Sporting News*, December 4, 1989: 52.

12 Ibid.

13 Sheldon Ocker, "Alomar More Than Lives Up to Hype," *The Sporting News*, July 2, 1990: 12.

14 Paul Hoynes, "It's Unanimous! Indians Catcher Alomar Is Rookie of the Year," *Cleveland Plain Dealer*, November 8, 1990: 1F.

15 Paul Hoynes, "Deep Thunder Alomar Homers Twice at Bottom of Order," *Cleveland Plain Dealer*, July 21, 1995: 1D.

16 Nancy Armour (Associated Press), "Sandy Ready to Teach," *Elyria* (Ohio) *Chronicle-Telegram*, March 3, 2003: C4.

17 Terry Pluto, "Playing, Coaching for Tribe 'Paradise,'" *Cleveland Plain Dealer*, April 3, 2013: C3.

18 Ibid.

19 "Alomar Draws Praise From Former Mate," *The Sporting News*, March 19, 1990: 30.

# LUIS ARROYO

## By Rory Costello

**L**UIS ARROYO WAS A CHUNKY little Puerto Rican southpaw whose out pitch was the screwball. He spent just four full seasons in the majors, plus parts of four others, from 1955 through 1963. He enjoyed modest success overall as a big-leaguer, but he had one outstanding season. That was 1961, when he helped the New York Yankees win their 19th World Series title by posting a 15-5 record out of the bullpen with 29 saves.[1]

Arroyo also spent 19 seasons in the Puerto Rican Winter League (PRWL) from 1946-47 to 1964-65. As of 2017, he ranked third in league's history in wins (110), innings pitched, and games pitched.[2]

Luis Enrique Arroyo Lugo was born in Peñuelas, Puerto Rico on February 18, 1927. Over the years, various stories hinted at an earlier birthdate, but census records support 1927. His parents were Felipe Arroyo González, a laborer on a sugarcane plantation, and Modesta Lugo de Arrazo. Luis was the third of five children in the family. Before him were sister Felícita and brother Ramón; after him came two more brothers, Miguel and Américo.

"Tite" (as Arroyo was known in his homeland) is a common Spanish nickname for Enrique. Another of Arroyo's nicknames at home was *El Zurdo de Tallaboa*, or The Tallaboa Lefty. That was a reference to the section of Peñuelas where his family lived. Starting in 1944, Arroyo pitched in Double A (as Puerto Rico's top local amateur level was known) for the Tallaboa Athletics.[3] His brother Ramón was his catcher.[4] Arroyo led the league in ERA in 1946 and earned a spot on the Puerto Rican roster at the Central American Games in Barranquilla, Colombia.[5]

Peñuelas is on the southern coast of Puerto Rico, just a little bit west of one of the island's leading cities, Ponce. When Arroyo turned pro in the winter of 1946-47, it was with the Ponce Leones. Because his family needed the money, he left high school in 1947 for a bonus of $500 — reportedly only the second bonus given to a player in the PRWL.[6]

The team Arroyo joined became league champions for the fifth time in six winters. The manager was George Scales, a tough, smart Negro Leaguer. The staff included one of the league's most successful pitchers, Tomás "Planchardón" Quiñones. A fellow rookie on the mound was José "Pantalones" Santiago (no relation to another future major-leaguer, José "Palillo" Santiago). Arroyo lost in both of his appearances that season. He also went just 1-4 in the winter of 1947-48, though his ERA improved from 4.19 to 2.46 (he pitched 44 innings in 10 games).

Arroyo first played in the U.S. minors in 1948. In 1955, after the pitcher had broken into the majors with the St. Louis Cardinals, St. Louis sportswriter Bob Broeg described how it came about. "In the spring of 1948 Ponce financed a trip to George Stirnweiss' Baseball School in Florida and there he was spotted by President Bob Doty of the Greenville (S.C.) club of the Class D Coastal Plain League. In mid-season, Doty transferred to Greensboro, N.C. of the Carolina League and took Arroyo with him."[7] Arroyo posted a 14-16 record overall, with a 3.90 ERA in 249 innings. The subsequent winter in Ponce was fairly similar (2-2, 3.66 in 15 games).

In 1949, however, the 22-year-old's performance took a big step up. He remained with Greensboro, going 21-10 with a 3.67 ERA (the Carolina League had gone from Class C to Class B). Arroyo also got a new nickname: Yo-Yo. As Bob Broeg wrote, "It seems that it was as close as the drawling Carolinians could get to pronouncing his last name."[8] The highlight of his season was a no-hitter against Burlington on July 25.[9]

That December, the Cardinals selected Arroyo in the minor league draft. He then went on to record the first of his six seasons with double-digit wins in the PRWL. He was 11-5 with a sparkling 1.82

ERA for the Leones. The league champion Caguas Criollos added him to their roster as a reinforcement for the 1950 Caribbean Series, held at old Sixto Escobar Stadium in San Juan. Although Carta Vieja of Panama was the upset winner of the tournament, Arroyo got two of Puerto Rico's four victories. On February 23, he beat Negro Leaguer Terris McDuffie (representing Venezuela) in an exciting duel. Caguas won 2-1, as pinch-hitter Wilmer Fields—called in from the coaching lines—hit a two-run homer in the bottom of the ninth.[10] Just three days later, Arroyo beat McDuffie again, 3-2.

The Cardinals moved Arroyo all the way up to Triple A for 1950, but he pitched mainly out of the bullpen. In 33 games (eight starts) for Columbus (Ohio) of the American Association, he was 4-4, 4.11. During the winter of 1950-51, though, he set a personal high in Puerto Rico with 13 wins. He lost eight and his ERA remained sharp at 2.48. He was runner-up in the All-Star voting among Puerto Rican fans, who gave the most ballots to scrappy American catcher Clint Courtney.[11]

The summer of 1951 was lackluster for Arroyo: 3-2, 5.52 in 24 games split between Columbus and Rochester, another Triple-A club in the St. Louis chain. His Puerto Rican season was good, but not great (10-10, 3.09). He got into another Caribbean Series, though, this time reinforcing the San Juan Senadores in Panama City.

Arroyo did not play in the U.S. in either 1952 or 1953. In the spring of 1952, he developed a sore arm. According to another 1955 feature in *The Sporting News*, "after a succession of rainouts, and fearing that his pitching staff would go stale, [Columbus manager Harry] Walker arranged to use a high school gym where his battery men could warm up. Arroyo bore down for about 20 minutes one afternoon, then took a hot shower and, without putting on a jacket, walked out into the cool mist and rain. Next day, he found that he couldn't raise his arm."[12]

He was not entirely idle during those two years, though—he played in the Dominican Republic. Professional baseball had resumed there in 1951, after a hiatus of 14 years, but the new Dominican League's first four seasons took place in the summer before it switched to the winter. In two seasons with the Escogido Leones, Arroyo was 14-14, with ERAs of 1.61 and 2.84.

Meanwhile, he remained active at home. The 1952-53 winter was one of Arroyo's worst (4-8, 4.77), but he rebounded to 7-7, 2.52 in 1953-54. He later spun a tall tale for the benefit of a New York sportswriter that he had visited an old man in the mountains of Puerto Rico who practiced natural medicine, and that a hot poultice made of leaves from a certain tree brought his shoulder back to life.[13] "I threw the bull good," Arroyo said with a smile in 1962 as he rolled a fat perfecto cigar between his fingers.[14]

When Arroyo returned to the U.S. in 1954, he did a big favor for Pedrín Zorrilla, owner of the Santurce Cangrejeros. As recounted in Thomas Van Hyning's book *The Puerto Rican Winter League*, the Crabbers had a 19-year-old outfielder named Roberto Clemente, who was then under contract with the Brooklyn Dodgers. "At Zorrilla's request, Arroyo accompanied Clemente on the latter's first stateside

*L to R: Arroyo with Whitey Ford.*

spring training trip. According to Arroyo, he flew with Clemente to Miami, purchased two bus tickets for the trip to the Dodgers' camp and checked Roberto into a hotel before leaving the next morning for the St. Louis training camp in Daytona. Arroyo then sent the bill to Pedrín Zorrilla."[15] A little over a year later, by which time Clemente had become a Pittsburgh Pirate, Arroyo correctly predicted, "He's going to help the Pirates win some games."[16]

Meanwhile, perhaps because he'd been away from the U.S. for so long, the Cardinals assigned Arroyo only to Class A. With Columbus (Georgia) of the South Atlantic League, he went 8-6, 2.49. He earned promotion to the Double-A Texas League, going 8-3, 2.35 for Houston. Again the peak moment of his season was a no-hitter; this one came on August 11 in Dallas. The Associated Press account of this game was notable because it mentioned that Arroyo featured a screwball, which he had learned from Rubén Gómez. Later accounts when Arroyo was with the Yankees made it sound like he came up with the screwball at that point, but the trail of evidence shows that it had long been part of his repertoire.

The winter of 1954-55 was Arroyo's last of nine with Ponce. It was also his nadir at home: 3-11, 4.95. He had a poor spring too, but nonetheless, he made the big club with St. Louis in the spring of 1955. The Cardinals wanted another lefty on their staff besides Harvey Haddix and Paul LaPalme.[17]

Arroyo was a winner in his major-league debut, a start on April 20 at Cincinnati's old Crosley Field. Johnny Temple greeted him with a leadoff single, then Arroyo threw a wild pitch, walked Wally Post, and ran a 3-0 count on Gus Bell. But after coach Dixie Walker paid a visit to the mound and settled him down, Arroyo got out of the inning unscathed. He walked six and allowed five hits — but no runs — in 7 2/3 innings, and Herb Moford got the last four outs. "I'm going on 29 and have a big family," said Arroyo. "I was worried about failing all spring. All of sudden, Dixie make me realize that no use worrying. I either do or I don't."[18]

Arroyo won his first six decisions, and his record stood at 10-3, 2.44 at the All-Star break. NL manager Leo Durocher named Tite to his pitching staff; that year Arroyo and Vic Power became the first Puerto Ricans to make it to the All-Star Game. Arroyo did not appear in the Midsummer Classic, though — the only player on Durocher's roster who got no action.[19] Fifty years later, he recalled, "The game went to extra innings and I was ordered to warm up [in the bottom of the 12th], but somebody [Stan Musial] hit a homer and the game was over. I was left longing to pitch."[20]

Arroyo's second half was also a letdown; he went just 1-5 the rest of the way, and by season's end, his ERA was 4.19. Even when he was going well, he was prone to the long ball; he gave up 22 in 159 innings.

For the 1955-56 winter ball season, Arroyo joined San Juan. He bounced back to 9-5, 3.64 with the Senadores. Spring training 1956 brought word of a "new" addition to his arsenal. Arroyo was talking about the screwball, which Al Hollingsworth — a Cardinals scout and San Juan's manager — had helped him develop in Puerto Rico. Arroyo expressed a lot of confidence in the pitch.[21] He was ineffective in spring training, though, so the Cardinals sent him down to Triple-A Omaha.

After five appearances there, Arroyo was traded to Pittsburgh in early May for another pitcher, veteran righty Max Surkont. He was "acquired to add balance to a Pirate mound staff top-heavy with righthanders."[22] During the rest of 1956, Arroyo was up and down between Pittsburgh (3-3, 4.71 in 18 games) and Hollywood of the Pacific Coast League (7-5, 2.81 in 16 games). One oddity came on August 10, when he was charged with a loss for Pittsburgh — and he wasn't even on the roster. The game had actually begun on July 1, but the Sunday afternoon contest had been suspended after eight innings because of Pennsylvania curfew laws. A few days later, Pittsburgh optioned Arroyo to Hollywood, and he didn't return until September, over a month after the suspended game had been completed.

Arroyo had a good winter in 1956-57 with San Juan (11-9, 3.20). His manager was Ralph Houk, who was later his skipper with the 1961 Yankees. He made a very strong impression on Houk, as discussed in *Puerto Rico's Winter League*. Houk said after the 1961 big-league season, "That man showed me five years ago he could pitch... he wants to pitch and that's why he's having some success in the big leagues."[23]

Arroyo then spent all of the '57 season with the Pirates. He worked often—54 games, including 10 starts—but the results were forgettable (3-11, 4.68). Even one of the highlights, a win at Wrigley Field on May 14, showed what kind of a year it was. After Ron Kline got knocked out in the fourth inning, Arroyo came on to pitch five innings in long relief, striking out nine. But he gave up two-run homers in both the eighth and ninth innings, so Elroy Face had to get the last out.

At home in 1957-58, Arroyo again performed respectably for San Juan (8-8, 2.64), but Pittsburgh kept him at Triple A for all of 1958. By then, Columbus, Ohio was affiliated with the Pirates—and Arroyo was almost strictly a reliever in the U.S. He started only four more games in his Stateside career. In 61 games for Columbus, he went 10-3, though his ERA was on the high side at 4.01.

In December 1958, the Pirates traded Arroyo to the Cincinnati Redlegs for a fellow Puerto Rican, Nino Escalera. At the time, he was in the middle of another typical workmanlike winter for San Juan (9-6, 3.17). After the Puerto Rican season ended, he served as a playoff reinforcement for Águilas Cibaeñas in the Dominican League.

In those years, Cincinnati's top farm club was the Havana Sugar Kings. Arroyo found the warm Spanish-speaking atmosphere conducive, and he pitched very well. The Reds called him up for about a month, and he got into 10 games from early June through early July (1-0, 3.95). Then Fred Hutchinson replaced Mayo Smith as manager in Cincinnati. Arroyo later said, "[Hutchinson] let me go without even a look."[24]

He picked up where he left off with Havana. Though his record was 8-9 for the year with the Sugar Kings, he posted a minuscule 1.15 ERA in 117 innings across 41 games. He also was part of the team's exciting run through the minor-league playoffs, capped with a victory in the Little World Series, played mostly in Havana because of a cold snap in Minneapolis.

Arroyo had one of his best winters at home in 1959-60: 11-4, 2.36. He returned to Havana to begin the 1960 season, but the club was forced to relocate to Jersey City, New Jersey that July. The veteran lefty continued to pitch well (9-7, 2.27 in 39 games)—and scouts for the Yankees were watching. On July 20, 1960, New York purchased Arroyo's contract from Jersey City. He thus became the first Puerto Rican to play for the Yankees in the majors.[25]

As a Newspaper Enterprise Association feature put it that August, "the Yankees...were hurting for pitching, especially in relief since Ryne Duren lost control of his hard one...Yankee pitching had struck rock bottom when Bill Skiff, chief of scouts, watched the Bronx club's Richmond branch play across the river. Skiff had his eye on Arroyo for two years, or since the Reds sent him to the International League."[26]

Arroyo described how greater command of his best pitch got him back to the top level. "I grip the ball with the first two fingers between the seams and twist the wrist so it rotates and breaks away from a right-hand and into a left-hand batter. At first I had trouble getting a piece of the plate with the screwball, but now I get it over any time I want to."[27]

Right around the same time, Arroyo also told the Associated Press about a variant of the pitch—"I call it a back-up scroogie," he said. "That's a screwball that breaks the other way, which is the way an ordinary curve breaks. I keep it away from right-handed batters and inside to left-handed batters." Manager Casey Stengel, in a typical phrase, called it "a whoosh-whish pitch."[28]

That feature opened by saying, "He's fat. He's old. He's little. But Luis Arroyo is a big man in the New York Yankee scheme of things when he answers Stengel's call for a relief pitcher."[29] Arroyo worked often and well for the Yankees during the rest of the 1960 season. He went 5-1, 2.88 with seven saves in 29 games.

In the fall of 1960, Arroyo also appeared for the first time in the U.S. postseason. He pitched two-thirds of an inning in Game Five of the World Series against one of his old clubs, Pittsburgh. The Pirates knocked Art Ditmar out of the box in the second inning that day, and though Arroyo prevented any further scoring in the second, he allowed a run in the third inning before Stengel removed him for Bill Stafford. Bob Turley, who started Game Seven, thought that Casey should have summoned Arroyo to face Hal Smith in the pivotal eighth inning.[30] Instead, Jim Coates stayed in and Smith hit a three-run homer.

Arroyo had his last full season at home with San Juan in 1960-61, and it was one of his best: 10-2, 1.64 in 71 1/3 innings across 29 games. He was named league MVP. San Juan won the championship and went on to represent Puerto Rico in the Inter-American Series in Caracas. (The Caribbean Series went on hiatus after 1960 because Cuba withdrew.) Arroyo reported late to spring training for a most unusual reason — Puerto Rico imposed a 10-day quarantine after a bubonic plague threat in the Venezuelan capital.

About a month into camp, Jesse Gonder (then a rookie catcher for the Yankees) lined a ball off Arroyo's pitching wrist. The result was a fractured ulna.[31] It kept Arroyo out of game action for a little over a month; the enforced rest was something he later viewed as a blessing in disguise. As the 1961 season developed, Arroyo became the main man in the Yankees' bullpen, which had been a big question mark.[32] He appeared in 65 games — then a club record — finishing 54 games and saving 29, which led the American League. He made the All-Star team for a second time (though again he did not pitch in the game) and was named AL Fireman of the Year.

Arroyo was very good at getting batters to hit ground balls — he gave up just five homers in 119 innings in 1961. Catcher Yogi Berra said, "The screwball works two ways for Luis. For one thing, it's a difficult pitch to hit. And, for another, the hitter seems to be always looking for it, enabling Luis to fool 'em with his fast one or his other curve." Arroyo concurred. "I keep the hitters guessing and I can usually get my

*Arroyo as manager of San Juan.*

stuff over the plate. There's not much more to pitching than that."[33]

That August, he added more about his belief that he had become a true pitcher, not just a thrower. He said, "I believe I have finally become a big-leaguer. . .Now I feel I belong. A fellow is not a big leaguer just because he is in the big leagues. He must make contributions and I think I have made these contributions."[34]

Whitey Ford especially appreciated Arroyo's support. A *Sports Illustrated* article that July quoted the staff ace: "If I win 25, I'm going to hold out for $100,000 and split it with Luis." Arroyo said he'd settle for 60:40.[35] When Ford got his 20th victory of the season — for the first time in his superb career — he merrily proclaimed in the clubhouse, "Beer for everybody on me. . . and make it two for my boy, Luis."[36] That was the tenth of 13 saves Arroyo picked up for Ford, who indeed went on to win 25 that season. In addition to inviting Arroyo to finish his 1961 Cy Young Award acceptance speech, Whitey kept his word, giving the closer a financial boost. Many years later, Arroyo recalled, "I must have made six trips [to the States] to do commercials with Whitey and I made around $30,000."[37]

The Yankees won the 1961 World Series in five games over the Cincinnati Reds. Arroyo finished up in Game Two, which was Cincinnati's only victory. He was the winning pitcher in Game Three, throwing scoreless innings in the eighth and ninth while New York came back behind solo homers from Johnny Blanchard (an old batterymate in San Juan) and Roger Maris.

After the Series concluded, as Arroyo discussed in *Puerto Rico's Winter League*, Yankees general manager Roy Hamey gave the pitcher $10,000 not to play winter ball—double what Arroyo indicated he would earn with San Juan. Along with his World Series share, a bonus that was reported at $5,000,[38] and the pay from the ads with Whitey Ford, Tite made more than he ever had in his life. Yet in retrospect, he thought it was a mistake.

"I'm almost 35 at the time, had a few drinks, ate a little too much. . .[though I did] do some throwing, running. Before you know it, I'm overweight, and I know I made a mistake by not playing that winter. I asked them [New York] to let me pitch 40 innings. I tell you that decision—I have myself to blame too—cost me my ten years in the big leagues. I only got six years and two months. But I can't say that Hamey was trying to hurt me, maybe protect me. I followed a routine for 14 years and never had a sore arm."[39] (This last sentence is at odds with accounts of what happened in 1952-53.)

Arroyo actually did wind up getting into five games for San Juan, pitching 11 innings. He also appeared in the Inter-American Series again with one of two Puerto Rican entries, Mayagüez. But after his superb performance in 1961—which earned him a salary raise from $8,500 to $20,000—he fell off in 1962. He was able to pitch just 33 2/3 innings in 27 games for the Yankees. He was 1-3, 4.81 with seven saves. He was out of action with a strained elbow from late April. According to Yankee historian Alan Blumkin, Arroyo sustained this injury at Detroit's Tiger Stadium on April 13. That game was played in a windy and wet 36 degrees.[40]

Arroyo finally went on the 30-day disabled list on May 21. He returned in late June but barely pitched in September. The Yankees kept him on the World Series roster, and gave him a full winners' share—but the closest he got to entering a game was when he warmed up in the ninth inning of Game Six with New York trailing, 5-2.[41]

In spring training 1963, Arroyo issued remarks consistent with his recollection for *Puerto Rico's Winter League*. He was a firm believer that winter ball made him strong and ready for the big-league season. Of the previous year, he said, "I rest in the winter and then my arm has no life in it. I could tell from the start. Those bone chips were nothing. I've been pitching with them for ten years. . I went to the Yankees and asked for their permission to pitch winter ball again. I explained my feelings to them. They agreed it was worth a try."[42]

Arroyo was effective in limited duty for San Juan in 1962-63 (0-1, 2.87 in 28 1/3 innings pitched). He got into only six games for the Yankees in April and May 1963, though, and was sent down to Triple-A Richmond in June. New York recalled Al Downing, who pitched very well in the majors for the remainder of the season. Arroyo pitched in 35 games for Richmond, and his marks (2-2, 4.60) did not warrant a recall. The Yankees announced the veteran's retirement on September 27, 1963, with one game still to go in the regular season. Arroyo's lifetime record in the majors was 40-32 with a 3.93 ERA and 45 saves in 244 games.

As part of the announcement, the Yankees made Arroyo a scout, assigning him to cover Puerto Rico and the Caribbean. His contract took effect in February 1964.[43] Tite played on in the winter, though—he got into 17 games with San Juan in 1963-64. The Senadores—starring Roberto Clemente—won the league championship. After that, Arroyo also pitched again in the Inter-American Series, this time for the Nicaraguan club Cinco Estrellas.[44]

Arroyo then had bone chips removed from his elbow in March 1964, and he went about his scouting duties. But as he told Frank Eck of the Associated Press later that year, he had a comeback in mind. In

September he threw pain-free with some high-school kids in Ponce, and he hoped to be in good enough shape to try to go to spring training and join Pedro Ramos in the Yankees' bullpen.[45]

Arroyo issued a word of caution, though—despite saying he'd still be using his bread and butter pitch. "When you throw the screwball you must throw the ball with an unnatural motion. It's no good for youngsters to use the screwball. It puts too much of a strain on the arm."[46]

Arroyo's last mound action was three games for San Juan in the winter of 1964-65 (he also served the club as a coach). His final totals in the PRWL were 110-93 with a 3.04 ERA in 364 games. In 1722 1/3 innings, he struck out 942 batters.

Nothing further came of the comeback; in early 1965, Arroyo was part of a crew of instructors that went to Mexico in a three-week clinic sponsored by Major League Baseball. In addition to his scouting duties for the Yankees, he also became a manager in Puerto Rico. He was Ponce's skipper for three straight winters starting in 1965-66. The Leones featured players from the Yankees (Roy White and Horace Clarke) and the Cardinals (Steve Carlton and Nelson Briles). According to *Puerto Rico's Winter League*, the St. Louis front office was leery of sending Carlton to winter ball for fear of injury, but Arroyo convinced them. It was an important step in the prize prospect's development.[47]

Arroyo led Caguas for two seasons (1968-69 and 1969-70)—missing out on the back-to-back championships that Ponce won. After that, he rejoined Ponce as a coach in 1970-71. Arroyo also served as general manager for the Leones during at least two seasons, in 1975-76 and again in 1993-94, after Pantalones Santiago became owner of the club.

In addition, Arroyo was a manager during three summers in Mexico. In 1967 and 1968, he was with Reynosa. In 1978, he started the season with Poza Rica, but the team went through three managers that year (which is not uncommon in the Mexican League).

Over the years, Arroyo was willing to teach other pitchers about the screwball. One example was another lefty reliever named Terry Enyart, who got into two games in the majors with the Montreal Expos in 1974. Enyart had relied on the scroogie previously but got Arroyo's advice while in Triple-A in 1977. Arroyo also taught southpaw Chuck Cary the screwball when Cary was pitching in Puerto Rico in the winter of 1988-89. It helped Cary make it back to the majors with the Yankees from 1989 through 1991.

Plus, Arroyo was responsible for the comeback of another lefty screwballer, Guillermo Hernández, in 1995. Hernández had been out of the majors since 1989 and had not pitched in the minors since 1991. Arroyo contacted the 40-year-old reliever, who was pitching coach for a semi-pro team in Puerto Rico. Hernández got into 22 games for the Yankees' Triple-A team, Columbus (though it did not go well).[48]

Arroyo was still scouting for the Yankees at that time, but he retired shortly thereafter. By one local account, he brought some notable Puerto Rican talent to New York.[49] Before the amateur draft extended to U.S. territories in 1989, the Yankees signed major-leaguers such as Otto Vélez (1969) and Edwin Rodríguez (1980). They found a real plum in Bernie Williams (1985), and after the draft took effect, they selected another major star, Jorge Posada, and Ricky Ledée in 1990. Based on other published sources, however, SABR's Scouts Committee gives direct credit to Arroyo only for Ledée.[50]

In July 2010, Arroyo returned to New York to take part in the Old-Timers' weekend festivities. He was taken ill during the Friday night cruise that was part of the fun, and it turned out to be a mild heart attack. He went to the hospital and so missed the Old-Timers' Game. He made a full recovery, however, and returned home to Peñuelas, where the municipal stadium is named for him. He made it back to Yankee Stadium for the 2012 edition of the Old-Timers' Game.

In his mid-eighties, Arroyo remained a keen observer of the baseball scene. In January 2012, shortly after Jorge Posada announced his retirement, Arroyo commented on the diminished presence of Puerto Rican talent. "The Yankees haven't invested not because they don't have the money, but because there isn't good talent in Puerto Rico. Good ballplayers aren't coming out now…there isn't the material, that's how I see it. It's always been said that the Yankees don't like Latino ballplayers. But it's not that way. The Yankees have always had good Latino prospects."[51]

According to his obituary in the *New York Times*, Arroyo was married at least twice.[52] As of 1960, he and his wife, Judith (who was a schoolteacher) had five children ranging in age from several weeks to 10 years. At least three of them were sons, but the names of only two were shown: Luis Jr. and Harold.[53] Another son was named Paicky and a daughter was named Milagros.[54]

Arroyo remained one of Puerto Rico's most celebrated and best-loved baseball players. He received various honors over the years.

- The Puerto Rican Baseball Hall of Fame inducted him in 1992, as part of its second class.
- In 2002, the mayor of Guaynabo, Puerto Rico announced that El Museo del Deporte de Puerto Rico (The Puerto Rican Sports Museum) would open in the San Juan suburb in 2003. The announcement came at the Caribbean Series in Caracas, and though Arroyo could not make it because of passport trouble, hundreds of people honored him at a ceremony.[55]
- The Puerto Rican Winter League dedicated its 2006-07 season to Arroyo.
- In January 2008, the Puerto Rican Sports Museum held the first Puerto Rican Yankees Festival. Arroyo called the honor one of the greatest he had received and talked about how the quality of the Yankees organization impressed him from the moment he joined.[56]
- More recently, another Latino Baseball Hall of Fame was established in the Dominican Republic. In 2012, Arroyo was one of eight inductees in the third class, joining Bernie Williams in representing Puerto Rico.

As late as 2013, Arroyo returned to Yankee Stadium for Old-Timers' Day. He died on January 13, 2016, aged 88, after being diagnosed with cancer the previous month.[57] His passing prompted many fond memories from Yankee teammates.[58] Luis "Tite" Arroyo was buried in Cementerio Municipal de Peñuelas, a day after many of his fellow Puerto Rican ballplayers joined his family in his hometown's Municipal Theatre to honor his memory.[59]

## SOURCES

In addition to the sources cited in the Notes, the author also consulted:

*Internet resources*

www.ancestry.com (1930 and 1940 census records)

Vázquez, Edwin. "Luis Tite Arroyo de Puerto Rico," 1-800-Béisbol website (http://www.1800beisbol.com/baseball/deportes/historia_del_beisbol/luis_tite_arroyo_de_puerto_rico)

www.paperofrecord.com (various small items from *The Sporting News*)

*Books*

Crescioni Benítez, José A. *El Béisbol Profesional Boricua* (San Juan, Puerto Rico: Aurora Comunicación Integral, Inc., 1997).

Antero Núñez, José. *Series del Caribe* (Caracas, Venezuela: Impresos Urbina, C.A., 1987).

## NOTES

1. Under the rule that applied in 1961, he was credited with 19 saves. Save figures mentioned in this story reflect retroactive recalculations.
2. Rubén Gómez and Juan Pizarro are the leaders in wins and innings pitched. Gómez and Julio Navarro are the leaders in games pitched.
3. Junior Lugo Marrero, "Luis 'Tite' Arroyo: Con sitial entre los grandes del diamante," *La Perla del Sur* (Ponce, Puerto Rico), unknown date (http://www.periodicolaperla.com/index.php?option=com_content&view=article&id=1874:con-un-sitial-entre-los-grandes-del-diamante&catid=92:portada-deportes&Itemid=318)
4. Bob Broeg, "Cardinals' Arroyo Still Giving the Bird to Prophet [Birdie] Tebbetts," *The Sporting News*, May 25, 1955: 9-10.
5. Lugo Marrero.
6. Broeg, "Cardinals' Arroyo Still Giving the Bird to Prophet Tebbetts"
7. Ibid.
8. Ibid.
9. "Arroyo Hurls Full-Length No-Hitter for Greensboro," *The Sporting News*, August 3, 1949: 38.
10. Santiago Llorens, "Panama Wins the Caribbean Pennant in Special Playoff," *The Sporting News*, March 8, 1950: 25.

## PUERTO RICO AND BASEBALL: 60 BIOGRAPHIES

11  Santiago Llorens, "Yankee Rookie Tops Star Poll in Puerto Rico," *The Sporting News*, January 3, 1951: 25.

12  Herb Heft, "April Flopper Luis Now Cards' Stopper," *The Sporting News*, June 29, 1955: 5.

13  Ibid.

14  Til Ferdenzi, "Round Man Arroyo Racks Up Goose Eggs," *The Sporting News*, April 25, 1962: 5.

15  Thomas Van Hyning, *Puerto Rico's Winter League* (Jefferson, North Carolina: McFarland & Company, 1995), 102.

16  Al Abrams, "Sidelights on Sports," *Pittsburgh Post-Gazette*, June 3, 1955: 20.

17  Heft,

18  Ibid.

19  Jack Hernon, "Roamin' Around," *Pittsburgh Post-Gazette*, July 25, 1955: 19.

20  Omar Marrero, "50 años de participación boricua," ESPN Deportes, July 12, 2005 (http://espndeportes.espn.go.com/story?id=344735)

21  "Luis Arroyo Ready to Use Screwball," Associated Press, March 8, 1956.

22  "Cardinals Trade Arroyo to Pirates for Surkont," Associated Press, May 8, 1956.

23  Van Hyning, 60-61.

24  "A Simple Twist of the Wrist Made Luis Arroyo a Yankee," Newspaper Enterprise Association, August 11, 1960.

25  It could have been Vic Power several years before, but the Yankees traded him to the Athletics (then still in Philadelphia) in December 1953. The alleged reasons included disapproval of Power's flashy approach and lifestyle.

26  "A Simple Twist of the Wrist Made Luis Arroyo a Yankee"

27  Ibid.

28  "Luis Arroyo: He's Fat, Old, Little but Key Man for Yanks," Associated Press, August 11, 1960.

29  Ibid.

30  Allen Barra, *Yogi Berra: Eternal Yankee* (New York, New York: W.W. Norton & Company, 2009), 274.

31  "Yankees May Lose Service of Reliefer Luis Arroyo," Associated Press, March 15, 1961,

32  For more detail, see William J. Ryczek, *The Yankees in the Early 1960s* (Jefferson, North Carolina: McFarland & Company, 2008), 69-70.

33  "Who's the Proudest All-Star? It's Luis Arroyo of New York," United Press International, July 29, 1961.

34  Joe Reichler, "Luis Arroyo Now Rates Himself a Big Leaguer," Associated Press, August 7, 1961.

35  Walter Bingham, "Whitey Throws for 30," *Sports Illustrated*, July 24, 1961.

36  Milton Richman, "Ford Gets 20th Victory with Some Help from Luis Arroyo," United Press International, August 11, 1961.

37  Van Hyning, 101.

38  "Luis Arroyo Gets Bonus from Yanks," Associated Press, October 12, 1961.

39  Van Hyning, 101. Arroyo had made the decision not to play winter ball during the summer (see also Reichler.),

40  E-mail from Alan Blumkin to Rory Costello, January 14, 2016. Eddie Jones, "Lary, Tigers Top Yankees, 5-3," *Toledo Blade*, April 14, 1963. The Tigers' starter, "Yankee Killer" Frank Lary, won that day. However, Blumkin believed the miserable weather may well have worsened the shoulder problems that derailed Lary's career. In addition, Lary tore a muscle in his knee while running the bases.

41  "Tasty Tidbits, *The Sporting News*, October 27, 1962: 26.

42  "Arroyo Traces Skid to Easy Winter Life," Associated Press, March 24, 1963.

43  "Yanks Retire Luis Arroyo," Associated Press, September 27, 1963.

44  Horacio Ruiz, "Estrellas Cops Latin Title Behind Top-Notch Hurling," *The Sporting News*, February 22, 1964: 27.

45  Frank Eck, "Arroyo Hopes to Be Pedro's Partner in Yank Bull Pen,:" Associated Press, December 5, 1964.

46  Ibid.

47  Van Hyning, 20.

48  Jack Curry, "Yanks Sign Ex-M.V.P. but He's 40," *New York Times*, March 7, 1995.

49  Carlos Rosa Rosa, "Distanciados Los Yankees," *El Nuevo Día* (San Juan, Puerto Rico), January 30, 2012.

50  Scouts of record: for Otto Vélez—José Seda, for Edwin Rodríguez—Jack Sanford and Carlos Pascual, for Bernie Williams—Roberto Rivera and Fred Ferreira, for Jorge Posada—Leon Wurth.

51  Rosa Rosa, "Distanciados Los Yankees"

52  Bruce Weber, "Luis Arroto, Baseball's Best Reliever in '61, Dies at 88," *New York Times*, January 14, 2016.

53  "A Simple Twist of the Wrist Made Luis Arroyo a Yankee"; Heft.

54  Weber.

55  "Former Yankee Luis Arroyo inducted into Latin Hall of Fame," Associated Press, February 6, 2002.

56  "Emotivo junte de Yankees Boricuas," *El Nuevo Día*, January 13, 2008.

57  "Two-time All-Star pitcher Luis Arroyo dies at 88," Associated Press, January 14, 2016.

58  Anthony McCarron, "Yankees remember Luis Arroyo as Whitey Ford's 'pickup guy'," *New York Daily News*, January 16, 2016.

59  Carlos Rosa Rosa, "Peñuelas le rinde honor a Tite Arroyo," *El Nuevo Día*, January 15, 2016.

# BENNY AYALA

## By Rory Costello

**B**ENIGNO AYALA LIVES UP TO HIS given name, which means "kind" or "friendly." Following a productive career as a role player, he has bestowed greater gifts on the baseball world, through his work with the Baseball Assistance Team (BAT). Quite a few of his fellow Puerto Rican pros have fallen on hard times since they left the game. "There are really sad stories," said Ayala in 2009. "And most of them are unknown, because ballplayers are proud. They don't like to ask."[1] Ayala played five full seasons in the majors and parts of five others from 1974 to 1985. He qualified for a good pension and does not have to worry about life's necessities—now he is a voice for those in need.

In his playing days, the outfielder wasn't known for his defense, but he was a pretty fair batting threat in platoon. In its glory years, the Baltimore organization understood the importance of "deep depth," as manager Earl Weaver called it in 1979. Pitcher Steve Stone detailed the concept in *Tales from the Orioles Dugout*.

"They were a team that pretty much understood that the spare parts of a baseball team determine whether you win or lose. It's going and getting ... [a] Benny Ayala. And then it's up to the manager after you get Benny Ayala to realize that ... when they put soft-tossing lefthanders in the game, Benny was good for two hits. Earl put him in a situation where he could be successful. So Hank Peters went and got him, and Earl used him correctly."[2]

Ayala came to the plate 951 times in his big-league career, and 86 percent of those appearances were against lefties. It's no surprise that 35 of his 38 regular-season homers came off southpaws—as did his crowning blow as a pro, his two-run shot off John Candelaria in Game Three of the 1979 World Series.

Benigno Ayala Félix was born on February 7, 1951, in Yauco, a town in southwestern Puerto Rico. He was the first of two sons born to Benigno Ayala and Lillian Félix (there was also a half-brother). The island has sent well over 200 men to the majors over the years, yet only two others have hailed from Yauco: Mario Ramírez (1980-85) and Mike Pérez (1990-1997). Benny himself did not start playing baseball until the age of 11, but in retrospect, he saw some benefits from it. In 2010, he said, "If you start late, you don't get bored. And when you grow, you have to go through a process of adjustment. I asked guys like Tom Seaver and Rusty Staub about it."

On January 28, 1971, the New York Mets signed Ayala as a free agent (the amateur draft did not include Puerto Rico until 1990). The scout was Nino Escalera, who covered Latin America for the Mets. "I was in my first year at Rio Piedras Junior College. Whitey Herzog came to Puerto Rico. He was with the Mets at the time. Many years later, Nino told me and Angel Cantres that Whitey said, 'Go as high as $125,000.' He didn't give us the money—he gave us $7,000! Nino's about 80 years old now, and you know what else he told me? 'Benny, out of all the guys I signed, you're the only one who has helped me.'"

Ayala's first pro team in the US was Pompano Beach in the Florida State League. He hit .279 with 8 homers and 34 RBIs in 63 games, which won him promotion to Visalia in the California League (high A). In the winter of 1971-72, he played in the Puerto Rican Winter League for the first time. "Nino Escalera was a coach for the San Juan Senadores, Roberto Clemente's team. Angel Cantres went to San Juan after he signed with the Mets, but I didn't. I said, I'll see what I can do in the US, then I'll see who's interested. I'll go to a club where I can develop. Arecibo was in the cellar. Cantres had more competition with San Juan."

Returning to Visalia in 1972, Ayala hit 19 homers, second on the club behind Ike Hampton's 21. He also had 66 runs batted in, one fewer than Greg Harts (who, like Hampton, appeared very briefly with the

Mets). Visalia is an agricultural town with a large Hispanic population, but there were plenty of times when Ayala didn't feel welcome. "We lived in a bad neighborhood called 'Sin City' but it was the only thing we could afford. People threw rocks at us. I remember waiting in a barbershop, and when my turn came, they said, 'We don't cut that kind of hair.' The team owners were good people, though. I remember they owned a chain of hot-dog stands."

Ayala continued to climb the ladder steadily. In 1973 he was with Memphis (Double A). Serving frequently as a designated hitter, he led the team in home runs (17) and was second in RBIs (68). That winter he led the Puerto Rican league in homers for the first time, as his 14 tied with Jerry Morales. Benny also tied Jay Johnstone for the league lead in RBIs with 46 and hit .340. To emphasize how strong that circuit was then, the four men who finished ahead of him in the batting race were George Hendrick, Chris Chambliss, Mickey Rivers, and José Cruz, Sr. Yet Ayala won the MVP award.

Ayala did well in spring training 1974, hitting homers off veterans like Woodie Fryman and Bob Gibson. He wasn't quite ready, though, and Cleon Jones did not take well to an experiment in center field. Near the end of camp the Mets sent Ayala down to their top affiliate, Tidewater. Here too he was the club leader in homers (11) and RBIs (40). The big club called him up in August after putting pitcher Jack Aker on the disabled list. He still has the bat he borrowed from Joe Nolan, his teammate with the Tides and later the Orioles.

With that bat, on August 27, Ayala made a memorable big-league debut at Shea Stadium. Batting sixth in the lineup, he stepped in against Houston's Tom Griffin (a righty!) with one out and nobody on in the second inning. He pulled a "high fosboll"—as he kept repeating on Ralph Kiner's postgame show, *Kiner's Korner*—down the line in left field. The ball stayed inside the foul pole, and Ayala became the 40th major leaguer to homer in his first big-league at-bat. He was the first to do so in the National League since Cuno Barragan in 1961 . . . which of course made him the first Met too (not to mention, the first Puerto Rican).

A contributor to the Ultimate Mets fan website provided some extra color. "We were sitting in the left field mezzanine at Shea among this group of 10 or 12 of Benny Ayala's cousins and extended family who were thrilled to see him in his first major-league game. When he homered in his first at-bat they went BERSERK, hugging and kissing everyone around, including me and my father of course. It was a great memory that I was able to recount with my dad that always drew a smile."

The rookie did not live with family, however, and although fellow Puerto Rican Félix Millán was present, he remembers that his most helpful teammates were John Milner and Cleon Jones. Manager Yogi Berra also did not stack up well against Earl Weaver in Benny's estimation. "He was always laughing, he didn't pay too much attention to the game."

Ayala did not see any big-league action in 1975. The Mets acquired Dave Kingman in February, which severely impaired his chances of making the big club. In fact, he played just 65 games for Tidewater, missing a big chunk of the early season after Rochester's Bob Galasso broke his hand with a pitch.

In the winter of 1975-76, Ayala led the Puerto Rican league in homers once again with 14 in 60 games. He finished in a four-way tie for second in RBIs with 39. Coming off this very strong effort, Benny made the Mets roster in spring training 1976. The team's new manager was Joe Frazier, his skipper at Visalia, Memphis, and Tidewater. Ayala was not in the lineup on Opening Day, but started the next two games. He would get just two more starts over the remainder of April and May, however, and he got only 3 hits in 26 at-bats (including a pinch-hit homer off Jack Billingham, his last off a righty in the majors). New York then called up Jack Heidemann and sent Ayala back to Tidewater, where he hit just .225 with 12 homers and 48 RBIs.

On March 30, 1977, New York traded Ayala to the St. Louis Cardinals in exchange for second baseman Doug Clarey, whose big-league career comprised nine games scattered across the '76 season. Ayala spent the bulk of 1977 with New Orleans in the American Association, where he had a good year (.298/18/73). The Cardinals called him up in September, but he got into just one game, singling in three at-bats.

The Cardinals had a new Triple-A affiliate in 1978, Springfield, but Ayala spent only part of the season there—he went to Columbus in the Pittsburgh organization on loan. As the *Pittsburgh Post-Gazette* wrote that August, "Columbus was so short of talent that it borrowed players from other minor-league clubs. Players like Hector Torres, an infielder, and Benny Ayala, an outfielder who has a problem. He can't catch a fly ball."[3] Ayala hit .340 for the Clippers in 59 games, though, lifting his overall mark for the year to .299. He totaled 11 homers and 56 RBIs.

On January 16, 1979, Ayala got the best break of his career. The Cardinals traded him to Baltimore for Mike Dimmel, another player whose big-league career was quite limited (39 games from 1977 to 1979). Benny had considered going to play in Japan with the Taiyo Whales, but Doc Edwards, his manager in Puerto Rico, was also the manager at Baltimore's Triple-A team, Rochester.[4] Edwards persuaded Benny to stay, farm director Clyde Kluttz liked what he saw too, and the Orioles called him up at the end of April after Doug DeCinces got hurt.

Earl Weaver used Ayala sparingly in '79, but he benefited from the AL's designated-hitter rule. In 86 at-bats across 42 games, he hit 6 homers, drove in 13, and hit .256. Benny had his only two-homer game in the majors on June 10 at Memorial Stadium. Both were solo shots off his former Mets teammate, Texas Rangers lefty Jon Matlack.

Weaver did not use Ayala in the American League Championship Series, but he got six at-bats in four games during the World Series. He singled off John Candelaria in his first at-bat in Game Three before reaching the Nuyorican for his homer. That blow brought the Orioles within a run at 3-2, and they proceeded to knock out Candelaria in the fourth inning. During that rally, righty Enrique Romo came out of the bullpen, and so Al Bumbry hit for Ayala.

The Associated Press write-up said, "Ayala also didn't know he was starting until he saw the lineup posted in the clubhouse. Ayala admitted that he never knows when Weaver is going to use him. 'He doesn't play me against certain lefthanders,' Ayala said. 'It's mostly if I can hit a certain lefthander.'" Many observers thought the lineup was unconventional, but Earl said, "It was one that helped us get here in the first place. . . . Benny has done that for us a number of times."[5]

Ayala enjoyed his best season in the majors in 1980 (.265/10/33 in a career-high 76 games). Always thinking positively, he said, "I don't mind my role here. I always have a chance to swing the bat with the Orioles and the way Earl uses me is decent." Frank Robinson, then a Baltimore coach, said, "Benny uses his time wisely, watching and studying the pitchers. He's not afraid to ask somebody about a certain pitcher either."[6]

Ayala's most dramatic hit that year may have come on September 5 at Memorial Stadium. This could have been the game described in a 1996 article in the *Los Angeles Times* about Earl Weaver's golden hunches. "One day, Weaver walked up to [pitching coach Ray] Miller and said, 'Ray, Benny Ayala. Don't forget that, Benny Ayala.' That night, Ayala hit an eighth-inning pinch homer. 'It just made sense to me in those days . . . to know if I had a hitter sitting on the bench in a situation that was hitting that pitcher good,' Weaver said. 'So I made up my lineups accordingly.'"[7] The three-run blow off Oakland lefty Bob Lacey brought the Orioles within a run at 6-5, and they won it 8-7 with another three runs in the bottom of the ninth.

In the strike season of 1981, Ayala served mostly as a platoon DH with Terry Crowley. During 1982 he was part of a three-man contingent in left field with John Lowenstein and Gary Roenicke. In his book *Weaver on Strategy*, Earl said, "By matching your bench-players' strengths to your starters' weaknesses, you can create a "player" of All-Star caliber." He likened the trio's total output to having a Reggie Jackson in the lineup.[8]

That July Ayala told Steve Wulf of *Sports Illustrated*, "I try to think ahead of time. Say, we are playing Chicago in two weeks. I think how the lefthander pitched me the last time. Sitting on the bench I have a lot of time to think. I try not to be surprised." Another line in the same article showed his Zen-like calm. On May 19 he hit a three-run homer after a rain delay of an hour and 21 minutes. "When asked if he thought he was in a tough spot, having to face a two-strike count after sitting for so long, Ayala replied, 'Not really. I just felt like I was pinch-hitting for myself.'"[9]

Wulf's piece was strewn with juicy quotes on Ayala. Earl Weaver said, "He's so good he knocks himself out of games. I'll start him against a lefthander, and he'll hit a three-run homer off him. Then they'll bring in a righty, and Benny's back on the bench." According to Lowenstein, Ayala was "the most profound player on the Orioles. 'He will sit there, arms folded, for eight innings. If he's going to hit, I'll ask him what he's looking for. He'll say, 'Something white. Coming through.'"[10] Indeed, Ayala (like many Caribbean players) didn't walk or strike out much—he got his hacks.

"I always try to take three swings," Ayala said that summer. "I don't think the hitter should give the pitcher a strike by taking." With the arrival of Dan Ford, Ken Singleton had moved from right field to full-time DH, leaving Benny with spot duty. Yet as always, he stayed positive. "Sure I would like to play more. But the important thing is to stay ready and then do your job when you're called on."[11]

In 2010 Ayala said, "I suffered a lot in the big leagues. It was hard for me to accept my role, but I accepted it quietly. If I don't play every day, I have it in my mind that I have to work harder. Rod Carew asked me one time, 'Benny, why are you over there by yourself? Don't you want to talk?' I told him I don't have time. I worked. I studied, so when I get that opportunity against Ron Guidry, I can say, 'I'm ahead of you.'" Benny did far better than most against "Louisiana Lightning"—9-for-28. Changeup artist Geoff Zahn was just his meat (11-for-30 with two homers), but the lefty whom Ayala owned was Mike Caldwell (11-for-21 with three HRs).

Benny remained in his reserve role with the O's in 1983, but his effectiveness diminished, as he hit just .221. "I was a little disappointed with Joe Altobelli [who succeeded Weaver], he didn't give me a chance. Then when he knows he needs me for the postseason, he put me up against John Montefusco, a righty with that overhand curve."

Ayala hit a sacrifice fly in his only at-bat in the ALCS against the White Sox, capping the three-run 10th-inning rally that won Game Four and the series for Baltimore. Benny also made his lone at-bat in the 1983 World Series count. In the seventh inning of Game Three, pinch-hitting for Jim Palmer, he lined a single to left off Steve Carlton, past a diving Mike Schmidt. Rick Dempsey scored the tying run. Benny then scored the go-ahead run, which would stand up as the margin of victory.

When asked about having a World Series ring, Ayala said, "Juan González turned down $150 million from Detroit because he thought there wasn't a chance for a ring. He should be in the Guinness Book of Records for that!

"You're on top. You're a champion. Even now, I'm signing autographs, and people request that I put '1983 World Series Champ' after my name. I'm lucky that I played with legends—six Hall of Famers."

In 1984 Ayala joked about his infrequent playing time. After getting just four at-bats in the month of June, he said, "I'm an eclipse player. You don't see me very often."[12] He hit just .212 for the year, and the Orioles announced in late September that they would not offer him a contract for 1985. Al Bumbry and Ken Singleton were also part of the housecleaning.

Spring training also came and went without any offers. Even Ayala thought it might be the end of the line. "So what's left?" he said. "Mexico. And I don't look at myself as a Mexican League player."[13] Looking back, he thought he should have paid his own way to camp, as he remembers players like Rob Picciolo and Kurt Bevacqua did.

On April 19, 1985, though, the Cleveland Indians signed the veteran to a minor-league deal. Although he went just 7-for-46 with the Maine Guides (Portland), the Indians called him up in May. Just days after he made it back, he missed a fly ball against the Boston Red Sox—but then drove in the game-winning run. Manager Pat Corrales said, "Benny looked a little ugly in left field, but he was Robert Redford at the plate."

Ayala spent the rest of the season with Cleveland, hitting .250 (19-for-76) in 46 games. "When I learned to hit to right field, I was 34 years old. I was a lowball hitter. I liked to uppercut, even in street fights!" His last big-league homer came off Jimmy Key at Toronto's Exhibition Stadium on September 4. The Indians made him a free agent in November 1985, and Ayala's big-league career ended.

In December 2009, Benny responded to blogger Bo Rosny's request for stories about his baseball cards. One anecdote captured a key part of his approach to the game. "In one of them the picture was taken in Chicago that I like a lot; Brooks Robinson [then an Orioles announcer] told me that I was looking good. That was a perfect day to take the picture. He said, 'Looking good, Benny, in case you have a bad game today.'

"After that I always shave before the game, good haircut, shine shoes, complete clean uniform, brand-new hat. In case I have a bad game, always looking good."[14]

In the winter of 1985-86, Ayala returned to the Puerto Rican Winter League after several seasons away. He regretted the hiatus. "After I established myself with the Orioles, I didn't go back. Relatives told me I was a little bored with the game. It was foolish. I should have played. I could have gone over 100 homers, I'd be one of the few there." He finished with 68 homers in his PRWL career.

In 1989 Ayala came back to play with the West Palm Beach Tropics of the Senior Professional Baseball Association. One of his teammates was Tim Stoddard. He recalled, "I went there, I'm a low-mileage player. How can a player like me be injured? I hit very good, but one day I chased a fly ball and didn't get it. [Manager] Dick Williams said, 'We aren't going to stick with you.'"

After his playing days finally ended, Ayala got an interview with Doug Melvin about a job in the Orioles chain but went back home to Puerto Rico. For a couple of years he was batting coach with Arecibo, "but there was not much money, $1,200 a month, and I was nearly killing myself driving." After that, "I managed a couple of amateur teams, but they were not easy to handle."

Ayala was married in 1971 to Esperanza "Eppie" Martínez. "I was always visiting her when I was in college. I was in love. I didn't like school much!" The Ayalas had four children: sons Benigno III, Luis Mario, and Melvin, plus daughter Jesica. As of 2010, there were eight grandchildren in the family.

In recent years, Ayala's main endeavor became his professional network. His goal: to help retired Puerto Rican players in such areas as pensions, health insurance, celebrity baseball clinics, training clinics for children, and more. In November 2007 Benny (in tandem with the Calero & Sullivan Baseball Management firm) held a groundbreaking meeting with 118 former pros from the island and the Major League Baseball Players' Alumni Association. As a result, the Baseball Assistance Team was able to offer financial and medical support to a number of men who needed it. Ayala also sets up memorabilia signings to bring the players some additional money. His network, as of 2010, included 250 pros.

Ayala's role as BAT's liaison to the Puerto Rican community brings him and his fellow *boricuas* much joy. He helped his old teammate Angel Cantres after Angel lost a leg following a work-related accident in 2001. After former minor-league pitcher Jacinto Camacho received a new artificial leg to replace his homemade prosthesis, he walked off the plane home to greet his family and completely forgot about his wheelchair. "Times like these are when I know that the work I do with BAT really makes my life worthwhile," Ayala said.[15]

In the summer of 2009 Ayala also reached out to former big-league outfielder Ricky Otero. Otero, who had fallen into alcohol and drug addiction, was living homeless in Cancún, Mexico. Benny was able to get him into a rehab program in New York, and Ricky was reportedly doing well as of early 2010.

Benny Ayala is a cheerful and chatty man, but his baseball memories feature a serious undercurrent. He says, "Earl Weaver respected you as a major-leaguer. Some people had to be on the field first, but still I feel, 'Here they treat everyone the same.' I was very proud to wear that big-league uniform, with that Orioles name up front."

*Grateful acknowledgment to Benny Ayala for his memories (telephone interview, May 2, 2010). All quotations that are not otherwise attributed come from this interview. Continued thanks to SABR member Jorge Colón Delgado (Puerto Rican statistics).*

## SOURCES

In addition to the sources cited in the Notes, the author also consulted retrosheet.org, ultimatemets.com, and caleroandsullivan.com, as well as Crescioni Benítez, José A., *El Béisbol Profesional Boricua* (San Juan, Puerto Rico: Aurora Comunicación Integral, Inc., 1997).

## NOTES

1. Carlos Rosa Rosa, "Benigno con el prójimo," *El Nuevo Día*, October 16, 2009.
2. Louis Berney, *Tales from the Orioles Dugout* (Champaign, Illinois: Sports Publishing LLC, 2004), 147.
3. Charley Feeney, "Columbus Turmoil Might Spell Peterson's Demise," *Pittsburgh Post-Gazette*, August 8, 1978: 13.
4. Steve Wulf, "It's the Right Idea for Left," *Sports Illustrated*, July 12, 1982.
5. Associated Press, "Baltimore Offense Is Ignited," October 12, 1979.
6. Ken Nigro, "Hitting Or Sitting, Ayala Happy," *The Sporting News*, August 2, 1980: 37.
7. Jason LaCanfora, "Beyond tantrums, was hidden Weaver," *Los Angeles Times*, August 4, 1996.
8. Earl Weaver and Terry Pluto. *Weaver on Strategy* (New York: Collier Books, 1984), 26.
9. Wulf, op. cit.
10. Ibid.
11. Ken Nigro, "Benny Always Fit as Bird in Pinch," *The Sporting News*, August 9, 1982: 27.
12. Robert W. Creamer, "They Said It," *Sports Illustrated*, August 27, 1984.
13. Associated Press, "Indians won't be sending Ayala to Mexico," May 19, 1985.
14. http://borosny.blogspot.com/2009/12/one-more-card-story-from-benny-ayala.html
15. Baseball Assistance Team, Winter 2008 newsletter (mlb.mlb.com/mlb/downloads/y2009/bat/bat_winter_2008_newsletter.pdf)

# CARLOS BAERGA

## By Joseph Wancho

**IN JUST HIS THIRD SEASON IN THE** major leagues, Carlos Baerga was a leader on the field. The Cleveland Indians second baseman broke into the big leagues as a third baseman in 1990. But he was moved to second, where he found a home. There was never a question about Baerga's ability to hit. He collected 205 hits in 1992, including 32 doubles and 20 home runs, and produced 105 RBIs. Those numbers added up to a .312 batting average and his first selection to the All-Star Game.

But on March 23, 1993, Baerga stepped outside the white lines to become a leader of the club off the field. The day before, the Indians were given a day off by manager Mike Hargrove. Their spring training was held in Winter Haven, Florida. The players took advantage of the free day. Some groups took their families to Disney World, others went to Universal Studios. Others stayed closer to the spring-training complex.

Tim Crews came over to the Indians via free agency from Los Angeles to Cleveland. He owned a ranch close to Winter Haven, and invited the team to his home for a picnic. Steve Olin and Bob Ojeda took Crews up on his offer. Toward the end of the day, Crews, Ojeda, and Olin climbed into Crews' 18-foot bass boat, and circled around Little Lake Nellie. Indians trainer Fernando Montes observed the trio from where the boat departed. A neighbor's dock, which extended more than 50 yards, sat on the far side of the lake. As Crews accelerated, the front of the boat rose up, blocking their vision. As soon as the boat planed out, it was now the under the dock. It was too late. The accident occurred in three feet of water. "We heard this loud thump and a crash," said Montes. "And it was silence, utter silence. I knew without any hesitation that Steve Olin had passed."[1] Crews was also dead and Ojeda was badly injured.

The next day, Cleveland's vice president of public relations, Bob DiBiasio, was looking for a player who would talk to the media about the boating tragedy. "Everybody on the team was in tears," said DiBiasio. "Nobody wanted to step forward and discuss what happened."[2] Carlos Baerga stepped forward, volunteering to be the team spokesman. "I was brokenhearted," he said, "but I had a responsibility to the two good people we had lost. They were part of my life. I told God, 'Give me words, because I know it's going to be hard for me.'"[3]

Carlos Obed Baerga was born on November 4, 1968, in Santurce, Puerto Rico. He was the oldest of four children born to José and Baldry Baerga. José worked in the credit office of Puerto Rico's largest newspaper, *El Nuevo Dia*. José managed Carlos's little league teams. At 8, Carlos was holding his own against boys 10 to 12 years old. When he reached 14, Baerga was mixing it up on the diamond with adult amateurs in their 20s and 30s in the Puerto Rican Double A League. When Baerga reached 16, he was playing in the winter leagues against major leaguers.

"I remember my father saying, 'Don't come back home if you don't have your uniform dirty,' Baerga once recalled. "Ever since, I have put it in my mind to play hard. He always pushed me. My father always watches me, he's always behind me."[4]

Longtime Indians bullpen coach Luis Isaac (1987-2008) watched Baerga grow in his native Puerto Rico. "I knew right away he'd be a big-league player," said Isaac. "Even when he was little, he was the type of kid who wanted to play two games a day. He'd be telling the other kids on the field what to do. He always played with that kind of intensity."[5]

José worked with his son on becoming a switch-hitter so that he could play every day no matter who the pitcher was. Carlos, a natural left-handed hitter, worked hard to sharpen his skill from the right side of the plate. "I've still got to practice it every day," he said in 1995. "But it has helped me. I see a guy like Randy Johnson pitching and I can't imagine having to face him left-handed. The same goes for David Cone and facing him right-handed."[6]

Word of Baerga's ability spread around the island, and soon professional scouts arrived to get a look at the 14-year-old. Luis Rosa, a scout for the San Diego Padres, got Baerga to sign for a $65,000 bonus in 1985, when he turned 17 years old. (Rosa had a keen eye for talent. At the time Baerga signed, 32 of Rosa's players had made their way to the big leagues.)

Although Baerga seemed destined for big-league stardom, there was one problem. The Padres already had a second baseman in-waiting, Roberto Alomar. Baerga started his playing career at Class-A Charleston in the South Atlantic League. "They asked me to take him with me and when (rookie level) Spokane opened up (in mid-June) he'd go there," said Charleston manager Pat Kelly.[7] Baerga, who did not speak English that well, would ask Kelly, "Coach, why me no play?" Kelly would explain to Baerga that he had to play his more experienced players. Baerga would nod, as if he understood, but he returned the next day, asking the same question. This went on for about a week. "Finally, I put him in as a pinch-hitter, and he got a hit, of course," said Kelly. "So I started him the next day, and he went like 4-for-4, and they were all (line drives). So he stayed with us the whole year."[8]

Baerga showed that he could handle the bat on the minor-league level. He was still somewhat raw, but he was still just a teenager in his first three years in the minors. Because Alomar was the second baseman of the future for the Padres, it became evident that a new position would have to be found for Baerga, even though he felt the most comfortable at second base.

When Baerga reported to Double-A Wichita in 1988, he was switched to shortstop. In 1989 he was promoted to Triple-A Las Vegas and was placed at third base. Although he made 32 errors while manning the hot corner for Las Vegas, Baerga was in the lineup to hit. He hit .275 with 28 doubles, 10 homers, and 74 RBIs. He was somewhat of a free swinger, and his strikeouts easily tripled his walks.

The Cleveland Indians were shopping outfielder Joe Carter at the 1989 winter meetings. Carter's contract was up in 1990, and the Indians knew they would not be able to re-sign him. Carter made no secret of his desire to leave the Indians, preferably to a contender, and a lucrative contract would also be nice.

The Indians found a suitor in the Padres. The teams dickered over whom the Padres would send the Indians' way for the star slugger. The Indians insisted that Baerga be included in the deal. The Padres viewed Baerga as their third baseman of the future. But the Indians' persistence won out, and they received Baerga, catcher Sandy Alomar Jr. (Roberto's brother), and outfielder Chris James for Carter. "I managed against Carlos in the Pacific Coast League in 1989," said Mike Hargrove. "On my report at the end of the year, I recommended that we should try to acquire him. So did my coaches, Rich Dauer and Rick Adair."[9]

The Indians hired John McNamara to manage in 1990. Cleveland was putting together a solid nucleus of young talent, and it began with Baerga and Alomar. The two newcomers were blended with Albert Belle, Cory Snyder, Jerry Browne, and Brook Jacoby. Tom Candiotti, Greg Swindell, and Buddy Black anchored the starting rotation.

Alomar was a star right away. He was named the starting catcher on the 1990 AL All-Star team, won the Gold Glove, and was voted Rookie of the Year. Baerga would have to wait a bit for his time to come. Browne was entrenched at second base and Jacoby manned third. The Indians had signed Keith Hernandez to play first base. But Hernandez suffered through various injuries and played in only 42 games. His injuries offered the break that benefited Baerga; Jacoby moved to first base and Baerga became the new third baseman. "From the time he got to Cleveland, Carlos was the heart and soul of the Indians," said batting coach José Morales. "We sent him down to Triple A for two weeks in his rookie year, and team spirit just sank. When he came back, it was like a kid returning to his family. He brings an energy, a unity to the team."[10]

Baerga hit .266 his rookie season. On September 20 at Yankee Stadium, the 5-foot-11, 165-pound infielder went 4-for-5 with three doubles (a career high) and a triple with three runs scored and three RBIs. The barrage came the day after his first child, a daughter, was born. "Baerga is a hitting machine and maybe his wife should have a baby every night," said McNamara.[11] Although the Indians finished with a 77-85 record, they found themselves in fourth place in the AL East. It was something to build on for the young Tribe.

Indeed, Baerga's enthusiasm for the game was unbridled and was contagious. He was a fan favorite for his all-out hustle. But in his second season, the Indians proved unable to build on the success from 1990. McNamara was fired (Hargrove replaced him) and the team topped 100 losses.

But the pieces were beginning to come together. Charles Nagy became the leader of the pitching staff. Kenny Lofton was acquired from Houston to solidify center field and bat leadoff. Paul Sorrento was acquired from Minnesota to provide a left-handed bat and he was an above-average first baseman. The Indians worked to sign Belle, Alomar, Nagy, Belle, Lofton, and Baerga to long-term deals, selling them on the talent of the core team.

Baerga made their investment pay off. In back-to-back seasons (1992 and '93) he hit more than 20 home runs, drove in more than 100 runs, and batted over .300. He was the first second baseman to achieve these numbers in consecutive seasons since Rogers Hornsby turned the trick in 1921 and 1922.

Baerga entered the record books on April 8, 1993. He hit two home runs in the seventh inning against the New York Yankees, one from each side of the plate. He connected off Steve Howe for a two run-shot, then hit a solo home run off Steve Farr. The Indians scored nine runs in the inning on their way to a 15-5 victory. "It's exciting," said Baerga. "They told me I set a record when I got back to the dugout after the second homer, but I didn't believe them. When I got to the clubhouse after the game, Bobby DiBiasio, our public-relations man, told me I'd set a record."[12] Baerga's record night did not surprise Hargrove. "The beauty about him is that there's no way to pitch him. He hits to all fields," the manager said.[13]

Baerga made the All-Star Game for the first time in 1992 and repeated in 1993. The Indians finished with identical 76-86 records in both seasons.

In 1994 the Indians said goodbye to Cleveland Stadium and relocated to the new Jacobs Field, across downtown. The baseball-only venue was a boon for the Tribe. The Indians had brought in veteran leadership in the offseason, signing Eddie Murray and Dennis Martinez. They traded for shortstop Omar Vizquel. Manny Ramirez and Jim Thome arrived through the farm system. The results were favorable. The Indians were one game behind Chicago in the new AL Central when the season ended on August 12 because of the players strike. Although the development was a big disappointment to Tribe fans, baseball fever had indeed returned to the North Coast.

The strike wiped out the 1994 postseason and bled over into the 1995 season. Baerga finished the 1994 season with 19 home runs, 80 RBIs, and a .314 batting average.

After play resumed in late April of 1995, Cleveland broke through its 41-year stretch of not appearing in a postseason game. The Indians won 100 games and Baerga, batting third in the potent Cleveland lineup, was third on the team with 90 RBIs. He batted .314. Cleveland swept Boston in the ALDS and topped Seattle in six games in the ALCS. The Indians met the Atlanta Braves in the World Series. The old adage that good pitching will defeat good hitting proved accurate, as the Braves captured the world championship in six games.

Baerga hit .400 in the ALCS and drove in four runs in both the ALCS and the World Series. He knocked in the first two runs in the Indians' 5-2 victory in Game Two of the ALDS and three runs in their 7-6, 11-inning Game Three win in the World Series. All told, he hit .292 in the 1995 postseason.

The one constant in Baerga's career to this point was his desire to play winter ball in his native Puerto Rico. He was lauded by Puerto Rican fans for his work in the community as well as his work on the diamond. He often held clinics and his enthusiasm for the game was infectious. "They won't even let you take batting practice," Baerga said, referring to the young fans. "They come right onto the field for autographs."[14]

Baerga was also a fan favorite in Cleveland. His all-out effort between the lines and his effervescent personality off it endeared him to hard-working, blue-collar town. Thus the backlash the Indians front office received when they traded Baerga on July 29, 1996, was not unexpected. The Indians swapped Baerga and utility infielder Alvaro Espinoza to the New York Mets in a trade-deadline swap for infielders Jeff Kent and José Vizcaino. Baerga's numbers were on the downside (10 home runs, 55 RBIs, .267 batting average) through 100 games. The Indians cited Baerga's weight gain. (He was said to have been 20 to 25 pounds overweight in spring training.) His work ethic and priorities were also questioned by the Indians brass. Baerga suffered a slight fracture in his right ankle and played in only about 10 games in the winter league. He used the winter league to stay in shape, hence the weight gain. He was also battling a badly sprained left wrist and a strained groin.

"When you get close to the trading deadline, you never know what's going to happen," said New York GM Joe McIlvaine. "To be honest, when they dropped Baerga's name, I was a little surprised. I thought, 'Here's a chance to get a good, quality player.' And we did it. I don't think a year ago we could've acquired Carlos Baerga."[15]

The presence of second baseman Edgardo Alfonzo on the Mets created a question of where Baerga would be stationed. As it turned out, an abdominal strain limited Baerga to 26 Mets games, mostly at first base, and a .193 batting average.

Bobby Valentine took over for Dallas Green as the Mets manager with a month to go in the 1996 season. Over the next two seasons, Baerga recaptured his second-base spot. Alfonzo was moved to third. Manager Valentine, who at times could be as subtle as a sledgehammer, would comment about Baerga's approach to hitting as "an embarrassment."[16] Baerga felt the pressure to produce, feeling that he needed to prove his worth every day. But he did not have a strong lineup like the one in Cleveland to back him up. His batting average was .274 over the 1997 and 1998 seasons, but his power numbers were dismal. The ball was not jumping off his bat as it once had.

One longtime major-league executive explained Baerga's decline this way: "Carlos is a God-given good hitter, and sometimes a player like that takes a lot for granted, doesn't stay on top of his physical conditioning and mental preparation. And there's no doubt in my mind that is what happened to him. I mean, he's always had a thick body, but last year, well, he just got plain heavy. I think it's all related (to his weight and conditioning). I was really surprised the Mets took him. No ... I was shocked."[17]

The Mets did not pick up Baerga's option year in 1999. The rest of his career was a composite of being signed, being waived, and riding the bench. St. Louis signed him for the 1999 season, but waived him at the end of spring training. Cincinnati signed Baerga, but sent him to Triple-A Indianapolis before the season, and released him after two months. In a bit of déjà vu, San Diego signed Baerga, and then traded him back to the Indians for the balance of the 1999 season.

Baerga signed on with Tampa Bay for 2000, but his contract was voided before the season began. He signed with Seattle for 2001, but was released before the start of the season. He bided his time in independent leagues and for Samsung in the Korean League. Baerga eventually made his way back to the big leagues as a role player with Boston (2002), Arizona (2003-2004), and Washington (2005). After the 2005 season Baerga retired with a lifetime batting average of .291, 1,583 hits, 134 home runs, and 774 RBIs.

Baerga worked for ESPN as a Spanish-language broadcaster for ESPN. He also helped coach the Puerto Rican National Baseball team. He also became the owner of the Bayamon Cowboys in the Puerto Rican Winter League.

Baerga married the former Miriam Cruz. They had two children, Karla and Carlos. In 2013 Baerga was inducted along with former Indians GM John Hart into the Cleveland Indians Hall of Fame. As of 2016 he was an ambassador for the Indians, making community appearances and spreading good will.

In 2016 Baerga threw out the first pitch in Game Two of the World Series at Progressive Field. He was, of course, cheered enthusiastically as he threw a perfect pitch to home plate.

## NOTES

1. ESPN, Outside the Lines, "*Indians Boating Tragedy,*" March 18, 2003. espn.com/page2/tvlistings/show155_transcript.html.
2. Frank Lidz, "Slick With the Stick," *Sports Illustrated*, April 5, 1994: 66.
3. Ibid.
4. Rick Lawes, "Baerga Has Big Talent," *USA Today Baseball Weekly*, January 13-26, 1993: 4.
5. Paul Hoynes, "Rock Solid: Carlos Baerga Is Part of the Foundation on Which the Indians Built a Winning Club," *Cleveland Plain Dealer*, July 3, 1995: 8-D.
6. Ibid.
7. Lawes.
8. Ibid.
9. Hoynes, July 3, 1995: 9-D.
10. Lidz.
11. Russell Schneider, "Tribe Rolls to Victory," *Cleveland Plain Dealer*, September 21, 1990: 1-E.
12. Paul Hoynes, "Baerga's Blasts Rip Yankees: Two-HR Inning Sets Mark," *Cleveland Plain Dealer*, April 9, 1993: 1C.
13. Ibid.
14. Lidz, 64.
15. Ray McNulty, "Net Heist Brings Baerga," *New York Post*, July 30, 1996.
16. Buster Olney, "Benching Doesn't Sit Well With Baerga," *New York Times*, April 23, 1997: B11.
17. Michael P. Geffner, "The Sound and the Fury," *The Sporting News*, May 5, 1997: 18.

# JUAN BENÍQUEZ

## By Jonathan Arnold

JUAN BENÍQUEZ WAS ONE OF MANY great position prospects for the Red Sox in the early 1970s, beginning his career as an infielder. After switching to the outfield he was faced with a logjam of star talent, and had to leave Boston to finding regular playing time. Through it all, he managed to play parts of 17 seasons for eight American League teams. He played in a World Series, won a Gold Glove, received votes for Most Valuable Player, and hit three home runs in one game.

Juan Jose Beníquez Torres was born on May 13, 1950, in San Sebastian, Puerto Rico. His father, Jose Julian "Pepe" Beníquez-Font, was an outstanding athlete whose sports included baseball, basketball, volleyball, and track and field. His mother, Clemencia Torres, remained at home to raise the children, one of who was Jose Juan "Pepito" Beníquez, who never went pro but played for the hometown club, Patrulleros de San Sebastian.[1]

Juan began his own career with the Patrulleros at the age of 16 and played for them until scout Pedro Vasquez signed him to the Red Sox at the tender age of 18. He played in Winter Haven, Florida, in Class A in 1969, hitting .261 in 120 games, and in Double-A in 1970 for Winston-Salem (92 games) and Pawtucket (56 games), showing some power with 13 homers for the two teams combined. In 1971 Beníquez played for the Triple-A Louisville Colonels and batted .279. That earned him a call-up to the big leagues in September.

In 1969 Beníquez married Irma Gonzalez. They had two children, Irma Nanette and Juan Jose Jr.

Beníquez made his major-league debut as a shortstop only three years after signing, on September 4, 1971, coming in to play in the eighth inning and grounding out in the ninth. But he had a great game the next day, in his first major-league start, batting 3-for-4 with two doubles and driving in two runs as the Red Sox beat the Cleveland Indians, 8-1.

Beníquez played a lot of shortstop for the rest of 1971, alternating with incumbent Luis Aparicio. He finished the season with a .298 batting average with four runs batted in and three stolen bases in 57 at-bats. However, he also made six errors in just 15 games. He didn't make the team out of spring training in 1972, but was called up from Louisville in June when Aparicio was disabled with a broken finger, and played daily until he set a modern major-league record with six errors in two consecutive games in July (making it a total of seven for three consecutive games). At Louisville he played in 66 games and hit .296. Aparicio returned in August, and Beníquez rode the bench for the rest of the season. He did play in the 1972 season finale, which the Red Sox won, but the strike-shortened schedule ended with the Red Sox a scant half-game behind the division-winning Detroit Tigers.

Beníquez was slated as the Sox utilityman for 1973, but Mario Guerrero's strong spring training won him the slot, and Beníquez was assigned to Pawtucket (now Boston's Triple-A team) where he started off at shortstop but was ultimately moved to the outfield. He spent the entire season at Pawtucket refining his outfield play. He hit .298, sufficient to lead the International League in batting. Pawtucket won the league championship.

In 1974 Beníquez was the Red Sox center fielder on Opening Day, and ended up sharing the position with Rick Miller, playing in 106 games (91 in center field), and batting .267 with an on-base percentage of .313. He normally hit first or second in the batting order, and stole 19 bases while being caught 11 times.

The 1975 Red Sox outfield was a logjam from the start. To incumbents Beníquez, Miller, Dwight Evans, and Bernie Carbo were added rookies Fred Lynn and Jim Rice. Despite this, Beníquez won a job in the spring, starting the first four games of the season (two in left field, two in center field) as the team's leadoff hitter. With the emergence of Rice and Lynn early in the season, Juan soon found himself in a reserve role. Manager Darrell Johnson used his entire roster, so Beníquez played in 78 games, mostly in the outfield (44 games), but he also filled in at third base (14 games) and as designated hitter (20 games). He stole seven bases and was caught stealing 10 times on a team that did not run a lot. Beníquez had a solid .291 batting average, but a mediocre .760 OPS (on-base percentage plus slugging average), reflecting his meager two home runs for the year.

With Rice hurt and inactive, Beníquez batted leadoff in all three games of the Red Sox' ALCS sweep against the Oakland Athletics, as the DH. He went 2-for-4, scoring one run and driving in another in Game One. He singled in Rick Burleson in the seventh, then proceeded to steal second, then third; he scored after Billy North muffed Denny Doyle's sacrifice fly. He ended up hitting .250 for the series.

In the World Series against the Cincinnati Reds, without the designated hitter in effect, Beníquez played in just three games. He was a surprise starter in Game Four, leading off and playing left field, as Carl Yastrzemski moved to first and Cecil Cooper was benched. Beníquez managed one single in that game, but was held hitless in three at-bats in Game Five. His final appearance was as a pinch-hitter for Rick Miller, leading off the bottom of the ninth in Game Seven, where he flied out to right field as the Sox lost to the Reds in a classic World Series.

After the 1975 season it was clear that Beníquez would not have a big role in the future of the team. Right or wrong, he had also acquired the tag of having an "attitude problem." In November he was dealt, along with pitcher Steve Barr and a player to be named (who proved to be pitcher Craig Skok), for future Hall of Fame pitcher Fergie Jenkins. For Texas, Beníquez was the biggest part of the deal, and he became the regular center fielder in 1976. As a Ranger, he led the American League in putouts (410) and assists for an outfielder (17) in 1976. In 1977 he was rewarded with the Gold Glove for his center-field play and he hit .269 with 10 home runs and 26 stolen bases while being caught stealing 18 times.

After three years starting with Texas, in the winter of 1978 Beníquez was part of a 10-player deal, in which Texas sent him, Mike Griffin, Paul Mirabella, minor-leaguer Greg Jemison, and hot minor-league left-hander Dave Righetti to the New York Yankees in exchange for Domingo Ramos, Mike Heath, Sparky Lyle, Larry McCall, Dave Rajsich, and cash. Beníquez played in only 62 games for the Yankees, mostly in the outfield, hitting four home runs and driving in 17 runs while hitting .254. He was dealt the following winter to the Seattle Mariners. After one season in which he hit only .228 in 70 games, he was granted free agency and signed with the California Angels.

After a couple of tough years in California (including hitting a mere .181 in 1981), Beníquez finally found the hitting stroke he had shown as a minor leaguer, hitting over .300 every year between 1983 and 1986, the last of which was for the Orioles. In 1984 for the Angels, he hit eight home runs and batted .336 playing outfield. He received two votes in the MVP balloting that year. During his one year in Baltimore, he had one of the more unlikely three-home run games, as he hit fully half of his six home runs on June 12, in a losing cause against the Yankees.

Dealt to Kansas City in October 1986, and then to Toronto in July 1987, Beníquez hit just .251 with eight home runs and 47 RBIs combined for the season.

In January 1988 Beníquez (and six other players) were granted free agency by a judge who ruled that the owners had conspired to hold down players' salaries after the 1985 season. He elected to remain with the Blue Jays, but played in just 27 games in 1988 before being released. His career over, he held the record for having played for eight American League teams.

After parts of 17 years in the big leagues, an American League championship ring, a Gold Glove, and experiences all over the country, Juan Beníquez could retire with a lot to be proud of. But he was not through. In 1989 he hit .359 for the St. Lucie Legends of the short-lived Senior Professional Baseball Association. With that league's demise the following season, he ended his career in Organized Baseball.

Beníquez, however, had never stopped playing ball in Puerto Rico. He played for 22 seasons, from the winter of 1968-69 to that of 1990-91. Four seasons were with the Arecibo Wolves and 18 with the Santurce Crabbers. He hit for a career average of .273 with 1,039 base hits in Puerto Rican baseball (only six players have hit 1,000 or more — the others being Luis Márquez, Carlos Bernier, Nino Escalera, Sandy Alomar, Sr., and José Pagan.)

After he retired, Beníquez managed Superior baseball at San Sebastian, and in the Winter League he managed the Mayaguez Indians and coached for other teams.

In 1998 he was inducted into the Puerto Rico Sports Hall of Fame, and in 2013 to the Santurce Sports Hall of Fame.

## SOURCES

An earlier version of this biography appeared in *'75: The Red Sox Team That Saved Baseball* (edited by Bill Nowlin and Cecilia Tan, and published by Rounder Books of Cambridge, Massachusetts, in 2005).

Baseball-Reference.com.

Retrosheet.org.

BaseballLibrary.com.

Thanks to Rod Nelson for information about Pedro Vasquez.

## NOTES

1  Considerable material has been added to supplement the original Juan Beníquez biography, thanks to SABR member Edwin Fernandez Cruz.

# CARLOS BERNIER

## By Charles F. Faber

**H**E WAS A VERY GOOD BALLPLAYer. Certainly good enough that he posted some outstanding numbers during a long and distinguished minor-league career. Probably good enough that he could have had a substantial major-league life. But Carlos Bernier managed to play only one season in "The Show." As Steve Treder wrote, "The baseball career of Carlos Bernier was in fact deeply intertwined with many of the most interesting and complicated issues of mid-20th century professional baseball: integration, racism, and the changing relationship between major league and minor league baseball in the 1950s and 1960s."[1] These factors, together with personality issues, combined to prevent the kind of career that his undeniable talent promised. He ended his life, tragically, at the age of 60, with his potential unfulfilled.

Carlos Bernier Rodríguez was born in Juana Diaz, on the southern coast of Puerto Rico, a few miles east of Ponce. At the time of Bernier's birth, the area produced rum from locally grown sugar cane. During Bernier's childhood, however, the Puerto Rican sugar cane industry suffered a sharp decline. Juana Diaz became known as *La Ciudad del Mabi*, in honor of a fermented beverage made from the bark of the mabi tree.

Little is known of Carlos's childhood. There is no record of his having played high-school baseball. He probably learned the game on the sandlots of his native area. Early in his professional career he played in the Manitoba-Dakota League. He claimed to be a teenager when his pro career started. Like so many players of his era, he lied about his age, thinking his chances of making it in the pros were greater if he appeared younger than his real age. He told baseball scouts that he was born in 1929, not 1927. As an independent circuit, the Mandak League was not recognized by Organized Baseball. Standard baseball references carry very little data on its teams or players.

*The Sporting News* did not cover the Mandak League. The first mention of Bernier in the self-proclaimed "Baseball Bible" came in a report of the 1948 Puerto Rico League championship series.[2] With the score tied in the 10th inning of the seventh and deciding game, Mayaguez left fielder Bernier committed an error that led to his team's defeat. Bernier played 19 years in Puerto Rico, mostly for Mayaguez in the winter league after spending the summers playing minor-league baseball in the United States

In 1948, 21-year-old Bernier got his start in Organized Baseball with the Port Chester (New York) Clippers in the Class-B Colonial League. Although the Clippers were affiliated with the St. Louis Browns, Bernier was the property of the local club rather than the parent organization.[3] According to Joe Guzzardi, in 1948 Bernier was, along with Jackie Robinson, Larry Doby, and Hank Thompson, one of Organized Baseball's four black players.[4] Evidently, Guzzardi overlooked Dan Bankhead and Roy Campanella, both of whom played in O.B. in 1948. (Willard Brown had played in the majors in 1947, but he was back in the Negro Leagues in 1948.)

Bernier did not have an outstanding season with Port Chester. A switch-hitter, he hit for neither average nor power, but he walked 54 times and stole 24 bases, enabling him to score 72 runs in only 104 games. Far more important than his statistics was an incident that occurred that season: He was struck by a pitch, which fractured his skull and caused him to suffer from chronic headaches the rest of his life.[5] The headaches were sometimes blamed for the quick temper that kept him in hot water much of the time. It was not just headaches that got him in trouble. Jackie Robinson was able to endure the slurs and indignities that came with being a racial pioneer. Bernier was different. He was not one to take racial taunts lying down, whether from opponents, teammates, fans, or umpires. He was competitive and ag-

gressive on the ballfield, and was suspended many times throughout his career.

Ron Samford, a longtime teammate of Bernier's, both in Puerto Rico and the Pacific Coast League, was quoted as saying, "Bernier had the ability to be a ten-to-fifteen-year major league career. His temper got the best of him."[6] Sportswriter John Schulian wrote, "Carlos Bernier had a temper as big as his chaw of tobacco."[7]

Bernier's son, Dr. N. Bernier-Collazo, explained his father's behavior:

> He lived in an era when it was fashionable to discriminate; in fact, many states upheld laws that discriminated against people of color. My father's only shortfall was that he did not handle the injustices of society with the same grace as a Jackie Robinson or a Roberto Clemente. He was quite angry at the injustices and faced them head on, even if it meant challenging a white minor league umpire who made a racial slur. I have often wondered how different life would have been for him with all his talents if he had played now (2004), instead of then. His career would have been spent primarily in the majors, rather than in the minors. ... Despite his extremely competitive demeanor on the field, he was a gentle soul off the field with the greatest qualities; kindness, compassionate, generous, responsible, and loving. ... Many people don't know what a wonderful person he was because they only witnessed his exploits and his aggressive style of play on the field.[8]

During Bernier's first season in the Colonial League, he drew his first suspension. League President John A. Scalzi meted out a six-day suspension and fined Bernier $25 for his part in a rhubarb with an umpire.[9] Many more suspensions were to follow during Bernier's career. Port Chester won the 1948 regular-season title in 1948 and followed up by taking the final playoff series. One highlight of the playoffs was an inside-the-park home run by Bernier at Poughkeepsie on September 19. He then returned to his native land to play for Mayaguez in the Puerto Rico League. He made his presence known, hitting two home runs in a game against Aguadilla on November 4. Mayaguez won the league championship, giving Bernier the distinction of having played for championship clubs in both the summer of 1948 and the winter of 1948-49.

After the 1948 season, the Port Chester Clippers disbanded, but Bernier remained in the Colonial League, the property of the Bristol (Connecticut) Owls. At the beginning of the 1949 season, the Owls sent him to Indianapolis of the Triple-A American Association. He didn't stay in Indiana long. After two pinch-running appearances, the Indians returned him to Bristol. Bernier gave up on switch-hitting and infield play and became a full-time right-handed batter and outfielder. He had a terrific season, leading Bristol to the pennant, hitting .336, leading the league with 136 runs scored and setting a league record for stolen bases with 89. But not all was sweetness and light. On July 25 Bristol manager Al Barillari fined Bernier $50 for what he called "two stupid plays that cost us the game with Bridgeport."[10] According to the manager, Bernier missed a bunt sign in the previous night's game and then was thrown out attempting to steal. In the winter Bernier again played for Mayaguez in the Puerto Rico League and tied the circuit's record for stolen bases in one season with 33.

In 1950 Bernier was back with Bristol and got off to a great start. On May 4 he established a league record by stealing six bases in one game. He stole second base four times and third twice, but was foiled in his attempt for seven thefts when he was thrown out trying to steal home in the ninth inning of the game against Bridgeport.[11] In 52 games for Bristol Bernier stole 53 bases and scored 67 runs. On July 14 the financially struggling Colonial League disbanded. Before the league collapsed, however, the Owls sold Bernier to St. Jean (Quebec) of the Class-C Provincial League. At the time of the sale, Bernier was leading the Colonial League in both stolen bases and home runs. He found the Canadian league to his liking. In 64 games for St. Jean he hit .335 with 15 home runs, scored 69 runs, and stole 41 bases, giving him a total of 94 steals for the two clubs.

In 1951 Bernier played for the independent Tampa Smokers in the Class-B Florida International League. He led the league in steals, triples, and runs scored. As frequently happened wherever he played, Bernier led his club to the pennant. His performance in Florida earned Bernier a big promotion. In 1952 he leaped all the way up to the top of the minor-league hierarchy with the Hollywood Stars of the Open Classification Pacific Coast League. Already known as "The Comet" for his speed on the basepaths, Bernier lit up the Southern California landscape. He hit .301 (third best in the league) and led the PCL in runs scored with 105 and stolen bases with 65. Once again he led his team to the league championship. He was named the PCL's rookie of the year.

Pittsburgh promoted Bernier to the majors in 1953. He became the first black player to join the Pirates. (Some sources credit Curt Roberts with being Pittsburgh's first black player, classifying Bernier as neither black nor white, but as Puerto Rican, as though Puerto Ricans were a separate race. Of course, biologically nobody really is black or white. Race is a sociological concept, not a biological one. Bernier considered himself black and deserves the distinction of being designated Pittsburgh's first black player.)

Bernier made his major-league debut at Forbes Field on April 22, 1953, at the age of 26. He entered the game in the eighth inning as a pinch-hitter for pitcher Paul La Palme, with the Pirates trailing Jim Hearn and the New York Giants 4-0. In his first at-bat he was hit by a pitch, advanced to third base on two consecutive singles, and scored the Pirates' first run of the game on an outfield lineout by Ralph Kiner. Bernier made his first major-league hit three days later at Connie Mack Stadium. In the seventh inning he hit a single off Curt Simmons in Pittsburgh's 7-6 loss to the Phillies.

On May 2 Bernier made headlines in the sports pages by hitting three triples in one game, tying a major-league record that has been frequently tied but never broken. In the game against the Cincinnati Reds at Forbes Field, Bernier hit a triple off Bud Podbielan in the fourth inning, followed by triples off Herm Wehmeier in the sixth and seventh. His line for the game read 4-for-5, with three runs scored and three runs batted in. Of course, he couldn't keep up that pace and slipped badly, losing his starting position later in the season. His final major-league appearance came at Ebbets Field on September 22, 1953. With the Pirates trailing the Brooklyn Dodgers 5-4 in the ninth inning, he entered the game as a pinch-hitter for Dick Smith. Brooklyn pitcher Clem Labine retired him on a grounder to shortstop. Bernier's major-league career was over at the age of 26. He finished with a batting average of only .213. Although he stole 15 bases, he was caught stealing 14 times.

During the winter of 1953-54, *The Sporting News* asked baseball writers to rate players on various characteristics. The scribes named Carlos Bernier Pittsburgh's most temperamental player.[12] Events of 1954 served to strengthen that impression.

Bernier was on the Pirates' spring-training roster in 1954, but was optioned conditionally to Hollywood shortly before Opening Day. He hadn't been long on the Coast before his temper flared. On April 30 he "staged a stormy scene at San Francisco after being picked off second base and was banished by umpire Cece Carlucci."[13] A more serious incident occurred on June 13 in a game between the Stars and the Los Angeles Angels. While trying to steal second base, Bernier was tagged out by shortstop Bud Hardin, who claimed that Bernier deliberately kicked him in the shins. Bernier accused Hardin of tagging him with more force than necessary. Players from both clubs rushed to the aid of their teammates. With the help of police, the umpires restored order. However, when Bernier returned to the dugout he said something that caused the Angels first baseman to charge him. The melee threatened to escalate until cooler heads prevailed. Numerous fights broke out in the grandstand with participants being ejected. After hearing a report from the umpires, PCL President Pants Rowland fined Bernier $50 and suspended him indefinitely.[14]

In the first day after his suspension was lifted, Bernier stole three bases. He was back to his own fiery self again. On August 11 in the eighth inning of a game against San Diego, Bernier was called out on strikes by umpire Chris Valenti. Bernier's temper flared. He bumped the umpire, who ordered him off the field. Bernier then slapped Valenti in the face with his left hand. The arbiter did not retaliate. Jack Phillips rushed over from the on-deck circle and restrained his angry teammate. After the game Bernier sought out Valenti, and with tears streaming down his face apologized for his actions. The two men shook hands.[15]

The next day Rowland suspended Bernier for the rest of the regular season and the playoffs. Hollywood president Rob Cobb expressed his disappointment over Bernier's conduct: "I hope Bernier, whom all of us in the front office have repeatedly urged to control his temper, realizes the seriousness of the suspension and that he profits by his mistake. A player of his ability will be mighty hard to replace."[16]

A few weeks later it was reported that Bernier had signed a contract to play with the Licey club in the Dominican Republic League, a circuit not affiliated with Organized Baseball. George M. Trautman, president of the National Association, the governing body of the minor leagues, reportedly wired Bernier that he would be placed on the disqualified list, barring him from winter league ball, unless he quit the Licey team immediately.[17]

Despite Trautman's warning, Bernier played for Licey. He participated in all five games of the league playoffs. He was tossed out of Game Four after a dispute over a decision by the second-base umpire.[18] Bernier appealed to Trautman to lift the ban so he might play ball in his native Puerto Rico this winter. He assured the president that he would behave himself and never again get into arguments with umpires.[19] The ban was lifted. In a nonbaseball note, on October 2 Bernier remarried his ex-wife, Emma Betances.

Bernier played winter ball in Puerto Rico, went to spring training with the Pirates, and became a member of perhaps the first all-Puerto Rican outfield on a major-league club when he joined Román Mejías and Roberto Clemente in the Pittsburgh outer garden for a game against the Phillies at Clearwater on March 13, 1955.

Bernier was back in Hollywood for the opening of the 1955 season. In early June Carlos's mother, 65-year-old Rosario Bernier, came to California from Puerto Rico for a visit with her son. It was her first trip to the United States mainland. Inexplicably, *The Sporting News* account of her visit focused on Ms. Bernier's smoking habits rather than on any of the other aspects of her visit that would seem more pertinent.[20] Carlos claimed to have turned over a new leaf. He said, "I learn my lesson. I'm a good boy now. I cause nobody no trouble no more."[21] He kept his promise during the 1955 PCL season and led the league in stolen bases. However, he got involved in fisticuffs in a game between Mayaguez and Caguas in Puerto Rico that winter. In a play at the plate Bernier was nearly hit in the head by a throw from Caguas first baseman Vic Power. Bernier claimed Power had deliberately thrown at him. The two got into a fist fight, which escalated into a brawl involving most players from both clubs, as well as many fans, who swarmed the field to join in the melee. Puerto Rico League President Ernesto Juan Fonfrias fined Bernier $100 for his part in the scuffle.[22]

The 1955 Puerto Rico League All-Star game was played in San Juan's Estadio Sixto Escobar on December 12. Proceeds from the annual game go to a special fund to buy toys for the poor children of the island. A series of track and field events preceded the 1955 game. Not surprisingly, Carlos Bernier won the 100-meter dash.

Bernier continued to star in the Pacific Coast League for several years, but never made it back to the majors. Perhaps his reputation as a troublemaker deterred the big-league clubs from taking a chance on him. Bernier led the PCL in batting average in 1961, in on-base percentage in 1961 and 1963, in runs scored in 1958, in triples in 1956 and 1958, in walks in 1959 and 1963, in hits in 1958, and in stolen bases in 1955 and 1956. Some of these accomplishments occurred while he was playing for Hollywood, but most came after the club moved to Salt Lake City in 1958. He got off to the best start of his career that first season in Utah, hitting over .400 throughout the spring. He had a streak of hitting safely in 35 consecutive games in April and May. Bernier was selected to play in the Pacific Coast League All-Star game. After the season, the National Association of Baseball Writers named him to their all-Triple-A All-Star team.

Bernier's numbers declined slightly in 1959, so he was demoted to the Columbus Jets, Pittsburgh's affiliate in the Triple-A International League. After 35 games in Ohio he was acquired by the Indianapolis Indians, a Philadelphia Phillies affiliate in the same circuit. In May 1961 he was sold to Hawaii, and he was back in the Pacific Coast League. Bernier still couldn't keep out of trouble. He was fined $100 for threatening and abusive language directed toward umpire Cece Carlucci in a game at Portland on July 3. Otherwise he had a terrific season. He won the PCL batting championship by hitting .351 for the Islanders, the highest batting average of his career. He was selected by National Association of Baseball Writers to the 1961 Class-AAA All-Star team. He followed this up with three more good seasons in the islands, hitting .313, .300, and .294 in 1962, 1963, and 1964, respectively.

In 1965 Bernier plied his trade south of the border, playing for the Reynosa Broncs in the Class-AA Mexican League. In his final season he hit .281 in 87 games. He then retired at the age of 38, having played 17 years in the minors, one year in the majors, and probably 19 seasons of winter ball in his native Puerto Rico.

After Bernier retired, he was plagued by financial insecurity and medical and emotional problems.[23] He was homeless near the end, and hanged himself in a garage in his hometown of Juana Diaz on April 6, 1989.

Carlos Bernier has not been forgotten. In 2004 he was inducted into the Pacific Coast League Hall of Fame. In 2012 the Orlando Cepeda Chapter of the Society for American Baseball Research commemorated Bernier's 85th anniversary with a celebration of his life at Los Autenticos Club in Juana Diaz. More than 130 people attended the event, which featured an exhibition of Bernier memorabilia and photos.[24]

## NOTES

1  Steve Treder, "Carlos Bernier," hardballtimes.com/carlos/bernier, August 25, 2004.

2  Santiago Llorens, "Puerto Rican Playoffs Won by Caguas Club," *The Sporting News,* March 17, 1948.

3  Treder.

4  Joe Guzzardi, "Carlos Bernier, More Than a Footnote," *Pittsburgh Post-Gazette,* April 14, 2013.

5  "Obituaries: Carlos Bernier," *The Sporting News,* May 29, 1989.

6  baseball-reference/bullpen/Carlos_Bernier.

7  Ibid.

8  Treder.

9  "First Colonial Suspension," *The Sporting News,* August 11, 1948.

10  *The Sporting News,* August 10, 1949

11  *The Sporting News,* May 17, 1950.

12  C.C. Johnson Spink, "The Low Down on Majors' Big Shots," *The Sporting News,* January 6, 1954.

13  *The Sporting News,* May 12, 1954.

14  *The Sporting News,* June 23, 1954.

15 John B. Old, "Bernier Slaps Ump, Banned for Rest of '64," *The Sporting News*, August 18, 1954.

16 Ibid.

17 "Suspended Bernier Warned Not to Play in Dominican," *The Sporting News*, September 1, 1954.

18 Albert Mlagon, "Bernier in New Ump Clash; Heaved in Dominican Game," *The Sporting News*, September 8, 1954.

19 Santiago Llorens, "Bernier Asks Lift of Ban; Seeks to Play Winter Ball," *The Sporting News*, October 13, 1954.

20 Jeane Hoffman, "Hollywood's Fiery Bernier Had Cigar-Smoking Mamma," *The Sporting News*, June 15, 1955.

21 "Bernier Back as Good Boy," *The Sporting News*, April 6, 1955.

22 "Power, Bernier Fined $100 After Puerto Rican Scrap," *The Sporting News*, November 23, 1955.

23 Guzzardi

24 Edwin Fernandez-Cruz, "SABR Day 2012 – Puerto Rico," sabr.org/sabrday/2012/puerto rico.

# HIRAM BITHORN

## By Jane Allen-Quevedo

**W**HILE MUCH MYSTERY SURrounds the life and career of the first Puerto Rican to play major-league baseball, there's no question that Hiram "Hi" Bithorn's entrance into the big leagues raised his island's self-esteem as well as opened the door for future Puerto Rican baseball players to realize their dreams, too. With the passage of time, memories of the "Tropical Hurricane"—as some called him—reside primarily with the old-timer players and fans who saw him pitch in the 1930s and 1940s. Even though the largest stadium on the island bears his name, today many residents of his homeland know little about Hiram Bithorn.[1]

He was a talented athlete. Standing 6 foot 1 inch and weighing about 200 pounds, Bithorn commanded attention when he took the mound, began his distinctive windup, raised his long left leg high in the air, and followed through with a powerful right-hand pitch over home plate, striking out one batter after another. He had remarkable control and delivery of a straight-line 90- to 95-mile-per-hour fastball that at least one time resulted in a hand injury that required a change of catchers.[2] But, it would take more than technical skill and brawn for this Latino baseball player to make it to the big leagues in the 1940s.

Historically, Latinos had been playing in the major leagues since the early 1900s,[3] and while earlier Puerto Rican players may have had the right stuff for the big leagues, until Bithorn came along, the color of their skin was deemed too dark for the all-white clubs of that time. Born March 18, 1916, in an area of San Juan called Santurce, Bithorn came from a family of Danish-German-Scottish and Spanish descent.[4] He had light olive skin, spoke English, and his name did not sound Latino. Besides, he had a mean pitch.

Hiram's father, Waldemar G. Bithorn, was a municipal employee while his mother, Maria Sosa, was a public school teacher. Hiram, the fourth of five Bithorn children, had three brothers, Waldemar, Fernando, and Rafael, and a younger sister, Maria Angelica.

According to Jorge Colon Delgado, baseball historian of Puerto Rico, the Bithorns were an exceptional family that traveled frequently to the United States.[5] His mother taught her children English, and at one time produced a radio program called "*Abuelita Borinqueña*" ("Puerto Rican Grandmother.")[6] Hiram attended Central High School in Santurce. His brothers Waldemar and Fernando, 11 and 10 years his senior, encouraged and assisted in training him to become an athlete. Even though during his childhood Hiram lost the big toe on his right foot in some kind of railway accident, the absent digit did not stop him from excelling in sports.[7]

In 1935, he played in the Third Central American and Caribbean Games in El Salvador, helping his island teammates bring home a silver medal in volleyball and a bronze in basketball. By this time, however, he had already begun making a name for himself in baseball. One game in particular occurred in the town of Guayama in 1932. Bithorn was on a team of *nativos* playing against Richmond, a team of white players, including first baseman, batting phenomenon, and future Hall of Famer Johnny Mize. That day 16-year-old Bithorn pitched a 10-1 game for the *nativos*.[8]

In Bithorn's day, attending baseball games in Puerto Rico and rooting for the home team was as much a social event as a sporting event. This is where people gathered to pass the time, catch up with the latest news and gossip as well as support the young athletes of their island. But it was a time when Puerto Ricans did not have a good self-image, believing that anything of value must come from outside. Bithorn's success would help change that perception.[9]

Most games in San Juan were played in Sixto Escobar in El Escambron, where local fans filled the benches and even climbed into the trees outside the ballpark to secure a good vantage point to watch Bithorn at work.[10] It was just a matter of time before he'd get a chance to play in the United States, and eventually in the major leagues. The opportunity came in 1936 when two individuals saw something special in him.

That year the Newark Eagles (created with the 1936 union of Brooklyn Eagles and Newark Dodgers) of the Negro National League had gone to San Juan ahead of an exhibition series against the Cincinnati Reds. While warming up with some practice games against the local Puerto Rican teams, the Eagles were impressed with Bithorn's performance on the mound. When one of their star pitchers, future Hall of Famer Leon Day, had an attack of appendicitis,[11] the Eagles invited the Puerto Rican to join their short-handed pitching squad against the Reds, a team led by future Hall of Famer Kiki Cuyler.[12]

That is how it happened that on March 1, 1936, 20-year-old Bithorn pitched his first game against a major-league club. For seven innings, he allowed Cincinnati only one run, but when the Reds scored three runs in the eighth inning, the Eagles brought in a relief pitcher to save the game.[13] The Eagles took the game, and Bithorn would get the break he needed to play in the United States.

Frank Duncan, catcher for the Eagles in that series, is credited with helping the Puerto Rican polish his pitching technique, while outfielder Ted Norbert recommended him for a contract with the Class-B Norfolk Tars of the Piedmont League.[14] Bithorn would spend six seasons in the minor leagues, moving up midseason 1937 to the New York Yankees' Class-A Binghamton Triplets. Midseason 1938 he continued to improve, advancing to the Newark Class-AA team, also affiliated with the Yankees. In his first two seasons in the minor leagues, he pitched 16-9 and 17-9 respectively.

Author Nick C. Wilson shares an unusual story from Bithorn's minor-league days with Norfolk. After winning the first game of a doubleheader on a Thursday evening, he took a seat in the stands to watch the second game, still wearing his uniform.

As it turned out, the game dragged on inning after inning until the entire Norfolk pitching squad was depleted. Manager Johnny Neun looked into the grandstand and called Bithorn to pitch the rest of the game. Finally, at two a.m. on Friday, Norfolk drove in two runs in the 15th inning, and as Wilson reports, "Bithorn had won back-to-back games on two different days without removing his uniform."[15]

After each season in the States he returned to Puerto Rico to play in the Winter League, wearing the San Juan Senators uniform. Initially, because of his minor-league record in the United States, the Puerto Rican Professional Winter League classified him as *blanquito* (white), and then briefly changed it to *refuerzo* (outsider) before finally allowing him to play as a *nativo*.[16] When San Juan manager Juan Torruella resigned only two weeks into the 1938 winter season, the *Senadores* chose 22-year-old Bithorn as manager, making him the youngest manager in the history of the Puerto Rican Professional Winter League.[17]

Hiram moved to the Pacific Coast League in 1939 where he acquired the nickname "Tropical Hurricane" or just "Hurricane" Bithorn. He played three seasons in the Class-AA clubs Oakland Oaks and Hollywood Stars, achieving win-loss percentages of .481 (1939), .370 (1940), and .531 (1941). He closed the 1941 season with a 17-15 record. Two of those games were shutouts.

The Hollywood Stars that Bithorn played with was the second club by that name to make its home in the movie industry community, the first having moved to San Diego in 1936 to become the San Diego Padres. Owners of the second Hollywood Stars, formerly the San Francisco Missions, determined to make the team a popular civic venture. To do this they formed the Hollywood Baseball Association and sold small shares of stock to local civic leaders as well as movie stars and moguls, promoting the club as "the Hollywood Stars baseball team, owned by the Hollywood stars."[18]

Baseball players and movie stars appeared together in print advertisements as well as social and promotional events. Fraternizing among baseball players and movie stars was all part of the Hollywood environment in which the Puerto Rican found himself. According to family members, Hiram did well socially in Hollywood, and in particular, befriended actress Ida Lupino. Although there is no evidence to support the story that the two were romantically involved, it is at least interesting to note that the Bithorn name appears in her 1943 movie, *The Hard Way*. In one of two shots of a newspaper page, the name of the character Laura Britton reads Laura Bithorn, doubtless a nod to Lupino's baseball-player friend.[19] By the time the movie came out, the Hurricane was already playing in the major leagues.

At the end of the 1941 season, the Chicago Cubs drafted Bithorn from the Hollywood Stars, along with Cuban-born Salvador "Chico" Hernández, from the Texas League's Tulsa Oilers, thus forming the third Spanish-speaking pitcher-catcher battery in major-league history.[20] Not only did Bithorn and Hernández speak the same language, photographs reveal a striking similarity of physical features. Former Cubs shortstop Lennie Merullo described the two as very popular "big handsome guys."[21] They were born within three months of each other (Hernández on January 3, 1916, in Cuba, and Bithorn on March 18, 1916, in Puerto Rico). The pitcher stood only one inch taller and weighed only five pounds more than the catcher. Bithorn made his major-league debut with the Cubs on April 15, 1942, at Sportsman's Park in St. Louis. Hernández made his the following day, April 16, 1942, also in St. Louis. Bithorn pitched two innings and allowed no hits in his debut game, which the Cubs lost, 4-2.

When playing teams with no Spanish-speaking players, Bithorn and Hernández openly conversed in Spanish on the field, calling out signals in what *The Sporting News* once called "Castilian Signal Code." Of course, the scheme worked only when no other Spanish-speaking players or coaches were in the game. New York Giants manager Mel Ott may not have had a player to translate what the pitcher and catcher said to each other, but he had a Spanish-speaking coach in the legendary Cuban-born Adolfo "Dolf" Luque who understood every word.[22]

Bithorn pitched 171 1/3 innings in 38 games in 1942 with 9 wins and 14 losses, achieving a 3.68 ERA. The next year he pitched his career high of 249 2/3 innings, allowing only 227 hits in 39 games, 19 of which were complete games. He ended the season with 18 wins and 12 losses, and a 2.60 ERA. With seven shutouts to his credit, he led the 1943 National League, making him the second Latino to do so, the first being none other than Adolfo Luque in 1921 (3), 1923 (6), and 1925 (4). Today Bithorn continues to hold the record for highest number of shutout games by a major-league pitcher from Puerto Rico.[23]

Merullo described Bithorn as a hard thrower with a great curveball. "He had a natural sinker that he would throw from a low three-quarter position. When he pitched, we knew as infielders we were going to get a lot of work. He was always good, but you knew you were going to be busy."[24]

Noteworthy are Bithorn's 1943 wins against the reigning world champion St. Louis Cardinals. Even though the Cardinals would go on to win the pennant, Bithorn allowed them only two runs in 32 innings.

Teammates and family members remember Bithorn as good-natured guy and even somewhat of a prankster. Prior to the 1943 season, columnist Ed Burns commented, "He has been full of fun and wisecracks all spring...."[25] Cubs first baseman Phil Cavaretta said he was a hard worker, very quiet and dedicated to the game.[26] *El Imparcial* writer Eduardo Valero recalled the time Bithorn came out of the dugout sporting an umbrella in protest of the umpire's delay in stopping play due to rain.[27] Merullo remembered him as a happy guy with a playful nature who could take a ribbing from his teammates.[28]

Despite his success as a major-league baseball player, Bithorn lived under a cloud of rumors and gossip regarding his racial ancestry. Simply the fact that he was Latino was enough to raise doubts in some minds and fuel suspicion that he might be a mulatto. Ever since the early 1900s, when the first Latinos were recruited to play organized baseball in the United States those responsible for policing baseball's color line during the Jim Crow era had sought evidence of a player's "whiteness" or Castilian blood line as a qualification for admission to a major-league team.[29] The Cubs were satisfied that Bithorn was white, and in fact, published his biographical information stating he was of Danish and Spanish heritage.[30] Nonetheless, Bithorn endured ethnic stereotyping and harassment from opposing players, fans, and managers, including New York Giants manager Leo Durocher, who discovered the limit of taunting the pitcher would take.

Durocher was hurling derogatory names at Bithorn as fast as the Puerto Rican could pitch hardballs on July 15, 1943. In the scenario Cavaretta remembered, the pitcher called for a time-out in the sixth inning, but instead of conferring with the catcher as he would be expected to do, Bithorn remained on the mound, staring straight at the batter. In a slightly different account reported in *New York Age*, the Cubs manager pulled Bithorn from the game, which sent the pitcher into a "frenzy of indignation." In both versions of the story, Durocher's diatribe of dirty words and racial slurs stopped abruptly when Bithorn shot the ball straight at him into the dugout, sending his target to his knees to avoid getting hit. It may have brought smiles to the faces of many observers, but Durocher and the commissioner of baseball, Ford Frick, failed to see the humor in it." Bithorn received a $25 fine and reprimand.[31] Major league commissioner Judge Kenesaw Mountain Landis subsequently issued a public statement denying any "ban in organized baseball against the use of colored players, either by rule or by agreement or by subterfuge."[32]

The question of Bithorn's racial heritage would emerge again more than 30 years later when Hall of Fame journalist Fred Lieb revealed in his 1977 autobiography *Baseball as I Have Known It*, an incident that occurred in St. Louis in late 1946 or early 1947. He said a man whom he did not know invited him to a performance of an all-black dance troupe and made a point of introducing him to one of the dancers, who claimed her mother and Hi Bithorn's mother were sisters. Afterward Lieb speculated that this meeting had been intentionally arranged in order to "tell me something," but he concluded, "... I have since been assured by a Puerto Rican baseball authority that Bithorn was not black, despite my curious experience."[33]

Author David Maraniss confirms, "That Bithorn had white skin meant very little to fans in San Juan . ... But it meant everything to the men who ran organized baseball in the States. It was the only reason they let him play."[34]

Unlike other Latino players from Central America and the Caribbean, as a Puerto Rican, Bithorn was a U.S. citizen (as per the Jones Act of 1917), and thus eligible for the draft during World War II. While his request for a draft deferment was denied, the War Department reclassified him to 1-A. Inducted November 26, 1943, Bithorn served most of two years at the San Juan Naval Air Station in Puerto Rico where he was player-manager of the post's baseball team.[35]

After his discharge on September 1, 1945, he reported to Chicago Cubs for the final weeks of the season, but did not play.[36] Four months later, on January 3, 1946, Bithorn and Chicago native Virginia Arford were married in Mexico. The next month he injured his hand while playing in the Puerto Rican championship games, delaying his return to the Chicago Cubs for the 1946 season.[37] He appeared on the mound in only 26 games in 1946 to garner six wins and five losses, primarily as a reliever.

Clearly, Bithorn was no longer the promising player who had pitched over 249 innings and seven shutouts in 1943. He'd gained about 25 pounds, and according to some, emerged from the military a changed man, grumpy, argumentative, and no longer the baseball star he had been before his military stint.[38] While some have speculated as to what may have happened, the real cause of his changed personality and lost skills remains something of a mystery (though arguably a nagging arm problem must have been a contributing factor). Reports that he suffered a "nervous breakdown" while in the Navy are flatly denied by family members today.[39] With his baseball career clearly on a downslide, the Cubs traded him to the Pittsburgh Pirates, but he never played for them. He was then selected off waivers by the White Sox, but plagued by that sore arm, he played only two games with the club.

His major-league career ended with his final game, the first of a doubleheader against the Philadelphia Athletics on May 4, 1947, at Comiskey Park. Bithorn pitched only one inning and allowed one hit, but got the 8-7 win over Philadelphia. Playing in 105 games during four seasons (1942, 1943, 1946, 1947), he accumulated a major-league win-loss record of 34-31 and a 3.16 ERA. He pitched 509 2/3 innings and allowed 517 hits while playing in the big leagues.

Sore arm or not, Bithorn was not ready to give up baseball. Returning briefly to the Class-AAA Hollywood Stars, he managed to pitch four games, achieving one loss and no wins. He finally underwent arm surgery and missed all of the 1948 season. Back to the game in 1949, he pitched one game with the Class-AA Oklahoma City team and 12 games with the Class-AA Nashville club. He spent the final years of his baseball career playing and/or umpiring in Mexico and the Class-C Pioneer League.[40]

Hiram and Virginia lived in Chicago when their only child, Hiram Jr., was born in May 1951. In the meantime, Bithorn's mother, along with his sister and family had moved to Mexico City where Maria Angelica attended university. Plans were made for Hiram to sponsor the baptism of her one-year-old son, David Hiram Arechiga, during the year-end holidays. However, fearing the trip would be too difficult for her and the baby, Virginia and seven-month-old Hiram Jr. remained in Chicago while Bithorn headed out on the 1,685-mile journey alone.

Driving a 1947 Buick, he crossed the U.S.-Mexico border and traveled to the extreme southern part of the state of Tamaulipas to the town of El Mante along Federal Highway 85. Here he met his untimely death by a policeman's bullet to his stomach. Exactly what happened that night remains a mystery, but apparently he stopped in El Mante to get a hotel room. While some reports say he had no money to pay for the room, another says he had $2,000 in U.S. currency with him.[41] The policeman, Corporal Ambrosio Castillo Cano, claimed Bithorn attempted to sell his car to raise money for the hotel room, but had no license or registration papers for it. How he could have

made it all the way from Chicago to Mexico without a license, registration, or money remains another puzzling piece of the Bithorn mystery.

According to Castillo's version, he got into the car with Bithorn and ordered him to drive to the local police station. A fight ensued, and fearing for his life, the policeman shot the Puerto Rican. Bithorn was then transported by ambulance to a hospital 84 miles away in Victoria, and within an hour of arrival, the 35-year-old was pronounced dead of internal hemorrhage. While various sources give his date of death anywhere from December 27, 1951, to January 1, 1952, the most generally accepted date of December 29, 1951, is the one documented by an Associated Press reporter in Mexico. In Chicago, Virginia learned of her husband's demise in a radio report, which she confirmed with a phone call to the *Chicago Tribune*.[42]

Bithorn's family never bought the policeman's story, believing he actually wanted to steal Bithorn's car and personal belongings. Castillo's story grew more convoluted as he attempted to place blame on the Puerto Rican. He even told Mexican officials that Bithorn admitted to being a member of the Communist Party and that he was on an important mission. Strangely, Puerto Rico's newspapers said very little about his death, and no Puerto Rican journalists went to Mexico to investigate.[43] However, Bithorn's family insisted on an FBI investigation. Castillo was indicted on January 11, 1952, convicted, and sentenced to eight years for the murder.[44]

Outraged over the death and crude burial of the baseball player in Mexico, Puerto Rican officials and Bithorn's family demanded that his remains be returned to the island for a proper Christian burial. At the request of Governor Luis Muñoz Marin and San Juan Mayor Felisa Rincón de Gautier, the U.S. ambassador to Mexico, William O'Dwyer, arranged with Mexican government officials for the transfer by air carrier. Bithorn's decomposing body, covered with mud and still in the clothes in which he was killed, arrived in Puerto Rico on January 12, 1952. The next day, about 5,000 people filed past his casket on the field at Sixto Escobar Stadium prior to burial in Buxeda Cemetery, Isla Verde, only a short distance from his birthplace in Santurce, Puerto Rico.

As a symbol of respect for their former teammate and manager, the *Senadores* played the rest of the season wearing black patches on their sleeves. Ten years later, in 1962, the city of San Juan memorialized the island's first major leaguer by naming its new 18,000-seat baseball park the Hiram Bithorn Stadium, a fitting tribute to the pioneer who opened the door for all the other Puerto Rican ballplayers who realized their dreams, and each in his own way contributed to the island's legacy in major-league baseball.

Bithorn's wife, Virginia, who later remarried, died in 2011 in Arizona.[45]

## NOTES

1 Autografo.tv/hiram-bithorn. 2012.
2 Autografo.tv/hiram-bithorn.
3 Adrian Burgos, Jr., *Playing America's Game* (Berkeley: University of California Press, 2007), 269-270.
4 Michael Bithorn interview by author, February 17, 2014.
5 Autografo.tv/hiram-bithorn.
6 Michael Bithorn interview by author, February 23, 2014.
7 Autografo.tv/hiram-bithorn.
8 Autografo.tv/hiram-bithorn.
9 Autografo.tv/hiram-bithorn.
10 Autografo.tv/hiram-bithorn.
11 Autografo.tv/hiram-bithorn.
12 Nick C. Wilson, *Early Latino Ballplayers in the United States* (Jefferson, North Carolina: McFarland & Company, Inc., 2005), 145.
13 Wilson, 146.
14 Wilson, 146.
15 Wilson, 146.
16 Burgos, 309.
17 Autografo.tv/hiram-bithorn.
18 SABR Research Journals Archive, "The Hollywood Stars."
19 Interviews by author: Michael Bithorn, February 23, 2014, and David Hiram Arechiga, March 25, 2014.
20 The first was a pair of Cubans, pitcher Oscar Tuero and catcher Mike Gonzalez, St. Louis Cardinals, 1918, and the second was Cuban Adolfo "Dolf" Luque and Tampa-born Al López, Brooklyn Robins, 1930.

21. Nick Diunte. Examiner.com. "Bithorn led the way for Puerto Ricans in the majors." Retrieved January 29, 2013.
22. Burgos, 171.
23. Autografo.tv/hiram-bithorn.
24. Diunte.
25. Wilson, 148.
26. Wilson, 147-148.
27. David Maraniss *Clemente: The Passion and Grace of Baseball's Last Hero* (New York: Simon & Schuster Paperbacks, 2006), 28.
28. Diunte.
29. Burgos, 98.
30. Wilson, 147.
31. Wilson, 148.
32. Burgos, 172.
33. Fred Lieb, *Baseball as I Have Known It* (New York: Coward, McCann & Geoghegan, 1977), 260.
34. Maraniss, 28.
35. Gary Bedingfield., www.baseballinwartime.com. March 29, 2008.
36. Wilson, 148.
37. Bedingfield, op. cit.
38. Autografo.tv/hiram-bithorn.
39. Maraniss, 30. Family interviews, 2014.
40. Bedingfield.
41. Andrew Martin, "Hi Bithorn: Puerto Rico's Baseball Pioneer," *The Baseball Historian*. Retrieved January 29, 2014.
42. Jorge Colon Delgado, www.elnuevodia.com/blog-titulo-852202. December 29, 2010.
43. Autografo.tv/hiram-bithorn.
44. Wilson, 150.
45. Obituary in *The Arizona Republic*, May 20-22, 2011.

# BOBBY BONILLA

## By Mark Souder

*"He's a quality player who's getting better all the time. A year ago, he played on talent alone. Now he's doing it on talent and know-how. His potential is unlimited."*

– Pittsburgh Pirates manager Jim Leyland[1]

**NO WORD BETTER DESCRIBES** Bobby Bonilla's baseball career than "potential." He was selected as an All-Star six times. Bonilla won three Silver Slugger Awards while a Pirate. Toward the end of his career, he helped lead the Florida Marlins to an improbable World Series triumph. In spite of all this success, Bonilla seemed trapped inside a bubble of bigger expectations.

Standing 6-feet-3 and weighing 210 to 240 pounds, Roberto Martin Antonio "Bobby" Bonilla was always a big man from the time he began playing professional baseball. He was similar in build to two former Auburn University football players, Frank Thomas and Bo Jackson, who like Bonilla tantalized Chicago White Sox fans with their potential to put a big hurt on every baseball. Bonilla was not a finesse hitter, or even a traditional home-run hitter. "He simply muscled the ball with the brute strength of an offensive tackle, which he resembled in appearance," one writer explained.[2]

There is great irony in the pressure for Bonilla to achieve even more than he did. When Bobby was born on February 23, 1963, the area dominated by the Jackson Houses of the South Bronx was not a neighborhood full of high expectations. Puerto Rican families, mostly low income, were pouring into the Bronx in huge numbers. The Bronx has been the political bulwark of nationally ground-breaking Puerto Rican politicians including Herman Badillo, Fernando Ferrer, and Jose Serrano. The Bronx is the second largest population area of Puerto Ricans, behind only San Juan, Puerto Rico.

Bonilla is of Afro-Puerto Rican heritage, his parents having moved to the Bronx from Puerto Rico. Roberto Sr. was an electrician and Regina, his mother, was a psychologist. They divorced when Bobby was 8. He, his twin sisters, Socorro and Milagros, and his brother, Javier, grew up living with their mother. His father lived only five minutes away. Bonilla said that "he was always there if I needed him."[3] Both parents worked to instill values in him though actions and words. His father took Bobby on electrical jobs to demonstrate how hard he had to work as well as the dangers of his job, and then, according to Bonilla, would ask, "Is this what you want to do?" and Bobby would reply "No, Dad, I'll work at my baseball a little harder."[4]

His home area was the infamous 40th Police Precinct, known for its homicides and robberies and not many success stories. Bonilla said that he "had my sports." "It kept me away from the drugs, the gangs," he told Ross Newhan of the *Los Angeles Times*.[5] Amidst the chaos, Bobby focused on baseball. He told *People* magazine that he "played sports 24 hours a day. In a place like the South Bronx, you have to dream or else you'll get caught up in the mess."[6] His life in the Bronx led to one of his oft-repeated phrases when people asked him if criticism, booing fans or batting slumps were "pressure." He'd say: "This isn't pressure. Pressure is growing up in the South Bronx."[7]

Not only did Bobby have his family to keep him focused, but he had an extraordinary high-school baseball coach, Joe Levine. Beyond just helping develop Bonilla as a high-school player, Levine put him in the position to launch an improbable and extraordinary major-league career. The coach attended a seminar at which a high-school all-star team was being assembled to play in Scandinavia in

the summer of 1980. High-school senior Bonilla was selected for the team, but did not have the money needed to go. His coach started a "Bobby Fund" to assist Roberto Sr. in paying for the summer trip. It is no wonder that Bonilla considered Coach Levine a second father.[8]

The coordinator and instructor for the trip was legendary baseball scout Syd Thrift. Thrift had spent nearly 20 years as the scouting coordinator of Pittsburgh Pirates, Kansas City Royals, and Oakland Athletics but had left baseball and was working during this nine-year stretch as a real estate agent. Here's how Thrift described the trip: "It was the season of the midnight sun. We all slept in one big room. There were no shades on the windows and the sun never set. It was the most bizarre thing you ever saw."[9] But it gave Thrift plenty of daylight to see Bobby Bonilla's potential.

Upon returning, Thrift called one of his old bosses, Pirates minor-league director Branch Rickey Jr., and within weeks of returning, Bonilla was at the Pirates' spring home in Bradenton, Florida for a tryout.[10] Bonilla was not an instant success story in minor-league baseball. He spent his first two years with the Pirates' rookie league team, hitting barely above the Mendoza line though occasionally flashing his potential power. At age 20, in 1983 at the Class-A level, Bonilla began to show improved skills so the Pirates advanced him to Nashua of the Double-A Eastern League in 1984. There he again slightly improved his power, average, and speed even though he had risen to a higher level in the minors.

In 1985 Bonilla was invited to spring training with the Pirates in Bradenton. He was getting his breakout chance, but Bonilla broke his leg in a collision with Bip Roberts while chasing a foul popup. He could have given up but did not. Bonilla credited his wife, Millie, his high-school sweetheart, with "keeping his head straight." "I was a big baby in a lot of ways," Bonilla said. "I had to learn to cope while wanting to be home. I earned $650 a month and spent $200 calling Millie. She picked up a lot of the slack. She kept my head straight."[11] The Pirates sent him back down to Class A with Prince William (Carolina League). There he met Barry Bonds, who was to become his closest friend in baseball.

In the winter of 1983-84, Bonilla had played his first baseball in his parents' native home of Puerto Rico. He was still a raw minor-league player when he joined the Senadores de San Juan. Mako Oliveras had taken over as manager and immediately liked the personable Bonilla. Since Bonilla had nowhere to stay, Oliveras asked his mother if Bobby could stay with them. He did so for two winters, where he loved the food and became part of their family.[12]

Bonilla played four additional seasons in the Puerto Rican Winter League. Before the 1984-85 season, the Indios de Mayaguez traded shortstop Adalberto Pena and pitcher Orlando Lind to San Juan for Bonilla. Assistant general manager Jorge Aranzamendi, based upon all the major-league scouting reports he had access to, supported going after prospect Bonilla because of his potential. While Pena helped lead San Juan to a championship, Bonilla was not a regular starter on Mayaguez until 1985-86.[13] Bonilla credited the Puerto Rican Winter League with advancing his skills. He had short high-school baseball seasons in New York City, so he entered minor-league ball without much game experience. After his spring-training injury in 1985, and his demotion back to Class A, the winter of 1985-86 was of great importance to his major-league career. His solid statistics during the last 39 games of the season at Prince William reflected improving skills that resulted in his starting for Mayaguez.

Based upon his broken leg and partial season in Class A, the Pirates had left Bonilla off their 40-man roster in the fall. They presumed that no team would select him in the Rule 5 draft because it would require placing an inexperienced, possibly damaged player on the 25-player roster for the season or potentially losing him. The Chicago White Sox had the advantage of being able to select the unprotected Bonilla after he had demonstrated recovery not only in a few months of minor-league baseball but also with the Indios in winter ball. For $50,000 the White Sox received a soon-to-be major-league star.

Bonilla astoundingly jumped from Class A to the majors without missing a beat. In 75 games for the White Sox, his .256 batting average slightly exceeded his best year in the minors and his on-base percentage and slugging average were roughly equal to his previous bests. No wonder Bonilla said that playing Puerto Rican Winter League baseball was particularly important to him because he skipped Triple A. Puerto Rico had been a critical training ground to maturing and developing his skills.

Bonilla had a friend who had never forgotten him: Syd Thrift. Thrift had been enticed back into baseball by the Pirates, who appointed him general manager. Thrift hired the White Sox third-base coach, Jim Leyland, to be the manager. In midseason the Pirates reacquired Bonilla for pitcher Jose DeLeon. In 2013 ESPN ranked each major-league team's best deadline trade. For the Pirates, it was receiving Bonilla for DeLeon.[14]

Bonilla returned to Indios de Mayaguez for the 1986-87 winter season. Post-season he was selected play for the Puerto Rican entry in the 1987 Caribbean Series held in Hermosillo, Mexico along with other major-league players Candy Maldonado and Juan Nieves, as were future stars Roberto Alomar and David Cone. Because of his Puerto Rican heritage, in the winter leagues and for the national team, Bobby Bonilla was classified as a Puerto Rican native player.[15] In retirement Bonilla has continued to support baseball efforts in Puerto Rico, including the Puerto Rico Baseball Academy that produced Houston Astros star Carlos Correa.[16]

In 1987 for the Pirates, Bonilla showed the first signs of a major breakout. He hit .300 (his previous high had been .269), topped 10 home runs for the first time, and slugged .481. He played his last year of winter ball for Mayaguez in 1987-88. In 1988 Bonilla hit 24 home runs and had 100 RBIs. The Pirates excelled as well, as Thrift built a powerhouse upon the ruins of the cocaine-devastated Pirates. From 1988 to 1991, Bonilla averaged 24 home runs, 38 doubles, 102 RBIs, and a 4.4 WAR. While Bonds was the top star with a Wins Above Replacement (WAR) average of 7.9, Bonilla was among the best players in the majors. In 1988, at the start of Bonilla's outburst, Philadelphia Phillies third baseman Mike Schmidt said, "He's the best all-around third baseman in the league."[17]

The Pirates had become the dominant team in the majors, winning three straight division titles in 1990, 1991, and 1992. Bonilla finished second in the National League's 1990 MVP voting (behind teammate Bonds) and third in 1991 (Bonds was second to Terry Pendleton of the NL Champion Atlanta Braves). The Spring 1991 issue of *Topps Baseball Card* magazine featured Bonilla and Bonds on the cover, calling them the "Killer B's."[18] Topps correctly realized that the double B's of Barry Bonds and Bobby Bonilla, combined with their first-second and second-third place MVP finishes, and the Pirates' natural bee-colored black and gold uniforms, made the duo the perfect "Killer B's" of all time.

Bonilla was not with the Pirates during the 1992 championship season. His life had started to take a bad turn during the 1991 season as his coming free agency began to raise dissatisfaction about money. Bonilla had always been known for having a "neon" smile. *People* magazine stated: "Perhaps not since Ernie ('It's a great day for a ballgame') Banks retired from the Chicago Cubs 17 years ago has baseball seen a man with a sunnier disposition swing a meaner bat." A teammate said it was nice to come to the ballpark and see his smiling face.[19]

Money had become a proxy for not only skill but respect. The Pirates had been a home to African American stars, and had fielded the first all-black lineup in 1971, anchored by Puerto Rican legend Roberto Clemente and Willie Stargell. However, Bonilla felt that teammate Andy Van Slyke and others were given large contract offers while the Pirates would not meet his request. The Yankees were interested in either Bonds or Bonilla but were rumored to prefer Bonilla because of his upbeat attitude.[20]

However, it was not the Yankees, but the New York Mets that brought Bobby Bonilla home to New York City. The Mets signed Bonilla to the highest dollar contract ever in the major leagues at the time, $5 million for five years. New York is considered a tough sports town, with many opinionated sports journalists competing for the attention of millions of opinionated and passionate sports fans. Bonilla, as the newly minted richest man in baseball, was going to have a bullseye on his head even if he performed well.

Barry Bonds accurately framed the difference between himself and his good friend. "I can handle New York because I don't get my feelings hurt the way Bobby does. I don't give a __ what people write about me or say. Bobby does. He's too sensitive. I told him before he went there that he wasn't going to be able to deal with it but he didn't believe me. Now, he believes me."[21]

Bonilla's return home started like the dream he hoped it would be. On February 3, 1992, he and his wife established the Millie and Bobby Bonilla Public

School Fund. Bronx Borough President Fernando Ferrer proclaimed the day Bobby Bonilla Day, stating what a great pleasure it was "to welcome back the four-star slugger of the South Bronx." Surrounded by Mets officials and teacher union representatives, Bonilla pledged to donate $500 for each RBI he got for sports equipment and incentive programs to the Bronx schools he attended. It was expected to be around $50,000 because Bonilla had become a reliable 100 RBIs-a-year player. Lehman High School was not represented at the ceremony because the principal had fired Bonilla's beloved former coach Levine. Instead, Levine spoke at the ceremony and the *New York Times* noted that he would be the "unofficial administrator of the fund."[22]

From there, things went downhill. Bonilla sank back to the mediocre performance level of his first year—he was hitting only .130 in May—only now he was the highest paid player in baseball. He improved but still drove in only 70 runs, largely because the weak Mets lineup had 31 percent fewer runners for him to potentially drive in.[23] Regardless of the reasons, fans were focused upon his underperformance compared with his record-breaking salary. He was scalded in New York, where he took to wearing earplugs, and his baseball homecoming to Pittsburgh was a disaster, including having a bottle thrown at him. The Mets imploded. Then it got worse.

The days of fawning sports reporters was over. The adoring public was no longer so adoring but more sarcastic. The title of the book *The Worst Team Money Could Buy* suggests the views of the author about the 1992 Mets.[24] The generally ebullient Bonilla was already upset with the world and upset with himself. He said later that he perhaps should have handled the criticism better, but when he was called out for lying about his attempt to reverse an error call on what he thought was a hit, the festering wounds to his pride were picked open. The powerful Bonilla physically intimidated the less imposing author/*New York Daily News* baseball reporter Klapisch by threatening to "show him the Bronx."[25] It was ironic since Bonilla had specifically separated himself from the more violent part of the Bronx his entire life, but the image of sunny Bobby never quite recovered.

After his poor performance in 1992, Bonilla recovered to have a solid season for the Mets in 1993, as well as in the strike-shortened seasons of 1994 and the first half of 1995. He was named to the NL All-Star team in 1993 and 1995. His statistics averaged over a full season were just shy of his annual performances in Pittsburgh. But now his personal image had been damaged, and his contract had raised expectations to levels he could not achieve.

In late July of 1995 the Mets traded their All-Star slugger to the Baltimore Orioles for two minor-leaguers. Bonilla, clearly glad to escape, drove to Baltimore that night in order to be in the lineup against the White Sox.[26] He hit extremely well for the Orioles in 1995, batting .333 with a slugging average of .544 and an RBI rate of 123 in a 162-game season. He followed that with another solid season in 1996. Bonilla was one of the reasons the Orioles made the 1996 American League playoffs as the wild-card team. He hit a game-sealing grand slam in the first game against the Cleveland Indians, and then homered again in the decisive fourth game. Baltimore defeated the Indians three games to one but was easily subdued by the Yankees in the ALCS.

When his season concluded, Bonilla was again a free agent. He signed with the Florida Marlins, where he was reunited with his former Pirates manager Jim Leyland. In 1997 he batted .297 with 39 doubles, 96 RBIs, and 17 homers. The Marlins' owner, Wayne Huizenga, had decided to open his checkbook, not only for Bonilla but also for Moises Alou, Alex Fernandez, and Jim Eisenreich. The Marlins made the NL playoffs as the wild-card team. It was Bonilla's fourth trip to the playoffs. This time the Marlins won the World Series, against Cleveland.

After the World Series victory, Huizenga, a trash magnate, trashed his team. He sold, failed to re-sign, or traded most of the key players. The Marlins went from first to worst, finishing 1998 with a 54-108 record. In May 1998 Bonilla was traded, along with Gary Sheffield and three others, to the Los Angeles Dodgers for Mike Piazza and Todd Zeile, who were then flipped as well. Bonilla's glory days were gone. His hitting collapsed (.249 for the season) and he was bounced to the Mets for Mel Rojas after the season.

At this late stage of his career, Bonilla was not a hitting asset but was more like a good-luck charm. For the 2000 season, he signed with the Atlanta Braves. They won their ninth straight division title. He was not re-signed. For 2001, at age 38, he played in 93 games for the St. Louis Cardinals, who won the NL wild-card slot. They were eliminated by the eventual World Series champion Arizona Diamondbacks. Bonilla's stellar playing career ended much as it had begun. It was an arc, beginning in 1981 with the Pirates Rookie League team, for which he hit .217, and finishing with a .213 batting with the Cardinals 20 years later.

However, it did not end the baseball legend of Bobby Bonilla. In 1999, his last year with the Mets, Bonilla had agreed to have his contract bought out and accepted deferred payments that would begin in 2011 and continue until 2035. On July 1 of each year he receives a check for $1,193,248.20 from the Mets on what the media refers to as "Bobby Bonilla Day." Some refer to him as the "Patron Saint of Bad Contracts," and others refer to players who also are receiving deferred paychecks long after retirement as the "Bobby Bonilla All-Stars."

Since Bonilla has not played for the Mets since the last century, the fact that his annuity exceeds the salary, for example, of any of the 2016 Mets' top four pitching stars—Noah Syndergaard, Jacob DeGrom, Matt Harvey, and Steven Matz—causes lots of tsk-tsking by the media and fans. Of course, when Bonilla was slugging away as a youngster for the Pirates he was not earning the big money either. More importantly, even though the Mets will have paid Bonilla $29.8 million for the 2000 season in which he was not on the team, the deal was both logical at the time and worked out well for the Mets. The biggest problem was scam artist Bernie Madoff. Mets owner Fred Wilpon was one of the investors Madoff defrauded of $17 billion for which he was sentenced to 150 years in prison. Wilpon had been receiving 10-15 percent annual gains. Had he earned even 10 percent on the $5.9 million owed Bonilla in 2000, by 2035 Wilpon would have netted a $49 million profit. In attempts to recover losses, Wilpon was sued but found innocent of any crime. He was guilty only of a combination of misplaced trust and economic ignorance.[27]

The cash freed up by the Bonilla deferred deal resulted in the signing of Derek Bell, Todd Zeile, and Mike Hampton. They helped lead the Mets to the National League title in 2000. Hampton earned the MVP of the NL Championship Series by pitching 16 shutout innings. When Hampton then signed with the Colorado Rockies, the Mets received as compensation a young ballplayer named David Wright, who developed into one of the 10 best Mets players ever.[28]

Bonilla had one other unique side of his personality: He had some minor success as an actor. Bonilla, Bonds, and Pedro Guerrero all had bit parts in the 1993 baseball movie *Rookie of the Year*. The movie is the story of a 12-year-old boy who, after hurting his arm, finds that the surgically repaired arm enables him to throw a baseball over 100 miles per hour. This results in his being signed by the Chicago Cubs and sparking them to a World Series victory. He reinjures his arm and returns to Little League baseball, only sporting a World Series ring.

The brief appearance of Bonilla is in one of the scenes that adds the patina of authenticity to the movie. The first is the day at Wrigley Field, filmed at the ballpark, when young Henry Rowengartner (Thomas Ian Nicholas) returns an opposing team's home run toward the field, only it goes to the catcher at home plate on the fly. Later, after his shaky early start, the "rookie" pitcher becomes a key part of the Cubs turnaround. Showing actual baseball players Bonilla, Guerrero, and Bonds swinging mightily, and late, on the alleged fastballs of the 12-year-old pitcher was a shortcut way to establish Henry's importance to the Cubs success. The ballplayers in the scene were billed as "The Big Whiffers."

The movie had mini-cult status among Cub fans desperate to win. Nicholas was invited to toss out the first pitch at a Cubs game in 2010, and to sing the National Anthem in 2015. After the Cubs won Game Seven of the 2016 World Series, he tweeted out the final shot from *Rookie of the Year*, when he held his World Series ring up to the camera.

The personable Bonilla was also interviewed on nontraditional baseball shows including the *Late Night With David Letterman* and *Lauren Hutton and...* He also appeared in three television series. In 1994 Bobby was "Ronnie Holland" in the episode "The Friendly Neighborhood Dealer" on the Fox series *New York Undercover*. The series ran from 1994 to 1998, starring Michael DeLorenzo and Malik Yoba as NYPD detectives. DeLorenzo, like Bonilla, was of Puerto Rican descent and from the Bronx.

In 1995 Bonilla appeared on *Living Single* in an episode titled "Play Ball." The series was carried five years by Fox, ranking among the top five shows among African-Americans. Among its stars were Queen Latifah, Kim Fields, and Kim Coles. In 1998 Bonilla and Tony LaRussa appeared in the episode "The American Game" on the HBO television series *Arli$$*. While it was critically panned, *Time* magazine reported that so many viewers claimed *Arli$$* was the sole reason they subscribed to HBO that it remained on the year for seven seasons.

By any standard, young Roberto Martin Antonio "Bobby" Bonilla of the South Bronx achieved his potential.

## SOURCES

In addition to the sources cited in the Notes, the author utilized Baseball-Reference.com for all baseball statistics and the website IMDb.com for information on Bonilla's movie and TV career.

## NOTES

1 Ross Newhan, "An Act of Piracy: Getting Bonilla Back Was a Steal," *Los Angeles Times*, July 8, 1988.

2 Bob Klapisch and John Harper, *The Worst Team Money Could Buy* (Lincoln: University of Nebraska Press, Bison Books, 2005), 75.

3 Newhan.

4 Ibid.

5 Ibid.

6 Eric Levin and Mary Huzinec, "Save That Ball, Boys—The Way Bobby Bonilla's Going, It'll Be Valuable," *People* magazine, July 18, 1988.

7 Ken Rappoport, *Bobby Bonilla* (New York: Walker and Company, 1993), 91.

8 Kenneth Shouler, "Swinging for the Fences," *Cigar Aficionado*, July/August 1998; Newman, "Act of Piracy."

9 Ibid.

10 Shouler.

11 Newhan.

12 Thomas E. Van Hyning, *Puerto Rico's Winter League: A History of Major League Baseball's Launching Pad* (Jefferson, North Carolina: McFarland, 1995), 29.

13 Ibid.

14 proxy.espn.com/blog/sweetspot/tag?name=bobby-bonilla.

15 Van Hyning, 111.

16 "MLB to Start Puerto Rico Summer League for 14-17-Year-Olds," Fox Sports, June 19, 2014.

17 Levin and Huzinec.

18 While some have included Sid Bream and Jay Bell among the Pirates' "Killer B's" and others later stretched the term to the powerful Houston "B's" (Jeff Bagwell, Craig Biggio, and Derek Bell), the term fit perfectly on Bonilla and Bonds.

19 Ibid.

20 Jon Heyman, "Yankees Are Targeting Bonds or Bonilla," *Newsday* (Long Island, New York), January 13, 1991.

21 John Feinstein, *Play Ball: The Life and Troubled Times of Major League Baseball* (New York: Villard Books, 1993), 26.

22 Bruce Weber, "Bobby Bonilla Puts His Bat to Work," *New York Times*, February 4, 1992.

23 Neil Paine, "Bobby Bonilla Was More Than the Patron Saint of Bad Contracts," FiveThirtyEight.com, September 30, 2016.

24 Klapisch and Harper.

25 Rappoport, 286.

26 Buster Olney, "All-Star Slugger Acquired From Mets for Minor-Leaguers Ochoa and Buford Orioles Get Their Cleanup Man: Bonilla," *Baltimore Sun*, July 29, 1995.

27 theundefeated.com/features/bobby-bonilla-was-more-than-just-that-mets-contracts-538/; Serge Kovaleski and David Waldstein, "Madoff Had Wide Role in Mets' Finances," *New York Times*, February 1, 2011; and Darren Royal, "Why the Mets Pay Bobby Bonilla $1.19 Million Every July 1," ESPN; July 1, 2016.

28 Mel Antonen, "Deferred Payment: Mets Owe Bobby Bonilla Nearly $30 Million From 2011-2035," *USA Today*; updated July 1, 2010; Ted Berg, "The Annual Deferred Payments to Bobby Bonilla Actually Worked Out Quite Well for the Mets," *USA Today*, July 1, 2015.

# IVÁN CALDERON

## By Daniel Potter

**T**HERE ARE MANY WAYS TO GAIN attention as a professional baseball player, and over the course of his career, Iván Calderón got plenty of attention.

At first, it was as a five-tool prospect for the Seattle Mariners; a can't-miss kid with tremendous power and raw talent who tore through the minor leagues. A short-time after arriving in Seattle, Calderón got pegged as a slacker who didn't hustle or work hard. It was a reputation he didn't deserve, based more on ethnic stereotypes than actual events on the field. In truth, he was playing hurt, having severely injured his shoulder diving for a ball. Those who played with him say Calderón was extremely dedicated to his craft. White Sox batting coach Walt Hriniak went so far as to call him one of the hardest workers he'd ever had.[1]

Calderón was known as a flamboyant and flashy player, a big man with big gold chains and big smile. He wore thousands of dollars' worth of jewelry both on and off the field in a time when such a thing was frowned upon by much of baseball's old-school establishment.

"I'm not worried about him on the field," his manager at Montreal Buck Rodgers said of Calderón in 1991. "I just hope he doesn't get mugged off the field."[2]

Eventually, Calderón became known as one of the best left fielders of his time, a clutch hitter with gap-to-gap power and a keen eye for the strike zone. The Montreal Expos thought so highly of his ability that they traded Tim Raines, arguably the best player in franchise history, to the Chicago White Sox to get him.

By the end of his career, Calderón had earned a far less desirable reputation, but one not uncommon to professional athletes. He was considered injury-prone. And unlike his previous reputation as a "lazy" player, the injury label was well-deserved. Calderón suffered several significant injuries over the course of his 10-year big league career, most notably that nagging shoulder injury from which he never fully recovered.

And Calderón will also be remembered for the grisly way in which he died. In December of 2003, at the age of 41 and nearly 10 years after retiring from baseball, Calderón was shot and killed execution-style in a bar near his home in Puerto Rico. Initial reports indicated he was killed by a man to whom he had loaned money as a bail-bondsman, but to this day, his murder remains unsolved.[3]

Iván Calderón Perez was born on March 19, 1962 in Fajardo, Puerto Rico, a coastal city on the northastern tip of the island. His father, Eliseo, worked in construction but struggled to support his family of six on just $120 a month.[4] Iván Calderón excelled in both baseball and volleyball at Mediana Alta Intermediate School in nearby Loiza before dropping out at the age of 14 play baseball full time.[5] He says he grew up idolizing Roberto Clemente and other Puerto Rican stars and recognized from an early age that baseball could be a good way to support himself and his family.

"I saw the players from Puerto Rico—Roberto Clemente, Vic Power, Orlando Cepeda—all leave the island to play baseball in America," Calderón said. "They had lots of money, nice cars, good clothes and jewelry. A lot of people told me when I was 16 I played good."[6]

One of those who most likely praised Calderón's play was Seattle Mariners scout Luis Rosa, who is credited with signing the then 16-year-old as an undrafted free agent on July 30, 1979.[7]

Calderón began his professional career in 1980, with the talent-laden Bellingham Mariners in the Northwest League. The 18-year-old quickly proved he belonged, batting a whopping .370 in his first 31 games. He cooled off, but still finished with a .318 batting average and a league-leading nine triples. The slugging left fielder was one of eight future big leagu-

ers on the Bellingham M's that season, a squad that finished a league-best 45-25.

Calderón's success continued the following season with the Wausau Timbers, another talent-rich Mariners farm club that dominated its league. He was one of the Timbers most dangerous hitters, finishing second on the club with 20 home runs while batting .306, driving in 62 runs, and stealing 26 bases. It was the first of two seasons in Wausau for Calderón, who followed up his 1981 season with an even better 1982, slamming 24 home runs, driving in 89 runs and batting .286.

A promotion to the Double-A Chattanooga Lookouts in 1983 did little to slow Calderón's progress. Just 21 years old, Calderón was one of the youngest players in Double A but still managed to make the Southern League All-Star squad. He earned high praise from his manager, Bill Haywood.

"He's a potential superstar. He hits the ball as well as anybody in the big leagues," Haywood told *The Sporting News*. "He's got big league speed, a big league arm, a big league bat. I pray that nothing happens to him. If it doesn't, he'll be up there a long time."[8]

Calderón finished the season tied for the lead in hits (170) and leading the league in triples (15), and in the top 10 in nearly every other offensive category including batting average (.311), runs (92), and RBIs (80).

By 1984, Calderón was one of the Mariners' top prospects and among a young corps of players general manager Hal Keller wanted to retain.[9] The 22-year-old opened that season with the Mariners' Triple-A Salt Lake City Gulls, and quickly established himself as one of the best hitters in the Pacific Coast League. He was batting .365 when Seattle came calling, promoting him to the big leagues on August 10. Inserted as the Mariners' starting center fielder, Calderón struggled at the plate over the next two weeks, managing just five hits in 24 at-bats before a wrist injury shut him down for the remainder of the season. It was the first of several significant injuries Calderón suffered over the course of his career.

Both Calderón and the Mariners were generating a lot of buzz during the spring of 1985. After all, the team had the top two rookies in the league in 1984 in first baseman Alvin Davis and pitcher Mark Langston along with several promising young Mariners who made their big-league debuts in 1984, including Jim Presley, Danny Tartabull, and Calderón. Add pitchers Mike Moore, Matt Young, Ed Vande Berg, and Edwin Nunez, and there was every reason to believe the Mariners might have a winning record for the first time in franchise history. It was not to be. The Mariners (74-88) finished sixth of the seven teams in the American League Western Division.

Despite winning six games of their first seven games, the Mariners once again proved incapable of sustaining any momentum, and finished the year a disappointing 74-88. For Calderón, 1985 was a microcosm of things to come. He made the opening day roster for the first time in his career, but the residual effects of his wrist injury limited him to mostly pinch-hitting duties. Calderón began getting regular playing time in mid-May, and by the middle of the summer, he was one of Seattle's top hitters and a leading candidate for Rookie of the Year. That all ended during the two-day players' strike in early

August when it was discovered that Calderón had been playing with a broken wrist, ending his season.[10] He finished the year batting .286 with eight home runs in 67 games.

After the season, Calderón's wrist had improved enough to allow him to return to the Puerto Rican winter league where he was among the league's best performers. His strong play continued into spring training in 1986, earning Calderón the starting job in right field. He hit safely in eight of Seattle's first nine games, but it was the only highlight in what was to become another disappointing year for both Calderón and the Mariners.

The team struggled, and in early May, manager Chuck Cottier was fired and replaced by veteran skipper Dick Williams. The fiery Williams and his young right fielder clashed almost from the start. Things came to a head in mid-May, when a Kansas City scout was quoted as saying Calderón didn't have "the heart to be a good big leaguer."[11] It was an all-too common criticism of Latin players of the time, a criticism many now feel had racist undertones. Mariners general manager Dick Balderson tried to use the quote as motivation for Calderón, sitting him and his agent down to discuss the issue.[12] It didn't work. The talk only soured the relationship between the club and its young right fielder and on May 26, Calderón was sent down to Triple A, ending his career in Seattle.

"I wasn't wanted in Seattle," Calderón said. "Dick Williams sent me down. He didn't like me: I don't know why. I asked if they could trade me, and they did."[13]

That trade came in June of 1986, when the Mariners dealt Calderón to the Chicago White Sox for catcher Scott Bradley. Bradley had a solid career in Seattle, but by the end of the 1987 season it was clear that Chicago got the better part of the deal.

Calderón played briefly for the Sox in July, August, and September before returning home for another season in the Puerto Rican winter league. He led the league in home runs and was named MVP of the all-star game. White Sox GM Larry Himes visited Calderón in Puerto Rico, telling the young slugger the team was counting on him to provide much-needed punch in the lineup.

Chicago manager Jim Fregosi echoed that sentiment during spring training, saying he was eager to see what Calderón could do with 500 big league at-bats over the course of a season.[14] For the first time in his big-league career, Calderón was receiving some very public positive reinforcement from his employers, and he rewarded them with what would be the best season of his big-league career.

By mid-May, he was one of the most productive hitters in the White Sox lineup before a severe ankle-sprain forced him onto the disabled list. Calderón was hitting .286 with four home runs at the time, apparently not good enough to endear himself to the old-school establishment that ran the game.

A column in *The Sporting News* on June 1 claimed that several front-office executives believed Calderón was getting the least out of his ability of any big-league player. One unnamed G.M. even went so far as to say that he was "...too-laid back, too lazy. He has the potential to be a star, but he'll never make it big."[15]

Calderón quickly proved his detractors wrong. On May 31, he returned from the DL in a big fashion, belting two home runs against the Boston Red Sox. By season's end, Calderón wound up leading the White Sox in nearly every offensive category including batting average (.2933, to Harold Baines' .2930), hits (159), doubles (38), home runs (28), and runs scored (93). His 1987 season also included one of the best catches ever caught on film, when he climbed the left-field wall in Tiger Stadium to rob Alan Trammell of a home run.[16]

One thing that wasn't widely reported at the time was the fact that Calderón had been playing with a nagging left shoulder injury for the past few seasons, an injury he had suffered while making a diving catch several years earlier.[17] The injury prompted countless cortisone shots and several surgeries, the first of which was performed in August of 1988. That surgery shut down what had already been a very frustrating season for the young slugger.

Things turned around for Calderón in 1989, although he was never the power threat he'd once been.

Once again, he led the team in virtually every offensive category including average (.286), hits (178), doubles (34), home runs (14), RBIs (87), and runs scored (83).

It was much of the same for Calderón the following season, when he helped the surging White Sox challenge the Oakland A's for the division title. Calderón was a key component in the Chicago offense, finishing the year with 44 doubles (George Brett and Jody Reed each led the league with 45), batting .273 and knocking in 74 runs. He stole a career-high 32 bags, and improved tremendously as a fielder, a part of his game that didn't go unnoticed by Sox manager Jeff Torborg.

"You don't have to defend for Iván in late innings," Torborg said. "If anything, you'd want to use him to defend for someone. He told me last September he didn't like being a DH. I said, 'Prove it to me next spring'. And he did."[18]

Still, after the 1990 season, the White Sox dealt Calderón to the Expos for Raines. It was a difficult transition for Calderón, who was not only replacing a Montreal icon, but was also in the midst of a very public contract negotiation.

Still a year away from free-agency, the 29-year-old Calderón was looking to cash in on his recent success with a long-term contract. His agent, Jaime Torres, said they were looking for a contract in the neighborhood of four years and $9 million.[19] "We have told (the Expos) that if we don't have a multi-year contract signed before arbitration, then Iván will leave Montreal after the 1991 season," Torres said.[20]

In the end, Calderón didn't get his four-year deal, but he did get nearly $8 million spread out over three seasons. And while he didn't exactly endear himself to Montreal fans or management before the season, Calderón gave them plenty to cheer about once games got underway, earning the team's player of the month honors in April and May.[21] Named to the All-Star team in July (his only All-Star appearance), Calderón wound up starting in place of injured Mets slugger Darryl Strawberry. He responded with a single and stolen base.

By season's end, Calderón was again one of the more productive left fielders in baseball, hitting .300 with 19 homers, 75 RBIs, and 31 stolen bases. He was limited to pinch-hitting duties for the final month because of his nagging left shoulder. Calderón underwent surgery on the shoulder on September 27 to repair what was described as a "well-defined labrum tear and a partially torn bicep tendon."[22]

The Expos had high hopes that Calderón's shoulder would rebound in 1992, but it wasn't to be. He received several cortisone shots beginning in spring training and hit fairly well when he was able to be on the field. But those days were not often enough. In mid-June, Calderón was placed on the disabled list for the third time that season.

"Right now there is no power there, no nothing," he said in June[23] In July, he said, "I know there is something wrong because every time I move my shoulder I can feel it clicking,"[24]

He had surgery on the shoulder again in late June and was able to return to the field in September, ending the year on a positive note. He batted .309 in

25 September games, serving mostly as the starting left fielder.

Those numbers were good enough to prompt the Boston Red Sox to trade for Calderón in the offseason, although the return the Expos got showed just how far his stock had fallen. Montreal received journeyman pitcher Mike Gardiner and minor-league starter Terry Powers.

The aging, injured slugger played regularly for the Red Sox over the first few months of the season, but batted in the low .200's with almost no power. Boston released Calderón in mid-August. The White Sox signed him for the final month of the season, hoping he would help them down the stretch. Chicago did win the division, but Calderón didn't contribute much in the nine games he played and was not included on the team's postseason roster. He played in the big leagues again, although he did DH for Santurce in the Puerto Rico winter league after the season, and even made the all-star team.[25]

In Puerto Rico, he began raising roosters for cockfighting (legal Puerto Rico.) He was also said to have worked as an informal bondsman, lending money to friends and acquaintances, a decision many believed contributed to his murder.[26]

Rubén Sierra and Bernie Williams were among those who attended Calderón's memorial service in Puerto Rico.[27] Sierra was described as a business partner of Calderón's. Williams remembered Calderón for taking him under his wing as a teenager in the winter league.

"I'll never forget the time Iván Calderón gave me one of his gloves during the 1985-86 season, when I practiced with Caguas," Williams said.[28]

Calderón's death was mourned in Chicago, where he had most of his big-league success. Ken Harrelson, who dealt for Calderón during his only season as a general manager, said the flamboyant outfielder was a competitive player and popular teammate in the White Sox clubhouse.

"I loved him from the first time I saw him," Harrelson said.[29]

Calderón had lost touch with most of his teammates over the years, but was remembered in the way most ballplayers want to be.

"You'd look at Iván with all the jewelry and picture a guy who was flashy and wouldn't work, but it was the complete opposite," White Sox teammate Greg Walker said. "He was a tough out, a middle-of-the-lineup guy who played the game right."[30]

Calderón was survived by his wife, Elisabeth Figueroa, and their two children. He had five other children from previous relationships.[31]

## SOURCES

In addition to the sources noted in this biography, the author also used baseball-reference.com, retrosheet.org, baseball-almanac.com, Topps baseball cards, Score baseball cards, and Donruss baseball cards. Thanks to Rod Nelson of SABR's Scouts Committee.

## NOTES

1 Teddy Greenstein, "Sox's Calderón Was a 'Gamer,'" *Chicago Tribune*, December 29, 2003.

2 "N.L. East: Montreal Expos," *The Sporting News*, March 25, 1991: 44.

3 Associated Press, "Robbery Ruled Out in Death of Baseball Player," *Puerto Rico Herald*, December 29, 2003.

4 Sharon Robb, "Calderón Looking to Rule the Roost with New Team," *Sun-Sentinel* (Fort Lauderdale, Florida), March 14, 1991.

5 *White Sox Media Guide*, 1987.

6 Sharon Robb, "Calderón Looking To Rule The Roost With New Team."

7 Noel Piñeiro Planas, "Muere el ex Buscador de Talento de Béisbol Luis Rosa," primerahora.com, August 6, 2014, at primerahora.com/deportes/beisbol/nota/muereelexbuscadordetalentodebeisbolluisrosa-1027086/

8 "Minor Leagues: Class AA Notes," *The Sporting News*, August 1, 1983: 41-42.

9 Peter Gammons, "AL Notes," *The Sporting News*, November 14, 1983: 48.

10 Bill Plaschke, "A.L. West: Seattle Mariners," *The Sporting News*, August 19, 1985: 18.

11 "A.L. West: Seattle Mariners," *The Sporting News*, May 19, 1986: 21.

12 Ibid.

13 Joe Goddard, "Calderón in the Picture," *The Sporting News*, October 5, 1987: 21.

14 Ibid.

15 Moss Klein, "A.L. Beat," *The Sporting News,* June 1, 1987: 24.

16 "A.L. West: Chicago White Sox," *The Sporting News,* August 10, 1987: 21. See also "CWS@DET: Calderón Climbs Fence to Rob Trammell," Youtube, youtube.com/watch?v=3j3KyTvnhv8

17 "A.L. West: Chicago White Sox," *The Sporting News,* May 9, 1988: 17.

18 "A.L. West: Chicago White Sox," *The Sporting News,* July 16, 1990: 14.

19 "N.L. East: Montreal Expos," *The Sporting News,* February 4, 1991: 38.

20 "N.L. East: Montreal Expos," *The Sporting News,* January 28, 1991: 36.

21 *Montreal Expos Media Guide,* 1992.

22 Ibid.

23 "N.L. East: Montreal Expos," *The Sporting News,* June 22, 1992: 17.

24 "N.L. East: Montreal Expos," *The Sporting News,* July 29, 1992: 16.

25 Thomas E. Van Hyning, *The Santurce Crabbers: Sixty Seasons of Puerto Rican Winter League Baseball* (Jefferson, North Carolina: McFarland & Co. Inc., 1990), 170.

26 *Toronto Star,* December 30, 2003: C14.

27 *Toronto Star,* December 31, 2003: E07.

28 Van Hyning, 209.

29 Greenstein.

30 Ibid.

31 *Toronto Star,* December 30, 2003: C14.

# JOHN CANDELARIA

## By Steve West

YOU COULD SAY THAT JOHN Candelaria's story is a tale of heartbreak, or a tale of unfulfilled promise, or a tale of self-destruction, and you might be right every time. On the other hand, how unlucky can a person be if he managed to pitch in the major leagues for 19 seasons? The Candy Man would ignore all that talk about being star-crossed, and tell you that he spent his life the way he wanted, not how others thought he should. As he said several times during his career, "Life is to enjoy. It's a mystery to be lived, not a problem to be solved."[1]

John Robert Candelaria was born on November 6, 1953, in Brooklyn, New York, to Puerto Rican parents. His father, also named John, was born in Arecibo, Puerto Rico, in 1932, and his mother, the former Felicia Bauza, was born in Rio Piedras, Puerto Rico, in 1934. Both moved from Puerto Rico when they were children to New York, where they met and began a family. John had a brother, Michael, and two sisters, Maria and Dolores. As a child John learned to throw and catch from his father, who played amateur baseball in the New York area. His father saw his talent early: "This kid really has it," he told his family when John was just 5 years old.[2] But John's parents divorced and his father moved back to Puerto Rico when John was 6. His father worked as a car salesman, but John knew little of him once he left, relying instead on his mother, a homemaker, who would closely follow his career as an athlete.

Growing up in Brooklyn, John was a Yankees fan, although with money tight he didn't attend too many games. "I didn't go unless there was a doubleheader," he said. "I used to sit in the bleachers for 75 cents."[3] He played baseball at LaSalle High School, where he attracted attention from scouts during his freshman season, but he felt that he was being worn out by pitching so much, and so he quit baseball. He switched to basketball, where he became the school's all-time leading scorer and second all-time rebounder (to Lew Alcindor, later known as Kareem Abdul-Jabbar[4]), and his performances on the court attracted college scouts from across the country. He was selected to play for Puerto Rico in the 1972 Olympics, but suddenly decided that he would rather play baseball instead, believing that he could be in the major leagues in baseball before he would even be out of college if he were playing basketball.[5] Candelaria performed well enough in his return to baseball that he was scouted by Pittsburgh Pirates scout Dutch Deutsch,[6] who remembered him from his first year in high school, and was drafted in the second round of the 1972 draft by the Pirates. Candelaria was in Puerto Rico, preparing to play basketball in the Olympics, when Pirates officials arrived to sign him. They brought Roberto Clemente with them to act as translator, and Clemente told him in Spanish to reject their offer of $15,000, that he was worth much more.[7] He did, and Clemente's advice proved sound, as Candelaria eventually signed for $40,000.[8]

After signing with the Pirates Candelaria was sent to Charleston (South Carolina) of the Class-A Western Carolinas League for the remainder of the 1973 season, going 10-2 despite feeling the effects of not having pitched regularly for so long. In his best start he threw a one-hitter—allowing the hit to the opposing pitcher in the sixth inning. Moving to Salem (Virginia) of the Class-A Carolina League in 1974, he went 11-8, but suffered from back pain throughout the season. This injury would become a recurring motif during his career. Candelaria sometimes claimed that it began when he slipped on the mound during a start in 1974, but at other times he said it came from a childhood injury, and Pirates doctors even suggested the problem dated back to when he was born.[9] At various times he also said that an operation to fuse the bones in his spine might help with the pain he often felt while pitching, but that it would end his baseball career.[10]

After the 1974 season Candelaria went to Puerto Rico to play winter ball for Bayamon, and learned from the veteran players there. "They taught me to spot my pitches and to use my curveball with more success," he said.[11] He pitched winter ball in Puerto Rico for three seasons.

Candelaria had one start for Charleston (West Virginia) of the Triple-A International League at the end of the 1974 season, and was assigned there again in 1975. He broke out, running his record to 7-1 with a 1.77 ERA. "His control is super. ... He is throwing consistently harder than he did when I first saw him two years ago," Charleston manager Steve Demeter said.[12] When left-hander Ken Brett went on the disabled list the Pirates needed a starter, so Candelaria got the call and made his major-league debut on June 8 in Pittsburgh, in the first game of a doubleheader against the San Francisco Giants. He pitched six innings and impressed, even though he gave up all the runs in a 3-1 loss. He stayed in the rotation, and on June 20, before 47,867 at Shea Stadium, he pitched in New York for the first time, where with a large group of family and friends watching, Candelaria earned his first major-league win by throwing his first complete game to beat the New York Mets, 5-1. "It was something special. Something I'll always remember," he later said.[13]

Despite his early success, Candelaria knew he hadn't made the big time just yet. "I've got a lot to prove," he said.[14] But he pitched well enough to stay with the team, finishing 8-6 with a 2.76 ERA. He ended the season pitching in the playoffs, starting Game Three of the NLCS in Pittsburgh, which the Cincinnati Reds won in 10 innings to complete their sweep of the then best-of-five postseason series. Even so, Candelaria struck out 14 batters in 7⅔ innings, an NLCS record that was not surpassed until 1997. "He's 6-5 and he's all arms and legs," said Pete Rose, although Candelaria was actually 6-7 (and 210 pounds).[15] Rose also said that it was "the greatest pressure game I've seen any pitcher pitch."[16]

Returning with the Pirates in 1976, the 22-year-old Candelaria showed composure beyond his years as he pitched in the rotation all season. "He has all the tools. ... He knows what he is doing on the mound," said Pirates manager Danny Murtaugh.[17] "He is a finished major-league pitcher despite his youth."[18] He did get one relief appearance when on May 26 he threw three shutout innings to get his first career save. But his highlight came on August 9 at home against the Los Angeles Dodgers. That night the Pirates held "Candy Night" and handed out candy bars to the crowd of 9,860, honoring the player who was now nicknamed the Candy Man, after the popular Sammy Davis Jr. song. Candelaria responded to the honor by throwing a no-hitter to beat the Dodgers, 2-0. He was perfect for every inning except the third, when he walked a batter and two others reached on errors to load the bases, but he got out of the jam and sailed the rest of the way home. (Many years later Candelaria admitted that one winter he needed to work out, and the game ball from his no-hitter was the only ball he had, so he practiced with it against a concrete wall and destroyed it.[19])

In 1977 Candelaria was feeling much more comfortable as a major leaguer. He had bought a home in Monroeville, just east of Pittsburgh, and in March he signed a multiyear contract with the Pirates. Even though he had some shoulder problems during spring training, and was having more back pain after slipping on the mound in Montreal in July, he pitched the full season and pitched well. He capped off his season by winning his last four starts to finish at 20-5, the only time he would win 20 games in his career. He won the ERA title at 2.34 (best in the major leagues), although he only finished fifth in Cy Young Award voting, the only season he got any votes for that award. Candelaria was also selected for his only All-Star team in 1977. (He didn't get into the game.)

Candelaria came into spring training 21 pounds lighter in 1978, hoping it would help his back, but he ended up with other problems. A sore left elbow in August had him skipping a few turns through the rotation, and he ended the year at 12-11. In 1979 he had numerous little injuries, not only from the back pain, but from a minor automobile accident on July 31, and then late in the season he pulled a muscle in his ribcage. He had helped the team return to the postseason with his 14-9 record, and started Game One of the NLCS, giving up two runs in seven innings as the Pirates won, 5-2, in 11 innings, starting their three-game sweep of the Cincinnati Reds.

In the World Series Candelaria started Game Three against Baltimore and struggled after being staked to a 3-0 lead, giving up two runs in the third inning before a 67-minute rain delay, and when he returned after the delay he allowed all four batters he faced to reach base (one on an error) before being pulled and taking the loss. But the Pirates fought back from a three-games-to-one deficit, and Candelaria started Game Six, in which he controlled the Orioles batters. He threw six shutout innings, allowing just two runners to get as far as second base, before being lifted for a pinch-hitter. Kent Tekulve came in and closed out the final three innings, the pair combining on a shutout that tied the World Series. "It's a tribute to him that he can pitch in pain the way he did tonight," Tekulve said.[20] The next night the Pirates did it again, beating the Orioles, 4-1, to become world champions.

In 1980 Candelaria came back to earth, and despite throwing the most innings of his career (233⅓) he had his first losing record at 11-14, and his highest ERA to that point at 4.01. The 1981 season was much worse, though, when on May 10 he felt something in his arm when he threw a pitch in a cold and wet game in St. Louis. Initially diagnosed with a torn biceps tendon, Candelaria turned to Dr. Paul Bauer, an expert in body mechanics. Bauer said he did not have a torn tendon, but rather nerve problems in his shoulder, and said Candelaria needed rehab and changes in his pitching motion. Candelaria went along with this idea, missing the rest of the season while working in Bauer's lab in San Diego, watching himself pitch on videotape and adjusting the way he pitched. It all worked; he avoided surgery and came back feeling better than ever. "I believed in myself, but they're the ones who showed me what to do. Without them I don't think I'd be pitching today."[21]

Candelaria returned in 1982 and pitched well all season, although no longer able to go as long as he did earlier in his career. He had said earlier that "I'm not a nine-inning pitcher. The back just aches too much for me to pitch nine innings."[22] Now it showed; he completed just six games in the next three seasons (he had completed 11 in 1976 alone). In those years he also talked more about long-term contracts, but enmity was growing between Candelaria and the Pirates front office. He would snipe about management, and they would snipe back, a pattern that continued for the rest of his time in Pittsburgh. (At one point he called the general manager an "idiot" and a "bozo.") He said he would never re-sign with the Pirates, although he suggested that the length of the contract would be the most important factor. Sure enough, he soon signed a new four-year contract with the Pirates, which made him happy again, at least for the short term.

Candelaria had a tumultuous personal life, making what might be considered poor choices numerous times. He had married and divorced twice in the 1970s. His first marriage was to a woman who had three children from her prior marriage. He successfully fought a paternity suit after blood tests proved a child was not his, and the papers for his second divorce were served between innings of a game he was pitching in Pittsburgh.[23] He finally settled down in his relationship with a flight attendant, Donna Hall, and the couple had two children, Amber born in 1982 and John in 1983. But tragedy soon struck, with John Jr. nearly drowning after falling in the family pool in Sarasota, Florida, on Christmas Day of 1984. The child spent months in the hospital and then at home, all the time in a coma, before he died in November 1985. Candelaria was naturally devastated, and spent most of the year with his mind on far more important things than baseball.

During that time Candelaria had problems on the field as well. He had bone chips removed from his elbow in October 1984, and the team decided in 1985 to move him from the rotation to the bullpen, in part due to the surgery and in part due to concerns over his mental condition while dealing with his son. Candelaria initially complained about the move, saying he wanted his contract renegotiated, but after having some success he reconsidered. "Relieving isn't as bad as I thought it would be ... I'm more involved in the games than I used to be," he said.[24]

Candelaria was always considered an oddball, a player who may have been a little too crazy at times. "There's the starting pitcher for tonight, hat on backward, leaning out the window screaming at people, talking to the grass, thinking about the hitters," as a teammate once described a bus ride to the ballpark in New York. A more astute analysis of Candelaria's style might be the following: "He wasn't particularly sharp. He didn't do anything extremely well. But when it was all over, he was the winner. Typical."[25] When asked once what he would be doing if he wasn't playing baseball: "I'd probably be living in an apartment building in Brooklyn and working for UPS. That would be fun, too."[26] Fun seemed to be his style, with a live-and-let-live attitude to both life and baseball. "If I ever lose the boy in me, what's the sense? I plan to be doing silly things when I'm 50. I just want to be remembered as footloose and fancy free."[27]

Eventually the Pirates tired of Candelaria's antics and insults, and let it be known that they were ready to move him. Several teams were interested, and he was traded to the California Angels in August of 1985, along with pitcher Al Holland and outfielder George Hendrick, for outfielder Mike Brown and pitchers Pat Clements and Bob Kipper. Candelaria still took some parting shots at the Pirates, saying he had been mishandled by manager Chuck Tanner. "I never should have been in the bullpen there," he said.[28] Switched into the rotation for the division-leading Angels, he pitched well, going 7-3, but the Angels fell just one game short of the Kansas City Royals in the AL West at the end of the season.

In 1986 Candelaria had pain in his elbow in the spring, and managed just two innings in his first start before succumbing to the pain. Surgery to remove bone spurs put him out for three months, although he returned and did well, going 10-2 with a 2.55 ERA, the second lowest of his career. This time the Angels won their division, and Candelaria, with relief help from Donnie Moore, pitched well to win Game Three of the ALCS against the Boston Red Sox, giving up one run in seven innings. "I'm throwing it better than I have in seven or eight years. ... I'm just trying to stay inside myself," he said.[29] But coming back in Game Seven, Candelaria had a rough outing, although badly hurt by his defense. He gave up three runs in the second and four in the fourth, when Jim Rice ended his misery with a three-run home run. All of the runs were unearned—both of those innings had begun with an error—but it made no difference as Roger Clemens and Calvin Schiraldi held the Angels batters down and the Red Sox easily won. After the season, Candelaria was named the AL Comeback Player of the Year by *The Sporting News*.

Perhaps due to his personal problems from the last few years coming back to haunt him, Candelaria struggled with injuries and off-field trouble during 1987. On April 17 he was arrested for DUI after running a stop sign ("It was my off day. ... It's nobody's business but mine," he said, earning the ire of anti-drunk driving campaigners), and on May 14 he got a second DUI arrest.[30] The Angels put him on the disabled list the following day for personal reasons, but he returned just two weeks later. In late June they put him back on the DL and checked him into rehab, where he spent more than a month dealing with his problems. "A lot of people assume that since you play this game, you should be happy. Sometimes it's not that way. We're all humans and we all have our problems - regardless," he said.[31] He returned to the team in early August, but they traded him to the New York Mets in mid-September for minor-league pitchers Shane Young and Jeff Richardson. The Mets, chasing the St. Louis Cardinals in the NL East for a playoff spot, had just lost starter Ron Darling to a torn ligament, and immediately traded for Candelaria, who went 2-0 in three starts but the team fell three games short anyway.

Candelaria signed with the New York Yankees as a free agent for 1988, saying that they had guaranteed him a spot in the rotation, something the Mets wouldn't do. "Every kid fantasizes about pitching for his hometown team," he said.[32] In a stunning attack on the Angels during spring training, he told a reporter that Don Sutton had set him up for his first DUI arrest the prior year, claiming that Sutton had called police on him because Sutton wanted his spot in the rotation ("He later told me it was out of concern for my well-being," Candelaria said.)[33] He also slammed Angels manager Gene Mauch, calling him a control freak and saying, "He isn't a very good manager, and I think he knew that I knew that."[34] Then he suggested that rehab was the team's idea, and he didn't want to do it but was forced to, before finally admitting that "I have no one to blame but myself for what was a very tough and frustrating year."[35] The Angels declined to respond to Candelaria, although they reminded reporters that his tirade was similar to when he left the Pirates.

Things didn't go much better with the Yankees, though, as Candelaria argued with manager Lou Piniella during the season and told reporters he wanted out. Even though he was pitching well with a 13-7 record, when he came down with knee pain in August, he was done for the season, although Yankees doctors suggested he should be able to play.

He had surgery for cartilage damage in his knee in October, and although he started 1989 in the rotation he returned to the disabled list in May for more knee surgery, missing another three months. When he returned it was to the bullpen for a few weeks, before being traded once again, this time in late August to the Montreal Expos for third baseman Mike Blowers. The Expos were hoping to add veteran talent for the stretch run, and Candelaria spent the last month of the season in their bullpen. But the Expos chose not to go to salary arbitration with Candelaria, so he once again was a free agent at the end of the year.

Candelaria signed with the Minnesota Twins for 1990, spending almost all his time there in the bullpen, compiling a 3.39 ERA along the way. Traded in July to the Toronto Blue Jays for second baseman Nelson Liriano and outfielder Pedro Munoz, he was used out of the bullpen but also for a couple of spot starts, and struggled, going 0-3 with a 5.48 ERA as the Blue Jays finished two games behind the Boston Red Sox in the AL East.

Yet again a free agent, Candelaria signed with the Los Angeles Dodgers in 1991, his eighth team in six years. Happy to be close to the Orange County home his family had lived in since moving to the Angels in 1985, he took the role of left-handed reliever, pitching in 59 games, the highest total of his career, even though he threw only 33⅔ innings. He returned to the Dodgers in 1992 with the same role, and in 1993 went back to where it all began, signing a one-year contract with the Pirates to be their left-handed reliever. Initial reports of his new-found work ethic—"I've mellowed out a lot. Let's put it that way"[36]—were ruined by his arrest for DUI in Sarasota, Florida, during spring training. He stayed with the team, but struggled, and eventually was released by the Pirates in July with an 8.24 ERA. With minimal interest from other teams—and perhaps not much interest from Candelaria himself—at age 39 his career was over.

As his career came to an end, Candelaria was regularly asked to look back at what he had accomplished. Numerous writers had written about him over the years, and many had said that he was a classic example of wasted potential. The general idea was that he would prefer to sit in the clubhouse and smoke and drink coffee, rather than working out or getting ready for baseball, and this rankled Candelaria. He had after all won 55 more games than he lost (career record of 177-122), and wondered just what he had to do to be considered a success. "I have been successful, I am successful, and I will be successful. Who is to say who has potential and what somebody else's potential is?"[37]

Candelaria tried various things after he retired from baseball, including owning an advertising agency in Pittsburgh. Ultimately, though, he found he preferred solitude. "I am a loner. That's the way I like it. It's what I choose."[38] He moved several times, finally settling in North Carolina, where as of 2016 he lived quietly.

## NOTES

1. Douglas S. Looney, "The Mad Hatter of Pittsburgh," *Sports Illustrated*, June 14, 1982.
2. Gene Wojciechowski, "It Took Him Tirade After Tirade to Obtain a Trade," *Los Angeles Times*, March 31, 1986.
3. Charley Feeney, "Candy Could Frost Bucco Cake With 20 Big Wins," *The Sporting News*, March 19, 1977: 40.
4. Charley Feeney, "Sweet-Throwing Candy Man Makes Bucco Mouths Water," *The Sporting News*, May 29, 1976: 16.
5. A.L. Hardman, "Candelaria's Proper Decisions Include 6-0 Charleston Start," *The Sporting News*, June 7, 1975: 36.
6. Michael I. Cohen, "Scouting Report," *The Sporting News*, August 2, 1975: 4.
7. Roy Blount Jr., "Another Keel Haul in the East," *Sports Illustrated*, July 14, 1975.
8. Charley Feeney, "Kid Candelaria Helps to Lift Shadows on Pirates' Mound," *The Sporting News*, July 12, 1975: 16.
9. Looney.
10. Charley Feeney, "Candy Man Can, And Does, Set Buc Mark," *The Sporting News*, August 28, 1976: 7.
11. Hardman.
12. Ibid.
13. Feeney, "Candy Man's Pitching Sweetens Bucco Outlook."
14. "Candelaria Keeps Cool," *The Sporting News*, August 16, 1975: 36.
15. Earl Lawson, "Reds' Playoff Sweep Dims Candelaria's Flame," *The Sporting News*, October 25, 1975: 13.
16. Looney.
17. Feeney, "Sweet-Throwing Candy Man Makes Bucco Mouths Water."
18. "Candy 'Poisons' Giants," *The Sporting News*, May 15, 1976: 32.
19. Bill Plaschke, "Dodgers: Memories Not Enough to Satisfy Candelaria," *Los Angeles Times*, March 6, 1991.
20. Lowell Reidenbaugh, "Candy Sweet Pitching in Pain," *The Sporting News*, November 3, 1979: 41.
21. Armen Keteyian, "To Save His Arm, a Pitcher Should Use His Head and Study Mechanics," *Sports Illustrated*, October 17, 1983.
22. Charley Feeney, "Nicosia Waits, Watches and Catches Pirate Eyes," *The Sporting News*, May 26, 1979: 12.
23. Looney, "The Mad Hatter of Pittsburgh."
24. Charley Feeney, "Candelaria Relieved He's Staying in Pen," *The Sporting News*, May 20, 1985: 18.
25. Looney,
26. Ibid.
27. Ibid.
28. Tim Rosaforte, "Can Vs. Candy Man: A Battle For Control," *Orlando Sun-Sentinel*, October 10, 1986.
29. Ibid.
30. Mike Penner, "Candelaria Arrested For Allegedly Driving Under the Influence," *Los Angeles Times*, April 18, 1987.
31. Mike Penner, "Candelaria Back With Angels, Set to Make New Start," *Los Angeles Times*, July 25, 1987.
32. Ross Newhan, "Angel Memories Still Trouble Candelaria," *Los Angeles Times*, March 1, 1988.
33. Ibid.
34. Ibid.
35. Ibid.
36. John Mehno, "Pittsburgh Pirates," *The Sporting News*, March 8, 1993.
37. Looney.
38. Wojciechowski.

# ORLANDO CEPEDA

## By Mark Armour

WHEN ORLANDO CEPEDA stood on the podium in Cooperstown, New York, on July 25, 1999, it is likely that no man had followed a more difficult path to the Baseball Hall of Fame, or that any man was any happier to attain the honor. Cepeda had escaped the slums of Puerto Rico to attain stardom at a very young age, and he overcame numerous injuries during his career, and even worse personal difficulties after leaving baseball. Although he had two remarkable comeback seasons in his baseball career, he had his biggest and most impressive comeback years later, when after a decade of humiliation he again stood on a ball field and listened to the roar of a crowd.

To know Orlando, one must first know his father. Pedro "Perucho" Anibal Cepeda, born in 1906, was one of the greatest ballplayers the island of Puerto Rico ever produced, starring in leagues in the Dominican Republic and Puerto Rico from the mid-1920s until 1950, when he was 45. He came up as a shortstop, and his strong hitting (he won numerous batting titles) and aggressive baserunning earned him the nickname "The Babe Cobb of Puerto Rico."[1] Perucho resisted many overtures to play in the Negro Leagues because he did not want to endure the segregated culture of the United States. So he stayed home, earning no more than $60 a week as a ballplayer and a bit more working for the San Juan Water Department.

Orlando Manuel Cepeda Pennes was born in Ponce, Puerto Rico, on September 17, 1937, to Carmen Pennes, a tiny (4-feet-11), beautiful woman, and Perucho Cepeda. (Per the custom in many Latino countries, each parent contributed half of his double surname, with the father's half being used in everyday life.) Orlando Cepeda was preceded by Pedro, born four years earlier, and he also had sisters born to his father's girlfriends, sisters whom Cepeda grew close to. Although surrounded by love, Cepeda grew up in stifling poverty — his father made little money, and often gambled what he made — and by crime and drugs, habits Orlando participated in. "What saved me," he later wrote, "was baseball — and the talent I inherited from my father. Had it not been for baseball and the legacy of Perucho Cepeda, I could have followed my boyhood pals into a world of crime, violence, and hate."[2]

His family moved a few times before settling in Santurce, a district of San Juan. The son of a baseball star, Cepeda had a childhood dominated by the game, including visits from famous ballplayers — like Satchell Paige, his father's friend. Orlando played a lot of baseball, but suffered the first of his many knee injuries playing basketball when he was 15. During his long recovery, he grew six inches and added more than 40 pounds to his previously scrawny frame. "Before I was in the hospital we had a short wall. I couldn't hit over it. But afterward, whoosh!"[3] He soon grew to 6-feet-1 and 210 pounds, and was playing mainly first base.

In late 1953 the 16-year-old was scouted by Pete Zorrilla, who ran the Santurce Crabbers in the Puerto Rican Winter League. Zorrilla asked his friend Perucho if Orlando could serve as the Crabbers' batboy and work out with the club. The next winter, Zorrilla arranged for the young Cepeda and a few other islanders (including future big-league teammate Jose Pagan) to go to a New York Giants tryout camp in Melbourne, Florida. Because they were all underage, and had never left the island, they were accompanied by the 20-year-old Roberto Clemente, on his way to spring training with the Pirates. Cepeda impressed at the camp, and signed a contract that included a $500 bonus.

Just days before Orlando's first professional game, with the Salem Rebels of the Appalachian League, the 49-year-old Perucho died after a long bout with

malaria. Cepeda returned home and used his bonus money for the funeral. He returned to Virginia but struggled on and off the field. "I lived in the black part of town, and on Sunday mornings I'd hear the people singing gospel music in the church across the street. I'd sit by the window in my room listening, and I'd cry from misery and loneliness."[4]

After a month with Salem, where he hit just .247 with one homer, he was released but picked up by the Giants' Kokomo, Indiana, club. The 17-year-old starred there, batting .393 with 21 home runs in just 92 games. The next year, in St. Cloud, Wisconsin, all Cepeda did was win the Northern League Triple Crown, with 26 home runs, 112 RBIs, and a .355 batting average. In 1957 he made it all the way to Minneapolis, the Giants' Triple-A affiliate in the American Association. It was at that spring that he first met Felipe Alou, a Dominican outfielder who became a lifelong friend. Alou was demoted to the Eastern League, but Cepeda became the club's first baseman and had another fine season: 25 home runs, 108 RBIs, .309 average. "If he ever learns the strike zone," said Red Davis, his manager, "he'll be murder up there. He's tough enough now."[5] Cepeda drew just 27 walks, and he would always be known as a free swinger.

In 1958 the Giants moved from New York to San Francisco. After winning the World Series in 1954, the club had slid to sixth place in both 1956 and 1957. But help was on the way. When Cepeda arrived at spring training in 1958, he was joined by fellow prospects Felipe Alou, Leon Wagner, Willie Kirkland, Willie McCovey, Jim Davenport, and Jose Pagan. The Giants had an opening at first base because Bill White was serving a two-year stint in the Army. Whitey Lockman had held the position in 1957, but manager Bill Rigney asked him to work with the 20-year-old Cepeda that March. The youngster had a tremendous spring, crushing home runs, fielding his position well, and running the bases. "Hey, Rig," said Lockman one day to Rigney. "This kid Cepeda is three years away." Rigney was startled, until Lockman added, "from the Hall of Fame."[6]

On April 15, 1958, the Giants hosted the Los Angeles Dodgers at Seals Stadium, in the first major-league game ever played in California. Cepeda played first base and batted fifth, joining right fielder Kirkland and third baseman Davenport, also playing their first big-league games. The Giants prevailed, 8-0, behind Rubén Gomez, with Cepeda hitting his first home run, off Don Bessent. This was the start of a magical season for the 20-year-old, as he hit .312 with 25 home runs and a league-leading 38 doubles. After the season he was the unanimous winner of the NL Rookie of the Year award.

Cepeda and San Francisco were a perfect fit. While Willie Mays had starred in New York before the Giants moved west, the provincial San Franciscans considered Cepeda to be one of theirs. And the feeling was mutual. "Right from the beginning, I fell in love with the city," Cepeda said. "There was everything that I liked. We played more day games then, so I usually had at least two nights a week free. On Thursdays, I would always go to the Copacabana to hear the Latin music. On Sundays, after games, I'd go to the Jazz Workshop for the jam sessions. At the Blackhawk, I'd hear Miles Davis, John Coltrane. … I roomed then with Felipe Alou and Rubén Gomez, but I was the only one who liked to go out at night. Felipe was very religious and quiet, and Rubén just liked to play golf, so he wasn't a night person. But I was single, and I just loved that town."[7]

Cepeda's stardom, which he sustained, was considerably complicated in 1959 by the arrival of Willie McCovey, another young hitting phenom who, like Cepeda, played first base. Though Cepeda had another great year in 1959 (27 homers, .317), McCovey's extraordinary four months in Phoenix (29 homers, .372) forced the Giants' hand. When McCovey debuted on July 30 (hitting two singles and two triples), Cepeda played third base. After four games there, manager Bill Rigney moved Cepeda to left field, which he played for the rest of the season.

The Giants spent most of the next five years dealing with the problem of having two All-Star first basemen. Though McCovey had a great two months in 1959, he was plagued by inconsistency and struggles against left-handed pitchers for a few years. Cepeda, regardless of his position, kept playing and kept hitting. But his reluctance to play the outfield became a matter of controversy. "I just wasn't ready mentally," Cepeda said years later. "I know I could've played left field if I'd put my mind to it, but I was only 21 years old and very sensitive. Friends and other players kept telling me I should demand to play first. It was all pride with me. And ignorance."[8]

"I could understand his reluctance," Rigney recalled. "But Cepeda was the better athlete, so I thought he could make the move to another position more easily. But he would come up to me and say, 'Bill, I'm the first baseman not the left fielder.' What could you do? He was the most popular San Francisco Giant. It was very hard not to like Orlando Cepeda. But this became an unresolvable situation."[9] McCovey was back in the minor leagues briefly in 1960, which got Cepeda his first-base job back, and the two shuttled between the outfield and first base in 1961. In 1962 manager Al Dark moved McCovey to left field and Cepeda was back at first base. Cepeda kept hitting, but McCovey did not become a consistent star as long as he and Cepeda remained teammates.

Most of Cepeda's offensive seasons look alike, but his 1961 stands out as a singularly great year; he led the league with 46 home runs and 142 RBIs while hitting .311. Baseball held two All-Star games each season from 1959 to 1962, and Cepeda was named to the team all eight times, starting in five of them. In his career he was named to 11 All-Star teams, playing in nine of them but hitting just 1-for-27. Although he continued to play, Cepeda hurt his right knee in a home-plate collision in 1961 and never had another day without pain.

After a few years of criticism for their underachieving, the Giants broke through in 1962 to win their first pennant in San Francisco. After tying the Dodgers at 101-61 through the regular schedule, they prevailed in a best-of-three pennant playoff, before falling to the New York Yankees in seven games in the World Series. Cepeda had another excellent season, batting .306 with 35 homers and 114 RBIs. The season was not without its problems—he was fined by Dark in August for not hustling, then hit just .231 with three homers after August. In the regular season final, Dark benched him, though Cepeda had four hits the day before in a doubleheader. He played in all three playoff games (3-for-13 with a home run) and hit just 3-for-19 in the World Series.

Cepeda's final years in San Francisco were clouded by his terrible relationship with Dark. Cepeda believed that Dark did not like blacks or, especially, Latinos. Dark did not approve of the Giants' many Latino players speaking Spanish, and he believed their loud Latino music and laughter to be indicative of not taking the game seriously.[10] Moreover, Dark developed his own plus-minus rating system, in which he gave people positive or negative points for what they did on the field. While Mays, unsurprisingly, led the 1962 team with over 100 points, Cepeda came in at negative 40. "There are," said Dark, "winning .275 hitters and losing .310 hitters."[11] That Dark kept such a system and publicly used it to denigrate one of his players is astonishing.

In the remaining two years of his stewardship of the Giants, Dark had run-ins with Cepeda numerous times for what the manager believed was a lack of hustle and what Cepeda claimed was a hurt knee. "The knee hurt me all the time," said Cepeda, "and I always aggravate it when I slide or stretch or even hit. Some people think that because we are Latins — because we did not have everything growing up — we are not supposed to get hurt. But my knee was hurt. Dark thought I was trying not to play. He treated me like a child. I am a human being, whether I am blue or black or white or green. We Latins are different, but we are still human beings. Dark did not respect our differences."[12]

Through it all, Cepeda continued to hit. He batted .316 with 34 home runs in 1963, then .304 and 31 in 1964. Through the first seven years of his career, he had hit .309, with a .353 on-base percentage and .537 slugging percentage. His 222 home runs were three more than Henry Aaron had through his first seven seasons. At the end of the 1964 season, Cepeda was still just 27 years old.

His return to first base full-time in 1962 surely helped his knee, but when he reported to spring training in 1965 he could barely put any weight on it. New manager Herman Franks, like Dark, felt that Cepeda was dogging it, so Cepeda tried to tough it out. After hobbling through the spring, Cepeda was used mainly as a pinch-hitter for the first month of the season (three singles in ten at-bats) before finally going on the disabled list in May. He returned as a pinch-hitter in August, but finished just .176 in 34 at-bats for the year. After the season he had surgery on his right knee.

When he returned in the spring of 1966, McCovey was finally fully entrenched at first base. Playing mostly left field, Cepeda started slowly but was hitting .286 with three homers in 19 games on May 8. On that date, he was traded to the St. Louis Cardinals for pitcher Ray Sadecki. Though Cepeda was shocked and upset by the trade, he was joining a team that had a gaping hole at first base, the only position he wanted to play. In fact, Cepeda never played the outfield again. Batting cleanup for the rest of the year, he homered in his first game and finished the season hitting .301 with 20 home runs in 123 games.

After years of discomfort in San Francisco, Cepeda was beloved by his teammates and manager Red Schoendienst. He became a jokester in the clubhouse, and his taste for jazz and Latin music earned him the nickname Cha Cha. Cepeda noted the change. "You know," he said, "if I do all this in San Francisco they would give me a funny look all the time and everyone would think there is something wrong with me."[13] In 1967 he completed his comeback in style, hitting .325 with 25 home runs and a league-leading 111 runs batted in. After two straight losing seasons, the Cardinals rolled to the NL pennant and victory over the Red Sox in the World Series. After the season Cepeda was unanimously named the league's Most Valuable Player.

After his MVP season in 1967, the 30-year-old Cepeda followed up with the worst full season of his career, batting just .248 with 16 home runs. The 1968 Cardinals returned to the World Series, this time losing to the Detroit Tigers in seven games. After hitting poorly in the Series in both 1962 and 1967, this time Cepeda hit .250 and slugged two home runs.

Cepeda returned to spring training in 1969 hoping for a comeback year with the Cardinals. But on March 17, he received the unwelcome news that he had been traded to the Atlanta Braves for star catcher-first baseman Joe Torre. Cepeda loved St. Louis and his teammates, and he was uncomfortable with the idea of playing in the South. In the end, he enjoyed his time in Atlanta, which reunited him with his good friend Felipe Alou and allowed him to play with the great Henry Aaron.

His first year in Atlanta was a struggle personally and professionally (.257 with 22 home runs) but a big success for the team, which finished first in the NL West in the first year of divisional play. Cepeda hit .455 in the playoff series against the Mets, with a home run off Nolan Ryan in Game Three, but the Mets swept the three-game series. Cepeda came back with a vengeance in 1970 (.305, 34 home runs, 111 RBIs), though the Braves dropped to fifth place.

Cepeda started 1971 as well as ever — on June 1 he was slugging .584 with 13 home runs, among the league leaders in both categories. Later that month, in the act of getting up to answer the telephone at home, his left knee—up until then, his "good" knee—collapsed. The Braves doctor told him the knee was "finished."[14] He hobbled out to first base for a few weeks before finally shutting it down in late July. He underwent another knee surgery in September and went home to Puerto Rico.

A hobbled Cepeda showed up in the spring wanting to play. He played only twice in April, hit .350 (but with little power) playing half-time in May, and hit just .182 in June. On June 29 he was traded to the Oakland A's for pitcher Denny McLain, another recent MVP who looked to be nearing the end of the line. He pinch-hit three times for Oakland, before shutting it down. After the season he was released. With two bad knees, Cepeda's career looked to be finished.

On January 11, 1973, the American League agreed to a three-year trial run of the designated-hitter rule, allowing a batter to hit in place of the pitcher throughout the game. Along with its strategic consequences, there was suddenly a place in the game for good hitters who could not play the field. A week later the Red Sox signed Cepeda with this role in mind. For the 1973 season, Cepeda played 142 games, never once playing in the field. He hit .289 with 20 home runs and 86 RBIs, and was the first recipient of the Designated Hitter of the Year award (later named the Edgar Martínez Award).

Just before the 1974 season, new manager Darrell Johnson decided he wanted to make room for younger players, and he released Cepeda and veteran shortstop Luis Aparicio, surprising most observers. Cepeda was crushed, and remarkably was unable to find another job. He played briefly in Mexico before finally being signed by the Kansas City Royals in August. He hit just .215 in 107 at-bats before drawing another release. This time he was finally through after 17 seasons and 379 home runs.

Cepeda had married Annie early in his career and fathered Orlando Jr., but after years of his infidelity, and at least one child with another woman, they divorced in 1973. He married Nydia in 1975 but his behavior did not improve. In December 1975 he was arrested for taking delivery of 170 pounds of marijuana. Although he admitted to being a marijuana user, he claimed that he was expecting only a small amount for himself, and that he was not a dealer. Puerto Rico had made Cepeda a hero after the tragic death of Roberto Clemente three years earlier, but his arrest made him a pariah on the island. He and his family received death threats. He lost all of his money on his legal case, which caused him to miss child-support payments and led to more legal trouble. He finally stood trial in 1978, was found guilty, and was sentenced to five years in prison. He served ten months in a minimum-security facility in Florida.

Upon his release Cepeda continued to struggle. Still shunned at home, he had trouble finding and keeping work. He got a job as a minor-league hitting coach for the White Sox, but failed to show up a few times and was let go. In 1984 he, Nydia and their two children moved to Los Angeles so he could conduct baseball clinics, but after a few months of fighting, his family moved back home, leaving Orlando with Orlando Jr., who had joined him in LA.

Orlando credited his embrace of Buddhism in the 1980s for turning his life around. It allowed him to take responsibility for the mess he had made of his life, to get control of his shame and his anger, and to

help him find a path forward. He also met Mirian Ortiz, a Puerto Rican woman who eventually became his third wife. He and Mirian moved to the Bay Area, close to where his baseball journey had begun 30 years earlier. In 1987 he took part in a Giants Fantasy Camp in Arizona. "Of all the ex-players we had there," recalled a team official, "Orlando was the approachable idol. I couldn't believe it; I kept waiting for the flaws to show in that great personality. But there were no flaws. He is such a genuine person, such an emotional person, that you feel like hugging him. You get this sense that people just want to love him. I asked him if he'd be interested in coming back to work for the Giants."[15]

The next year Cepeda started by making trips for the team to scout or help with instruction. In the 1989 NLCS, he was asked to throw out the first ball before the third game, listening from the pitcher's mound as the cheers rained down on him. For more than 25 years Cepeda acted as a humanitarian ambassador for the club, showing up wherever and whenever they wanted him to, including inner-city schools throughout the country. He also made appearances in Puerto Rico, his native island that once again embraced him.

In 1999 Cepeda was inducted into the Baseball Hall of Fame, 25 years after his last at-bat. "I wasn't ready to get in before," he said. "I still had work to do in healing myself."[16] That same year the Giants retired his number 30. In September 2008 the Giants unveiled a statue of Cepeda outside the 2nd Street entrance of AT&T Park. "When things like this happen to you, that's when I say to myself, 'Orlando, you're a very lucky person,'" Cepeda said after seeing his bronze likeness, holding a ball and first baseman's mitt.[17]

As of 2014, Cepeda lived in Fairfield, 35 miles northeast of San Francisco, with Mirian, and still worked for the Giants. He had five sons, Orlando Jr., Malcolm, Ali, and Karl and Jason.

## NOTES

1. Orlando Cepeda and Herb Fagen, *Baby Bull: From Hardball to Hard Time and Back* (Dallas: Taylor Publishing, 1998), 2.
2. Cepeda and Fagen, 7.
3. Robert Creamer, "Giants—A Smash Hit in San Francisco," *Sports Illustrated*, June 16, 1958.
4. Ron Fimrite, "The Heart of a Giant," *Sports Illustrated*, October 16, 1991.
5. Cepeda and Fagen, 31.
6. Roy Terrell, "The Sa-fra-seeko Kid," *Sports Illustrated*, May 23 1960.
7. Fimrite, "The Heart of a Giant."
8. Ibid.
9. Ibid.
10. Peter Bjarkman, *Baseball With a Latin Beat—A History of the Latin American Game* (Jefferson, North Carolina: McFarland, 1994), 138.
11. Richard Boyle, "Time of Trial for Alvin Dark," *Sports Illustrated*, July 06, 1964
12. Mark Mulvoy, "Cha Cha Goes Boom, Boom, Boom!" *Sports Illustrated*, July 24, 1967.
13. Ibid.
14. Cepeda and Fagen, 161.
15. Fimrite, "The Heart of a Giant."
16. William Nack, "From Shame to Frame," *Sports Illustrated*, July 26, 1999.
17. John Shea, "Cepeda Honored With His Own Statue at the Ballpark," *San Francisco Chronicle*, September 7, 2008.

# PEDRO A. CEPEDA (PERUCHO)

By Edwin Fernández

**PEDRO CEPEDA, BETTER KNOWN** as Perucho, was the first player considered a superstar in Puerto Rican professional baseball. He began playing baseball when there was no formal professional baseball league on the island. About 5-feet-11-inches tall, he could play in various positions, both in the infield and the outfield, and was a consistent hitter who could bat for power and average, and was a good defensive player. In addition to Puerto Rico, he played in Venezuela and the Dominican Republic. He never wanted to play in the Negro Leagues of the United States. According to his son Orlando, "Although he was invited to participate, he declined. He was very proud, and he thought that playing [on the racially segregated mainland] was an offense to his sense of justice."[1]

Pedro A. Cepeda-Ortiz, also known as "The Bull," was born in Cataño, Puerto Rico, on January 31, 1906. His parents were Rafael Cepeda and Asunción Ortiz. Don Rafael worked in construction as a mason. Perucho, his son, used to help him in those labors. His mother, Asunción Ortiz, dedicated her time to raising her four children, Pedro, Jesus, Rafael, and Berta. Perucho Cepeda was married to Carmen Pennes and fathered two children, Pedro and Orlando. He also had other children, the product of other relationships.

Cepeda began playing baseball in his hometown in amateur tournaments. He played professional baseball from 1928 to 1950. In 1928 he signed his first contract, with the San Juan Athletics. He had very good speed on the bases. Many compared him to Ty Cobb because of his aggressiveness and the way he used to slide.

In 1929 Cepeda played for the Sandino club in the Dominican Republic, and batted .429. In 1930 he played in Venezuela with Macon and Cincinnati. He returned to Venezuela in 1932 to play in Valencia, with Selección in 1934, Gavilanes in 1935, Maracaibo Centauros in 1939 and 1940, and with Santa Marta in 1941.

In 1937 Cepeda joined one of the best baseball teams of all time, the Trujillo Dragons of the Dominican Republic, who signed many of the best players of the Caribbean and Negro Leagues. Cepeda was the shortstop, and among his teammates were Sam Bankhead, Cy Perkins, Silvio Garcia, Josh Gibson, Satchel Paige, and Cool Papa Bell. The latter three were future members of the Baseball Hall of Fame in Cooperstown. The team was created to promote the re-election campaign of the Dominican dictator Rafael Leonidas Trujillo. In its first year it won the Dominican professional baseball league championship. Perucho was the only Puerto Rican player on the team, which was organized by Satchel Paige.

In Puerto Rico Cepeda played with Guayama of the new Semiprofessional Baseball League in 1938. Guayama won the league championship in 1938 and 1939. Perucho was its shortstop and cleanup hitter, winning the batting title both seasons with robust averages of .465 in 1938 and .383 in '39, edging Josh Gibson (.380) in 1939. He lost the 1939 home-run championship to Gibson by one homer and finished tied in triples with Ed Stone, with 8. On November 5, 1939, he was the first player to collect six hits in a league game and on April 4, 1940, became the first with a seven-RBI game.

In the 1940-1941 season, Cepeda finished third in batting, at .421, but topped legendary players Buck Leonard, Roy Campanella, and Monte Irvin. In the first four years of the league, Cepeda racked up 293 hits in 713 at-bats (.411). He led the league in RBIs during its first three seasons, and remains the only player to lead three years in succession. He also has the distinction of being the only Puerto Rican to hit .400 in two different positions, shortstop (1938-39) and first base (1940-41).

Cepeda played from 1938 to 1950 (11 seasons) in the Puerto Rico Professional Baseball League. He played for the Guayama Brujos for the first four years, then played two seasons with the San Juan Senators, one with the Mayagüez Indians, one with the Santurce Cangrejeros and two seasons with the Caguas Criollos. He missed the 1948 and 1949 seasons, the came back in 1949-1950, his last season, with the Ponce Leones. His lifetime average was .325, the third best in the league, trailing only Willard Brown (.350) and Pancho Coímbre (.337). At the end of his career, in 1,589 at-bats, he had 516 hits, 70 doubles, 31 triples, 14 home runs, 247 runs scored, and 300 RBIs. His slugging average was .434.

In the fall of 1947 an all-star team from Puerto Rico was assembled to play several games against the World Series champion New York Yankees, who were touring several Latin American countries. Perucho's son, Orlando, recalled, "My father went 4-for-4 in one of those games against the pitchers Vic Raschi and Allie Reynolds."[2]

In the late 1940s Alex Pompez, the owner of the New York Cubans of the Negro American League, announced that he had signed Perucho Cepeda, but Cepeda refused to play in the United States because of the racism that prevailed at the time. Son Orlando said that his father's temperament was very volatile and that he could not have tolerated the experience.

Perucho Cepeda never earned more than $60 per week as a player. He worked with the San Juan Water Authority in the 1940s while playing at in the Puerto Rican Professional Baseball League. With that, he had to support two families. One of them was comprised of his wife and two sons, Pedro and Orlando.[3]

Perucho Cepeda died in San Juan, Puerto Rico, on April 27, 1955. Two weeks earlier his son Orlando signed a professional contract with the New York Giants. Orlando used his $500 signing bonus to defray his father's funeral expenses. "Peruchin," as Orlando Cepeda was later known, became a superstar in major-league baseball, as well as Puerto Rican baseball, and in 1999 he was inducted into the Baseball Hall of Fame, the selection made by the veteran committee. Perucho never saw his son play professionally. According to Orlando, he had seen him play once, in an amateur game.

Cepeda has said several times that his father was better player of the two. He said the first time he saw his father play was in a professional Puerto Rican League game between Mayagüez and Santurce at Sixto Escobar Stadium on January 5, 1946. In that game Perucho hit a home run and, while playing second base for Santurce, had 11 assists in a game in which Santurce hurler Luis Raul Cabrera struck out 16 Mayagüez batters.[4]

Perucho Cepeda has been inducted in six other halls of fame: Latin American Hall of Fame, Puerto Rican Sports Hall of Fame, Cataño Hall of Fame, Guayama Hall of Fame, Professional Baseball Hall of Fame of Puerto Rico, and the Latino Baseball Hall of Fame.

Pedro Vázquez, a prominent Puerto Rican sports journalist, said at the time of Cepeda's death: "There were no flaws in Perucho Cepeda, the athlete. There was no weakness in Perucho Cepeda the man. Before his figure, glory cannot pass without bowing."5

## SOURCES

In addition to the sources cited in the Notes, the author also consulted Baseball-Reference.com and the following:

Colón Delgado, Jorge. *Dream Team del Béisbol Boricua 1938-2013* (San Juan, Puerto Rico: Professional Graphics), 2013.

## NOTES

1. Orlando Cepeda with Bob Marcus, *High & Inside, Orlando Cepeda's Story* (South Bend, Indiana: Icarus Press, 1983), 7.
2. Ibid.
3. Cepeda with Marcus, 8.
4. Interview with Orlando Cepeda by the author, April 2017.
5. Jorge Colón Delgado, "Perucho Cepeda: un siore espectacular," beisbol101.com, 2014.

# ROBERTO CLEMENTE

## By Stew Thornley

**R**OBERTO CLEMENTE'S GREATness transcended the diamond. On it, he was electrifying with his penchant for bad-ball hitting, his strong throwing arm from right field, and the way he played with a reckless but controlled abandon. Off it, he was a role model to the people of his homeland and elsewhere. Helping others represented the way Clemente lived. It would also represent the way he died.

Jackie Robinson's breaking of the color barrier opened the way not just for African Americans in organized baseball but to many others whose skin color had excluded them. By the 1960s Clemente had emerged as one of the best of the players from Latin America.

Clemente came from Puerto Rico, which had established its own baseball history extending back to the late 1800s, at about the same time that the island became a possession of the United States.[1] Puerto Rico shares its love of baseball with many of the countries in and along the Caribbean Sea. Professional leagues formed and thrived in the winter in these areas, including Venezuela, Mexico, and the Dominican Republic.

Puerto Rico has produced many great players, such as Pedro "Perucho" Cepeda—because he was black, Perucho never got to play in the major leagues in the United States. His son Orlando did and eventually made the Hall of Fame.

The greatest Puerto Rican player, however, was Roberto Clemente.

Roberto Clemente Walker was born on August 18, 1934, to Melchor Clemente and Luisa Walker de Clemente in Carolina, which is slightly east of the Puerto Rican capital of San Juan. Roberto was the youngest of Luisa's seven children (three of whom were from a previous marriage).[2]

Melchor was a foreman overseeing sugar-cane cutters. He also used his truck to help a construction company deliver sand and gravel to building sites. Luisa was a laundress and worked in different jobs to assist the workers at the sugar-cane plantation. Roberto contributed to the family income by helping his dad load shovels into the construction trucks. He also earned money by doing various jobs for neighbors, such as carrying milk to the country store. Roberto used his money to buy a bike and to purchase rubber balls. He liked to squeeze the balls to strengthen his hands.[3] Many people commented on the size of young man's hands. He had strong hands, and it was clear at an early age that he had athletic ability.

Roberto had not just ability but a deep love of sports, especially baseball. He attended games in the winter and watched the star players from the United States mainland. One of his favorites was Monte Irvin. Irvin played for the Newark Eagles in the Negro National League in the summer and for the San Juan Senadores of the Puerto Rican League in the winter. Irvin remembers kids hanging around the stadium. "We'd give them our bags so they could take them in and get in for free," he said. Irvin didn't know Clemente was among the kids until Clemente told him years later, when both were in the major leagues. Clemente also told Irvin that he was impressed with his throwing arm. "I had the best arm in Puerto Rico," said Irvin. "He loved to see me throw. He found that he would practice and learn how to throw like I did."[4] Roberto began playing baseball himself. He wrote in his journal, "I loved the game so much that even though our playing field was muddy and we had many trees on it, I used to play many hours every day. The fences were about 150 feet away from home plate, and I used to hit many homers. One day I hit ten home runs in a game we started about 11 a.m. and finished about 6:30 p.m."[5]

When he was 14 years old Roberto joined a softball team organized by Roberto Marín, who became very influential in Clemente's life. Marín noticed Roberto's strong throwing arm and began using him at shortstop. He eventually moved him to the outfield. Regardless of the position he played, Roberto was sensational. "His name became known for his long hits to right field, and for his sensational catches," said Marín. "Everyone had their eyes on him."[6]

Roberto also participated in the high jump and javelin throw at Vizcarrondo High School in Carolina.[7] It was thought that he might even be good enough to represent Puerto Rico in the Olympics. Throwing the javelin strengthened his arm and helped him in other ways, according to one of his biographers, Bruce Markusen: "The footwork, release, and general dynamics employed in throwing the javelin coincided with the skills needed to throw a baseball properly. The more that Clemente threw the javelin, the better and stronger his throwing from the outfield became."[8]

Roberto said that throwing the javelin in high school was only part of the reason he developed a strong arm. "My mother has the same kind of an arm, even today at 74," in said in a 1964 interview. "She could throw a ball from second base to home plate with something on it. I got my arm from my mother."[9]

Although he had great all-around athletic ability, Roberto decided to focus on baseball, even though it meant forgoing any dreams of participating in the Olympics. He began playing for a strong amateur team, the Juncos Mules.

In 1952, Clemente took part in a tryout camp in Puerto Rico that was attended by scout Al Campanis of the Brooklyn Dodgers. Clemente impressed Campanis with his different skills, including his speed. The Dodgers did not sign Clemente then, but Campanis kept him in mind.

Also in 1952, Clemente caught the eye of Pedrín Zorrilla, who owned the Santurce Cangrejeros, or Crabbers, of the Puerto Rican League. The Juncos team was to play the Manatí Athenians in Manatí, where Zorrilla had a house on the beach. Roberto Marín advised Zorrilla to go to the game. Afterward, Zorrilla offered Clemente a contract to play with the Cangrejeros.

Clemente was barely 18 years old when he joined the Cangrejeros. As a young and developing player, he was brought along slowly by the team's manager, Buzz Clarkson. Clarkson had had an outstanding career in the Negro Leagues in the United States and played many winters in Puerto Rico. Like many great black players, Clarkson's best years were behind him by the time he got his chance to play in the majors in 1952 at the age of 37. Two other such players were Willard "Ese Hombre" Brown and Bob Thurman, who were top hitters in the Negro Leagues. Both were outfielders (with Thurman also doing some pitching) on the Santurce team that Clemente joined in the winter of 1952-53.

"Clemente looked up to Bob Thurman," wrote Thomas Van Hyning. "Clemente pinch-hit for Thurman in a key situation and doubled off Caguas's Roberto Vargas to win the game, earning congratulations from Thurman."[10] Despite the big hit, Clemente did not play much his first winter in the Puerto Rican League.

He began playing more in 1953-54 and even played in the league's All-Star Game. (The star of the All-Star Game was Henry Aaron of the Caguas Criollos, who had four hits, including two home runs, and drove in five runs.) By midseason, Clemente's name was appearing along with Aaron's in the list of the Puerto Rican league leaders in batting average. Clemente finished the season with a .288 batting average, sixth best in the league.

The Brooklyn Dodgers had remembered Clemente from the tryout he had had in front of Al Campanis in 1952.[11] Buzzie Bavasi, the Dodgers' vice president, said that during the 1953-54 season a scout in Puerto Rico told him the Dodgers could sign Clemente.[12] Other major-league teams had noticed Clemente, too. One was the New York Giants, the Dodgers' great rivals. Brooklyn outbid the Giants and Clemente agreed to sign. The Milwaukee Braves also made an offer, one that was reportedly much more than the Dodgers', but Clemente stuck with his decision.[13] He knew that New York City had a

large Puerto Rican population and looked forward to playing there.

On February 19, 1954, Clemente signed a contract with the Dodgers, who had to make a decision on what to do with him. The Dodgers had signed him for a reported salary of $5,000 as well as a bonus of $10,000.[14] Rules of the time required a team signing a player for a bonus and salary of more than $4,000 to keep him on the major league roster for two years or risk losing him in the offseason draft.[15] Many bonus players of this period were kept at the major-league level, pining on the bench for two years rather than developing in the minors. The Dodgers chose to have Clemente spend the 1954 season with the Montreal Royals in the International League, even though it meant they might lose him at the end of the season.

Buzzie Bavasi had the power to determine Clemente's fate. In 1955, Bavasi told Pittsburgh writer Les Biederman that the Dodgers' only purpose in signing Clemente was to keep him away from the Giants, even though they knew they would eventually lose him to another team.[16] Some writers said an informal quota system was in effect in the early years following the breaking of baseball's color barrier, but this is not supported by the facts.[17] In his biography of Clemente, Kal Wagenheim wrote that the Dodgers would never start all five of their black players in the same game. The box scores prove that is false. (There are other reasons to question the existence of a quota, although it is beyond the realm of this article to fully explore the issue.)[18]

In a 2005 e-mail message to the author, Bavasi wrote that while there was no quota system, race was the factor in the club's decision to have Clemente play in Montreal: "The concern had nothing to do with quotas, but the thought was too many minorities might be a problem with the white players. Not so, I said. Winning was the important thing. I agree with the [Dodgers'] board that we should get a player's opinion and I would be guided by the player's opinion. The board called in Jackie Robinson. Hell, now I felt great. Jackie was told the problem and after thinking about it awhile, he asked me who would be sent out if Clemente took one of the spots. I said George Shuba. Jackie agreed that Shuba would be the one to go. Then he said Shuba was not among the best players on the club, but he was the most popular. With that he shocked me by saying, and I quote: 'If I were the GM, I would not bring Clemente to the club and send Shuba or any other white player down. If I did this, I would be setting our program back five years.'"[19]

So Clemente went to Montreal to play for manager Max Macon. Most accounts say the Dodgers were trying to "hide" Clemente in Montreal by playing him rarely, hoping that other teams wouldn't notice him and wouldn't draft him at the end of the season.

Several biographers, among them Phil Musick, Kal Wagenheim, and Bruce Markusen, provide examples to back up the contention that Clemente was hidden. However, a game-by-game check of Montreal's 1954 season indicates that many of the examples are incorrect.[20]

Wagenheim and Markusen go so far as to claim that Clemente did not play in the Royals' final 25 games of the season, another claim that is not correct. In fact, by the final part of the season, Clemente was playing regularly against left-handed starting pitchers.[21]

Montreal manager Max Macon, until his death in 1989, denied that he was under any orders to restrict Clemente's playing time. "The only orders I had were to win and draw big crowds," Macon said.[22]

It is true that Clemente, after an initial period when he was being platooned over the first 13 games of the season, played little over the first three months of the season. This was hardly unusual for a 19-year-old in his first season of organized baseball.

Also, for much of the year, the Royals had a full crop of reliable outfielders in Dick Whitman, Gino Cimoli, and Jack Cassini. In addition, the Dodgers sent Sandy Amoros down to Montreal early in the season, and Amoros hit well enough for the Royals that he was recalled by Brooklyn in July. The crowded outfield situation didn't leave a lot of playing time for a newcomer like Clemente. He was often used as a late-inning defensive replacement for Cassini.

When he did play, he struggled. In early July his batting average was barely over .200. Part of that may be attributed to his infrequent playing time; it's hard for a batter to get in a groove and hit well when he doesn't play regularly. On the other hand, it's hard for a player to get regular playing time if he's not hitting well.

Macon said he didn't use Clemente much because he "swung wildly," especially at pitches that were outside of the strike zone: "If you had been in Montreal that year, you wouldn't have believed how ridiculous some pitchers made him look."[23] Clemente got more chances against left-handed pitchers. Macon was known for platooning, and Clemente often split time in the lineup with Whitman, a left-handed hitter.

Through June and July Clemente often went long stretches without seeing any action. Then, on July 25, he entered the first game of a doubleheader against the Havana Sugar Kings in the ninth inning. The game was tied and went into extra innings. With one out in the last of the 10th, Clemente hit a home run to win it for the Royals.

Macon rewarded him by starting him in the second game of the doubleheader, Clemente's first start in nearly three weeks. For the rest of the season Clemente started every game in which the opposition started a left-handed pitcher. He had a few more highlights during this time. Near the end of July, he came to bat in the top of the ninth inning of a scoreless game in Toronto. Clemente doubled and went on to score to put Montreal ahead. The Royals won the game, 2-0.

The next time the Royals were in Toronto, three weeks later, Clemente helped them win in a different way. Montreal had an 8-7 lead over the Maple Leafs in the bottom of the ninth. Toronto had a chance to tie the score, but Clemente threw out a runner at home plate to end the game.

Late in August he had two triples and a single at Richmond, although the Royals still lost the game. A week later he hit a home run to win the game for Montreal and give the Royals a sweep of a doubleheader against Syracuse.

Teammate Jack Cassini said, "You knew he was going to play in the big leagues. He had a great arm and he could run."[24] When Clemente began playing regularly against left-handers, the Royals rose in the standings and finished in second place. Clemente batted .257 in 87 games in his only season in the minors.

By the end of the 1954 season, it had become clear to Bavasi and the rest of the Brooklyn organization that other teams were interested in Clemente. However, Bavasi said he still wasn't ready to give up. The Pirates, by having the worst record in the majors in 1954, had the first pick in the November draft. If Bavasi could get the Pirates to draft a different player off the Montreal roster, Clemente would remain with the Dodgers organization. Each minor-league team could lose only one player.

Bavasi said he went to Branch Rickey, who had run the Dodgers before going to Pittsburgh. After Bavasi declined Rickey's offer to join him in Pittsburgh, Bavasi said, Rickey told him that, "Should I need help at anytime, all I had to do was pick up the phone." Bavasi said he used this offer to get Rickey to agree draft a different player, pitcher John Rutherford, off the Royals' roster. However, Bavasi was dismayed to learn two days later that the deal was off and that the Pirates were going to draft Clemente.

"It seemed that [Dodgers owner] Walter O'Malley and Mr. Rickey got in another argument and it seems Walter called Mr. Rickey every name in the book," explained Bavasi. "Thus, we lost Roberto."[25]

When he was drafted by Pittsburgh, Clemente was in Puerto Rico playing for the Santurce Cangrejeros and on his way to his best-ever winter season. He again played with Bob Thurman, but the Santurce outfield had a new addition in 1954-55. It was Willie Mays, who had just led the New York Giants to the World Series championship and was named the National League's Most Valuable Player. An outfield of Clemente, Mays, and Thurman ranks as one of the best ever in the Puerto Rican League. By mid-season Santurce manager Herman Franks was calling Clemente "the best player in the league, except for Willie Mays."[26]

Clemente and Mays had been providing some real highlights. In late November, the Cangrejeros were behind by a run going into the ninth inning of a game against Caguas-Guyama. Clemente led off the ninth with a single, and Mays then hit a two-run homer to give Santurce a 7-6 win. Not long after that, the pair starred in another 7-6 win. Mays hit two home runs and Clemente one home run in an 11-inning win over Mayaguez.

Both players homered in the league's All-Star Game on December 12, leading their North team to a 7-5 win. By this time, Mays, Clemente, and Thurman were the top three players in the league in batting average, and Santurce moved into first place.[27]

While things were going well on the baseball diamond, there were other problems for Clemente. On New Year's Eve of 1954, one of his brothers, Luis, died of a brain tumor. Shortly before that, Clemente had been in a car accident that damaged some of his spinal discs. The back injury hampered him for the rest of his baseball career.[28]

Back on the field, Santurce finished first in the Puerto Rican League. The top three teams advanced to the playoffs, so the Cangrejeros had to win another series to capture the league title. They did that, defeating Caguas-Guyama four games to one. Clemente had four hits, including two doubles, and drove in four runs in the first game of the series, which Santurce won. Caguas-Guayama won the next game, but the Cangrejeros then won three in a row to finish the series. As champions of the Puerto Rican League, they advanced to the Caribbean Series.

The Caribbean Series was played in Caracas, Venezuela, in February of 1955. In addition to Santurce, teams from Cuba, Panama, and Venezuela participated. It was a double round-robin tournament. The team with the best record at the end would be the champion.

The Cangrejeros won their first two games and then faced Magallanes of Venezuela. The game went into extra innings. Clemente singled to open the last of the 11th inning, and Mays followed with a home run to win the game, 4-2.

One more win would clinch at least a tie for the title for Santurce. The Cangrejeros' fourth game was a rematch against Almendares of Cuba, a team they had defeated in their first game. Almendares opened up a 5-0 lead, but Santurce battled back to win. Clemente drove in two runs to help in the comeback.

Santurce played Carta Vieja of Panama with a chance for the championship. Clemente had a triple as the Cangrejeros scored three times in the top of the first. In the third, Clemente had another triple as Santurce scored four runs to take a 7-0 lead. Santurce won the game, 11-3, to wrap up the championship.

It was the second Caribbean Series title for Santurce in three years. Clemente had been a part of the team that had won the championship in 1953, but he did not play in the series. This time he was a key member of the team that won. Santurce shortstop Don Zimmer, who was voted the Most Valuable Player of the Caribbean Series, said, "It might have been the best winter club ever assembled."[29]

Soon afterward, Clemente was in training camp with the Pittsburgh Pirates, hoping to earn a spot in the major leagues. The Pirates had been keeping an eye on Clemente over the winter. Rickey said, "He can run, throw, and hit. He needs much polishing, though, because he is a rough diamond."[30]

The Pirates were loaded with outfielders when they began spring training in Florida in March of

1955. Clemente would have plenty of competition for a spot on the team. After the first week of training camp, Clemente earned some good words from Pirates manager Fred Haney. "The boy has the tools, there's no doubt about that. And he takes to instruction readily. Certainly I have been pleased with what I have seen," Haney said. "He has some faults, which were expected, but let's wait and see."[31]

Clemente's chances were helped when Frank Thomas, the Pirates' best outfielder, held out for more money and missed the first part of spring training. Thomas then got sick and missed more time. Clemente took advantage of this opportunity and made the team.[32]

Clemente's original number with the Pirates was 13, but early in the season he switched to 21, a number that became strongly associated with him. It is reported that Clemente chose the number because his full name, Roberto Clemente Walker, has 21 letters.[33]

Clemente didn't play in the first three regular season games. However, he was in the starting lineup, playing right field, for the first game of a doubleheader on Sunday, April 17, 1955, against the Brooklyn Dodgers at Forbes Field in Pittsburgh. Clemente came to the plate with two out in the bottom of the first inning for his first at-bat in the major leagues. He hit a ground ball toward the shortstop, Pee Wee Reese. Reese got his glove on the grounder, but he couldn't field it cleanly. Clemente had his first hit. He followed that by scoring his first run to give Pittsburgh a 1-0 lead. However, Brooklyn came back to win the game.

Clemente started the second game of the doubleheader, this time in center field and batting leadoff. He had a double, but the Pirates were unable to score and trailed the Dodgers, 3-0, going into the last of the eighth. Clemente got another hit, a single, as part of a two-run rally that closed the gap, but the Pirates still lost.

In Pittsburgh's next game, in New York against the Giants, Clemente hit an inside-the-park homer, but the Pirates lost again. At this point, their won-lost record was 0-6. Pittsburgh lost two more games before winning its first of the season. The Pirates went on to finish in last place in the National League for the fourth year in a row. However, Branch Rickey insisted that young players such as Clemente would help turn the team around.

Early in the 1955 season, the new players were leading the Pirates' offense. Clemente was leading the team in batting average over the first three weeks. On the base paths he was even more exciting. "When he starts moving around the bases he draws the 'Ohs' and 'Ahs' of the folks in the ball park," wrote Jack Hernon in *The Sporting News*.

Hernon added, "The fleet Puerto Rican was a stickout on defense."[34] Forbes Field, the home of the Pirates, was a classic ball park that had opened in 1909. The outfield fence was a brick wall. It was only 300 feet from home plate to the wall down the right-field line. But the wall jutted out and changed directions. Clemente learned the angles and how to play balls that caromed off the fence. He could corral long hits quickly and, with his great arm, opposing baserunners were careful on trying to take an extra base.

Less than a third of the way through the season, Clemente already had 10 assists, and he also made some outstanding catches. "The Pittsburgh fans have fallen in love with his spectacular fielding and his deadly right arm," wrote Les Biederman, a reporter who covered the Pirates.[35]

Clemente's rambunctious style in the field could be costly, though. In May, he made a nice catch in St. Louis, but he hurt his finger and ran into the wall. The injury caused him to miss a few games.

Clemente's hitting slumped as the season went along, in part because he still had trouble laying off pitches that were out of the strike zone. However, he became known as a good "bad-ball hitter," able to make good contact on bad pitches. Jack Cassini, who had played in the minors with Clemente the year before, said, "He could hit. He didn't need a strike. The best way to pitch him was right down the middle of the plate."[36]

Clemente played 124 games for the Pirates in 1955 and had a batting average of .255. He walked only 18 times. Drawing bases on balls would never become a strong point for him. While it wasn't a sensational rookie season, Clemente had earned a spot in the Pirates' outfield. More than that, his exciting style of play made the fans look forward to seeing more of him.

Clemente returned to Puerto Rico in the fall of 1955. It had been reported that he might not play winter ball in his homeland and instead would begin college and study engineering.[37] However, Clemente ended up back on the diamond, playing another season for Santurce.

Back on the mainland in 1956, Clemente had a new boss in Pittsburgh. Bobby Bragan had taken over as manager from Fred Haney. Bragan appeared to be well-liked by the players, although he quickly demonstrated his strictness. In the second game of the season, Clemente missed a signal for a bunt and Bragan fined him.[38] He also fined another player, Dale Long. Biographer Kal Wagenheim wrote, "This harsh action worked like a shot of adrenalin. The club was soon fighting for first place in the league. Dale Long hit eight home runs in as many games. Clemente moved his batting average up to .348, fourth best in the league."[39]

The Pirates were in first place in mid-June, but an eight-game losing streak dropped them to fifth and ended their pennant hopes. Even so, they avoided last place for the first time since 1951 and they were showcasing one of the major league's most exciting players. In the outfield, Clemente had 17 assists, a sign of his strong throwing arm. At the plate, his .311 batting average was third-best in the National League. Two of his biggest hits were game-winning home runs. On Saturday, July 21, the Pirates trailed the Reds, 3-1, in the top of the ninth but had two runners on base as Clemente came to the plate. The Cincinnati pitcher was Brooks Lawrence, who had already won 13 games that season and hadn't yet lost. Clemente changed that, hitting a three-run homer, to give the Pirates a 4-3 win and spoil Lawrence's perfect record.

The following Wednesday, the Pirates were at home, playing the Chicago Cubs. Chicago led, 8-5, but Pittsburgh loaded the bases with no out. With Clemente due up, the Cubs brought in a new pitcher, Jim Brosnan. On Brosnan's first pitch, Clemente hit a long drive to left-center field. Hank Foiles, Bill Virdon, and Dick Cole raced around the bases toward home plate with the runs that would tie the game. Clemente also tore around the diamond. Manager Bobby Bragan was coaching at third base and held up his arms, giving Clemente the signal to stop at third. With no one out and good hitters coming up, Bragan figured they'd still get Clemente home with the winning run and didn't want to take the chance on him being thrown out at the plate. However, Clemente ignored his manager, kept running, and was safe at home. The inside-the-park grand-slam home run won the game for the Pirates.[40]

Bragan, who had fined Clemente earlier in the season for missing a sign, wasn't happy about Clemente deliberately disobeying this one. However, he decided not to fine him.[41]

Clemente's hits were the usual way for him to reach base because he rarely walked. He drew only 13 bases on balls in 1956, and at one point went 50 games without walking.[42] Branch Rickey wasn't concerned: "His value is in not taking bases on balls because he can hit the bad pitches. If I tried to teach him to wait for a good pitch, I'd simply make a bad hitter out of him. The cure would be worse than the disease. He'll cure his own ailments simply by experience."[43]

At the end of the season, Clemente headed home to play another season for Santurce in the Puerto Rican League. However, a couple of significant events took place between Christmas and New Year's Day. First, Santurce owner Pedrín Zorrilla sold the team. A few days later, the new owner of the Cangrejeros traded several players, including Clemente, to Caguas-Rio Piedras. The trade was extremely unpopular and even caused the Santurce manager, Monchile Concepcion, to resign.[44]

Clemente was leading the league in batting average and had gotten at least one hit in 18 consecutive games when he was traded. He continued his hitting streak, which reached 23 to set a new Puerto Rican League record. His streak was snapped when he was held hitless in a game by Luis "Tite" Arroyo, a longtime friend and teammate on the Pirates who was pitching for the San Juan Senadores in the winter.[45] Clemente finished with a batting average of .396.

His batting eye was certainly sharp, but Clemente's back was continuing to bother him, and he reported a day late to spring training in 1957 as a result. Bobby Bragan made light of the backache because Clemente had always played well even when he had some aches and pains. "The case history of Clemente is the worse he feels, the better he plays," reported *The Sporting News*, which quoted Bragan as saying, "I'd rather have a Clemente with some ailment than a Clemente who says he feels great with no aches or pains."[46]

Clemente's ability to play through pain and perform well may have contributed to charges that he wasn't really hurt. However, this time the back problems forced him to miss the first two games of the season. In all, Clemente played in only 111 games for Pittsburgh in 1957 and his batting average dropped to .253. The back problems lingered into the winter, and Clemente didn't play in the Puerto Rican League until mid-January of 1958.

The Pirates had finished last in 1957, but they made a big jump in 1958 under manager Danny Murtaugh. Clemente, who was feeling better physically, helped them get off to a good start in their opening game. He had three hits, one of which tied the game in the eighth inning against Milwaukee. The Pirates eventually won in 14 innings.

Clemente continued to hit well. He had three hits again in a 4-3 win in Cincinnati on April 25. One was a single in the sixth inning when the Pirates were trailing, 1-0. Clemente eventually scored to tie the game. The next inning he broke the tie with a three-run homer.

Another game-winning home run came in Milwaukee on August 4. Clemente broke a 3-3 tie with two out in the top of the ninth with a home run off fellow Puerto Rican Juan Pizarro, who had also been a winter teammate.

A little over a month later, Clemente had an even more spectacular game, although he didn't hit any homers. He had three triples, tying a National League record, in a 4-1 win over Cincinnati on September 8.

Clemente batted .289 in 1958. From right field, he continued to terrorize opposing baserunners, finishing with 22 assists. Fans loved it when a ball was hit his way with runners on base, rising in anticipation of seeing him uncork a strong throw.

Led by Clemente, the Pirates climbed from last place all the way to second, eight games behind the Milwaukee Braves.

Clemente didn't play winter baseball in Puerto Rico in 1958-59. He wore a different uniform, for the United States Marine Reserves. He fulfilled a six-month military commitment at Parris Island, South Carolina, and Camp LeJeune, North Carolina. The rigorous training program helped Clemente physically. He added strength by gaining ten pounds and said his back troubles had disappeared.[47]

When he reported to the Pirates in the spring of 1959, he complained of a sore right elbow. In May he made it worse when he hit the ground hard while making a diving catch. A few nights later, he had to be taken out of a game because he couldn't throw overhanded. He missed more than a month and continued to feel pain after he returned to the lineup.[48]

Clemente played in only 105 games and batted .296 as Pittsburgh dropped to fourth place. But he and the Pirates were primed for better things in 1960.

For the first time in several winters, Clemente played a full season in the Puerto Rican League in 1959-60. He was on a new team, having been traded to the San Juan Senadores, and he had a batting average of .330. Clemente and the Pirates hoped that he was ready for a big season back in Pittsburgh.

Another encouraging sign was that he was free of injuries. Feeling good and tuned up from his winter play, Clemente got off to a great start in 1960. In the Pirates' second game, at home against the Reds, he went three-for-three and drove in five runs as Pittsburgh won, 13-0. By the end of April, Clemente was batting .386. In 14 games, he had scored 12 runs, driven in 14, and hit three home runs. But he was just warming up. In Cincinnati, he had a home run and four RBIs on the first day of May. The 13-2 win was Pittsburgh's ninth straight and the team was in first place.

The Pirates cooled off a bit, but Clemente stayed hot. In May, he had 25 RBIs in 27 games, raising his season total to 39. He helped Pittsburgh regain the top spot in the National League standings and was named the league's Player of the Month by *The Sporting News*.

The Pirates battled for first with the San Francisco Giants and then the Milwaukee Braves. On the first Friday night in August, the Pirates were locked in a scoreless battle with the Giants at Forbes Field. Vinegar Bend Mizell was pitching for Pittsburgh and getting great help from his outfielders. Bill Virdon made a couple of good catches. Then Willie Mays led off the seventh inning for San Francisco with a long drive to right. Clemente chased the fly, reached out, and caught it, robbing Mays of an extra-base hit as he crashed into the outfield wall. He hurt his knee and also ended up with a gash in the chin that needed five stitches.[49]

Clemente stayed in the game the rest of the inning, but he was replaced by Gino Cimoli to start the eighth. Pittsburgh eventually won, 1-0, starting a four-game sweep of the Giants. Clemente missed the rest of the series as well as another three games.

He was out for a week. The day after he returned, he had a big game against the St. Louis Cardinals. St. Louis had beaten the Pirates the previous two nights and the Cardinals were in second place, only three games behind Pittsburgh. The Cardinals took the lead with a run in the top of the first inning. In the last of the first, Pittsburgh tied the game when Clemente singled home Dick Groat.

With the score still tied, Groat opened the third inning with a double, and Clemente followed with a homer. Clemente had another run-scoring single in the fourth as Pittsburgh won the game, 4-1. Clemente batted in all four of his team's runs.

The Pirates swept a doubleheader from the Cardinals the next day to open up a six-game lead. No one came close to them the rest of the way. Except for one day, the Pirates had been in first place since May 29.

Clemente finished the 1960 season with a .314 batting average and hit 16 home runs, more than doubling his previous high. He also made the National League All-Star team for the first time.

Pittsburgh's first pennant since 1927 put them in the World Series against the New York Yankees. Despite being outscored 46-17, the Pirates split the first six games to force a decisive seventh game.

New York came back from a 4-0 deficit to carry a 7-4 lead into the last of the eighth. The Pirates rallied, helped by a bad hop that turned a probable double-play grounder into a base hit. One run was in and Pittsburgh had runners at second and third with two out when Clemente came to bat against the Yankees' Jim Coates. Clemente swung and topped the ball toward first base. Coates couldn't get to it, and it was left to Moose Skowron to field it. Skowron had no chance of beating Clemente to the base, and Coates's pursuit of the ball left the bag uncovered. Clemente zipped safely across the base, his helmet flying off, while the two Yankees watched helplessly.

Clemente's hit drove in another run and the Pirates took a 9-7 lead when Hal Smith followed with a three-run homer. New York came back in the top of the ninth to tie the game, setting the stage for one of the most dramatic moments in Pittsburgh sports history—a Series-winning home run by Bill Mazeroski leading off the last of the ninth.

Clemente had had a hit in each of the seven games in helping the Pirates win the World Series.

Returning to his homeland following the 1960 season, Clemente skipped the first part of the Puerto Rican League season, but then joined the San Juan Senadores in the second half. Even after he became a star in the major leagues, Clemente continued playing winter ball well past the time that he needed to keep his batting eye sharp. He felt an obligation to the people of his homeland, who otherwise would not have a chance to see him play. Clemente is perhaps the most inspirational figure the island has ever known, and he took that responsibility seriously.

He frequently stood up for himself and his fellow Latin players, speaking out against injustices he saw. He approached this in the same manner in which he played—with a passion, sometimes an anger, which drove him on and off the field.

Much of his anger was justified. Although the game became more open to Latins after the breaking of the color barrier, certain attitudes and prejudices toward these players remained. Latin players were often accused of being lazy or faking an injury if they missed a game because they were hurt or ill. Clemente knew first-hand the feeling of being called a hypochondriac. He suffered through many ailments in his career and he burned when his manager or reporters didn't believe him when he said he was hurt.

One of Clemente's biographers, Kal Wagenheim, wrote, "The legend of his hypochondria became part of baseball's folklore. He claimed so many ills—and performed so well despite them—that his plaints evoked skepticism or laughter." Wagenheim also noted that Clemente had problems in the 1960s with Pirates manager Danny Murtaugh, who "reportedly accused him of feigning an injury and fined him for not playing."[50]

Beyond the injuries and claims of hypochondria, Clemente maintained that Latin players often did not receive the recognition they deserved. Once again, Clemente was an example of this. After helping the Pirates win the National League pennant, and then the World Series championship, Clemente finished eighth in the voting for the league's Most Valuable Player. Clemente thought he should have gotten more votes and finished higher in the balloting.

Each slight, whether at him or a fellow Latin, he took personally. He spoke out often, although some of the claims he made about being mistreated weren't always entirely correct.

Phil Musick, a reporter who covered the Pittsburgh Pirates during the final years of Clemente's career, said, "He was anything but perfect. He was vain, occasionally arrogant, often intolerant, unforgiving, and there were moments when I thought for sure he'd cornered the market on self-pity. Mostly, he acted as if the world had just declared all-out war on Roberto Clemente, when in fact it lavished him with an affection few men ever know."

However, Musick added, "I know that through all of his battles ... there was about him an undeniable charisma. Perhaps that was his true essence—he won so much of your attention and affection that you demanded of him what no man can give, perfection."[51]

Clemente did eventually receive the respect he sought. Toward the end of his career, fans and reporters recognized his greatness on the field. More than that, they knew of his caring nature for all people.

Clemente said he rarely set goals, but that he did once: "After I failed to win the Most Valuable Player Award in 1960, I made up my mind I'd win the batting title in 1961 for the first time."[52]

Clemente did exactly that, leading the National League with a .351 batting average. He hit 23 home runs, scored 100 runs and drove in 89. He led National League outfielders with 27 assists and won a Gold Glove for his fielding excellence for the first time. Clemente would win a Gold Glove every year for the rest of his career.

In Puerto Rico, Clemente played winter ball less often. He skipped the 1962-63 season altogether. It was the first time he hadn't played in the Puerto Rican League other than the time he was in the Marine Reserves in 1958-59.

However, Clemente was back for a full season with San Juan in 1963-64. The Senadores finished third during the regular season but won the league play-offs and represented Puerto Rico in the International Series, which was played in Managua, Nicaragua. Author Thomas Van Hyning reports, "Clemente was a fan favorite and made a lot of fans in Nicaragua."[53] Clemente developed a fondness for the country and its people and would return again.

The race for the Puerto Rican batting title involved two National League stars—Clemente and Orlando Cepeda—and a young player on the verge of stardom in the American League, Tony Oliva. Back on the mainland in 1964, Oliva and Clemente led their respective leagues in batting average. Oliva, who credited his winter-league experience with helping his development as a hitter, had a .323 average in his first full season in the majors.[54] Clemente's .339 average was good for his second National League batting title.

The winter of 1964-65 was an eventful one for Clemente. He married Vera Cristina Zabala. He also began managing. In December of 1964, Clemente took over as manager of the San Juan Senadores. He still played, although less often. In his first game as manager, Clemente had two doubles off Dennis McLain of Mayaguez. "He drove in two runs with his second double and raced home on a wild throw, but twisted his left ankle slightly and left the game," reported Miguel J. Frau in *The Sporting News*.[55]

Clemente later suffered a more serious injury. He was mowing the lawn at his home when a rock flew out of the mower and hit him in the thigh. He missed some games as a player, but when the league's All-Star Game was played, Clemente felt obligated to make an appearance. He pinch-hit and singled, but he aggravated the injury. "I felt my thigh ligament pop and something like water draining inside my leg," he said. Clemente had partially severed a ligament in his thigh, and he had to have surgery.[56]

The injury, combined with a fever, left Clemente weak, and he got off to a slow start in 1965 with the Pirates. Under new manager Harry Walker, the team also began poorly, losing 24 of their first 33 games. A 12-game winning streak followed, lifting Pittsburgh in the standings. Clemente got hot over this stretch, hitting .458 during the winning streak. The Pirates never overcame their slow start and finished third. Clemente led the league in batting average for the second year in a row and the third time in his career.

No one knew, though, that he was on the verge of his best season ever.

In addition to his other skills, Clemente was increasing his walk total in the mid-1960s. Early in the 1966 season, the Pirates were in Chicago, trailing the Cubs by a run. Clemente came to bat with two out and no one on base in the ninth inning. Cubs reliever Ted Abernathy got two strikes on Clemente. The Pirates were on the verge of losing, but Clemente remained patient. Abernathy's next three pitches were outside the strike zone, and Clemente laid off them. The count was full. Clemente stayed alive by fouling off the next eight pitches. Finally, Abernathy missed again and Clemente was on base with a walk. Willie Stargell followed with a double and Clemente came home with the tying run. Pittsburgh won the game in extra innings.

The win kept the Pirates in first place. They stayed in the pennant race all season, battling the San Francisco Giants and Los Angeles Dodgers. At the end of August the Pirates and Giants were tied for first. On September 2, Clemente hit a three-run homer off Chicago's Ferguson Jenkins that helped Pittsburgh beat the Cubs and take over sole possession of first place. It was the 2,000th hit of his career and his 23rd homer of the year, equaling his previous career high. In addition, it gave him 101 runs batted in, the first time he had ever reached 100 RBIs in a season.

He ended the season with career-highs in home runs (29) and RBIs (119). The Pirates finished third behind the Dodgers and Giants, but Clemente edged out Los Angeles' Sandy Koufax for the Most Valuable Player award.

Clemente had another outstanding season in 1967. He led the league with a .357 batting average for his third batting title in four years and his fourth overall. In addition to 209 hits, Clemente walked or was hit by a pitch more than 40 times, and he reached base at least 40 percent of the time for the first time in his career.

After having taken the previous winter off, Clemente played occasionally in the Puerto Rican League in 1967-68 and had a batting average of .382. Back on the mainland, things did not go well for him in 1968. The Pirates' opener was delayed two days because of the assassination of Martin Luther King. Clemente homered in the first game, but his batting average fell to .222 at the end of May. He said he was having trouble swinging the bat because he had injured his right shoulder in a fall at his home in Puerto Rico in February of 1968. He added that he might retire from baseball if the shoulder didn't get better.[57]

He improved over the last part of the season and finished with a .291 batting average, his lowest since 1958. Clemente didn't play winter ball and rested his body. He felt good when spring training began in 1969, but then he hurt his left shoulder as he tried to make a diving catch and went back to Puerto Rico for treatment. Clemente returned in time for the start of the regular season, but for the second year in a row he got off to a slow start. In the latter half of May, after going hitless in the first game of a series in San Diego, his batting average had fallen to .225.

Clemente claimed something else happened—a strange and scary incident. He did not tell the story in public until a year later, but Clemente said he was kidnapped while in San Diego. According to Clemente, he was walking back to the hotel where the Pirates were staying after going out to eat. He said four men forced him into a car at gunpoint. They took him to an isolated area and took his wallet and his All-Star Game ring. "This is where I figure they are going to shoot me and throw me in the woods," he told Pittsburgh writer Bill Christine more than a year after the incident. "They already had the pistol inside my mouth." Two of the men spoke Spanish, and Clemente talked to one of them in Spanish. After that, the men returned Clemente's money and ring and brought him back to his hotel. They even gave Clemente back the bag of chicken he had purchased at the restaurant. He said he did not report the incident to the police.[58]

Despite the harrowing event, Clemente finished the series in San Diego by getting three hits against the Padres and raised his batting average above .300 by mid-June. For a while it looked like he might lead the league again. He didn't, but Clemente still finished the season with a batting average of .345. The Pirates didn't do as well, finishing third in the new East Division of the National League.

After a slow start in 1970, the Pirates caught fire as they moved from Forbes Field, where they had played since 1909, to Three Rivers Stadium. Pittsburgh and New York fought for first place through July, with Chicago staying close. The Pirates were hanging in without Clemente. He was hit in the wrist with a pitch on July 25 and, except for one pinch-running appearance, was out of the lineup for more than a week. He returned on August 8 and had a double and a home run against the Mets.

Later in August, Clemente had five hits in each of two straight games. The first one came on a Saturday in Los Angeles. Clemente already had four hits as he came to the plate in the top of the 16th inning. He singled, stole second, and later came scored the go-ahead run as the Pirates beat the Dodgers, 2-1. The next day, the Pirates won again, 11-0. Clemente had five of Pittsburgh's 23 hits in the game.

He had raised his average to .363, tops in the National League. However, he played little in September because of a bad back and did not win the batting title. The Pirates still won the National League East Division and advanced to the playoffs. Scoring only three runs in three games, however, they were swept by the Cincinnati Reds.

That winter, Clemente played for the last time in the Puerto Rican League. Although he played in only three games during the regular season, he appeared in one of the playoff series. In addition, he managed the San Juan Senadores in 1970-71. The Senadores' opening game that season was against Santurce, which was managed by Frank Robinson. Both Robinson and Clemente had been mentioned as possibilities to be the first black manager in the major leagues.

After he got off to a slow start with the Pirates in 1971, he said, "My biggest mistake was managing in Puerto Rico that past winter. I had more responsibilities and did not get my rest. The long bus trips out of town, I have to make them because I am the manager. They take something out of me."[59]

Willie Stargell took the lead with Pittsburgh in 1971. He set a major league record by hitting 11 home runs in April and continued his great hitting throughout the year. Stargell finished with 48 home runs and 125 runs batted in.

Although Stargell had emerged as the team's star player, the team leader was still Clemente. He was receiving the recognition he had sought, and he was also showing he could continue playing with the same flair and hustle, even as he approached his 37th birthday. Clemente got off to a bad start, but he got hot in May and went on to finish the season with a .341 batting average. He was still outstanding in the field. In mid-June, Clemente preserved a shutout for Steve Blass, and a victory for the Pirates, on back-to-back plays. Pittsburgh held a 1-0 lead over Houston in the last of the eighth inning. The Astros had a runner on first with one out when Cesar Cedeno hit a soft liner to right field. Clemente hustled in and made a sliding catch of the ball before it could hit the turf. Bob Watson then hit a much harder drive toward the corner in right. Clemente raced toward the ball and made a twisting leap, grabbing the ball and robbing Watson of a two-run homer. Clemente crashed into the wall, bruising his ankle and elbow and cutting his knee. Astros manager Harry Walker, who had managed Clemente in Pittsburgh, said it was the greatest catch he ever made. Because of Clemente's catch, the Pirates maintained their lead and then padded it with two more runs in the ninth. Blass finished with a 3-0 win but said, "That shutout belongs to Clemente."[60]

The win gave the Pirates a 3 ½ game lead over the New York Mets and St. Louis Cardinals. Pittsburgh increased its lead to 9 ½ games at the All-Star break in July. The Pirates had several players in the All-Star game, including two starters—Willie Stargell in left field and Dock Ellis, who pitched. Clemente entered the game as a replacement for Willie Mays in the fourth inning. Later in the game, he hit his first home run in an All-Star Game.

Pittsburgh went on to win the East Division and beat San Francisco in the league playoffs to make it back to the World Series, against the Baltimore Orioles. Clemente turned the event into a showcase for his greatness.

Baltimore took the first two games before the series shifted to Pittsburgh. Clemente drove in the first run of the third game with a fielder's choice. The Pirates added another run, but Baltimore came back on a home run by Frank Robinson to cut the lead to 2-1. Clemente led off the last of the seventh by grounding back to Mike Cuellar, who had briefly pitched for Clemente's San Juan team in the Puerto Rican League the previous winter.[61] However, Clemente hustled down to first so hard that Cuellar hurried his throw and threw wildly. Clemente reached base on the error and, after Stargell walked, Bob Robertson hit a three-run homer. Pittsburgh won, 5-1.

The next game was the first night game in the history of the World Series. The Orioles got off to an early lead with three runs in the top of the first. Pittsburgh came back with two in the bottom of the inning, and the Pirates rallied again in the third. With one out, Richie Hebner singled. Clemente then hit a long drive to right. It cleared the fence and looked like a home run to put the Pirates ahead. However, the ball was ruled foul after the umpires had a long discussion. The ball was foul, and Clemente had to resume his at-bat. He couldn't come up with another long ball, but his single sent Hebner to second. One out later Al Oliver singled, scoring Hebner to tie the game. The score stayed at 3-3 until the Pirates pushed another run across in the seventh inning. Pittsburgh won the game, 4-3, and tied the World Series, 2-2.

The Pirates won again the next day as Nelson Briles held the Orioles to two hits. Clemente had a run-scoring single in the fifth inning to cap Pittsburgh's scoring as the Pirates won, 5-0.

The Series shifted back to Baltimore, but Pittsburgh had the lead. Just as he had done in the 1960 World Series, Clemente had at least one hit in each of the games. In the sixth game, with two out in the top of the first, he tripled off the fence in left-center field. However, Willie Stargell struck out, and Clemente was stranded at third.

By the time Clemente came up again in the third inning, the Pirates had a 1-0 lead. Clemente made the score 2-0 by hitting a home run to right field. The Orioles came back and tied the game in the seventh. In the last of the 10th inning, Brooks Robinson hit a sacrifice fly that scored Frank Robinson, giving Baltimore the win and extending the series to a seventh game.

Cuellar and Pittsburgh's Steve Blass were the starters in Game Seven, and both were sharp. Cuellar retired the first 11 Pittsburgh batters before Clemente came up with two out in the fourth. Cuellar threw him a high curve ball, and Clemente drove it over the left-center field fence. Clemente's second home run of the series gave Pittsburgh a 1-0 lead.

The Pirates got another run in the eighth inning, which they needed. In the bottom of the eighth, Baltimore got the first two runners on base. Blass was able to work out of the jam with only one run scoring, leaving Pittsburgh in the lead. Blass retired the Orioles in order in the last of the ninth. Clemente's homer had given the Pirates a lead they never gave up. Pittsburgh won the game, 2-1, and the Pirates were again champions of the world.

The Pirates had a number of pitchers who stood out, but when the voting was complete for the outstanding player of the World Series, the award went to Clemente. He had 12 hits, including two home runs, for a .414 batting average in the seven games.

There was no doubting his greatness nor his influence on the champion Pirates. Clemente had played in the All-Star Game, the World Series, had won the Most Valuable Player award, and had led the National League in batting average four times. He still had another milestone in his sights. "I would like to get 3,000 hits," he said in 1971.[62]

The Pirates had a rough start in 1972 and were in last place in May. They climbed in the standings and by the last half of June had taken over first place for good. Clemente was also doing well even though he had an intestinal virus that caused him to miss a few games. By the end of June, his batting average was .315, and he was making good progress toward the mark of 3,000 hits. On July 9, he got his 78th hit of the season, leaving him only 40 short. However, the virus returned, and Clemente left the Pirates to go back to Pittsburgh for treatment. He was out of the lineup for two weeks, then came back and got a big hit in a Pirates win on July 23.

Clemente missed another four weeks with strained tendons in both heels. Over a 40-game span between July 9 and August 22, he started only one game. Fortunately, the Pirates were still playing well and opened up a big lead in the National League East Division, but the illness and injuries had slowed Clemente in his drive toward 3,000 hits.

At the end of August he had 30 hits to go. He hit well in September and was within striking distance by the final week of the season. On Thursday night, September 28, he got his 2,999th hit off Steve Carlton of the Phillies. Because the game was in Philadelphia, he was taken out so he could get his 3,000th hit before the home fans.

Even this event would not happen without a bit of controversy as the Pirates opened a series against the New York Mets in Pittsburgh. Facing Tom Seaver in the first inning, Clemente hit a chopper up the middle. Second baseman Ken Boswell bobbled the ball, and Clemente reached first. Official scorer Luke Quay ruled the play an error. Seaver allowed only two hits, neither to Clemente, in winning his 20th game of the season. After the game, Clemente complained about the scoring decision and later made accusations that official scorers through the years had deprived him of two batting titles. Part of the outburst was a result of Clemente thinking (erroneously) that the scorer in the game was Charley Feeney, a local sportswriter who Clemente thought had deprived him of hits on borderline calls in the past.[63]

The next afternoon Clemente struck out in the first inning. The game was scoreless when he came up again, leading off the fourth. He hit a long fly toward left-center field. The ball hit the fence on one bounce, and Clemente cruised into second with a double, the

3,000th hit of his career. The Pittsburgh fans stood and applauded Clemente, who raised his cap to show his appreciation. That hit started a three-run rally, and the Pirates won the game, 5-0. Bill Mazeroski pinch hit for Clemente in the fifth inning.

Clemente played in only one of Pittsburgh's final three games as he rested for the playoffs. The Pirates played Cincinnati and looked like they were on their way back to the World Series. Pittsburgh carried a 3-2 lead into the last of the ninth inning of the decisive fifth game. However, Johnny Bench tied the game with a home run, and the Reds scored the winning run on a wild pitch.

As usual, Clemente went back to Puerto Rico. Although he didn't play baseball, he managed a Puerto Rican team that went to the Amateur Baseball World Series in Nicaragua. The Puerto Rican team finished third in the tournament.[64]

Clemente was back home a few weeks later when the city of Managua was racked by a massive earthquake on December 23. He had gotten to know people during his visits to Nicaragua. He was concerned about the people there and wanted to help.

Clemente got busy organizing a committee to raise money and get other items, such as medicine and food, that could be sent to Nicaragua. Through Christmas, he worked on the relief efforts. He finally decided he would go on one of the cargo planes that were flying the supplies to the stricken area.

A little after 9 p.m. on New Year's Eve, as others in Puerto Rico were celebrating, the plane took off. Besides Clemente, four other people were on board. Almost immediately, the plane had problems, and the pilot tried to return to the San Juan airport. Before the plane could make it back, however, it crashed into the Atlantic Ocean about a mile from the coast.

The fate of the people on board was not immediately known. But it soon became clear. The five men on the plane, including Roberto Clemente, were dead.[65]

People, not just baseball fans, mourned the loss of Clemente, who left behind his wife, Vera, and three sons, Roberto, Jr., Luis Roberto, and Roberto Enrique.

Normally, a player cannot be inducted into the Baseball Hall of Fame until at least five years after he stopped playing. Because of the circumstances, an exception was made for Clemente. A special election was held, and he received enough votes to be elected. In the summer of 1973, Clemente became the first player from Latin America to be inducted into the Hall of Fame.

There were other honors. An award, established in 1971 to honor a player for his accomplishments on and off the field, was renamed the Roberto Clemente Award.

Clemente had dreamed of establishing a Sports City for young people in Puerto Rico. He had a vision for a place where young people could come and play as well as read and learn other skills they would need in life. Vera Clemente continued her husband's work, aided by son Luis, and while the project remains uncompleted, the Foundation that was established works to support clinics, sports activities, and similar efforts.

Although he is gone, all sorts of reminders of Clemente still exist. More than anything, Roberto Clemente left behind memories of how he played the game on the field and how he lived his life off it.

## SOURCES

Retrosheet (http://retrosheet.org) provided game-by-game details of Clemente's performance. The information used was obtained free of charge from and is copyrighted by Retrosheet.

## NOTES

1 Peter C. Bjarkman, *Baseball with a Latin Beat: A History of the Latin American Game* (Jefferson: North Carolina: McFarland & Company, Inc., Publishers, 1994), 262.

2 Kal Wagenheim, *Clemente!* (New York: Praeger Publishers, 1973), 15.

3 Bruce Markusen, *Roberto Clemente: The Great One* (Champaign, Illinois: Sports Publishing, Inc., 1998), 4.

4 Telephone interview with Monte Irvin, June 30, 2005.

5 "Roberto Hit Ten HRs in 'Day-Long' Slugfest," *The Sporting News*, July 6, 1960: 6.

6 Wagenheim, 24.

7 "Starred in Javelin, Jumps Before Turning to Diamond," *The Sporting News*, July 6, 1960: 6.

8. Markusen, 8.

9. Les Biederman, "Pride Pushes Clemente: 'I Can Hit With Best'," *The Sporting News*, March 28, 1964: 11.

10. Thomas E. Van Hyning, *The Santurce Crabbers: Sixty Seasons of Puerto Rican Winter League Baseball* (Jefferson, North Carolina: McFarland & Company, Inc., Publishers, 1999), 39.

11. Frank Graham, Jr., "Spanish-Speaking Al Campanis Lures Latin Talent for Dodgers," *The Sporting News*, January 12, 1955: 21.

12. E-mail correspondence with Buzzie Bavasi, June 3, 2005.

13. Santiago Llorens, *The Sporting News*, January 20, 1954: 23.

14. *The Sporting News*, March 3, 1954: 26.

15. The bonus rule in effect at that time is chronicled in Brent Kelley, *Baseball's Biggest Blunder: The Bonus Rule of 1953-1957* (Lanham, Maryland: The Scarecrow Press, Inc., 1997).

16. Les Biederman, "Dodgers Signed Clemente Just to Balk Giants," *The Sporting News*, May 25, 1955: 11.

17. Wagenheim, 35; Markusen, 33-34.

18. The claim that the Dodgers would not start five blacks in the same game was made by Wagenheim on page 35 of *Clemente!* Box scores of Brooklyn Dodgers games in 1954 from *The Sporting News* indicate four instances in which Jim Gilliam, Jackie Robinson, Don Newcombe, Sandy Amoros, and Roy Campanella were all in the starting lineup: July 17, August 24, September 6 (second game), and September 15.

19. E-mail correspondence with Buzzie Bavasi, June 3, 2005.

20. Phil Musick, *Who Was Roberto? A Biography of Roberto Clemente* (Garden City, New York: Doubleday & Co., 1974). See also Wagenheim and Markusen.

21. The game-by-game analysis of the 1954 season was done through box scores of Montreal Royals games, published in *The Sporting News* in 1954, and cross-checked by SABR member Neil Raymond from box scores in Montreal newspapers.

22. Musick, 89.

23. Musick, 89.

24. Telephone interview with Jack Cassini, June 20, 2005.

25. E-mail correspondence with Buzzie Bavasi, June 3, 2005.

26. "Jack Hernon, "Backward Buccos Refuse to Go Overboard on Rookie," *The Sporting News*, January 12, 1955: 18.

27. Pito Alvarez de la Vega. "Mays, Gomez & Co. on Top in Puerto Rico: Santurce Takes Over Lead from Caguas; Willie Ups Swatting Average to .423," *The Sporting News*, December 22, 1954: 24.

28. Wagenheim, 43.

29. Interview with Don Zimmer, July 2, 2005.

30. Jack Hernon, "Clemente a Gem in Need of Polish," *The Sporting News*, February 9, 1955: 4.

31. Jack Hernon, "Haney's Sizeup on Bob Clemente 'Much to Learn'," *The Sporting News*, March 16, 1955: 30.

32. http://www.bioproj.sabr.org/bioproj.cfm?a=v&v=l&bid=1187&pid=14117 Frank Thomas biography by Bob Hurte; Jack Hernon. "Holdouts Thomas and Law Absent as Bucs Start Drills" *The Sporting News*, March 9, 1955: 33.

33. *The Sporting News*, March 16, 1955: 27; "Uniform Numbers Range from 1 to 81," *The Sporting News*, April 13, 1955, 28; Thomas E. Van Hyning. *Puerto Rico's Winter League: A History of Major League Baseball's Launching Pad* (Jefferson, North Carolina: McFarland & Company, Inc., Publishers, 1995), 53.

34. Jack Hernon, "Haney's Young Bucs Shaking off Buck Fever," *The Sporting News*, May 11, 1955: 11.

35. Les Biederman, "Clemente, Early Buc Ace, Says He's Better in Summer," *The Sporting News*, June 29, 1955, 26.

36. Telephone interview with Jack Cassini, June 20, 2005.

37. Les Biederman, "Clemente, Early Buc Ace, Says He's Better in Summer."

38. "Bragan Cracks Down Early, Fines Clemente, Long $25," *The Sporting News*, April 25, 1956: 21; Les Biederman, "Bear-Down Bragan Means Business, Buc Fans Learn," *The Sporting News*, May 2, 1956: 7.

39. Wagenheim, 67.

40. Irving Vaughan, "7-Run Cub 8th Isn't Enough! Pirates Win, 9 to 8, on Clemente Homer," *Chicago Tribune*, Thursday, July 26, 1956: 6, 1.

41. "Clemente Ignored Stop Sign on 'Slam,' But Escaped Fine," *The Sporting News*, August 8, 1956: 18.

42. Les Biederman, "Clemente in 50 Games Without Walk," *The Sporting News*, August 8, 1956: 18.

43. Oscar Ruhl. "Rickey Rates Clemente as Top Draft Dandy," *The Sporting News*, March 20, 1957: 15.

44. Pito Alvarez de la Vega, "New Owner Peddles Trio of Santurce's Stars to Flag Rival," *The Sporting News*, January 9, 1957: 21.

45. Pito Alvarez de la Vega, "Bilko Released in Economy Move; Clemente Sets 23-Game Hit Mark," *The Sporting News*, January 16, 1957: 21.

46. "Clemente, Best When Ailing, Reports Late with Backache," *The Sporting News*, March 13, 1957: 10.

47. "Clemente to Start Six-Month Marine Corps Hitch, Oct. 4," *The Sporting News*, September 24, 1958: 7; "Buc Flyhawk Now Marine Rookie," *The Sporting News*, November 19, 1958: 13; *The Sporting News*, January 21, 1959: 9.

48. "Clemente Put on Disabled List and Baker Released by Bucs," *The Sporting News*, June 3, 1959: 3.

49. Bob Stevens, "Little Things Add Up to Big Plunge for Snoozing Giants," *The Sporting News*, August 17, 1960: 13, 18.

50. Wagenheim, 106.

51 Musick, 14-15.

52 Les Biederman, "Clemente—The Player Who Can Do It All," *The Sporting News*, April 20, 1968: 11.

53 Thomas E. Van Hyning. *Puerto Rico's Winter League: A History of Major League Baseball's Launching Pad*, 66.

54 Interview with Tony Oliva, June 5, 2005.

55 Miguel J. Frau, "Puerto Rico: Senators Dip As Clemente Grabs Reins," *The Sporting News*, January 9, 1965: 27.

56 "Clemente May Have Trouble As Result of Thigh Injury," *The Sporting News*, February 13, 1965: 25.

57 Les Biederman, "Shoulder Sore; Clemente Says He May Retire," *The Sporting News*, August 24, 1968: 18.

58 "Clemente Reveals Close Call with Kidnapers," *The Sporting News*, August 22, 1970: 24.

59 "Clemente Laments Managing," *The Sporting News*, May 15, 1971: 14.

60 Charley Feeney, "Greatest Catch? This One by Roberto Will Do," *The Sporting News*, July 3, 1971: 7.

61 Phil Jackman, "Orioles Shrug Off Cuellar's Winter Ball Woes," *The Sporting News*, December 26, 1970: 36.

62 Charley Feeney, "Clemente Sets 3,000 Hits As Wish on 37th Birthday," *The Sporting News*, August 28, 1971: 9.

63 Charley Feeney, "Roberto Collects 3000th Hit, Dedicates It to Pirate Fans," *The Sporting News*, October 14, 1972: 15.

64 "Veteran Cuban Team Captures Amateur Title; U. S. Runner-Up," *The Sporting News*, December 30, 1972: 46.

65 "Baseball Mourns Loss of Buc Star Clemente," *The Sporting News*, January 13, 1973: 42.

# FRANCISCO "PANCHO" COIMBRE

## By Joseph Gerard

*"Baseball is in the heart of all Latin people. They feel in baseball. They think in baseball."*

— Pancho Coimbre

**BASEBALL IN PUERTO RICO HAS A** long and storied history; many fans of the game on the island are willing to regale one another at the drop of a hat about the careers and exploits of such well-known stars as Roberto Clemente, Orlando Cepeda, Roberto Alomar, Carlos Baerga, and Juan González. But less is spoken about the early years of professional baseball on the island, and the many greats of the game who paved the way for their successors.

One of the most important figures in the early history of professional baseball in Puerto Rico was Francisco Luis "Pancho" Coimbre, who was born on January 29, 1909, to Guillermo Coimbre and Zoila Atiles in Coamo, a city in the south-central region of Puerto Rico. Coamo is approximately 42 kilometers east of Ponce, where Coimbre eventually settled and became a local legend for his exploits as a member of the Leones de Ponce, a founding team of the *Liga de Béisbol Profesional de Puerto Rico* (LBPPR).

The LBPPR was founded as a semiprofessional league in the winter of 1938-1939, and became an official professional league in 1941. Coimbre played 13 seasons in the LBPPR, and his team won five championships during that period. He also had a relatively brief but distinguished career in the American Negro Leagues, excelling for the New York Cubans in the 1940s, and for various clubs in Mexico, the Dominican Republic, and Venezuela.

Like many young boys growing up in Puerto Rico in the early 1900s, Coimbre played local sandlot ball, with his first exposure to organized baseball coming when he joined his high school team in Ponce. There he was tutored in the ways of the game by a seminal figure in the development of Latin American baseball, Pedro Miguel Caratini, a player and manager on the island who went on to fame as "the father of Dominican baseball" as manager of the Tigres del Licey.

Coimbre excelled in both baseball and track in high school, but his ability to compete in school athletics was interrupted by a bureaucratic entanglement when he transferred from his school in Ponce to one in Caguas. When he attempted to participate in an athletic competition there, the Puerto Rico Instruction Department withheld its permission, asserting that Coimbre was registered in a different region of the island. Apparently the Coimbre family took legal action, as a court case commenced, the first ever involving public school athletics in the island's history.

Perhaps deterred by these difficulties and his resulting ineligibility, Coimbre returned with his family to Ponce, but his attempt to participate in athletics was derailed once again when the Instruction Department accused Coimbre of having accepted remuneration while a student-athlete. Once again the matter ended up in court, with Judge Roberto Todd Jr. deciding in Coimbre's favor as a result of limited evidence.

While playing ball in high school, Coimbre came to the attention of Felipe "Pipo" Maldonado, the owner of the Leones de Ponce, a team in the amateur Liga Insular. While he excelled as a second baseman and pitcher in high school, Coimbre became the Leones' right fielder when he wasn't pitching; in his first game with the team, he got four hits. He played for the Leones through the 1928 season, when they won the island championship against the club from Guayama.

Coimbre's first baseball experience outside of his native country occurred in 1927, when he played ball in the Dominican Republic for the amateur Sandino team in Santiago de los Caballeros. Coimbre came to the attention of Emilio "Millito" Navarro, a ballplayer and Ponce native, who recommended him to the Magallanes squad in the *Asociación del Béisbol Venezolano*. Coimbre played in Venezuela for Magallanes in 1929.

In 1930-31, Coimbre played for the Tigres del Licey in Santo Domingo, as well as for the Leones, but in 1932, at the age of 23, he went to work as a security guard in a penal institution, where he played on a local semipro team. His need for reliable employment apparently gave way to his desire to play baseball, as he accepted an offer to play once again in Venezuela, this time for the Santa Marta club located in La Guaira. He returned to the Dominican Republic and played for Licey in 1933 and 1934 before returning to Venezuela in 1935 to play for the Pastora team in Maracaibo.

The LBPPR was formed the following year and quickly established itself as a prominent winter ball venue featuring the talents of many exceptional major league, Negro League, and Latin American players. Coimbre played the inaugural winter league season for his native Ponce before traveling to New York City, where he was recruited to play for the Puerto Rican Stars, a barnstorming team that played throughout the Northeast. There he was noticed by Alejandro Pómpez, the legendary owner of the New York Cubans, who signed Coimbre to join the Cubans for the 1940 season.

Coimbre had immediate success with the Cubans, and Pompez brought him back for the 1941 season. Coimbre established himself as one of the finest players in the Negro National League, representing the East as the starting right fielder in the annual Negro League All-Star Game at Comiskey Park in Chicago, and finishing the season with a batting average of .353. The Cubans won the second half of the season but fell to the Homestead Grays in the championship series.

Coimbre returned to Ponce to play for the Leones in the 1941-42 season, leading his team to a record of 30-13 and the league championship. The Leones featured several veterans of the Negro Leagues, including Howard Easterling, Barney Morris, Max Manning, and the team's manager, George Scales. They repeated as champions in 1942-43, and Coimbre won the batting title with a .342 mark.

Coimbre did not play in North America in 1942 – the year when light-skinned, European-looking Hiram Bithorn became the first Puerto Rican in the majors – but returned to the Cubans for the 1943 season. He hit for an average of .428 and was once again selected as the starting right fielder for the East in the annual All-Star game.

The 1943-44 Ponce Leones were one of the finest teams in the history of Latin-American baseball, compiling a record of 37-7 and winning the LBPPR championship by 15 games. Once again managed by George Scales, the roster included Sam Bankhead, Millito Navarro, and pitcher Tomás Quiñones. Coimbre batted .376 for the year, and went on to hit .318 for the Cubans in 1944, with a .421 slugging percentage.

Afterwards, he returned to Ponce and led the LBPPR in hitting with a .425 average (45 for 106), the seventh-best mark in league history for batters who had at least 100 at-bats. The Leones won their fourth straight league title. In those days, the league had four teams and divided its season into two halves. Ponce was very consistent, winning both halves in three of four years. Thus, there was only one playoff series during this run, in 1942-43 against Santurce.

The summer of 1945 brought several changes for Coimbre. Instead of playing in North America, he began the year playing in Barranquilla, Colombia for the El Torices club, but an injury reduced him to a coaching role. He went on to play for Puebla of the *Liga Mexicana del Béisbol;* on a basic batting line of 5 homers, 85 RBIs, and a .346 average in 89 games, he finished fourth in total bases, seventh in hits, and eighth in batting average. It was his only season in Mexico.

Coimbre returned to the New York Cubans in 1946, and recorded a batting average of .357 and a slugging percentage of .510, in what turned out to be his final season in the Negro Leagues.

The Ponce Leones won their fifth and final championship with Coimbre on their roster in the winter of 1946-47. However, an injury to his knee as a result of an errant pitch resulted in hospitalization and subsequent physical therapy for Coimbre, and limited his play in 1947. The following year, he went to New York City to visit family and friends, with intentions to sign on with either the Baltimore Elite Giants or the New York Black Yankees. Instead, he was contacted by the Sherbrooke Athlétiques of the independent Canadian Provincial League, and subsequently joined Cuban players Claro Duany, Adrián Zabala and fellow former New York Cuban Rodolfo Fernández on the Sherbrooke roster. The Athlétiques won the league championship that season, finishing with a record of 61-37; Coimbre, still hobbled by injury, managed to appear in both infield and outfield positions. He even won two games as a pitcher.

Coimbre continued to play for Ponce in the LBPPR through the 1950-1951 season, when he finished with just 19 at-bats. He often acted as a designated hitter due to his injuries. He retired as a player after being hit by a pitch during a game against the Santurce Cangrejeros. Coimbre was prepared for the next phase of his career; he had already managed the Puerto Rican national team in 1947 and 1948, when they participated in the Amateur World Series in Colombia and Nicaragua. He formed his own barnstorming team in 1949, which included Dick Seay and Rubén Gómez, and toured Puerto Rico and the Dominican Republic.

After his retirement as an active player, Coimbre managed the Criollos de Caguas/Guayama in the LBPPR, and worked in an administrative role for the Indios de Mayagüez during their tours of Cuba. During this period, he coached amateur baseball in Puerto Rico, leading the Juana Díaz team to the island championship. He also taught baseball in Ecuador, and managed the juvenile team of Bolivia in 1966.

Coimbre was employed by the Pittsburgh Pirates as a scout for a period of 25 years, and recommended that the Pirates claim Roberto Clemente from the Dodger organization. Clemente was very aware of Coimbre as well, and aspired to achieve greatness as a means of respecting the great Puerto Rican player who helped blaze the trail for him.

There was a last spooky connection between Coimbre and Clemente, as author Steve Wulf wrote in *Sports Illustrated* in 1992. Wulf quoted Puerto Rican baseball man Luis Mayoral: "There was a pregame ceremony on the day after his 3,000th hit, on October 1, 1972. We gave him two awards, the Governor's Cup and a clod of earth from the field in Puerto Rico where he used to play. A picture went out over the wires, and when you looked at it, Roberto had such a sadness to his face. He looked almost gray in the black-and-white picture. I remember showing the picture to Pancho Coimbre... Pancho took one look at the picture and said, '*Este hombre está muerto.*' This man is dead. Three months later Pancho's premonition came true."[1]

How great a player was Coimbre? Certainly his best-known – and unparalleled – accomplishment was his record of not striking out over a period of three seasons, covering 550 at-bats, in the LPBBR, from the 1939-40 season through the 1941-42 season. In three other seasons, 1943-44, 1944-45 and 1948-49, Coimbre struck out only once each year. Over the course of his career in the LPBBR, he struck out only 20 times in 1,915 at-bats, while drawing 187 walks. (The data are patchy, however; Coimbre's strikeout totals – though probably minimal – are not available for the 1938-39 season. Walk totals are probably a good deal higher, because data are missing for five seasons.)

Coimbre's career batting average at home was .337, second only to Hall of Famer Willard Brown and ahead of Perucho Cepeda, Roberto Clemente, and Orlando Cepeda. He recorded a slugging percentage of .463, with 24 home runs.

John Holway credits Coimbre with a Negro League career batting average of .377 in 616 at-bats, which places him fifth on the all-time list (again, availability of data is a caveat). He hit for a .453 average in 1943, his finest year. It is likely that Coimbre benefited somewhat from playing against weaker competition in the NNL during the war years. But when considering Coimbre's performance, it is important to realize that he was already 29 years old when the LPBBR came into existence, and that he played in the Negro National League from age 31 through age 34. Clearly, many of Coimbre's peak years were spent playing for various amateur and semi-professional teams in the Caribbean and South America, and it is quite reasonable to presume that his totals would have been far greater had his professional career begun earlier, and had he played those seasons in the LPBBR and the NNL instead.

Coimbre's batting averages indicate the type of hitter he was; he did not possess above-average power, but he was a supremely talented contact hitter. He has been compared to Tony Gwynn and Rod Carew in that regard; perhaps only Joe Sewell is comparable with regard to striking out so rarely. Millito Navarro said, "He was the type of player that when you needed a hit, he didn't let you down."[2] Coimbre had an excellent stolen base record in his career (though unfortunately the Puerto Rican data are incomplete here too). Given his history as a track star in his youth, it is certain that he had good speed, which certainly contributed to his high batting average and his excellent defensive reputation.

It is clear that Coimbre was widely respected by his peers and those who saw him play. In 2008, his close friend Millito Navarro – then 102 years old – called him "my favorite player" and "an extraordinary player."[3] Satchel Paige stated "Coimbre could not be pitched to. No one gave me more trouble than anyone I ever faced, including Josh Gibson and Ted Williams."[4] Roberto Clemente said "It's a shame he [Coimbre] couldn't play in the major leagues due to the color barrier. I've always insisted Pancho would have been one of the best ever."[5]

Pancho Coimbre was married to Antonia Napoleonis. They had at least three children, as the 1940 census shows: two sons named Rafael and Francisco Luis Jr., plus a daughter named María. Francisco Jr., who was also an outfielder, played three seasons (1958; 1960-61) in the lower levels of the Pirates chain. He had a promising first year in the U.S., batting .316, but sat out the summer of 1959

with a leg injury. The younger Coimbre followed the family tradition by playing for the Ponce Leones, starting in the 1957-58 season. His father was then manager – though he resigned after the Leones were shut out in both ends of a doubleheader in December 1957 – and later a member of the coaching staff.

Francisco Coimbre Sr. passed away tragically on November 4, 1989, at the age of 80, when he was trapped in his home in Ponce after a fire broke out in his kitchen. Many homes in Puerto Rico have bars across the windows, and this, combined with a padlocked front door, prevented his escape. (He was living alone, according to coverage in Miami's *El Nuevo Herald*, suggesting that he was a widower.) Coimbre was buried in Ponce, and a national day of mourning was held in Puerto Rico to mark his passing. Subsequently, a small museum honoring his memory, as well as those of other local sports figures, was opened in Ponce.

Coimbre was one of 94 initial candidates under consideration by the 2006 Special Committee on the Negro Leagues, but failed to make the final ballot of 39 players, 17 of whom were elected to the Baseball Hall of Fame in Cooperstown.

He was elected to the Puerto Rican Baseball Hall of Fame in its inaugural year of 1991, as well as the Latin American Baseball Hall of Fame on its first ballot in 2010.

## SOURCES

In addition to the sources cited in the Notes, the author also consulted ancestry.com, baseball-reference.com, baseballthinkfactory.org, and various issues of *The Sporting News*, as well as the following books:

Treto Cisneros, Pedro, editor. *Enciclopedia del Béisbol Mexicano* (Mexico City: Revistas Deportivas, S.A. de C.V.: 11th edition, 2011)

Crescioni Benítez, José A. *El Béisbol Profesional Boricua* (San Juan, Puerto Rico: Aurora Comunicación Integral, Inc., 1997)

Holway, John. *The Complete Book of Baseball's Negro Leagues* (Winter Park, Florida: Hastings House, 2001)

McNeill, William F. *Black Baseball Out of Season: Pay for Play Outside of the Negro Leagues* (Jefferson, North Carolina: McFarland & Co., 2012)

Revel, Dr. Layton and Luis Muñóz. *Forgotten Heroes: Francisco "Pancho" Coimbre* (Carrollton, Texas: Center for Negro League Baseball Research, 2009)

Riley, James A. *The Biographical Encyclopedia of the Negro Baseball Leagues* (New York, New York: Carroll & Graf, 2012)

Roque-Vicens, Cruz. *Francisco Coimbre: Una Estrella del Béisbol de Todos los Tiempos* (Puerto Rico)

## NOTES

1 Steve Wulf, "Arriba Roberto," *Sports Illustrated*, December 28, 1992.

2 Danny Torres, "Navarro an ageless ambassador," MLB.com, June 5, 2008.

3 Ibid.

4 Leslie A. Heaphy, *The Negro Leagues, 1869-1960* (Jefferson, North Carolina: McFarland, 2002), 178.

5 Thomas E. Van Hyning, *Puerto Rico's Winter League* (Jefferson, North Carolina: McFarland & Co., 2004), 78.

# ALEX CORA

## By Scott Cummings

"That is one of finest at-bats that I have ever seen!" announced Vin Scully on May 12, 2004. "And then to top it all off with a home run, that is really shocking." Los Angeles Dodgers shortstop Alex Cora just hit a home run off Chicago Cubs right-hander Matt Clement in an 18-pitch at-bat. Cora justly took a curtain call from the Dodger Stadium crowd. Scully agreed, "Yeah take a bow, Alex! You deserve it and then some!"[1] The scoreboard at Dodger Stadium flashed a message: "Now that's an at-bat!"[2]

Alex Cora, infielder from a Puerto Rican family, graduated from the University of Miami and was drafted by the Los Angeles Dodgers. He had achieved a rare feat.

José Alexander Cora, known as Alex, grew up in a Puerto Rico baseball family. Brother Joey (José Manuel), older by 10 years, was an infielder for 11 years with San Diego, the Chicago White Sox, Seattle, and Cleveland. Alex was born on October 18, 1975, in Caguas, Puerto Rico. He attended Bautista High School and soon after graduating in June 1993 he was drafted in the 12th round of the free-agent draft by the Minnesota Twins. Instead he enrolled at the University of Miami and in each of his three seasons playing for the Hurricanes, Cora helped lead the team to the College World Series. (In 1996 the Hurricanes went to the final, losing to Louisiana State, 9-8, despite Cora's three hits and three RBIs.) That season *Baseball America* rated Cora the best defensive player in the college game.[3] He was inducted into the University of Miami Hall of Fame in 2006.

Cora's college efforts were rewarded when, on June 3, 1996, the Los Angeles Dodgers drafted the 6-foot, 200-pound left-handed batter in the third round. Brother Joey was already in his ninth major-league season, playing second base for the Seattle Mariners.

Alex rose rapidly through the Dodgers farm system: Vero Beach in the High-A Florida State League for the rest of the 1996 season, San Antonio of the Double-A Texas League in 1997, and Triple-A Albuquerque (Pacific Coast League) in 1998. In June of 1998

he was called up to the Dodgers and made his major-league debut on June 7 in a game at Seattle, whose leadoff batter was brother Joey, playing second base. With the Dodgers leading 7-1, Alex replaced Eric Young at second base in the bottom of the eighth. He led off in the top of the ninth and was caught looking at three strikes. Brother Joey was 2-for-5.

For the next two seasons Alex bounced between Albuquerque and the Dodgers. He came up for good in 2000, when he played in 109 games, batting .238 with 4 home runs and 32 RBIs. Cora was a regular for the Dodgers through 2004, playing mostly shortstop in 2000 and 2001 then second base after his double-play partner Mark Grudzielanek was traded to the Chicago Cubs. In 2003, he led the National League by turning 112 double plays and in putouts with 286.

Cora's home run to climax an 18-pitch at-bat on May 12, 2004, was a rare feat in major-league baseball. Of his battle with Matt Clement, a stalwart of the Cubs pitching rotation, Cora said, "It was tough; he was throwing good pitches. When they put it on the scoreboard [as the string of consecutive fouls built], that put me under a little bit of pressure. I had to stand back and regroup." He drove a 2-and-2 pitch into the bullpen in right to put the Dodgers up 4-0 in the seventh.[4] How rare is an 18-pitch at-bat? Paul Swydan in an article in *Hardball Times* commenting on a 14-pitch at-bat wrote that an 18-pitch at-bat happened only four times in the major leagues from 1988 to 2013. Cora's at-bat was one of the four times.[5]

Cubs manager Dusty Baker called it a "heck of an at-bat," but didn't necessarily approve of the way Cora reacted. "He kind of spoiled it a little bit at the end by flipping the bat," Baker said. "He won the battle already, so you don't rub it in. But that's

modern stuff, I guess." The next day, May 13, Alex Cora was hit by a pitch.[6]

That 2004 season was the last one in which Cora played 100 or more games, though he hung around in utility roles until 2011. The Dodgers made the playoffs in 2004, Cora's first postseason appearance. He played in all four games in the NLDS against the eventual National League champion St. Louis Cardinals. He tripled and drove in a run in Game One, but had only one other hit in 16 plate appearances.

After the 2004 season Cora signed a two-year free-agent deal with the Cleveland Indians. Indians general manager Mark Shapiro said, "Alex is overqualified to be called a utility player and has the upside to be a starter. He should get a chance to start 50, 60 games."[7]

Cora played in 49 games for Cleveland and batted .205. On July 8, 2005, he was traded to the Boston Red Sox for Ramon Vázquez. In Boston, Cora was seen as the backup shortstop for Édgar Rentería. The shortstop position had been a revolving door for the Red Sox since Nomar Garciaparra left in a July 2004 trade-deadline deal with the Chicago Cubs. Cora played in 47 games with Red Sox, batting .269 and helped hold the door, completing the remainder of the 2005 season with the Red Sox after a .205 mark with the Indians. He reached the postseason again, but played only briefly in the 2005 ALDS, with Renteria getting the bulk of the work. The Red Sox were swept 3-0 by the eventual World Series champion Chicago White Sox.

Cora remained with Boston in 2006. Rentería had been a major disappointment for the Red Sox and he had been traded in the offseason to the Atlanta Braves. Cora played 96 games at shortstop, batting .238 with one home run and 18 RBIs. He was a free agent after the season but re-signed with Boston on a two-year, $2 million deal. The team had, however, signed Julio Lugo to be the primary shortstop so Cora was assigned a backup role. In 2007 the Red Sox beat Cleveland in the ALCS and swept the Colorado Rockies in the World Series. Cora played only briefly in the postseason, working in late-inning defense in three games. In his one plate appearance, in the ninth inning of Game Three of the World Series, he executed a sacrifice bunt to advance baserunner Mike Lowell.

Again backing up Julio Lugo in 2008, Cora was 2-for-11 in the postseason as the Red Sox defeated the Los Angeles Angels of Anaheim in the Division Series and fell in seven games to the Tampa Bay Rays in the ALCS.

A free agent again after the 2008 season, the 33-year-old Cora signed a one-year, $2 million deal with the New York Mets for 2009. He was 33 at the time and batted .251 while playing 82 games for the 70-92 Mets. He re-signed with the Mets for 2010. Batting .207, he was released on August 7.

Ten days later, Cora signed as a free agent with the Texas Rangers, but played in only four games and was released on September 17.

In February 2011 Cora signed a one-year deal for $900,000 with the Washington Nationals. He was 35 and nearing the end of his career. The deal included an invitation to spring training, but it was lowest salary he had received since 2002 with the Dodgers. Cora batted .224 in 91 games in a backup role. The Nationals did not re-sign him after the season.

After the season with the Nationals, Cora played winter ball in Puerto Rico and contemplated retirement. He even announced his retirement officially once winter ball ended. However, the St. Louis Cardinals offered Cora a minor-league contract with an invitation to spring training,[8] and he accepted the offer. But he played poorly in spring training and was released on March 25.[9] He signed another last-ditch effort with the Detroit Tigers, but was released again, and retired as a player.

Cora took a year off from the game, but returned to other work in February 2013. ESPN hired him as a studio analyst for *Baseball Tonight* and *Sports Center*, and as a Spanish-language broadcaster for ESPN Deportes.[10]

Cora interviewed for the San Diego Padres' managerial opening, and also interviewed for manager of the Texas Rangers during the 2014 offseason. Media reports linked him to other big-league manager openings in Seattle, Miami, and Washington.[11]

On March 2, 2016, Cora was named general manager of Puerto Rico for the 2017 World Baseball Classic. In the press release, Cora said, "No matter what happens in the future, if I am leader of Major League Baseball or general manager, as people always say, I think being a team manager Puerto Rico goes beyond that. It is a unique experience, you do not dream to be general manager of your country."[12]

On November 16, 2016, Cora was named the bench coach for the Houston Astros.[13]

## SOURCES

The author consulted Alex Cora's player file at the National Baseball Hall of Fame Library, and relied upon baseball-reference.com.

All collegiate baseball states were provided by Hurricane Sports.com.

## NOTES

1  Link to video m.mlb.com/video/topic/6479266/v21317087/chclad-alex-cora-wins-18pitch-battle-with-a-homer.

2  *New York Daily News*, May 16, 2004.

3  *Baseball America*, June 10-23, 1996.

4  Amalie Benjamin, "An At-Bat for the Ages," boston.com, January 13, 2009. Retrieved August 26, 2016.

5  Paul Swydan, "Just How Rare Is a 14-Pitch Plate Appearance?" *The Hardball Times*, May 16, 2014. hardballtimes.com/tht-live/just-how-rare-is-a-14-pitch-plate-appearance/.

6  espn.go.com/mlb/recap?gameId=240512119.

7  Associated Press, "Indians Agree to $2.7 Million Deal With Cora," ESPN.com, January 18, 2005. espn.com/espn/wire/_/section/mlb/id/1969953

8  "Cora Joins Cards on Minor League Deal," MLB.com, February 6, 2012.

9  Associated Press, "Cardinals Release Alex Cora & Koyie Hill," via KTVO-TV website, March 25, 2012.

10  Kristen Hudak,"Alex Cora Joins ESPN as MLB Analyst in Multiplatform Role," ESPN MediaZone, February 19, 2013.

11  espn.com/mlb/story/_/id/13896267/alex-cora-interviews-san-diego-padres-manager-position.

12  todaysknuckleball.com/mlb-news/alex-cora-will-be-puerto-ricos-gm-for-wbc/.

13  m.mlb.com/news/article/208927892/astros-name-alex-cora-as-bench-coach/.

# JOEY CORA

## By Alan Cohen

*"El problema de'ser un bien deportista, es que hay que perder para probarlo" (The problem with being a good sportsman is you must lose to prove it)*

From a sign on 22-year-old Joey Cora's room posted by his sister Iris in 1988.[1]

*"He was everything to me. As far as baseball and discipline and being a man, he was the one who taught me."*

Joey Cora speaking of his father, José, in April 1990.[2]

*"He was the first infielder I ever saw who practiced diving for balls. He was one of those guys who got to the park very early and worked his tail off to stay ready for any situation. He went all out, all day and had a lot of fun doing it. He gave us a lot of laughs and was tight with Ozzie Guillen. It was great to see them win a World Series together."* - Matt Merullo, 2017.[3]

JOEY CORA WAS THE SECOND CHILD and first of two sons born to José Cora and his wife, Iris, in Caguas, Puerto Rico. José Manuel Cora Amaro was born on May 14, 1965, in Caguas, Puerto Rico. Brother Alex came along 10 years later. Their older sister became a medical technologist. Their younger sister, Iris, was born in 1968. When his father took a position with Gillette, the family moved to New York not long after Joey was born. However, they were in New York for only a short time before returning to Puerto Rico, where his father started and served as president of the local Little League. Joey first made his mark in Little League at age 7, playing with and against much older youngsters. His father took a position with the Sports Recreation Department of Puerto Rico and went on to become a scout for the Texas Rangers. Once José Jr. (Joey) joined the Padres, José Sr. did as well.

At 16, Joey graduated from Baptist College of Caguas (a high school) and was courted by the Yankees, Phillies, and Brewers. But his family had other ideas and Joey took his track-and-field skills and 3.97 grade-point average to the University of Puerto Rico. "The only reason I didn't get the 4.0 is because of the 'B' I got in Christian Education, and the reason I got the 'B' was we had to go to chapel every Thursday and I didn't go."[4]

American Legion ball became Joey's ticket to a career. While playing at a tournament in Ohio, he was scouted by Vanderbilt coach Roy Mewbourne and offered a scholarship to play baseball. Not versed in English, Joey headed to Vanderbilt with an English dictionary. A scholar in any language, Joey quickly learned English and compiled a 3.50 grade-point average in his first semester. He elected to major in math.

While at Vanderbilt, Cora was named to the American Baseball Coaches Association All-South Region Team as a shortstop in 1984. He was only a sophomore at the time. That summer he ventured north to play for Chatham in the Cape Cod League; he was a league all-star selection at second base. He also was selected as the league's MVP, after finishing second in the league in batting.[5]

In 1985, his junior year at Vanderbilt, Cora led the Southeast Conference in triples with six, and was named to the All-SEC team at shortstop. His efforts in the classroom were recognized when he was named to the SEC's Athletic All-Scholastic Team. He batted .403 and stole 51 bases. By that point, Cora had broken 10 school records for hits and stolen bases. He was named to the second team Converse All-American team. (Only Barry Larkin was better at the shortstop position.) In the draft that June, Cora was the first-round pick (23rd overall) of the defending National League champion San Diego Padres.

In the rookie Northwest League, Cora batted .324 with 3 homers and 26 RBIs with Spokane. His career seemed to be on the fast track and a promotion was on the horizon when his season was interrupted after a collision at second base. An oncoming runner decided that Cora's knee was a better target than the base and Cora required surgery that ruined his hopes of an early promotion. After playing for Leones in the Puerto Rican Winter League, he joined the Beaumont Golden Gators of the Double-A Texas League for the 1986 season.

An incident that season almost finished off Cora's career before it had begun. In early June Joey's father was battling colon cancer and had surgery. Joey left his Beaumont teammates to be with his father and family. A week later, he returned to his team, and his head admittedly was not in the game. After a game in which he went hitless at San Antonio on June 21, Cora and teammate Sandy Alomar Jr. were accosted while waiting for the team bus in the parking lot. Under normal circumstances, Cora would have just walked away, but these were not normal circumstances. Words were exchanged, a fight broke out, and Cora's teammate Eric Hardgrave was knocked to the ground. The leader of the gang of outsiders, Jose Puente, stabbed Cora twice. Joey was seriously injured and was tended to by team trainer Ray Suarez. Cora had to have part of his small intestine removed.

Hospitalized, he missed most of the balance of the season, returning to Beaumont in mid-August.[6] In the 81 games he played, he batted .305 with 24 stolen bases. Both father and son emerged from the ordeal, with Joey having learned a life lesson. "It affected me that, in a way, off the field I had to be more careful with where I was and what I was doing. As far as playing the game, no, it didn't affect me, but off the field, it definitely changed me. Because I took a lot of what was happening on the field and in the game, and I was taking it off the field wherever I was. It changed me a lot, actually."[7]

Cora made his debut with the Padres the next season. Before the season, scout Dick Hager, reflecting on the adversity of Cora's first two professional seasons, said, "I don't recall just how many knife wounds he received, but for a while he was in serious condition. The kid is a real gamer. He can play. We don't know whether he is ready to play in the majors, but Larry Bowa (the Padres manager) plans to find out."[8] Unfortunately for Cora, the chemical reaction of the no-longer-combative player and the ever-combustible manager Bowa would be such as to ultimately prolong Cora's apprenticeship.

On Opening Day, April 6, 1987, Cora was at second base, batting eighth for the Padres. In his first at-bat, facing Mike Krukow, he lined out to shortstop. In the top of the eighth inning, in his third at-bat, he singled with one out, stole second base, and scored on a single by Marvell Wynne. Tied, 3-3, the game went into extra innings. Cora's bunt single in the top of the 12th inning put him at first base with one out, but he was caught stealing and the Giants won the game in their half of the inning. Cora played in each of the Padres' first 54 games, but was batting only .234 when he was sent down to the minors on June 4. His fielding and immaturity caused more problems than his tired bat. He had committed nine errors, including two in the same game on a pair of occasions. He also was perceived as being uncooperative by the coaches. His reaction was to say, "I'm listening. Sometimes they tell you things that you don't feel comfortable doing. You're not confident because you have not done it their way before. And I've got to practice it before I go out and use it in a

game. Like bunting. They're trying to teach me a new way, but I think too much. It doesn't come natural to me. If I go to the minors, I've got to practice, practice until it becomes natural."[9] So, to the minors he went. He played his next 81 games at Triple-A Las Vegas, batting .276, before returning to the Padres in September. For the Padres, he batted .237 with 13 RBIs and 15 stolen bases.

Cora had arthroscopic knee surgery during the offseason and the following spring was assigned back to Las Vegas to get "more playing time." Manager Bowa and the local media had been highly critical of Cora's defense while he was with the club in 1987. Cora accepted the demotion, saying, "It's all right, I guess. I just have to play when I get a chance. I like it like this. I don't have to talk a lot. I can be by myself and be myself. I'm ready for Triple-A."[10]

The experience with Bowa in 1987 had been traumatic. "It was terrible," he told a sportswriter in 1989. "Larry said so much, all the time. I did not want to come to the ballpark. And when I got there, I didn't want to be there. I got so down and lonely. I went home every night and tried to cook, to help me forget."[11] Cora remained in Las Vegas for the 1988 season, as well as most of 1989. After batting .296 with 21 extra-base hits and 31 stolen bases in 1988, he batted .310 in 1989 with 29 extra-base hits and 40 stolen bases. In 1989, he put together a 37-game hitting streak, and at the end of the season he was named to the Pacific Coast League All-Star team. In September Cora got his second bite of the big-league apple, playing for new manager Jack McKeon. He batted .316 in 12 late-season games. In the offseason, there was bad news on the home front as his father died from hepatitis on October 5, 1989.

Playing for Ponce in the Puerto Rican Winter League, Cora batted .293 with 15 thefts. Ponce was managed by Padres third-base coach Sandy Alomar,[12] and the Padres were impressed enough to keep Cora in "The Show." But the 1990 season was one of frustration. After playing in only 31 of his team's first 77 games, he was once again sent back to Las Vegas, where in 51 games he batted .351 with 22 extra-base hits and 15 stolen bases. During his time with the Padres, he showed himself to be the ultimate team player, going behind the plate for the final two innings of the game on June 14 after each of the Padres catchers went down with injuries. Listed generously at 5-feet-7 and 150 pounds, Cora was not a catcher out of Central Casting, but he played an errorless two innings while setting up the target for pitcher Mark Grant. In the offseason between 1990 and 1991, while playing winter ball, Cora fractured his ankle in a collision while chasing a pop fly. The Padres were unsure of his status for 1991, and eventually, after a good spring training, he was traded along with Kevin Garner and Warren Newson to the Chicago White Sox for pitchers Adam Peterson and Steve Rosenberg. Cora reacted to the trade by saying, "This is the team I've always been with, since '85 when I was drafted. They made my family happy and everything. They gave me a shot in the big leagues. I've been through a lot with these guys. I love them very much, but life goes on and you have to do what you have to do."[13]

Cora spent the entire 1991 season with the White Sox. After spending the early part of the season backing up Scott Fletcher at second base, he was inserted into the lineup, getting his first start and first multi-hit game on May 17. It took some time for him to find a consistent stroke, but manager Jeff Torborg saw Cora as a player who "seems to be able to make things happen." Those things included a spectacular fielding play to end a game on June 10. In the bottom of the 13th inning at Texas, with two outs and the White Sox clinging to a 3-2 lead, Cora, going to his left, grabbed a groundball that had deflected off the glove of first baseman Dan Pasqua and threw a strike to catcher Matt Merullo to nip pinch-runner Mario Diaz and end the game. Joey said, "I look at it as a job I have to do. Whatever they ask me to do, I'll do."[14]

From June 8 through June 21, Cora batted .395 over a 13-game stretch to raise his average from .229 to .321. But once again injury interrupted his season. He sprained his right knee sliding into third base in the ninth inning of a game against the Texas Rangers. Subsequently, the White Sox filled the bases, and Cora came home with the tying run on a walk to Robin Ventura. After the game, he was placed on the

15-day disabled list.[15] After his return from the DL, Cora was unable to match his performance prior to the injury. He finished the season with a .241 batting average.

In 1992 Cora only got into 68 games with the White Sox. In the offseason, Chicago had acquired Steve Sax and his $3.5 million salary from the Yankees. Cora, in his limited appearances, batted .246. "I am not a superstar or anything," Cora said. "I'm the just the kind of player who's going to be there doing what I did last season (1991)—be a backup, work hard. They call you, go and do the job. That'll be my role. I really enjoy it. I'm that type of guy—a kamikaze type of guy. Wherever they put me, I'll go after it hard. Whatever they ask me to do, I'll be ready."[16]

And ready he became. As Sax only batted .236, and was second on the team with 20 errors, he and his big contract would wind up on the bench the following spring. An injury to heir-apparent Craig Grebeck during the last weekend of spring training gave Cora an opportunity that he did not waste. For Cora, 1993 was a breakout season. He played in 153 games and batted .268. The smallish Cora hit his first two career homers and had 51 RBIs. He stole a career-high 20 bases and had a career-high 13 triples. He led the league in sacrifices with 19. Paired with Ozzie Guillen, Cora improved his fielding, and through the first 29 games he was involved in 22 double plays.

On April 20, 1993, Cora was at his acrobatic best. This time, the folks in Baltimore witnessed the unfathomable. In the fourth inning, the Orioles had loaded the bases with two out. The Sox tried to pick off the runner at second base, but the ball bounced off Guillen's glove. Cora pounced on the ball and his side-arm throw to Ron Karkovice nailed Chris Hoiles trying to score from third base. The game remained tied, 1-1, and the Sox went on to win 2-1 in 14 innings with Cora, after walking, scoring the winning run.[17]

But Cora's main contribution to the team had nothing to do with the type of statistics that fly off the page. Batting in front of Frank Thomas, he was adept at working deep into counts. From the on-deck circle, Thomas thus got a good look at a pitcher's repertoire and was ready when he made it to the plate.[18] Ready enough to win the first of two MVP awards. He also had many chances to drive in Cora who, via hit or walk or hit by pitch, reached base 231 times during the season. Cora still led the league with errors by a second baseman with 19. The White Sox won the AL West and Joey advanced to the postseason for the first time. His bat grew cold in the playoffs; he batted only .136 as Chicago was eliminated by Toronto in the American League Championship Series.

In the strike-shortened 1994 season, Cora played in 90 of his team's 113 games and batted .276. Other than a trip to the DL in early July, he never had more than one day off between starts. His injury, as usual, came at the worst possible time. He had been on a tear, going 27-for-74 (.365) during June to raise his average for the season to .287. The injury occurred in a game against Kansas City on June 29. Leaping for a line drive, he pulled a muscle in his rib cage.[19] At the time of the strike in August, the White Sox led the AL West by one game, a lead that was wiped out along with the season.

Before the 1995 season the White Sox let Cora go to free agency and he signed with the Seattle Mariners. He was with Seattle for four seasons, during which his salary increased from $425,000 to $1.7 million. In Seattle, he became known not only for his dedication on the field but for his work with the Joey Cora Children's Foundation.

With Seattle in 1995, Cora raised his batting average to .297 and was once again in the postseason. In August, he batted .392 with 10 extra-base hits and 10 RBIs in 23 games, and the Mariners took a 7½-game lead into September. They would need every bit of that as the fight for the division championship went down to the last weekend with Seattle winding up tied with the California Angels. In a one-game playoff for the division championship, Cora had three productive at-bats as the Mariners won, 9-1, behind Randy Johnson. He singled during a rally in the fifth inning that plated Seattle's first run, was hit by a pitch and scored during a four-run outburst in the seventh, and drove in a run with a sacrifice fly in the eighth inning.

Seattle lost the first two games of the Division Series against the wild-card Yankees in the Bronx. In Seattle, the Mariners won Game Three, 7-4, and Game Four, 11-8, with Cora going 2-for-4 and scoring two runs. With Seattle trailing 5-0, Cora led off the third inning with a bunt single and scored on an Edgar Martínez homer as the Mariners erupted for four runs. In the decisive eighth inning, Cora again reached on a bunt and again came home on an Edgar Martínez homer. This one was a grand slam. In Game Five Cora gave Seattle a 1-0 lead with a third-inning home run off David Cone. The game went into extra innings and New York took a 5-4 lead in the top of the 11th. Cora led off the bottom of the inning with his third bunt single in two games. After a single by Ken Griffey Jr., Edgar Martínez doubled both runners home and Seattle advanced to the League Championship Series.

In the LCS, the Mariners lost to Cleveland in six games. Although Cora had only four hits in the series, he had a key hit in Seattle's Game Three win. The game went into extra innings and, in the 11th Cora led off with a single. He scored on a three-run homer by Jay Buhner, giving Seattle a 2-1 edge in the Series. But Seattle would not win another game in 1995.

In 1996 Seattle slipped to second but Cora had another good year, batting .291. His 37 doubles were the best in his career to that point, as were his six home runs. He had 43 multiple-hit games. The Mariners were nine games out of the league lead on September 11, when they launched a 10-game winning streak to make things tight. During that stretch, Cora had two homers and three RBIs in seven games. But although the Mariners pulled to within one game of the division lead, they were unable to close the deal, losing six of their last eight games.

In 1997 Seattle won its division for the second time in three years, but lost the best-of-five Division Series to Baltimore in four games. For Cora, it was a banner year. He had career highs in batting average (.300), doubles (40), home runs (11), and RBIs (54). Most impressive was his setting a franchise record by hitting in 24 consecutive games. The streak lasted from May 2 through May 29. Cora batted .475 during the streak, raising his average for the season from .247 to .374. In the 24th game, he kept the streak alive with an infield hit with two outs in the ninth inning. Once the streak concluded, he proceeded to reach base in another dozen games, making his on-base consecutive streak 36 games. His hit streak stood as the record for switch-hitters in the American League until 1998. The franchise record stood for 10 years until Ichiro Suzuki hit in 25 straight games in 2007. (Ichiro set the current Seattle standard by hitting in 27 consecutive games in 2009.)

In 1997 Cora was named to the All-Star team for the only time in his career. He was one of eight players born or raised in Puerto Rico to be chosen for the 1997 game. He entered the game as a pinch-runner in the fifth inning and replaced Roberto Alomar at second base. He had a fielding gem in the sixth inning when he dived to grab a grounder and rob Tony Gwynn of a base hit. In his only at-bat, Cora hit a fly ball to left field in the seventh inning. Cora's teammates praised his selection for the squad. Ken Griffey Jr. said, "Before he was chosen, we were all asked if Joey Cora was an All-Star, and we all said he deserves to go. He's worked hard at this sport. He's a quiet player, but he's a spark plug. It is fun just to watch him every day, diving for balls, hustling."[20] Cora himself relished being honored as an All-Star. "I get excited when I play a regular season game, but an All-Star Game, this is it," he said. "Until you're here, you don't understand. There's no way I would trade this for anything."[21]

In the losing 1997 Division Series, Cora was not a factor, going 3-for-17. The following season would be his last as a player. He was batting .283 with 6 homers, 26 RBIs, and 13 stolen bases when the soon-to-be free agent was traded to Cleveland on August 31 for infielder David Bell. Despite their high-powered offense, the Mariners had fallen on hard times. At the time of the trade they were 11 games below .500 and trailed the first-place Angels by 12½ games. In 24 games with Cleveland, Cora batted .229. Cleveland won the Central Division and went as far as the LCS in the postseason, losing to the Yankees in six games. Cora's postseason performance was disappointing. He played in six games and went 1-for-17.

In the offseason, Cora signed with Toronto as a free agent, but after faring poorly in the field in six exhibition games, the 33-year-old on March 11 decided to retire.

After his playing days, Cora stayed in baseball in a variety of positions. He coached at Daytona, the Cubs affiliate in the Florida State League, in 2000. He joined the Mets organization in 2001 and managed at Kingsport, Tennessee, in 2001 and 2002. In 2003, he managed Montreal's Class-A affiliate in Savannah. In 2004 friend and former double-play partner Ozzie Guillen hired Cora as the third-base coach with the White Sox. He stayed with the White Sox through 2011 and received his first World Series ring in 2005 after the White Sox swept the Houston Astros. He became the bench coach in 2007 and served in that capacity until Guillen was fired toward the end of the 2011 season. In 2012, when Guillen took over as manager of the Marlins, Cora became the bench coach in Miami.

After the 2012 season, Guillen was fired by the Marlins, and Cora spent the next three seasons out of professional baseball. In 2013, he worked as an analyst with MLB, and in the following two seasons, he stayed at home with his family.

In 2015, the Mariners invited Cora back to Seattle to throw out the first pitch on Opening Day.

In 2016, at the invitation of Larry Broadway, the Pirates' farm chief, Cora joined the Pittsburgh organization, managing their Double-A affiliate in Altoona, Pennsylvania. He was named the Pirates' third-base coach for the 2017 season. In 2003 Broadway had played for Cora at Savannah. Thirteen years later, Broadway reached out to his old mentor.[22]

Cora has had a lifelong dream. "My dream wasn't to be a major-league baseball player. My dream always, when I was little, was to be a big-league manager."[23] Maybe that dream will come true.

## SOURCES

In addition to the sources cited in the Notes, the author used Baseball-Reference.com and the Joey Cora player file at the National Baseball Hall of Fame Library.

## NOTES

1   Barry Bloom, "Coras Hang Tough During Rough Times," *San Diego Union Tribune*, April 4, 1988: Baseball-4.

2   James Posner, "Cora Making Most of Second Chance," *San Diego Union Tribune*, April 26, 1990: E-1.

3   Matt Merullo email to author, March 10, 2017.

4   Chris Jenkins, "The Drive to Excel: At 21, Cora Won't Rest in His Quest for perfection," *San Diego Union-Tribune*, April 26, 1987: H-1.

5   *Boston Herald*, August 19, 1984: 72.

6   Chris Jenkins.

7   Doug Padilla, "Tragic Incident Becomes Life Lesson for Cora," *Chicago Sun-Times*, October 19, 2005.

8   *New Orleans Times Picayune*, March 29, 1987: C-20.

9   Tom Friend, "Is Joey Cora Stubborn, or Is He Scared? Only He Knows for Sure," *Los Angeles Times*, May 22, 1987: 1.

10  Bill Plaschke, "Padre Notebook Joey Cora: 'The Forgotten Man' Knows He's Heading Down," *Los Angeles Times*, March 16, 1988: 3.

11  Bill Plaschke, "No Fist in His Glove: Joey Cora Doesn't Want to Fight, He Just Wants a Chance," *Los Angeles Times*, March 9, 1989: 1.

12  Phil Collier, "Angels Stockpile Pitchers in Bid for Hitter," *San Diego Union Tribune*, January 14, 1990: H-15.

13 Barry Bloom, *San Diego Union Tribune*, April 2, 1991: C-3.

14 Alan Solomon. "Cora Not 'Starter' Yet, but Boss Is Impressed," *Chicago Tribune*, June 12, 1991: B-9.

15 John Mulka, "Cora's a Bright Spot for Gloomy Sox," *Northwest Indiana Post-Tribune*, June 23, 1991: C7.

16 Alan Solomon, "On 2nd Thought … Cora, Grebeck Adjust," *Chicago Tribune*, March 15, 1992: B6.

17 Joey Reaves, "Cora Play Gives Sox a Huge Lift: Arm, Legs Trip Orioles in 14," *Chicago Tribune*, April 21, 1993: B3.

18 Bill Jauss, "Cora Takes a Long Look at His Contributions," *Chicago Tribune*, August 26, 1993: B12.

19 Dan Binkley, "Cora Goes on DL—Grebeck Returns," *Chicago Sun-Times*, July 1, 1994.

20 Claire Smith, "Worthy of the Honor, Based on Enthusiasm Alone," *New York Times*, July 9, 1997.

21 Ibid.

22 Alan Saunders. "New Coach Joey Cora Embraces Mental Approach—Pirates," *Allegheny Times* (Beaver, Pennsylvania), November 16, 2016: B-1.

23 Kevin Thomas. "On Baseball: Joey Cora Has a Big-League Resume and a Minor League Job," *Portland* (Maine) *Press-Herald*, August 18, 2016.

# JOSÉ CRUZ DILAN SR. (CHEO)

## By Jane Schupmann Hewitt

"One of the best and most underrated players I have ever seen"

—Joe Morgan, Hall of Famer

"A Puerto Rican legend whose brilliance equals that of the stars"

—Honduran sportswriter Greg Moraga

**G**ROWING UP IN HOUSTON IN THE 1970s and '80s, every kid idolized Astros left fielder José Cruz. They dreamed of watching him, meeting him, and getting his autograph. One of the most popular players in the history of the franchise, Cruz is equally adored in his native Puerto Rico, as widely known as the great Roberto Clemente. His consistently solid work ethic, good character, and respect for the game and his fans have won him admiration from young and old alike.

Nothing exemplifies these traits more than the story of young fan-turned-ballplayer, Dave Dellucci. On a Fox Sports *Diamondbacks Live* pregame show on April 26, 2012, interviewer Todd Walsh introduces Arizona Diamondbacks outfielder Dave Dellucci to his childhood hero, José Cruz, now the Houston Astros first-base coach. Dellucci tells the heartfelt story of driving to his first major-league baseball game, in Houston with his uncle from Baton Rouge, Louisiana. About 5 years old, Dave was carried on his uncle's shoulders down the sidelines to meet some Astros ballplayers. The player who signed his miniature baseball bat that day was José Cruz. Little David never forgot. He began rooting for "Cheo" Cruz and developed a stronger interest in baseball as a result. When possible, Dave always chose to wear Cruz's number 25 when he played. He was thrilled to be introduced to his idol, José Cruz, and Cruz was touched by Dellucci's story. He said he always liked "being good to everybody," and could never "say no to the kids."[1]

Born in Arroyo, Puerto Rico, on August 8, 1947, José was the eldest of three brothers who must have been born to play baseball. He was an all-around athlete at Arroyo High School, excelling in track, basketball, softball, and baseball. Cruz signed with St. Louis Cardinals scout Chase Riddle out of high school in 1966.[2]

After paying his dues with minor-league teams in St. Petersburg, Florida (Class A), Modesto, (A), and Little Rock (Double A), Cruz was called up to St. Louis for his major-league debut on September 19, 1970. He played in six games and got his first major-league hit, a single, off the Philadelphia Phillies' Rick Wise on September 19. He started the 1971 season with the Triple-A Tulsa Oilers of the American Association, managed by Hall of Famer Warren Spahn. He roared to a .327 average in the first 67 games with the Oilers, and was called up to the majors for good.

In 1973 spring training, Cheo found himself in an all-Cruz outfield for the Cardinals, playing an exhibition game against the New York Yankees. Younger brothers Cirilo (Tommy, b. 1951) and Hector (Heity, b. 1953) had been signed by the Cardinals in 1969 and 1970, respectively, and would make their major-league debuts in the 1973 season. While a good many brothers have played professional baseball, the Cruz trio was one of only a handful of sets of three or more baseball brothers to be in uniform at the same time. Cardinals manager Red Schoendienst was impressed with them, telling sportswriters, "They're good ballplayers. [If] they have six brothers back home, and if they come to town, I'll play them, too."[3]

José Cruz was not destined to stay long in St. Louis. He was sold to the Astros in a cash deal on October 24, 1974. Cruz debuted for the Astros on April 7, 1975, in the Astrodome, going 3-for-4 with a home run and three RBIs in a 6-2 victory over the Atlanta Braves. The Astros' spacious Astrodome was a pitcher's haven, especially against the Astros weak offensive lineup.

That bland offense began to shape up, though, and Cruz was a large part of its success. In 1977, he emerged as the best hitter on the team, batting .299 with 17 home runs, 87 RBIs, and 44 stolen bases. Fans loved how J. Fred Duckett, the Astros public-address announcer, drew out Cruz's name when he came up to bat, and they joined in a chorus of "CRUUUUUUUUUUUUUZ!" This created a great relationship between the two; José appreciated Duckett's gesture, and when he left the Astros, he gave Fred one of the bats from his last game, signing "Cruz" with about 15 U's, according to Duckett.[4]

Tal Smith, often called the architect of the Astros for his role in constructing both the team and the Astrodome, had returned to the Astros in 1975, bringing Bill Virdon with him as manager. His challenge was to build a talented nucleus of young players mixed with experienced veterans. He wanted pitching, speed, and defense—necessities in the spacious Astrodome. Smith didn't need "stars." He wanted versatility and flexibility.

To outfielders José Cruz and Enos Cabell, called the "glue of the team" by sportswriter Jack Hand of the *Houston Chronicle*, and an already talented pitching staff including Larry Dierker, J.R. Richard, Dave Roberts, and Joe Niekro, Smith added other versatile talent, including Cesar Cedeño, pitcher Joaquin Andujar, and a strong veteran presence in Joe Morgan.[5] Cruz and Morgan were like-minded, both interested in the team win, not personal recognition. Virdon brought a new level of efficiency to the team, expecting every player to run all-out to first base, even the pitchers. "This started a new mindset, a changing of the guard," said Cabell when he appeared on a panel at the SABR convention in Houston in 2014.

Cheo Cruz was already a leader in that philosophy, frequently sacrificing personal stats to move runners ahead. "I always play for the team," Cruz said. He never tried to pull the ball because the Dome "wasn't a place for home runs." Cruz's batting coach on the Astros, Deacon Jones, observed that, "Cheo worked tirelessly at hitting to the opposite side," which made him one of the best clutch hitters in baseball. In fact, in Smith's opinion, the 1980 outfield was "the absolute best in character and performance."[6]

Cruz had hit in 15 straight games early in the 1979 season, from April 21 to May 9, raising his batting average from .267 to .340. He led the Astros in many offensive categories that year: batting average (.289), games (160), doubles (33), home runs (9), RBIs (72), and walks (72), as well as in game-winning RBIs (14). In 1980 he was selected to play in his first All-Star Game, was voted Astros team MVP, and received his second straight Roberto Clemente Award.[7]

However, the 1980 season held misfortune, too. Midway through the season the Astros suffered the tragic loss of phenomenal young pitcher J.R. Richard to a stroke. And though Cruz's memories of the Astros-Phillies playoffs were unforgettable, as the first-ever championship series for the Astros franchise and himself (he batted .400 and received a record three intentional walks in Game Three of the 1980 NLCS), the outcome was dismal. The best-of-five series included four extra-inning games, two controversial plays in Game Four,[8] and in Game Five, with the Astros six outs from the World Series, Cruz having helped tie it up at 7-7, doubles by Phillies Del Unser and Garry Maddox led to a heartbreaking 8-7 loss in the 10th.

In 1981 Cruz continued to excel, leading National League batters throughout the strike-interrupted season.[9] He led Astros teammates in games played, at-bats, runs scored, hits, and RBIs. He had a great defensive year in his second full season in left field. Cruz hit in three out of five Division Series games against the Los Angeles Dodgers, with the Astros winning two home games to start but losing the last three in Los Angeles. He was named Puerto Rico's 1981 Pro Athlete of the Year.

The 1982 and 1983 seasons showed Cruz to be one of the most durable Astros, rarely missing a game. By the end of the 1982 season, he was among the top six in every Astros category for career offense; his .291 was second all-time to Bob Watson in batting average and he ranked third to Cedeño and Morgan, with 213 stolen bases. In 1983, he put together a monumental season, going down to the wire in a battle for the National League batting title. He hit a scorching .375 in July, and averaged .341 for the second half of the season. While he came in third for the batting title at .318, he tied Andre Dawson of the Montreal Expos for most NL hits (189), was sixth in on-base percentage (.385), seventh in RBIs (92), and ninth in slugging percentage (.463). The 1983 season saw Cruz drive in his 1,000th run, on his 36th birthday, August 8, and rap out his 1,800th hit two days later

Cruz continued to excel in 1984, again finishing the season at the top of National League offensive categories; he tied for fifth in hitting (.312), third in triples (13), fifth in hits (187), sixth in runs scored (96) and on-base percentage (.381), seventh in RBIs (95), and ninth in walks (73). He became the Astros team MVP for a record fourth time. For the second consecutive season he was named to *The Sporting News* Silver Slugger team as one of the National League's top three offensive outfielders. He passed Joe Morgan's former franchise record for triples (63) with 68, and tied the club record for runs scored in one game (4).

By 1985, Cruz had finally been discovered by baseball fans across America. It seemed that everywhere the Astros played, some reporter wanted to do a story on him. At least one writer referred to him as "the most underrated ballplayer of the last decade."[10] But fame was so new to the always genial Cruz that he even complained a bit about the overwhelming presence of the press to surprised Astro teammates and staff. What was remarkable was that, at age 37, his career seemed to be getting better. Astros manager Bob Lillis asserted that Cruz continued to have the body of a younger man because he was continually in shape. After playing in the Puerto Rican winter league he came back to spring training ready to go, said Lillis.[11] Cruz said, "That's all mental. I've been playing winter ball for 15 years. Then I take two or three weeks off and I don't even need spring training." Lillis liked the fact that Cruz was willing to play

anywhere. He didn't want to have a day off, said Lillis. He just loved to play.[12]

Latin players had often had trouble getting recognition, even stars like Clemente, and Cruz was no exception. Writers hesitated to tackle the possible language barrier, and multiple players named Cruz (including his brothers Hector and Tommy) added confusion. But *Chicago Tribune* sportswriter and columnist Robert Markus concluded, "People have been adding the numbers and they add up to stardom."[13]

Cruz turned 38 at the end of the 1985 season, leading the franchise batting lists, but starting to show his age. In August 1986, he was hot, hitting .327 and driving in 17 runs for the Astros. That season he had enough stamina left to aid the Astros playoff efforts, but by 1987 a much younger Gerald Young was competing for his spot in left field. Many Astros fans were disappointed when Cruz was not able to complete his career in Houston; when his contract was not renewed he played a final partial season with the New York Yankees. When he left the Astros, he was first or second in virtually every offensive category. His 80 triples (as of 2017) remained a franchise record.

Cruz also holds a few rather extraordinary distinctions: Out of 7,448 at-bats, he was hit by a pitch only three times in his career in Houston (once each in 1975, 1982, and 1983). He seemed to have developed a unique ability to avoid getting hit.[14]

The second noteworthy record involves a play resulting in major-league baseball's millionth run scored.[15] Major League Baseball was tracking the scoring of this milestone run. As players closed in on the milestone, the clock times of run-scoring were being monitored across the major leagues. In the second inning at San Francisco's Candlestick Park on May 4, 1975, Astros first baseman Bob Watson walked, then stole second during José Cruz's at-bat. Cruz also walked. Then Astro Milt May hit a home run off San Francisco Giants pitcher John Montefusco, scoring both Watson and Cruz. Watson crossed the plate at precisely 12:32 P.M. with the millionth run, followed by Cruz and May, who almost crossed paths, which would have nullified the run. Watson reached home only three seconds before Cincinnati Reds shortstop Dave Concepcion scored from his homer off Phil Niekro of the Atlanta Braves in Cincinnati.

As Cruz's career drew to a close, baseball fans and writers attempted to evaluate his impact on the game. Some, like Puerto Rican baseball writer/historian Edwin Kako Vasquez, simply said that Cruz was a "great natural ballplayer," and that he had many fine attributes, the best of which are "his good character, his great friendship, and the fact that he is always ready, always prepared."[16]

Others, like Bill James, who in 1987 introduced the concept of "park effects" in his annual *Baseball Abstract*, tried to analyze Cruz's stats and determine the effect of the Astrodome on his hitting. He concluded that the playing field is not level when it comes to the effects of home ballparks on player statistics. In other words, Cruz's offensive numbers would have been much better if he had not had to hit in the Astrodome, since his on-the-road statistics were considerably better than at home. Astros fans had long before figured this out: Cruz was a much better hitter than most people realized.[17]

The writers of Total Baseball also developed an objective method for evaluating hitters, called the Total Player Rating (TPR). It is expressed in a number that attempts to show how a player performs either above or below what an average player might produce. It is also adjusted for park effects. Cruz's TPR of 28.7 is not only very good, but places him at number 139 on the all-time major-league player list, and above several already in the Hall of Fame. While many may not have voted Cruz into the Hall of Fame, few would dispute that he never received the credit he deserved.[18]

In 1992 José Cruz's number 25 was retired by the Astros, and in 1997, he was named first-base coach when Bob Lillis became manager. However, now came the time for Cheo's sons to share a little of the limelight. Baseball had always been a family affair in the Cruz house, and now Cruz and his wife of 30 years, Zoraida (Vasquez), had time to watch sons José (Cheito or Little Cheo) Jr., and José Enrique shine — first, at Rice University, where both sons excelled in baseball. After some years of taking classes around their baseball careers in order to keep a promise made to their mother, both Cheito and Enrique graduated in May 2013 with degrees in sports management.[19] José Jr. had been drafted in the first round in 1995 by the Seattle Mariners, and played in the major leagues for 12 years.

Enrique Cruz, drafted in 2003 by the New York Yankees, moved around for eight seasons in the minors, and then became the director of Cruz Baseball Camps. Both sons played in the Puerto Rican winter leagues. In 2003-04 Cheo Cruz was voted Manager of the Year for piloting the Ponce Lions (and both sons) to the Roberto Clemente Professional Baseball League Championship[20] and later to victory in the 2004 Caribbean World Series. One of Enrique's favorite moments was when he and José Jr. hit back-to-back home runs during the 2003 winter season,[21] a repeat of an earlier feat when father José Sr., playing for Houston, and Uncle Cirilo "Tommy" Cruz, playing for the Chicago Cubs, both hit homers in the same game on May 4, 1981.[22] When Carlos Beltran was traded to the New York Mets at the end of the 2004 season, Cheo suggested that the Astros sign his son Cheito to fill his spot in the outfield.[23] In the 2006 World Baseball Classic, José Sr.

coached the Puerto Rican national team, including José Jr., to the second round.

In 1992 Cheo Cruz's number 25 was retired by the Astros. It was a special day for Cruz, but did not signal the end of the Cruz family's contribution to baseball. They have contributed six players to US professional baseball,[24] Cheo and brothers Hector and Tommy, sons Cheito and Enrique, nephew Cirilo (Hector's son), and possibly more, with grandson Trei (son of José Jr.) a middle infielder playing at Rice University, scheduled to graduate in 2017, and attempting to "keep the Cruz legacy going."[25]

The 2017 baseball season marked José Cruz's 34th campaign with the Astros. He played 13 seasons in the outfield, coached for 13 more, spent five years as a special assistant to the president and then as a community outreach executive.

## SOURCES

In addition to the sources cited in the Notes, the author also consulted baseball-reference.com, CallthePen, LatinoBaseball.com, MLB.com, SABR.org, YouTube.com, and the following:

*Puerto Rico Herald,* puertoricoherald.org/PRBtnArch/PRBtnArch2002/PRSportsBeat.

AstrosDaily.com, astrosdaily.com/files/team/cruz/cruz.html.

Moraga, Greg. "José "Cheo"Cruz, leyenda boricua que brillo igual a los Astros." CatrachoSports.com, June 14, 2015.

Special thanks to my daughter, Mary K. Moritz, for assistance with Spanish translation.

## NOTES

1 See entire Walsh/Dellucci/Cruz interview at: youtube.com/watch?v=Psoi5btQK9k.

2 Riddle since 1963 had been the Cardinals' scouting supervisor for the Southeastern United States, Puerto Rico, and Latin America.

3 Samuel O. Regalado, *Viva Baseball!: Latin Major Leaguers and Their Special Hunger* (Chicago: University of Illinois Press, 1998), 154.

4 David Barron, "J. Fred Duckett Remembered for Cruuuuz Intro," *Houston Chronicle,* June 26, 2007.

5 Joe Morgan had been signed to the Colt .45s in 1963, and appeared two years later in the lineup for the renamed Astros' first game in the Astrodome, April 9, 1965, vs. the New York Yankees. Traded to the Cincinnati Reds in 1971, where he helped win two World Series in 1975 and 1976, he was reacquired from Cincinnati by the Astros in 1980.

6 All quotations from a panel at the SABR convention in Houston in 2014.

7 The Roberto Clemente Award is presented each year to the major-league player who most exemplifies baseball, sportsmanship, and local humanitarian work. Each of the 30 clubs selects a team winner, who then becomes a candidate for the national award. Cruz won the team award in 1979 and 1980.

8 Both were disputes over trap-or-catch situations. See entire Game Four at: youtube.com/watch?v=-2kkfWUozz4.

9 The strike began June 12, 1981; an agreement was reached on July 31; and play resumed with the All-Star Game on August 9, followed by the remaining regularly scheduled games. A total of 713 games had been canceled. See also: thesportsnotebook.com/downloads/download-the-story-of-the-1981-mlb-season/ for a summary of the unusual and not-quite-fair split-season format adopted by MLB after the strike to determine playoff teams.

10 Robert Markus, "Meet Best Cruz of All, Houston's Jose," *Chicago Tribune,* May 26, 1985. articles.chicagotribune.com/1985-05-26/sports/8502020814_1_jose-cruz-houston-astros-left-fielder-bob-lillis

11 Ibid.

12 Ibid.

13 Ibid.

14 "Cruz Control: Avoiding the Plunk," astrosdaily.com/files/team/cruz/cruz.html.

15 Jonathan Fraser Light, *The Cultural Encyclopedia of Baseball* (Jefferson, North Carolina: McFarland and Co., Inc., 1997), 627.

16 Enrique Vasquez, Tribute to Cruz on Television, Houston Channel 7, in Spanish: youtube.com/watch?v=Dd4q41oxWr0 Uploaded on May 15, 2009. Retrieved on November 11, 2016.

17 "The Astrodome: Where Fame Went to Die," AstrosDaily.com: Jose Cruz Tribute, astrosdaily.com/hall/Cruz_Jose.html.

18 Ibid.

19 Richard Justice, "Cruz Family to Enjoy a Proud Day Together," MLB.com, m.mlb.com/news/article/47139994/jose-cruzs-sons-jose-jr-and-enrique-to-graduate-from-rice-university/.

20 The Liga de Béisbol Profesional Roberto Clemente or LBPRC was formerly known as the Puerto Rico Baseball League, or Liga de Béisbol Profesional de Puerto Rico, and is the main professional baseball league in Puerto Rico.

21 Playing for the Caguas Creoles (las Criollos de Caguas).

22 Lyle Spatz, ed., *The SABR Baseball List and Record Book: Baseball's Most Fascinating Records and Unusual Statistics* (New York: Scribner, 2007), 64.

23 Jose de Jesus Ortiz, "Cruz Suggests Astros Pursue His Son in Trade," *Houston Chronicle,* January 14, 2005.

24 The Cruz family is tied with several on the list of five or more family members in baseball, including the Perez and Alomar families, with six; fewer than 20 other families have more than six. Baseball-Reference, baseball-reference.com/bullpen/Largest_Baseball_Families.

25 Mark Berman, Houston's Fox 26, September 24, 2015. fox26houston.com/sports/24283728-story.

# JOSÉ CRUZ JR.

## By Thomas J. Brown Jr.

**JOSÉ LUIS CRUZ JR., A SWITCH-HIT**-ting major-league outfielder for 12 years, grew up around baseball. "It's pretty much been baseball all my life," said Cruz as he reflected on his adolescence as the son of major leaguer José Cruz Sr. "People ask me if it was exciting, growing up with a father in the majors, and two uncles. Maybe now, I guess, looking back. Back in those days, it was just normal."[1]

Cruz was born on April 19, 1974, in Arroyo, Puerto Rico, on the south coast of the island. His father is not his only major-league connection. He is also the nephew of former big leaguers Héctor and Tommy Cruz. Cruz hung around the ballparks as he grew up. He studied his father and his uncles. He learned from an early age how to carry himself as a player and studied the give-and-take in the clubhouse.[2]

"I remember one time getting knocked out by a foul ball during the Caribbean World Series, literally knocked out, when I was five years old," he told the authors of a book on baseball fathers and sons. "Later I was able to see my dad's last hit in the big leagues. It was a grand slam. It was a great way to end a career."[3]

When Cruz started playing baseball as a youngster, his father and uncles played a big role in helping him to develop his skills. He learned a lot from his family: "I remember driving in the car with [my father and uncles] to and from games. My dad was driving, my uncle was in the passenger seat and I was in the back seat. We used to go through all different kinds of scenarios, matchups and lineups. What's the right way to get an out? What's the wrong way?"[4]

Cruz grew up in Bellaire, Texas, a suburb of Houston, while his father played for the Astros. He At Bellaire High School he led the baseball team to a number-one national ranking during the 1992 season, his senior year.[5] The Atlanta Braves selected him in the 15th round of the 1992 amateur draft but Cruz chose to attend college.

Cruz attended Rice University from 1992 to 1995 and led the Owls in hits, home runs, and RBIs during the 1993 and 1994 seasons, and in runs and doubles in 1994. On February 9, 1995 Cruz had a school-record 10 RBIs in a game against Southwest Texas State. (As of 2017 the record still stood.) Cruz was a three time All-American at Rice.[6]

Cruz was the Seattle Mariners' first-round pick in the 1995 amateur draft, the third overall pick that season. Seattle gave Cruz a team-record $1.3 million signing bonus and placed the young player on a fast track to the majors.

After signing his contract, Cruz played in just three games for the Mariners' short-season team, the Everett AquaSox. He had five hits in 11 at-bats before being moved to the Riverside Pilots of the high-A California League. With the Pilots he had 29 RBIs in 35 games. After the season, Cruz played winter ball for Santurce in Puerto Rico, a club that was managed by his father.

With the Lancaster JetHawks, the new Mariners farm team in the California League, at the start of the 1996 season, Cruz improved his batting average 68 points to .325 and had 43 RBIs in 53 games, earning himself a promotion to the Port City Roosters in the Double-A Southern League. Against the faster competition his batting average fell but he drove in 31 runs in 47 games. The Mariners promoted him once more: He finished the season in Triple A, with the Tacoma Rainiers of the Pacific Coast League. Cruz struggled against the higher caliber pitchers in the league and his batting average dropped to .237.

The Mariners sent Cruz back to the Rainiers in 1997. His confidence improved and so did his statistics. He raised his batting average to .268 in 50 games before the Mariners called him up in May. Cruz made his major-league debut on May 31, 1997. Playing left field alongside Ken Griffey Jr., he was hitless but drove in a run with a groundball. Cruz

played in 49 more games before he was traded on July 31 to Toronto for pitchers Paul Spoljaric and Mike Timlin. At the time of the trade, Cruz had 12 doubles, 12 home runs, and a .541 slugging percentage.

The trade was a surprise since the Mariners had such high expectations for Cruz. But they decided that they needed pitching more than hitting.[7] In Toronto, Cruz hit 14 home runs in 55 games as he split his playing time between left field and center field. His play for both teams earned him a second-place finish behind Nomar Garciaparra in the balloting for the Rookie of the Year Award.

Cruz started the 1998 season with Toronto's Triple-A team, the Syracuse SkyChiefs, in the International League. After 40 games there, he was recalled and became one of the Blue Jays' regular outfielders, again splitting his time between left field and center field. In 105 games he batted .253 with 11 home runs.

The Blue Jays sent Cruz back to Syracuse to start the 1999 season but recalled him after just 31 games. He played in 106 games for the Blue Jays and hit .243 with 14 home runs and 14 stolen bases.

The next season, 2000, was Cruz's breakout year as a major leaguer. He started in center field in all 162 Blue Jays games. He led the league's outfielders with 407 putouts and flashed power with 32 doubles and 31 home runs, though his batting average was still in the .240s. He was voted the Blue Jays' MVP by the Toronto chapter of the Baseball Writers Association of America.

In the offseason Cruz played for the Cangrejeros de Santurce, which swept the Caribbean Series. Cruz was the MVP of the series. He hit .385 with 5 doubles and 10 RBIs. "That Caribbean Series was extremely special. It was all about the team and country," he said in a 2015 interview.[8]

In 2001 Cruz continued to play well defensively and offensively, raising his batting average to .274, hitting 34 home runs, and stealing 32 bases. He was caught stealing only five times, an 86.4 percent rate for the season.[9]

Cruz's offense slipped in 2002. He played in 124 games for the Blue Jays, losing five weeks to injury in August and September. He hit just 18 home runs and stole only seven bases and his batting average slid 29 points to .245. After the season the Blue Jays let him go to free agency, and Cruz signed with the San Francisco Giants in January 3002.

With the Giants in 2003 Cruz batted .250 with 20 home runs. He won his only Gold Glove that season, logging 18 outfield assists and a .994 fielding percentage. But Cruz may be remembered in San Francisco for dropping an easy fly ball in the 2003 Division Series against the Florida Marlins. With the series tied at one game apiece and the game in extra innings, the Giants scored a run in the top of the 11th to take a 3-2 lead. Jeff Conine led off for the Marlins with a fly ball to right field. It looked as though it would be the first out of the inning, but Cruz dropped the ball when he closed his glove too soon and the ball bounced off of the heel of the glove.[10] The Marlins went on to win the game 4-3 win and take 2-1 series lead. "We lost a game we should have won. That's it," Giants manager Felipe Alou said.[11]

A free agent again after the season, Cruz signed with Tampa Bay and smacked 21 home runs in 2004. But on February 6, 2005, Cruz was traded to the Arizona Diamondbacks for Casey Fossum.

Cruz played for three teams in 2005. He started the season with the Diamondbacks. He had played in only 64 games because of injuries when he was traded on July 30 to the Boston Red Sox for two minor leaguers. The Red Sox put him on waivers 10 days later and the Los Angeles Dodgers picked him up. Although Cruz was injured for most of the year, he ended the season on a tear, hitting .301 with six homers for the Dodgers.

Cruz was picked to play for Puerto Rico in the 2006 World Baseball Classic. He helped Puerto Rico reach the second round of the tournament as he hit .353 with a .476 on-base percentage in five games. When Cruz was asked about his experience playing for his birthplace, he said: "It was amazing. It was the most fun playing baseball I had as a professional."[12]

Throughout his career, Cruz always emphasized that the importance of his family's Puerto Rican heritage. "[T[he older I get, the prouder I am of the whole family thing," he said. "I look at it from a father's perspective because I'm a father too. I'm very privileged and very blessed to be a part of [the Cruz family]. Both my father and I were able to help put the game of baseball in such a high place in Puerto Rico. We grinded it out and gave it our all—and that's what we try to show to my kids."[13]

Cruz played for the Dodgers again in 2006. Injuries continued to limit his play and Cruz started just 86 games before the Dodgers released him on August 1, 2006. Cruz did not play for the rest of the 2006 season. In December he signed with San Diego. He played in 91 games for the 2007 Padres but his weakness at the plate led to his release on July 31. Cruz signed a minor-league contract with the New York Yankees on August 18 and finished the season playing in 16 games with the Scranton/Wilkes Barre Yankees.

Cruz played for the Ponce team coached by his father in the Puerto Rico Winter League in 2007 and 2008. He described the experience as a family reunion, since he also played with his cousins and uncle. His cousin Enrique was a player in the Mets organization at the time. Alberto, another cousin, was playing in the minor leagues with the Astros. His uncle Tommy was the hitting coach on the Ponce team. "We rode together in the same car to games. We had a lot of fun, talked a lot of baseball and about life … about how much baseball had done for us and about growing up in Arroyo," Cruz wrote in an article about the experience.[14]

The Houston Astros signed Cruz as a free agent in November 2007. It was a homecoming of sorts for Cruz, since his father had been such an important player for the Astros over the years, and had lobbied multiple times for the team to sign him. Cruz started seven times in the outfield in 2008 but hit just .122 with one double, one RBI, six runs scored, and nine strikeouts.[15] The Astros released him on June 1 and he retired as a player.

In 2012 Cruz joined ESPN as a baseball analyst. In an interview about his career shortly after taking the job, Cruz reflected on the rewards and challenges of being a major leaguer: "I think the scrutiny of being an everyday player in the MLB along with the traveling were the toughest parts of being a pro. The good parts were that you got to play baseball in the best stadiums of the world. … [It's the] [g]reatest job."[16]

When Cruz was drafted by the Mariners in 1995, he lacked credits for his degree in sports management. As part of his contract with the Mariners, the club had agreed to pay a portion of his education costs if he decided to finish his degree. Cruz finally decided to finish up the required classes for his degree in sports management from Rice University in 2012. He graduated in May 2013 along with his younger brother, Enrique. Cruz said his mother, Zoraida, was the impetus for his return to school. "She said, 'All I want is for you to graduate from college. That's my request.' That stayed with me through the years."[17]

While keeping his ESPN job, Cruz in 2012 took a job with the Major League Baseball Players Association to provide assistance and counsel for Spanish-speaking players. MLBPA president Tony Clark said of Cruz at the time: "José's playing career, background in the game and his desire to support our fraternity of players makes him the ideal candidate for a role in the union's player services department."[18]

Cruz and his wife, Sarah, have two sons Trei, 18, and Antonio, 17 and a daughter Alisa Loren, 15.

Cruz told the authors of the book on baseball fathers and sons that he counted his family's relationship to baseball as one of the most important parts of his life. His father's advice and coaching was special to him in many ways. "He taught me to have fun with the game and enjoy what you are doing. He would often say that people lost sight of that. Even to this day, he stresses that fact — to enjoy what you are doing."¹⁹

## SOURCES

In addition to the sources cited in the Notes, the author also utilized the Baseball-Reference.com and Retrosheet.org websites for box scores, player, team, and season pages, pitching and batting game logs, and other material pertinent to this biography. FanGraphs.com provided some the statistical information used in this biography.

## NOTES

1. Larry Stone, "All in the Family — Mariner Prospect Owes Much o Parents' Influence," *Seattle Times*, March 26, 1997.
2. Ibid.
3. Kevin Neary and Leigh Tobin, *Major League Dads: Baseball's Best Players Reflect on the Fathers Who Inspired Them to Love the Game* (Philadelphia: Running Press, 2012), 57.
4. Den Cafardo, "Double Duty: Jose Cruz Jr. Joins Baseball Tonight, Beisbol Esta Noche," ESPN Frontrow.com, May 2007.
5. Neary and Tobin, 57.
6. Rice Owls Baseball 2016 Baseball Factook, grfx.cstv.com/photos/schools/rice/sports/m-basebl/auto_pdf/2015-16/prospectus/prospectus.pdf, accessed March 15, 2017.
7. Barrett Hansen, "Deadline: 7 Worst Deadline Deals in Mariners History," Bleacher Report.com, July 29, 2011.
8. David Venn, "Cruz Fondly Recalls Puerto Rico's Legendary Title Teams," MLB.com, January 31, 2015.
9. Clayton Ritcher, "Cruz Missile — Interview With Jose Cruz Jr.," Baseball Hot Corner.com, May 10, 2012.
10. Michael Almonte, "A Missed Catch 10 Years Ago," Sports Media101.com, August 17, 2013.
11. Henry Schulman, "Giants Drop the Ball, Face Elimination / Cruz Error, Blown Chances Doom Them in 11 Innings," SFGate.com, October 4, 2003.
12. Ritcher.
13. Cafardo.
14. Jose Cruz Jr., "Cruz Cherishes Baseball Winters of Family Fun," *San Diego Union Tribune*, May 21, 2007.
15. David Coleman, "Astros History: Cheito's 38-Game Career in Houston," CrawfishBoxes.com, May 12, 2012.
16. Ritcher.
17. Richard Justice, "Cruz Family to Enjoy a Proud Day Together," MLB.com, May 10, 2013.
18. "Jose Cruz Jr. Joins MLBPA Staff," MLB.com, February 25, 2013.
19. Neary and Tobin, 57.

# IVÁN DE JESÚS SR.

## By Richard A. Cuicchi

**I**VÁN DE JESÚS SR. IS OFTEN REMEMbered as being involved in the worst trade in the Philadelphia Phillies history, but the stigma associated with that trade didn't actually define his playing career. He is otherwise known for being a durable, serviceable shortstop for the Chicago Cubs and the Phillies and for making two World Series appearances with the Phillies and St. Louis Cardinals.

De Jesús filled the bill for what major-league clubs generally expected from their shortstops during his era. He was the prototypical shortstop: a solid fielder, a threat at stealing bases, and an average hitter who wasn't generally relied on for offensive production.

While future Hall of Famers Roberto Clemente and Orlando Cepeda were among the first to bring national attention to Puerto Rican players in the major leagues in the late 1950s, De Jesús later became part of a steady wave of Puerto Ricans to reach the major leagues. A case could be made for De Jesús being the best major-league shortstop to come from Puerto Rico.[1]

Thirty-seven years after De Jesús broke into the majors, his son, Iván De Jesús Jr., also a native Puerto Rican, made his major-league debut in 2011.

De Jesús was born in Santurce, Puerto Rico, on January 9, 1953, the second of four children of Fundador and Teodora (Alvarez) De Jesús. His father was an electrician. Santurce was a hotbed of baseball in the Puerto Rican Winter League. The parents were fans of the local Santurce baseball team, often listening to their games on the radio and taking their children to the games.[2] De Jesús eventually played for the popular team himself for 12 seasons, like many American and Latin major leaguers who played winter ball in Puerto Rico after the regular major-league baseball season ended.[3]

De Jesús' family interests in baseball translated to his playing little league baseball at Las Lomas, in the Babe Ruth league at Caparra Terrace, and with an amateur team in Guaynabo. He attended Gabriela Mistral High School in San Juan and Margarita Janer High School in Guaynabo. He played on varsity baseball teams, while also participating on track and field teams. De Jesús credits his early development in baseball to Alejandro Cruz, a teacher and coach at Margarita Janer.[4]

De Jesús drew interest from Corito Varona, a Cuban scout for the Dodgers organization, because he held his own in local amateur leagues against players as old as 25.[5] Not having completed high school, he was signed at age 16 by the Los Angeles Dodgers on May 23, 1969. At the time of his signing, only 35 Puerto Ricans had reached the major leagues.[6]

His first professional team was actually the San Juan Senadores of the Puerto Rican Winter League in 1969, when Roberto Clemente was his manager. De Jesús said of his experience with that team, "I didn't get any at-bats during the season, but I had a good opportunity to learn from the great Clemente. He had such a positive impact on all of the players. Apparently he liked me, because he invited me back the next winter-ball season to play for the team, after I had played my first season in the minor leagues."[7]

The 17-year-old De Jesús made his stateside pro debut with Class-A Daytona Beach in 1970 and then spent three additional seasons at the Class-A level. He initially had trouble with the English language and getting adjusted to living in the United States, but he credited fellow Dodgers farmhands Orlando Alvarez and Henry Cruz with helping him get acclimated. He also acknowledged Dodgers minor-league infield coach Monty Basgall and Dodgers player Manny Mota with assisting in his early player development in the minors.[8]

His highest batting average during those first four seasons was .244, while he struck out in nearly one-fourth of his at-bats. However, he showed an ability

to steal bases. He advanced to Triple-A Albuquerque in 1974 after having a good showing in spring training. His 1974 season was his best to date; as he seemed to mature at the plate, hitting .298 and cutting down on his strikeout rate. He got a late-season call-up to the Dodgers and made his major-league debut against the Cincinnati Reds on September 13, 1974, at age 21. His first major-league hit came off Houston Astros pitcher Ken Forsch on October 2.

With five minor-league seasons under his belt through the 1974 season, it became time for the Dodgers to decide what De Jesús' future would be with the organization. He had played well enough at the Triple-A level in 1974 such that he was considered by Dodgers vice president of player personnel Al Campanis to replace shortstop Bill Russell whom the Dodgers would move to center field, the position at which he originally broke in.[9] However, Russell, a six-year major leaguer and a National League All-Star in 1973, ultimately wasn't shifted from shortstop.

The 5-foot-11, 175-pound De Jesús split the 1975 season between Albuquerque and Los Angeles, when Russell spent time on the disabled list from April 13 to May 6 and then again from May 11 to June 30. De Jesús shared starts at the shortstop position with Rick Auerbach while Russell was out. For the season, De Jesús struggled at the plate, batting only .184 in 87 major-league at-bats and 63 games. With Albuquerque he hit .271 in 62 games.

Early in the 1975 season the Dodgers were considering trading Russell with Bill Buckner to the St. Louis Cardinals for Reggie Smith. The trade would have cleared the way for De Jesús to become the Dodgers' regular shortstop, but injuries to the players involved squashed the deal.[10] De Jesús recalled that it was also rumored he would be going to the Cardinals.[11]

Campanis commented about De Jesús in the 1976 Dodgers media guide, "This young man has fast feet and all other physical aspects to become a super star defensively. If he can hit .270 in the major leagues he could become one of the next great ones."[12]

De Jesús started the 1976 season with the Dodgers, but was unimpressive again at the plate in the few starts he got, and was optioned to Albuquerque. There he proceeded to have his best minor-league season with a .304 batting average, 7 home runs, and 64 RBIs.

By now, with Russell apparently entrenched in the shortstop position,[13] the Dodgers decided their future wouldn't include De Jesús, who became trade bait in their quest for an outfielder. On January 11, 1977, he was traded with Bill Buckner and minor leaguer Jeff Albert to the Chicago Cubs for Rick Monday and Mike Garman.

A new team seemed to be just what De Jesús needed, as he became an immediate starter for the Cubs in 1977 and ran off a string of five seasons as the regular shortstop. Regarded as a solid defender in the minors, he also attracted notice for his all-around defensive play with the Cubs.[14] He formed a formidable double-play combination with second baseman Manny Trillo. De Jesús set a franchise record in 1977 for most assists by a shortstop (595).

De Jesús was the stolen-base leader with the Cubs in four of his five seasons with them. He finished fourth in the National League in 1978 with 41 steals, and led the league that season in runs scored (104). He stole a career-best 44 bases in 1980.

In a full-time role, De Jesús became more of a complete player. The right-handed batter emerged as a respectable hitter, with batting averages of .266, .278, .283, and .259 in his first four seasons with the Cubs. On April 22, 1980, De Jesús had a personal-best five hits against the St. Louis Cardinals. His hitting barrage that day included hitting for the cycle in his first four at-bats in the slugfest won by the Cubs, 16-12.

After the 1978 season De Jesús was touted as one of the most improved players in a coming wave of top stars. Asked whether there was any player on the club he wouldn't trade, Cubs GM Bob Kennedy responded, "Yes, there is one man, and that's De Jesús."[15] Broadcaster Tony Kubek said of the underrated De Jesús, "He scared the Dodgers when they had him because he struck out so much, but he's made himself a better hitter and he's right up there as a fielder."[16]

But the Cubs were going nowhere during De Jesús' tenure. They didn't have a winning campaign in the five years (1977-1981) he played there. Their best season was an 81-81 record in 1977. In the 1981 strike-interrupted season, they posted a dismal .369 winning percentage in 106 games. De Jesús' batting average plummeted to .194 that year.

On January 27, 1982, De Jesús was traded to the Philadelphia Phillies for Larry Bowa and Ryne Sandberg. The trade has been referred to as one of the worst in Phillies history, because they dealt away a future Hall of Famer in Sandberg, who then had only six major-league at-bats under his belt. The trade affected the futures of the Cubs and Phillies over the next 10 years.[17]

De Jesús recalled that he was ecstatic about going from a losing team to a competitive, winning team like the Phillies. He said, "All of a sudden my teammates were Pete Rose and future Hall of Famers Mike Schmidt and Steve Carlton. I was able to rejoin my double-play partner from the Cubs, Manny Trillo. And then in 1983 we added two more future Hall of Famers in Joe Morgan and Tony Perez. The trade was a big break for me."[18]

De Jesús batted .239 with a career-high 59 RBIs for the second-place Phillies in 1982. They won the National League East Division in 1983 by six games over the Pittsburgh Pirates. The Phillies were led by pitcher John Denny, who had a Cy Young Award season, and Phillies third baseman Mike Schmidt, who finished third in the National League MVP voting on the strength of his 40 home runs and 109 RBIs. De Jesús batted .254 with 4 home runs and 45 RBIs.

The Phillies defeated De Jesús' former team, the Los Angeles Dodgers, in the National League Championship Series. De Jesús contributed three singles and three walks during the series. The Phillies then faced the Baltimore Orioles in the World Series, losing in five games. De Jesús collected only two hits in 16 at-bats. His error in the seventh inning of Game Three allowed the Orioles to score the go-ahead run.

De Jesús recalled of his appearance in the World Series: "It was the highlight of my career. Even though we lost to the Orioles, I think about all the players who put in long careers and never made it there."[19]

The Phillies slipped to being a .500 club in 1984, 15½ games behind the division-winning Cubs. Except for the strike-shortened season of 1981, De Jesús had his lowest offensive production since he became a

starter. His play in the field also declined, as the Phillies finished near the bottom of the National League in fielding.

De Jesús fell out of favor with the Phillies, who began trying to unload him during the offseason, with the Expos expressing some interest.[20] He went to spring training with the Phillies but lost his shortstop position to third-year player Steve Jeltz. Just before Opening Day the Phillies traded De Jesús and pitcher Bill Campbell to the St. Louis Cardinals for Dave Rucker.

At age 32, De Jesús became the Cardinals' backup at third base, and at the shortstop position held by Ozzie Smith. He was primarily used as a defensive replacement, starting only 11 times in 59 games. The Cardinals won the National League East Division and defeated the Los Angeles Dodgers in the Championship Series, but lost to the Kansas City Royals in seven games in the World Series. De Jesús didn't factor into the Cardinals' postseason plans; he was hitless in his only plate appearance in the World Series.

De Jesús bounced around for the remainder of his career, never landing a full-time major-league roster spot. In 1986, 1987, and 1988, he played in the major leagues with the Yankees, Giants, and Tigers, but his primary playing time in those seasons occurred in the minors. At age 35 in his 15th season, he played in his last major-league game on July 15, 1988, with the Tigers.

For his career De Jesús batted .254 in 1,371 games. He had 21 home runs, 324 RBIs, and 595 runs scored, while stealing 194 bases. He was a durable player, never having to go on the disabled list.

De Jesús began a 23-year managing and coaching career in 1990. "After I finished playing, I was still young enough to be active in the game, and I wanted to give back to the younger players just as others had done for me when I first began pro baseball," he said. "I wanted to pass down what I had learned in my 19 years as a professional player."[21]

De Jesús managed for 10 seasons in the minors for the Dodgers, Mariners, and Astros and coached in the minors for eight seasons. He spent three years as a special assistant to Cubs manager Lou Piniella before becoming a base coach for the Cubs in 2010 and 2011. De Jesús also managed teams in the Puerto Rican Winter League and served as a coach for the Puerto Rican squad in the 2006 and 2009 World Baseball Classic tournaments.

DeJesús has been married twice, to Annie Nunez and to Marta Rondon. He has three children: Joanne, Marvett, and Iván Jr.[22] In an interview with *The Sporting News* in 1974 De Jesús said he looked forward to having a son who would also play in the majors.[23] His wish/prophecy became true: Iván Jr. was the second-round draft pick of the Dodgers in 2005 and made his major-league debut on April 1, 2011, with the Dodgers.

Iván Sr. remarked about his son growing up, "I allowed Iván Jr. to spend time with me at the ballpark when he had breaks in school, especially during spring training. I was able to teach him the right ways to play. He worked real hard at his game, and I'm very proud of him."[24] An infielder like his father, Iván Jr. connected the time he spent with his father while coaching in the minors as creating his own love for baseball.[25]

De Jesús was what the baseball industry calls a lifer, beginning as a 17-year-old professional player learning the game from his fellow countrymen and eventually spending his post-playing career teaching others in the minors and in Puerto Rican winter ball as a coach and manager. In between, he put in 15 seasons as a major leaguer, including eight years as the capable starting shortstop for the Cubs and Phillies.

## SOURCES

In addition to the sources mentioned in the Notes, the author also consulted:

Baseball-Reference.com.

Coleman, Coleman, Ernie Harwell, Ralph Kiner, Tim McCarver, Ned Martin, and Brooks Robinson. *The Scouting Report: 1983* (New York: Harper & Row, 1983), 542.

Pietrusza, David, Matthew Silverman, and Michael Gershman, eds. *Baseball: The Biographical Encyclopedia* (New York: Total Sports Illustrated, 2000), 278.

1981 Chicago Cubs Official Roster Book: 9.

1985 Philadelphia Phillies Media Guide: 32.

2010 Chicago Cubs Media Guide: 26.

2012 Houston Astros Media Guide: 210.

## NOTES

1. An overall number-one draft pick and highly-rated prospect, Puerto Rico-born Carlos Correa made his major-league debut in 2015, was named the National League Rookie of the Year, and was immediately touted as of the best major-league shortstops. He could eventually challenge De Jesús in the consideration for the best shortstop to come from Puerto Rico.
2. Iván De Jesús Sr. telephone interview with author, September 21, 2016. (De Jesús interview)
3. Thomas E. Van Hyning, *The Santurce Crabbers* (Jefferson, North Carolina: McFarland & Company, Inc., 1999), 211.
4. De Jesús interview.
5. De Jesús interview.
6. Baseball-Reference.com.
7. De Jesús interview.
8. De Jesús interview.
9. Gordon Verrell, "Everyone Eyes De Jesús of Dodgers," *The Sporting News*, January 25, 1975: 43.
10. Gordon Verrell, "Ferguson Can Be Had, Dodgers Hint," *The Sporting News*, November 15, 1975: 38.
11. De Jesús interview.
12. 1976 Los Angeles Dodgers Media Guide, 13.
13. Bill Russell had been the Dodgers shortstop since 1972 and went on to be part of the Dodgers infield, with Steve Garvey, Davey Lopes, and Ron Cey, that played together for 10 seasons. Bill Buckner had a similar situation; he was unable to displace Garvey at first base and was included in the trade to the Cubs with De Jesús.
14. Jerome Holtzman, "Cub Fans Sniffing Honey After 32-Year Drouth," *The Sporting News*, June 18, 1977: 7.
15. George Vass, "These Are the Seven Most Improved Young Players," *Baseball Digest*, November 1978: 16.
16. Joe Goddard, "These Are the Majors' 20 Most Under-rated Players," *Baseball Digest*, December 1978: 28.
17. Tyler Conway, "Iván De Jesús: Everything You Need to Know About Former Top Prospect," *Bleacher Report*, August 25, 2012. bleacherreport.com/articles/1311169-ivan-de-jesus-everything-you-need-to-know-about-former-top-prospect. With Sandberg, the Cubs became division winners in 1984 and 1989, their first postseason teams since 1945. The Phillies suffered a postseason drought from 1984 to 1992, which coincided with Sandberg's prime years with the Cubs. Because Sandberg went on to have a Hall of Fame career, Phillies fans retrospectively speculate about what their team's success would have been had they had retained him during that period.
18. De Jesús interview.
19. De Jesús interview.
20. Bill Conlin, "A Have-Nots' Shopping List at Houston," *The Sporting News*, December 3, 1984: 58.
21. De Jesús interview.
22. De Jesús interview.
23. Carlos Salazar, "Patient De Jesús Helping Dukes Dazzle With DPs," *The Sporting News,* August 24, 1974: 43.
24. De Jesús interview.
25. Robert Bondy, "De Jesús Jr. Credits Dad for His Love of Baseball," MLB.com, June 19, 2015. m.mlb.com/news/article/131264212/ivan-de-jesus-jr-credits-dad-for-his-love-of-baseball/.

# CARLOS DELGADO

## By Paul Hofmann

**THE COMMONWEALTH OF PUERTO** Rico has produced 257 major-league baseball players, including Hall of Famers Roberto Clemente, Orlando Cepeda, Roberto Alomar, and Iván Rodríguez. Although the list of Puerto Rican-born players is long and impressive, no other player from the islands has hit more home runs than Carlos Delgado. During a 17-year career with the Toronto Blue Jays, Florida Marlins, and New York Mets, Delgado slugged 473 home runs and accumulated 1,512 RBIs.

Carlos Juan Delgado Jr. was born on June 25, 1972, in El Prado section of Aguadilla,[1] Puerto Rico, to Carlos "Cao" Delgado and Carmen Digna Hérnandez.[2] Both his father, "Don Cao," and his grandfather, Asdrúbal "Pingolo" Delgado, were well-known figures in the town. Carlos's father was a drug and alcohol counselor while his mother worked as a medical laboratory assistant. Like many young boys growing up in Puerto Rico at that time, Carlos's boyhood hero was Roberto Clemente. Having both parents employed in social- and-human service jobs and a hero like Clemente undoubtedly had an impact on Carlos's development as a social activist and his deep commitment to social justice and charitable work in his adult years.

Carlos attended Agustín Stahl Middle School and José de Diego High School in Aguadilla.[3] After his junior year of high school, the Texas Rangers, New York Mets, Montreal Expos, Cincinnati Reds, and Toronto Blue Jays all expressed an interest in signing Delgado. Ultimately, the 16-year old catcher signed with the Blue Jays primarily because he felt the organization, which had become a perennial contender, had an established track record of developing young talent from the Caribbean, including Blue Jays greats George Bell and Tony Fernandez, both of whom hailed from the Dominican Republic.

While Carlos's parents recognized their son's athletic ability when he was still young, the Delgados placed a high value on education. His parents fully supported their son's desire to pursue his dream to play professional baseball, but only if he had a backup plan in the event he failed. Delgado's deal with the Blue Jays included a $90,000 signing bonus and a promise that the team would pay for his college education if he ever decided to pursue one. That was all his parents needed to hear.

After completing his senior year of high school, Delgado—just two weeks shy of his 17th birthday—was sent to St. Catharines, Ontario, to join the Blue Jays' New York-Pennsylvania League affiliate. In 31 games, he hit just .180 with no home runs and 11 RBIs. Delgado, however, was full of youthful exuberance and was never one to hang his head. John Cerutti remembered Delgado from spring training that year: "He always had a smile on his face. Whenever anybody wanted to do extra work and throw on the side, Carlos would jump up and say, 'I'll catch you.'"[4]

Delgado returned to St. Catharines for a second year of seasoning with the short-season Class-A Blue Jays and made great strides at the plate while he began showing some of the promise that Blue Jays general manager Pat Gillick envisioned. In 67 games he hit .281 with 6 home runs and a team-leading 39 RBIs and .471 slugging percentage. For his efforts he earned a spot in the NYPL all-star game and was named the R. Howard Webster Award Winner for the St. Catharines club.[5]

Following his success at St. Catharines, Delgado began the 1991 season with the Myrtle Beach Pelicans of the Class-A South Atlantic League. In 132 games he hit .286 with 18 home runs and 70 RBIs. While the Blue Jays were impressed enough with his bat to promote him to the Triple-A Syracuse Chiefs as a late season call-up, his defensive skills were not progressing as quickly. He committed 19 errors behind the plate for the Pelicans.

Delgado continued to advance through the system and spent the 1992 season with the Dunedin Blue Jays of the Class-A Florida State League. There he had a breakout year that cemented his status as a top prospect. The left-handed-hitting catcher had grown to 6-feet-3, is listed as weighing 215 pounds, and topped the circuit in nearly every offensive category including hits, doubles, home runs, slugging percentage, on-base percentage, and runs batted in. He finished the year with a .324 average, 30 home runs, and 100 RBIs.

After his outstanding year at Dunedin, *Baseball America* pegged Delgado its number-4 overall prospect entering the 1993 season and the Puerto Rican backstop was promoted to the Knoxville Smokies of the Double-A Southern League. He was the Smokies' primary catcher and hit .303 with a Southern League-leading 25 home runs and 102 RBIs. At this point the Blue Jays continued to see Delgado as the eventual successor to catcher Pat Borders and called him up to Toronto when the rosters expanded in September.

On October 1, 1993, at Camden Yards in Baltimore, Delgado made his major-league debut when he entered the game as a defensive replacement for catcher Randy Knorr in the bottom of the sixth inning. In the top of the eighth he made his first major-league plate appearance and drew a one-out walk off Orioles right-hander Todd Frohwirth. Two days later, in the final game of the season, Delgado made his only other appearance of the year when he pinch-hit for future Hall of Famer Paul Molitor in the top of the eighth inning. Delgado ended the inning with a pop fly to shortstop.

Delgado earned a roster spot with the Blue Jays in the spring of 1994, and in an effort to get his bat into the lineup, manager Cito Gaston inserted him in left field. His success was immediate and the power he demonstrated turned lots of heads in Toronto. In his first 13 games Delgado belted eight home runs and drove in 18 runs. Among his home runs were a pair of majestic shots, the second of which banged off the window of the Hard Rock Café in right-center field. The homer, estimated to have traveled 445 feet, was one of the longest ever hit at the Sky Dome.[6] Delgado's early success was short-lived and he managed to hit only .183 with one home run and six RBIs in his next 30 games before being optioned to Syracuse.

Delgado later commented on his struggles at the plate during this stage of his career. "I learned the hard way. When I started hitting home runs, I thought, I can hit these pitches. Then I started thinking, if I can do this, I can hit the pitch four inches outside or four inches up. I expanded the zone and got myself out. Pitchers are smart. If they find out they don't have to throw strikes, they won't."[7]

Delgado split the 1995 season between Toronto and Syracuse. He started the season in the Blue Jays lineup but was mired in a slump that left his batting average at .154 after 14 games and he was once again optioned to Syracuse. He continued to demonstrate that he could handle Triple-A pitching. In 91 games with Chiefs he hit .318 with 22 home runs and 74 RBIs. It was during this time that Delgado's transi-

tion to first base began in earnest. He returned to the Blue Jays in September and played in 23 games during the final month of the season. Despite hitting only .169 during this stretch, he continued to get valuable experience in the field. His days as a catcher were behind him.

After a 56-88 fifth-place finish in 1995 (AL East), the Blue Jays World Series championships of 1992 and 1993 were fading in the distance of the rear-view mirror. Delgado, who earned a spot as the Jays' primary designated hitter during spring training, was among a cast of younger players that included Shawn Green, Alex Gonzalez, and Tomas Perez whom the Jays attempted to blend with an aging nucleus to bring the club back into contention. During his first full season in the majors, he established himself as an integral part of the Jays' future plans. He finished the 1996 season with a .270 average, 25 home runs, and 92 RBIs.

Delgado always had raw, natural power and a knack for hitting long home runs. Just as he had done in April of 1994, he displayed his immense power in a July 6, 1996, tilt against Detroit at venerable Tiger Stadium. In the top of the third, Delgado cleared the right-field roof and deposited a 2-and-1 offering from Omar Olivares onto Trumbull Avenue — the 29th player to clear the grandstand at Tiger Stadium.[8] He later added a three-run blast to deep left field to lead the Jays' 15-0 rout of the Tigers.

Blue Jays broadcaster Buck Martinez, who covered and managed Delgado in Toronto, witnessed these early displays of unrestricted power. "He had power that you don't see very often," Martinez said. "The first time we saw him we went, 'Oh my God, this is Carlos Delgado.' We had heard about him."[9]

While Delgado was a professional's professional on the field, baseball did not define who he was as a person. According to teammate and close friend Shawn Green, "What separates him from other superstars is that he doesn't have a big ego."[10] This was evident when Delgado volunteered to surrender his number-21 jersey in deference to then three-time Cy Young Award winner Roger Clemens, who had signed with the Blue Jays in December of 1996.[11]

The change in uniform number did little to slow Delgado's development as a rising star. While his batting average dipped slightly to .262 in 1997, he had 20 more extra-base hits than in the previous season and by the end of the year was the Blue Jays' everyday first baseman, filling the void created when John Olerud was traded to the New York Mets during the previous offseason. The 1997 season was the first of 10 consecutive seasons in which Delgado hit 30 or more home runs — a feat that as of 2017 put him in a select group with only five other players.

The 1998 season marked the beginning of six consecutive seasons in which Delgado drove in 100 or more runs and solidified his spot as a bona-fide superstar. During this six-year stretch, he compiled a .295 average, hit 237 home runs, and drove in 741 runs, with a .585 slugging percentage and .998 OPS. In 1999 he hit a career-best 44 home runs. His two finest seasons came in 2000 and 2003, the years he made his two All-Star Game appearances.

Delgado entered the 2000 All-Star break with a .363 batting average, 28 home runs, and 80 RBIs. He was a legitimate Triple Crown candidate when he made his All-Star Game debut at Turner Field in Atlanta. He entered the game as a defensive replacement at first base in the bottom of the fourth inning and later doubled off Astros' All-Star right-hander Darryl Kile in the top of the sixth inning. After the All-Star break he hit only 13 home runs the rest of the season. He finished the year with a .344 average, a league-leading 57 doubles, 41 home runs, 137 RBIs, .664 slugging average, and 1.134 OPS — one of the greatest offensive seasons in Blue Jays history. He finished fourth in AL MVP balloting behind Jason Giambi, Frank Thomas, and Alex Rodríguez.

The 2003 season was another All-Star- and MVP-type year for Delgado. Unlike his initial All-Star Game appearance, he started the 2003 midsummer classic, held at U.S. Cellular Field in Chicago. In his first at-bat he flied out to left field to end the bottom of the first. In the bottom of the third he lined a single to left off Philadelphia southpaw Randy Wolf to drive in Ichiro Suzuki with the game's first run. In his final at-bat, he struck out swinging to end the fifth inning. While Delgado continued to pile up All-Star-caliber numbers, he never again played in another All-Star Game.

On September 25, 2003, Delgado became the 13th major-league player in the modern era to hit four home runs in a single game.[12] He hit a three-run home run in the first inning off Jorge Sosa, the 300th of his major-league career, and then touched Sosa again to lead off the fourth inning. Delgado hit his third home run off Joe Kennedy while leading off the sixth. His fourth was the most impressive, a towering blast off Lance Carter that landed above the Sky Dome's restaurant in right center. Delgado's effort was distinguished from the 12 previous four-home-run games (and the subsequent one) by the fact that he was the only player to hit four home runs with only four plate appearances in the game.[13] He finished the 2003 season with a .302 average, 42 home runs, and a major-league-leading 145 RBIs. The effort earned Delgado a second-place finish to Alex Rodríguez in the AL MVP Award voting.

At this point a veteran of 11 major-league seasons, Delgado was one of the most respected players in baseball. When the United States invaded Iraq in March of 2013, he decided he was unable to publicly support the US military action. Delgado stood for "God Bless America" through the 2003 season but as the 2004 season opened, he vowed not to do so.[14] In an act of a simple protest against the war, Delgado chose to remain in the dugout while "God Bless America" was being sung. This was not the first time Delgado had expressed his political views. A year earlier he publicly opposed the US Navy's use of the Puerto Rican island of Vieques as a weapons-testing ground.[15] On the field Delgado had an injury plagued "off year" in which he finished with a .269 average, 32 home runs, and 99 RBIs.

After the 2004 season, the Blue Jays were facing some payroll constraints and were not interested in re-signing their first baseman at the price he would command on the open market. As a free agent, Delgado was seriously courted by the Baltimore Orioles, Florida Marlins, New York Mets, and Texas Rangers.[16] On January 26, 2005, he signed a four-year, $52 million contract with the Florida Marlins. The Marlins were in the process of building support for a new ballpark in Miami and drafted a contract that called for Delgado to receive only $4 million in the first year and included a club option for year five.[17]

Miami seemed like the perfect fit for Delgado. He liked the idea of playing in a city with a large Spanish-speaking fan base and for a team that had a strong young pitching rotation. With Juan Pierre and Luis Castillo hitting in front of him and Miguel Cabrera offering protection behind him, it seemed as though the Marlins were poised to make a run at a third World Series title. The 2005 season did not unfold as the Marlins planned and they finished tied for third, seven games behind the NL East champion Atlanta Braves.

Delgado was a $4 million bargain for the 2005 season. He hit .301 with a team-leading 33 home runs (tied with Cabrera) and 115 RBIs. The Marlins were acutely aware that Delgado's salary was set to quadruple over the next three years and frustrated that they were unable to put together a deal to finance a new ballpark. On November 24, 2005, the Marlins sent Delgado and the remaining $48 million of his contract to the New York Mets for first baseman Mike Jacobs, pitching prospect Yusmeiro Petit, minor-league utilityman Grant Psomas, and $7 million.[18] In acquiring Delgado, the Mets were filling a dire need at first base and bringing in a veteran clubhouse presence. From his perspective, he was happy to be joining fellow Puerto Rican Carlos Beltran on a team that had the ability to contend.

The Mets' new first baseman enjoyed another solid season in 2006, his first year in New York. On August 22 he eclipsed the 30-home run plateau for the 10th consecutive season and hit his 400th career home run when he slugged two homers off the Cardinals' Jeff Weaver. The second, Delgado's 400th, was a fifth-inning grand slam. Delgado batted .265 with 38 home runs and 114 RBIs during the season and along with Beltran and David Wright (who both drove in 116 runs) led the charge that ended the Atlanta Braves' 14-of-15-year stranglehold on the NL East. After 1,711 major-league games, Delgado was finally headed to the playoffs.

The Mets easily dispatched of the Los Angeles Dodgers in the Division Series. Delgado led the way in Game One, going 4-for-5 with two RBIs, including a solo home run off Derek Lowe in the fourth inning and a run-scoring single off Brad Penny in seventh. The Mets held on to win the game, 6-5, and went on to sweep the Dodgers in three. Delgado hit .429 in the series.

The Championship Series against the Cardinals was an epic seven-game encounter. Delgado had a feast-or-famine series. He batted .304 with three home runs and nine RBIs over the course of the series, but all three home runs and nine RBIs came in just two games. He hit a pair of home runs off Cardinals right-hander Chris Carpenter as he drove in four runs in Game Two, and added his third home run and five RBIs in Game Four. Ultimately, the Cardinals won the NLCS and went on to sweep the favored Tigers in the 2006 World Series.

In 2006 Delgado was recognized for his humanitarian and charitable efforts when he was given the Roberto Clemente Award. Over the years Delgado has been true to his hero's legacy. He has assisted Puerto Rico's youth through his nonprofit organization Extra Bases, participated in initiatives to improve the islands' public-education system, visited hospitalized children, and donated video-conferencing equipment to the local hospital in Aguadilla.

Delgado got off to a slow start in the 2007 season. He ended the month of April with a .188 average and was still sitting at .227 with 12 home runs and 44 RBIs as June ended. He did find his stroke during the second half of the season but his power numbers were down. From July 1 on Delgado batted .297 and finished the season at .258 with 24 home runs and 87 RBIs. Perhaps the sole highlight of the first half of his season came on May 9 when he took the Giants' Matt Morris deep and hit a home run into San Francisco's McCovey Cove.

The 2008 season was a bounce-back year for Delgado. He played in 159 games, his most since 2003. His power returned as he belted 38 home runs and drove in 115 runs. All indications suggested that the first baseman was healthy and had returned to form. As expected, the Mets exercised their $12 million option for the 2009 season.

Unlike previous springs, Delgado started the 2009 season hitting well. In his first 26 games he hit .298 with 4 home runs and 23 RBIs before his season was cut short by a hip injury. On May 18 the Mets announced that Delgado required surgery to remove a bone spur and a torn labrum in his hip.[19] The prognosis was that he would be out for approximately 10 weeks and the Mets expected him to return in July to resume his quest to join the exclusive 500-home-run club. However, Delgado was unable to return during the 2009 season and he filed for free agency in November.

Delgado experienced a setback while playing winter ball in Puerto Rico and had a second hip operation in February 2010. In August of 2010 he signed a minor-league contract with the Boston Red Sox. He played five games with the Pawtucket Red Sox before aggravating his hip once again. A short 16 months earlier, it seemed certain that Delgado was destined to hit 500 home runs. Now his career was over.

Despite his gaudy offensive numbers, which compare favorably to many who have been enshrined in Cooperstown—he ranks 32nd on the list for career home runs and 55th on the list for RBIs—and four top-10 finishes in league MVP voting, Delgado's Hall of Fame candidacy ended before it ever get started. Appearing on the ballot for the first time in 2015, he received only 21 votes (3.8 percent) and was removed from future consideration by the Baseball Writers Association of America. ESPN's Jayson Stark reacted by stating, "Carlos Delgado is the best player in history to get booted off the Hall of Fame ballot after his first year."[20]

Reflecting on his exclusion from the Hall of Fame, Delgado diplomatically stated, "I'm a little disappointed, to say the least. I was hoping to be able to get enough votes to stay on the ballot for the following year, because I knew coming in this was going to be a strong group of players. Sometimes there's things in life you can't control. This is one of them. I'm not going to let it overshadow what I've done in my career."[21]

As of 2017 Delgado resided in his hometown of Aguadilla, Puerto Rico, with his wife and two children. He enjoyed keeping a low profile, spending time on the computer, listening to music, watching movies, and enjoying his cigars.

## NOTES

1. Aguadilla was first made famous by Christopher Columbus, who landed there on November 19, 1493, on his second voyage to the New World. Delgado's hometown is located on the island's northwest coast, about two hours from the capital city of San Juan.
2. "Carlos Delgado," jockbio.com/Bios/Delgado/Delgado_bio.html.
3. "Carlos Delgado," aclu.org/sites/default/files/pdfs/humanrights/Carlos_Delgado.pdf.
4. "Carlos Delgado, What They Say," jockbio.com/Bios/Delgado/Delgado_quotes.html.
5. Each year, the Toronto Blue Jays organization, with consultation from their minor-league coaches, bestow the R. Howard Webster Awards to the MVPs of each minor-league affiliate.
6. "Jays Rookie Hits Restaurant Again," *Pittsburgh Post-Gazette*, April 6, 1994: D-4.
7. "Carlos Delgado: My Say," jockbio.com/Bios/Delgado/Delgado_mysay.html.
8. "Blue Jays 15, Tigers 0," apnewsarchive.com.
9. Ian Harrison, "How Carlos Delgado fell short of Cooperstown," June 12, 2015, sports.vice.com/en_us/article/how-carlos-delgado-fell-short-of-cooperstown.
10. "Carlos Delgado: What They Say."
11. Roger Clemens went on to win the Cy Young Award an unprecedented seven times.
12. Bobby Lowe of the Boston Beaneaters (May 30, 1894) and Ed Delahanty of the Philadelphia Phillies (July 13, 1896) both hit four home runs in a single game in the nineteenth century.
13. Shane Tourtellotte, "Holland and Granderson," April 20, 2012, hardballtimes.com.
14. William Rhoden, "Sports of the Times; Delgado Makes a Stand by Taking a Seat," *New York Times*, July 21, 2004. Retrieved from nytimes.com.
15. Ibid.
16. "Carlos Delgado Weighs Options; Former Tiger Clark Picks Diamondbacks," *Argus-Press* (Owosso, Michigan), January 25, 2005: 10.
17. "Delgado Inks Deal with Marlins, *Seattle Times*, January 25, 2005.
18. Associated Press, "Marlins Seal Deal, Trade Delgado to Mets," November 25. 2005. Retrieved from espn.com.
19. Anthony DiComo, "Delgado Has Surgery; 10 Weeks to Recover," May 19, 2009, m.mets.mlb.com/news/article/4814480.
20. Jayson Stark, "Delgado Deserved Better in HOF Voting," January 8, 2015, espn.com.
21. Brendan Kennedy, "Carlos Delgado Shut Out of the Baseball Hall of Fame," *Toronto Star*, January 6, 2015.

# ED FIGUEROA

## By Rory Costello

**THE NEW YORK YANKEES WON** three straight American League pennants from 1976 to 1978, becoming World Series champions in the latter two years. Yet even devoted fans might have trouble recalling which pitcher got the most victories for the Bronx Bombers over this period. It wasn't Catfish Hunter or Ron Guidry—it was Ed Figueroa, the only native of Puerto Rico (as of 2017) to have a 20-win season.[1]

Figueroa relied on a good sinking fastball and a variety of breaking pitches. As Guidry described him, "Figgy was a good pitcher. He wasn't an overpowering guy. He was always around the plate. He wasn't flashy, wasn't dominant, wasn't a strikeout guy. He just won."[2] Unfortunately, elbow problems ended his run of success after just four seasons.

Eduardo Figueroa Padilla was born on October 14, 1948 in Ciales, Puerto Rico. He was the eldest of seven boys and three girls born to Otilio Figueroa and María Padilla. Although well over 200 *boricuas* have made it to the majors, Figueroa is the only one from Ciales, a mountain village about 30 miles southwest of San Juan. However, he lived there for only two months.

Young Eduardo started playing baseball in Little League at the age of nine. When he was 11, his team won the championship in Puerto Rico. At age 14, he went to the Babe Ruth World Series in Farmington, New Mexico. As he told author Brian Jensen in 1999, "I've been a winner all my life in whatever I've done."[3]

After that, Figueroa graduated to La Liga Bithorn, named for Hiram Bithorn, the first major-leaguer from Puerto Rico. He played for Cidra, a town south of San Juan, along with future Cub Jerry Morales.[4] In June 1966, the 17-year-old Figueroa and Morales played on the Puerto Rican national team.[5] They took part in the Central American Games, which were held in San Juan that year, and won a silver medal behind Cuba.

The following month, Figueroa signed with the New York Mets. He was one of the club's first prospects to come out of Latin America. The scout was Nino Escalera, who covered the region for the Mets from 1966 to 1981. Figueroa pitched four games in Rookie League and Class A ball in 1966. Joined again by Jerry Morales, he then made his debut in the Puerto Rican Winter League (PRWL) as a reliever with the Caguas Criollos. Caguas is just east of Cidra in the San Juan metro area.

Figueroa first showed promise in 1967. With Winter Haven in the Florida State League, he was 12-5 with a 2.05 ERA. Nolan Ryan, later his teammate in California, was briefly on the same roster. The young Puerto Rican was happy on the field—but not off it, as he told author Dave Klein in 1977. Among other things, he encountered prejudice as a barber refused to cut the hair of an African-American teammate.[6]

In 1968, Figueroa pitched for Raleigh-Durham in the Carolina League, but his season fizzled out. A 2008 feature by Anthony McCarron for the *New York Daily News* told the story. "He was called to take a draft physical in Puerto Rico. The Mets said go for a week and come back, but he stayed with his girlfriend for three weeks. 'When you're 18 [*sic*], you don't know what you're doing,' Figueroa says.

"The day he returned, he pitched and hurt his arm. Then the Marines called, the Mets released him and Figueroa spent the next year in Vietnam. 'I didn't know what the heck I was doing there, but I was there. I learned that life, it's beautiful to be alive. I saw a lot of people dead there. When I got out of there, I was happy I was out, happy I was alive.'"[7]

In a 1976 feature, longtime Yankees beat writer Phil Pepe offered some more detail on the pitcher's military service. Figueroa served 10 months total, including two with the infantry "in country," before he was granted a hardship discharge. He told Pepe,

"The Marine training helped me when I eventually returned to baseball."[8]

When Figueroa got back home at first, though, he did not feel confident about playing again in the U.S., as he told Dave Klein. He had made plans to play in the Mexican League, but Pedrín Zorrilla—owner of the PRWL's Santurce Cangrejeros and a scout for the Giants going back to their New York days—convinced him otherwise. "He said I could be a pitcher, that the Giants wanted me, that I would make a big mistake to give up and not try again. I said to him I did not want to go back to the United States. But he told me the Mexican League was not for me."[9]

Having missed nearly two full seasons, Figueroa took two more to re-establish himself in Single-A and Double-A. Following the 1971 season, *The Sporting News* wrote that he "showed extreme promise" with his combined record of 18-9, including a 2.08 ERA in 104 innings after promotion to Amarillo in the Texas League.[10] As a result, he finally reached Triple-A in 1972 with Phoenix. Although his ERA was over 4, he had a 10-2 record. "There was talk the Giants wanted to bring me up," Figueroa recalled in 1976. "But my mother died that August…We have a very close family so I went home and didn't play the rest of the year."[11]

Figueroa regressed when he returned to Phoenix in 1973 (1-5, 5.54 in 65 innings). That July, San Francisco traded him to the California Angels for shortstop Bruce Christensen and pitcher Don Rose. He finished the year in better form with the Angels' top farm club, Salt Lake City.

A big breakthrough in Figueroa's development came that winter at home. He had spent the past five Puerto Rican seasons with the Arecibo Lobos, none especially remarkable, though he did post a 2.80 ERA in 1972-73. Before the season, he came back to Caguas along with Manuel Muñíz in return for shortstop Iván de Jesús, then just 20 years old.[12] Figueroa was 10-3, 3.47 for the Criollos, tying for the league lead in wins. Ernie McAnally of Ponce and the Montreal Expos edged him in voting for pitcher of the year.[13]

Figueroa made the Angels staff out of spring training in 1974. He started the season in the bullpen and pitched seldom—only 10 times before the Fourth of July. After Dick Williams replaced Bobby Winkles as manager, the rookie finally got his first start on July 6. He lost a 1-0 decision to the Indians at Anaheim Stadium, despite allowing just six hits and going all the way.

Six days later, he got his first big-league win, shutting out Boston on 10 hits at Fenway Park. Williams—who got his first win in California after 10 straight losses—said, "Even though he gave up a lot of hits, he never was in any real trouble. He did a good job, particularly at keeping the ball down. He's a good competitor. We looked up his statistics and found he did better starting than in relief, so we gave him a chance."[14]

Figueroa finished with a 2-8 record in 25 games, but his 3.67 ERA was not bad. He then followed up with his best season at home. He went 10-3 again for Caguas, leading the league in wins by himself, and his 2.35 ERA ranked fifth. "The league helped me become a major league pitcher," Figueroa told author Tom Van Hyning. "It gave me seasoning and confidence."[15]

Although he started the 1975 season at Salt Lake, Figueroa said in 2008 that it still might have been his best year overall. Crediting Angels pitching coach

Billy Muffett, he became a sinker/slider pitcher.[16] Figueroa told Phil Pepe, "I'd say those two pitches, plus the confidence I gained by pitching regularly at California, enabled me to have a winning season."[17] He was 16-13 with a 2.91 ERA for a team that "was one of the worst in baseball...We had no hitting."[18] That season, he earned the nickname "Señor Stopper"[19] — 15 of his wins came after the Angels had lost. Figueroa actually had a better year than Nolan Ryan in '75, but teammate Frank Tanana emerged to lead the league in strikeouts.

On December 11, 1975, Yankees general manager Gabe Paul made another in his sequence of brilliant trades that helped lift the team back to pennant-winning status. He sent Bobby Bonds to the Angels and received both Mickey Rivers and Figueroa in return. The headline in the *Los Angeles Times* said "Angel Offense: More Security With Bonds"—but the *Christian Science Monitor* rightly observed, "The Yankees, in terms of youth and potential, got a lot from California for Bonds."[20] Bonds had a disappointing, injury-marred 1976, and though 1977 might have been his career year, he was traded again that December. Meanwhile, Rivers and Figueroa were vital parts of the Yankees' 1976-78 run. Plus, while Paul said he hated to let Bonds go, the deal also allowed him to trade Doc Medich and obtain another key cog: Willie Randolph.

The Bonds swap was not received well in New York. As Phil Pepe wrote in 1977, "Remember the flak that was stirred? Remember how people criticized the deal? Figueroa was a tough sell to Yankee fans and know-nothing television critics." But the club liked how well he had pitched against key divisional rivals Baltimore and Boston. "He's going to be one of the best pitchers in baseball in the next few years," predicted Gabe Paul and George Steinbrenner.[21] They were right.

Figueroa (sporting a fierce-looking mustache by then, as did many of his Yankee teammates) won a club-high 19 games in 1976. He might have reached the 20-win plateau two years earlier than he eventually did, but he missed a couple of turns in August with a stiff elbow, lost his last two decisions, and then a rainout canceled his last start of the season. Right around that time, the *Christian Science Monitor* said, "When it comes to using only the corners of home plate, Ed Figueroa is a craftsman."[22]

Figueroa's postseason record was not impressive. He was 0-2, 8.10 in four starts in the AL Championship Series of 1976-78, all against the Kansas City Royals. In Game Five of the 1976 ALCS, though, he pitched seven steady innings and left with a 6-3 lead. Grant Jackson then gave up a game-tying homer to George Brett (who hit an astounding .610 against Figueroa in his career during the regular season and .592 overall). An inning later, Chris Chambliss brought New York the pennant with his memorable homer off Mark Littell. In the 1976 World Series, Figueroa went eight innings and allowed five runs as the Cincinnati Reds completed their sweep in Game Four.

On New Year's Day 1977, the *New York Times* reported that Figueroa was seeking a five-year contract for $2 million. He wound up settling for four years and $500,000.[23] For such a modest amount, especially on George Steinbrenner's team, Figueroa gave the Yankees 16 more victories in 1977, despite assorted aches and pains. An intriguing insight into his mindset was revealed 30 years later during the filming of the ESPN miniseries *The Bronx Is Burning*. "To stroll on the set...is to take a remarkable walk back in time. Inside the Yankee clubhouse, no detail goes unchecked...In pitcher Ed Figueroa's [locker] sits a yellowed paperback copy of *Politics in Africa*."[24]

Though the Yankees gave Figueroa an early 4-0 lead kin Game Four of the ALCS, manager Billy Martin pulled him in the fourth inning. Figueroa was charged with four runs and got no decision. Martin then passed Figueroa over in the 1977 World Series, believing that the pitcher had not yet recovered from nerve damage in his right index finger. This prompted a dispute, and Figueroa considered leaving the team early. He later called the rumors that he had "jumped" a misunderstanding. Figueroa said, "I asked Billy if I could go home and he said go ahead. Then I thought about it and decided it would be a bad move on my part. . .I want to be part of the club until the series is over."[25]

Ed and Billy just didn't see eye to eye. The pitcher asked several times to be traded out of The Bronx Zoo before Martin resigned under fire in July 1978. "Boy, was he [Figueroa] glad when mellow Bob Lemon replaced Martin as manager of the Yankees. 'Billy thinks he knows pitching. He doesn't know s—-. He hurts pitchers because he doesn't know how to use them. And he screws pitchers up because he wants to call all the pitches.'"[26] "Billy was always lying to me," Figueroa said in September 1978.[27] He had more blunt words the next month: "He treated me like dirt, a second-class citizen. He has told people I'm gutless and cannot pitch under pressure. He never said anything good about me."[28]

Conversely, Figueroa said of Lemon, "He treats me like a man. He lets me pitch to the hitters my way. I have more confidence with him."[29] He added, "Lemon was a pitcher himself. He has a feeling for what it's about."[30] Figueroa always insisted he performed best in the classic four-man rotation. There's an irony here. Billy Martin gained a reputation for burning out starters, especially later when he managed Oakland. Yet reportedly he did not want to let Figueroa work on three days' rest—though he did say in late May, "I can't control the weather and the schedule." The most reasonable—not to mention prophetic—remark came from Yankees president Al Rosen. "He's 5-2 and he's started nine times in our 41 games. At that rate he'll start 33 or 34 times and be 20-8. That's what you expect from a premier righthander and he is one."[31]

It's also hard to blame Martin for the bout of arm soreness Figueroa endured in late June and early July, when he missed a couple of turns and got a cortisone shot. Nonetheless, Bob Lemon consistently gave Figueroa the ball every fourth day—and at least in '78, it paid off. When Figgy got his 20 wins that year, he was 11-2 after Martin left, winning eight of his last nine starts as the Yankees and Red Sox staged their gripping fight for the AL East. Victory number 20 clinched a tie for the division title, but then Rick Waits beat Catfish Hunter in the Yankees' 162nd game, setting up the one-game playoff won by Bucky Dent's homer.

Unfortunately, despite his brilliance down the stretch, Figueroa got knocked out of the box in the second inning of both Game Two of the ALCS and the World Series opener. Following his poor showing in the latter game, he beefed about not getting high strike calls from NL umpire Ed Vargo (back then there was a perceived difference between the leagues' strike zones).[32] This was rich, coming from a sinkerball pitcher, but Lemon reasoned with him. Figueroa realized, "After I got shelled by the Dodgers, he talked to me about it. I was getting my fastball too high. I deserved to be chewed out. I can take that."[33] The skipper stuck with Figueroa in Game Four; a Yankee comeback left him with no decision.

For reaching the 20-win milestone that year, Figueroa got a hero's welcome in Puerto Rico. He threw out the first ball to open the PRWL season (although he did not play that winter and the next two). Governor Carlos Romero Barceló held a luncheon in Figueroa's honor, and former Governor Luis Muñóz Marín invited the pitcher to his home. On December 2, WKAQ Telemundo made Figueroa's life story—"Ciales to Yankee Stadium"—the first in a series of TV documentaries entitled "Diary of a Winner."[34]

However, Figueroa was never effective again in the majors after 1978. Author Bruce Markusen summed it up well in 2008: "Over a four-year span, he averaged 248 innings per season, a substantial workload that became exacerbated by an awkward motion. In his wind-up, Figueroa tucked his left leg and left arm in toward his mid-section; by the time he put himself in position to deliver the pitch, he was throwing the ball across his body. It was a fun delivery to imitate (as I know well from hours of throwing a ball up against a boulder outside of my house), but it sure did appear to put extra stress on the arm and shoulder. Figueroa's arm problems began in 1979; by 1981, he was fully cooked."[35]

In 1979, Figueroa fell out of the rotation in May. He started just four games in June and two in July amid a stint on the disabled list. In mid-August, he finally had bone spurs and chips removed from his elbow. The following season went from bad to worse. As he tried to rebound from surgery, his sinker lacked its former zip. Figueroa was especially unhappy about going to the bullpen. The Yankees sold his contract to the Texas Rangers in late July, as Yankees executive Cedric Tallis said, "All parties concerned felt it was time for a change."[36] With the Rangers, Figgy was 0-7 in eight starts.

Figuerpa returned to the Puerto Rican Winter League after three seasons away but was ineffective in seven games. He re-signed with the Rangers on a minor-league deal in March 1981 and was assigned to Triple-A Wichita. He said he didn't start the season "in the right frame of mind. . .I was mad at myself, and mad at baseball."[37] Texas released him in late May.

Figueroa then put aside past acrimony and called up Billy Martin about a job. Billy, who had become manager of the Oakland A's, "decided Figueroa was worth a risk and signed him for Tacoma," the team's Triple-A farm club. That June, Figueroa said, "I've got a lot of confidence I can pitch again in the big leagues. I'm looking forward to the day when my chance comes. If I didn't think I could pitch in the big leagues again, I wouldn't be here. I'd be in San Juan with my family and working in my trucking business." He added, "If I pitch good in Tacoma, Billy thinks I can help the club in Oakland. I'd like to pitch again for him."[38] That was exactly how it turned out; Figueroa did pitch rather well in the Pacific Coast League and got into his last two games in the majors with the A's that September.

In 1982—following removal of another bone spur in his elbow that January—Figueroa pitched five forgettable games with Modesto (Class A) and Tacoma. Also, according to the *Modesto Bee*, "his attitude stirred team resentment."[39] Figueroa *was* nursing hard feelings. That year he also published a memoir called *Yankee Stranger*, in which he sounded off about the obstacles that Latino players commonly faced. "We Latins do not get what we should in baseball: not the money, recognition, publicity, or honors. They usually just give everything to the American players before any Latin players are considered." Even after his 20-win season, "not one baseball magazine that came out in the spring of 1979 had my picture in it, nor were there any stories."[40]

Back in Puerto Rico for the winter of 1982-83, however, Figueroa earned Comeback Player of the Year honors. With Santurce, he led the league in ERA at 2.93.[41] However, he then turned down a $200,000 minor-league offer from the Brewers. "I threw $200,000 away that year. . .I should've tried another year. I just retired."[42] That was only in the U.S. minors, though—Figgy finally did appear in the Mexican League with the Yucatán Leones, more than a decade after Pedrín Zorrilla convinced him to stay away.[43] In 54 innings across nine starts, he posted a 4-5, 3.50 record.

Figueroa also made five more appearances with Santurce in the winter of 1983-84. Across 15 seasons and 188 games in the PRWL, he won 46, lost 40, and had a 3.61 ERA.

Figueroa was a pitching coach for Caguas in at least one season, 1987-88. There he helped Cincinnati Reds flamethrower Rob Dibble break through to the majors. "Ed Figueroa. . .told him to be himself, cut it loose, throw as hard as he could for as long as he could."[44]

Figueroa's career on the mound did not truly end until 1990. At age 41, he played for the Gold Coast Suns of the Senior Professional Baseball Association in the 1989-90 season. He was 1-10 with a 6.86 ERA, leading the league in losses.[45] He got his lone win on a chilly Thursday night in Pompano Beach before just 254 fans. The manager, Earl Weaver, showed his old Baltimore form, getting ejected for the second time in the season's 12th game. "It was a classic Weaver argument. He turned his cap backward, the better to get in [umpire] Shulman's face."[46]

After leaving the minors, Figueroa focused on his trucking company, United Maritime Transport, which he had bought when his arm problems started. He and his first wife raised three children: Eduardo Jr., Vanessa, and Brandon. Figueroa later got remarried to Diana Jove on November 14, 1999.

After about 14 years, Figueroa sold the trucking firm and got into the restaurant business. He established two Mexican joints called Lupi's, one in Old San Juan and the other near the San Juan airport (though in 2009, they were put up for sale). Brian Jensen's interview with Figgy in his book *Where Have All Our Yankees Gone?* provided much detail and many personal quotes on the pitcher's post-baseball career, as did Anthony McCarron's story in the *Daily News*.

Figueroa served as pitching coach for the Puerto Rican national team in 2003, although Cuba knocked them out in the regional qualifying tournament for the Athens Olympics. That year, the Caguas Criollos retired his uniform number, 19. Since then, in addition to further appearances at the Yankees' Old-Timers' games (his last visit came in 2008), he has provided analysis on broadcasts of PRWL games.

Yes, the flashy dominant strikeout guys overshadowed Ed Figueroa even when he was at his best. He was never named to an All-Star team. Even so, only four pitchers won more games from 1976 to 1978: Jim Palmer, Steve Carlton, Dennis Leonard, and J.R. Richard. At times Figgy was described as "temperamental," but it is more accurate to say that he was proud. If he couldn't pitch on his terms, or gain due recognition, that pride could be wounded. "I used to have a lot of pride," he admitted while trying to come back in 1982. "I think I used to have too much."[47]

Yet that pride also manifests itself in a positive way. Figueroa looks back fondly on his time in New York and the fans there. In January 2008, he attended the first Puerto Rican Yankees Festival at the Museum of Puerto Rican Sports in Guaynabo (the San Juan suburb where Figueroa lives). He said, "I played five years with the organization and the minute I put on the uniform I felt different. It's something you never forget."[48]

*Thanks to Ed Figueroa for his input and to Benny Ayala for the introduction.*

## SOURCES

Figueroa, Ed and Dorothy Harshman. *Yankee Stranger* (Smithtown, New York: Exposition Press, 1982).

Jensen, Brian. *Where Have All Our Yankees Gone?* (Lanham, Maryland: Taylor Trade Publishing, 2004: 93-97).

Crescioni Benítez, José A. *El Béisbol Profesional Boricua* (San Juan, Puerto Rico: Aurora Comunicación Integral, Inc., 1997).

Treto Cisneros, Pedro, editor, *Enciclopedia del Béisbol Mexicano*, Mexico City: Revistas Deportivas, S.A. de C.V., 11th edition, 2011.

www.retrosheet.org

www.baseball-reference.com

http://demo.museodeldeportedecaguas.org

www.meta.pr (information on 1966 Central American Games)

www.extrarealtypr.com

## NOTES

1 John Candelaria, who played basketball for the Puerto Rican Olympic team, won 20 in 1977, a year ahead of Figueroa. But as Figueroa said, "He doesn't count…he was born in New York City." (Wire service reports, September 19, 1978)

2 Cecilia Tan, *The 50 Greatest Yankee Games* (Hoboken, New Jersey: John Wiley & Sons, 2005), 129.

3 Brian Jensen,. *Where Have All Our Yankees Gone?* (Lanham, Maryland: Taylor Trade Publishing, 2004), 95.

4 Benjamin López Feliciano, "Breve historia del béisbol en Cidra 1962-1968." *Periódico La Cordillera* (Cidra, Puerto Rico), unknown date (http://www.lacordillera.net/index.php?option=com_content&view=article&id=288:breve-historia-del-beisbol-en-cidra-1962-1968&catid=43:columnistas&Itemid=110)

5 Thomas Van Hyning, *Puerto Rico's Winter League* (Jefferson, North Carolina: McFarland & Co., 1995), 104.

6 Dave Klein, *On the Way Up* (New York: Julian Messner, Inc., 1977), 89.

7 Anthony McCarron, "Where Are They Now? In Puerto Rico, ex-Yankee Ed Figueroa is Still Cookin'," *New York Daily News*, December 6, 2008.

8 Phil Pepe, "Now Lynn Knows Why Yanks Got Figueroa," *The Sporting News*, January 24, 1976: 51.

9 Klein, 91.

10 Pat Frizzell, "Don't Sell Giants Short, Kids Look Extra Sharp," *The Sporting News*, December 18, 1971: 58.

11 Alan Friedman, "Ed Figueroa: The Yankees' Anonymous Star," *Baseball Digest*, October 1976: 96.

12 Van Hyning, 107.

13 "McAnally, Ayala Are Class of Puerto Rican League," *The Sporting News*, February 16, 1974: 43.

14 "Williams' First Angel Win: It Was Long Time Coming," Associated Press, July 14, 1974.

15 Van Hyning.

16 Pepe.

17 Ibid.

18 McCarron.

19 "Figueroa Stops Another Losing Streak — Yanks'," *Los Angeles Times*, August 23, 1975: C1.

20 Phil Elderkin, "Bonds Gives Angels a Star," *Christian Science Monitor*, December 18, 1975: 22.

21 Phil Pepe, "Figueroa Makes Pitch for Super-Star Class," *The Sporting News*, June 4, 1977: 12.

22 Phil Elderkin, "Yankees' Figueroa Has Rival Batters Hitting into Ruts," *Christian Science Monitor*, September 29, 1976: 12.

23 "Figueroa Looks to Future, Sees He's Worth $2 Million," *New York Times*, January 1, 1977: 25. "Figueroa Gets 4-Year Pact for an Estimated $500,000," *New York Times*, February 3, 1977: 54.

24 Jeff Pearlman, "Has ESPN Hit a Home Run with *The Bronx Is Burning*?" *TV Guide*, July 9, 2007.

25 "Yanks Hope to End Tough Season," United Press International, October 18, 1977.

26 Kevin Nelson, *Baseball's Even Greater Insults* (New York: Fireside Books, 1993), 178.

27 "Lemon Restores Fresh Figueroa," United Press International, September 17, 1978.

28 Will Grimsley, "Anger Will Be Wearing Pinstripes," Associated Press, October 14, 1978.

29 "A dDefinite Twist of Lemon," Associated Press, September 19, 1978.

30 Grimsley.

31 "Yanks' Figueroa Wants to Leave," United Press International, May 28, 1978.

32 "Figueroa Hampered by Control Problems," Associated Press, October 11, 1978.

33 Grimsley.

34 Phil Pepe, "It's Time to Hail Yanks' Figgy as Biggie," *The Sporting News*, January 6, 1979: 40.

35 Bruce Markusen, "Card Corner — Ed Figueroa," Bronx Banter website (http://bronxbanter.baseballtoaster.com/archives/1091587.html) August 11, 2008.

36 "Texas Rangers Purchase Ed Figueroa from the Yankees," United Press International, July 27, 1980.

37 "Ed Figueroa is Confident, but the Numbers Don't Back Him," Associated Press, June 25, 1981. See also "Figueroa Not Smiling Much at Wichita," United Press International, May 13, 1981.

38 Ibid.

39 Bob Slocum, "Modesto A's Revel in Championship," *Modesto Bee*, June 22, 1982: D-4.

40 Quoted in Samuel Regalado, *Viva Baseball!* (Urbana: University of Illinois Press, 1998), 165.

41 Van Hyning, 107-108.

42 McCarron.

43 "Tom Lasorda Elogia el Juego de Guerrero," *El Nuevo Herald* (Miami, Florida), May 30, 1983: Sports-8.

44 Hal McCoy, "Dibble Strikes Back, Unloads on Old Regime," *Dayton Daily News*, April 1, 1990: 4D.

45 Tom Jones, "The Best and Worst of the Senior League," *St. Petersburg Times*, December 31, 1990: Sports-4.

46 "Figueroa Hurls Gold Coast Past Orlando," *Orlando Sentinel*, November 17, 1989: C6. "Weaver Ejected, Misses 3-1 Victory," *Miami Herald*, November 17, 1989. "Mad Hatter Weaver Gets Tossed Again," *South Florida Sun-Sentinel*, November 17, 1989.

47 Bob Slocum, "Figueroa Starts Over Again tonight," *Modesto Bee*, April 16, 1982: E-1.

48 Carlos Rosa Rosa, "El 'Puerto Rican Yankees Festival'," *El Nuevo Día* (San Juan Puerto Rico), January 13, 2008T

# RUBÉN GÓMEZ

## By Thomas E. Van Hyning

**R**UBÉN GÓMEZ WAS THE SECOND pitcher from Puerto Rico to reach the majors—and the first to start and win a World Series Game. He led the New York Giants to a 6-2 win in Game Three at Cleveland on October 1, 1954. A limber 6 feet even and 170-175 pounds, Gómez was amazingly durable. He pitched in just 10 big-league seasons—but no one is even close to his 29-year career in the Puerto Rican Winter League (PRWL).[1] From 1947 through 1977, he amassed 174 regular-season wins and 27 postseason wins in the PRWL, all but one with the Santurce Cangrejeros (Crabbers). These are marks that will never be broken. All told, "El Divino Loco"—the Divine Crazy—won over 400 games as a pro.[2]

**Rubén Gómez: Career Won-Lost Snapshot**

|  |  | Regular Season | Postseason |
|---|---|---|---|
| Major Leagues | 1953-60; 1962; 1967 | 76-86[3] | 1-0 |
| Puerto Rican Winter League | 1947-1977 | 174-119[4] | 27-10[5] |
| U.S./Canadian minor leagues | 1949-52; 1960-63 | 69-36 | NA |
| Mexico | 1964-67; 1971 | 19-21 | NA |
| Dominican Republic | 1952; 1961; 1964 | 7-3[6] | 6-1[7] |
| Venezuela | 1966 | – | 2-1 |
| Semi-pro (Canada) | 1968-70 | 27-5[8] |  |
| Total |  | 372-270 | 36-12 |

NA: not available. See endnotes for further clarifications.

Despite his World Series win, Gómez's biggest pro baseball thrill came in Havana, Cuba. On February 22, 1953, his game-winning hit lifted Santurce to a Caribbean Series title for Puerto Rico over Cuba. His six career victories in this tournament (a matter of great regional pride) are tied for the most ever with Cuba's Camilo Pascual and Venezuela's José "Carrao" Bracho.

Rubén Gómez Colón was born in the Aguirre community of Arroyo, Puerto Rico, on July 13, 1927. He was the fifth child of Luis Gómez and Dolores Colón (aka Doña Lola). Rubén's siblings were Luis ("Wiso"), Lillian, Rafaelina and Baby. Rubén was influenced by his stepfather, Don José Jacinto Barclay, who was of English descent. Barclay was an educated fellow who ran a few departments within the sugar cane industry of Aguirre, according to his grandson, Rafael Gómez.[9]

The Guayama Brujos (Witches) were Rubén's favorite PRWL team, winning back-to-back titles in the league's initial seasons: 1938-39 and 1939-40. Rubén—who loved to play and watch baseball, and to fish—studied the warm-up tosses of Guayama's Satchel Paige before the Sunday twin-bills in 1939-40. Paige "warmed up using cigarette packets as a home plate, and threw strike after strike over that tiny object," said Rafael Gómez.[10] Rubén's other favorite Brujo hurler was lefty Barney "Brinquito" Brown, who was with Guayama in 1941-42.

Rubén graduated from George Washington High School in Guayama in 1945 after starring in volleyball, track & field, and baseball—mainly as a center fielder. His mentor was coach Cándido Fortier, who first taught the young man the fine art of pitching. Gómez enrolled at the University of Puerto Rico (UPR) on an athletic scholarship. He earned it by his success in the 300-meter run, the 4 x 100 meter relay, the high jump and the pole vault.

UPR played the island's top amateur (AA) baseball teams—Juncos and Humacao. Pepe Seda, the UPR baseball coach, was also the San Juan Senators' GM and a Caribbean scout for the New York Yankees. San Juan and the Santurce Crabbers were after Gómez's services in 1947. Luis "Maquenco" Soler, a Crabbers scout, and Monchile Concepción, their third base coach, loved Rubén's talent. After many visits to the Gómez household, Santurce owner Pedrín Zorrilla convinced Doña Lola to let Rubén sign with his Crabbers. Pedrín became a guide, mentor and father figure to Rubén.

The 1947-48 Santurce Crabbers featured outstanding imports from the Negro Leagues: Willard Brown, Bob Thurman, Earl "Mickey" Taborn, John Ford Smith, and Satchel Paige. They gave advice to the younger Puerto Rican players, and took them under their wings. Gómez was particularly impressed with Willard Brown: "Brown still holds the all-time record of 27 homers in 60 games [set that season]," Gómez reminisced. "It was our era…we had a great time together." Rubén married his first wife, María Teresa Carlo, early in his Santurce career.

Gómez got his nickname of "El Divino Loco" from friends and Santurce teammates for two reasons: his highway speeding habits and crazy (yet safe) driving off the field; and, he could not be intimidated on the mound. His best friend on the club was Luis Raul Cabrera, aka "Cabrerita." Cabrera understood that his mantle as the team's "bread and butter" pitcher and nemesis of arch-rival San Juan would be passed on to Gómez. Cabrera's sidearm deliveries were like those of Kent Tekulve, the reliever who emerged with the Pittsburgh Pirates in the 1970s.

Vic Harris, Santurce's manager in Gómez's first three winter seasons, appreciated his versatility — #22 could start, relieve, play the outfield, pinch-hit or pinch-run. Gómez's first post-season game for Harris was a win at Ponce in Game Three of the 1948-49 semi-finals. Cabrera won Games One and Five as Santurce advanced to the finals against Mayagüez. Gómez hung on for an 8-7 win in Game Two and pitched well in long relief in Game Five. "Those Mayagüez hitters (Wilmer Fields, Johnny Davis, Alonzo Perry, Luke Easter, Artie Wilson) were so good," said Gómez. "I had to pitch with my heart as well as my talent."

Gómez added a screwball to his repertoire of fastballs, curves, sliders and a change-up (drop), after hitting against Barney Brown (by then with Ponce) in 1947-48. Brown's pitches tailed away from the right-handed hitting Gómez. Not only could he handle the bat, Gómez made heads turn with his terrific fielding ability. Island sportswriters called him a 10th player on the field due to his speed covering first on a 3-to-1 play and ability to field bunts. Rafael Bracero, an island sportscaster, marveled at Rubén's ability in both the infield and outfield. "Rubén made basket catches in the outfield look easy," said Bracero. "He was as good a fielder on the mound — or even better — than Greg Maddux."[11]

Gómez finished degree requirements at UPR in the spring of 1949 before playing in the U.S. minor leagues for the first time. Gómez (5-1) and Cabrera (11-1) pitched superbly for the 1949 Bristol (Connecticut) Owls, an unaffiliated team in the Class-B Colonial League. Puerto Rican star Carlos Bernier told them about the opportunity. The Owls bested Waterbury in the semis and Bridgeport in the finals. Rubén pitched four more games with Bristol in 1950, but he didn't get along with the business manager there and asked to be traded. He landed with the St. Jean (Quebec) Braves in the Class-C Provincial League. The Havana Cubans, a Washington Senators farm club which had many prominent Cuban pitchers, drafted Gómez from St. Jean in December 1950. He got into four games for Havana, managed by Adolfo Luque, in 1951. However, he spent most of the 1950 and 1951 seasons with St. Jean, going 14-4 and 13-8. During this time, Rubén became fluent in French.

Gómez averaged 12 wins per PRWL season from 1949-50 through 1954-55, and won the 1951-52 League MVP Award. Frank Thomas, who played with San Juan in 1951-52, said that Gómez was the "league's best pitcher." Santurce dethroned Caguas in 1950-51 to win their first league title and Caribbean Series. They won the former on a walk-off homer by Jose "Pepe" Lucas. Rubén recruited Lucas, a Dominican, to play for Santurce in the late 1940s, during a baseball tournament in Santo Domingo. They became close friends and fishing buddies. Lucas's February 16, 1951 homer became known as the "Pepelucazo"—comparable in island lore to Bobby Thomson's homer off Ralph Branca on October 3, 1951. Gómez won two February 1951 Caribbean Series games, both over Panama's Spur Cola Colonites; he saved one versus the host Magallanes (Venezuela) Navigators. Santurce won the four-team round robin at 5-1, to edge the Havana Reds (with Hoyt Wilhelm) by one game.[12] Gómez earned a spot on the Series All-Star team.

The Yankees had kept their eye on Gómez—their Triple-A club in Kansas City drafted him in December 1951. Casey Stengel, the Yankees' manager, took time off from a February 1952 vacation in the U.S. Virgin Islands to watch Gómez shut out San Juan, 1-0, in Game Two of the 1951-52 finals. That helped assure the pitcher's assignment to Kansas City—but he wasn't happy there. Rubén remembered, "I pitched a win for Kansas City; they didn't use me for a month [even after he'd recovered from a broken little finger on his pitching hand]. So I went to play [summer] ball with Licey in the Dominican Republic and the Yankees suspended me. At the end of that season, I bought out my contract for $3,000 by giving money to another person who gave the cash to them."[13]

Yet despite such infrequent action with Kansas City, Gómez still attracted the attention of the New York Giants. Chick Genovese, the manager of the Giants' Triple-A club in Minneapolis, filed a positive report on the pitcher. But over and above that, Pedrín Zorrilla—a good friend of Giants owner Horace Stoneham—was a Caribbean bird dog for the club.

Gómez's 1952-53 season in the PRWL featured duels with San Juan righty Cot Deal and two lefties—Harvey Haddix and Don Liddle—in City Championship match-ups. Deal reinforced Santurce for the 1953 Caribbean Series, and Liddle became Rubén's teammate with the 1954 New York Giants.[14] One duel on October 21, 1952—ended with a 4-0 shutout by Haddix—was the first pro game by Roberto Clemente, the 18-year-old Santurce outfielder, who played a few innings in left field.

Gómez got permission to travel to away games in his own car, instead of the team bus, due to motor coach car sickness. Billy Hunter, a Santurce teammate in 1952-53, recalled a harrowing experience seated next to Rubén in his sports car going to Mayagüez. Gómez's mountain turns at 90 miles per hour were scary. Even scarier were crosses at the roadside marking the site of fatal accidents. Hunter was relieved upon arriving in Mayagüez. Hunter, 40 years later, noted that Puerto Rico was the only place he played where fans exploded firecrackers during a game.

Pedrín Zorrilla helped Rubén sign a $10,000 contract with the 1953 Giants, plus a $5,000 signing bonus, in Santurce's team office, on February 5, 1953. Gómez then shut out Ponce, 1-0, with an 11-inning gem to open the best-of-five semifinals. The Crabbers swept Ponce, and bested San Juan, four games to two, to win the PRWL title. Santurce, with players from other teams—Cot Deal, Vic Power, José Santiago, Luis Márquez, Joe Montalvo—swept the Caribbean Series, with a key Game Three win over Havana. Cot Deal recalled, "They led us by two runs (5-3). I had been the relief pitcher in the seventh and when Buster Clarkson, our manager, left me in to hit, the Havana fans really let the Puerto Rican fans have it. They let up a bit when I doubled. Márquez followed with a single. Junior Gilliam singled. The Cuban fans were not so vociferous at this point. Pellot [Power] singled, putting the tying and winning runs on second and third. Rubén Gómez, who had run for Willard Brown, was left in to hit. The scorecard had him as a pitcher, which brought the hooters and hecklers back to life. They didn't know what manager Clarkson and those of us from Puerto Rico knew…Gómez singled sharply in the ninth to score the tying and winning runs. Grand Stadium became awfully quiet."[15]

Gómez, who homered in Santurce's opening game win over Chesterfield of Panama, called the game-winning hit versus Cuba the highlight of his pro career: "Nothing can top that one," said Gómez. "It's the only time a [professional] team from Puerto Rico won the Caribbean Series in Cuba."

This momentum continued into spring training in Arizona in 1953. In a game against Cleveland early that camp, Gómez fanned three straight hitters: Larry Doby, Luke Easter, and Harry "Suitcase" Simpson. Gómez remembered, "I called my wife, María Teresa, and told her 'We're in the big leagues! They're going to give me a new number (28) to replace 72.'" Their only child at the time was Rubén, Jr. Rafael was born shortly after the 1954 World Series. Nilka was their third and last child. Rubén's wife preferred to be called Teresa when she introduced herself to the author in 1965.

In August 1953, *The Sporting News* ran a full-page feature about Gómez headlined, "Giants Plucked a Peach in Puerto Rico." It was a streaky year, but he got help from pitching coach Freddie Fitzsimmons, especially with the slider. He won the confidence of manager Leo Durocher, who tended not to be fond of rookies. Cincinnati manager Rogers Hornsby, who'd watched the Caribbean Series, told Durocher that Gómez was the best pitcher he'd seen from the region. Casey Stengel told the Yankees brass that they'd made a mistake.

By season's end, Gómez had gone 13-11, 3.40 with three shutouts. He earned 1953 major-league All-Rookie team honors. Underscoring how strong the PRWL was then, that squad also included ex-Santurce teammates Jim Gilliam and Billy Bruton; San Juan's Ray Jablonski and Harvey Haddix; and Caguas (1953-54) hurler Bob Buhl.

Santurce finished last in 1953-54 when Gómez and Tom Lasorda were the team's best starters. Mickey Owen, 1953-54 Caguas player-manager, struck gold when Gómez replaced Buhl on Caguas's roster for the 1954 Caribbean Series. Gómez won his start against Venezuela to help Caguas win it. Owen, the catcher, said, "He was a pleasure to catch. I think he had 10 strikeouts."

Leo Durocher's 1954 New York Giants won the NL pennant by five games over the Brooklyn Dodgers. Gómez's best season in the majors helped: a 17-9 record and 2.88 ERA, fueled by four shutouts. "I was in a groove most of that season," said Gómez. "I established a friendship with Willie Mays and knew Don Liddle and Monte Irvin from winter ball. I was 13 when Irvin first came to Puerto Rico (with San Juan) so it was a joy being Monte's teammate in New York." Durocher and his team became the talk of the town after sweeping the favored 111-43 Cleveland Indians in four straight Series games.

Game Three of the 1954 World Series had a paid attendance of 71,555, the most fans Rubén ever pitched in front of. *The Sporting News* wrote, "Game 3 started with a distinct Latin-American flavor as far as the starting pitchers were concerned. [Mike] Garcia, the California-Mexican, opened against Gómez, Durocher's Puerto Rican." It was a first for both World Series starters to be of Hispanic descent—Gómez and Garcia had a pre-game chat in Spanish. Garcia asked Rubén how his wife was doing and whether Rubén signed his [1954-55] winter contract.

Tris Speaker threw out the first pitch; Danny Kaye sang the national anthem; Cleveland manager Al López had his photo taken with Speaker (player-manager of the World Series champion 1920 Indians) and Lou Boudreau (player-manager of the 1948 champs). Dusty Rhodes's two-run pinch-hit single gave him a pinch-hit in his third straight Series game, tying Bobby Brown's 1947 record with the Yankees. Gómez allowed two runs on four hits, one a solo homer by Vic Wertz, on a hanging screwball. Hoyt Wilhelm got the last five outs to preserve it. Vernon "Lefty" Gomez, ex-Yankee pitcher with a 6-0

World Series mark, was there, saying, "I rooted for the Giants; a Gómez has never lost a World Series game."16

Rubén received a hero's welcome when his Pan Am flight arrived in San Juan on October 11, 1954. He went to a reception hosted by Doña Felisa Rincón de Gautier, San Juan's mayor. Willie Mays arrived five days later to play for the 1954-55 Crabbers, considered by Don Zimmer—who became their star shortstop after his release from Mayagüez—to be "the best winter league team ever assembled."17 Herman Franks, Leo Durocher's third base coach, wrote the foreword for the history of the Santurce franchise 45 years later. Franks recalled, "The 1954-55 Santurce club with a little more pitching depth could have won it all in the major leagues. Rubén Gómez, Sam Jones and Bill Greason were three terrific starters. Can you imagine the power on that Santurce club with George Crowe, Buster Clarkson, Bob Thurman, Roberto Clemente and Willie Mays? The old Sixto Escobar Stadium had some distant fences, but it wasn't anything for that gang…don't think the new stadiums had or will ever have the feeling of Sixto Escobar Stadium."

Gómez went 13-4 for Santurce in the regular season. He also won the All-Star game; two final series games versus Caguas; and Game One of the Caribbean Series over Cuba's Almendares Blues, 6-2, with 34,000 onlookers at Caracas's University Stadium, on February 10, 1955. Gómez retired Almendares' last 10 hitters and fanned seven in his complete game. Cuban shortstop Willy Miranda said, "Santurce hitters are a threat but the real deal is Rubén Gómez…chico, what a pitcher, that Rubén Gómez!" Santurce won the Caribbean Series for the third time in five years and Crabbers' shortstop Zimmer was voted Series MVP. Gómez had a no-decision in Game Four on February 13 against Cuba, a Santurce win.

From April 13, 1954 through February 13, 1955, Gómez pitched 418 total innings: 230 major-league innings (including the World Series) plus 188 winter ball frames (including the All-Star Game and post-

season). Gómez went 35-13 overall in that span 18-9 for the Giants and 17-4 for Santurce!

That workload may well have taken something out of him, though. Gómez got off to a slow start in 1955, and in June, *The Sporting News* reported that the Giants were considering banning or curtailing his winter-ball play. The article recognized the pitcher's hero status in his homeland, and how he put out all the time, believing that Puerto Rican competition was on a level with the game in the States.

Gómez loved playing year-round and never did stop. He may have paid a price—the rest of his major-league career was sub-par except for a 15-13 record with the 1957 Giants. He disagreed, however, that the lack of vacation had taken a toll. "The more I throw, the better I like it," he said in 1959. He admitted to not liking cool early-season weather up north, but attributed his up-and-down performance to not staying in the rotation on a steady basis.

The best-remembered outing from this time is probably the game in Milwaukee on July 17, 1956, when Joe Adcock of the Braves chased Gómez off the field after getting nicked on the wrist by an inside pitch. Adcock had a history of serious injuries after being hit by pitches, and he also claimed that Gómez had yelled at him on his way to first base. Gómez could be wild, and he was not averse to knocking batters down—as he evidenced with Carl Furillo of Brooklyn in 1953. He insisted in 1958 that he was no headhunter, though (this after a bench-clearing episode with the Pittsburgh Pirates).

Gómez did pitch the first big-league shutout west of St. Louis when he blanked the Los Angeles Dodgers, 8-0, on April 15, 1958. Valmy Thomas—his Santurce catcher for 13 seasons—caught that gem. The U.S. press noted that he found himself in manager Bill Rigney's doghouse with some frequency, though—and he got the stereotyped Latino labels "moody" and "temperamental."

On the plus side, Gómez won his sixth Caribbean Series game (2-1 over Almendares) in February 1959. Orlando Cepeda and Jackie Brandt were Santurce's top hitters that season. On the way to the league championship, however, Mayagüez fans vandalized Gómez's beloved red Corvette after a dispute broke out during a semi-final game.[18] Gómez, an avid race car driver and mechanic, spent many hours at the Caguas Speedway doing practice laps, working with pit crews, etc.[19]

By then, Gómez was a member of the Philadelphia Phillies. He had been traded– along with Valmy Thomas—for Jack Sanford in December 1958. Phillies manager Eddie Sawyer said about Gómez, "With the kind of stuff he has, he ought to win 20 games…maybe the change of scenery will make a big difference." Gómez's big-league career nosedived after the deal, though. He hurt his knee early in the 1959 season and could make only sporadic starts. After mid-July he was sent to the bullpen, and he became just a spot starter in the majors.

Gómez pitched for Luis Olmo—one of his best friends in Puerto Rico—who managed the 1959-60 and 1960-61 Crabbers. He also enjoyed the hospitality of Rafael Leónidas Trujillo—the Dominican dictator—when he pitched in the postseason for the 1960-61 Escogido Lions. That team, managed by Pepe Lucas, had ties to the Trujillo regime. Back in Puerto Rico, Rubén bet Santurce teammate Bob Gibson (1961-62) that Gibson couldn't lift a 1953 Pontiac off the ground. But he lost that bet and gave Gibson a case of beer.

The Phillies sent Rubén down to Buffalo in June 1960, and he pitched part of that season on loan to Baltimore's Triple-A club, Miami. Buffalo sold Gómez to Cleveland's farm club, the Jacksonville Suns, after the 1961 season. "When we bought Gomez, the Buffalo management said he wouldn't win eight games," said Suns owner Bobby Maduro. On the contrary, the veteran went 8-0, 2.28 in the early part of 1962. Cleveland recalled him in June, but later traded him to Minnesota.

Sam McDowell, the Indians' fireballer, was Rubén's Santurce teammate in 1962-63. He recalled that manager Ray Katt—an ex-teammate of Gómez with the 1954 Giants—tore his heel during a team fight with the opposition (Caguas) and lost his (managing) job with the 1963 Cleveland Indians "because Katt was on crutches for six months."

The Twins released Gómez in January 1963, and soon thereafter the Cleveland organization re-signed him. At Jacksonville that year, he taught Mike Cuéllar to throw a screwball. Years before, he had taught the pitch to his fellow Puerto Rican, Luis "Tite" Arroyo, and it became Arroyo's bread and butter. Juan Marichal also added the scroogie to his repertoire with the help of Gómez. Bill James and Rob Neyer ranked Gómez tenth on their list of the best screwballs.

Gómez earned extra cash reinforcing the 1963-64 Licey Tigers—managed by Vern Benson, who was Santurce's skipper in 1961-62—in the post-season. Rubén pitched six-plus innings in a Licey win over Águilas Cibaeñas, a team featuring Felipe Alou, Willie Stargell, and Cookie Rojas.

Gómez then pitched in Mexico for the first time. He was with Monterrey for one game in 1964, which appears to be the only one he pitched that summer, though *The Sporting News* indicated that Jalisco had obtained him. He pitched well for Preston Gómez in Santurce's 1964-65 title season, with a semifinal win over San Juan.

Back in Mexico, Gómez joined Puebla in 1965 (4-2, 2.84 in 16 games). After a good season for

Santurce (7-3, 1.92), Rubén traveled to Venezuela as a postseason reinforcement in 1965-66. First, he was 0-1 in two games with Magallanes; then he joined La Guaira, going 2-0 with a save to help the Sharks become league champions.

Gómez enjoyed his best Mexican season with Veracruz in 1966, when he was 10-4 with a sparkling 1.24 ERA in 16 games (13 starts). Rubén and his son, Rafael, spent summers in Mexico. Rafael recalled that Vinicio Garcia, the Veracruz skipper, was nice and helpful to him and his dad. Gómez—always fit and with a smile—came to the Robinson School in Santurce (1965-66) to pick up Rafael. He (Rubén) played baseball games with the children, and pitched for both teams. One of the students, a girl named Terrie Epstein, idolized Gómez. She remembers his aqua and white Corvette, like the one in the TV show *Route 66*, and a maroon one that looked like something out of the movie *Bonnie and Clyde*. "Wherever Rubén was, people seemed to gravitate toward him," said Terrie.

Earl Weaver became the Crabbers' manager in October 1966. Rubén had 15 quality starts for Weaver before blanking the Arecibo Wolves, 5-0, to open the semis. Tito Stevens, *San Juan Star Sportswriter* (another Robinson School alumnus) noted that Gómez had not walked a batter in his last three regular season games plus this playoff win. Gómez turned the final series against Ponce around with a 7-0 win in Game Three, after Santurce lost the first two. Rubén fanned seven Lions and walked only one. Ponce's Roy White, a switch-hitter, opted to hit right-handed that evening due to Gómez's tantalizing screwball. Santurce, whose line-up included Orlando Cepeda and Tony Perez, won the finals on a three-run homer by Paul Blair in Game Six.[20] Weaver said, "It was just like winning any other championship including the World Series." He complimented the island's baseball fans: "outstanding—similar to those who follow the Yankees or Mets."

The 1967 season featured a last return to the majors with Philadelphia. Phillies manager Gene Mauch had seen him pitch in Puerto Rico and was impressed enough to offer the 39-year-old an invitation to camp as a situational reliever. Mauch said, "You wouldn't believe what great physical condition this man is in. If Chi-Chi Olivo at his age can get people out, then Gomez certainly can." Gómez won a job and got into seven games (without a decision) in April and early May. When the Phillies acquired Dick "Turk" Farrell, however, they returned Gómez to Veracruz.

Wherever else Gómez went, though, playing winter ball for Santurce remained a constant. Rafael Gómez enjoyed arriving at Hiram Bithorn Stadium with his dad by 5 p.m. before a night game and the great view from the Santurce bullpen. He met his dad's teammates and opponents; in 1967-68 they included San Juan's Johnny Bench, the catcher with the rifle arm. Another was Santurce's Reggie Jackson, the loop's top home run hitter (20) in 1970-71. "I was (like) a team mascot," remembered Rafael. "Went (with dad) to the 10th Inning Lounge in Santurce where he and others relaxed."

Frank Robinson succeeded Weaver as Santurce's skipper. Rubén (9-1, 2.05) and Jim Palmer (5-0) were two of his best pitchers for the 1968-69 Crabbers, a 47-22 first-place team that lost in the semis to fourth-place San Juan, managed by Sparky Anderson. Anderson said, "Santurce was loaded. They had the best club with Scott, Gotay, Cardenas, Foy, Hendricks, Blair, Palmer, Pizarro, Gómez. Puerto Rico helped me be around that many big leaguers at that time. All the clubs had at least six or seven big leaguers. We had Tony Taylor, Cardenal, Beauchamp, Kekich, Cuellar, Orlando Peña."

From 1968 through 1970, Gómez pitched summer ball in the Saguenay Senior League of Quebec with the Chicoutimi Bombardiers. He was the star pitcher, 12-0 in 1968 and 9-1 in 1969. Rubén played golf from the late 1960s on (with Luis Olmo) and returned to Quebec as a golf pro. He sold insurance—as did Olmo. Gómez returned to Mexico in 1971, going 1-7, 4.50 for Poza Rica and Sabinas.

Gómez pitched for Santurce through the mid-1970s, making a final Caribbean Series (in relief) appearance in February 1971, against Mexico's Hermosillo Orange Growers, at Bithorn. Maury Wills managed Hermosillo; Frank Robinson led

Santurce; and Manny Mota was Licey's player-manager. Roberto Clemente, San Juan's 1970-71 manager, used Rubén for two innings in the 4-1 win by the local stars over the imports.

Frank Robinson was unable to manage Santurce in 1971-72 and Gómez stepped in to manage the team to a third-place finish—it was the only winter in 30 years in which he did not play a game. He appreciated the fine play of the Crabbers' Don Baylor, league batting champ, and Dusty Baker. Gómez exhorted Rogelio (Roger) Moret—the Guayama native—to have a good season. Moret pitched his heart out, with a 14-1 ledger, five shutouts and 1.81 E.R.A. Ponce ousted Santurce in the semi-finals.

Gómez pitched in relief for the 1972-73 champion Crabbers; Ron Cey played third base. Rubén's final shutout in PRWL play—an 8-0 blanking of San Juan—came on December 20, 1973 at Bithorn Stadium. That night, Gómez's screwballs got the best of a Senators line-up with Chris Chambliss, José Pagán, and Rusty Torres. Mickey Rivers gave Rubén the only run he needed with a leadoff homer in the first. All the 4,135 fans gave #22 a standing ovation. Frank Robinson gave Rubén one start in 1974-75;[21] ditto for Jack McKeon in 1975-76.[22]

Rubén signed a 1976-77 contract with the Bayamón Cowboys (formerly San Juan). Dickie Thon—on Bayamón's practice squad at 18—recalled: "Gómez did not appear too happy at this stage of his career."[23] The 49-year-old closed out his PRWL career with the last eight of his league-record 417 appearances.

Gómez coached the 1980-81 Crabbers, along with Orlando Cepeda and Juan Pizarro. Cookie Rojas managed Santurce to a fifth-place finish. Catcher Gary Allenson recalled team meetings—with the first 45 minutes in Spanish, and the final five minutes an English translation. The 1981-82 Crabbers got off to a 14-6 start, but Rubén resigned after Santurce suffered 10 losses in their next 12 games. Iván de Jesús, Ed Figueroa, and Pat Tabler were on this team. By this time, Gomez was married to his second wife (from the U.S. mainland), and they adopted a Dominican child (Gabriela) with the help of Pepe Lucas, in Santo Domingo.

In the summer of 1985 the author visited a longtime family friend who was very ill. Hu Barton recalled the night he had car problems on a highway in Puerto Rico's mountains. Out of nowhere, an athletic-looking young man—Rubén Gómez—in an expensive sports car came to the rescue. Hu bought a case of beer and they had a few laughs.

Rubén threw out the first pitch to open the 1990-91 PRWL season—"First time in 18 years Santurce won the title," Gómez said, with a smile. He was inducted into the Puerto Rico Professional Baseball Hall of Fame in 1991, as part of its first class. In 1997, he entered the Guayama and Sons of Santurce Halls of Fame. Rafael Gómez gave the plaque to his dad at the latter one. "The committee paid for my trip expenses," he recalled. "Dad was moved by the local people; always had time to teach a child, sign an autograph, share a soda—he belonged to the world." Rubén and Ricky Ledée each received the 1998 Pedrín Zorrilla Award from Pedrín's widow, Diana.

Gómez was hospitalized in 2001 after a battle with cancer. A doctor from Mexico requested permission to attend his operation. When Gómez asked why, the doctor replied, "I was the boy who sold you the winning lottery ticket." While pitching in Veracruz, Rubén had won a $35,000 prize. When he tried to share the winnings with the kid's family, they refused. So Gómez went to a local bank and set up a trust fund for him.

In 2002, Rafael Gómez played catch with his 75-year-old dad one last time. They were in Rafael's home in a Philadelphia suburb, as he recalled. "I bought two new gloves and a ball and jokingly said, 'Is there anything left in your rusty arm? C'mon—let's throw for old times' sake.' My neighbors are watching an old man and his son playing catch—ridiculous for them, *heavenly* for us. As soon as the glove entered Dad's hand, his demeanor changed...and he asked me to hunker down and catch some strikes—what a way to throw consecutive strikes."

Rubén Gómez passed away at San Juan's Oncological Hospital of Centro Medico, on July 26,

2004. He was 77. He was interred at the Guayama Municipal Cemetery.

The Veterans Committee voted Gómez into the Latino Baseball Hall of Fame on February 9, 2011, in a ceremony at Altos de Chavón, Dominican Republic.[24] His Crabbers number, 22, is on permanent display on Hiram Bithorn Stadium's outfield fence along with 21 (Roberto Clemente) and 30 (Orlando Cepeda).

*With thanks to Rafael Gómez, a former classmate of the author's, and to Rory Costello for additional research.*

## SOURCES

*Interviews and correspondence*

E-mails, text messages and phone conversations with Rafael Gómez, January–February 2013.

E-mails to and from Terrie Epstein O'Regan, ex-school classmate in Santurce, January 2013.

Phone conversation with Doug Davis, ex-batting practice pitcher for Santurce, February 7, 2012.

Phone conversations and e-mail correspondence with Ellis "Cot" Deal, 2011 and 2012.

Personal interview with Gary Allenson, Smith Wills Stadium, Jackson, Mississippi, July 1998.

Conversation with Rafael Bracero, WAPA TV Sportscaster, Guaynabo, Puerto Rico, November 18, 1997.

Conversation with Paul Blair, Smith Wills Stadium, Jackson, Mississippi, July 1997.

Personal interview with Sparky Anderson, prior to Detroit spring training game, Lakeland, Florida, March 1993.

Personal interview with Tom Lasorda, before a Los Angeles Dodgers spring training game, Vero Beach, Florida, March 1993.

Conversations/interviews with Rubén Gómez, San Juan, Puerto Rico, January 1992 and 1993.

Personal interview with Frank Robinson, Camden Yards, Baltimore, Maryland, August 19, 1992.

Personal interviews with Víctor Pellot Power and Bob Thurman, Ponce, Puerto Rico (October 20, 1991).

Personal interview with Dickie Thon, Veterans Stadium, Philadelphia, September 15, 1991.

Mail correspondence /phone conversations with Bob Bruce, Mike Clark and Harvey Haddix (January 1992); Billy Hunter and Don Liddle (February 1992), Mickey Owen and Bob Turley (January 1992), Vern Benson and Roger Freed (January 1993), Jack McKeon (February 1993). Mail correspondence with Bill Skowron (February 1992), Sam McDowell (July 1997) and Earl Weaver (July 1997), and Herman Franks—October 1998—October 1999.

*Books*

Though not used as a source for this biography, *El Béisbol* by John Krich (1989) includes a delightful chapter entitled "El Divino Loco," a firsthand account of Krich's travels in Puerto Rico with Gómez.

Jorge Colón Delgado, *La Maquinaria Perfecta*. Colombia, S.A.: Panamericana Formas e Impresos S.A., 2007.

Jorge Colón Delgado, *Pedrín Zorrilla: El Cangrejo Mayor*. Colombia, S.A.: O.P. Graficas, 2011.

Rafael Costas, *Enciclopedia Beisbol Ponce Leones, 1938-1987*. Santo Domingo, Dominican Republic: Editora Corripio, 1989.

Rob Neyer and Bill James, *The Neyer/James Guide to Pitchers: An Historical Compendium of Pitching, Pitchers and Pitchers*. New York: Simon & Schuster, 2004.

Thomas E. Van Hyning, *Puerto Rico's Winter League: A History of Major League Baseball's Launching Pad*. Jefferson, North Carolina: McFarland & Co., 1995.

Thomas E. Van Hyning, *The Santurce Crabbers: Sixty Seasons of Puerto Rican Winter League Baseball*. Jefferson, North Carolina: McFarland & Co., 1999.

Gary Gillette and Pete Palmer (editors), *The ESPN Baseball Encyclopedia*, Fifth Edition, New York: Sterling Publishing Co., Inc., 2008.

Lloyd Johnson and Miles Wolff (editors), *Encyclopedia of Minor League Baseball*, Third Edition, Durham, North Carolina: Baseball America, 2007.

Pedro Treto Cisneros (editor), *Enciclopedia del Béisbol Mexicano*, 11th edition, Mexico City: Revistas Deportivas, S.A. de C.V., 2011.

*Puerto Rico Enciclopedia Manual*, Sixth Edition, Hato Rey, Puerto Rico: Publicaciones Puertorriquenas, Inc., 2007.

*Paloviejo en los Deportes*. Statistical Summary of the 1966-67 Puerto Rico Baseball Season, Camuy, Puerto Rico: Barcelo Marques & Co., October 1967.

*Magazine and newspaper articles*

Antonio R. Concepción Velásquez, "Rubén Gómez." *El Vocero Revista del Sabado* (San Juan, Puerto Rico), January 16, 1999.

Jaime Córdova, "Rubén 'El Divino Loco' Gómez." *Claridad*, October 1-7, 1999.

"Dodgers Arrange Pact with Venezuelan Club," *The Sporting News*, March 7, 1951.

Joe King, "Giants Plucked a Peach in Puerto Rico," *The Sporting News*, August 5, 1953, 3.

Bill Ladson, "Robinson remembers San Juan," MLB.com, April 11, 2003.

"Mr. Rhodes Does It Again, Backing Gómez' 4-Hitter. *The Sporting News*, October 13, 1954.

Allen Lewis, "Phils' Four Starters Best in Baseball, Mauch Boasts," *The Sporting News*, March 4, 1967: 9.

Allen Lewis, "Phils Given Scare over Gomez Deal," *The Sporting News*, December 17, 1958, 17.

Allen Lewis, "Gomez Billed to Boost Phil Spring Sprint," *The Sporting News*, March 18, 1959, 21.

Gabrielle Paese, "Rubén Gómez, Puerto Rico's Legendary Pitcher, dies at 77. *Puerto Rico Herald* (San Juan, Puerto Rico), July 30, 2004.

"Giants May Ban Winter Ball for Pitcher Gomez," *The Sporting News*, June 22, 1955, 21.

"Novatos Estrellas de las Mayores," *El Mundo* (San Juan, Puerto Rico), October 27, 1953.

*The Sporting News*, February 20 and 27, 1952; October 13, 1954; February 23, 1955; February 25, 1959.

*The San Juan Star*, January 30, 1967.

Websites:

Baseball-reference.com

http://www.factualhelp.com/article/1954_Cleveland_Indians_season

http://www.salondelafamadelbeisbollatino.com.

## NOTES

1. Four players are tied with 22: Juan Beníquez, Julio Navarro, Juan Pizarro, and Héctor Valle. Gómez played more PRWL seasons (29) than Roberto Clemente (15) and Orlando Cepeda (13) combined.

2. The Santurce portion only (regular and postseason): 200-128, .610. Puerto Rico totals: 201-129, .609. Known non-Puerto Rico record: 207-153, .575. Overall pro career: 408-282, .591. Note also that Gómez won at least one Puerto Rican all-star game and possibly more.

3. 1,454 innings in 289 games (205 starts), 677 strikeouts, 574 walks, 15 shutouts, 4.09 ERA.

4. 173-118 in 28 seasons with Santurce, 1-1 in one season with Bayamón. 2,486 innings in 417 games (breakdown between starts and relief appearances is not available), 1,390 strikeouts, 756 walks, 32 shutouts, 2.97 ERA.

5. 10-5 in semifinals; 11-3 in finals; 6-2 in seven (7) Caribbean Series. Excludes all-star games.

6. Licey Tigres, 1952 (the Dominican League played in the summer during the first four years of its modern era).

7. Subject to full confirmation. In addition to the 1952 summer playoffs with Licey, Gómez was a playoff reinforcement for Escogido Leones (1961) and Licey (1964).

8. Two seasons are documented, 1968 and 1969. Years ago, the author was told that Gomez won as many semi-pro baseball games in Canada as postseason games in/for Puerto Rico (27). After going back to some work papers, a 6-4 semipro record in 1970 appears to be a solid estimate

9. Arroyo (founded on December 25, 1855) is in southeastern Puerto Rico, east of Guayama. Arroyo means "small creek"—travelers used to stop there to freshen up before continuing their journey. Sugar cane was its major economic driver. Samuel Morse, the telegraph inventor, introduced wired communication to Latin America with the Puerto Rico Telegraph system in the late 1850s. Morse's oldest daughter (Susan) married a Danish merchant (Edward Lind) who worked at and later owned the Sugar Cane Hacienda La Enriqueta in Arroyo. Samuel Morse wintered in Arroyo. His first Caribbean telegraph was transmitted in Arroyo on March 1, 1859. The father of Arroyo native José Cruz—who played many years of winter ball and with the Houston Astros—worked with Mr. Barclay in Arroyo's Sugar cane industry.

10. Guayama, where Gómez is buried, has sentimental value to the Gómez family. Satchel Paige set the league's all-time single-season records of 19 wins and 208 strikeouts—both still standing—with Guayama in 1939-40, when he was league MVP. The 39-17 Witches swept San Juan in the playoff finals. Barney Brown, the 1941-42 League MVP according to league historian Jorge Colón Delgado (other sources list Josh Gibson), had a 16-6 record in 1941-42 for the 29-15 Witches. His catcher was Quincy Trouppe. Gómez saw Santurce's Josh Gibson pulverize the ball (.480, with 13 homers) that winter. Teams were allowed three (3) imports—stateside or Cuban players. That limit increased to five (5) by the late 1940s; six (6) by 1952-53 and 10 in the 1960s and 1970s.

11. Rubén Gómez lived in the Barrio Obrero section of Santurce from the late 1940s through the mid-1950s; on the same street where Rafael Bracero was born. Barrio Obrero was a "hotbed" of rabid Santurce Crabbers followers at that time of high PRWL attendance levels. Bracero, who stood out as a San Juan fan in that part of Santurce, played sandlot ball with Rubén's brother-in-law, Nano.

12. George Scales was Santurce's manager in 1950-51, at a time when MLB teams began sending top prospects and managers to Cuba and Puerto Rico. To name just a few, Hoyt Wilhelm, Bill Virdon, Jackie Brandt played in Cuba. American imports who played in Puerto Rico in the 1950s included Bill Skowron, Lew Burdette, Harvey Haddix, Ray Jablonski, Hank Aaron, Bob Buhl, Sandy Koufax, Elston Howard, Bob Cerv, Don Zimmer, Tom Lasorda, Bill White, Al Worthington, Pete Burnside, Ronnie Samford, Jim Landis, Maury Wills. Harry Craft (1953-54, 1954-55) and Ralph Houk (1956-57) managed San Juan. Santurce later (1966-71) had a formal working agreement with the Baltimore Orioles; Mayagüez with Detroit; San Juan with Pittsburgh (due to the Roberto Clemente connection), and so on.

13. Rubén Gómez was not comfortable with George Selkirk, manager of the 1952 Kansas City Blues. Víctor Pellot, aka Vic Power, and Bill Skowron were two Blues stars who later had fine MLB careers. Pellot/Power told me the Yankees groomed Elston Howard to be their first African-American player and that he (Power) was used as trade bait during an 11-player deal between the Yankees and A's. Skowron mentioned (to me) that Gómez was one of the PRWL's top pitchers during his (Skowron's) 1950-51 season with Ponce.

14 San Juan and Santurce shared Sixto Escobar Stadium from 1939-40 to 1961-62. Their head-to-head games were part of the "City Championship" Series, conceived in 1939-40. Gómez had a 33-14 won-loss record versus San Juan during his first eight PRWL seasons. A lot of money was bet on the outcomes of these contests. Don Liddle recalled that he received $300 in cash shortly after beating Santurce and Rubén in 1952-53. Some gambler made his way on the field and deposited the money in his back uniform pocket before moving on. Bob Turley, San Juan's ace pitcher (1953-54) also had fond memories of pitching duels versus Gómez at Escobar Stadium. Gómez's career totals versus San Juan in the regular season were 51-24, with 17 shutouts.

15 Ellis "Cot" Deal's e-mail of February 12, 2011 included an account of his week-long Caribbean Series experience in Havana, Cuba, February 1953. His brother flew to Puerto Rico from Oklahoma to pick up Cot's two children, so Cot Deal and his wife could travel to Havana. Cot received a 1953 DeSoto sedan from the San Juan franchise and its fans.

16 *The Sporting News*, October 13, 1954. Total paid attendance at the 1954 World Series was 251,507. The winning player's share: $11,118. Losing player's share: $6,713.

17 Don Zimmer was visibly moved when we conversed about the 1954-55 winter season, prior to a Boston—Kansas City spring training game in Florida, March 1992. Zimmer had vivid memories of his Santurce teammate Rubén Gómez, whom he faced in the National League, when Brooklyn played the New York Giants. Zimmer managed the 1967-68 San Juan Senators in Earl Weaver's second season at the Santurce helm. Johnny Bench was San Juan's catcher.

18 According to pitcher Bob Bruce, this 1958 Corvette Classic was torn apart and its tires were cut after Gómez hit Mayagüez outfielder Joe Christopher with a pitch and Orlando Cepeda went to the first base to catch a foul fly and got pelted with oranges. A furious Cepeda threw the ball into the stands and hit a kid in the mouth, who bled profusely. Santurce's Jackie Brandt was ejected. The police barricaded the visiting clubhouse.

19 Rafael Gómez recalled the time Juan Manuel Fangio, the Formula One driver from Argentina, visited the Caguas Speedway in 1958. Fangio had won the 1957 German Grand Prix and was doing promo work in Puerto Rico. Rubén challenged Fangio to a "race" and—according to Rafael—won!

20 Paul Blair's three-run homer came off a spitball thrown by Ponce's John Boozer. Blair told me that he "hit the dry side of that Boozer pitch, and Boozer cheated by throwing it." That ninth-inning homer quieted the Ponce home fans. According to Blair, Santurce was confident they would win Game Six, and did not pack for a Game Seven in Ponce. Santurce players boarded the team bus and it made the rounds through various sections of Santurce to cheering multitudes. I wrote this on February 1, 2013, exactly 46 years after hearing the radio broadcast of this game. Rubén Gómez's screwball is considered the 10th best of all-time per Rob Neyer and Bill James.

21 Frank Robinson enjoyed managing Gómez in Puerto Rico. They became friends even though Gómez had hit him with a pitch during the 1956 NL season. Robinson was a minor-league roommate of Bob Thurman. When Baltimore promoted Earl Weaver from first base coach to manager in the summer of 1968, Robinson met (in Baltimore) with Santurce owner Hiram Cuevas, to express interest in the Santurce managing job. They agreed to a contract during lunch for a $2,000 monthly salary. Doug Davis, who threw some batting practice (BP) for Santurce in the mid-1970s, recalled the time that Santurce coach Pochy Oliver threw BP to Frank. Rubén relieved Pochy. Frank dropped his bat and moved away. Davis said, "Rubén was old—(but) still had a hell of a breaking ball and a two-seam fastball that moved in on you. Guys were looking for a fastball...he could junkball you to death!"

22 McKeon's 1975-76 Crabbers took Caguas to a seventh game in their semi-final series. McKeon loved Puerto Rico and gave the team's younger players a chance to play more. Gómez pitched just four games for McKeon, with six-and-two/thirds innings, and a 2.90 ERA. Jack McKeon was the last Santurce manager in Gómez's 28 years as a Crabbers player.

23 Dickie Thon's grandfather, Freddie Thon, pitched and played the outfield for San Juan in the 1940s, including Gómez's first two years in the PRWL. Freddie managed San Juan to the 1951-52 league title. Dickie won PRWL batting crowns for Bayamón in 1980-81 and 1981-82, when Gómez coached and managed Santurce. Gómez's career managing record with Santurce was 50-49. Dickie hit the Caribbean Series-winning homer for Santurce in February 1993. Frankie Thon, Dickie's brother, is a longtime general manager in the PRWL. Freddie Thon, Jr. was San Juan's batboy in the 1940s, when Monte Irvin and Larry Doby starred for them.

24 Others inducted in 2011 by the Veterans Committee: Héctor López (Panama), Vidal López (Venezuela), Adolfo Luque (Cuba), Horacio Martinez (Dominican Republic), Jose Luis Chile Gómez (Mexico), Oscar Negro Prieto (ex-owner, Caracas Lions). Younger ex-MLB players inducted: Rico Carty (Dominican Republic), Andres Galarraga (Venezuela), Dennis Martinez (Nicaragua), Edgar Martínez (Puerto Rico), Manny Sanguillen (Panama), Luis Tiant (Cuba), and Fernando Valenzuela (Mexico). Cookie Rojas and Pedrín Zorrilla were inducted in 2013.

# JUAN GONZÁLEZ

## By Edwin Fernández

JUAN GONZÁLEZ PLAYED IN THE American League during an era of power hitters like Cal Ripken Jr., Albert Belle, Cecil Fielder, Ken Griffey Jr., Frank Thomas, and Rafael Palmeiro. Among them, Igor, as he was nicknamed in his native Puerto Rico, excelled, with the high point of his 17-year career in 1998, when he was was the Most Valuable Player in the American League.

Juan A. González-Vázquez was born into a working-class family on October 20, 1969, in Arecibo, about 50 miles west of San Juan. His father, Juan González-Claudio, better known as Chon, was a schoolteacher and his mother, Iris Vázquez-Salgado (Doña Lelé), was a housewife. They both grew up in Vega Baja, a town halfway between Arecibo and San Juan. Juan also grew up in Vega Baja. From a young age, he liked baseball, but also played basketball and volleyball and was a fan of wrestling. Dave Winfield and Roberto Clemente were among his idols. Both played right field, the position where González most often played in the big leagues.

González almost became a Yankee. Yankees scout Roberto Rivera attended a game to observe González. Bernie Williams, playing right field, chased after a ball with such energy, threw it in so quickly, and so impressed Rivera that he ended up signing Williams for the Yankees instead of González.[1]

Juan had barely turned 16 and was taller than the other prospects of his time. Big-league scouts had already noticed his power and his strong arm. Several teams were interested, the finalists coming down to Toronto and Texas. Rangers scout Luis Rosa signed González on May 30, 1986. At the time, Puerto Rican players did not have to go through the major-league amateur draft. González signed for $140,000, said to be the most any team had offered a Puerto Rican player.[2]

Asked about his nickname, Igor, González said he always liked wrestling and his favorite wrestler performed under the name Mighty Igor. González started calling himself Igor the Great, and his friends and family began to call him Igor.[3]

As González grew up, drugs and crime rendered Altos de Cuba, the barrio where his family lived, not a desirable place, and so his parents moved when Juan was 12. His parents always instilled moral values in him. He grew up always believing what his parents said: "If you do honest work, you'll live a good life."[4] For Juan, playing baseball was something honest.

The Rangers sent González to their Gulf Coast League (Rookie) team in Sarasota. His teammates included Sammy Sosa, a Dominican slugging prospect. González batted .240, with no home runs and 36 RBIs. Omar Minaya, then the Rangers' scout for Latin America, wrote of González: "Juan has a great physique, who must develop it properly. His two most impressive qualities are the way the ball jumps from his bat and his ability to drive in runs. He must play in a league where he can hit home runs."[5]

In 1987, playing for Gastonia of the Class-A South Atlantic League, González hit his first professional home run. He finished the season with 14 home runs and 74 RBIs. He was chosen for the league all-star team. The following year, 1988, he played with Port Charlotte in the high Class-A Florida State League. On April 20, he injured cartilage in his left knee and was sidelined for about eight weeks. He hit .256, with 8 homers in 77 games.

In 1989, playing for the Tulsa Drillers in the Double-A Texas League, González had a breakout year, connecting for 21 homers and batting .293. Again he was named an all-star. And he was called up to the big leagues.

On September 1, the 19-year-old González debuted with the Rangers. Playing against the Kansas City Royals, he went 0-for-2. On September 4, he collected his first big-league hit, off Minnesota

Twins lefty Shane Rawley. His first homer came on September 18, at the expense of right-hander Scott Bankhead of the Seattle Mariners. He played in 24 games, batting .150 with the one home run and seven RBIs. Speaking of his first month with Texas, he said, "I was very happy. I would not say I was nervous, but I was desperate to prove what I could do on the field. I was very proud of Puerto Rico, the Barrio Altos de Cuba, Vega Baja, as well as my parents and sisters."[6]

The following year, 1990, González started the season with Triple-A Oklahoma City (Pacific Coast League). He had a big year, with 29 homers and 101 RBIs in 128 games. In September, he was recalled to the Rangers, and this time he was in the majors to stay. He played in 25 games and hit four home runs.

González also played in parts of eight seasons in the Professional Baseball League in Puerto Rico. He wore the flannels of the Ponce Lions (1986-1989), Caguas Criollos (1989-1990, 1994-1995), Santurce Crabbers (1992-1994), San Juan Senators (1996-1997), and Carolina Giants (2006-2007). Although his participation was limited in Puerto Rico, there were some important moments. In his first three seasons with Ponce, he played in only 16 games. In 1989-1990 he moved to Caguas, where he played his first full season. In 1991-92 he did not play baseball in Puerto Rico. He returned in 1992-1993, with the Santurce Crabbers, and was voted the Most Valuable Player of the tournament. He played for the Crabbers again in 1993-94.

In 1994-1995, González played with the Caguas Criollos in the regular season, but for the Caribbean Series, the Puerto Rican champion San Juan Senators took him on as a replacement. The Series was held in San Juan and proved to be one of the most memorable in Series history. Because of the 1994 strike in the major leagues, many Puerto Rican players took part, several of them with San Juan, which was dubbed the Puerto Rican Dream Team. The squad was unbeaten in six games and inflicted on their archrivals, the Dominican Republic, one of their most humiliating defeats, 16-0. In that game the starting pitcher for the Dominicans was future Hall of Famer Pedro Martínez. The Puerto Rican squad had, besides González, Roberto Alomar, Bernie Williams, Carlos Delgado, Edgar Martínez, Rubén Sierra, Carmelo Martínez, Carlos Baerga, and Rey Sánchez. This team has been compared to teams like the 1954-55 Santurce Crabbers, who had in their roster Willie Mays, Roberto Clemente, Luis Olmo, Bob Thurman, and Don Zimmer, among others, and with the Mayagüez Indios of 1949, who had players like Luke Easter, Artie Wilson, Wilmer Fields, Carlos Bernier, and Billy Byrd.

González's first full big-league year was 1991. Playing in 142 games, he hit 27 home runs and drove in 102 runs. He likely would have won the Rookie of the Year award, but he'd had too many at-bats in his first two seasons to qualify.

In 1992 González had a big year for the Rangers. He was the American League home-run leader, with 43, drove in 109 runs, and won his first Silver Bat. On June 7 he had a three-homer game. His offense captured the attention of Rangers fans who watched him battle Oakland's Mark McGwire for the home-run crown right to the final day of the season, October 4. The two were tied with 42 home runs. McGwire was homerless, while González went 3-for-4, with a

home run and three RBIs. He became the first Puerto Rican player to win the American League home run title and the second to win it in the major-leagues.[7]

Bobby Valentíne was González's manager in his first years with Texas, but was replaced in midseason 1992 by Toby Harrah, who once referred to González as a troublemaker.[8] Kevin Kennedy took over as manager in 1993 and 1994. Valentíne had helped González fit into the big leagues. Kennedy had worked in Puerto Rico and become acquainted with Latino players.

In 1992 González's first son, Juan Igor (Jay), was born to González and his second wife, Jackie. (He and his first wife, Jackeline Ortiz, were divorced.)

In 1993, the season before González hit free agency, he was earning $525,000. Texas GM Tom Grieve offered him a $14 million, four-year contract. But González sat tight, believing he could get a more lucrative deal.[9] He came through with a season, batting .310 with a league-leading 46 homers and 118 RBIs. His .632 slugging percentage also led the American League. For the first of three times, he was named to the AL All-Star team. He was 0-for-1 in the All-Star Game, but won the Home Run Derby the day before, out-homering Ken Griffey Jr., Cecil Fielder, Dave Justice, and Barry Bonds.

Before the 1994 season, González signed a seven-year, $45 million contract with the Rangers. It became a difficult year. In April he was affected by the death of his half-brother, Juan Alberto. The Rangers began play in the new Ballpark in Arlington, which had a much larger outfield and hurt his home-run production. In 107 games before the player's strike ended the season in August, he batted .275 with 19 homers and 85 RBIs. This was the only year in which he played more than 80 games and did not hit at least 20 home runs. He was injured several times during the season.

In 1994 González married for the third time. His bride was Elaine López, sister of former catcher Javy López and a member of the Puerto Rico volleyball team.

In 1995 González endured pain in his legs and back, until a personal trainer, Ángel Presinal-Doñé, helped ease his ailments. He played in 90 games, 83 of them as the designated hitter, and batted .295 with 27 homers.

González had the first of his two MVP seasons in 1996 and helped lead the Texas Rangers to the postseason for the first time. Despite losing 28 games to injury, he played in 134 games and batted .314 with 47 home runs and 144 RBIs. (Albert Belle led the league with 147 RBIs.) He was again an All-Star. In Puerto Rico, he was declared the Professional Athlete of the Year. In addition, he won his third Silver Slugger Award. In July he was named the American League Player of the Month, when he hit .407 with 15 home runs and 38 RBIs. In the American League Division Series González was 7-for-16 with five homers and nine RBIs, but the Rangers were ousted by the Yankees, three games to one.

In 1996 González married Olga Tañón, a merengue singer, his fourth marriage. Their daughter, Gabriela Marie, was born in 1998. After they were divorced two years later, Gabriela was diagnosed as suffering from Sebastian syndrome, a very rare blood disorder. In addition to Juan Igor and Gabriela, González fathered another son, Igor, from his relationship with Liza Ferrer.

In January of 1997, while playing with San Juan in Puerto Rico winter ball, González suffered a fracture in the ligament of his left thumb. Surgery kept him from joining the Rangers until May 2. Still, he was able to play in 133 games, batting .296 with 42 home runs and 131 RBIs. It was the fourth year that he had hit 40 or more home runs and his fifth with more than 100 RBIs. He was declared the American League player of the month in September (.337, 10 home runs, 26 RBIs). He was also the Player of the Year for the Rangers. The Fort Worth Hispanic Chamber of Commerce named him its Man of the Year and the Texas Rangers nominated him for the Roberto Clemente Award for his humanitarian work.

Fully healthy in 1998, González played in 154 games, 116 of them in right field. He batted .318, with a career-high 50 doubles, 45 homers, and a league-leading 157 RBIs. At the All-Star break González had 101 RBIs; the only other player to achieve this was Hank Greenberg (103 in 1935). González was again an All-Star. On September 19 he hit his 300th home run, setting an AL record for the fewest games it took to accomplish the feat. He won the MVP Award for the second time, the first Latin American player to win it twice. He received his fifth Silver Slugger Award. *The Sporting News*, *Baseball Weekly*, and *USA Today* also named him the MVP, and he was named to the All-Star team of both *The Sporting News* and Associated Press. The Rangers reached the postseason again; this time they were eliminated by the Yankees in three games. González was 1-for-12.

That year González donated $50,000 toward the construction of a children's baseball park in Dallas. (The Rangers matched the contribution.) The ballpark bears his name. He also helped the victims of Hurricane George in Puerto Rico. His $25,000 donation was matched by the Rangers and catcher Iván Rodríguez. Fans and media voted him the winner of the Hank Aaron Award, given to the season's best hitter.

The 1999 seasons was also productive for González. On July 3, in a game against the Seattle Mariners, he tied a record with three sacrifice flies. On September 24, against Oakland, he hit three homers for the third time in his career. As for the All-Star Game, he said that "if the fans did not choose him [in their vote], he was not going to participate."[10] Not selected by fans, he refused to attend the game, which brought on criticism by the press, though several fellow players praised him. The Rangers entered the postseason for the third time but failed again when the Yankees defeated them in three games. González went 2-for-11. He hit a home run in the second game, which was the only run Texas scored in the series.

After the season the Rangers traded González to the Detroit Tigers with two other players for six Tigers. Detroit's new Comerica Park had dimensions not very friendly for batters like González. The Tigers offered González an eight-year contract worth $151.5 million, which would make him the highest-paid player ever. He declined to sign the contract, saying, "That park is too big for my batting style."[11] He added, "It is better to play at ease and be happy than to have all that money. … Money does not assure you of happiness."[12]

González was not happy with the Rangers for trading him, but said he was treated well in Detroit and promised to do his best to try to win. Sammy Sosa, in Arizona, while training with the Chicago Cubs said, "You have to know how to treat Juan. He really is a person of great sensitivity and if you know how to treat him as a person, he is the greatest."[13]

González was hampered by injuries in 2000 and was limited to 115 games. On April 14 he hit Comerica Park's first home run. His year-end numbers were a .289 batting average with 22 home runs and 67 RBIs. (In 2002, the Tigers announced they would shorten the left- and center-field distances at the ballpark. Tigers teammate Robert Fick said, "If this had happened before, Juan González would (still) be in Detroit."[14]

One bright moment for González in 2000 came in an interleague game in Pittsburgh, where he played right field. He said, "To play in right field of Three Rivers Stadium, where the national hero Roberto Clemente played, made me very happy."[15]

After the 2000 season, González was a free agent for the first time. On January 9, 2001, he signed with the Cleveland Indians for one year and $10 million. He had a fine season, batting .325, his second-best career average, hitting 35 homers and driving in 140 runs, the eighth time he had at least 100 RBIs and the seventh time he hit more than 30 home runs. On June 22, with his 380th homer, he passed Orlando Cepeda as the home-run leader among Puerto Rican players. On July 10 he played in his third All-Star Game. (He was named to the team by fan vote.) The Indians lost the Division Series to Seattle in five games. González batted .348 with two homers and five RBIs. He won another Silver Slugger Award and had the highest batting average in the American League (.392) while playing as a designated hitter. He was only 31 years old, and looked to be on the road to Cooperstown.

On January 8, 2002, incoming Rangers general manager John Hart, who had come from Cleveland, signed González for $24 million for two years. Fate played another trick. On April 4 he was injured in

the fourth game of the season, tearing a ligament in his right thumb. He played in only 70 games, batting .282, with 8 home runs, and 35 RBIs. (One of his homers, hit in a game against Anaheim on June 5, was number 400.) González was limited again in 2003, playing in 82 games, but batted .294 with 24 home runs and 70 RBIs.

Injuries continued to plague González. A free agent again after the 2003 season, he signed with the Kansas City Royals for 2004, but played in only 33 games. After the season he signed with the Indians for 2005 but had only one at-bat. At the age of 35, his career was over. He retired with a .295 lifetime batting average, with 434 home runs, 388 doubles, 1,061 runs scored, 1,404 RBIs and a career .561 slugging percentage.

Despite his height of 6-feet-3 inches and a listed weight of 220 pounds, González was an excellent fielder. Over the course of his career he played all three outfield positions. His .983 career fielding percentage compares favorably with other great right fielders such as Hank Aaron, Frank Robinson, and Dave Winfield. His manager in Cleveland, Charlie Manuel, once said, "I've always known that Juan is an excellent player. But the thing that surprised me most about him is his work in the outfield. He covers a lot of ground, has strong hands and a strong and precise arm."[16]

González played in 2006 with the Long Island Ducks of the Atlantic Independent League, batting .323 in 36 games. That year he returned to play in Puerto Rico with the Carolina Giants. He batted .369 in the playoffs as the Giants won the championship. In the Caribbean Series he batted .385 and was selected to the all-star team as a DH.

González's charitable work drew the applause of President George W. Bush, once an owner of the Rangers. Bush said, "I admire in Juan, more than his abilities as a player, the genuine interest he has in helping youth and the less fortunate."[17] González was invited twice to the White House when Bush was president.

In retirement González settled in Puerto Rico and helped coach and finance teams and tournaments in Puerto Rico and Texas. In Puerto Rico, he participated actively with the AA baseball team of Vega Baja. He played briefly with an amateur team in the El Maní neighborhood of Mayagüez.

In 2011, eligible for election to the Hall of Fame for the first time, Gonzalez was named on 5.2 percent of the ballots. In 2012 he failed to reach the requisite 5.0 to remain on the Baseball Writers Association of America ballot. If he is eventually elected, it will have to be by the veterans committee.

In the 2017 World Baseball Classic, González was a coach for the Puerto Rico team.

González was inducted to the Latino Baseball Hall of Fame in 2013 and to the Puerto Rican Sports Hall of Fame in 2012.

## SOURCES

In addition to the sources cited in the Notes, the author also consulted Baseball-Reference.com and Baseball-Almanac.com.

## NOTES

1. Remarks at Williams' 2012 induction into the Latino Baseball Hall of Fame, as noted by the author, a board member of the Hall.
2. 2 Luis Rodríguez Mayoral, *Juan González, Igor de las Américas* (Fort Worth, Texas: Sprint Press, Inc./Jim Hicks, 2003), 15.
3. Evan Grant, *Juan Gone!* (New York: Sports Publishing, Inc., 1999), 8.
4. Grant, 7.
5. Ibid., 14.
6. Rodríguez Mayoral, 22.
7. In 1961, Orlando Cepeda won the National League title.
8. Rodríguez Mayoral, 33.
9. Rodríguez Mayoral, 32.
10. Rodríguez Mayoral, 78-79.
11. Rodríguez Mayoral, 86.
12. Rodríguez Mayoral, 87.
13. Rodríguez Mayoral, 88.
14. Rodríguez Mayoral, 90.
15. Rodríguez Mayoral, 89.
16. Rodríguez Mayoral, 102.
17. Rodríguez Mayoral, 114.

# JOSÉ HERNÁNDEZ

## By Marlene Vogelsang

IN HIS 15 YEARS IN THE MAJORS, JOSÉ Antonio Hernández Figueroa spent time with nine different ballclubs, including two stints with the Chicago Cubs. Born on July 14, 1969, in Rio Piedras, Puerto Rico, Hernández came from a baseball family, counting Luis Figueroa (Pirates, Blue Jays, and Giants) among his cousins, and Orlando Gomez (longtime minor-league manager) as his father-in-law.

In a June 2016 interview, when asked about what team he identifies with, he remarked, "Probably the Cubs, because that was my prime years, I played from '94-'99. But I've got different places I can probably mention. In Milwaukee, I made the All-Star Game, I can mention, probably, the few months I played in Atlanta, just a bunch of good guys on the team. We went all the way to the World Series. All the teams I went to, I enjoyed being on the team. I consider myself a nice guy, and everybody liked me"[1]

Hernández, who batted and threw right-handed, debuted at age 22, on August 9, 1991, with the Texas Rangers. Over his career he had a .252 batting average and hit 168 home runs, driving in 603 runs in his 1,587 games. Although primarily a shortstop, he played every position except pitcher. In 1999 he was a member of the National League champion Atlanta Braves. In 2002 he was a member of the National League All-Star team. His final game was with the Philadelphia Phillies on October 1, 2006.

Hernández attended Maestro Ladi High School, in Vega Alta, Puerto Rico, where he played baseball, basketball, and volleyball. He graduated in 1987. He studied at the Inter-American University, in Bayamon, Puerto Rico.

Scout Luis Rosa signed Hernández for the Texas Rangers as an undrafted free agent on January 13, 1987. He debuted at shortstop in the rookie Gulf Coast League, hitting just .173, and struck out 25 times in 52 at-bats. However, the next year, he played third base and led the Gulf Coast League in fielding percentage (.950). Although his strikeout rate dropped (36 in 162 at-bats), his batting average, .160, declined.

Hernández continued developing in the minors. One of his teammates with the Gastonia Rangers of the Sally League in 1989 was his countryman, Hall of Famer Iván Rodríguez. In 1990, playing shortstop with the Port Charlotte Rangers of the Florida State League, he led the league's shortstops in fielding percentage at .959.

In 1991, after short stints in the Double-A Texas League with the Tulsa Drillers and 14 games in Triple A with the Oklahoma City 89ers, Hernández was promoted to the big-league club on August 9. He hit safely in each of his first four at-bats, but his numbers for his 45 games that season weren't remarkable. In 107 plate appearances, he batted .184 and drove in only four runs, scoring eight times.

The Rangers placed Hernández on waivers and he was claimed on April 3, 1992, by the Cleveland Indians. They placed him with the Double-A Eastern League's Canton-Akron Indians, playing shortstop. He hit .255 with 108 strikeouts. He was called up to Cleveland in September and played in three games. A lackluster Puerto Rican League winter season with the Ponce Lions found him batting just .227.

Hernández started the 1993 season with Canton-Akron, playing 45 games and batting .200. On June 1 the Chicago Cubs acquired him on June 1, sending pitcher Heathcliff Slocumb to the Indians. Hernández spent the rest of the season with Orlando and the Iowa Cubs, and made the Cubs roster in 1994 as a backup for Steve Buechele at third base and Shawon Dunston and Rey Sánchez at shortstop. He showed steady improvement over the next several seasons with Chicago. In 1996 Hernández began to play more regularly, and in 1997 he batted a solid .273 as the Cubs' main bench player.

Hernández still spent his winters in Puerto Rico, playing winter ball. In the 1997-98 winter season, he hit 20 home runs to break Orlando Cepeda's league record for home runs by a Puerto Rican. Hernández played for the Mayaguez Indians that season, and won the league's MVP award. *Baseball America* named him shortstop for the Winter Leagues All-Star Game. In 1998 he played with the Santurce Crabbers in the Caribbean Series, leading the Series in home runs and RBIs. The club finished second, after an error he made in Game Four cost them the Series win. *Baseball America* accorded him another order, naming him Winter League Player of the Year.

In 1998 Hernandez spent time around short and third, as well as in left field and center field. He batted .254 with 23 home runs. He started 1999 as the Cubs' shortstop, and was batting .272 with 15 home runs when on July 31 he was traded, along with pitcher Terry Mulholland, to the Atlanta Braves for pitchers Micah Bowie, Rubén Quevedo, and Joey Nation.

Hernandez was the Braves' main shortstop after the trade. He went 4-for-18 in the playoffs; his two-run single in Game Six of the Championship Series against the New York Mets was a significant contribution to Atlanta's 10-9 victory. His two-run double in the third inning of Game Three of the World Series against the Yankees gave the Braves a 4-1 lead, but Braves pitchers were unable to hold the lead.

After the season Hernández was a free agent and signed a three-year, $10 million deal with the Milwaukee Brewers. He played third and shortstop in 2000, and was

the Brewers' regular shortstop in 2001, when he had career highs in home runs (25) and RBIs (78). He also led the National League with 185 strikeouts.

Hernández had a big 2002 with the Brewers, batting .288 with 24 home runs, 72 runs scored, and 73 RBIs. However, he became the center of controversy when his manager, Jerry Royster, benched him for eight of the last 11 games, when with 188 strikeouts he was one short of matching the record then held by Barry Bonds. (That record was broken by Adam Dunn, who struck out 195 times in 2004.)

The 2003 season found Hernández with Colorado, signed over the winter in a slow free-agent market. Rockies general manager Dan O'Dowd had wanted him from the beginning, but could not afford the contract Hérnandez had just finished with Milwaukee. Other offers were not forthcoming, and Hernández finally accepted the Rockies' offer, which guaranteed him $1 million including a $300,000 signing bonus. He said, "It wasn't an easy decision to sign the contract, but my wife and I say, 'This game is not about money. It's about a chance to play the game every day.'"[2]

It was the first of five consecutive one-year free-agent signings for Hernández.

Hernández played for the Rockies until June 20, when he was traded to his old Chicago Cubs team for Mark Bellhorn. He hit just .188 with the Cubs and a month later was traded to the Pittsburgh Pirates on July 23 in a deal that sent outfielder Kenny

Lofton This deal turned out great for the Cubs, while Hernández struggled in Pittsburgh, too. For the year, he hit .225 with just 13 home runs while striking out 177 times. It was his last season as a starting player.

The Los Angeles Dodgers picked up Hernández as a free agent in 2004, a relative bargain at $875,000, and he enjoyed a good year in a role of utility player. "It's nice to be here," Hernández commented. "I'm not playing every day, but I enjoy watching from the bench because this team is fun to watch. (Manager Jim Tracy) gives everyone a chance to play. … I just thank God I made the right decision to sign here."[3] He hit .289 with 13 home runs and 61 strikeouts in 211 at-bats. Hernández made his third trip to the playoffs but had just one at-bat (a walk) as the Dodgers fell to St. Louis in the Division Series.

A free agent again in 2005, Hernández was picked up by Cleveland Indians and batted .231 in 84 games. Jim Tracy, now managing Pittsburgh, picked him up for the 2006 season. Again Hernández struggled early, but improved by midseason. He was hitting 267 when he was acquired by the Philadelphia Phillies for cash in late August, in part due to a season-ending injury to Philadelphia center fielder Aaron Rowand. That moved up Shane Victorino and called for a veteran presence on a young bench. Assistant GM Rubén Amaro Jr. said "We're pretty pleased at this point to be able to get a guy of this caliber. He's been around a long time and has been through the wars. He's excited and looking forward to being here."[4]

Hernández signed a minor-league contract with the Pirates in 2007, promising him $900,000 if he made the big-league club. He was considered a favorite to be Pittsburgh's utilityman but lost the job to Don Kelly. He did not make the team, and his major-league career was over. The Pirates assigned him to Indianapolis, where he hit .242. He was unconditionally released on March 30, 2008. The well-traveled journeyman played for the Leones de Yucatan in 2008 Mexican League baseball, and hit for a .298 batting average. That same year, 2008, he helped Puerto Rico win the Americas Baseball Cup. In 2009 he appeared in 17 games for Yucatan. He was 39 years old, and it was his last year as a player.

In 2010 Hernández joined the Gulf Coast League Orioles as a coach. He moved to the Delmarva Shorebirds in 2011, the Frederick Keys in 2012, and in 2013 joined the Triple-A Norfolk Tides as third-base coach.

In a 2016 interview he spoke of the challenges of coaching at third base, "just making decisions, I think — when you're supposed to stop the guy, or the situation of the game, sometimes it's tough. …"[5] He said he enjoyed what he was doing with Norfolk: "I'm enjoying what I'm doing every day: just come to the park and see these guys. We are having lots of fun." But he said he would also enjoy coaching at the big-league level.[6]

Hernández and his wife, Melanie (Gomez) Hernández, live in Puerto Rico in the offseason. He is an avid golfer, and enjoys golf as a distraction from the ballpark.

## SOURCES

In addition to the sources cited in the Notes, the author also consulted baseball-almanac.com, baseball-reference.com, mlb.com, and the Giamatti Research Center at the National Baseball Hall of Fame.

## NOTES

1 David Hall, "Tides Report. A Few Words With Third Base Coach José Hernández," *Norfolk Virginian Pilot*, June 18, 2016. pilotonline.com/sports/baseball/norfolk-tides/tides-report-a-few-words-with-third-base-coach-jose/article_5c5e77c0-dddb-566c-a77f-54232887bef.html.

2 Tracy Ringolsby, "Hernandez Is Focused on the Opportunity," *Rocky Mountain News* (Denver), February 13, 2003.

3 Tony Jackson, "Disposition for Position," *Los Angeles Daily News*, June 7, 2004.

4 Ken Mandel, "Phils Acquire Hérnandéz From Bucs," MLB.com, August 22, 2006.

5 David Hall.

6 Ibid.

# ROBERTO HERNÁNDEZ

## By Alan Cohen with Matt Merullo

*"As a reliever, you've got to have amnesia. Not only with the bad days, but with the good days. You may get them out one, two, three today, but you've got to forget about it immediately, because that may not happen tomorrow."*

– Roberto Hernández, 2007[1]

*"(In the 1989 Instructional League), Roberto (Hernandez) and (pitching coach) Rick Peterson worked hard like the rest of the staff always did under 'Pete' but, Roberto really took it a step further than most guys and made himself figure it out.' Obviously, he did, overcoming a life-threatening injury and going on to pitch for 20 years in the bigs. I love Roberto's whole story because it's a great one—from PR to NYC to Storrs and S.C. He did whatever it took—and was great friend and teammate along the way.*

*"To this day, he has always been the guy I tell people about when they ask me 'who was the toughest guy to catch?' Not from that day in the bullpen (when I first caught him in the Instructional League in 1989) but in games at both the minor- and major-league level when his stuff was just beginning to really explode early in his career. His fastball took off in all directions and his split was both hard and late-breaking. He threw heavy, heavy balls that could ruin your thumb if you caught it wrong, he was deceptive but what I respected the most about him was he never made excuses and was accountable."*

—Matt Merullo, October 1, 2016.

**ROBERTO HERNÁNDEZ WAS BORN** in Santurce, Puerto Rico, on November 11, 1964.

When he was 2 years old, his family—parents, two brothers and two sisters—moved to New York City. He grew up a Mets fan and, at age 16, even had a tryout at Shea Stadium. They wouldn't be calling him back until more than 20 years had elapsed. As a catcher, he followed Thurman Munson of the Yankees and cried when he heard the news of Munson's untimely death in a plane crash. Roberto was 14 years old at the time. After three years at Chelsea High School in New York, he received a scholarship to attend New Hampton High School in New Hampshire. Due to poor grades, he had to repeat his junior year, but he worked on his grades as well as his form as a catcher, and completed his secondary studies during the 1983-84 academic year.[2]

After high school, Hernandez went to the University of Connecticut. Although he was a pitcher in his professional career, the talented Hernandez was mostly positioned behind the plate at Connecticut in 1985. During the spring of 1985, Connecticut played a series of games in the Carolinas. Future teammate Matt Merullo remembers their first encounter: "I met Berto when he came to play UNC with the UConn baseball team. He was a freshman like me and was their starting catcher. I was DHing that day and during one at-bat, he started talking to me and I immediately liked him. I paid close attention to him and wondered what UConn was doing with him back there. He looked out of place and was young. He caught fine and had good energy but he was so tall and lanky that it took a while for him to release the ball. But when he did, it was a bazooka. Guys would be safe by a mile then have to get out of the way of a bullet."

Hernandez starred in the first game of the Big East tournament against Georgetown. He slammed a two-run homer early on and in the 10th inning, with the game tied, really showed his mettle. He had been victimized by the Hoya running game, and three stolen bases were taken at this expense. However, in the top of the 10th, he gunned down Georgetown's Glen Bruckner. In the bottom of the inning, he singled and was on board when Mike Pingree homered as UConn won its first game in the tourney, 11-9.[3]

After the 1985 season, Connecticut coach Andy Baylock was able to find Hernandez a place in the Valley League in Virginia. It was in this summer league that he pitched regularly for the first time, striking out 14 batters in his first start. He attracted the interest of college scouts and before long had a scholarship offer from the University of South Carolina at Aiken. Connecticut was not in a position to offer Hernandez significant scholarship money, and after getting approval from the UConn athletic director, Hernandez transferred to Aiken.

In 1986 at Aiken, he pitched regularly and he took a 9-2 record into the NAIA tournament in Lewiston, Idaho. When not pitching, he was the team's designated hitter, and on May 11, 1986, he had three homers as Aiken won the district championship, and homered as his school won the regional playoffs to advance to the NAIA tournament. For the season, he wound up batting .315 with a team-high 18 homers. In the tournament, he extended his pitching record to 10-2 with a four-hit, 9-2 win over St. Francis of Joliet, Illinois, as his team finished in third place. He finished the season with 97 strikeouts in 94 innings pitched.

That season, his path once again crossed with that of Merullo. Merullo remembered, "The next fall (1985) I was jogging in the outfield just before a game against USC-Aiken and their starting pitcher was also jogging prior to his mound warm-up. We got close to each other in shallow center and I recognized him as that catcher from UConn. We had a big smile for each other and I knew he was excited to put the shinguards away and use that cannon on the mound. Being from a scouting background, I knew he had made the right career move. He just looked the part out there and the velocity was obvious without any gun. I really don't recall that game, just meeting him again in the most unlikely place ... but it made sense."

*Baseball America* rated Hernandez as the 19th best player in the country going into the 1986 draft. He was the number-one draft pick (16th overall) of the California Angels in 1986 and was signed by Al Goldis.

Injuries plagued Hernandez during his first two minor-league seasons, and in 1988 he was 9-10 with a 3.17 ERA for Quad Cities in the Class-A Midwest League. He was off to a slow start in 1989 at Midland in the Double-A Texas League. After registering a disappointing 2-7 record at Midland, he was demoted to Palm Springs in the Class-A California League and eventually that season, the Angels lost interest. However, Chicago White Sox general manager Larry Himes had received positive reports on Hernandez. On August 4, the Angels traded him to the White Sox. Hernandez finished the season at South Bend in the Midwest League. The following season, he was back in Double-A, this time with Birmingham in the Southern League.

It was in the Instructional League that Hernandez once again he crossed paths with Merullo.

Matt remembered:

"Now it's the fall of '89, Instructional League in Sarasota. I made my debut with Chicago that April, was sent down when Fisk came back and suffered a broken hand that caused me to miss a lot of playing time. I was set to go to winter ball in the Dominican Republic after tuning up some in Florida. The new GM in Chicago was Larry Himes. He was another former catcher, turned scout then GM and had been with the Angels. He makes a deal for Roberto, who hadn't done much in the minors but was a good 'project.' Roberto shows up in Instructs and just so happens to throw his first bullpen session for 'the brass' with me catching him. I squatted down and caught sinkers and tailing fastballs with about six guys standing behind Roberto watching every move like they were biting into gold to see if it was real. They didn't like what they had sunk their teeth into. There wasn't much on the ball and the delivery was way out of sync.

"Then our pitching coach, Rick Peterson, steps in and asks him to come to a set position on the mound, stare at my catcher's mitt then 'close your eyes and make the pitch.' I called 'Time out! What? You wanna catch him?' The first pitch hissed through the air harder than anything he'd thrown, only it was off the corner of the bullpen fence about six feet to my upper left. I learned a lot that day. It was the first time I ever caught a pitcher with his eyes closed. The first of many. It was like putting a train back on the tracks. Roberto's body was going one way and his arm was making up for it by throwing a strike with no power behind it. I didn't even try to catch the ball but I noticed it had real life on it. It literally took off. The brass behind Peterson scratched their heads in both frustration and amazement as they witnessed a huge velocity jump in a matter of minutes. Peterson got Roberto to feel where his momentum was going and Roberto started making the adjustment to get his body under control and moving in the right direction. He was still a project of sorts but he was on his way. By the next year, he was in Double-A Birmingham and again I was catching him. I had a knee injury in winter ball that forced me back on the depth chart and I found myself playing with two kids named Frank Thomas and Robin Ventura in a league where I was an all-star two years before!"

Hernandez was invited to spring training with the White Sox in 1991, and did well. He was not sent down until the final week of spring training when Chicago decided to go with Brian Drahman as the 10th and final member of the mound staff.[4]

In 1991 Hernandez began the season at Triple-A Vancouver (Pacific Coast League) and posted a 4-1 record in seven starts. As early as spring training, he had felt numbness in his right hand. In June he sought medical help, and a doctor in Vancouver de-

termined that Hernandez had blood clots. Surgery was performed by Dr. James Yao on June 4 to transfer veins from his inner thigh to his right forearm. "I was under the knife for 10½ hours one day and five hours the next. That's the hardest thing I've ever had to do in my life. I had to go back under the next day because it did not take. The vein they took out of my leg and implanted in my arm did not take. It opened up and I was bleeding internally. It felt like I was on fire."[5] Although the doctor in Vancouver told him that he would never pitch again, Dr. Yao was more encouraging, saying that his chances were 50-50. Hernandez's rehabilitation started in late June and bordered on the miraculous. He resumed pitching in July, throwing six innings in a Rookie League game in Sarasota. He then posted a 2-1 record with a 1.99 ERA in four starts at Birmingham. The key to his success was developing a slider in lieu of a curveball that had been described as "big and sloppy" by White Sox minor-league pitching coordinator Dewey Robinson.[6]

Late in the 1991 season Hernandez was summoned to Chicago and made his major-league debut on September 2, starting and pitching seven innings as the White Sox defeated Kansas City, 5-1. That evening the press box was full, as Bo Jackson was returning to action after surgery. Hernandez allowed only one hit and struck out four. He was simply spectacular, retiring the first 16 batters he faced and taking a no-hitter into the seventh inning before it was broken up by Bill Pecota. "At the time, I was kind of ticked. If I was going to give it up, I was going to give it up to George Brett or Danny Tartabull," Hernandez said.[7] Reflecting back on his surgery he said, "The doctors said I couldn't come back, but I have a strong will to compete. I've been through a lot so I take nothing for granted."[8]

His next two starts were not successful. He was knocked out in the second inning on September 7 and the third inning five days later. He spent the balance of the season in the bullpen and had no decisions after his win on September 2. His ERA ballooned to 7.80 by the end of the season.

In the offseason, Hernandez pitched winter ball for Mayaguez, Puerto Rico, which won the Caribbean World Series.

The move to the bullpen was permanent. In early May of 1992, he was sent back to Vancouver. Working exclusively in relief, he went 3-3 with a 2.61 ERA before returning to the White Sox in June. On June 21 against Detroit, Alex Fernandez started for Chicago and was done in by a five-run fourth inning. Hernandez came into the game with his team trailing 5-1, one out, and a runner on first. Hernandez stopped the bleeding and pitched through the eighth inning. By the time he left the game, the White Sox had scored five runs to take a 6-5 lead. In his 4⅔ innings Hernandez struck out seven batters and allowed only one hit as he got his second career win. Opposing manager Sparky Anderson said, "I didn't know that kid, but he's got a great arm." White Sox catcher Ron Karkovice said, "I knew he felt good out there. He was throwing all three pitches (fastball, slider, and forkball) for strikes."[9]

Manager Gene Lamont had a deep bullpen in 1992 and three pitchers, Bobby Thigpen, Scott Radinsky, and Hernandez, each had more than 10 saves. By season's end, however, Hernandez had assumed the role of closer, finishing the last 15 games in which he appeared, saving nine and winning two. Knowing that his role could change day by day, he was philosophical: "It doesn't matter who closes, we just pull for each other. Whatever role they want to use me in is fine with me."[10] From the All-Star break through Labor Day, he was 3-2 and converted five of eight save opportunities, posting a 1.44 ERA in 31⅓ innings. "I'm just having fun out there," Hernandez said. "I'm getting ahead of hitters. Before this year and earlier in the year, I was having trouble throwing strikes and getting ahead of people."[11]

Hernandez finished the season at 7-3 with 12 saves and his ERA of 1.65 was the best on the team. In 38 games from June 21 through the end of the season, his ERA was 1.53, and he struck out 63 batters in 64⅔ innings. The White Sox were in third place down the stretch and were within 6½ games of the lead when Hernandez got his eighth save on September 9. They were unable to get any closer and finished 10 games behind the first-place Oakland A's. Hernandez was selected as the White Sox Rookie of the Year and received the Bill Veeck Newcomer Award from the Chicago Baseball Writers Association.

The next season, the White Sox won their division and advanced to postseason play for the first time in 10 years. Hernandez was a key. Manager Gene Lamont said, "He's unfazed by the big situations. Everybody knew he had the stuff to do it. But you never really know how someone will react when you make him the (closer). Everybody can't do it. You never know how situations will get to a guy. If he fails, how will he do next time? Every time he's failed, he's done fine."[12] For the 1993 season, Hernandez was in 70 games and recorded 38 saves. In the League Championship Series, which Chicago lost in six games to Toronto, Hernandez pitched in four games and was not scored on. He earned the save in Game

Four as the White Sox evened the series, but Chicago lost the final two games and was eliminated.

Over the next four seasons, Hernandez became one of the preeminent closers in the league. But on occasion the road was bumpy. In the strike-shortened 1994 season, he temporarily lost his closer role when he blew consecutive saves on June 15 and 17, and was ineffective in a White Sox loss on June 20. His ERA stood at 7.33. After the three poor outings, Hernandez said, "I have to find where I was prior to this madness. It's like everything that could happen has happened. The thing I have to do is forget about what happened and try to start over."[13] And start over he did. After missing eight games, he returned to action. In his remaining 19 appearances, his ERA was 1.74 as he saved seven games and posted a 3-1 record. For the year, his won-lost record was 4-4, but his ERA, due to the June debacle, skyrocketed to 4.91. He saved 14 games but blew six other opportunities. Twice he was taken off the hook as the White Sox came back to win.

In 1995, although Hernandez registered 32 saves, there were 10 blown saves, four during his second June swoon in as many seasons. To maintain a high strikeout ratio and be effective, he needed to spot his fastball and be effective with his breaking pitches. His 84 strikeouts in 59⅔ innings gave him a career high and all-time White Sox reliever record of 12.7 strikeouts per nine innings pitched. The record stood for 16 years until broken by Sergio Santos in 2011. Hernandez learned not to carry over a poor performance to the next day. "It's hard for me to live with myself (after a blown save). You see your teammates go out there, battle for eight innings, and then I come in in the ninth and blow that game. I've learned to put it behind me for that day, but it doesn't change the fact that I let him down."[14]

In 1996 Hernandez increased his save total to 38, was named to the All-Star team for the first time, and finished sixth in the Cy Young Award voting. After blowing a save on Opening Day, he reeled off 20 consecutive saves (and one win) during 27 appearances where his ERA was 0.59. At the end of this stretch the White Sox had a 41-23 record and were within a half-game of the division-leading Mariners. In his first All-Star Game appearance, he pitched a scoreless eighth inning. But his notoriety from that game had little to do with his pitching. While posing for the team picture before the game, the platform tilted and the next thing anyone knew, Hernandez's forearm had come into contract with the nose of Cal Ripken Jr., the guy with (at the time) 2,239 consecutive games. Ripken's nose was bloody and broken, and "Robbie (Alomar) and Brady (Anderson) offered to get me a bodyguard when I got to Baltimore."[15] Ripken, all bandaged up, was able to start the game and later continue his streak.

On the verge of his becoming a free agent after the 1997 season, the White Sox sold Hernandez to the San Francisco Giants for the stretch drive. At the time of the trade, he was 5-1 with a 2.44 ERA and 161 career saves. After a 1996 season during which he had 38 saves and a 1.91 ERA Rodríguez had seen his salary jump to $4.62 million. But with free agency looming, the White Sox was not sure if they could keep Hernandez in the fold.

When the White Sox traded Hernandez to the Giants, he joined a contender, serving as setup man for closer Rod Beck, as the Giants won the NL West. After six years in the American League, National League audiences got to see his fastball, which was sometimes clocked at more than 100 mph. One of his victims, Todd Hundley of the Mets, said, "This guy was throwing BB's. I don't see anyone throwing harder than this guy."[16]

Down the stretch, when Beck became erratic, Hernandez was pressed into service as the closer. On September 17, he pitched two innings to get the save against Los Angeles as the Giants pulled to within a game of the division-leading Los Angeles Dodgers. Two days later, against San Diego, he preserved the lead as the Giants, who had moved into the division lead the night before, maintained their one-game lead. On September 24 Hernandez gained his fifth win since joining the Giants. He entered the game against Colorado with the score tied 3-3 and pitched the final two innings as the Giants broke the tie and won 4-3, reducing the magic number to two. In his last appearance of the regular season, Hernandez was back in the role of setup man, pitching the eighth inning and turning over the ball to Beck as the Giants clinched the division.

Many of the Giants players had come from other organizations and Hernandez, during the stretch run, remarked, "We are a team of outcasts." Of his role, Hernandez said, "Some situations are better for (Beck), some are better for me. I'm comfortable in the position I'm in. I'm a rover from the sixth inning until the ninth. I don't consider it a sacrifice. I call it being a team player."[17]

In 28 games with San Francisco, Hernandez went 5-2 with four saves (bringing him to 31 for the season), nine holds, and a 2.48 ERA. But in the postseason, he had little success. In Game One he entered the contest with the score tied. There were none out and two runners on base in the ninth inning. After getting two outs, he yielded a walk-off single to Florida's Edgar Renteria. In Game Two he again entered the game in the ninth inning but was unable to record an out as the Marlins fashioned two singles, a walk, and a stolen base into the game-winning run in a 7-6 victory. In the decisive third game, he entered with his team trailing 4-2 in the eighth inning and was charged with two runs as the Giants were eliminated, 6-2.

Hernandez's time with the Giants was short. After the season, he became a free agent and signed with the Tampa Bay Devil Rays, who were new in the American League in 1998. He set a personal high with 43 saves in 1999, blowing only four for the 69-93 Rays, and saved 101 games over three years. In 1999, he was named to the All-Star team for the second time. But despite his efforts, the Rays were years away from success, and it was time for him to move on.

Before the 2001 season there was a three-team trade involving Kansas City, Oakland, and Tampa Bay sent Hernandez to Kansas City. He toiled in Kansas City in 2001 and 2002 and racked up 54 saves, making him the first Latin player to achieve 300 saves. When he recorded number 300 on May 25, 2002, he became the 15th major leaguer to accomplish the feat. The Royals, like the Devil Rays, were not a contender and if Hernandez was to return to the postseason, it would be with another team.

That other team wound up being the Atlanta Braves. Hernandez was once again a free agent after the 2002 season and he signed with the Braves, where he became a setup man. In 2003, he appeared in the postseason for the third time. He pitched a scoreless ninth inning as the Braves lost the opener of the Division Series to the Cubs. After the Braves lost in five games to the Cubs, it was "a bad taste walking off the field, packing up, and knowing there aren't more games."[18]

Over the next three years, Hernandez made this way the Phillies (2004) and the Mets (2005). With the Mets in 2005, reunited with coach Rick Peterson, the then 40-year-old went 8-6 with four saves and an ERA of 2.58 while appearing in a team-leading 67 games. In 2006, after beginning the season with the Pirates and recording his last save, he was traded back to the Mets and returned to the postseason for the fourth time.

By that point, Hernandez was no longer a closer, but embraced his newfound role as set-up man and elder statesman. "I do miss closing, but I've learned to replace the satisfaction I got from that with trying to help get the lead to the closer, and also talking to and helping the young kids in the bullpen," he said.[19]

How much longer would Hernandez pitch? He signed with the Cleveland Indians before the 2007 season, and that spring said, "It's inevitable that I will have to retire some time. I'd love to play until I'm 50. [He was 42 at the time.] I may not make it, but I'm having a hell of a time trying."[20]

In June 2007, when the 42-year-old Hernandez was released by the Indians, his place was secure. He was 11th in career saves with 326 and had appeared in 988 games. Was there anything left in his arm that would propel him to 1,000 career appearances. The Los Angeles Dodgers thought so and signed him on July 6. He pitched in 22 games and became one of 16 pitchers, as of 2016, to have appeared in more than 1,000 games. With the Dodgers, he was 0-2. He pitched for the last time (number 1,010) on September 25 against Colorado. He allowed three hits and a pair of runs, but he struck out his last batter, Troy Tulowitzki. It was the 945th strikeout in Hernandez's career, and gave him a strikeout rate of 7.939 per nine innings.

Hernandez has been married to his wife, Yvonne, since his early days in the minor leagues. They have three children.

During his career and into his retirement, Hernandez was involved in his community in New York and was honored as a "Good Guy in Sports" by *The Sporting News* from 2000 through 2002. In his retirement, he stayed active in a number of projects, including Gloves for Kids and Project Warmth.

Just before retiring, Hernandez spoke of his resolve outside of baseball: "I think that as an athlete and coming up from New York City, and living a life as an inner-city kid, there's a lot of things you want, but you can't have your you can't reach. We try to help as many people as we can, athletically or economically. Like a mentor basically. Like a concerned parent, because I have three kids of my own."[21]

## SOURCES

In addition to the sources included in the Notes, the author used Baseball-Reference.com, the Roberto Hernández player file at the National Baseball Hall of Fame, and the following:

Gay, Nancy. "Artful Reliever Graces Giants," *San Francisco Chronicle*, August 21, 1997: B1.

*Greenville* (South Carolina) *News*.

Interviews:

Andy Baylock—October 10, 2016.

Matt Merullo—October 1, 2016.

## NOTES

1. Jim Ingraham, "Hernandez Getting Better with Age," *Lorain* (Ohio) *Morning Call*, March 15, 2007: C4.
2. Tyler Kepner, "Saving the Best for Next to Last: Roberto Hernández Now Calls the Eighth Inning His Domain," *New York Times*, May 20, 2005: D2.
3. George Smith, *Hartford Courant*, May 18, 1985: C5.
4. "Hernandez Looking to Crack White Sox' Starting Rotation," *Southern Illinoisan* (Carbondale, Illinois), March 8, 1992: 22.
5. Murray Chass, "After Aneurysm Surgery, There's Reason for Hope," *New York Times*, May 24, 1996: B13.
6. Alan Solomon, "Changeover Sure Changed Hernandez," *Chicago Tribune*, September 3, 1991: B9.
7. Solomon, "Hernandez's 1-Hit Debut Is Royal Dazzler," *Chicago Tribune*, September 3, 1991: B1.
8. Joe Mooshil, "Hernandez Pitches Three-Hitter in Debut," *Salina* (Kansas) *Journal*, September 3, 1991: 9.
9. Solomon, "Sox Talk About Winning—and Do It," *Chicago Tribune*, June 22, 1992: B3.
10. Dave Van Dyck, "Chicago White Sox," *The Sporting News*, August 17, 1992: 39.
11. Solomon, "Healthy Arm Hernandez's Idea of Happiness," *Chicago Tribune*, September 4, 1992: B12.
12. Joe Illuzzi, "Chisox Count on Hernandez," *New York Post*, September 3, 1993.
13. Van Dyck, "Chicago White Sox," *The Sporting News*, June 27, 1994: 34.
14. Jerome Holtzman, "Sox's Hernandez Ready to Mix It Up to Straighten Out," *Chicago Tribune*, March 24, 1996.
15. Thomas Boswell, "A Little Break but Still No Bend," *Washington Post*, July 10, 1996: C1.
16. Jonathan Mayo, "Hernandez Is One Giant Pickup," *New York Post*, August 27, 1997.
17. Steve Marantz, "Harmonic Convergence," *The Sporting News*, September 29, 1997: 31-32.
18. Todd Zalecki, "Putting It All in Words: A New Phils' Reliever Can Always Find Pleasure in Talkin' Baseball," *Philadelphia Inquirer*, February 21, 2004: E7.
19. Ingraham.
20. Ibid.
21. Jayson Addcox, "Hernandez Makes Saves, On, Off Field," MLB.com, August 6, 2007.

# WILLIE HERNÁNDEZ

## By Gary Gillette

**IN 1973, JASON MILLER'S ANGST-EN**abled play *That Championship Season* won both a Pulitzer Prize and a Tony Award. The drama, set in Scranton, Pennsylvania, focused on the 25th-anniversary reunion of the players and the coach of a high-school basketball team that won the state championship. Full of booze, brooding, bigotry, bitterness, betrayal, and bruised feelings, neither the now-middle-aged players nor their retired coach can cope with the way their lives have played out since their collective moment of sweet triumph.

A world away from the limelight of the Big Apple, an 18-year-old Puerto Rican ballplayer signed his first professional contract on September 11, 1973, exactly one year after the first preview of *That Championship Season* had been staged by the New York Shakespeare Festival on Broadway.

Miller's masterwork was produced by Joseph Papp, a giant of the American theater. Hernandez's masterwork was produced by Sparky Anderson, a giant of the national pastime.

Willie Hernández, an inexperienced 19-year-old pitcher, made his professional debut in April 1974 with Spartanburg, South Carolina, the Philadelphia Phillies' affiliate in the old Western Carolinas League. When Miller's *Championship Season* closed after 700 performances on Broadway that same month, Hernandez had just begun working on the "screenplay" for his dramatic championship season: The first scene in the first act had the hero lead his Class-A loop in starts (26), complete games (13), innings (190), and strikeouts (179) against only 49 walks. His 11-11 ledger could only partially mask his dominance, which included a 2.75 earned-run average.

The young pitcher's next stop was at Double-A Reading, like Scranton a small, declining industrial city in the interior of the Keystone State, about 100 miles south of Scranton through the hardscrabble anthracite coal belt of eastern Pennsylvania.

Robert Mitchum, Martin Sheen, Stacy Keach, Bruce Dern, and Paul Sorvino starred in the 1982 Cannon Films movie *That Championship Season*, written and directed by Miller. That was the year that Hernandez notched 10 saves for the first time, graduating from the obscurity of middle relief to a top-notch setup pitcher with the Chicago Cubs.

High-school basketball is worlds away from major-league baseball, and snowbound Scranton will never be mistaken for sunny Puerto Rico. Still, gritty Scranton displays more than a passing resemblance to its much larger Rust Belt cousin Detroit, where Hernandez would rise to fame and fortune. And the movie's theme has some resonance with the career of Guillermo Hernandez.

In 1983 Dern won a Silver Bear at the prestigious Berlin International Film Festival for his celluloid performance as Scranton Mayor George Sitkowski. Meanwhile, Hernandez was earning rave reviews for his mound performances with Philadelphia. On July 3, he tied the National League relief record by fanning six consecutive batters; in the final game of the 1983 World Series, he punched out three Baltimore Orioles hitters in a brilliant three-inning hitless relief performance.

Describing Hernandez's award-winning 1984 performance is easy: The left-hander became Detroit's closer and completely stifled opponents while racking up 35 saves in 37 opportunities (including the postseason). The only glitch came on the final weekend of the season after Detroit had clinched, when Hernandez was inserted into a one-run situation with a runner on third simply to get work. A sacrifice fly tied the game and registered a meaningless blown save, ending Hernandez's then-major-league record 32 consecutive saves.

Setting a major-league record normally gets harder over time, but Hernandez's record is far more impressive than that of a later titlist, Eric Gagne, who blitzed his way to 84 straight saves from 2002 to 2004. The majority of Gagne's saves were the piece-of-cake one-inning, no runners-on-base variety; the Dodgers' right-hander recorded more than three outs in only 18 percent of those appearances—only once going as much as two innings. By contrast, Hernandez pitched more than one inning in 66 percent of his save chances, going two or more frames 18 times. He did multi-inning stints in nonsave situations, including a four-inning outing. He also hurled four innings to earn a richly deserved save.

Hernandez's statistics in '84 were truly astounding: 80 games, 68 games finished (both major-league-leading totals), a 9-3 record, 140⅓ innings, 96 hits, only six (!) home runs, 28 non-intentional walks, 112 strikeouts, a 1.92 ERA. His 140⅓ IP turned out be the fourth-highest relief workload of the 1980s.

The All-Star, AL Pitcher of the Month for July, Cy Young Award winner and Most Valuable Player, and Sporting News American League Pitcher of the Year became only the second Detroit hurler to win a Cy Young Award (Denny McLain being the first). He set Tigers records for games finished and appearances by a pitcher while becoming only the second Tigers pitcher to top 30 saves (John Hiller, the first). Appropriately, Hernandez threw the final pitches of the AL East-clinching game, the American League Championship Series-winning game, and the last game of the World Series.

From the first Cy Young Award (1956) to 2009, only nine relief pitchers won the award. There weren't really full-time relief pitchers until after World War II; it is probably certain that the Philadelphia Phillies' Jim Konstanty would have copped the award in 1950 if there were one at the time. So counting Konstanty, only 10 relief pitchers have managed to rise to the heights that Willie Hernández achieved in 1984. Three of them are in the Hall of Fame: Rollie Fingers, Dennis Eckersley, and Bruce Sutter. Detroit's relief ace became only the second bullpen hero to be honored with both the MVP and the Cy Young Awards (the third if you count Konstanty). Hernandez was also the first player from Puerto Rico to win the award and, 25 years later, remained the only Latino hurler to take home that trophy. In a 2005 poll by *La Prensa*, published for Hispanics living in the Detroit-Toledo corridor, Hernandez was voted the fourth best Latin "lanzador relevista" (relief pitcher) of the 20th century.[1]

**Cy Relievers Team Lg Year**
Eric Gagne LA NL 2003
Dennis Eckersley* OAK AL 1992 MVP
Mark Davis SD NL 1989
Steve Bedrosian PHI NL 1987
Willie Hernández* DET AL 1984 MVP
Rollie Fingers* MIL AL 1981 MVP
Bruce Sutter CHN NL 1979
Sparky Lyle* NY AL 1977
Mike Marshall* LA NL 1974
Jim Konstanty* PHI NL 1950 MVP (pre-Cy Young)
* won pennant (pre-1969) or division (1969-2009)

Of the nine Cy Young firemen, Hernandez's career most closely resembles that of Konstanty, an undistinguished reliever for the Phillies in the late 1940s before a good season in relief in 1949. Then, in 1950, the Whiz Kid Phillies streaked to a surprise National League pennant with Konstanty having his career year as closer. The right-hander earned his first and only All-Star nod on the way to becoming the first relief ace to win the MVP. Afterward, however, Konstanty slumped and had only two good seasons in relief in his remaining six years in the majors. Hernandez, likewise, made his first All-Star team in 1984. He pitched for another five seasons, turning in one very good year and a second good one before retiring.

While Hernandez experienced a peak that few other pitchers ever achieve, he was not the dominant reliever of the era. Looking at the top 10 relievers in terms of saves from 1984 to 1986, Detroit's closer ranks only fifth—and this is counting only Hernandez's peak years. Hernandez does, however, top the list in terms of how well he shut down enemy batsmen, holding hitters to an extremely low OPS+ (slugging average plus on-base average adjusted for league and park) of 61 (39 percent below league average).

| Pitcher | SV | G | GF | W-L | IP | H | BB | SO | ERA | OPS+ | Ages |
|---|---|---|---|---|---|---|---|---|---|---|---|
| Dave Righetti | 106 | 212 | 181 | 25-21 | 310 | 263 | 117 | 265 | 2.53 | 68 | 25-27 |
| Jeff Reardon | 99 | 193 | 156 | 16-24 | 263.2 | 221 | 89 | 213 | 3.35 | 84 | 28-30 |
| Lee Smith | 97 | 200 | 175 | 25-20 | 289 | 254 | 109 | 291 | 3.27 | 83 | 26-28 |
| Dan Quisenberry | 93 | 218 | 197 | 17-19 | 339.2 | 355 | 52 | 131 | 2.57 | 79 | 31-33 |
| Willie Hernandez | 87 | 218 | 185 | 25-20 | 335.2 | 265 | 71 | 265 | 2.60 | 61 | 29-31 |
| Rich Gossage | 72 | 157 | 127 | 20-16 | 246 | 208 | 73 | 199 | 2.96 | 76 | 32-34 |
| Bruce Sutter | 71 | 145 | 124 | 14-14 | 229.2 | 217 | 61 | 145 | 2.90 | 97 | 31-33 |
| Jesse Orosco | 69 | 172 | 131 | 26-18 | 247 | 188 | 103 | 215 | 2.55 | 73 | 27-29 |
| Donnie Moore | 68 | 161 | 128 | 16-18 | 240 | 214 | 61 | 172 | 2.51 | 72 | 30-32 |
| Dave Smith | 65 | 171 | 121 | 18-16 | 212.2 | 168 | 59 | 131 | 2.37 | 70 | 29-31 |

*The Sporting News* columnist Peter Gammons wrote that the Tigers' biggest worries heading into the 1984 season were third base and relief pitching. As predicted, the hot corner proved problematic for Detroit all summer, but worrying about late-inning relief soon evaporated. In midseason *Detroit News* scribe Jerry Green, who had covered his first major-league game a quarter-century earlier, in 1959, was surprised when voluble Tigers manager Sparky Anderson—"looking for headlines"—started talking up Hernandez as an MVP candidate.[2] (Relief pitching was then viewed as much less important; try finding the handful of entries for saves records in the 464 pages of lists in the *1995 Official Baseball Record Book*. Another example is the 1990 book *Baseball's Dream Teams*, which had no relief pitchers picked for the its all-decade teams through the 1980s—nor were any given honorable mention.)

In his over-the-top fashion, Anderson summarized the 1984 season after Detroit had won its world championship. Legend has it that he said, "First, I thanked God. Then I thanked Hernandez. ..." Anderson said, "If Hernandez isn't the Most Valuable Player in the American League, there is no justice."[3]

In high school Hernandez starred while playing first base and the outfield, but he didn't try pitching until the summer of 1973—a departure from the typical developmental pattern of major-league pitchers, who very often star as both hitters and pitchers in high school. He graduated from Martin Hernandez High School in Aguada in 1973, signing his first professional contract with the Phillies shortly thereafter on September 11.

Despite his youth and lack of experience, Hernandez that summer made the Puerto Rican national team, which won a silver medal in the Intercontinental Cup and both silver and bronze medals in the Baseball World Cup (two separate competitions).

The promising amateur was scouted and signed for a $25,000 bonus by Phillies scout Rubén Amaro Sr. in Amaro's first year as a scout. Hernandez spent three full seasons in the minors as a starting pitcher, progressing quickly to Triple A in the middle of his second season. In 1976, however, he posted a 4.53 ERA in Oklahoma City, after which Philadelphia left the 22-year-old off its 40-player winter roster. Wisely, the Cubs snatched the unprotected youngster in the 1976 Rule 5 draft.

With Chicago, Hernandez made his big-league debut in the second game of 1977, on April 9, pitching 2⅓ innings in relief and surrendering one hit. The rookie went 8-7 with a 3.03 ERA in 110 innings as future Hall of Famer Bruce Sutter completed his first full season as the Cubs' closer. Hernandez's sophomore campaign in 1978 was solid (8-2, 3.77, 59⅔ innings), but he suffered a rocky third year in the bigs (4-4, 5.01, 79 IP) in 1979. Things got worse in 1980 (1-9, 4.40, 108⅓ IP), causing a trip to Triple A in 1981, with Hernandez both starting and relieving before being recalled in August after the midseason strike.

The left-hander rebounded in 1982, going 4-6 with a 3.00 ERA in 75 innings over 75 games.

On May 22, 1983, the Phillies reacquired Hernandez, sending veteran starter Dick Ruthven and pitching prospect Bill Johnson to Chicago.

Hernandez got the win when the Phillies clinched their 1983 National League East title on September 28 against the Cubs. *The New Phillies Encyclopedia* said that "the Phillies could never have clinched without him."4 The budding star didn't see action in the NLCS, but appeared three times for the losing Phillies in the five World Series games, facing 14 hitters and allowing only two to reach, via a walk and hit batsman. In Game Five the unheralded reliever served notice that he had come of age, pitching three perfect frames (sixth through eighth). However, Philadelphia failed to take advantage of the opportunity to stage a comeback as Baltimore prevailed, 5-0.

In the American League, Detroit's brain trust was watching and planning for 1984. The league in the mid-1980s was full of dangerous left-handed batters; six of the 10 leading hitters in slugging and OPS in '84 were lefties. The Tigers concluded after their 1983 second-place finish that they couldn't win without adding a top-notch southpaw to their staff. (Closer Aurelio López had completely smothered righty hitters in '83, but lefties posted a .786 OPS against him.) Hernandez filled that need; his ascent to stardom was enhanced by Sparky Anderson's need to shut down enemy lefties.

While the trade that brought Hernandez to Detroit at the end of spring training in 1984 is famous among Tigers fans, it is not really an issue among Phillies partisans—not rating as one of the franchise's worst deals as enumerated in *The New Phillies Encyclopedia* in 1993. Partly that is because the deal didn't go as Philly had planned. John Wockenfuss had a decent year primarily as a backup first baseman and catcher in the City of Brotherly Love in 1984, hitting .289 with an .807 OPS in 86 games. Fading quickly at 36, Wockenfuss was released in mid-August of 1985 while hitting a "buck-62" (in the parlance of the day).

Outfielder Glenn Wilson, whose "power potential" was the key for Philadelphia, played four seasons

there in the prime of his career (ages 25-28). Wilson flopped badly in 1984, recovering in 1985 to drive in 102 runs and make the All-Star team for the only time. But his RBI production tailed off to 84 in 1986, and sank to 54 in 1987, ending his career at Broad and Pattison Streets in South Philly. Wilson hit only 49 homers in 2,102 at-bats for the Phillies.

Legendary Hall of Famer Christy Mathewson wrote in 1912, "There are two ways of fooling a batter. One is literally to 'mix 'em up,' and the other is to keep feeding him the same sort of a ball, but to induce him to believe that a curve is coming."5 In 1984, Willie Hernández did both to perfection.

Like many pitchers, Hernandez learned key elements of his craft from aging veteran moundsmen. Early on, his repertoire was pretty standard: fastball, curveball, slider, change. Because he didn't throw exceptionally hard, and because his changeup wasn't that good, he had a lot of trouble with right-handed power hitters.

Former Cy Young winner Mike Cuellar taught Hernandez the screwball as an alternative offspeed offering when the two Latino lefties played in the Puerto Rican winter league in 1983. Though the new pitch gave Hernandez another arrow in his quiver, he didn't rely on it until he was with Philadelphia, where Latino catcher Bo Diaz kept calling for it. (While the screwball hadn't yet faded from pitchers' repertoires in the mid-1980s, Latino pitchers threw it much more frequently, so Diaz had experience catching it.)

While Hernandez's famous screwball was crucial to his dominance in 1984, the pitch that elevated him from a good pitcher to an MVP was the cut fastball, with which he pounded right-handed hitters inside. Surprisingly, Hernandez didn't start depending on either pitch until 1983.

Hernandez learned how to throw the cutter—which, unlike the screwball, was becoming much more popular in the 1980s—with Chicago in the spring of 1983 from another Cy Young winner, veteran Ferguson Jenkins, at the end of his Hall of Fame career. By throwing what looked like a standard fastball on the inside part of the plate, Hernandez suckered righty hitters into swinging at something they thought would be right in their wheelhouse. But breaking the cutter in on their hands, Hernandez induced weak popups or grounders. He was also pushing righties off the plate, setting them up for a down-and-away screwball that they couldn't handle. "All of a sudden, I could pitch inside," said Hernandez when interviewed by *Sports Illustrated* in 1984.[6]

Like many other top relievers with devastating out pitches, Hernandez used his scroogie mostly when ahead of the batter since it would often break out of the strike zone. His fastball was average in velocity, though his delivery had enough deception for his heater to earn the time-honored "sneaky fast" label. Hernandez's Number 3 pitch, a decent curveball, was employed primarily against left-handed hitters.

Hernandez was neither preordained as Detroit's closer nor immediately handed that coveted job after his first few performances with the Tigers. In April 1984, Aurelio López appeared in nine games, saving two and finishing four. In May he was called upon 11 times, finishing all 11 games while saving five. During those two months, Hernandez appeared in 22 games, finishing 18 and recording the same number of saves as López.

In his first appearance of the year, on April 3, López pitched a scoreless eighth inning before Hernandez followed up with a scoreless ninth. But that was with Detroit holding an 8-1 lead, so it really was just a tune-up for both relievers. In López's second appearance, he pitched four innings of one-run ball against Chicago in relief of starter Dave Rozema, fanning four and picking up the win. Hernandez again followed López, pitching a scoreless ninth in a nonsave situation. López's third outing didn't go so well after he replaced staff ace Jack Morris in the eighth with an 8-2 lead, allowing two runs. Hernandez followed with a scoreless ninth in another nonsave situation.

The next time López didn't finish a game, he entered the fray with Detroit holding a 4-0 lead over Chicago and pitched a scoreless eighth. The Tigers scored five runs in the bottom of the frame and with a 9-0 lead, Anderson asked Hernandez to finish. On April 27, López pitched 4⅔ scoreless innings, entering with one out in the 10th to bail Hernandez out of a jam. Detroit finally fell to Cleveland in the 19th.

May was similar. At the beginning of June, here's how the "competition" between Detroit's dynamic duo stood. Try to tell them apart without a scorecard:

| Category | Pitcher 1 | Pitcher 2 |
|---|---|---|
| Games | 22 | 20 |
| Games Finished | 18 | 15 |
| Wins | 2 | 4 |
| Losses | 0 | 0 |
| Saves | 7 | 7 |
| Innings | 41 | 41⅔ |
| Strikeouts | 34 | 31 |
| ERA | 2.63 | 1.73 |
| Opponents' BA | .221 | .177 |
| Opponents' OPS | .571 | .552 |

Pitcher Number 1: with the slightly inferior statistics overall. Pitcher Number 2 (López) had one blown save (Hernandez had none), but López had two more wins, a lower ERA, and lower opponents' batting stats. Over the whole of 1984, 71.5 percent of

López's saves qualified as either "tough" or "long"; for Hernandez, it was 62.5 percent.

Hernandez didn't take the team lead in saves for good until June 8. Detroit's meteoric 35-5 start meant the Tigers were bludgeoning their hapless opposition with such regularity that save opportunities were hard to come by. Yet the fact remains that López was Detroit's closer until mid-May and then became co-closer until a week into June. Only then did the veteran Mexican fireballer become the setup pitcher for the Puerto Rican sniper who would win the Cy Young and MVP. In April 2009, Hernandez acknowledged what most fans and writers had forgotten, telling Steve Kornacki of Booth Newspapers, "I shared closing with Aurelio López, who was a great closer, too. But … I was real consistent and Sparky named me the stopper. … Nobody wanted to face me."[7]

Even though the Tigers couldn't be blamed for Hernandez's treatment in the National League—where he bridled at being stuck principally behind Sutter and Lee Smith in Chicago and Al Holland in Philly—Hernandez's pride and ambition were already simmering before the '84 season finished. "If Detroit can't give me the money I want, they might as well trade me to a team that will. Heck, if I'm the MVP, I may be able to ask for the world," he told *Sports Illustrated* writer Jaime Diaz. "I'm hungry to make some money."[8] Detroit gave Hernandez a generous contract extension after hard negotiations, though the pitcher's public comments probably contributed to the future fan backlash.

The problem with Hernandez's post-1984 career—trite as it seems—was that it was no longer 1984. The reigning MVP had an excellent year in 1985, but to many fans it seemed pallid by comparison to 1984. Anyone who ever bit their fingernails to the nubs with Todd Jones on the mound in the ninth inning for the Tigers in the 2000s would wish Hernandez could time-travel. But without the benefit of hindsight, 8-10 with 31 saves in 40 chances ain't 9-3 and 32 out of 33, and Hernandez's stock in Motown began to fall. The failure of Detroit to repeat in '85 was largely blamed on its bullpen, with Hernandez and López the key targets.

In 1986 Hernandez went 8-7 with 24 saves in 30 chances; tellingly, however, he was nicked for almost a hit per inning, with enemy hitters batting .251 off him as opposed to .201 in 1984-85. Making things worse was the lusty booing the erstwhile hero was getting at Tiger Stadium. By November 1986, Anderson was talking about a "bullpen by committee."[9]

Hernandez lost his monopoly on the closer's job in 1987 due to two stints on the DL in April and May. Anderson auditioned younger hurlers Mike Henneman and Eric King in the role. Hernandez blew five saves in 13 chances that year, allowing more hits than innings pitched for the first time since 1981. After the aging Detroit club squeaked past Toronto to win the AL East, Anderson called on the veteran lefty only once in the five-game American League Championship Series. In Game One Hernandez entered in the eighth with the bases loaded and the game tied. The formerly invincible fireman was treated rudely by the Twins, allowing two hits and three inherited runs while retiring no one—getting credit for one-third of an inning pitched only because a fourth runner was thrown out at the plate. Though Sparky rang the bullpen six times in the last three games as Detroit was upset by Minnesota, he never called for Hernandez.

Perhaps smarting over his reduced role, and definitely reminiscent of the Bobby/Roberto Clemente episode a couple of decades earlier, the proud Hernandez demanded early in 1988 to be addressed henceforth as Guillermo, his birth name, rather than its anglicized diminutive Willie. Though completely unnecessary, even that reasonable request generated controversy. Adding to the unhappiness with Hernandez was his dumping a bucket of ice water on popular *Detroit Free Press* columnist Mitch Albom in spring training that year. After the incident, Hernandez stopped talking to the media until midseason. Initially a big deal, the dousing became the subject of humorous TV commercials run by the newspaper and later made its list of fun facts for its 178th birthday in 2009.[10]

In a way, the end in Detroit for Hernandez was fitting, given that his arrival coincided with what was expected to be a dynasty. The former MVP rebounded somewhat, allowing only 50 hits in 67⅔ innings while blowing seven saves in 17 opportunities in 1988. But the hero of 1984 also threw the last pitch in a game that effectively crushed the Tigers' hopes for one last hurrah before the aging club completely fell apart. Though Detroit ultimately finished only one game back of Boston in the AL East, the closeness was really due to the Red Sox' 4-9 tailspin in the final two weeks, plus the Tigers winning their last three games after being eliminated while Boston dropped its last three.

At 7:38 P.M. on September 11, 1988, the Yankees' Claudell Washington clouted a homer to right-center off Hernandez in the bottom of the 18th inning to give New York a 5-4 win in a six-hour contest that broke the Bengals' backs. Hernandez had already pitched two full innings in relief of closer Mike Henneman, who had hurled seven innings after relieving starter Doyle Alexander.

Detroit had taken the lead with a run in the top of the 18th. After walking Rickey Henderson to begin the final frame, Hernandez was victimized by Washington, who said, "I knew it was gone when I hit it."[11] The heartbreaking loss was the 10th in 11 games and dropped Detroit into a second-place tie, 3½ games behind eventual division winner Boston. "It could break (the Tigers') backs," said Henderson about New York's four-game sweep of Detroit.[12] After 1988 the Mayo Smith Society wrote, "Tiger fans have a love/hate relationship with Hernandez, who probably receives more abuse from the boo-birds than any other player on the team."[13]

The final unhappy season played out as Detroit collapsed to 103 losses in 1989, punctuated by Hernandez's making two trips to the disabled list with left-elbow tendinitis, although he managed to log 15 saves in 17 opportunities in only 32 appearances. Hernandez pitched his last game in the majors on August 18, coughing up a two-run homer to the Yankees at Tiger Stadium while in a nonsave situation. The proud warrior was absent from combat for the rest of the year.

After being released by the Tigers on December 22, 1989, Hernandez made several attempts to stage a comeback. The first was with Oakland in the spring of 1990; it lasted all of two days before Hernandez voluntarily left camp because of a sore arm. Athletics manager Tony La Russa complimented Hernandez, saying, "That took guts. He walked away from guaranteed money."[14]

The second attempt came with Philadelphia, which invited the former Phillies hurler to the club's spring camp in 1991 as a nonroster player. After failing to make the cut with Philadelphia, Hernandez appeared in eight games with Triple-A Syracuse in the Blue Jays' organization. Four years later, a 40-year-old Hernandez tried out for a Yankees' replacement team in the bitter spring of 1995. Saying he'd do whatever he could to make a comeback, the veteran with the serious hardware on his trophy shelf at home took

the practice field with a bunch of fringe ex-major leaguers and a gaggle of nobodies.

New York manager Buck Showalter expressed the prevailing attitude that spring, saying, "We wanted to know why" when he heard that Hernandez was interested in trying out.[15] The retired pitcher had been seduced by Luis Arroyo, a Yankees scout, former star relief pitcher, and fellow Puerto Rican, who had contacted Hernandez about making a comeback. Showing again his defiant streak, Hernandez said when he reported, "Nobody is going to take my chance away. If I want to play baseball again, nobody is going to stop me."[16] Hernandez even went to Triple-A Columbus in the Yankees' system after the strike was settled. But the magic of 1984 was nothing but a memory, as International League hitters pounded the former Cy Young Award winner in his 22 games in relief before Hernandez hung up his spikes for the final time.

After giving up the game he loved, Hernandez involved himself in several business ventures as well as coaching youth and semipro baseball. He also participated in the Tigers' 2009 fantasy camp in Lakeland, Florida. He raised cattle on a ranch in Santo Domingo, Dominican Republic. But the ex-pitcher suffered from various ailments, including asthma, diabetes, and several strokes. He underwent heart surgery in 2009.

In September 2009, the Westport Country Playhouse in the tony Connecticut suburbs of New York City staged a revival of Miller's play. Later that month, Guillermo Hernandez signed autographs and posed for photos with hundreds of fans on the concourse at Comerica Park in Detroit when the Tigers celebrated the 25th anniversary of their 1984 championship season. According to Guillermo Jr., his father had been "driving me crazy" because "[h]e was so excited to come back to Detroit again and see everyone."[17]

Many aging ex-ballplayers make a point of not going to or watching ballgames to express their bitterness with or disappointment in the way they were treated or in the way the game has changed. Not Hernandez, who followed the Tigers closely and returned stateside periodically, mostly to appear at Tigers, Phillies, or Cubs events.

"Even when they have a bad ballclub, I follow them, because they gave me good memories," Hernandez said in 2009. "I played for three different teams, but I want to be known as a Tiger, and I will always be a Tiger."[18]

Unlike Jason Miller's five fictional angry men, there was not a trace of anger or angst in Hernandez when he reflected upon his championship season—nor should there be.

Guillermo Hernandez Villanueva was born on November 14, 1954, in Aguada, Puerto Rico. Aguada, a small city on the northwest coast of the island about 90 miles west of San Juan, is one of the earliest settlements in Puerto Rico, dating its founding to 1508/10. It is sometimes called La Ciudad Del Descubrimiento (City of Discovery), referring to the widely held belief that Christopher Columbus landed at Aguada in 1493 when he "discovered" Puerto Rico. During the Colonial era, the busy port of Aguada was a stopover for ships of the Spanish Empire sailing between Spain and South America.

The son of Dionicio, who worked in a large local sugar cane *centrale* (factory), and Dominga, a domestic, Hernandez was the second youngest child in a large, poor family with eight siblings. (Sugar cane was the primary cash crop of Puerto Rico in the first half of the twentieth century before the island commonwealth began to convert its economy from agriculture to manufacturing.) His parents encouraged their children to be active in athletics—and they were rewarded when their son reached the pinnacle of success in the majors.

Hernandez married the former Carmen Rivera in 1978. They had two children together, but later divorced. Guillermo Hernandez had five children and one grandson.

## SOURCES

In addition to the sources cited in the Notes, the author also consulted the following sources:

Publications

# PUERTO RICO AND BASEBALL: 60 BIOGRAPHIES

Anderson, Sparky, with Dan Ewald. *Bless You Boys: Diary of the Detroit Tigers' 1984 Season*. (Chicago: Contemporary Books, Inc., 1984).

Balzer, Howard M. *Official 1979 Baseball Register* (St. Louis: The Sporting News Publishing Company, 1979).

Campbell, Dave, Denny Matthews, Brooks Robinson, and Duke Snider. *The Scouting Report: 1984* (New York: Harper & Row Publishers, 1984). The 1985 and 1986 editions were consulted as well.

Carter, Craig. *Official Baseball Record Book, 1985 Edition* (St. Louis: The Sporting News Publishing Company, 1985).

Cantor, George. *Wire to Wire: Inside the 1984 Detroit Tigers Championship Season* (Chicago: Triumph Books, 2004).

Coleman, Jerry, Ernie Harwell, Ralph Kiner, Tim McCarver, Ned Martin, and Brooks Robinson. *The Scouting Report: 1983* (New York: Harper & Row Publishers, 1983).

*Detroit Tigers Press/TV/Radio Guide*, 1985-1989 editions (Detroit: Detroit Tigers, 1985-89).

Dickson, Paul. *The Dickson Baseball Dictionary*, third edition (New York: W.W. Norton & Company, 2009).

Dierker, Larry, Jim Kaat, Harmon Killebrew, and Jim Rooker, *The Scouting Report: 1987* (New York: Perennial Library, 1987).

Dickson, Paul. *Baseball's Greatest Quotations: An Illustrated Treasury of Baseball Quotations and Historical Lore*, revised edition (New York: Collins, 2008).

Enders, Eric. *The Fall Classic: The Definitive History of the World Series* (New York: Sterling Publishing, 2007).

Gillette, Gary, and Pete Palmer. *The ESPN Baseball Encyclopedia*, fifth edition (New York: Sterling Publishing Co., Inc., 2008).

Hoppel, Joe. *Official Baseball Guide, 1984 Edition* (St. Louis: The Sporting News Publishing Company, 1984).

James, Bill, John Dewan, and Project Scoresheet. *Bill James Presents The Great American Baseball Stat Book*, first edition (New York: Ballantine Books, 1987).

James, Bill, and Rob Neyer. *The Neyer/James Guide to Pitchers* (New York: Fireside Books, 2004).

James, Bill, Don Zminda, and Project Scoresheet. *Bill James Presents The Great American Baseball Stat Book, 1988 Edition* (New York: Villard Books, 1988).

Johnson, Lloyd. *Baseball's Dream Teams* (New York: Crescent Books, 1990).

Marcin, Joe, Larry Wigge, Carl Clark, and Larry Vickrey. *Official Baseball Guide for 1978* (St. Louis: The Sporting News Publishing Company, 1978).

Pietrusza, David, Matthew Silverman, and Michael Gershman. *Baseball: The Biographical Encyclopedia* (Kingston, New York: Total/Sports Illustrated, 2000).

Porter, David L. *The Biographical Dictionary of American Sports: G-P* (Westport, Connecticut: Greenwood Press, 2000).

Quigley, Martin. *The Crooked Pitch* (Chapel Hill, North Carolina: Algonquin Books, 1984).

Reichler, Joseph L. *The Baseball Encyclopedia*, sixth edition (New York: Macmillan Publishing Company, 1985).

Seaver, Tom, with Rick Hummel and Bob Nightengale. *Tom Seaver's Scouting Notebook 1989* (St. Louis: The Sporting News Publishing Company 1989).

Siegel, Barry. *Official Baseball Register, 1982-89 Editions* (St. Louis: The Sporting News Publishing Company, 1982).

Siwoff, Seymour, Steve Hirdt, and Peter Hirdt. *The 1985 Elias Baseball Analyst* (New York: Collier Books, 1985). Also 1986.

Sloan, Dave. *Official Baseball Guide, 1985 Edition* (St. Louis: The Sporting News Publishing Company, 1985).

Spatz, Lyle. *The SABR Baseball List & Record Book* (New York: Scribner, 2007).

Sumner, Benjamin Barrett. *Minor League Baseball Standings* (Jefferson, North Carolina: McFarland & Company, Inc., 2000).

Articles

"AL Insider," *USA Today*, July 18, 1988.

Bernreuter, Hugh. "Detroit Tigers 1984 Hero Willie Hernández Brings Memories to Dow Diamond Saturday," mlive.com, August 28, 2009.

Brussat, Frederic, and Mary Ann Brussat. "Film Review/That Championship Season," SpiritualityandPractice.com (undated).

Felber, Bill, and Gary Gillette. "The Changing Game," in John Thorn and Pete Palmer's *Total Baseball*, seventh edition (Kingston, New York: Total Sports Publishing, 2001).

Gage, Tom. "Hernandez Tigers New Bullpen Ace," *The Sporting News*, April 2, 1984: 23-24.

Gage, Tom. "Ex-Tiger Hernandez Joins Yankees as Replacement Player," *Detroit News*, March 7, 1995.

Gillette, Gary. "Requiem for the Tigers," in *The 1989 Baseball Abstract* (Kirkwood, Missouri: Mad Aztec Press, April 1989), 149-151.

Henning, Lynn. "Tigers' 35-5 start in 1984 Still Has Power to Amaze," *Detroit News* online edition. May 21, 2009.

"Hernandez Leaves Phils in 3-Way Deal," *Chicago Tribune*, March 25, 1984.

Joy, Emilia Badillo. "The Sugar Industry of Puerto Rico," PReb.com.

Kornacki, Steve. "Brotherhood of 1984 World Series Champion Tigers Lives On," mlive.com, September 28, 2009.

McClary, Mike. "The 1984 Hernandez/Bergman Trade Revisited," DailyFungo.com, March 28, 2008.

Meixell, Ted. "Glenn Wilson Comes Back With Desire to Be Best/Phillies: At Spring Training," *Allentown Morning Call*. April 1, 1985.

Rothstein, Mervyn. "Joseph Papp, Theater's Champion, Dies," *New York Times*, November 1, 1991.

# PUERTO RICO AND BASEBALL: 60 BIOGRAPHIES

"Sports People/Phils Invite Hernandez," *New York Times*, February 22, 1991.

Stertz, Bradley A. "It's Probably Not Too Smart for Us to Publicize This Kind of Revenge," *Wall Street Journal*, March 14, 1988.

Welch, Chuck. "'84 Tigers Celebrate Series Anniversary at Fantasy Camp Game," LakelandLocal.com, January 29, 2009.

Websites

Detroit.Tigers.MLB.com.

SABRpedia.org (Society for American Baseball Research's online encyclopedia).

welcome.topuertorico.org/city/aguada.shtml.

welcome.topuertorico.org/economy.shtml.

BaseballIndex.org.

Baseball-Reference.com.

ibdb.com (Internet Broadway Database).

imdb.com (Internet Movie Database).

MapQuest.com.

WestportPlayhouse.org.

Interviews & Communications

Carlton, Russell (coordinator, baseball media relations, Detroit Tigers). Email messages to author.

Craig, Roger. Telephone interview by author.

Green, Jerry. Telephone interview by author.

Kornacki, Steve. Telephone interview by author.

Nelson, Rod. Email messages to author.

Palmer, Pete. Email messages to author.

Shea, Stuart. E-mail messages to author.

Unpublished sources

Society for American Baseball Research Who-Signed-Whom Database.

24-7 Baseball Modern Player Register, 1975-2009.

24-7 Baseball Relief Pitcher Reports, 1984-89.

24-7 Baseball Salary Database, 1982-2008.

24-7 Baseball/ESPN Baseball Encyclopedia Disabled List-Injury Register.

## NOTES

1. Raquel Julich, "Un Poquito De Beisbol Con Sabor Bilingue/Major League Baseball: 100-Plus Years of Legends," LaPrensaToledo.com, 2005.

2. Peter Gammons, "Hernandez Deal May Put Tigers on Top," *The Sporting News*, April 9, 1984: 14.

3. "Hernandez Wants $1 Million a Year," *The Sporting News*, October 29, 1984: 48.

4. Rich Westcott and Frank Bilovsky, *The New Phillies Encyclopedia* (Philadelphia: Temple University Press, 1993), 95.

5. Christopher Mathewson, *Pitching in a Pinch* (CreateSpace, 2015, reprint of 1912 Knickerbocker Press edition), 9.

6. Jaime Diaz, "He's Giving Batters the Willies," *Sports Illustrated*, September 19, 1984.

7. Steve Kornacki, "Unknown by New Tigers Teammates, Guillermo Hernandez Lifted Detroit to 1984 World Championship," mlive.com, April 5, 2009.

8. Jaime Diaz.

9. Dave Desmond, "Eric King," *Los Angeles Times*, November 27, 1986: D28.

10. Peter Gavrilovich, "178 fun facts for the Detroit Free Press' 178th birthday," *Detroit Free Press*, May 5, 2009.

11. Joe Sexton, "Yanks Defeat Tigers in 18th," *New York Times*, September 12, 1988: C1.

12. Ibid.

13. Paul Cox, *Tiger Tracks 1989: An In-Depth Review of the 1988 Detroit Tigers* (London, Ontario: Mayo Smith Society, 1989).

14. "Around the Majors/Senior Arms," *Washington Post*, March 26, 1990.

15. Jack Curry, "Yanks Sign Ex-M.V.P. but He's 40," *New York Times*, March 7, 1995: B15.

16. Ibid.

17. Jo-Ann Barnas, "Year of the Tiger Relived," *Detroit Free Press*, September 29, 2009.

18. *Grand Rapids Press*, "Beloved Tigers Closer 'Willie' Hernandez Will Return From Puerto Rico for Whitecaps Event," August 27, 2009, at mlive.com/whitecaps/index.ssf/2009/08/beloved_tigers_closer_willie_h.html.

# SIXTO LEZCANO "EL DIAMANTE DEL NORTE"

## By Brian Wood

*Opening Day at Milwaukee's County Stadium, April 10, 1980. Visiting Boston scores two runs in the top of the inning to tie Brewers at 5 apiece. Bottom of the inning, two outs, bases loaded. Up to the plate steps Sixto Lezcano. A packed house of 53,313 screaming as one, urging Sixto to send them home with smiles on their faces.*

**D**IAL BACK THE CLOCK 26½ YEARS to Saturday, November 28, 1953. Sixto Joaquin Lezcano Curras was born in Arecibo, Puerto Rico, 50 miles west of the capital city of San Juan. Arecibo produced major leaguers Luis Olmo and Vic Power before him and is known as "El Diamante Del Norte" (The Diamond of the North).[1] Quite apropos since Lezcano would grace the diamonds of major-league baseball for 12 seasons. Properly pronounced "SEES toh,"[2] but "SIX toh" by most fans, Lezcano became a fan favorite through the years, as did his name itself. However, his career was noted for periods of poor attitudes.[3]

Félix Delgado[4] signed 16-year-old Lezcano to a contract with the Milwaukee Brewers for $5,000[5] when he was a student at Fernando Collegio San Jose High School[6] in San Jose, Puerto Rico, on October 1, 1970.[7] However, four years earlier, Delgado first tried to sign him as a 12-year-old, thinking he looked much older.[8] He later wore number 16 while with both the Brewers and Cardinals in honor of his age at the signing of his contract.[9] He worked his way through the Milwaukee farm system with stops at Newark, New York (short-season Class-A New York-Penn League), Danville (Class-A Midwest League), Shreveport (Double-A Texas League), and Sacramento (Triple-A Pacific Coast League). Brewers batting coach Harvey Kuenn noticed Lezcano's potential during winter instructional ball in 1971: "The kid can't miss. He can hit with power, run, and throw."[10]

Lezcano showed improvement each season, raising his home-run and RBI totals each year, culminating in 1974 with the Sacramento Solons when he hit 34 home runs, had 99 RBIs, batted .325, and was a late-season call-up to the Brewers. However, he was only third on the team in round-trippers behind Bill McNulty's 55 and Gorman Thomas' 51. Sacramento hit 305 home runs, a large number until you consider that the left-field foul pole sat a mere 233 feet from home plate. Hughes Stadium was primarily a football and track and field stadium and thus not suited for baseball.[11]

Brewers manager Del Crandall penciled Lezcano's name into the starting lineup on September 10, 1974. And did Sixto ever perform! He singled against the Baltimore Orioles' Dave McNally in his first career at-bat. He went 3-for-5, including a game-winning single in the bottom of the 10th. Lezcano scorched a line-drive single off reliever Grant Jackson, driving in Johnny Briggs from third base for a 6-5 Milwaukee victory.[12]

Lezcano's first home run came 10 days later, off John Hiller of the Detroit Tigers, a three-run shot to give the Brewers a 5-3 lead. Lezcano would patrol the outfield for Milwaukee for the next six seasons.

On May 1, 1975, the Brewers bombed the Tigers at County Stadium, 17-3, led by Hank Aaron's 4-for-4 day with two RBIs. In the third, Aaron drove in Lezcano with a single off Vern Ruhle to surpass Babe Ruth on the all-time RBI list with number 2,210.[13]

Lezcano developed a reputation for being a "hard head" during the 1975 season, leading to a clash of personalities with manager Del Crandall. His approach at the plate was one of going for the home run.[14] Lezcano felt Crandall had tried to give him too much advice and had confused him. This led to a certain amount of arrogance and with temper tantrums. In early August Crandall fined Lezcano twice (for $100 and $50) for his poor attitude and benched him for several games.[15] One of the fines was for smashing a water cooler in the dugout in Minnesota and hurting his hand. The friction with the manager came to a head when Crandall suspended Lezcano for a week at the end of the season. After using a number of pinch-hitters and runners during a game, Crandall asked Lezcano to pinch-run. Lezcano did not respond and continued to stand in place, smoking a cigarette.[16] Some viewed his actions as downright mutiny. Before the season ended, Lezcano went to Crandall's office and apologized for his behavior. Crandall was impressed with his sincerity. "After all, he knew I was going to be fired, so he didn't have to butter me up," the manager said.[17] He also had a long discussion with Bud Selig, the Brewers president, and general manager Jim Baumer who related, "He was almost apologetic as he told us he was wrong. He promised us he was going to be a different person and you've got to believe him. He'd never been a problem before in our organization."[18]

Lezcano had a new manager in 1976, Alex Grammas, fresh from a World Series title as third-base coach with the Cincinnati Reds. Lezcano again promised management that he would turn over a new leaf and not be the "rebellious youngster" from the previous season.[19] A thumb injury in spring training, led to a slow start. Lezcano's batting average slipped to a season low .265 in May. Grammas rested him for a week and he was able to bounce back, finishing the season at .285.[20]

During the 1976 season Lezcano became engaged to his hometown sweetheart. In addition, he became his niece's godfather on November 6.[21]

*Red Sox pitcher Dick Drago gets the sign from catcher Dave Rader. Here's the pitch ...*

Lezcano was also a frequent winter-ball participant, playing on three championship teams in Puerto Rico.[22] During the 1975-76 winter season, he changed his approach at the plate from trying for home runs to looking for a hit by getting good wood on the ball. He adjusted his stance so he could cover more of the plate. He acknowledged advice from his winter-ball teammates Félix Millan, Jerry Morales, Willie Montañez, and manager Jim Bunning.[23] In the 1976-77 winter season, Lezcano led the league in batting (.366) for Caguas Criollos,[24] or Country Boys.[25] The Criollos, who had a team batting average of .307, included future Hall of Famer Eddie Murray. Manager Doc Edwards later compared the team to many big-league clubs of the mid-'90s.[26]

On April 10, 1977, Lezcano provided all of the offense in a 2-1 victory over the New York Yankees, including a "called" shot in the ninth inning. After hitting a home run to tie the game, 1-1, in the fourth, Lezcano came to the plate in the top of the ninth inning and was overheard by the Yankees' Spanish-speaking batboy to say, "Yo voy saca reste" ("I'm going to take this one out").[27] And he did.

On May 20, 1977, Lezcano broke the American League record for most putouts by an outfielder with 10 in a nine-inning game.[28]

Lezcano's home run numbers went up in 1977, as did his strikeouts, in which he ranked as high as third in the AL during the season. However, starting on July 9, Lezcano reduced his strikeout ratio from 22.9 percent to 9.1 percent, including only 9 in his final 99 at-bats.

The Yankees' Mike Torrez broke Lezcano's left hand with a pitch on July 22. After a 49-game absence (save for one appearance as a pinch-runner), he returned to the lineup and banged out five home runs in his first 12 games. Of his hand, Lezcano said, "It still hurts. I'm getting paid and I don't like to get paid sitting. I like to get paid working."[29] It was the first time in his baseball career that he had been out for such an extended period. During the winter (1977-78), he passed up playing in the Puerto Rican winter league, the first time he had done that. He wanted to spend more time with his family in Puerto Rico and give his hand time to heal.[30]

After two years of consecutive sixth-place finishes, Bud Selig dispatched both manager Grammas and general manager Baumer, replacing them with Harry

Dalton (from the California Angels) and George Bamberger (from the Orioles). It was the start of Bambi's Bombers.[31] However, winning 93 games in 1978 was good enough for only third place in the AL East behind the Yankees and Red Sox.

Lezcano knocked out two grand slams in 1978, the first on Opening Day, April 7, against the Orioles' Tim Stoddard. It was the first of three consecutive games in which a Brewer hit a grand slam, the first time this occurred in the major leagues.[32] Gorman Thomas (April 8) and Cecil Cooper (April 9) followed Lezcano. Lezcano's second grand slam of the season was part of a five-RBI game against the Indians on August 24 in a 9-8 extra-inning win at County Stadium. The 1978 season was the Brewers' first over .500. They stayed above .500 for the rest of Lezcano's time in Milwaukee.

An early-season shoulder injury caused him to miss 10 games in April.[33] After he was named the Brewers' player of the month in May (.333, 8 home runs, 17 RBIs), Lezcano's contract was extended three years through the 1981 season.[34]

After the 1978 season, the Brewers had four regular outfielders—Lezcano, Larry Hisle, Gorman Thomas, and Ben Oglivie—and the case was being made to dispatch Lezcano in a trade. However, manager Bamberger thought highly of him, saying, "He's 25 years old and he's probably the best right fielder in baseball. The only guy close is Dwight Evans at Boston, and if you ask me which one I'd rather have, I'd take Lezcano."[35] The fact that he led AL right fielders with 18 assists may have prompted that statement. As it turned out, Hisle tore his rotator cuff 20 games into the season.[36]

Lezcano's best season came in 1979 when he socked 28 home runs, drove in 101 runs, and hit .321, all career highs. He was awarded a Gold Glove as the league's premier right fielder.[37] He was voted the Brewers' Most Valuable Player[38] and named the Puerto Rican professional athlete of the year.[39]

While sidelined with a thumb injury, he was married to fiancée Marianjelly on May 21.[40] On May 25, after returning from the injury, he knocked out two home runs and scored all three runs in a 3-2 Brewers win over the Oakland A's.[41]

In early June, hitting coach Harvey Kuenn said Lezcano had matured. "He's starting to know the strike zone better," Kuenn said. "He's not swinging at as many bad balls as he used to."[42] Lezcano reduced his strikeout ratio to a career-low 15.6 percent.

In the bottom of the 11th inning, on July 19, 1979, Lezcano homered off Blue Jays pitcher Tom Buskey for a 3-2 Brewer walk-off win.

"He is one of the most underrated ballplayers in the American League," said manager Bamberger.[43] "[He] can do everything. Some guys are superstars and they can only do two things. Not only does he play outstanding baseball, but when he wasn't playing, he was rooting for everybody else. That impressed me. His attitude is outstanding."[44]

Milwaukee won its last five games going into the All-Star break. Coming out, the Brewers won five more to tie the team record of 10 consecutive wins set in 1973 and earlier in the 1978 season from June 9-17. Lezcano hit four home runs in the first four games until he went down with a sore heel.[45] During this stretch, Lezcano's wife was admitted to a Milwaukee hospital due to pregnancy complications.[46]

Milwaukee improved to a then franchise record 95 wins and a second-place finish behind the Orioles in 1979.

*The 5'10" 165 pound Lezcano swings. ... It's a long fly ball to right field ...*[47]

Lezcano's postseason victory was the birth of his son Michael in October 1979.[48] Once again, he passed up winter ball.[49]

On Opening Day of 1980, April 10, he kicked off the season with two home runs. The first one was a two-run homer off Boston's Dennis Eckersley that tied the score; the second was his other Opening Day grand slam, a walk-off homer hit down the right-field line off reliever Dick Drago.

The Brewers slumped to 86 wins and a third-place finish in 1980. It was Lezcano's worst season to date. He was plagued by injuries, including a season-ending broken bone in his hand after he was hit by a pitch from the Tigers' Jerry Ujdur on August 31. His average dipped to .229 (from .321), the largest drop of any major-league regular,[50] making him expendable.[51] Lezcano's attitude also took a nosedive. Teammate Ben Oglivie noted that the 1980 Brewers team was marked by frustration and fault-finding and that Lezcano was one of the instigators.[52]

Lezcano became part of two blockbuster trades that helped both Milwaukee and St. Louis reach the 1982 World Series.[53] On December 12, 1980, he was sent to the Cardinals with a highly regarded prospect, outfielder David Green, and starting pitchers Dave LaPoint and Lary Sorensen for catcher Ted Simmons and the next two AL Cy Young Award winners, Rollie Fingers and Pete Vuckovich. All three new Brewers were key members of the 1982 pennant-winning team. All four of the new Cardinals (or players traded for them) made contributions to the 1982 Cardinals World Series champions.

Lezcano's 1981 season was marred by another injury, this time to his wrist, that sidelined him from mid-June to mid-August,[54] and a sore elbow that caused him to miss a number of games in September.[55]

Lezcano took a platoon role in St. Louis, batting primarily against left-handed pitchers despite hitting 100 points higher against righties.[56] After the season he demanded to be traded and Cardinals manager-GM Whitey Herzog obliged.[57] The Cardinals had a chance to unload troubled shortstop Garry Templeton with Lezcano to the San Diego Padres for shortstop Ozzie Smith and pitcher Steve Mura.[58] While Templeton was a key cog in the Padres' 1984 NL championship season, Smith was the final piece the Cardinals needed to win the 1982 World Series and the 1985 and '87 NL pennants. Lezcano did not mince words after his departure: "I'm pretty sure Whitey hasn't been in the World Series," comparing him to his Padres manager Dick Williams who had won two World Series Championships with the 1972 and 1973 Oakland A's. "Whitey won two [division titles] (with Kansas City) and was still fired. I wonder why?"[59]

Before the 1982 season, Lezcano became a father again when son Steven was born on February 18.

The 1982 season turned out to be a comeback year for Lezcano as he had his second-best offensive season with 16 home runs and 84 RBIs (both second on the team), a .289 batting average, 78 walks, a .388 on-base percentage, and a .472 slugging percentage. Despite missing 24 games to injuries,[60] he led the NL in assists (16, tied with Chili Davis and Lonnie Smith) and double plays (8) and made only three errors. "I thought I deserved a Gold Glove. I felt like I made more contributions than the guys who won them," said Lezcano during spring training in 1983.[61]

Lezcano had a spectacular day on July 31, going 6-for-7 with three home runs, two doubles, and seven RBIs in a doubleheader sweep of the Reds. He was named the National League Player of the Week twice during the season. On September 13 Lezcano was hit on the left hand by a Bob Welch fastball. The injury ended Lezcano's season and the Padres won just seven of their remaining 19 games, finishing at .500 in fourth place, eight games out of first place.

During the 1982-83 winter-ball season semifinal series between Lezcano's Santurce team and Arecibo, his hand was broken again by a pitch from Keith Creel, and was lost for the rest of the playoff season.[62]

Lezcano got off to a good start in 1983, batting .293 with six doubles, and 16 RBIs in the month of April.

However, after May 5 he fell into a slump, hitting .210 through the end of August. On August 31 Lezcano was dispatched to the Phillies in a trade involving five players to be named later.[63] He platooned with former Padres teammate Joe Lefebvre in right field and had a game-winning hit on September 11 with a pinch-hit single in the seventh inning in a 5-3 win over the Pirates. The win kept the Phillies a half-game behind first-place Montreal in the tight NL East race.

Commenting on his new role as a platoon player, Lezcano said, "All my life I've been a regular, and there's a certain adjustment you have to make when you're a platoon player. There's nothing wrong with platooning; with the personnel we have, we have to use everybody. Then if we make the playoffs and World Series, everybody will be ready. I've never been in a pennant race before, and it feels good. I feel like I've come out of a nightmare and gone into a dream, so I'm willing to do whatever it takes. Otherwise, I'll be home watching the World Series on TV."[64]

Because the Phillies acquired Lezcano before September 1, he was eligible to play in the postseason for the first time. Batting .308 in the NLCS, Lezcano went 3-for-4 including a two-run home run against Rick Honeycutt in the sixth inning of Game Four against the Dodgers, to ice the game and the series. In the seventh inning, he gunned down the Dodgers' Bill Russell trying to stretch a single into a double. Lezcano batted .125 in the World Series, starting two games in the five-game Series loss to Baltimore.

Lezcano had a respectable year in 1984 for the Phillies, who were unable to repeat as division champions (81-81, fourth place, NL East) as a pinch-hitter and part-time outfielder, hitting .277 with 14 home runs in 294 at-bats. On May 1 he hit two home runs and drove in five runs in a 7-4 victory over the Montreal Expos.

During the offseason, the Pirates signed Lezcano as a free agent. He commented, "Before I leave this game, I wanted to play for the team my idol played for. All Puerto Rican kids where I was growing up [Arecibo] idealized Roberto Clemente."[65] He opted for a two-year, $800,000 deal with Pittsburgh over offers from Oakland and Houston. Lezcano said he was frustrated with a lack of playing time on the Phillies, even though Pirates manager Chuck Tanner saw Lezcano as a fourth outfielder.[66] Lezcano batted just .207 for the 1985 Pirates with three home runs in 153 at-bats. What turned out to be his last major-league hit was a pinch single off the Cardinals' John Tudor on August 12.

Lezcano was released by the Pirates in April 1986 and spent time caring for his ailing wife in Puerto Rico.[67] He attempted a comeback the next year when he signed with the Yokohama Taiyo Whales of the Japan Central League. However, after hitting .217 in 20 games, Lezcano retired from the game. He reportedly told team officials, "I couldn't show power as in the past and I do not want to give trouble to the Whales anymore."[68]

In the years after his retirement as a player, Lezcano coached in the Royals and Braves organizations from 1993 through 2010, when he retired.[69]

In 1994 Lezcano was named manager of his old team, the Caguas Criollos, just four games into the winter season after Mike Easler was fired. Lezcano was later fired as well as Caguas finished in last place.[70]

On June 13, 2014, Milwaukee established the Brewers Wall of Honor with Lezcano being one of the initial honorees along with Hall of Famers Hank Aaron, Robin Yount, Paul Molitor, and Rollie Fingers.[71]

Sixto's cousin Carlos Lezcano played two seasons for the Chicago Cubs and managed more than 1,800 games in the minor leagues.[72]

*It's GONE!!! for a Grand Slam and the Brewers win the game 9-5!! Lezcano crosses the plate and his teammates mob him.*

This home run, on April 10, 1980, was Lezcano's second grand slam in an Opening Day game, a major-league record. In 2006 Brewers historian Mario Ziino selected the blast as the most memorable home run in Brewers history.[73]

## SOURCES

In addition to the sources cited in the Notes, the author also relied upon Baseball-Reference.com and Retrosheet.org.

## NOTES

1. "Arecibo, PR-Diamond of the North," eyetour.com/blog/arecibo/, retrieved August 18, 2016.
2. "Sixto Lezcano," cardboardgods.net/2007/09/12/sixto-lezcano/, September 12, 2007, retrieved August 18, 2016.
3. Witness his run-ins with Del Crandall and Whitey Herzog, among others.
4. Milton Richman, "Lezcano: Starting Over in NL," *Los Angeles Times*, April 5, 1981.
5. Phil Collier, "Everyday Action Is Lezcano's Goal," *San Diego Tribune*, March 27, 1982.
6. Sixto Lezcano fact page from Baseball Hall of Fame, September 1974.
7. Kyle Lobner, "Today In Brewer History: Happy Anniversary, Sixto Lezcano," m.mlb.com/video/topic/6479266/v7999465/41080-sixto-lezcano-hits-a-homeopener-walkoff, October 1, 2012, retrieved August 18, 2016.
8. Collier, "Everyday Action Is Lezcano's Goal."
9. Richman.
10. Lou Chapman, "Thomas and Lezcano Brighten Brewers' Future," *Milwaukee Sentinel*, September 28, 1974.
11. Baseball Oddballs, "Arena Baseball at Hughes Stadium," baseballoddball.blogspot.com/2013/02/arena-baseball-at-hughes-stadium.html, February 17, 2013, retrieved December 11, 2016.
12. Chapman, "Thomas and Lezcano Brighten Brewers' Future."
13. Herm Krabbenhoft has conducted research on RBIs and determined that Ruth should have been credited with an additional five RBIs (2,214). In this case, Aaron did not actually pass Ruth until May 15, when he hit a sacrifice fly off Texas Rangers starter Steve Hargan. (He added a three-run home run later in the game.) "40 Years Ago: Hank Aaron Sets new RBI Mark - 1976 Topps #1 Record Breaker." phungo.blogspot.com/2015/04/40-years-ago-hank-aaron-sets-new-rbi.html, April 30, 2015, retrieved August 18, 2016.
14. Lou Chapman, "Ex-Bad Boy Lezcano Brewers' Pride and Joy," *The Sporting News*, September 11, 1976.
15. Article in unknown newspaper, August 28, 1975, from Lezcano's Hall of Fame file.
16. Deane McGowen, *New York Times*, September 24, 1975.
17. Lou Chapman, "Lezcano Promises to Curb Tantrums," *Milwaukee Sentinel*, unknown date.
18. Ibid.
19. Ibid.
20. Chapman, "Ex-Bad Boy Brewers' Pride and Joy."
21. Ibid.
22. Lou Chapman, "Ex-Midget Lezcano Packs a Big Wallop for Brewers," *The Sporting News*, April 30, 1977.
23. Chapman, "Ex-Bad Boy Lezcano Brewers' Pride and Joy."
24. Thomas E. Van Hyning, "Dennis Martinez's Winter League Career," SABR, *The National Pastime*, 16, 1996: 51.
25. Keith Harmon, "In Wisconsin or Puerto Rico, Sixto's Still a Hero," 1977 Milwaukee Brewers Scorebook: 12B.
26. Van Hyning, "Dennis Martinez's Winter League Career."
27. Associated Press, "Sixto's KOs, 'Legal Balk' Foul Up Yanks," *Binghamton (New York) Press and Sun-Bulletin*, April 11, 1977.
28. "Record for Lezcano," unknown newspaper in Lezcano's Hall of Fame file, June 11, 1977. Note, this article stated the record occurred on May 21, 1977. Retrosheet states it happened on May 20, 1977.
29. Lou Chapman, "Sixto Shooting for Top Spot as Brewer Belter," *The Sporting News*, October 8, 1977.
30. Ibid.

# PUERTO RICO AND BASEBALL: 60 BIOGRAPHIES

31 Michael V. Uschan, United Press International, "In 1978 the Milwaukee Brewers Were Known as 'Bambi's...," April 28, 1986, upi.com/Archives/1986/04/28/In-1978-the-Milwaukee-Brewers-were-known-as-Bambis/2098515044800/ retrieved December 15, 2016.

32 "Sixto Lezcano," baseball-almanac.com/players/player.php?p=lezcasi01, retrieved August 18, 2016. See list at bottom of page.

33 "Sixto Lezcano Rightfielder," 1978 Seattle Mariners scorecard, from Lezcano's Hall of Fame file.

34 "Brewers Bits," *The Sporting News*, July 15, 1978.

35 Mike Gonring, "Brewers Nix Trade Talks Involving Sixto," *The Sporting News*, December 23, 1978: 48.

36 David E. Skelton, "Larry Hisle," SABR BioProject, sabr.org/bioproj/person/99d6b47d, April 25, 2014, retrieved December 15, 2016.

37 Of note, 1979 was Lezcano's worst season in defensive wins above replacement (dWar) with a -1.1. In fact, he had only two positive dWar seasons (1978, 0.2; 1982, 0.6). dWar is the defensive counterpart of wins above replacement (WAR).

38 Unattributed newspaper article, January 26, 1980, from Lezcano's Hall of Fame file.

39 Tom Flaherty, "MVP Lezcano Reaps Reward," *Milwaukee Journal*, February 16, 1980.

40 "Sixto Lezcano," Facebook, facebook.com/sixto.lezcano.75/about?lst=1655423404%3A100004230403197%3A1490929601, retrieved December 12, 2016.

41 Untitled recap associated with box score from May 24, 1979 game between Oakland and Milwaukee, from Lezcano's Hall of Fame file.

42 Mike Gonring, "Sixto's RBI Numbers Take Up Brewer Slack," *The Sporting News*, June 2, 1979.

43 Mike Gonring, "Lack of Acclaim Doesn't Bother Maturing Lezcano," *Milwaukee Journal*, May 15, 1979: 21.

44 Flaherty.

45 Mike Gonring, "Lezcano's Bat Fills a Big Void for Brewers," *The Sporting News*, August 11, 1979.

46 Ibid.

47 "4/10/80: Sixto Lezcano hits a home-opener walk-off", m.mlb.com/video/topic/6479266/v7999465/41080-sixto-lezcano-hits-a-homeopener-walkoff, retrieved August 18, 2016.

48 Rick Hummel, "Money Talk Disturbs Lezcano," *St. Louis Post-Dispatch*, April 18, 1981.

49 Flaherty.

50 Richman.

51 Lezcano's left hand was broken on a pitch from Mike Torrez of the Yankees on July 22, 1977. He was out of the lineup for a little over a month. Photo, NYP Holdings, Inc. via Getty Images, gettyimages.com/detail/news-photo/sixto-lezcano-screams-in-pain-after-his-hand-was-broken-by-news-photo/533001554, July 23, 1977, retrieved August 18, 2016. Note: The caption incorrectly states that the injury occurred on July 23.

52 "Dissension Brewers Problem?" unknown newspaper article, March 21, 1981, from Lezcano's Hall of Fame file.

53 Jenifer Langosch, "Players Recall Epic '82 'Suds Series'" m.mlb.com/news/article/25568000/, October 9, 2011, retrieved August 18, 2016; Dave Anderson, Trade That Brewed the 6-Pack Series," *New York Times*, October 12, 1982, nytimes.com/1982/10/12/sports/sports-of-the-times-trade-that-brewed-the-6-pack-series.html, retrieved August 18, 2016.

54 Bob Chandler, San Diego Padres press release dated March 12, 1982.

55 John Sonderegger, "San Diego Hopes Sixto Lezcano's Bat Makes a Comeback." *St. Louis Post-Dispatch*, undated article from 1982.

56 Phil Collier, "Lezcano Hikes Padres' Punch," *San Diego Union*, date unknown.

57 Sonderegger.

58 Relief pitcher Luis DeLeon was the player named to complete the deal, moving from the Cardinals to the Padres.

59 Sonderegger.

60 Untitled *San Diego Tribune* article, March 14, 1983, from Lezcano's Hall of Fame file.

61 Ibid. The three NL Gold Glove outfielders were Dale Murphy, Garry Maddox, and Andre Dawson.

62 Thomas Van Hyning, *The Santurce Crabbers: Sixty Seasons of Puerto Rican Winter League Baseball* (Jefferson, North Carolina: McFarland, 1999), 144.

63 Lezcano was traded with Steve Fireovid for the Phillies' Marty Decker, Ed Wojna, Darren Burroughs, and Lance McCullers.

64 Pohla Smith, "Sixto Lezcano, Who Says He's Still Trying to Learn..." September 11, 1983, upi.com/Archives/1983/09/11/Sixto-Lezcano-who-says-hes-still-trying-to-learn/6357432100800/, retrieved August 18, 2016.

65 Charley Feeney, "Lezcano Follows Clemente to Bucs," *The Sporting News*, February 4, 1985.

66 Ibid.

67 Associated Press, "Sixto Lezcano Quits Japanese Baseball," articles.latimes.com/1987-05-18/sports/sp-393_1_show-power, May 18, 1987, retrieved August 18, 2016.

68 Ibid.

69 "Brewer Player Retrospective—Sixto Lezcano," forum.brewerfan.net/viewtopic.php?f=63&t=33766, retrieved August 18, 2016.

70 David Nevard, "The Making of Mo Vaughn," buffalohead.org/nomomo.htm, 1999, retrieved December 11, 2016.

71 Bob Wolfley, "New Wall of Honor Brings Together Old Milwaukee Brewers," *Milwaukee Journal Sentinel*, June 13, 2014. archive.jsonline.com/sports/brewers/new-wall-of-honor-honors-old-milwaukee-brewers-b99290675z1-263126431.html, retrieved August 16, 2016.

72 Mark Schremmer, "Lezcano's Baseball Journey Lands Him in Joplin," *Joplin Globe*, January 25, 2015, joplinglobe.com/sports/local_sports/lezcano-s-baseball-journey-lands-him-in-joplin/article_c3c93711-d660-5ea2-ac96-d4c87fd2486a.html, retrieved August 18, 2016.

73 Drew Olson, "Blasts From the Past: A Look at Memorable Home Runs in Brewers History," May 13, 2006, onmilwaukee.com/sports/articles/brewhomers.html, retrieved August 18, 2016.

# JAVY LÓPEZ

## By Kyle Eaton

JAVIER TORRES "JAVY" LÓPEZ WAS born on November 5, 1970, in the city of Ponce, Puerto Rico. López was a right-handed-hitting catcher who played for the Atlanta Braves, Baltimore Orioles, and Boston Red Sox over his 15-year major-league career, though he is primarily known for his time with the Braves. López was a three-time All-Star and one-time Silver Slugger recipient, and in 1995 was a World Series champion, all with the Atlanta Braves. López is listed at 6-feet-3 and 185 pounds,[1] but by his own admission, his weight climbed to at least 248 pounds during his career.[2]

Javy was the second youngest of five children (two boys, Juan Eduardo and Javy, and three girls, Sandra, Betsy, and Elaine) in his household, and learned from an early age the value of hard work from his parents and his lower-middle-class upbringing. López's mother, Evelia Torres, held many jobs ranging from bank teller to teacher, but she eventually left the work force to better provide supervision and care for her children. This left Jacinto López, Javy's father, an auto-parts dealer, former employee of a credit union, and occasional car salesman, as the primary source of income for the family. The modest, four-bedroom house in which Javy grew up lies in close proximity to the other homes on his block, and lent itself perfectly to providing close familial and neighborly ties. The values growing up in this modest family created a bond that López has reflected upon.[3]

Javy's first swings came when he took an old bat and a bucket of rocks to the roof of his house and hit the rocks into the vacant lot across the street. Jacinto López recalled the stamina Javy displayed while doing this: "I'd be on the couch and he would be up there swinging at stones. I would say to myself, gosh, this kid never gets tired."[4] At 7 years old López began playing baseball at a neighborhood church on a concrete field with a rubber ball.[5] Whenever a bat or tape to make a ball could not be found, Javy and his friends improvised with broomsticks and soda-bottle caps. Any materials that could be feasibly used as a bat or ball were used.[6]

López did not know the idiosyncrasies of baseball but he did enjoy playing the game and began to develop a knack for it as well. His father took him to a recreational league when he saw his son's potential. Once the duo started playing catch, coaches took notice of Javy's potential and put him on a team. Javy demonstrated a strong arm, but lacked the touch or control to pitch, the agility to play shortstop, or the swiftness to patrol the outfield. But he hit well, so the coaches kept plugging him in at different positions until one worked for him. López benefited from baseball being a year-round sport in Puerto Rico. As soon as one season ended, López went to another team to play. The repetition and extra coaching were invaluable in developing his defensive skills, and it was by the time he made his third team that López began to find his way and started to feel comfortable on the diamond.[7] Baseball even taught López an early life lesson. His uncle bought him his first baseball glove and Javy left it on the patio one day. Someone stole the glove and Javy learned how to properly keep track of his belongings.[8]

By age 13 López still did not have a true position, but one of his managers, Johnny Rodriquez, tried him at catcher. López was not great at blocking balls or catching bad pitches, but his arm was strong enough to compensate for his rawness behind the plate; he threw out a plethora of runners on his first day as a catcher, and thus his position was found.

López's hard work was rewarded when he was signed as an amateur free agent by the Atlanta Braves in 1987.[9] He turned down offers from the New York Yankees, San Diego Padres, and Montreal Expos to sign with the Braves, who offered $45,000 while the Padres and Expos were offering $75,000. Jacinto

López explained: "TBS used to be the only station that showed games here, so we were Braves fans."[10] After López signed with the Braves, even more teams began to pursue him, but he honored his contract. López said, "You know what? Forget it! I'm going to be in Atlanta, on TBS!"[11]

For what it is worth, López might not have been the best athlete, or even the best baseball player in his family, at least for a time. His sister Elaine was at one point regarded as one of the best beach volleyball players in Puerto Rico, if not the best. Elaine also was married to former American League MVP Juan Gonzalez for a time, causing a fun debate on which member of the extended López family was the best baseball player.[12]

López started with the Braves' team in the Gulf Coast League (rookie) as a 17-year-old in 1988. Each subsequent year he advanced a level, and in September 1992 he made the jump from Double-A Greenville (Southern League) to the Braves. No stop was without trials and tribulations, but López continued to show promise. For example, López had 31 passed balls playing for Burlington, Iowa (Midwest League). López blamed his fear of the ball, the cold weather, and the pitchers lacking the ability to properly grip the ball in that climate.[13]

During his rise through the minors, López paused in 1991, while playing for Durham (Carolina League) to marry his childhood sweetheart, Analy Hernandez.[14]

Called up from Greenville, López made his major-league debut on September 18, 1992, at Atlanta-Fulton County Stadium, hitting a pinch-hit double off Houston's Rob Murphy in his first at-bat. He was 6-for-16 in a nine-game audition, then opened the 1993 season playing for the Triple-A Richmond Braves. Called up in August, he played in only eight games but hit his first major-league home run on August 21 at Wrigley Field against Chicago Cubs reliever Shawn Boskie.

By Opening Day of the 1994 season, the 23-year-old López had become the Braves' starting catcher, replacing Damon Berryhill. He performed well enough to earn a top-10 spot in the National League

Rookie of the Year balloting, and learned quite a bit about handling a major-league pitching staff—one with three future Hall of Famers, Greg Maddux, John Smoltz, and Tom Glavine.

It was, however, a starter from the back end of the rotation, Kent Mercker, who provided López his most memorable game in 1994. On April 8 the Braves were visiting the Los Angeles Dodgers for their fifth game of the season. Kent Mercker was on the mound for the Braves and López was behind the plate. Despite some first-inning trouble (two walks), López was able to guide Mercker out of the inning unscathed. Mercker finished the game with 10 strikeouts, four walks, and zero hits allowed. As of 2017 the game was the last no-hitter pitched by a member of the Braves.

After the strike-shortened season of 1994, and the late start to the 1995 season as the strike wound down, López solidified his spot in the starting lineup for the perennial playoff contender Braves. He improved in every major statistical category, and by the end of the season there was no doubt who the backstop of the future was for the Braves. In the postseason López helped the Braves slug their way past the Colorado Rockies and Cincinnati Reds, and provided one of the greatest plays of the World Series, against the Cleveland Indians.

In the bottom of the sixth inning López hit a line-drive, two-run home run off Dennis Martinez that gave the Braves a 4-2 lead, which they did not relinquish.

In the top of the eighth, the Indians' Manny Ramirez was on first and slugger Jim Thome was at bat. López had observed Ramirez's penchant for a large lead off the bag and decided to take a chance at stealing an out. López recalled, "McGriff looked at me, and I signaled to him by touching the ground and picking up the dirt. He signaled back by tugging on his pants."[15] On a 2-and-2 count, Alejandro Peña threw a pitch up and in, which Thome did not offer at. López flung the ball to Fred McGriff at first, catching Ramirez by surprise for the second out of the inning. Thome walked on the next pitch, and without López's pickoff throw, the eighth inning might have unfolded differently. "It was the best feeling in the world," López recalled.[16]

The Braves won the World Series in six games. Just nine days after López jumped into Mark Wohlers' arms as a World Series champion,[17] Javy and Analy welcomed the couple's first son, Javier Alexander, to the world. It was certainly about as good a two-week stretch anyone can hope to have.[18]

The 1996 regular season was a respectable one for López. He eclipsed the 20-home-run mark for the first time. But López again saved his best performances for the postseason. In the NLCS he helped guide the Braves back from a three-games-to-one deficit against the St. Louis Cardinals by going 13-for-24 with two home runs, five doubles, and three walks. López did not maintain this torrid pace in the World Series, which the Braves lost in six games after taking a 2-games-to-none lead over the New York Yankees. López was 4-for-25.

López was selected for the National League All-Star team in 1997 and 1998. He showed solid power, called a respectable game behind the plate. López finished the 1998 season with 34 home runs, two shy of Joe Torre's franchise record of 36 home runs by a catcher.[19] In both seasons the Braves were defeated in the NLCS.

In 1999 López suffered the first major setback in his career. López was having another strong year statistically, but in late July López suffered a torn ACL, and his season was finished.[20] Also that year López's mother died after having a stroke, and his father had quadruple bypass surgery. As Jacinto López recovered in the López family home, Javy decided to buy the house next door and moved in Jacinto's twin sister, Lourdes, where she helped take care of Jacinto and kept him company. López also decided to provide everything his father needed financially so he did not have to return to his high-stress job as a newspaper distributor. Professionally, López watched the Braves make another World Series run, but were swept by the Yankees. López wondered how much he could have helped the Braves in the Series. López was also coming to terms with his failing marriage, a brother addicted to drugs, and his sister Elaine's pending divorce from Juan Gonzalez. He acknowledged that the combination of all of these issues left López in quite a negative state of mind.[21] During this tumultuous time, López's second son, Kelvin Gabriel, was born.[22]

López returned with a solid 2000 season, but the decline in his game was starting to become evident. His batting and power numbers slipped in 2001 and 2002, and rumors that the Braves would move on from López became more and more audible. A team built around a pitching staff cannot afford to have a liability at catcher, especially a catcher paid as an All-Star-caliber player but who no longer performed as one, and this was on a team with growing budgetary concerns. One of the issues that plagued López throughout the 2002 season was a contentious divorce and the fear that López might become estranged from his two sons. The mental toll of the divorce and custody battle was tremendous, and were probably a strong factor in some of López's shortcomings on the field.[23]

Then … The 2003 season was undoubtedly López's best, statistically speaking. He was at a crucial juncture in his career. López was 32 years old and played a position in which players do not typically age gracefully. He had come off a dismal 2002 season, and faced the realization that the Braves had recently acquired their supposed catcher of the future in Johnny Estrada. Long gone were the All-Star campaigns of 1997 and 1998, and the postseason heroics of the mid-1990s. The reality was that López was a hit-first catcher with some pop who no longer could hit — or at least that was what the baseball world believed. López heard the critics, and in many regards he agreed with their assessment of the state of his game.

López entered the 2003 season with a new mental approach and a revamped conditioning program. No longer the flabby 248-pound catcher eating everything in sight, he was a lean 210-pounder who lifted weights multiple times per week instead of once or twice a month, the regimen he followed in previous seasons.[24] Whether these improvements were the result of hard work and determination or chemical enhancements, as was the theme of baseball of the period, could be debated for years to come. López even created some doubt on his new physique with interviews in which he was a little too coy about the subject. In an interview in 2010 he reflected upon 2003: "Well, everybody seen players getting big, hitting the ball harder, home runs and stuff. All of a sudden — boom — they got the big contract and everybody's like, 'You know what, did that, it worked for him, why not do it?'… I mean, how can I explain this? It's like if you're going to race cars, if you're going to race a car and some people are using nitro in the fuel [López laughed], and you see them winning all the time, and you're using regular gas — you know what? If they're using nitro and they've been winning, well, I'd be stupid enough not to use nitro, too."[25]

But the fact remains that López showed tremendous results from his lifestyle changes, regardless of how they were obtained, and slugged his way to an incredible 2003 season. Even the noticeable focus on his diet and conditioning did not create immediate benefits. López had to stop fighting his psyche in the batter's box — taking every out as an indictment of his abilities — and had to have faith in his natural abilities. Also, López opened his stance a bit, and began to reap the benefits. He made consistent and hard contact.[26] His new approach, conveniently in a contract season, created López's finest season in the big leagues with career highs in home runs (43), RBIs (109), batting average (.328), on-base percentage (.378), and slugging percentage (.687). López established the major-league record for home runs by a catcher, 42 (one of his home runs came via a pinch-hit against the Mets in July). He played in his third and final All-Star Game (he was the starting catcher for the National League) and was poised to cash in on his success in the coming free-agency period. But all of this success still did not mean that López would be catching one of the best pitchers of his generation, Greg Maddux.

One of the most discussed aspects of López's career was his professional relationship with Maddux. Attempting to explain why the most talented catcher on the roster was not catching Maddux, arguably the best pitcher in the league, article after article was published suggesting that, at least at some level, there was a rift between the two.

Both players downplayed the drama, but every time Maddux toed the rubber and López was not behind the plate, there would be a comment or question about it. In fact, between September 8, 1998, and September 28, 2003, if López caught a pitch from Maddux, it was because López entered the game late as a pinch-hitter, and manager Bobby Cox did not want to remove his ace pitcher from the game just yet.[27] Fueling the controversy was the fact that in 1994, when Maddux led the league with a 1.56 ERA, López caught 22 of his 25 starts. So, on paper at least, it seemed as if the two players could coexist in the same game.

Eddie Perez was a longtime backup catcher with the Braves and personal favorite of Maddux; he also downplayed the rift. Perez said a player knowing when he would get to play or have a day off was important for staying mentally sharp throughout the grind of the long season, and Maddux was able to provide this for two players, López and his backup, each season.[28] Even in the playoffs, Bobby Cox adhered to his distaste for pairing Maddux and López in the battery despite endless objections and questions from the media. It just seemed to be regarded as certain that López was not going to be catching Maddux, regardless of the magnitude of the situation.[29] After his career was over, López did admit that it bothered him that he did not catch Maddux in some of the biggest situations for the Braves. He wondered if the Braves could have won even more if he had caught Maddux, and he wondered how much more gaudy his own 2003 season would have been with the added at-bats from catching Maddux on a consistent basis.[30]

After his dominant 2003, López did test the free-agency waters and landed in Baltimore, which was attempting to revamp its offense. López played in a career-high 150 games, and batted .316. It was easily his second best season in the majors. Despite his impressive stats, López was on a losing team for the first time in his career and watched the postseason from home, but at least he was not watching alone.[31] The move to Baltimore coincided with another major happening in his life. On June 23, 2004, he married his second wife, Gina.[32]

The 2004 season was López's high-water mark with the Orioles, and in August of 2006 he was jettisoned to the Boston Red Sox for a journeyman player, Adam Stern. He played in 18 uneventful games before being released in September. López was re-entering the free-agency pool with much less luster than in his previous free-agency campaigns. López signed with the Colorado Rockies but was released before the 2007 season began. He tried a comeback with the Braves in spring training in 2008, but decided to retire when it became evident that he just could not hit the ball the way he once did and he was reassigned to the minor-league camp.[33]

López retired with a career batting average of .287, 260 home runs, a World Series ring, an NLCS MVP award, three All-Star team selections, one Silver Slugger Award, over $61 million in earnings, and an incredible pickoff throw in the 1995 World Series. He had played on 11 division winners, and had that magical 2003 season when he set the season record for home runs by a catcher.

López founded Bones Bats, a company that made hardwood bats, so that he would still have some connection to baseball.[34] He chose to use the word Bones instead of his name because he knew no player would buy a bat to use in the major leagues with another player's name on it. Appealing to major-league players with the bat did not work, and most of the sales were to the amateur ranks and dealers. Bones Bats did not prosper as López had hoped, but he felt strongly about his product and said he would continue to produce bats as long as he felt this way.[35]

López occasionally traveled to Florida to help coach the Braves young players during spring training. He was inducted into the Atlanta Braves Hall of Fame during the 2015 season.[36]

López and Gina settled in Suwanee, Georgia, in the Atlanta metropolitan area. They had two sons, Brody, born in 2014, and Gavin, born in 2010. He began to play in charity golf tournaments.[37] López also enrolled in Leadership Gwinnett to learn more about his community and its government, and to network with people outside of baseball.[38] He also spent more time at his longtime hobby of remote-control airplane flying.[39] López also strove to make at least two trips a year to his native Puerto Rico, especially for New Year's Eve, which was a time for rejoicing and celebration with his family and friends at his sister's home.[40]

## NOTES

1 Both baseball-reference.com and retrosheet.org list López at that height and weight.

2 Associated Press, "Javy López: What a Difference a Year Makes," *Augusta Chronicle*, June 28, 2003.

3 Javy López and Gary Caruso, *Behind the Plate: A Catcher's View of the Braves Dynasty* (Chicago: Triumph Books, 2012), 15-16.

4 "Braves: Javy López Returns to His Roots. Puerto Rico Welcomes Native Son Home," *Savannah Morning News*, April 15, 2003.

5 López and Caruso, 20.

6  "Braves: Javy López Returns to his Roots."

7  López and Caruso, 20-22.

8  "Braves: Javy López Returns to his Roots."

9  López and Caruso, 22-29.

10 "Braves: Javy López Returns to his Roots."

11 López and Caruso, 28.

12 I.J. Rosenberg, "Whatever Happened To: Ex-Brave Javy López," *Atlanta Journal-Constitution*, October 1, 2015.

13 López and Caruso, 32.

14 López and Caruso, 109.

15 I.J. Rosenberg, "Javy López Remembers Picking Off Manny Ramirez," *Atlanta Journal-Constitution*, October 1, 2015.

16 Gene Sapakoff, "Javy López Recalls 'Goofy' Maddux, Respect for Former Braves Coach Cox," *Charleston* (South Carolina) *Post and Courier*, January 28, 2014.

17 López and Caruso, 111.

18 Sapakoff.

19 Mike Berardino, "López Finally Grabbing Headlines," *South Florida Sun Sentinel* (Fort Lauderdale), September 13, 1998.

20 "Braves Lose López For Season," cbsnews.com/news/braves-lose-lopez-for-season/, accessed February 1, 2017.

21 López and Caruso, 103-104.

22 López and Caruso, 111.

23 Roch Kubatko, "Clearing His Mind, Though Not His Plate," *Baltimore Sun*, February 23, 2004.

24 Associated Press, "Javy López: What a Difference a Year Makes," *Augusta Chronicle*, June 28, 2003.

25 Craig Calcaterra, "Javy López on Steroids: 'I'd be Stupid Not to Use Nitro Too," Hardball Talk, http://mlb.nbcsports.com/2010/02/05/javy-lopez-on-steroids-i/, accessed December 14, 2016.

26 Associated Press, "Javy López: What a Difference a Year Makes."

27 Rafael Hermoso, "Baseball: If Maddux Is Pitching, López Isn't Catching," *New York Times*, October 5, 2002.

28 Mark Bowman, "For Perez, a Front-Row Squat at Maddux's Greatness," MLB.com, m.mlb.com/news/article/66355592/former-braves-catcher-eddie-perez-reflects-on-greg-madduxs-greatness/, accessed January 15, 2017.

29 Rafael Hermoso, "Baseball: If Maddux Is Pitching, López Isn't Catching."

30 Fox Sports South, "Javy López Q&A, Yardbarker.com, yardbarker.com/mlb/articles/javy_lopez_q_a/s1_10297_10268746?, accessed February 1, 2017.

31 Roch Kubatko, "Orioles, J. López Agree to Contract," *Baltimore Sun*, December 22, 2003.

32 López and Caruso, 116.

33 Associated Press, "Catcher Javy López Retires After Getting Cut by the Braves," *USA Today*, March 23, 2008.

34 Fox Sports South, "Javy López Q&A.

35 López and Caruso, 175-176.

36 "Javy López to the Braves HOF," NotintheHallofFame.com, notinhalloffame.com/home/news/4514-javy-lopez-to-the-braves-hof, accessed December 14, 2016.

37 I.J. Rosenberg, "Whatever Happened To: Ex-Brave Javy López."

38 López and Caruso, 177-178.

39 Bill Zach, "López Finds Escape Through His Planes," Online Athens, onlineathens.com/stories/111900/spo_1119000073.shtml#.WI-x97YrLR0, accessed January 31, 2017; Matt Hennie, "Javy López and His Multi-Million-Dollar Home," projectq.us/atlanta/javy_lopez_and_his_multi-million_dollar_home, accessed January 31, 2017.

40 López and Caruso, 16.

# MIKE LOWELL

## By Bill Nowlin

**M**IKE LOWELL WAS A NEW YORK Yankees prospect who won a world championship with the 2003 Florida Marlins (beating the Yankees). He then became part of a salary dump that saw him sent to the Boston Red Sox, where he picked up a second world champion ring and was accorded the honor of being named Most Valuable Player in the 2007 World Series.

He drove in 100 or more runs in three seasons, twice for the Marlins and once for the Red Sox.

The third baseman set and still holds both the best single-season fielding percentage record and the best career fielding record in Red Sox franchise history.

He's a four-time All-Star and won a Silver Slugger and a Gold Glove.

Mike's father, Carl Lowell, was a ballplayer, too, a right-handed pitcher who played on the Puerto Rican National Team in 1971. Though born in San Francisco, Carl Lowell was Cuban and remains the only Cuban pitcher to have beaten the Cuban national team. When he had the opportunity to meet the Cuban president, Carl Lowell chose to remain on the bus while the other Puerto Rican players had photographs taken with the Cuban leader. Mike's father-in-law, José López, reportedly spent some 15 years as a political prisoner under Fidel Castro.[1]

They weren't the first in the family to experience political persecution. Carl Lowell's grandfather and great-grandfather had both been placed in anti-German internment camps on the Isle of Pines for more than two years.[2] In fact, grandfather Carl Vogt-Lowell was an American citizen, born in Chicago, apparently imprisoned because of his Germanic surname. After being released from the prison camp, he returned to the United States and became a paratrooper near the end of World War II.[3]

His son was born Carl Lowell, in California, but returned to the island with his father and was raised as a Cuban. He played baseball there, but his family elected to move to Puerto Rico when Carl was 11. There Carl (or Carlos, as he was called) attended San Ignacio High School and won an academic scholarship to St. Joseph's University in Philadelphia. He played baseball at St. Joe's, too, a pitcher who threw a no-hitter, and became MVP of the team, and—after returning to Puerto Rico for dental school—he was named to the Puerto Rican National Team. He was later inducted into the Puerto Rico Athletic Hall of Fame.[4] It was when the Puerto Rican team played in the 1970 World Series of Baseball that he declined to be presented to Fidel Castro. And then in 1972, the team traveled to Cuba for a Friendly Series and played and beat the Cuban National Team, 5-4. Carl had pitched, and left with a 5-1 lead, scoring that fifth (and ultimately deciding) run himself.

Mike was born in San Juan, Puerto Rico, on February 24, 1974. His mother, Beatriz, was Cubana. When Mike was 4, the family moved to the Miami area, where his father ultimately established a dental practice in Coral Gables. "My upbringing, my culture, my customs are all Latino," Mike said in a September 2006 interview.[5] English became the dominant language in the Lowell home, though for family gatherings at holiday time, Spanish was more commonly spoken. Mike felt his English was a little better than his Spanish, grammatically, but he clearly fit in well with the Spanish speakers in the three big-league clubhouses where he plied his trade.

Carl Lowell took a half-day off from work on Wednesdays each week to take Mike and his brother to batting practice, and he coached Little League as well. And yet, Mike said in 2007, "What I appreciated most about my dad was he didn't push baseball on me." That said, when Mike showed an interest, "He was big on the mental side of the game. I remember him telling me, 'If you want to drive in the run, you've got to be the guy who wants it.'"[6] When

8-year-old Mike hit a game-winning homer one day in Little League, his father talked to him afterward, "Doesn't it feel great to get that hit? If you want to do that more often, you have to *want* to be the guy that's in that situation — because a lot of people say they want to be in that situation, but they don't want to be. … What's the worst that could happen? You make an out? Big deal. But if you *want* to be in that situation and you try your best, good things are going to happen."7

Mike graduated from Coral Gables High School, though he'd started high school at Christopher Columbus. He made the junior-varsity team there as a second baseman; one of his teammates was shortstop Alex Rodríguez. He began to sense he wasn't going to make the varsity, though, and so transferred to Coral Gables High.8

Mike had been drafted by the Chicago White Sox in the 48th round after high school, but elected not to sign. He became a freshman All-American at Florida International University, then played (and struggled) in a summer baseball league in Waynesboro, Virginia. The next summer he played for Chatham in the esteemed Cape Cod League. The FIU team, he said, was nationally ranked, at one point as high as eighth in the country. After he finished his junior year, he was drafted by the New York Yankees as their 20th-round pick in the June 1995 amateur draft. They settled on $20,000 plus the cost of tuition for his final two semesters of college. But they drafted him a catcher. He later said, "I had barely ever caught, and really had no desire to catch."9 It is worthy of note that Lowell graduated summa cum laude from FIU.10 His degree was in finance.

His first assignment was in Oneonta, New York, for the New York-Penn League Oneonta Yankees. He soon found himself playing third base, batting .260 in 72 games, with just one homer but with 18 doubles. He played in the instructional league, and then in 1996 played both for Greensboro and Tampa, batting .282 in both locations. Fielding was not always his forte; he committed 24 errors for Oneonta in 1995 and 34 for Greensboro and Tampa in 1996.

In 1997 Lowell broke out, batting .344 in 78 games for Double-A Norwich (Eastern League). Advanced to the Triple-A Columbus Clippers during the season, he didn't hit for as high an average (.276) but he hit 30 home runs for the season, 15 with Norwich and 15 with Columbus. He played in 126 games for Columbus in 1998, hitting 26 homers (and .304), earning himself a September call-up to the big leagues.

Lowell was right-handed, stood 6-feet-4, and weighed 195 pounds. The 1998 Yankees were on their way to a world championship, ultimately sweeping the San Diego Padres in four games in the World Series. It was a team that won 114 games. In September Lowell played in eight games. On September 13, his first at-bat produced a pop-fly single to center field at Yankee Stadium. A week later, he got into his second game and went 3-for-5, all singles. Those were his only four hits for the Yankees. He finished the tail end of the season 4-for-15 (.267) without a run batted in and with just one run scored. And he never played for the Yankees again. They had World Series MVP Scott Brosius and re-signed him for three more years.

On February 1, 1999, Lowell was traded to the Florida Marlins for three pitching prospects—Mark Johnson, Ed Yarnall, and minor-leaguer Todd Noel.

It was fortuitous. Lowell was pretty unlikely to break into the starting lineup for the Yankees at any time in the foreseeable future, whereas with Miami he was returning home and was positioned to earn a slot as a regular. Marlins GM Dave Dombrowski said, "He has a chance to be a premium third baseman for years to come."[11] And he had gotten married in the offseason, to Bertica López.

Eighteen days after the trade, during a routine physical for spring training, Lowell was taken aside, given some more tests, and diagnosed with testicular cancer. Two days later, on February 21, he had surgery which removed one of his testicles. Fortunately the cancer had not spread, and he was made aware that both Mike Gallego and John Kruk had beaten testicular cancer and gone on to big-league careers.[12]

Mike and Bertica had met at Coral Gables High School. Oddly enough, after they had become engaged, she herself had an ovary removed due to a cyst which proved to be benign. They were able to joke that with her having one ovary and Mike having one testicle, they were a "perfect fit."[13]

Mike's new father-in-law, José López, had been a political prisoner in Cuba for 15 years. There were some allowances for family, however, and during one visit to his family, he met a remarkable woman who married him while he was in prison. Bertica was conceived during a conjugal visit, her father spending the first three years of her life behind bars before he was released to Venezuela. The López family moved to Miami three years after that.[14]

The surgery was successful. Lowell underwent several radiation treatments as well; he lost 10 pounds in the first few weeks of treatment due to the associated vomiting. In just over five weeks, though, he was able to play in an exhibition game in Calgary, and hit two doubles and a home run.[15]

Lowell joined the Marlins, appearing in his first game on May 29. He was 0-for-4, but on May 30 was 2-for-3 with a single and a double and the first RBI of his career. That first base hit—the double to left-center off Cincinnati's Steve Parris and over the center fielder's head—broke the ice: "Okay, it was just a simple double, but, believe me, few hits in my career have offered such a sense of relief. I was back in it. All that cancer, radiation weakness was behind me now."[16] He drove in one or more runs in each of the four games after that as well. Lowell was perhaps not at full strength but played in almost every game for the rest of the season—97 in all—batting .253 with 12 home runs and 47 runs batted in.

That winter, Lowell was presented the 1999 Tony Conigliaro Award "given annually to the major leaguer who overcomes adversity through spirit, determination and courage."[17]

Mike and Bertica had two children, Alexis and Anthony.

Lowell got off to a very strong start in the 2000 season and after the team's first 21 games was batting an even .300 with 19 RBIs. Then he declined to play the April 25 game, as part of a work stoppage to protest the handling of the Elián González case, that of a 6-year-old Cuban refugee who was taken from his great-uncle's home in America to be returned to Cuba. His absence was approved by the ballclub; it was announced that "the Marlins organization gave its OK for front-office workers, players and coaches to be absent without pay. The team will close its downtown merchandise store for the day."[18] Lowell quoted as saying, "I've got problems with them (the US government) saying they're concerned with the kid's welfare, and they go in there like it's World War III."[19] Field manager John Boles, GM Dave Dombrowski, and team owner John W. Henry all approved of the form of protest.

Over the long course of the 2000 season, Lowell saw his average dip to .249 in late June and was still just at .250 in mid-July, but he built it back up to .270 by season's end, with 22 homers and 91 RBIs.

He drove in an even 100 runs in 2001 (with 18 homers and a .283 average), and then 92 more in 2002, the year he was first accorded All-Star status. One highlight of 2002 was participating in the first triple play in team history. It came in the third inning of a 1-1 game against the Montreal Expos on July 28.

There were runners on first and second and Vladimir Guerrero at the plate. On a 3-and-2 pitch, Guerrero slashed one to third base. Lowell saw baserunner Brad Wilkerson break from second toward third, which prompted him to get closer to the bag at third. He snagged it at ankle height and then stepped on the bag. "It was part good reaction, part self-defense," Lowell said. "It was cool."[20] Wilkerson pulled up helplessly and Lowell tagged him, and then took his time throwing to first since the other runner, José Vidro, had been off with contact, too, and was simply standing on second base.

In 2003 Lowell enjoyed both strong individual stats (a career-high 32 homers, helping produce 105 RBIs, and a second All-Star nod), but also the ultimate in team success: the Florida Marlins won the World Series. He was hit in the hand by a Hector Almonte fastball on August 30, and the resulting fracture almost caused him to miss the opportunity to play in the postseason, but he was able to come back just in time to get into one more game, on September 28 (1-for-4, with a double), and continue from there.

Lowell only had three plate appearances in the Division Series, without reaching base.

In Game One of the NLCS, against the Cubs at Wrigley Field, after Sammy Sosa's two-run homer in the bottom of the ninth had tied it up, the score stood 8-8 after 10 innings. Marlins manager Jack McKeon had already used the team's primary pinch-hitter, Todd Hollandsworth. Reliever Ugueth Urbina was due to lead off for the Marlins in the top of the 11th. McKeon asked Lowell to pinch-hit. On the sixth pitch of the at-bat, Lowell homered to center field off Mark Guthrie, the game-winning hit. Father Carl Lowell said he had "cried like a baby, because I had seen him go through the personal suffering" of missing almost the entire final month of the season, which could have cost the team a shot at the playoffs and probably did prevent Mike from finishing higher than 11th in the MVP balloting.[21]

The Cubs won the next three games, but come Game Five, now an elimination game, Florida's Josh Beckett shut out the Cubs on just two hits. Lowell won the game with another home run, a two-run shot off Carlos Zambrano in the bottom of the fifth.

It looked as though the Cubs were wrapping it up in Game Six, with a 3-0 lead at home through seven innings. The Marlins had only three hits to that point, but then exploded with an eight-run eighth that pushed the Series to a seventh game. In that eighth inning—it embraced the notorious Steve Bartman incident which robbed the Cubs of an out on a foul ball—Lowell came up with the score tied, 3-3, and runners on second and third with one out. He was walked intentionally, scoring three batters later on Mike Mordecai's three-run double.

Lowell had hit only .200 in the NLCS (4-for-20), but two of the hits were game-winning homers, and he had scored five times.

In the 2003 World Series against the New York Yankees, he was 5-for-23 at the plate, with two RBIs (both in Game Five), thanks to a single to center in the bottom of the fifth that boosted a 4-1 lead to 6-1. The final score was 6-4, with Lowell's two runs driven in being the difference in the game. More than 55,000 fans saw the Marlins' Josh Beckett shut out the Yankees at Yankee Stadium in Game Seven, limiting them to five hits in a tight 2-0 win. Beckett was named Series MVP. Mike Lowell earned a world championship ring.

There had been a medical scare during the '03 season. Lowell had hit 28 of his homers by the Marlins' 95th game, but a hip tweak and playing for more than three weeks with a strained groin prompted him to get an MRI. The doctors found what they feared was a recurrence of cancer; fortunately it turned out to be fibrous dysplasia, and a huge relief to the Lowell family.[22]

With a certain irony, the home runs coming so often—but then dropping off in the second half of the 2003 season—prompted whispering that perhaps Lowell had been taking steroids. He himself had wondered back in 1999 if he would need to, after the removal of a testicle, but doctors had advised him "my body would adjust—and if I did take testosterone or anything related to steroids, it would raise my testosterone levels to a point where my healthy testicle was going to be fooled into shutting down. That's where any talk of supplements ceased for me."[23]

At the end of the 2003 season, owner Jeffrey Loria signed Lowell to a four-year deal for $32 million. "I'm embarrassed to answer when people who don't know baseball ask me how much I make. I can't justify the money they pay me. Every time I look at one of my checks, I can't believe it," he told Jeff Miller of the *Miami Herald*. He never flaunted his wealth, though, and the family stuck to its values; when Mike offered to pay for his younger brother's and sister's school, his father said thanks but no thanks.[24]

In 2004 the Marlins finished third, just four games over .500 (83-79). Lowell had another very good year, another All-Star year (.293, 27 HR, 85 RBIs). His biggest day was April 21, with a three-homer game with four RBIs in an 8-7 12-inning win in Philadelphia. Lowell was popular with other players, too. Before the 2004 All-Star Game, third baseman Scott Rolen of the Cardinals talked about Lowell's world championship ring, but said, "He plays the game right. He has a great knowledge of the game. He goes out and competes every day. He understands the importance of running out there and being accountable and being on the field. He's a fun guy to watch." Then, to keep from getting too carried away with compliments, he added a further assessment: "He's a [jerk]. I think his head is kind of disproportional to the rest of his body."[25]

Lowell had a discouraging year in 2005. The positive was his defense. In 150 games, he committed only six errors, a .983 fielding percentage, and he won a Gold Glove.[26] On offense, however, he put up what he himself called "grim numbers": a .236 batting average, with just eight home runs. He drove in only 58 runs. "That was the reality of my '05 season," he wrote. "And these grim numbers were all the more inexplicable given that I was coming off perhaps the best year of my career in '04."[27] He'd maybe tinkered too much with his swing. It was reported that in August a contact lens he wore on his lead eye broke and he never found a suitable replacement, but Lowell himself says he had no problems with contacts that year.[28]

Inexplicable was a good word. After the season, he turned for advice to Gary Denbo, who had been one of his minor-league hitting coaches in his early days with the Yankees. Denbo was coaching in Japan at the time, but he talked with Lowell and urged him to get back to fundamentals, even to start using a batting tee again. Denbo then looked at some video Mike sent him, and when Denbo returned to Tampa, they worked together simply focusing on hitting balls up the middle.

In the meantime, on November 24, Lowell changed organizations. As he put it, the Boston Red Sox were "forced to take me in a trade with the Florida Marlins if they were going to get the blessed arm of Josh Beckett."[29] The Red Sox wanted Beckett badly. He was 25 years old, coming off a 15-8 season with the Marlins, and had been the World Series MVP for them in 2003. The Marlins told the Red Sox that if they wanted Beckett, they had to take Lowell, too, saving them $18 million for the final two years of his four-year contract. The two were traded, with Guillermo Mota, in exchange for four young players with potential: Jesus Delgado, Harvey Garcia, Hanley Ramirez, and Anibal Sánchez. It was a trade that worked well for both parties—Beckett excelled

for the Red Sox, a 20-game winner in 2007; Hanley Ramirez was Rookie of the Year in 2006, hit .300 in seven seasons in Miami, and won the NL batting crown in 2009. Though the Red Sox didn't know it at the time, they were not only acquiring the 2003 World Series MVP, but also—in Mike Lowell—the 2007 World Series MVP as well.

Lowell, of course, wanted to prove himself in 2006, and succeeded, starting with a home run on Opening Day in Texas. He put together a solid season, both on offense and defense, batting .284, hitting 20 home runs, and driving in 80 runs. His .987 fielding percentage in 2006 was (and remains) the best in Red Sox franchise history.

The short-season A ball minor-league affiliate Lowell Spinners scheduled a little fun during the year, changing their name for one night (July 28) to the Mike Lowell Spinners. They even tailored their jerseys for the game to read "Mike Lowell" on the front.[30]

The year 2007 was a magical year, though Lowell started shakily in the field with three errors in the second game of the season, and by the end of April he already had eight errors, two more than in the entire 2006 season. He committed 15 errors in all in 2007. By the end of April, though, he already had 20 RBIs.

There was no late-season injury this time to threaten his availability in the postseason. Lowell drove in 26 months in the month of September alone, helping the Sox seal the deal and clinch a playoff berth. He finished the season with 120 RBIs (a team record for a third baseman) and a .324 average.

The Red Sox swept the Division Series over the Angels, scoring 19 runs to their four. Lowell drove in one run in each of the three games. In the ALCS against the Cleveland Indians, it took seven games to win. Lowell drove in three runs in Game One (including the winning run) and three more in Game Two, a game lost when the Indians scored seven runs in the top of the 11th. Cleveland won three of the first four games, but then the Red Sox bounced back with three of wins of their own, lopsided ones at that. Lowell drove in one run in Game Six and one more in Game Seven, with a sacrifice fly that drove in the third run in an 11-2 win.

Then came the World Series against the Colorado Rockies. Josh Beckett won Game One with ease, 13-1, becoming 4-0 in the postseason. Curt Schilling won a 2-1 squeaker in Game Two, with Lowell's double in the bottom of the fifth breaking a 1-1 tie. In Game Three, in Denver, he drove in a pair in the top of the third. And in the final Game Four of the sweep, Lowell homered to lead off the top of the seventh, giving Boston a 3-0 lead at the time (the Red Sox won, 4-3.) "It was my third at-bat. … I looked for a sinker in and there it was. … I knew I hit it really well, with nice trajectory, but at that point I didn't take anything for granted because it was the World Series. I was looking at the left fielder and saw him running and subsequently slow down. That is a great feeling. But what I really, really enjoyed was that home-run trot." Harking back to the advice his father gave him when he was 8, he said, "This was the moment I had yearned for ever since that car ride with Dad. To be on the big stage at the big moment. It was also the culmination of years of what I call my visualizations."[31]

A number of players could have been awarded the MVP trophy, but it was presented to Mike Lowell. The *Boston Globe*'s Bob Ryan said he felt that Lowell merited it even before Game Four, then he scored the second run and then homered for the third run.[32] He'd hit .333 in the ALDS, .333 in the ALCS, and .http://sabr.org/bioproj/person/35b5cb46400 in the World Series, with 15 postseason RBIs.

Lowell's contributions in the regular season earned him fifth in league MVP voting.

Three of the 2007 Red Sox won World Series MVPs—Beckett (with the Marlins) in 2003, Lowell in 2007, and David Ortiz in 2013.

Lowell's contract was up at the end of the year. Fan sentiment was vocal at postseason events. "Bring back Lowell!" was the cry. In the celebratory parade, someone handed Jason Varitek a sign reading "Re-sign Lowell" and he held it throughout. Manny Ramirez yelled it repeatedly to fans along the route. The sentiment was so strong that the team almost had no choice. The Red Sox didn't waste time, and in mid-November signed him to a three-year, $37.5 million deal. He probably could have gotten a fourth year elsewhere; Peter Gammons reported both the Phillies and Dodgers had offered it. "How cool is that?" asked Curt Schilling. "Leaving years and dollars on the table to come back here for three more years, good stuff."33

The 2008 season was a struggle. Lowell lost a few weeks in August and early September, and in October had to undergo surgery to repair a torn labrum in his right hip. He hit .274 with 73 RBIs, and put up very similar figures in 2009: .290, with 75 RBIs. He homered 17 times in each year.

Just before spring training began in 2010, the Red Sox tried to trade him to Texas, agreeing to pay 75 percent of his salary because a damaged ligament in his right thumb had caused him to fail a physical. In 2010, with Adrian Beltre at third base and Kevin Youkilis at first, Lowell had what became his final year, appearing in only 73 games, batting for a .239 average with 5 homers and 26 runs batted in. In early September he announced his retirement. "It's been 12 outstanding years and I don't regret anything in my career," he said. "I'm super happy to spend time with my family, but I'm super happy to say I played baseball as my job. I wanted to do it since I was 6 years old. To have that chance has really been unbelievable."34

On October 2, the Red Sox held a "Thanks, Mike Night" at Fenway Park.

In 2011 he began as a studio analyst on the MLB Network, and as of the close of 2016 continues to work for the network.

Having retired from the daily grind of baseball provides opportunities to make up for some of the inevitably "lost time" with family. In mid-November 2016, Lowell says, "I am enjoying plenty of family time. Specifically, coaching my son's 12u baseball team. I am also enjoying watching my daughter as she entered high school and played volleyball there as a ninth grader."35

## SOURCES

In addition to the sources noted in this biography, the author also accessed Lowell's player file from the National Baseball Hall of Fame, the *Encyclopedia of Minor League Baseball*, Retrosheet.org, Baseball-Reference.com, and the SABR Minor Leagues Database, accessed online at Baseball-Reference.com. Most of the story regarding the political problems the family faced—and most of the information regarding Mike's upbringing in Cuba, Puerto Rico, and Florida come from his 2008 autobiography, *Deep Drive*.

## NOTES

1. Bill Nowlin, "Hot Season at the Hot Corner," *Diehard*, October 2006.
2. Mike Lowell with Rob Bradford, *Deep Drive* (New York: Celebra, 2008), 39.
3. *Deep Drive*, 40.
4. *Deep Drive*, 81. Also see caption on photograph in the photo insert opposite page 146.
5. Author interview with Mike Lowell, September 2006.
6. Nick Cafardo, "A Firm Grasp at Third," *Boston Globe*, March 18, 2007.
7. *Deep Drive*, 5, 6.
8. *Deep Drive*, 98-103. Alex Rodríguez transferred, too, to Westminster Christian High School.
9. *Deep Drive*, 112, 113.
10. Clark Spencer, "Home Schooled," *Miami Herald*, February 29, 2004.
11. Rod Beaton, "Yankees Get Pitching, Marlins Finally Get Lowell," *USA Today*, February 3, 1999.
12. Joel Sherman, "Lowell Undergoes Testicular Surgery," *New York Post*, February 23, 1999.
13. *Deep Drive*, 139.
14. *Deep Drive*, 41-43.
15. Fred Tasker, "Mike Lowell Remembers Vividly the Day the Fort Lauderdale Oncologist Told Him He Had Testicular Cancer," *Miami Herald*, June 13, 2002.
16. *Deep Drive*, 145.
17. Bloomberg News, "Lowell Is Honored," *New York Times*, December 14, 1999.
18. Associated Press, "Marlins Join Cuban-American Protest," AOL News, April 25, 2000.
19. Ibid. The Marlins lost the game to the Giants, 6-4, in 11 innings.

20 Ted Hutton, "For Lowell, Triple Play 'Was Cool,'" *South Florida Sun Sentinel*, July 29, 2002: 3C.

21 "Home Schooled."

22 Any family that has experienced good news of a medical nature can relate to Lowell's talking about the family dancing around his brother Victor's apartment, joyfully chanting "fibrous dysplasia" over and over, when three doctors concurred in that diagnosis. See *Deep Drive*, 13, 14.

23 *Deep Drive*, 154.

24 Jeff Miller, "A Bargain, Even at $32 Million," *Miami Herald*, December 4, 2003.

25 Mike Berardino, "1st Class at 3rd; Lowell, Rolen," *Sun-Sentinel*, July 13, 2004.

26 Lowell did pull off the first two hidden ball tricks of the 21st century — on September 15, 2004, getting Montreal's Brian Schneider, and on August 10, 2005, tagging out Luis Terrero of the Diamondbacks.

27 *Deep Drive*, 21.

28 Chris Snow, "Lowell Offers His Spin," *Boston Globe*, November 26, 2005. Mike Lowell e-mail to author, November 14, 2016.

29 *Deep Drive*, 7.

30 "Name Game," *USA Today*, July 18, 2006.

31 *Deep Drive*, 205-207.

32 Bob Ryan, "Exclamation Point Added," *Boston Globe*, October 29, 2007: E4.

33 "Red Sox Keep World Series MVP Lowell with Three-Year Deal," ESPN.com, November 19, 2007.

34 John Tomase, "As End Nears, Mike Lowell Looks Back at Career," *Boston Herald*, September 13, 2010.

35 Mike Lowell e-mail to author, November 14, 2016.

# CANDY MALDONADO

## By Tom Hawthorn

FRED MERKLE HAD HIS BONER AND Steve Bartman his bobbled foul ball. For Candy Maldonado, a momentary lapse and blinding lights contributed to a play less infamous but just as devastating for the unfortunate protagonist.

It was October 13, 1987, as Game Six of the National League Championship Series pitted Maldonado's San Francisco Giants (90-72) against the St. Louis Cardinals (95-67). The Giants needed just one more win to advance to the World Series for the first time in 25 years.

Tony Peña, leading off the bottom of the second inning for the hometown Cardinals, lined a Dave Dravecky pitch toward Maldonado in right field. The fielder charged in before sinking to his knees on the artificial turf as the ball sailed over his head. By the time the ball was returned to the infield, Peña was standing on third base.

One out later, with the Giants infield playing in, batter Jose Oquendo sliced a soft fly toward Maldonado. "Fly ball to right field and pretty shallow," Vin Scully told television viewers. "Maldonado makes the catch and Peña's going to come! Here's the throw, the play, he is …"

Maldonado raced about 15 steps toward the seats, his momentum taking him across the foul line as he caught the ball before quickly pivoting to face home plate. He made a strong, one-hop throw to catcher Bob Melvin, the ball arriving about 10 feet up the line as Peña sidestepped his counterpart. "He is … safe!" Scully declared.[1]

The Cardinals nursed that lone run to victory. After the game, Maldonado was disconsolate. "I just lost the ball in the lights," he said. "I tried to protect my face. I got the glove up but fell and missed it." Nor did the outfielder ignore his lapse on the throw home. "If I make a good throw, the man is out. We might still be playing the game."[2] Newspapers the next day showed Maldonado on his back like an overturned turtle, glove helplessly up in the air, the ball bouncing away. The Cardinals went on to win Game Seven and the Giants' promising season seemed to have turned on an outfielder's misplay.

Nine months later, lingering tensions between the teams erupted when a hard slide led to a bench-clearing brawl. With Will Clark on first base, Maldonado hit a grounder fielded by Cardinals shortstop Ozzie Smith, who tossed underhand to José Oquendo as Clark barreled through and beyond second base. Oquendo's response was to knee or kick Clark (the video evidence is inconclusive), whose rise from the dirt led to a flurry of pushing and punching. Smith punched Clark from behind. Seeing his teammate ganged up on by four Cardinals, including Oquendo, a fellow Puerto Rican, Maldonado raced from first base to throw a desperate, diving haymaker punch at Smith, bloodying his lip.[3]

Those lowlights in a 15-season career were more than matched by highlights, including several breathtaking throws, spectacular catches, and timely hits, most notably during the 1992 World Series, when he helped the Toronto Blue Jays win the first championship by a team not based in the United States.

In his career, Maldonado went from being a touted (but surplus) prospect to a struggling (and self-doubting) newcomer to a valued (but mercenary) hitter. He patrolled the outfield for seven major-league teams—the Los Angeles Dodgers (1981-85), Giants (1986-89), Cleveland Indians (1990, 1993-94), Milwaukee Brewers (1991), Blue Jays (1991-92, 1995), Chicago Cubs (1993), and the Texas Rangers (1995).

Cándido Maldonado y Guadarrama was born in Humacao, Puerto Rico, on September 5, 1960. His father, Cándido Maldonado de León, worked as a heavy-machinery operator, while his mother, Irene Guardarrama de Jesús, worked in a factory, later establishing her own food business. The young athlete moved to Arecibo on the island's north shore to play Little League baseball. He would eventually drop out of junior high school to pursue a baseball career. As he played in his homeland, he attracted the attention of scouts representing six major-league teams, though none was prepared to make an offer.

"I was kind of disappointed," Maldonado later said, "but I kept playing hard."[4]

After a game, he was approached by Ralph Avila, a scout for the Dodgers best known for his work in the Dominican Republic. The interest after so much rejection left the player unimpressed. "I gave him my name and all the details, but I didn't care anymore. After all those others, I was tired of wasting my time."[5]

The Dodgers liked the youth's whip-like batting stroke and strong right arm. He was signed as a non-drafted free agent on June 17, 1978, soon establishing himself as an exciting, power-hitting prospect at age 17 with the Pioneer League team in Lethbridge, Alberta. After another season split between Lethbridge and the Dodgers farm team in Clinton, Iowa, Maldonado graduated to the Lodi Dodgers of the California League, where he smacked 25 home runs in his first 121 games in 1980. He was leading the circuit in home runs, runs batted in, and total bases when his season ended prematurely after he suffered a spiral fracture of the pinky on his left (catching) hand while diving for a line drive. Sportswriters and official scorers named him a league all-star, while he also shared most valuable player honors with Jamie Cocanower, a pitcher.[6]

Maldonado feasted on Triple-A pitching after being promoted to the Albuquerque Dukes of the Pacific Coast League for the 1981 season. The outfielder whacked two homers and knocked in six runs in a 15-9 win over Phoenix on April 22. He was only getting warmed up. On April 30, he hit two round-trippers in his final two at-bats against the Tucson Toros. He was plunked in his first plate appearance the following night, and responded by hitting a solo shot in the fourth and a two-run homer in the fifth to power his team to a 7-5 success. The homers on four consecutive at-bats tied a league mark set by

Gus Zernial in 1948 and matched by Ted Beard five years after that.[7]

Maldonado didn't only do his slugging with a bat. On August 18, 1981, he was hit in the helmet by a pitch thrown by Rick Aponte of the Toros. Maldonado charged the mound, only to be tackled by trailing Toros catcher Tom Vessey. As both dugouts emptied, Maldonado's manager, Del Crandall, went after Aponte, who blocked a punch with his gloved hand. For his efforts, Crandall was punched in the nose by Toros first baseman Danny Heep. It was the fifth time in the season that Maldonado fought a pitcher.[8]

Maldonado and first baseman Mike Marshall gave the Dukes a mighty power duo and the pair received attention from *The Sporting News* and other newspapers as future stars. Both players were September call-ups, debuting in the majors at Dodger Stadium on September 7, 1981, two days after Maldonado's 21st birthday. The 6-foot, 180-pound outfielder replaced Dusty Baker in left field in the ninth inning of a 5-1 victory over the San Francisco Giants. The Candy

Man, as he was called, went just 1-for-12 with five strikeouts in his first stint with the Dodgers.

After a stellar 1981 campaign with the Dukes (.335, 21, 104), he returned to Albuquerque for more seasoning in 1982, once again recording strong numbers (.301, 24, 96) and again joining the parent Dodgers in September.

Meanwhile, Maldonado continued to play in the Puerto Rico Winter League with the Arecibo Lobos (Wolves), who took the league title in 1982-83. The Lobos went on to win the Caribbean World Series in Caracas, Venezuela, posting a 5-1 record. Against Mexico, Maldonado hit a two-run single in the eighth inning for a 2-1 victory. He also hit a three-run homer and saved another game with a leaping, over-the-fence catch. The heroics cemented his reputation among Puerto Rican fans, and to no one's surprise Maldonado was named the tournament's all-star center fielder.

A month later, Maldonado reported to training camp at Dodgertown in Vero Beach, Florida. At 22, he had been in the organization five years, still without a spot on the parent club. The Dodgers already had five outfielders. "Where am I going to put him?" lamented manager Tommy Lasorda.[9] Maldonado was asked to try third base as a potential backup to Pedro Guerrero, another player who had chafed at a long internship.

With his options running out, Maldonado figured he might be traded to another team. "I've got to realize that a lot of ballplayers are going through the same thing," he said. "I guess what makes the difference between being a kid and a man is having a little more understanding of what's happening around you, why this may not be for you."[10]

Maldonado split the 1983 season between Albuquerque and the Dodgers, where he replaced Ron Roenicke as a fifth outfielder. Maldonado recorded just 12 hits, including his first big-league home run, in 62 at-bats (.194), as both Lasorda and batting instructor Manny Mota blamed impatient aggressiveness at the plate for the poor showing. He got his first taste of the postseason, going 0-for-2 as a pinch-hitter as the Dodgers lost the best-of-five National League Championship Series in four games to the Philadelphia Phillies.

Maldonado would become one of those players who seemed always to be in the playoffs even as he bounced from team to team, seeing postseason action in 1983, '85, '87, '89, '91, and '92.

Maldonado spent the next two seasons full-time with the Dodgers before he was traded to the Giants for Mexican-born catcher Alex Trevino in December 1985. The Giants at first used him as a pinch-hit specialist. In his first month in San Francisco, the new acquisition registered eight hits, including two homers, in 10 pinch-hit appearances, knocking in six runs. That earned him a full-time spot in the lineup at last, and Maldonado hit 18 and 20 home runs in successive seasons.

On May 4, 1987, Maldonado, batting cleanup, hit for the cycle in game against the Cardinals at Busch Stadium. Maldonado was left stranded after hitting a third-inning triple. By the time he came to bat in the seventh, he was 1-for-3 and his team was trailing by 7-2. Maldonado homered off starter Danny Cox, who lasted only one more batter. Maldonado then singled in the eighth and doubled in the ninth as the Giants came from behind for a 10-7 victory.

Following their collapse in the 1987 Championship Series, the Giants returned to the playoffs two years later, eliminating the Chicago Cubs before being swept in the Earthquake Series by the cross-bay rival Oakland A's. Before the Series, Maldonado lamented a season-long slump in which his swing seemed to have deserted him. "I went through a lot of things that probably could have destroyed me, because (baseball) is something that I love," he said. "It's frustrating when you know you're not doing the job you can do and you see the other guys doing it all and you want to be a part of it."[11] In the end, Maldonado struck out four times in 11 at-bats, his only safety a pinch-hit triple off reliever Rick Honeycutt in Game Four. The outfielder signed as a free agent with the Cleveland Indians the following month. He hit a career high 22 homers for the Tribe in 1990 before signing with the Milwaukee Brewers just before the start of the 1991 season. In August, the Blue Jays pried him from the Brewers in exchange for minor leaguer Bob Wishnevski and a player to be named later, who turned out to be minor leaguer William Suero. Maldonado responded by hitting .277 in 52 games with 7 homers and 28 RBIs, though he sagged with a 2-for-20 run in the postseason.

Maldonado hit .272 with 20 homers for the Blue Jays in 1992. He had timely hits in the World Series, the first coming in the bottom of the ninth inning of Game Three against the Atlanta Braves at Skydome in Toronto. A series of managerial chess moves pitting relief pitchers against pinch-hitters led to a situation with the bases loaded and one out in a 2-2 game. Jimy Williams, acting in place of manager Bobby Cox, who had been tossed for throwing a helmet onto the field, called on Jeff Reardon to face Maldonado, who had a woeful 2-for-13 career record with seven strikeouts against the right-hander. Maldonado swing and badly missed two curveballs from Reardon, who then threw a third. The Candy Man was waiting for it. "I figured after the first two made me look so bad, he wasn't going to change," Maldonado said later.[12] The batter drove the ball to deep center for a game-winning single in the first World Series game played in Canada.

Maldonado's second hit in the Series came against left-hander Steve Avery in Game Six, a solo homer to left field in Atlanta in the top of the fourth inning to give the Blue Jays a 2-1 lead. Maldonado and the Jays went on to win the game, 4-3, in 11 innings, and the World Series.

He spent the next three more seasons wearing four different uniforms. Maldonado retired after the 1995 season with a .254 career average, 146 homers, and 618 RBIs in 1,410 major-league games.

Five years later, Maldonado joined the Spanish-language ESPN Deportes as an analyst and co-host of such shows as *Beisbol Esta Noche*. Among his contributions was a weekly online video, called *La Esquina de Candy* (Candy's Corner), in which he addressed newsworthy topics.

Maldonado has been inducted into the Salón de la Fama del Béisbol Profesional de Puerto Rico (Puerto Rican Baseball Hall of Fame) and the Pabellón de la Fama del Caribe (Caribbean Baseball Hall of Fame).

## SOURCES

In addition to the sources cited in the Notes, the author also consulted Baseball-Reference.com and Retrosheet.org. Thanks to Jorge Colon-Delgado and Candy Maldonado for helping with information for this biography.

## NOTES

1. *Tony Pena Scores on Candy Maldonado's Throw* [video]. Retrieved January 17, 2017. youtube.com/watch?v=2q6tH9KNSag.
2. Steve Wilstein, "Maldonado: 'I Feel Real Down,'" *Star Press* (Muncie, Indiana), October 14, 1987.
3. *Will Smith Takes on Ozzie Smith and Jose Oquendo* [video]. Retrieved March 13, 2017. youtube.com/watch?v=2hbxU2oSkNQ.
4. Paul Scherr, "Maldonado, Marshall Climb Fast on Dodger Ladder," *The Sporting News*, July 25, 1981: 38.
5. Ibid.
6. "Season Ends Early for Maldonado," *The Sporting News*, September 13, 1980: 57.
7. "The Candy Man," *The Sporting News*, May 23, 1981: 41.
8. "Dukes Duke It Out," *The Sporting News*, September 12, 1981: 69.
9. Gordon Edes, "Maldonado: What He Wants Is a Chance," *Los Angeles Times*, March 7, 1983.
10. Ibid.
11. "Giant Hopes Slump Is a Thing of the Past." *Press-Citizen* (Iowa City, Iowa), October 13, 1989.
12. *1992 World Series video* [video]. Retrieved April 3, 2017. youtube.com/watch?v=mDVND9PC8DQ.

# FÉLIX MANTILLA

## By Rick Schabowski

**V**ERSATILITY IS THE BEST WORD to describe Félix Mantilla's 11-year career, in which he won a world championship with the 1957 Milwaukee Braves, appeared in the All-Star Game, and played every position other than pitcher and catcher.

Félix (Lamela) Mantilla was born on July 29, 1934, in Isabela, a town in the northwest corner of Puerto Rico. His parents were Navidad, of Taino Indian and Spanish descent, and Juan, of African descent. Juan drove a taxi and Félix said that the family "never had much money, but you know, it never seemed to bother us."[1] Félix had two younger sisters, Judith, who graduated from the Interamerican University in San German, Puerto Rico, and Felicita, who became a police officer with the Puerto Rican Police Department.

Puerto Ricans love baseball. There are many different levels of leagues in the country. Mantilla began playing baseball when he was 9 years old, competing in police-sponsored leagues. He was such an excellent third baseman that he was promoted to what Puerto Ricans call Class-A ball, playing with older teammates. After a year he was promoted to Arecibo, a city about 45 miles from Isabela to compete in a Class-AA league. Later, he became a player on the Puerto Rican National team. Mantilla also played high-school sports, competing in softball, baseball, and track, running in the 100-meter event. One of Mantilla's greatest accomplishments was playing for the Puerto Rican National team that won the Amateur World Series in 1951, defeating Cuba 6-5.

At Caguas in the Puerto Rican league, Mantilla played for manager Luis Olmo, who spent six years in the major leagues with the Brooklyn Dodgers and Boston Braves. Olmo sent Mantilla to the Boston Braves' minor-league camp at Myrtle Beach, South Carolina. "I always wanted to be a big leaguer," Mantilla said. "I guess I looked pretty good at Caguas, so the (team) sent me to the Braves for a trial. They had a kind of working agreement."[2] Braves scout Hugh Wise was so impressed with Mantilla that he offered him a contract. Mantilla remembered signing the final contract and said, "It was for (a bonus of) $400, which seems paltry today, but back then, I can assure you, it was a fortune. Of course I grabbed it and signed." Asked how he spent his bonus, Mantilla said, "Are you kidding? My mother got it."[3]

Before leaving for the camp, Mantilla got a warning from his high-school principal. "The principal knew that I was going to the United States, and he told me, Félix, you might have some problems when you get to the US. You are going to go from San Juan to Miami, then from Miami to Myrtle Beach. Sometimes if you ride a bus, to avoid problems you have to sit in the back."[4] This was all new to Mantilla, since he didn't have to go through this in Puerto Rico, but he was grateful for the advice, and having about 10 Puerto Rican players accompany him on the trip made it a little easier.

The Myrtle Beach complex had four baseball diamonds, and in the middle was a tower for the coaches to observe. One day Mantilla was taking batting practice with the Class-C Eau Claire team, then "It was the seventh inning of the [Class-B] Evansville game, and they needed a third baseman. They sent me over, and I stayed with Evansville. It was a break for me."[5]

Another barrier Mantilla had to overcome was being able to communicate in English. "They wanted me to go for English lessons in Evansville, and I went to school, but they talked too fast," he said. "I picked up my English at the movies, Westerns. There were three or four movie theaters, but there was only one where colored people could sit in the balcony and watch."[6]

At Evansville (Three-I League) Mantilla played for manager Bob Coleman, of whom he said, "He liked me, and I liked the guy. He gave me a chance to play."[7] Mantilla had an impressive 1952 season, playing shortstop and batting .323, and was named the Three-I League's rookie of the year and its All-Star shortstop.

In the offseason, Mantilla played winter ball for Caguas in the Puerto Rican league, where one of his teammates, second baseman Henry Aaron, was moved to the outfield where, Mantilla said, "It seemed he was more at ease than he was at second."[8]

For 1953 Mantilla was promoted to the Jacksonville Braves of the Class-A South Atlantic League. He, Aaron, and Horace Garner integrated the team for the first time and helped as it finished in first place. (The Braves lost in the playoff finals.) Mantilla batted .278 and Aaron led the league in batting (.362). "Jacksonville was real bad. I'm talking about 1953, not now," Mantilla said. "They wouldn't boo you because you were playing bad; it was just because you were colored."[9]

Again he spent the offseason playing for Caguas, helping the team capture the Puerto Rican title. For 1954 "They were going to move me to what I think was the Atlanta Crackers at the time, but I wasn't too receptive to that idea, so they moved me to the Triple-A team in Toledo. ... It was pretty tough there too, though."[10] Mantilla batted .273 and hit 16 home runs. In a Memorial Day doubleheader sweep at Louisville, he accounted for eight of his team's 12 runs, belting two triples in the opener and a three-run homer in the nightcap. He had a 23-game hitting streak during the season. Still only 20 years old, Mantilla also spent the 1955 season at Toledo, batting .275

At Milwaukee's spring training in Bradenton, Florida, in 1956, Mantilla impressed manager Charlie Grimm, who said he had "one of the best pair of hands I ever saw."[11] For the start of the season he was sent to Sacramento of the Pacific Coast League, but was called up on June 15 to provide backup for shortstop Johnny Logan, who was in a batting slump. He made his major-league debut on June 21 against the Pittsburgh Pirates at Forbes Field, replacing Logan at shortstop. In his first at-bat he popped out to the second baseman. He made his first start on July 1, against the Chicago Cubs in the second game of a doubleheader at Wrigley Field, playing third base and leading off. He went hitless in four at-bats. Mantilla said he was "kind of nervous, but after one inning, I lost my nervousness."[12] He stayed with the Braves the rest of the season, batting .283 in 53 at-bats.

Mantilla earned a spot on the Braves' 1957 roster, impressing manager Haney, who observed that "At third, he's as quick as a cat and has that arm. He can make the pivot on the double play at second."[13] After the newly acquired Red Schoendienst was injured, Mantilla briefly filled in for him.

Mantilla suffered a bruised chest in a collision with outfielder Billy Bruton on July 11 and was sidelined for 18 days. (Bruton was sidelined for the rest of the season.) Mantilla returned to duty on July 29 at County Stadium with a pinch-hit bases-loaded walk that ended a wild extra-inning contest against the New York Giants. The come-from-behind victory kept the Braves in first place by a half-game over St. Louis. In mid-August he filled in at shortstop for Logan, who was recovering from an infected shinbone.

Playing in Milwaukee was an unbelievable experience, Mantilla said. "I remember in spring training, Humberto Robinson said, 'When you get to that city you won't believe it.' I didn't have any idea. I thought maybe it was like Puerto Rico where people got kind of goofy. But when I came here it was a different thing. When I was in the house I could hear at the back door someone was leaving milk. They used to bring a gallon every day for free. There was beer out there. ... We used to get Wisco 99 gas and a car from Rank and Son (a Milwaukee car dealer). I had never seen a place like this before. And the fans. If you lost a game they didn't boo you. Coming from a Latin country, when you started losing games you had to watch your back. The park was crowded every day. It was a good feeling every time you went to the ballpark. With the fans behind you, you can't lose."[14]

Mantilla played in four games in the Braves' World Series victory over the Yankees. As a pinch-runner he scored the tying run in Game Four. He

replaced second baseman Schoendienst (pulled muscle) in Game Five and started Games Six and Seven at Yankee Stadium. In Game Seven. Being on the field for the final out in Game Seven "was the greatest feeling of all time," he said. Mantilla called the World Series victory one of his memorable accomplishments.[15]

Mantilla demonstrated his versatility during the 1958 season, starting 27 games in center field, filling in for the injured left fielder Wes Covington, and also filling in at second base, shortstop and third base. One of his biggest disappointments was the Braves' loss to the Yankees in their World Series rematch, when Milwaukee squandered a three-games-to-one advantage.

At Caguas after the 1958 season, manager Ben Geraghty moved Mantilla from shortstop to second base to help facilitate his probable move to second base to replace tuberculosis-stricken Schoendienst in 1959. As it turned out, Mantilla played 60 games at second, one of six players to fill in for Schoendienst.

In Harvey Haddix's historic pitching feat on May 26, Mantilla became the Braves' first baserunner when he reached first on a throwing error by Pirates third baseman Don Hoak to lead off the 13th inning. Mantilla went to second base on Eddie Mathews' sacrifice and scored the winning run on Joe Adcock's blast. But the season ended on a sour note for the Braces, who were swept by the Los Angeles Dodgers in two games in a best-of-three pennant playoff. Mantilla started Game Two at second base but switched to shortstop after Johnny Logan was injured in the seventh inning. In the 12th inning with two out and Dodgers on first and second, Carl Furillo hit a grounder up the middle. "When the ball came over the pitcher's head," said Mantilla, "I thought I could pick it up and step on the bag. When I got it, I was past the bag and I knew I had to throw to first. I never thought of not throwing to first because I could've gotten him with a good throw. I was off balance when I threw, and that's why it bounced away."[16] Gil Hodges scored on the play, giving the Dodgers the pennant. Braves manager Fred Haney said of Mantilla, "He did the only thing he could, he didn't make a bad play. He was lucky to stop the ball at all."[17]

The 1960 season was another carousel at second base. The Braves were hoping for a return of Schoendienst after his bout with tuberculosis, but the 37-year-old struggled at the plate. Chuck Cottier and Mel Roach also played second base. Mantilla had 148 at-bats with a .257 average and played mainly at second base and shortstop in 63 games.

During the offseason, the Braves changed the makeup of their infield. They acquired Roy McMillan from the Reds to share duties at shortstop with Johnny Logan, and Frank Bolling from the Tigers to play second base. The handwriting was on the wall and Félix knew it, commenting, "They use me in 45 games, and then I see a newspaper got a list of the guys who might go in the draft, Bob Boyd, Al Spangler and me."[18] On October 10, 1961, Mantilla was selected by the brand-new New York Mets in the National League expansion draft.

Given the opportunity to play regularly for the Mets in 1962, Mantilla responded by batting .275 (second highest on the team) in 141 games. The Mets had a horrible season, going 40-120. It was a difficult transition going to a losing team; Mantilla said,

"I don't think anyone dreamed the team was going to be that bad. On paper, it didn't look that bad." Casey Stengel, he said, "would bring out the lineup to the umps before the game, then would go back into the dugout and go to sleep. I guess he couldn't bear watching."[19]

After the season Mantilla was traded to the Boston Red Sox for infielder Pumpsie Green, pitcher Tracy Stallard, and shortstop Al Moran. Red Sox manager Johnny Pesky was pleased with the acquisition of Mantilla. "I saw him in 1955 when I was coaching at Denver and he looked like a fine shortstop," Pesky said. "They say he plays a good third and second base. I could use Mantilla in three different positions."[20] Mantilla loved playing in Fenway Park; "it was a great park to see the ball real well. Everything seemed like it was green."[21] While playing for Boston he lived in the nearby Kenmore Hotel.

Mantilla didn't get much playing time during the 1963 season, appearing in just 66 games, but he batted .315. When Ed Bressoud suffered a severe heel sprain and bruise, Mantilla filled in for him, and he began playing second base the last two weeks of the season.

In 1964 he played more often (133 games), filling in at all the outfield positions and at second base, third base, and shortstop. Johnny Pesky had acknowledged before the season, "I should have used Félix Mantilla more (in 1963). He played well in the infield and outfield when I used him. ..."[22]

Mantilla delivered a walkoff two-run, pinch-hit home run in the bottom of the ninth in a 5-4 victory over the Kansas City Athletics on May 23. It was only his second home run of the season. On May 31 he came through again, slugging a pinch-hit double in the ninth inning to beat the Minnesota Twins, 4-3. While replacing an injured Tony Conigliaro in the lineup, Mantilla blasted three homers in two games against the Cleveland Indians on June 27-28. The home run barrage continued and by August 15 Mantilla had 20 home runs.

What caused this sudden power surge? Cleveland manager Birdie Tebbetts, who had also managed Mantilla at Milwaukee, had a theory: "When he went to the Polo Grounds, it became necessary to pull the ball, that he developed a swing that lifted the ball up. It's a swing that's perfect for Fenway and almost every park in our league. He has become probably the most improved man in a career I ever saw."[23]

Mantilla finished the season with 30 home runs in 425 at-bats, an amazing performance considering that he had clubbed only 35 home runs in his previous eight seasons in the majors. He drove in 64 runs, and batted .289. Not bad for a player who saw limited action the first month of the season. Mantilla was honored by the Boston Chapter of the Baseball Writers Association, which gave him the Comeback Player of the Year Award after the season.

Newly appointed Red Sox manager Billy Herman had big plans for Mantilla for the 1965 season, saying he planned to bat him in the fifth spot. "Félix hit 30 homers last year and I want him down where he can drive in the maximum number of runs," Herman said.[24] Mantilla came through with a big season, batting .289, driving in 92 runs, and blasting 18 home runs. He was picked as the American League's starting second baseman for the All-Star Game, his only All-Star Game appearance, and went 0-for-2.

Mantilla spent the offseason working for the Milwaukee police department along with major leaguers Bob Uecker and Don Pavletich in a program instituted by Judge Robert Cannon to help curb juvenile delinquency. Just before the start of the 1966 Mantilla was traded to the Houston Astros for infielder Eddie Kasko. Mantilla had hurt his arm and shoulder during spring training, and he thought the Red Sox decided that this was a good time to move him. He was puzzled that Red Sox told him the trade was for youth but Kasko was two years older.

For the Astros, Mantilla spent most of the first month of the season on the disabled list, then batted .219 with 22 runs batted in in 77 games (151 plate appearances). In the Astros' final game of the season, on October 2 against the Mets at Shea Stadium, Mantilla had a home run, a double, and three runs batted in in what turned out to be his last major-league game.

After the 1966 season, Mantilla asked the Astros for his release, which was granted. He considered playing in Japan, but in February 1967 he signed with the Chicago Cubs, who were closer to his home in Milwaukee. While in spring training with the Cubs, Mantilla tore his Achilles tendon during a timing drill. He realized his career was over.

Mantilla played a few games for a team in Sherbrooke, Quebec, but his legs were hurting. The team's manager was fired and Mantilla succeeded him and guided the team to a second-place finish. Mantilla wanted to continue as manager, but the ownership wanted a player-manager, Mantilla returned home to Milwaukee. He worked for the Boys' Club in Milwaukee. A Little League team that competes in the southside of Milwaukee was named after him.

Mantilla has two children from his marriage on September 17, 1953, to Delores Berry, whom he met while playing at Jacksonville. Félix Jr. is a retired attorney and Jose is a retired banker. Mantilla has been married to Kay since 1981, and they reside in the northwest side of Milwaukee. They have five grandchildren. Mantilla said he loves retirement because he can do what he wants to do, when he wants to.[25]

## SOURCES

In-person interviews with Félix Mantilla, November 3 and 8, 2012.

*Milwaukee Journal*

*Milwaukee Sentinel*

*San Francisco Chronicle*

*The Sporting News*

Baseball-Reference.com

Retrosheet.org

Baseball Hall of Fame Library: Player file for Félix Mantilla.

## NOTES

1. Jack Pearson, "The Kid from Puerto Rico decided he liked it here," *50 Plus*, May 2010.
2. Bob Wolf, "Mantilla Now Blocked by Logan at Shortstop but Has Bright Future," *Milwaukee Journal*, April 1, 1956.
3. Pearson, "The Kid."
4. Mantilla interview.
5. Vic Ziegel, "Mantilla Arrives," *Sport*, August 1965.
6. Ziegel, "Mantilla Arrives."
7. Mantilla interview.
8. Paul Green, "Félix Mantilla," *Sports Collectors Digest*, July 19, 1985.
9. Ziegel, "Mantilla Arrives."
10. Green, "Félix Mantilla."
11. Bob Wolf, "Braves' Talent Bin Overflowing With Nifty Kid Infielders," *The Sporting News*, March 21, 1956.
12. Mantilla interview.
13. Cleon Walfoort, "Pennant Rides on 'Félix the Cat,' Now the Club's Only Shortstop," *Milwaukee Journal*. Undated article from the Mantilla file at the Baseball Hall of Fame library.
14. Mantilla interview.
15. Ibid..
16. Ibid.
17. "Crestfallen Mantilla Says He Was Off Balance," *San Francisco Chronicle*, September 30, 1959.
18. Ziegel, "Mantilla Arrives."
19. Pearson, "The Kid."
20. Hy Hurwitz, "Wanted: Hungry Players, Pesky Tells Hub Hose," *The Sporting News*, February 2, 1963.
21. Mantilla interview.
22. Pesky Will Return in '64; Vows to Correct Mistakes," *The Sporting News*, October 5, 1963.
23. Ziegel, "Mantilla Arrives."
24. Larry Claflin, "Pleasant Surprise? Watch Morehead, Says Hub's Herman," *The Sporting News*, December 19, 1965.
25. Mantilla interview.

# LUIS ÁNGEL "CANENA" MÁRQUEZ SÁNCHEZ

## By Amy Essington

LUIS MÁRQUEZ WAS A MEMBER OF the generation of baseball players who integrated professional baseball in the 1940s and 1950s. Márquez played in many levels of segregated and integrated baseball including the Puerto Rican Winter League, the Negro Leagues, the Mexican Leagues, the minor leagues, and the major leagues. He integrated the Portland Beavers of the Pacific Coast League, along with Frank Austin, in 1949. Two years later, he became only the third Puerto Rican to play in the major leagues when he joined the Boston Braves. Although he never found the success in the majors that he had in other leagues, Márquez had a 20-year career in professional baseball.

He is the only Puerto Rican with batting titles in Negro League baseball (1947 Homestead Grays, .417), Puerto Rican baseball (1953-54 Mayaguez, .333), and Organized Baseball (1959 Dallas, Triple-A American Association, .345).

Of Spanish and African heritage, Luis Ángel "Canena" Márquez Sánchez was born on October 28, 1925, in a house on Calle Mercado in Aguadilla, Puerto Rico, to Matilde Márquez and Adela Sánchez. His father left when he was very young, and Adela married Manuel Acevedo Quinones. Luis was the oldest of five children, two boys and three girls. More information about his parents is not known. In 1944 Márquez played third base for the Puerto Rican national team in the Amateur World Series in Venezuela.[1] Aguadilla local Victor Navarro described Márquez as "something else," adding, "He put up great numbers in the league, but he was a warm, caring human being."[2] Márquez also exhibited both a sense of humor and humility when, after missing a team practice with Mayagüez during the 1945-46 season, he brought manager Joe Buzas "a big local pineapple, knowing Buzas loved fruit."[3]

The nickname "Canena" was bestowed on Márquez him by his mother, Adela, a name by which she had been known. After a truly hot start in a series in the 1944 Amateur World Series in Venezuela, he picked up the nickname "El Fogón Boricua."[4]

After he finished high school, an 18-year-old Márquez signed a professional baseball contract with Mayaguez. During his career, Márquez, who was quick and had a strong arm, played in both in the infield and outfield. The 5-foot-10, 174-pound player threw and batted right-handed. Márquez began his professional career with the Mayagüez Indios during the 1944-1945 season. In his first game, Márquez experienced both high and low points—he raced from second to home on an infield out, but he also made two fielding errors.[5] Márquez's career in Puerto Rican winter ball included time with the Mayagüez Indios (1944-1946, 1953-1956, 1957-1964), the Aguadilla Sharks (1946-1951), the San Juan Senators (1952-1953), and the Ponce Lions (1957-1958, and 1959-60, both stints as manager).

During his first professional season in Puerto Rico, Márquez batted .361 and tied with Alfonso Gerard for 1944-45 Rookie of the Year honors. The next season, he led the league with 10 triples, tying the league record, and, during the 1946-47 season, he set the single-season home run record with 14 round-trippers, breaking Josh Gibson's record by one.[6] During the 1953-1954 season, Márquez was the Puerto Rican Winter League's batting champion with a .333 batting average and was voted Most Valuable Player as well. He hit two home runs in the 1957 Caribbean Championship Series.

Over the course of 20 seasons in Puerto Rico, Márquez played in 4,018 games; scored 768 runs;

registered 1,206 hits which included 235 doubles, 66 triples, and 97 home runs; and batted .300. His totals of games played, hits, doubles, and runs scored are all league records. He was inducted into the Puerto Rican Baseball Hall of Fame in October 1991.

After his first season of winter ball in Puerto Rico, Márquez joined the New York Black Yankees in 1945. He then played for the Baltimore Elite Giants and the Homestead Grays of the Negro National League in 1946 and the Grays in 1947 and 1948. In 1947 and 1948, Márquez represented the Grays in both the Chicago and New York games of the Negro Leagues' East-West All-Star Game. In 1947 Márquez led the league in hitting with a .417 batting average, and he had 29 stolen bases. The following season, the second baseman changed positions, moving to the outfield, and also moved to the top of the batting order. James Riley's *Biographical Encyclopedia of the Negro Baseball Leagues* says Márquez had a .274 batting average the year his team won the Negro National League pennant and the Negro League World Series in 1948. After the Homestead Grays folded in 1949, Márquez's contract was transferred to the Baltimore Elite Giants, now of the Negro American League. By the time his Negro League career concluded, he had posted a .335 career batting average.[7]

The Brooklyn Dodgers' signing of Jackie Robinson on October 23, 1945, initiated the integration of baseball in the United States and allowed Márquez to move from the Negro Leagues into Organized Baseball. Márquez was one of the hundreds of players who participated in the process of integrating the minor and major leagues in the 1940s and '50s. This process included sorting out contracts that may or may not have existed with the teams of the collapsing Negro Leagues.

On February 3, 1949, newspapers reported the purchase of Márquez's contract with the Baltimore Elite Giants by New York Yankees general manager George Weiss.[8] Márquez was the first player of color signed by the Yankees, although he was not the player who ultimately integrated the team. He reported to the Newark Bears, the Yankees' affiliate in the Triple-A International League, at their spring-training camp in Haines City, Florida. Whether the Baltimore Elite Giants or the Homestead Grays owned his contract, however, was in dispute.[9] The Grays still made a claim to Márquez's contract and owner See Posey had offered Bill Veeck of the Cleveland Indians a 120-day option to purchase the contract.

The dispute over Márquez's contract was revealed in the midst of another contract disagreement between the Yankees and Indians. The Yankees accused the Indians of signing Artie Wilson of the Birmingham Black Barons, who was already under contract with them. The commissioner's office mediated the two disputes in the spring of 1949. Commissioner A.B. "Happy" Chandler's decision sent Márquez to the Indians and Wilson to the Yankees. Márquez had been playing with the Newark Bears, the Yankees' affiliate, and Wilson had been playing with the San Diego Padres, the Indians' affiliate. In 18 games in Newark, Márquez had one home run, three stolen bases, and a batting average of .246. Even though his preference was to remain in the Yankees organization, Márquez joined the Indians on May 13,

1949, and was optioned to the Portland Beavers of the Pacific Coast League.[10]

In the United States, Márquez spent most of his baseball career in the minor leagues. He joined the Beavers on May 27, 1949. After he had arrived by plane from New York, he went straight into left field for that night's game.[11] Márquez and his teammate Frank Austin were the first players of color on that team, though Art Pennington of the Chicago Giants later joined the Beavers in July.[12] During the 1949 season, Márquez hit .294 in 132 games and led the team with 32 stolen bases. He returned to Portland in 1950, played 194 games, hit over .300, and again led the club in stolen bases. As one of the players who were at the forefront of the integration of baseball, Márquez faced discrimination on and off the field.[13] Despite the discrimination, he made strong connections in the PCL. In 1957, when the three-time manager of the Portland Beavers, Bill Sweeney, died, Márquez served as an honorary pallbearer.[14]

In 1951 Márquez finally moved up to the major leagues when he was claimed by the Boston Braves in the Rule 5 draft prior to the season.[15] Márquez had joined the Braves one year after Sam Jethroe integrated it, but historian Adrian Burgos has noted that Márquez was the first Afro-Latino player signed by the Braves, and the second one overall (after Minnie Miñoso)[16] His major-league debut came on April 18, 1951, when he entered the game against the New York Giants as a pinch-runner for Jim Wilson.[17] Márquez's first hit, a triple, came on April 19 in the second game of a doubleheader against the New York Giants.[18] His first RBI followed the next day in a 2-for-4 performance against the Philadelphia Phillies; Márquez drove in the first run and scored the second in a 2-1 Braves victory. He scored the winning run on Max Surkont's sacrifice fly after singling, advancing to second base on a sacrifice, and stealing third. Márquez played in 68 games for the Braves in 1951, and he was frequently used as a pinch-runner. He hit only .196 and was successful on only half of his stolen base attempts, going 4-for-8 on the year.

The next season, Márquez returned to the minors, where he played in 136 games for the Milwaukee Brewers of the Triple-A American Association. His batting average was third best in the league at .345, and he had 14 home runs and 99 runs batted in. Márquez's contributions to the Brewers helped the team to win the American Association championship in 1952. During the 1953 season, Márquez played 130 games and batted .292 for another American Association team, the Toledo Sox. With Márquez on the roster, the Sox won the American Association championship and playoffs.

Márquez's performance merited a return to the major leagues in 1954, and he batted .083 in 17 games for the Chicago Cubs; after a trade on June 14, 1954, he hit .111 in 14 games for the Pittsburgh Pirates. He had only one base hit for each of the two teams, and the Pirates released Márquez to Toledo on July 14, 1954. Over the course of his major-league career, Márquez played a total of 99 games for three different teams and finished with a .182 batting average and an on-base percentage of .278. He drove in 11 runs, all during his 1951 season with the Braves.

From 1955 to 1958, Márquez returned to the roster of the Portland Beavers, with a 21-game stint with the Toledo Sox in 1955. In 1956 he represented the Beavers on the Pacific Coast League's All-Star team. During his time as a Beaver, Márquez accepted a Friday the 13th challenge of playing all nine positions in one 1957 game, which he completed by pitching the last three outs of the game.[19]

After his seasons in the Pacific Northwest, Márquez spent two seasons in Texas. In 1959 he was with the Dallas Rangers of the American Association, where he played in 142 games and won the batting championship with a .345 average. The next season he played in 144 games with the Dallas Fort-Worth Rangers of the American Association, batting .264.

In 1961, in Márquez's 17th year as a professional baseball player, he moved down to Single-A ball for the first time, playing in 19 games with the Williamsport Grays of the Eastern League. That season, he also played 18 games with the Dallas Fort-Worth Rangers.

After his final minor-league stints, Márquez moved south of the border for two seasons, and played for the Mexican League's Poza Rica Petroleros in 1962 and 1963. He excelled during his first season in Mexico, batting .357 with 28 doubles, 21 homers, and 91 RBIs in 126 games. His performance was not quite as strong in 1963, but he still hit .314 with 20 home runs and 72 RBIs in his final season.[20]

Márquez's career included three seasons in the Negro Leagues, 12 seasons in the minor leagues, two seasons in major-league baseball, and two seasons in the Mexican Leagues in addition to his years in the Puerto Rican Winter League. As a player, Márquez had a superstition of touching first or third base while trotting in from the outfield at the end of an inning. He later worked as a scout for Montreal Expos in 1969 and 1970, the first two years of the franchise's existence.

Following his short stint as a scout, Márquez worked for the Department of Sports in Aguadilla, and also coached both amateur and professional baseball. A first marriage to Lydia Babilonia was short-lived. He then married Olga Asis Rodríguez, who died in 1974. After her death, Luis went to live with and care for his mother. He and Olga had two children, Wanda and Gloria. In 2017, Wanda worked and gave sports talks at the ballpark that bears her father's name.

At the time of his death, Márquez was working with the Sports and Recreation Department in Aguadilla and in charge of Parque Colón.

His daughter Wanda's husband, Luis Ramos, shot Márquez twice with a handgun when Márquez confronted his son-in-law about the way he treated his daughter.[21] He was shot on the same street where he had been born, Calle Mercado.[22] Márquez was pronounced dead at the hospital in Aguadilla on March 1, 1988. He buried in Monte Cristo Memorial Park in Aguadilla. Reportedly because of a number of police "mistakes" of some sort, Luis Ramos was never convicted of a crime and as of 2017 was free in New York.[23]

The municipal baseball park in Aguadilla, Estadio Luis A. Canena Márquez, is named for the local man who had a 20-year career in professional baseball.[24] A bronze statue of Márquez is located in front of the stadium. Although he did not succeed in the majors, Luis Márquez was part of history as a member of a generation that broke down the racial barriers of professional baseball.

## SOURCES

Thanks to Carlos Delgado Sr., Pedro Julio Molinari, and Jorge Colón Delgado for assistance with this biography.

## NOTES

1. Thomas E. Van Hyning, *Puerto Rico's Winter League: A History of Major League Baseball's Launching Pad* (Jefferson, North Carolina: McFarland & Company, Inc., 1995), 118.

2. Van Hyning, 119.

3. Van Hyning, 179.

4. Email from Edwin Fernandez Cruz to Bill Nowlin, February 20, 2017. A fogón is a kind of hot stove.

5. "Luis L. Márquez," *1950 Beavers Scrapbook*, Dick Dobbins Collection on the Pacific Coast League, California Historical Society.

6. Van Hyning, 119. The following season (1947-48), Willard Brown, playing for Santurce, shattered the home-run record by hitting 27, which combined the totals from the previous records set by Márquez (14) and Gibson (13).

7 James A. Riley, *The Biographical Encyclopedia of the Negro Baseball Leagues* (New York: Carroll and Graf Publishers, 1994), 513.

8 See, for instance, "Yankees Buy Negro Player," *Oregonian* (Portland), February 3, 1949: 21.

9 "Luis L. Márquez," *1950 Beavers Scrapbook*.

10 Associated Press, "Cleveland Options Márquez to Portland," *Boston Traveler*, May 23, 1949: 32.

11 Al Wolf, "Haney's Comets Take 5th in Row," *Los Angeles Times*, May 28, 1949: B1.

12 Associated Press, "Coast Nine Signs 3rd Negro Player," *Omaha World-Herald*, July 16, 1949: 10.

13 John E. Spalding, *Pacific Coast League Stars: One Hundred of the Best, 1903 to 1957* (John Spalding, 1994), 115. Spalding states, "The Coast League was the scene of many fights between black and white players and Márquez was involved in two altercations in his first year in the league in 1949."

14 "Notables of Baseball at Sweeney Rites," *Los Angeles Times*, April 23, 1957: C1.

15 Al Wolf, "Sportraits," *Los Angeles Times*, January 20, 1951: B2.

16 Adrian Burgos, *Playing America's Game: Baseball, Latinos, and the Color Line* (Los Angeles: University of California Press, 2007), 273.

17 James P. Dawson, "Jethroe's 3-Run Homer in Ninth at Boston Tops Durocher Men, 8-5," *New York Times*, April 19, 1951: 51.

18 "Giants Split with Braves, Losing Wild Second Game in Tenth Inning," *New York Times*, April 20, 1951: 40.

19 "Pacific Coast League," *The Sporting News*, September 25, 1957: 40.

20 Pedro Treto Cisneros, *The Mexican League: Comprehensive Player Statistics, 1937-2001* (Jefferson, North Carolina: McFarland & Company, Inc., 2002), 185.

21 "Asesinan a ex pelotero Luis (Canena) Márquez," *Listen Diario* (February 2, 1988), article in Baseball Hall of Fame Library, player file for Luis Angel Márquez.

22 Email from Edwin Fernandez Cruz.

23 Ibid.

24 skyscrapercity.com/showthread.php?p=91051440.

# EDGAR MARTÍNEZ

## By Emily Hawks

**W**HEN MANY REFLECT ON THE 1990s Mariners, often the flashier stars jump to mind: Ken Griffey, Jr., Randy Johnson, Alex Rodríguez. However, few on those teams would disagree that the stalwart of the Mariners was a player who toiled just outside of the spotlight. Known as Gar, El Papa, or Papi, Edgar Martínez was the quiet, hard-working hitting machine who was the heart of the Mariners. Chants of "Eeeed-gaaaar" reverberated throughout the Kingdome during every Martinez at-bat, and Martinez's name became synonymous with the designated hitter position at which he excelled. A Mariner for his entire career, his legacy is strongly felt in Seattle even to this day (2017).

Edgar Martínez was born on January 2, 1963 in New York City to parents Jose Martinez and Christina Salgado Martinez.[1] When he was two years old, his parents divorced, and Martinez went to live with his grandparents, Mario Salgado and Manuela Rivera, in the Maguayo neighborhood of Dorado, Puerto Rico.

At eight years old, he watched the Pittsburgh Pirates win the 1971 World Series on television, led by Puerto Rican great Roberto Clemente. "After that series, I went outside my house and I started playing in the backyard," said Martinez. "I was hooked on baseball after that."[2] Martinez's parents reconciled three years later and summoned their three children back to New York. Though his brother and sister returned to his parents, Martinez opted to remain with his grandparents in Puerto Rico. "He locked himself in his room and wouldn't come out, didn't want to leave," said Martinez's uncle, Jose Juan Rivera. "I felt my grandparents needed me," Martinez explained. "I went with my feelings."[3]

Martinez grew up playing baseball with his cousin and future big-leaguer Carmelo Martinez. Carmelo was two years older, and they would often pitch to each other between games, throwing anything they could find: balls, rocks, even bottle caps. "Bottle caps were great training for hitting breaking balls, they curved so much," Carmelo recalled. "I'd go out with a broomstick and hit the rocks all over, try for open space," Edgar remembered. "I never broke windows or anything but the neighbors did complain."[4]

After graduating from Jose S. Alegria High School in Dorado, Martinez went on to attend American College in Puerto Rico, while also working the night shift in a pharmaceutical factory and playing semipro baseball. When Edgar was 20, Mariners scout Marty Martinez (no relation) held a tryout camp in Dorado. Though he had heard of Edgar's hitting abilities, he'd also heard that he lacked speed and power. Still, this did not deter him. "I never did listen much to other scouts," he said. "I had my own ideas on things." Edgar completed his tryout after working an eight hour night shift at the factory. His performance was enough to garner him a $4,000 offer to sign with the Mariners, yet he still required a little prodding from his cousin, Carmelo. "He was the one who kept saying 'take the chance, you can make it,'" Edgar said. "I did not know. Finally, I decided to try it. But Carmelo . . . he kind of made the decision for me."[5]

Martinez began his professional career with the Bellingham Mariners of the Northwest League. He started slowly, batting just .173 in 1983. But he was also contending with the culture shock of playing in the far northwest corner of the contiguous United States, bordering Canada. "When I got to Bellingham, I could only speak a few words of English, just enough to order in a restaurant," Martinez recalled. "And I couldn't believe people could live in such cold weather."[6]

He improved the following year with the Wausau Timbers of the Midwest League, hitting .303 and drawing 84 walks. Martinez split the 1985 season between the Double-A Chattanooga Lookouts of the

Southern League, where he hit .258 in 111 games, and the Triple-A Calgary Cannons of the Pacific Coast League, .353 in 20 games. Back in Chattanooga in 1986, he led the league third basemen with a .960 fielding percentage.

Martinez began the 1987 season in Calgary, where he batted .327 through 129 games, including 31 doubles and 10 home runs. After this strong performance, the Mariners called him up, and he made his big-league debut on September 12. He quickly became acclimated to big-league pitching, compiling a .372 average in the season's final 13 games. Martinez certainly enjoyed the change in lifestyle. "To me, everything is first class. We stay at the best hotels, we don't have to carry our luggage and you make better money in the big leagues," he observed shortly after his call-up. He aimed to make the best impression possible and was willing to do whatever was required of him to stay in the majors. "I think I can play utility, third, second, wherever they want to play me I try to do it."[7]

In 1988, Martinez joined the Mariners for spring training in Arizona, but was trimmed from the major league roster on March 22 and once again began the season in Calgary. His season began with a rough start. During a game in Tempe, a ground ball took a bad hop, struck him in the face, and broke his nose. The injury sidelined him for a few games, but he recovered splendidly, winning the 1988 Pacific Coast League batting title with a .363 average. He also performed creditably with the big-league club in limited service in September. Shortly after the season's conclusion, Martinez underwent a patellar scraping and debridement procedure on his left knee, which had been causing him discomfort throughout the season.[8]

In 1989, Martinez began the season with the big-league club in Seattle. Joining him in the Opening Day lineup were fellow rookies Ken Griffey, Jr. and Omar Vizquel. Martinez struggled early on and again split his time between Seattle and Calgary. The consistent playing time in the minors lifted him out of his rut. "When I was sent down I played every day and I found my rhythm," Martinez said. "[I] was more comfortable and secure with myself."[9] Unlike many players who became discouraged by living in

constant flux between the major and minor leagues, Martinez embraced his situation. "I saw other players who were very frustrated by playing in the minor leagues, but I was lucky," said Martinez. "I never got frustrated. I was doing what I really liked. I was just happy to be playing the game."[10] Cumulatively, he hit .345 in 32 games at Calgary, and .240 in 65 games with Seattle.

Following the 1989 season, Martinez returned to his native Puerto Rico to play winter ball. He won the Puerto Rican League batting title, hitting .424 through 43 games at San Juan and shared MVP honors with Carlos Baerga.[11]

On his return, Martinez agreed to a one-year, $90,000 deal with the Mariners, though the M's third-base job in 1990 apparently belonged to Darnell Coles. But after a stretch in which Coles committed five errors in six games, manager Jim Lefebvre moved him to the outfield, clearing the way for Martinez to take over at third. Which itself wasn't without incident: Lefebvre stuck with Martinez even after a horrendous game on May 6 when Martinez tied the American League record of committing four errors in a single game.[12] Lefebvre knew what he was doing. Martinez had become the reliable source of offensive production the team had been looking for, hitting .302 on the season, with an OPS of .830 in his first season as a "full timer." Many were also noticing his strong work ethic, including the Mariners' strength and conditioning coach and former Olympic shot putter Pete Shmock. "He has the kind of discipline I wish all baseball players had," Shmock said. "I'm proud of him, and he should be proud of himself."[13] Despite Martinez's excellent season, most media and fan attention was lavished on teammate Griffey, Jr., who had both flair and flashier power numbers. This didn't bother the humble Martinez. When asked about the disparity in the amount of publicity each player received, Martinez commented, "It's simple. Junior is one of the greatest players. He deserves the attention."[14] Martinez had played much of the season through knee pain, and immediately after the conclusion of the season, underwent arthroscopic surgery on his right knee to repair a torn ligament.[15]

Before the 1991 season, Martinez signed a two-year contract for $850,000 plus incentives.[16] He began the season on an offensive tear, hitting .412 through the month of April. Manager Lefebvre experimented with putting Edgar at nearly all spots in the lineup, including 67 games in the leadoff position later in the season. His strongest performance came in the cleanup spot, where he hit .380 in 71 at bats. He finished the season again hitting over .300 with an overall WAR of 6.1.

By 1992, Martinez began to get noticed in the baseball world at large. Offensively he seemed to be getting increasingly better, even in spite of a right shoulder injury that was causing a great deal of pain. He was selected to his first American League All-Star squad, going into the break hitting .328 with 14 home runs and 26 doubles. "Since I was a kid, playing in the All-Star Game was a dream," Martinez said. "I feel great to be selected. It is an honor."[17] The following month, the Mariners signed Martinez to a three-year, $10 million contract—the most lucrative in franchise history to that point.[18] Amidst the batting race in late August, Martinez realized he had finally been recognized as a competitor when a shipment of bats he ordered from Rawlings arrived, and every one of the dozen was in pristine condition, with the perfect cut of wood.[19]

As Mariners beat writer Bob Finnigan noted, "Over the years it was a common sight to see him sitting at his locker doing his daily eye exercises or pulling out his little kitchen scale, checking every bat of a new shipment, carefully writing the weight in ounces on the knob, and occasionally shaking his head over discrepancies."[20] To the ever-meticulous Martinez, those precise scale figures were a sign he'd made it big. However the pain in his shoulder cut his season short: it began impeding his play. "Most of the season it just hurt me to throw," Martinez said. "But lately it has bothered me swinging the bat."[21] He underwent arthroscopic surgery to remove bone spurs in his right shoulder on September 19. Martinez's .343 BA easily won the AL batting title, and indeed led the entire majors. He also tied Frank Thomas for the most doubles in baseball with 46, and won his first Silver Slugger award. The following offseason brought a mixture of joy and sorrow for Martinez. In October, he married Holli Beeler, a Seattle-area native and Seattle Pacific University student. The two met on a blind date after being set up by a mutual friend.[22] Soon afterward, however, he faced adversity in his personal life. "Shortly after [I got married], my grandfather passed away. I got the flu for a long time. My grandmother had a stroke," Martinez recollected.[23]

In January of 1993 the Mariners signed Edgar's cousin Carmelo to a minor-league deal and invited him to spring training camp. By that time, Carmelo had played nine seasons in the majors and had long been soliciting hitting advice from his younger cousin. "That was a strange feeling when Carmelo started to ask me for help. My cousin was my hero when I was a little kid," Edgar said. "He is the one who taught me to hit and is still the only batting coach I've ever had."[24]

Just before the 1993 season began, Martinez suffered a freak mishap in an exhibition game that would ultimately change the entire trajectory of his career. Four teams were set to play in the "Baseball Classic" at BC Place Stadium in Vancouver, British Columbia, as part of a preseason exhibition. The Mariners opened the series in a game against the Milwaukee Brewers on April 3. The venue had hosted a Guns 'N Roses concert earlier in the week, so the field's turf and dirt had been hastily installed. The dirt used to fill the cutouts surrounding the bases was loose and sandy, and it contained no clay for the players to gain grip with their cleats. "It was like playing in a sandbox, like playing on a beach," said manager Lou Piniella.[25] When Martinez stole a base in the fourth inning, he heard a pop in his leg. He hit the ground and lay there for two minutes until helped off the field by the trainers. Team doctor Larry Pedegana later diagnosed Martinez with a partial muscle tear above the left knee. Martinez would play only 42 games that season, with dismal numbers across the board (.237/.366/.378). It was by far his worst regular season. The event profoundly shaped Martinez's approach to the game in the future. After the obstacles he endured in his personal life the preceding offseason, Martinez recounted, "From the time I came to spring training I was behind and I felt I got hurt because I wasn't in good enough shape. After that I decided I would never let that happen again."[26]

The bad luck continued early in the 1994 season, however, as Martinez was hit by a pitch on Opening Day while facing Cleveland right-hander Dennis Martinez. "I thought, 'Not again,'" Martinez said. "I couldn't believe it was my first game."[27] Returning to play nearly a week later, he made three errors in a game. After a stint on the disabled list, Martinez went on to appear in 89 games of the strike-shortened season. He played 65 games at third base, 23 as designated hitter, and appeared once as a pinch-runner.

Martinez roared back into form in 1995. Playing nearly all games as a designated hitter, he had the best season of his career leading the American League in runs (121) and batting average (.356), he led the major leagues in doubles (52), on-base percentage (.479), and OPS (1.107). He also earned an impressive offensive WAR of 7.2. He was selected to his second American League All-Star squad, won a second Silver Slugger, and finished third in MVP voting. Martinez gave the Mariners a much-needed boost after star player Griffey, Jr. went on the disabled list on May 26. Twenty-five of his 29 home runs, and 97 of his 113 RBIs came after Griffey, Jr.'s injury.[28] Due in no small part to Edgar's achievements, the Mariners went on to win their first-ever AL West division championship.

In their playoff debut, the Mariners faced the Wild Card Yankees in the ALDS. Martinez swung a hot bat for the entire series, getting three hits in each of the first two games, for example, although the Mariners lost both contests. The M's battled back to win Game Three, in which Martinez buoyed the team with a grand slam. And they also captured Game Four, with Edgar contributing a three-run dinger in that victory.

With the series back in Seattle for the decisive fifth game, 57,411 frenzied fans packed into the Kingdome. The Yankees sent Game One victor David Cone to the mound, who held the Mariners

in check through seven innings. But in the eighth, down 4-2, the Mariners tacked on a run, and then added another in the ninth, sending the game into extra innings. After a dramatic relief appearance by Mariners ace Randy Johnson in the top of the ninth, the Yankees countered with former Cy Young winner Jack McDowell in the bottom half of the inning. Johnson gave up a run in the top of the 11th, and the Mariners went into the bottom half of the inning trailing 5-4. With everything on the line, Joey Cora and Griffey, Jr. singled and Martinez came to the plate with runners on first and third. Having fanned against McDowell in the ninth, Edgar was out for revenge. Reliever Norm Charlton recalled their encounter in the dugout, "I told him, 'You're going to get another chance.' He looked at me with the look in his eye that said, 'I know.'"[29]

Edgar did not waste his chance. On an 0-1 count, he laced a split-fingered fastball into the left-field corner. Cora scored easily, while Griffey, Jr. kicked into overdrive from first. As the entire team waved him in (along with third-base coach Sam Perlozzo), Junior slid safely into home, securing the Mariners their first Division Championship and sending the Kingdome into an eruption. Martinez had a monstrous series: hitting an electric .571, with two homers and 10 RBIs. "A professional is the best description I can use for him," Piniella said. It's the highest praise I can think of for a major-league baseball player." Griffey, Jr. added, "People are always asking about Edgar. What can you say? He's just Edgar. The man can hit."[30] Though the Mariners went on to lose the ALCS to Cleveland, the dramatic Game Five ALDS victory has not been forgotten. Even 20 years later, "The Double" is permanently etched in collective memory and franchise lore. It's depicted in a Safeco Field mural and was constantly re-lived for 15 years through the baritone voice of the late Ford C. Frick award-winning Mariners broadcaster Dave Niehaus.

Martinez, now being used almost exclusively as a DH, put up another solid All-Star year in 1996, hitting .327 In an unfortunate ironic twist, the only game he played at third base that season resulted in four cracked ribs and 21 games on the DL after a collision with catcher John Marzano.[31]

Adding a fourth All-Star appearance to his resume in 1997, and a third Silver Slugger to his trophy case, Martinez helped bring his team back to the playoffs, though they fell to the Orioles in four games in the ALDS. At the time, with ownership interests in limbo, great uncertainty surrounded the future of the Mariners. . "It looks to me like they want to change leagues," Martinez said after the season, a matter of some moment to a man who made his living as a superb DH. "Right now I have no clue if they want to keep me or if they want to trade me. I'd rather stay, but it's not up to me."[32]

Fortunately, the Mariners remained in the AL where Martinez continued to produce. Over the next two years he batted .327 and .330 and led the AL in OBP, something he accomplished three times in his career. Indeed, he excelled at getting on base: for two-thirds of his 18-year career, he earned an OBP over .400.

Near the end of the decade, eye problems connected to strabismus, a lifelong condition for Martinez, began bothering him. Strabismus affects eye coordination, and Martinez's right eye would wander, causing him to lose focus. He was first diagnosed with the condition in the minor leagues, but the problem tends to worsen with age. In 1999, Martinez began losing sight of pitches and seemed headed for the DL. He even confided in some people that he might have to retire. Early in his career, Martinez began incorporating 30 minutes of eye exercises into his pregame routine. When the trouble worsened, he invited team optometrist Douglas Nikaitani to his house for extra homework. The doc put charts on the walls and told Edgar to fuse them together while simultaneously batting tennis balls away. He added martial arts and math problems to the exercise, trying to push Martinez to his limits. These strange ministrations seemed to work. "I felt different," Martinez said. "I could see the ball more. I was able to pick up the rotation ... I felt I was improving, back to where I wanted to be again."[33]

In 2000 he led the AL in RBI (145), was selected to his fifth All-Star team, had a career-best 37 home runs, and finished sixth in MVP voting. He also hit .364 in the ALDS as the Mariners swept the White Sox, but they ultimately fell to the Yankees in the ALCS.

2001 was a magical year for the Mariners: the team tied the 1906 Cubs' record of 116 wins in a season. Martinez was one of eight Mariners selected to that year's All-Star Game, which took place on their home field. In the Division Series against the Indians, Martinez hit .313, but only .150 in their Championship Series loss to the Yankees. It would be his final playoff appearance.

A ruptured hamstring tendon behind his left knee shortened Martinez's 2002 season and he again underwent surgery in April. Whether Martinez, then approaching 40, would play another year was questionable. But the Mariners weren't quite ready to let the heart-and-soul of their team go, and signed him to a one-year deal. "We just had to get it done," said the Mariners' CEO Howard Lincoln.[34] Martinez rewarded the franchise's confidence, rebounding from his injury in 2003, hitting .294 with 24 home runs, .403 OBP, and a strong 3.3 WAR. Buoyed by his season, Martinez signed another one-year deal with the Mariners in November.

But around mid-August of the following year, with his team buried in the AL West cellar 29 games below .500, and Martinez hitting only .258, he decided to retire at season's end. His body was worn out and would no longer allow him to compete at his accustomed level. Unlike many stars he played with over the years—Griffey, Jr., Johnson, and Rodríguez, to name a few—Martinez played for Seattle his entire career. Though he was sometimes a quiet presence, especially when contrasted with big personalities like Griffey, Jr. and Jay Buhner, Martinez still knew how to have a laugh. He featured prominently in the always popular Mariners commercial campaigns over the years. Fan favorites included a commercial in which he taught other young Latino players to say "geoduck" (a clam which is a Pacific Northwest delicacy), another where he had a garage-door opener in his car that controlled the Safeco Field roof, and the legendary "light bat" commercial where he constructed a lamp out of a bat. "I never got the bat lamp," Martinez recalled, feigning sadness.[35] Still, what most fans and teammates remember was his unwavering work ethic. Mariners Vice President of Communications Randy Adamack remembered, "I can recall two years I came to the office the day before Christmas. The parking lot was empty except for one other car, Edgar's."[36]

It's little mystery why the city of Seattle renamed the street adjacent to Safeco Field "Edgar Martínez Drive." In fact, the city did not even wait for his retirement to do so, making the switch on "Edgar Martínez Day" at Safeco Field, the last day of his playing career. "Why wait?" said Seattle mayor Greg Nickels. "He's been a part of Seattle for so long, and his contribution has been unlike any other pro athlete, we thought it would be a great idea."[37] Commissioner Bud Selig—on hand that weekend to commemorate Ichiro Suzuki's breaking George Sisler's single-season hits record—called Martinez a role model for the game and announced that the annual Designated Hitter Award would forever be known as the Edgar Martínez Award. Teammate Bret Boone characterized him as "the greatest Mariner of all time."[38]

That point is scarcely arguable. He appears on the team leader boards in virtually every offensive category, leading in games played, on-base percentage, extra-base hits, doubles, RBIs, walks, runs, and total bases, and finishing second in OPS, overall WAR, batting average, hits, and home runs. Shortly after the season concluded, Martinez became the first Puerto Rican to be awarded the Roberto Clemente Award for his charitable work in the Seattle community. It was a fitting award for Martinez, who became interested in baseball largely because of Clemente. "Clemente was my idol as a child," he said, "and to get this award is very special to me."[39]

Though he retired from playing baseball, the always hard-working Martinez could not remain idle during his retirement. In addition to spending more time with his family—by then, he and wife Holli had three children: a son, Alex, and daughters, Tessa and Jacqueline—Martinez also launched a promotional merchandise agency called Branded Solutions. When asked why he didn't just retire to a life of leisure, spending his post-playing days on the golf course, Martinez said, "I tried that. But I felt the need to be productive. I feel energetic. I feel young. I wanted to do something."[40] Martinez and his wife also founded The Martinez Foundation, a charitable organization that provides scholarships and support programs to students of color who are pursuing teaching careers.

Martinez had always said that he might be interested in a return to the baseball world, but he wanted to wait until his children were older. "In 2005, on opening day, I had a baby in my arms watching the game," Martinez recalled 10 years later. "Now it's the right time. I really missed the game over all those years."[41] On June 20, 2015, the Mariners named Martinez as their new hitting coach. "For the last three years, I've wanted to get back into the game, obviously I wanted to do it with the Mariners," Martinez said. "I haven't seen so much talent on the Mariners for a long time . . . I think it's a great opportunity for me."[42]

While Martinez has certainly had a significant impact on the game, his Hall of Fame candidacy has been a hotly debated topic ever since his retirement. Martinez debuted on the ballot in 2010, receiving 36 percent of the vote. His tally held fairly steady for four years, but dropped a bit in 2014 and 2015 to about 25 percent. Many believe Martinez's late start to his career, coupled with the fact that he played primarily as a designated hitter, have held him back. One of the biggest supporters of Martinez's HOF candidacy is former teammate Randy Johnson, who was inducted in 2015. "The first person on my ballot who would get my vote is Edgar," said Johnson. "I've faced a lot of Hall of Fame hitters, and . . . Edgar is the best hitter that I ever saw."[43]

For fans in Seattle, Martinez will long be remembered as the heart of their team. While he was a superbly talented hitter who worked hard at his craft, his most important attribute may well be the quality of his character. He is perhaps best described by the late Dave Niehaus: "I've never heard anybody in any walk of life say anything ever halfway bad about Edgar Martínez. I've never heard a cross word from him. He has always had nice things to say about everyone, even in trying circumstances. He's a great human being."[44]

*All statistics from Baseball Reference, unless otherwise noted.*

## NOTES

1. David L. Porter, *Latino and African American Athletes Today: A Biographical Dictionary,* (Santa Barbara: Greenwood Publishing Group, 2004), 253.
2. Ian C. Friedman, *Latino Athletes,* (New York: Infobase Publishing, 2007), 133.
3. Larry Stone, "Martinez is Still the Talk of His Town," *Seattle Times,* October 4, 2004.
4. Bob Finnigan, "Double Play—Cousin Carmelo Talked Edgar Martínez into Taking a Chance, Signing with M's," *Seattle Times,* March 7, 1993.
5. Porter, *Biographical Dictionary,* 253; ibid.
6. Blaine Newnham, "Mister Muscle—Martinez Gives M's a Lift," *Seattle Times,* May 24, 1990.

7   Bob Sherwin, "Martinez, Diaz Help Save M's Moore from Embarrassment," *Seattle Times*, October 2, 1987.

8   Bob Sherwin, "Christensen Reassigned; 6 Others Get Ax," March 22, 1988; Bob Finnigan, "Parker's Bleeders Killed Mariners," *Seattle Times*, April 5, 1988; email, Rick Griffin to author, October 27, 2015, in author's possession. Griffin is the M's senior director of athletic training.

9   Bob Sherwin, "Majors Top Minors for M's—Martinez, Briley Show They Plan to Stay in Win Over Blue Jays," *Seattle Times*, June 19, 1989.

10  Blaine Newnham, "Mister Muscle."

11  Bob Finnigan, "Reynolds Looks Like a Million; Presley Looks Like a Red Sock," *Seattle Times*, January 14, 1990.

12  Jim Cour, "Mistakes Don't Rattle Martinez—M's Third Baseman Swings Hot Bat," *Seattle Times*, May 20, 1990.

13  Blaine Newnham, "Mister Muscle."

14  Ibid.

15  Bob Sherwin, "M's Finish Season with 7-4 Loss—Seattle 1 Victory Short of Matching Best-Ever Season," *Seattle Times*, October 3, 1990.

16  Bob Finnigan, "Valle Overcomes Contract Dispute to Report on Time," *Seattle Times*, February 23, 1991.

17  Bob Sherwin, "Edgar—All-Star Dream Comes True for Sore-Shouldered Martinez," *Seattle Times*, July 10, 1992.

18  Bob Sherwin, "M's Invest in Future—Martinez Signs for Hot Numbers: 3 Years, $10M," *Seattle Times*, August 14, 1992.

19  Bob Finnigan, "Make Way for Martinez—League's Top Hitter Finally Gets Noticed Outside Seattle," *Seattle Times*, August 25, 1992.

20  Bob Finnigan, "Edgar Was a One-Man Hit Parade—Injuries Sapped His Legs But Couldn't Derail Him," *Seattle Times*, October 4, 2004.

21  Bob Finnigan, "Edgar's Season May Be Finished—Shoulder Surgery Possible for Martinez," September 16, 1992.

22  Connie McDougall, "Rooting for the Home Team," *Response*, Winter 1997.

23  Finnigan, "Edgar was a One-Man Hit Parade."

24  Bob Finnigan, "Double Play."

25  Bob Finnigan, "M's Lose Edgar for Up to 6 Weeks—Martinez Sidelined After B.C. Mishap," April 4, 1993.

26  Bob Finnigan, "Edgar was a one-man hit parade."

27  Bob Sherwin, "Mariner Log—Edgar Gets a Scare in First Trip to Plate," *Seattle Times*, April 5, 1994.

28  Ibid., "Martinez Gets Summertime Due—Finishes 3rd in MVP Vote After Lifting Griffey-Less M's," November 17, 1995.

29  Bob Finnigan, "Miracle Mariners—Pair of Aces, Edgar's Clutch Hit Ends Series for the Ages in 11th," *Seattle Times*, October 9, 1995.

30  "What They're Saying About Edgar," *Seattle Times*, October 9, 1995.

31  "Mariners '96: A Look Back," *Seattle Times*, September 30, 1996.

32  Glenn Nelson, "Martinez Uncertain About Future—Wants to Stay, But Has No Say," *Seattle Times*, October 6, 1997.

33  Ken Rosenthal, "Martinez Keeps Hits Coming Despite an Eye Disorder," *Sporting News*, May 6, 2001.

34  Bob Finnigan, "Back in the Fold—Martinez Agrees to One-Year Deal with Mariners," *Seattle Times*, November 8, 2002.

35  Ibid., "Edgar was a one-man hit parade."

36  Ibid.

37  Art Thiel, "Seattle to Rename Street After Edgar Martínez," *Seattle Post-Intelligencer*, September 30, 2004.

38  Bob Finnigan, "A tip of the cap—Rangers 10, M's 4 | Seattle Honors Retiring DH with a Moving Tribute | Edgar Martínez Day", *Seattle Times*, October 3, 2004.

39  Steve Kelley, "Martinez Receives Clemente Award—'It Means a Lot'," *Seattle Times*, October 27, 2004.

40  Greg Johns, "Edgar's Life After Baseball," *Seattle Post-Intelligencer*, February 16, 2007.

41  Ryan Divish, "Mariners hire Edgar as New Hitting Coach," *Seattle Times*, June 21, 2015.

42  Ibid.

43  Jerry Crasnick, "Randy Johnson: Vote Edgar Martínez," *ESPN.com*, January 7, 2015, http://espn.go.com/mlb/story/_/id/12132849/randy-johnson-endorses-former-seattle-mariners-teammate-edgar-martinez-baseball-hall-fame.

44  Steve Kelley, "Loud Bat Belied the Quiet Pro Behind It," *Seattle Times*, October 4, 2004.

# ORLANDO MERCED

## By Justin Cabrera

**O**F THE MANY TALENTED PLAYERS involved in the successes of the early 1990s pennants won by the Pittsburgh Pirates, one player who flew under the radar was amateur free-agent signing Orlando Merced. Orlando Luis Villanueva Merced was born on November 2, 1966, to José R. and Sylvia Villanueva. Merced's parents were both originally from Puerto Rico, José from Yabucoa and Sylvia from Humacao, but later settled on the US mainland. José spent his early life in the military, then worked for the US Postal Service, and Sylvia was a professor at New York University. While they were still in Puerto Rico, Orlando caught the eye of Pittsburgh scout Howie Haak while at University Garden High School in San Juan.

Raised alongside the three sons of Hall of Famer and national hero Roberto Clemente, Orlando grew up a Pirates fan. At 18, having been passed over by scouts, Orlando decided to give up baseball and go to college. But one day in 1985 one of Clemente's sons, Luis, invited Orlando to the Clementes' house, where Luis was to sign a contract with the Pirates. While he was there a family friend, Victor Henriquez, urged Haak to also sign Orlando. Haak held a one-man tryout for Merced and did sign him.[1]

Merced and Luis Clemente were both assigned to the rookie-level Gulf Coast League. Playing mostly third base and shortstop, he hit .228 in 40 games. His fielding was woeful at shortstop; 22 errors in 19 games at the position. Nonetheless, the Pirates had sufficient faith in him to keep him in the system. (Luis Clemente, meanwhile, left Organized Baseball after one season.) In 1986 Merced played 92 games at Class-A Watertown (New York-Penn League) Macon (South Atlantic League).He continued to struggle at the plate, with a combined .191 average. Third base was also a struggle, and he played some games at first base and in the outfield,

Merced was plagued by injuries in 1987 and had only 19 plate appearances at Watertown and Macon. Eager to get back on the field in 1988, Merced batted.283 with 8 home runs and 15 stolen bases at Class-A Augusta (South Atlantic League) and Salem (Carolina League). He started the 1989 season with Double-A Harrisburg and late in the season was promoted to Triple-A Buffalo. In 129 at-bats for the Bisons Merced impressed with a .341 batting average and a .372 on-base percentage. He concentrated on hitting to all fields and relied less on pulling the ball. Merced spent most of 1990 with Buffalo, batting.262 with 9 home runs, 55 RBIs, and 14 stolen bases. At manager Terry Collins's recommendation, the Pirates called Merced up in late June and he played in 25 games for the team as a pinch-hitter and late-innings fill-in. In his major-league debut, Merced got a pinch-hit double off the Philadelphia Phillies' Ken Howell on June 27.

In 1991 the switch-hitting outfielder-first baseman played in 120 Pirates games, batted .275 and finished second to Jeff Bagwell in the National League Rookie of the Year voting. Merced was a disciplined hitter, demonstrated by his career .355 on-base percentage, and had a strong arm in the outfield, shown by his 65 career outfield assists. Merced's most intriguing skill, however, was his knack for performing well under pressure, with a career .300 batting average in high-leverage situations.

After playing every infield and outfield position in the minors, Merced found an opening at first base with the Pirates in 1991, after the incumbent, Sid Bream became a free agent after the 1990 season. Merced missed the final seven games of the 1991 season after spraining a ligament in his right foot.

After not starting a game since September 26, on October 12 Merced led off Game Three of the National League Championship Series against the Atlanta Braves with a home run off future Hall of

Famer John Smoltz. At the time, only three players had homered to lead off a playoff game (Bert Campaneris in 1973, George Brett in 1978, and Bob Dernier in 1984). Pittsburgh fell to the Braves, the second of three straight years the Pirates lost the NLCS.

Merced's performance fell off in 1992, his second season with the Pirates; his batting average fell to .247, with 6 home runs and 60 RBIs. After the season, several Pirates who had helped orchestrate the successes of the previous few years departed, notably Barry Bonds and Doug Drabek. This thrust the young Merced into a more demanding role, and he rose to the occasion, batting .313 with 8 home runs, 70 RBIs, a career-high OPS (on base percentage plus slugging percentage) of .857. Merced's success didn't translate to enough wins as Pittsburgh finished fifth in the National League East and missed the playoffs for the first time in four years.

Pittsburgh missed the postseason for the remainder of Merced's tenure with the team. During his seven seasons with the Pirates he hit 65 home runs, with 394 RBIs. In 1996, his last season with Pittsburgh, Merced batted .287 and had one of his best slugging seasons, with 17 home runs and 80 runs batted in. Nevertheless, after the season the Pirates sent Merced to the Toronto Blue Jays in a nine-player deal. By this time Merced had shown his defensive abilities and arm strength in right field, and started the season as the Blue Jays' everyday right fielder.

Merced joined a formidable offense in Toronto that included fellow Puerto Ricans Carlos Delgado, Benito Santiago, and Jose Cruz. Merced posted decent numbers in Toronto, with 9 home runs, an above-average on-base percentage (.352), and continuing to play a formidable right field. Toronto missed the playoffs, and Merced, now 30 years old, decided to test the free-agent market. Though his production was respectable, he went into free agency with a .266 batting average for the season and the fewest RBIs and hits in his career. Teams must have assumed he was on the decline. Merced had been paid $2.7 million in each of his past two years, but after nearly three months on the market, he signed

a one-year contract with the Minnesota Twins for $800,000. Merced played only 63 games with the Twins in 1998, posting a .289 batting average before being dealt to the Boston Red Sox on July 31 in a five-player trade.

The 1998 Red Sox were postseason-bound but Merced had few opportunities to perform; on September 1, the Red Sox released him. He wasn't unemployed long. Four days later the Chicago Cubs picked up his contract. In 10 at-bats with the Cubs, Merced hit .300 with a three-run home run. With the Cubs, Merced again found himself playing for a team that was eliminated in the playoffs by the Atlanta Braves. Merced did not see any playing time in the playoffs and the Cubs were defeated in a three-game sweep. On October 28 the Cubs let him go. On February 10, 1999, he signed with the Montreal Expos in a one-year, $560,000 deal that would send him back to Canada.

Once again Merced joined a number of Puerto Rico-born players, including Javier Vasquez and Jose Vidro. At 32 Merced became a part-time player, getting into 93 games and batting .268. The tremendous defensive play and throwing arm of Vladimir

Guerrero saw Merced pushed over to left field in Montreal for the first time in his career. The Expos finished the season in fourth place in the National League East, missed the playoffs, and on October 15 the team released Merced.

For 2000 Merced signed with the Orix Blue Wave of the Japanese Pacific League, playing in 23 games and at least well enough to warrant a minor-league deal with the Houston Astros in August. Over the rest of the season he played in 17 games for the New Orleans Zephyrs and batted .269.

The 34-year-old Merced's play and experience warranted him another contract from Houston in 2001. He earned $300,000 in just over 130 at-bats. Houston reached the playoffs in 2001 but was eliminated from contention by the Atlanta Braves. Merced went 0-for-1, fouling out to the catcher in his last postseason at-bat. He returned to Houston the following two seasons on one-year contracts and ended his major-league career in 2003 playing alongside his 1991 rival for the Rookie of the Year Award, Jeff Bagwell. Released by the Astros after the 2003 season, Merced signed a minor-league contract with the Pirates but was released in 2004 spring training. He left the major leagues with a career .277 batting average with 103 home runs.

After life in the majors, Merced took his love for baseball back to Puerto Rico in the 2004 season and continued playing in the Puerto Rican Winter League until 2005. In 2010 he became the hitting coach for the Jamestown Jammers, a Pirates farm team in the rookie-level New York-Penn League.

Merced started his managerial career with the Rojos del Aguila de Veracruz of the Mexican League in 2012 and later that year helped coach the Puerto Rican National team in the World Baseball Classic. As of 2017, Merced remained involved in baseball and was hitting coach of the Billings Mustangs, the Cincinnati Reds' rookie league team. When away from baseball, Merced spends time with his four children who live with their mother in Missouri. Merced's son, Rob, is a football standout at Kickapoo High School, well known for preparing young athletes for college football.

## SOURCES

In addition to the sources cited in the Notes, the author also consulted Baseball-Reference.com and the following:

greatest21days.com/2010/09/orlando-merced-pain-and-gain-18.html.

news.google.com/newspapers?id=PN8cAAAAIBAJ&sjid=IGQEAAAAIBAJ&dq=orlando-merced&pg=4973,6713036&hl=en.

news-leader.com/story/sports/high-school/2016/10/27/baseball-his-blood-football-his-mind-kickapoos-robbie-merced/92849322/.

Thanks to Edwin Fernandez for information on Merced's family background.

## NOTES

1   articles.latimes.com/1991-06-16/sports/sp-1554_1_orlando-merced.

# FÉLIX MILLÁN

## By Jane Allen-Quevedo

**B**ASEBALL FANS IN THE 1960S AND '70s could bet their Cracker Jack that second baseman Félix Bernardo Millán would put the ball in play when he stepped up to bat for the Atlanta Braves or New York Mets. In 6,325 plate appearances, the 172-pound right-handed batter whiffed only 242 times, establishing himself as the National League's toughest hitter to strike out in four of his 12 major-league seasons. Fans also remember the funny way Millán held his bat, choking up so high it looked as if he'd punch himself in the stomach when he swung at a pitch. He obviously did not choke the bat to produce home runs because he hit only 22 in his major-league career. He choked the bat to get hits and move up runners. In 1,480 games, he had 1,617 hits and a batting average of .279. Today some still consider Millán the best second baseman to ever play for the Braves and among the best to play for the Mets.[1]

Millán's story begins in the barrio of El Cerro del Calvario, in Puerto Rico, where he was born on August 21, 1943. An aunt started calling him "Nacho," mistakenly thinking it was the nickname for Bernardo, his middle name. By the time she learned it was short for Ignacio, Félix was already answering to Nacho, the name his family and friends from Yabucoa continued to call him. Millán was one of those kids who grew up in the sugarcane fields of the Caribbean batting a ball of string with a guava branch and dreaming of someday making it to the big leagues. "I prayed to God that I could make enough money to help my parents," he said in a 2010 interview.[2]

Millán was the third of 11 children born to Victor and Anastasia Millán of Yabucoa, Puerto Rico. One baby died at birth and another died at a very young age, leaving a family of nine children. Victor Millán worked at a sugarcane-processing plant during harvest season, earning about 35 cents an hour, while Anastasia took in laundry to help meet expenses. Often, however, there was not enough money to buy food for the large Millán family. To make a little spending money, young Félix found odd jobs such as shining shoes or picking a grass called *coitre*, which he sold for 10 cents a bag to people who raised rabbits.

An extremely shy kid, Félix was painfully embarrassed that he had no shoes to wear to school. To hide his bare feet from the other students he would stretch them as far under his seat as possible, living in constant fear of his teacher calling him to the front of the classroom. When he was 10 years old, his father sent him to live with his grandparents in the rural barrio of Juan Martín, where among other chores he took care of an uncle's fighting cocks. Living in the country meant the young boy walked almost an hour to and from school every day, giving him a lot of time alone in his own thoughts, usually dreaming of baseball and his hero Lou Gehrig. A baseball field was the one place his shyness disappeared.

In grade school Félix played in a league sponsored by the Yabucoa police department. For lack of high-school baseball in Puerto Rico, during his teen years he played on a local amateur team, where his agility and quick glove soon made him one of the most popular kids in school. Everyone wanted Nacho on their team. After graduating from high school in 1960, with no plans for his future and no money for college, he joined the US Army. He hated Army life, however. Away from Spanish-speaking Puerto Rico for the first time, he was lonesome and homesick. Things finally began to look up for Millán when he discovered that Army bases had baseball teams. After he made the team, Army life was not so bad for Félix. Letters from a young woman in Puerto Rico also helped. Sensing correctly that Félix missed his home land, a friend suggested that he write to a girl named Mercedes "Mercy" Garcia. In time the two were exchanging letters three or four times a week and were looking forward to his discharge in July

1962. Millán may have been anxious to meet Mercy, but her father was not so sure about him. Without their knowledge, he went to Félix's hometown to personally investigate Mercy's young suitor. There he discovered that everybody in Yabucoa knew Nacho Millán, the shy kid who dazzled hometown fans on the baseball field. Mercy's father not only allowed her to continue seeing Félix, he also said yes when the young man asked for permission to marry her. Félix and Mercy were married on December 21, 1962, two kids madly in love and sharing a dream of a career in professional baseball.

Baseball scout Félix Delgado spotted Millán playing first base in Puerto Rico's Double A[3] professional league and signed him for the Kansas City Athletics in 1964. Although Delgado soon switched him to second base, Millán started out playing first base with the Daytona Beach Islanders of the Class A Florida State League. After a year in the Athletics system, the Milwaukee Braves drafted Millán on November 30, 1964, and signed him for only $2,500. He was assigned to their Yakima (Washington) team in the Class-A Northwest League, where he met manager Hub Kittle. Millán remembered that at one point when he was batting under .200, Kittle personally took him aside and practiced with him every day until he was hitting over .300. He also credited Kittle for advising him to choke up on the bat.[4] Millán moved up the Braves' minor-league ladder quickly, playing in 35 games for Austin of the Double-A Texas League at the end of the 1965 season.

Millán joined the Braves in the spring of 1966, the club's first season in Atlanta after moving from Milwaukee. What he remembered most about his first day in Atlanta was meeting his future roommate, Hank Aaron. Approaching the new kid on the team, Aaron invited Millán to stay in his home rather than a hotel his first night in Atlanta. The next morning Aaron handed him a set of car keys. "Take my Camaro," Hank said. Not only did Aaron loan Millán his car, he asked to room with the Puerto Rican when they played on the road. The two were roommates throughout Millán's years with the Braves.

Millán, the 27th player from Puerto Rico to make it to the big leagues,[5] made his major-league debut on June 2, 1966, getting a single in his first at-bat off Bob Bolin of the San Francisco Giants. Manager Bobby Bragan had benched the struggling veteran second baseman Frank Bolling in favor of Millán, and Félix did not disappoint his skipper. Millán started 21 straight contests and had his first major-league four-hit game on June 7 at Shea Stadium in New York. However, a broken finger sidelined Millán in late June, and he then found it hard to return to the regular lineup with Bolling and Woody Woodward handling the position.

Millán knew something was amiss when new manager Billy Hitchcock invited him to breakfast after only 87 days in Atlanta and only three days shy of receiving a much-anticipated progression bonus. His heart sank as he listened to Hitchcock explain that he'd rather see him playing in the minors in Richmond than sitting on the bench in Atlanta. Brokenhearted, Félix knew better than to argue the point. Sitting across the breakfast table from Hitchcock, he listened politely and kept his mouth shut, not daring to say anything that might jeopardize his future in the big leagues. Millán did his job at Triple-A Richmond, hitting .306 for the remainder of the International League season.

As the 1967 season started, Millán was back with Atlanta, but struggled at the plate and, sporting a paltry .194 average, was sent down at the end of May. Back in Richmond, he teamed up with third baseman Bobby Cox and, as Laurence Leonard reported, the pair created a lot of interest in minor-league baseball, drawing huge crowds and leading their team to the International League pennant in 1967.[6] With a .310 batting average, he won the minor-league Player of the Year award.[7] The best thing that happened to Millán in Richmond was manager Lum Harris. Probably nobody in his baseball career believed in Millán more than Harris, who later claimed the Puerto Rican to be the best second baseman in the National League.[8]

Millán was recalled in early September, and raised his batting average to .235. Atlanta was floundering badly in seventh place near season's end and fired Hitchcock with three games remaining in 1967. Harris was named manager for the 1968 campaign a week later and took Félix with him. Soon the second baseman was getting a fair amount of attention by the press. "He can hit, he can hit and run, bunt for a hit, sacrifice and finagle a base on balls. He can run and slide and he can scramble back up and run some more," wrote Gary Ronberg.[9]

It was those skills that earned Millán the nickname Kitten or Kit for short. In his homeland they called him "El Gatito." The English moniker evolved to Cat, which stuck for the rest of his career. Félix "Cat" Millán had a way of playing the game without attracting a lot of attention. As Lum Harris told Ronberg, "He's the type of player that you never realize is around until the game is over. Then you look up and he's got two hits, an RBI, stolen base, and he's been in on two double plays."[10] During his first full season in the majors, Millán was batting .309 at midseason before finishing at .289, just missing the Top 10 in the league, during the "Year of the Pitcher."

From 1969 to 1971, Félix was named to three straight All-Star teams, playing in two of the midsummer classics (1969 and 1971). He also won Gold Gloves in the same years his children (a son, Bernardo, in 1969 and daughter, Femerlie, in 1972) were born. Millán was the first Brave to play in all 162 games of a regular season (1969), the same year he achieved career highs in RBIs (57) and home runs (6). Defensively, during the 1969 season he led National League second basemen with a .980 fielding average, 373 putouts, and 444 assists.

Never hailed as a home-run hitter, Millán hit his only major-league grand slam on April 8, 1969, against San Francisco Giants pitcher Gaylord Perry. That year he helped the Braves take the top spot in the National League West and go to the first-ever National League Championship Series. Although the Braves were favored to win the series, New York's Miracle Mets surprisingly won the pennant with a three-game sweep of the then best-of-five playoff. Millán hit .333 in the series. During the 1969 NLCS, Wayne Lockwood of the *San Diego Union* observed, "Millán does his job with a quiet competence in all departments that inspires respect from both sides of the diamond."[11]

In 1970 Félix batted a career-high .310 and scored 100 runs, also a career high. He became the first Brave to go 6-for-6 in a nine-inning game, a team record he held by himself for 37 years until Willie Harris tied it in 2007. The Braves second baseman completed a career high 120 double plays in 1971, had 8 triples, and struck out only 22 times in 577 at-bats, making him the National League's toughest batter to strike out for the first time.

Even though he won his second Gold Glove the following year, 1972, Millán played in only 125 games because of an injury, and his batting average slipped to .257. At the end of the season, the Braves chose to trade him for some much-needed pitching talent. Millán was not surprised by the Braves' decision to trade him, and he was elated when he learned where he was going. Manager Eddie Mathews tried to break the news carefully because he knew Félix was loyal to the Braves. As Millán told the story, Mathews apologized as he broke the news that he was going to the Mets. "What's there to be sorry for?" Félix thought. "Does he know how many Puerto Ricans live in New York?"

Millán was traded, along with pitcher George Stone, for pitchers Gary Gentry and Danny Frisella in what is considered to be one of the best trades the Mets ever made.[12] For Millán, from his first day with the club he felt as if he had been with them forever. While the Mets' 1973 season looked like another in a string of disappointing years after their 1969 world championship, Millán was having the best year of his career. His 16 hits and a batting average of .533 earned him the National League Player of the Week award on June 17. Millán was a key player in the Mets' remarkable turnaround in the last five weeks of the season. Winning 24 of their last 33 games, they managed to get 82 wins to squeak into the top spot of the NL East. By the end of the season Félix had regained his standing as the toughest man to strike out with only 22 strikeouts in a Mets season record of 638 at-bats. He also led the Mets in games played (153), runs (82), hits (185, a Mets season record), singles (155), triples (4), batting average (.290), hit by pitches (6), and sacrifice hits (18, a Mets season record). His .989 fielding average in 1973 was his career high and the third-best in the league that season.

New York sportswriters named Millán the team's Most Valuable Player. Beating the odds by taking the National League pennant three games to two during the best-of-five playoff over heavily favored Cincinnati, the Mets did what naysayers said could not be done and were on their way to the World Series again. But the 1973 Series against the Oakland Athletics was plagued with bad hitting and errors,[13] and the Mets' sure-handed second baseman was no exception. One of the key players responsible for getting the Mets to the World Series made what was probably the most embarrassing error of his career when he misjudged a groundball by Bert Campaneris, allowing it to pass under his glove for a crucial error during the third inning of Game One which led to both Oakland runs in a 2-1 loss for the Mets.

The Series went seven games before Oakland finally won it, with Millán batting just .188. After the World Series, Millán went home to Puerto Rico for what turned out to be the best of the 17 years he played winter ball with the Caguas Criollos. The team took the Puerto Rican League title for the first time since 1968 and went on to win the 1974 Caribbean Series, a feat it had not achieved in 20 years.

Back in the States, Millán continued to be the National League's toughest batter to strike out in 1974 and again in 1975, achieving that distinction four times in five seasons. In 1974 he broke his own record and led the National League with 24 sacrifice hits, and also led the Mets for the season in singles (121) and hit by pitches (8). Playing 162 games in 1975, he became the first Met to play every game in a regular season (a mark tied by John Olerud in 1999), thus repeating his 1969 achievement with the Braves. He also established Mets season records (all of which have since been broken) with career highs of 676 at-bats, 191 hits, and 37 doubles.

In his Mets career, Millán played nine games in which he had four or more hits. The most famous of these games included a dubious achievement on the part of teammate Joe Torre. Félix batted ahead of him on July 21, 1975, in a game against Houston. Millán hit

four singles, which Torre followed with four grounders to give the Astros four easy double plays. Torre set a National League record, hitting into four double plays in a single game, and afterward credited Félix for the "assists." "I'd like to thank Félix Millán for making all of this possible," Torre said.[14]

Millán continued to be the Mets' leader in several categories in 1976: 139 games, with 531 at-bats, 150 hits, 122 singles, and 7 hit by pitches. He tied for the team lead with 25 doubles and, among players with 500 at-bats, led the team with a .282 batting average. But Millán's major-league career literally came crashing to the ground on August 12, 1977, at Pittsburgh's Three Rivers Stadium. He had just entered the games as a defensive replacement in the sixth inning during the second game of a doubleheader against the Pirates, and the Mets' quiet, well-respected second baseman lost his cool in an on-field brawl when Ed Ott tried to break up a double-play attempt. The Pirates had runners on first and second when Mario Mendoza hit a grounder to shortstop Doug Flynn, who flipped the ball to Millán to try for a double play. All of a sudden Millán was on the ground with his face in the dirt, knocked down by Ott, who slammed into him like an NFL linebacker. Millán came up spitting and shouting and, with the ball still in his fist, punched Ott in the face. Millán said he fully expected a return punch. Instead, Ott picked him up and body-slammed him to the ground. The benches cleared, Ott was ejected by home-plate umpire Ed Sudol, and Millán was carried out on a stretcher with a broken clavicle, dislocated shoulder, and severely wounded pride. Ott was later fined $250 by National League President Chub Feeney.

When an offer came for Millán to play in Japan, he was ready to move. He played three seasons (1978-1980) with the Yokohama Taiyo Whales (now the Yokohama BayStars). In 1979 he helped them achieve their best season to date, finishing in second place in the Central Japan League. With a .346 hitting record in 1979, Millán was the first foreigner to claim Japan's batting title, and he received the Best Nine Award.[15]

Millán loved playing in Japan, and was well liked there. His quiet demeanor and dedication to the game helped him fit into the culture of Japanese baseball, where players are expected to put their team's interests ahead of their own.[16] However, Félix made a little known and highly unusual request of his managers in his last year with the Whales when he asked to be excused from Friday night and Saturday games for religious reasons. He wished to join his wife, a Seventh-day Adventist, in observing the Sabbath from sunset Friday to sunset Saturday. Initially the Whales said it was impossible but, in true Japanese fashion, agreed to discuss the matter. After a few days, they revealed a plan that avoided loss of face by either party, which is paramount in resolving differences in Japanese culture. Millán's name quietly disappeared from the Friday night and Saturday lineups, but he was expected to play every Saturday night and Sunday game. When the Whales released him after the 1980 season, Millán had made 1,139 plate appearances with only 52 strikeouts. He had also hit the second grand slam of his professional career. Even though he was approached informally by the club from Nagoya, Félix decided it was time to retire. That feeling lasted about as long as a trans-Pacific flight back to Puerto Rico, and he soon accepted an offer to play with the Red Devils of Mexico City. However, Mexico wasn't Japan, nor was it the big leagues. After only one year Millán returned to Puerto Rico to retire.

Although officially retired, Millán did not fully leave the game. As of 2014 he continued making appearances for the Mets and Major League Baseball, including trips to Italy and Taiwan as an MLB instructor. In the 1980s he worked as an infield instructor[17] for the Mets' rookie league in Port St. Lucie, Florida, and for a time worked as Latin American coordinator for the Mets' minor-league system. Millán played for the St. Lucie Legends of the Senior Professional Baseball Association in 1989, hitting .269 in 31 games. For a couple of years, he directed a baseball academy in Savannah, Georgia,[18] and as of 2014 continued to be involved with the Félix Millán Little League, established in New York in 1977.[19] He was named to the Braves 400 Club's All-Time Atlanta Braves Team in 2001.[20] As of 2014 he lived in Puerto Rico and Florida.

# PUERTO RICO AND BASEBALL: 60 BIOGRAPHIES

## SOURCES

In addition to the sources in the author consulted Baseball-Reference.com, Retrosheet.org, and the following articles:

Graczyk, Wayne, "BayStars continue burgeoning baseball tradition in Yokohama," The Japan Times Online, November 20, 2011. (japantimes.co.jp/text/sb20111120wg.html)

Hulka, James, "All-Time Braves Lineup," Bleacher Report, August 5, 2008. (bleacherreport.com/articles/44585-all-time-braves-lineup).

Leggett, William, "Mutiny and a Bounty," *Sports Illustrated*, October 29, 1973. sportsillustrated.cnn.com/vault/article/magazine/MAG1087941/index.html.

Madio, Vinny, "New York Mets All-Time Lineup," Bleacher Report, August 5, 2008. (bleacherreport.com/articles/44494-new-york-mets-all-time-lineup).

Ragus, Jonathan, "The Ultimate Mets Fantasy League," Bleacher Report, May 28, 2009. (bleacherreport.com/articles/186891-the-ultimate-mets-fantasy-league.)

Stowe, Rich, "MLB Power Rankings: Every Team's Greatest Second Baseman in History," Bleacher Report, June 1, 2011. (bleacherreport.com/articles/713346-mlb-power-rankings-every-teams-greatest-second-baseman-in-history).

## NOTES

1. Shale Briskin, "New York Mets: Top 10 Second Basemen in Team History," Bleacher Report, June 22, 2011 (bleacherreport.com/articles/736774-new-york-mets-top-10-second-basemen-in-team-history).

2. Félix Millán with Jane Allen Quevedo, *Tough Guy Gentle Heart* (West Conshohocken, Pennsylvania: Infinity Publishing, 2012), 129; Millán with Quevedo, El Pelotero con un corazón noble (Ringgold, Georgia.: Aspect Books, 2013), 106.

3. In this case, "Double A" does not refer to the minor-league classification used in Organized Baseball; it was the name of that particular professional league in Puerto Rico.

4. Ken Ross, "Hub Kittle," The Baseball Biography Project, Society for American Baseball Research (Retrieved November 7, 2010).

5. Baseball-Almanac.com

6. Laurence Leonard, "Ambitious Millan-Cox Duo Braves' Box-Office Beauts," *The Sporting News*, August 26, 1967: 31.

7. Gary Ronberg, "Félix Is One Sweet Ballplayer," *Sports Illustrated*, July 22, 1968. (sportsillustrated.cnn.com/vault/article/magazine/MAG1081411/index.htm).

8. Wayne Lockwood, "Félix Millan Close to Perfect Player," *Baseball Digest*, October 1969: 56-58.

9. Ronberg.

10. Ronberg.

11. Lockwood.

12. Barry Duchan, "Trades From the Past—Millan and Stone for Gentry and Frisella," Mikes Mets (mikesmets.com/2007/11/trades_from_the_past_millan_an.html).

13. Ron Fimrite, "Buffoonery Rampant," *Sports Illustrated*, October 22, 1973 (sportsillustrated.cnn.com/vault/article/magazine/MAG1087919/index.html).

14. Joe Torre and Tom Verducci, *The Yankee Years* (New York: Doubleday. 2009), 516.

15. Jim Albright, "Japanese Best Nine Winners," Baseball Guru (baseballguru.com/jalbright/best9.htm).

16. Robert Whiting, "You've Gotta Have 'wa,'" *Sports Illustrated*, September 24, 1979 (sportsillustrated.cnn.com/vault/article/magazine/MAG1095410/).

17. Paul Gutierrez, "Links in the Chain," *Sports Illustrated*, March 22, 1999 (sportsillustrated.cnn.com/vault/article/magazine/MAG1015386/index.html).

18. Victor Fernandes, "Millan Hoping To Produce Future Major Leaguers at Academy," *Savannah Morning News*, August 18, 1998 (savannahnow.com/stories/081898/SPTmillanfeature.html )

19. "Loisaida Little League," July 4, 2007 (nypress.com/loisaida-little-league/).

20. "Braves 400 Club's All-Time Atlanta Braves Team" (braves400.org/event_gameboree2001_alltime.html).

# BENGIE MOLINA

## By John Vorperian

FROM 1998 TO 2010, BENGIE Molina was a two-time consecutive Gold Glove Award catcher. Considered one of the slowest baserunners in his era, nevertheless in 2003 Molina was rated the best defensive catcher in the American League by *Baseball America*. He is the only player in baseball history to hit a home run but not be credited with a run. He played for the Anaheim Angels/Los Angeles Angels of Anaheim, Toronto Blue Jays, San Francisco Giants, and Texas Rangers. Molina closed out his major-league career with two World Series rings. His brothers José and Yadier were also major-league catchers who each have their own pair of World Series rings, unique among a trio of brothers in the record books.

Benjamin José "Bengie" Molina was born on July 20, 1974, Rio Piedras, Puerto Rico, to Benjamin Molina Santana and Gladys Matta Rosado. He was the couple's first-born. They then had two more sons, José and Yadier. Benjamin was employed as a machine operator on an assembly line for Westinghouse. Gladys tended the Molina household and also held a factory job with General Electric.

The Molina family lived in the town of Vega Alta located in the district of Dorado. The municipality has a nickname *El pueblo de los nangotaos*, the town of squatters. The town got the name in that workers squatted by the rail tracks waiting for trains to take them to the sugarcane fields.

Bengie's earliest recollection of baseball was at age 4 or 5. He remembered being in a dugout watching his father hit a walk-off home run for a semipro team. Benjamin was the inspiration, coach, and mentor to Bengie as well as his brothers to play and love the game of baseball.

At age 6, when he was old enough to play Little League, no team in his home town had an open roster spot. Benjamin stepped in, recruited other youngsters like Bengie who had been overlooked, and formed a squad that gained entry into a neighboring circuit. Bengie's father coached the team and named it Los Pobres (The Poor). The uniform colors were yellow and black, like the Pittsburgh Pirates and Roberto Clemente.

A national hero in Puerto Rico, Clemente was revered for his phenomenal athleticism, social activism, and charitable endeavors. Bengie recalled, "In many houses … including ours, the portraits of two famous men hung in honored spots among the family photos: Jesus, and Roberto Clemente."[1]

In the winter of 1966, Bengie's father, then a teenager, was taken by Jacinto Camacho, a baseball scout, to a Senadores game at Hiram Bithorn Stadium and was introduced to Clemente. The Hall of Fame player not only talked with Bengie's father in the clubhouse before and after the game but invited the teen to sit with him on the team's bench and continued the conversation during the actual contest. In telling this story about his father, Bengie said, "Nonplayers weren't permitted in the dugout during games. But it was Clemente. Who was going to argue?"[2]

Growing up, Bengie himself did idolize one particular major leaguer, the Cincinnati Reds' Pete Rose. Bengie favored "Charlie Hustle" because Rose played baseball the way Benjamin Senior was teaching his boys how to play the sport—with all-out effort.

By age 15, Bengie joined the Bayamon Post 48 American Legion team and also continued playing with Los Pobres. During this period the budding ballplayer was involved in no fewer than four organized games a week.

In 1990 the 16-year-old graduated with honors from Maestro Ladi High School in Vega Alta. June 1990 was the first year Puerto Rico became a part of major-league baseball's amateur draft. Until then youngsters on the island were signed as free agents. Bengie commented, "Every ballplayer in Puerto Rico raced a ticking clock. … [T]he youngest … sent to team-run baseball academies … until they were mature … to move onto the farm system. … If you weren't signed by 18 your best hope was … a college team in the States and hope you got noticed there."[3]

Nine players from his American Legion club, which won the Puerto Rican championship, were picked in that year's draft. Although Bengie had been invited and participated in several major-league tryouts during the year and was a pitcher, outfielder, and infielder, he was not among those selected. One bright spot that summer was that he took his first trip from the island. The Post 48 team journeyed to the mainland for the American Legion National Championship. They won the regionals held in Arkansas and moved onto Oregon to compete against other regional winners. The team got to the championship game but lost. Molina led the tournament in RBIs and stolen bases.

After the tournament, with his father's blessing and with the help of a family friend, the undrafted Molina went to Arizona Western College in Yuma, Arizona. He struggled in adjusting to college and the difference in climate. Although there were Puerto Rican players at the school, he had pangs of homesickness and loneliness. He also had to learn the English language. Nonetheless he persevered. As for baseball, he also had to learn a new key role. The Arizona Western roster had a dearth of shortstops. When one of the players from Puerto Rico informed Matadors coach John Stratton that Molina had played middle infield, Stratton asked the originally slated outfielder if he would switch to shortstop. Molina readily agreed. "He was really skinny," Stratton recalled. "And he was not a slow baserunner. He wasn't a burner, but he was very athletic and a decent runner."[4] In addition to shortstop, Bengie was a starting pitcher and a closer with an 85-87-mph fastball and had a good slider. In his first season, out of 14 freshmen, the team voted Molina Rookie of the Year.

In late May 1991, Molina went home to await the amateur draft. He joined Vega Alta Maceteros, a Double-A club in the Puerto Rico Baseball Federation. Its season ran from January to June with playoffs in July. The first week in June the player draft was conducted, but once again he remained undrafted.

Molina returned to Arizona Western. At the end of his second season with the Matadors, Bengie had a .385 batting average and a 2.90 ERA. He had been named All-Conference. The team voted him its MVP.

On June 1, 1992, the major-league amateur draft commenced. Bengie was living, working, and playing semipro baseball in Puerto Rico, and for a third time he was passed over and remained unselected. He chose not to return to Arizona Western that fall. Northern Alabama had made an overture to him but the scholarship offering fell through. Molina was finished playing baseball at the NCAA level.

His personal life took center stage. As a freshman, Bengie had met a young woman, also a freshman, who had sparked his interest. He and Joséfa dated frequently and steadily over the course of two years and in September 1992 Bengie flew to San Luis, Mexico, to see her family and ask her father for permission to marry her. The wedding took place in December 1992.

Bengie and his bride resided in San Luis. He took a job as a migrant field worker picking cauliflower in Yuma from sunrise to sunset. After the harvest, Molina worked at a Jack-in-the-Box fast-food restaurant located in his former college town handling the midnight-to-8 shift. Joséfa worked at the same location reporting for the morning shift and punching out at 2 P.M. In the meantime Bengie would have slept in their car, located in the eatery's parking lot. And the two would then return home together to Mexico to start the same routine all over again the very next day. Any down time Molina had, he did play baseball. But Bengie's father did not approve of this arrangement. Bengie's father was adamant that he should play ball in Puerto Rico. His father's firm belief was that major-league scouts would not look for talent in Mexico.

In March 1993 Bengie took his wife to Puerto Rico and they moved into his parents' home. He got a factory job, played Double-A baseball and attended weekly pro tryouts. By May 1993 he led the circuit in RBIs and was among the top five in home runs and batting average. But in late May he told his wife that his baseball career was over. The years of being passed over swelled his emotions raw. In a symbolic act, Molina took his blue Pony baseball spikes, knotted the shoelaces together, and tossed the pair over some tangled power lines.

Plans were that the couple would return to Yuma. He would take a job as a farm worker and study computers. Fate intervened.

His brother José insisted that Bengie come to his scheduled tryout before two California Angels scouts. Bengie told José it would be a waste of a time. But his brother would not relent and Bengie acquiesced. When José and Bengie arrived that morning at Parcelas Carmen Field in Vega Alta, indeed there were the Angels bird-dog duo and their mother. She had with her a scrapbook of newspaper clippings of Bengie's baseball exploits and she was being quite vocal to the scouts that they should give her oldest son a look. The Puerto Rican scout waved her off. But the American scout told Bengie to return at 3:00 P.M.

That afternoon, wearing Cheo's borrowed spikes, Bengie had a masterful round of batting practice. And then he was handed a catcher's mitt and told to get into a crouch and make some throws to second base. His brothers were catchers. Bengie had never caught before, but without hesitation, he took the glove from the scout got into position and threw.

At session's end, Angels scout Ray Poitevint, who once signed Hall of Famer Eddie Murray, was quite pleased but surprised that Bengie had never played catcher. He questioned Molina about that fact and said, "I can see you come from a baseball family. But I can't sign you to pitch or play third or outfield. You'll never get out of Single A the way you run."[5] The scout, who also discovered Dennis Martinez and Teddy Higuera, continued, "But I like your arm and I like your bat."[6]

Four days later, in May of 1993, the newly signed catching prospect was on a flight to the Angels' minor-league complex in Mesa, Arizona. He had inked

the deal on May 23; his bonus check netted less than $800.

After years of waiting for his opportunity to be selected by a major-league club, Bengie would say about this primary deal with the Angels, "I would have signed for nothing."[7]

On another occasions he said, "I don't care if I had to be a catcher, a ball boy, a water boy. I only wanted to be a part of the Big Show."[8]

The 18-year-old was assigned to California's Rookie level team, which had the right staff to provide a catching tutorial. He was managed by Bill Lachemann, who accrued six seasons as a minor-league catcher in the Dodgers organization. Molina received direct instructions about the finer techniques of being behind the dish by fellow Puerto Rican and an eight-season big-league catcher, coach Orlando Mercado, and by coach John McNamara, who had spent 14 minor-league seasons, initially with the

St. Louis Cardinals farm system as a receiver. In 27 games, Molina batted .263 with 10 RBIs.

Molina was moved up to the Angels' Low-A club for the 1994 season. At Cedar Rapids (Midwest League), the manager, Tom Lawless, used him as a designated hitter. At the plate, Molina had a .281 batting average, 3 home runs, and 16 RBIS in 48 games. On November 25, 1994, his first child, Kyshly, was born at a Bayamon, Puerto Rico, hospital.

The 1995 season was an up-and-down experience for the 20-year-old. Molina was promoted to the Angels' High-A club in Lake Elsinore (California League), where in 27 games he batted .385 with 12 RBIs. He was reassigned to Cedar Rapids, for which he played in 39 games and amassed a .293 batting average with 4 home runs and 17 RBIs. But his prospects of making the big leagues were diminished because Todd Greene, a 24-year old in Triple A, was having a banner year; he hit 40 homers, the most by a minor leaguer in a decade. The Angels saw him as their catcher of the future.

Molina opened the 1996 season with Midland in the Double-A Texas League. In 108 games he hit .274 and clubbed 8 home runs, with 54 RBIs. At season's end, he returned to Puerto Rico as he had been doing to work and play winter ball.

From 1993 to 1995, Molina was the bullpen catcher for Mayaguez. However, in '96 he made the roster as the third-string catcher. He credited the team's backup catcher with making him a better ballplayer: "That winter with Sal Fasano was like graduate school."[9]

Just a few years older than Molina, Fasano was a Kansas City Royal and had made his major-league debut on April 3, 1996. A journeyman in the big leagues from 1996 to 2008 and then a coach, Fasano was named Double-A Manager of the Year in 2011.

Fasano's teaching skills certainly came forward during that winter of 1996 and forever benefited Molina. The two would sit together in the Mayaguez dugout and Fasano would endlessly pepper Bengie with game scenario questions. Fasano showed Molina how to properly position himself behind the plate to give pitchers a bigger and better target as well as to get better calls from the umpires. "He told me to look confident when I called a pitch so the pitcher felt confident, too." Bengie also noted another lesson: "A good catcher sees all eight teammates, plus the batter and baserunners, as a single entity, an ensemble, and he adjusts to the shifting circumstances."[10]

"Too many catchers, not enough spots" was how Molina explained his demotion from Double A to Lake Elsinore for the opening of the 1997 season.[11] Midland's regular catcher was injured in midseason and the Angels moved Molina into that vacancy.[12]

After 1998 spring training, Molina, now 23, found himself assigned to Vancouver (Pacific Coast League), the Angels' Triple-A club. Now only one step away from the majors, he batted .293 with 22 RBIs in 49 games and was shocked and dismayed when at midseason he was sent back to Midland. This inexplicable transaction nearly caused Molina to quit baseball. However due to the strenuous intervention of Vancouver teammate Jovino Carvajal, a veteran minor leaguer, coupled with a telephone conversation with his father, Molina reconsidered and reported to the Double-A team. His decision paid off.

On September 21, 1998, at Edison International Field in Anaheim before 33,487, in the top of the ninth inning, Bengie Molina made his major-league debut. He was sent in to replace the purported catcher of the future, Todd Greene. Anaheim lost the game, 9-1, to the Texas Rangers. Molina got his first major-league at-bat on September 27 in a 4-2 road win over the Oakland Athletics. Angels manager Terry Collins sent the 5-foot-11, 190-pound right-handed batter in as a pinch-hitter in the eighth inning. Molina grounded out to third.

Three weeks after the season ended, Bengie and Joséfa's second child, daughter Kelssy, was born in Yuma.

In 1999 Molina came to the Angels camp ranked 11th among the organization's prospects. Yet, for the seventh straight year, he found himself in the minors on opening day, at Triple-A Edmonton (Pacific Coast League), where he batted .286 with 41 RBIs in 65 games. Then one night in August 1999, Edmonton skipper Carney Lansford and first-base coach Leon

Durham showed up at Molina's room to tell him to pack his bags — he was headed to The Show.

This time, it was not as a September call-up. Molina played in 31 contests, hit .257, drove in 10 runs, and got his first major-league home run. On August 19, 1999, in the third inning of a 9-2 Angels victory over the Chicago White Sox at Comiskey Park II, Molina smacked the homer off Chicago left-hander James Parque.

Bengie opened 2000 as the Angels starting catcher. Mike Scioscia, a former Dodgers catcher, had replaced Terry Collins as Anaheim's manager. Molina always felt that Collins had never sufficiently appreciated his abilities. Nonetheless, he was now Scioscia's and the Angels' first-string catcher.

With that ringing endorsement, in his first full season in the majors, Molina played in 130 games, the most by an Angels catcher in a decade. He hit .281, clubbed 14 home runs, and drove in 71 runs. At Scioscia's insistence, Molina did not play winter ball in Puerto Rico. He lived in Mexico with his nuclear family that offseason. He accepted a multiyear deal for four years with an option. Having subsisted at the league minimum, Molina took the team's overture, which resulted in $350,000 for 2001 and 2002, $1,425,000 in 2003, $2,025,000 in 2004, and $3,000,000 if the Angels picked up his option.

Although he was the regular catcher in 2001, Molina had some friendly family competition for the spot. His brother José made the team's roster as a backup. Hence the Molinas became the first pair of brothers to catch for the same major-league club since 1887, when Lave and Amos Cross did so for the Louisville Colonels (American Association). The Molinas became the 13th set of brothers to catch in the big leagues. The last grouping occurred in the 1940s when three sets of brothers were receivers, one pair being New York Yankees Hall of Famer Bill Dickey and his brother George, who played with the Red Sox and White Sox. In reflection Molina said, "This was our dream as kids — to play baseball in the majors. We never thought we'd be together on the same team."[13]

Under Scioscia, the Angels went from pretenders to contenders as they captured the 2002 American League pennant and then topped the San Francisco Giants in their first trip to the World Series. October 27, 2002, was a joyful day for the Molina tribe, as the Angels beat the Giants, 4-1, in Game Seven of the fall classic. Bengie Molina got his first championship ring. His brother José earned a ring, too. And back home on the island, Benjamin Senior, as a once second baseman, was inducted into Puerto Rico's amateur baseball Hall of Fame.

Bengie was named 2002 American League Gold Glove catcher, breaking Iván Rodríguez's 10-season (1992-2001) winning streak.

In 2003 Molina was having his best offensive year yet but his season was cut short by injury in early September. He batted .281 in 119 games, with 14 home runs and 71 RBIs. He received another Gold Glove.

On June 3, 2003, Molina enjoyed the opportunity to play his first major-league game in Puerto Rico itself; the game was held at Estadio Hiram Bithorn, the same venue where his father had met Clemente. Bengie Molina felt pressure to honor both his family and Puerto Rico. He could hardly have done better, starring in a 15-4 Angels rout of the Montreal Expos before 10,034 fans (including well over 100 who were Molina family and friends). Bengie drove in three runs and tied a personal career high with four hits, including a home run.

The promising year crashed to a halt on September 3, when Molina was severely injured in a 6-5 loss to the Minnesota Twins. With two outs in the bottom of the ninth, he caught a relay throw and had Twins pinch-runner Dustan Mohr out by a few feet. Mohr's only chance to be safe was to throw his shoulder into Molina's mitt and knock the ball out. Mohr had been a high-school linebacker and he hit with full force, fracturing Molina's wrist, popping the baseball loose, and allowing Shannon Stewart to round the bases unimpeded for the winning run. The next day Molina had surgery to repair fractured radius and ulna bones above his left wrist. He was out for the season.

Molina faithfully worked out during the winter, but concentrated solely on his legs as he was directed to refrain from upper-body workouts. He also failed to properly hydrate himself during these specific exercise sessions and as a result he endured hamstring problems that plagued his performance in exhibition games and early regular-season contests. At times he simply had to sit out games.

In 2004 Molina was in the last year of his four-year deal. The Angels held a $3 million option for 2005 that could be bought out for $100,000. Jeff Mathis, a 2001 first-round draft pick, was ranked the number-2 catching prospect by *Baseball America* and was slotted for Anaheim's Triple-A affiliate and possible promotion to the majors by 2005.

Molina went into self-imposed silence with the media until mid-August, but the Angels pitching staff spoke out in his defense. Closer Troy Percival said, "I can't tell you much about the National League, but in the American League no one stands above him."[14] Declared Jarrod Washburn, "I haven't seen all the catchers in baseball, but I think we're very spoiled. … [He] takes a lot of pride in studying … knowing everyone's game and going in with a solid game plan. There's not a lot of whole lot of shaking off [signs] when we're working together.[15]

Molina was consigned to the disabled list from August 3 with a broken right index finger. His season totals were .276 batting average, 10 home runs, and 54 RBIs in 97 games. And in November 2004 Angels exercised their option on him for the following year.

For the newly branded Los Angeles Angels of Anaheim in 2005, Molina hit a career-best .295 with 15 homers and 69 RBIs in 119 games. But in the offseason the team chose to sever ties. No contract offer was made and the Angels did not offer arbitration by the December 7 deadline; this opened the starting catching job to his brother José or Jeff Mathis.

On February 6, 2006, the Toronto Blue Jays signed Molina, 31, to a one-year, $5 million contract with an option for 2007.

Three days later, Molina lashed out at Angels management: "[T]he way they let me go without a notice, without calling me, that said a lot . … They just threw me like a piece of trash."[16] Angels GM Bill Stoneman disputed his accusations. Molina's agent, Alan Nero, said his client had wanted to be an Angel for his full career and "by expressing his feelings made the situation more negative than it is."[17]

On Opening Day April 4, 2006, before a hometown Rogers Centre crowd of 50,449, Molina homered off Johan Santana as the Jays beat the Minnesota Twins, 6-3. On April 12 at Fenway Park, he homered against David Wells in an 8-4 romp over the Red Sox. In the first inning of the April 22 game in Toronto, Boston southpaw Lenny DiNardo delivered up a home run to Molina as the Jays pecked the Red Sox, 8-1. Despite his offense, Toronto manager John Gibbons platooned Molina and Gregg Zaun as Blue Jays receivers for the remainder of the season. Over 117 games Bengie posted a .284 batting average, with 19 home runs and 57 RBIs. On October 29 he was granted free agency.

In baseball circles Bengie Molina got the nickname Big Money. That December, he signed a three-year deal with the San Francisco Giants for $16 million.

Molina clocked his 100th career home run on September 5, 2007, off the Colorado Rockies' Jorge Julio in a 5-3 win. The mark was overshadowed because in the same contest, fellow Giant Barry Bonds hit his 762nd home run.

Sixteen days later, Molina racked up his 500th career RBI in an extra-inning 9-8 home loss to the Cincinnati Reds. In the pregame ceremony, he was named the 2007 Willie Mac Award winner, named in honor of Hall of Famer Willie McCovey. The award, voted upon by Giants players, coaches, training staff, and fans, goes to on the Giants player who best exemplifies a fighting spirit and competitive desire to win.

In a doubleheader on May 25, 2008, Molina caught 16 innings against Miami in which he went 6-for-7 with four doubles and five RBIs.

On September 26 Molina became the first major-league player to swat a home run and not get credit for a run scored. In the sixth inning against the Los Angeles Dodgers, he hit a long fly ball at AT&T Park as described by Retrosheet.org:

"Bengie Molina's fly ball hit a few feet to the left of the 'Splash Hits' sign in right field; Molina held at first while Pablo Sandoval ran from first to third; Giants manager Bruce Bochy had told Emmanuel Burriss to run for Molina if he got on base, so Burriss immediately popped out of the dugout and replaced Molina; then Omar Vizquel said he thought the ball hit the green metal awning along the right-field wall, which is a home run; Bochy saw a baseball with green paint on it and went out to the field to show it to the umpires and asked them to discuss the play; crew chief Tim Welke decided to use the replay system and reversed the call from ball in play to home run; however, he would not allow the Giants to put Molina back in to run out his homer; Bochy protested the game, which became moot because the Giants won the contest; Molina was given credit for a home run and two RBI but no run scored; Burriss ran out the homer and was given credit for the run scored; when he returned to the dugout, Molina greeted him by saying 'Good Swing!'"[18]

Perhaps ironically, Molina had received his second consecutive Willie Mac Award before the game. He closed out 2008 with a .292 batting average, 16 home runs, and 95 RBIs in 145 games.

In 2008 the Molinas lost patriarch Benjamin Senior, 58, to a heart attack on a baseball field in Dorado, Puerto Rico. Bengie and his father had always remained close.

On February 14, 2009, Bengie remarried.

The 2009 San Francisco Giants finished 88-74 in the middle of the NL West Division. Molina played in 132 games, hit .265, homered 20 times and drove in 80 runs. He led the majors with 11 sacrifice flies. He threw out 23 percent of the runners attempting to steal, tying with his brother Yadier of the Cardinals as second-best in the National League. In assessing Bengie Molina, San Francisco special assistant Felipe Alou said, "He's a manager's dream, a catcher who can catch and bat cleanup. ... He's a great two-strike hitter, one of the best in the game."[19] In November 2009 Tim Lincecum won his second Cy Young Award. "Bengie's half the reason I'm here," the pitcher said.[20]

On January 19, 2010, "Big Money" re-signed a one-year deal with the Giants for $4.5 million. Like any team, San Francisco had stretches of losing streaks. Although they were leading in the NL West Division after a series of losses, on June 30 the Giants traded Molina to the Texas Rangers for relief pitcher Chris Ray and minor-leaguer Michael Main. Another factor in swapping the 34-year-old was the noted performance of rookie catcher Buster Posey. Posey was later named National League Rookie of the Year.

Molina made the record books again on July 16, 2010, when he became the first catcher to hit a grand slam and hit for the cycle in the same game. At Fenway Park, against the Boston Red Sox, batting eighth, Molina had four at-bats in which he hit a single, double, his grand slam, and a triple. After hitting the three-bagger, he incurred a leg injury and was taken out for a pinch-runner.

In Game Four of the 2010 American League Championship Series, the Rangers were losing to the Yankees, 3-2, in the sixth inning with two outs. Molina hit a three-run home run off left-hander A.J. Burnett. The homer enabled Texas to nab the game and the ALCS, and allowed the Rangers to go to their first World Series. There they faced the San Francisco Giants. Molina became the sixth player to play for the two World Series opponents in the same season. No matter which team won, he was guaranteed a World Series ring. Texas lost in five games. Molina was 2-for-11 (.182), with one RBI.

After the season Molina retired as a player. On December 14, 2012, he became an assistant hitting coach for 2013 with the St. Louis Cardinals, the same franchise for which his youngest brother, Yadier, was the regular catcher. Bengie returned to the Texas Rangers organization for the 2014 season as their first-base coach and catching instructor.

In February 2016, Molina continued with baseball as an Angels spring-training guest instructor.

## SOURCES

In addition to the sources cited in the Notes, the author also consulted Molina's player file at the National Baseball Hall of Fame, baseball-almanac.com, and baseball-reference.com.

## NOTES

1. Bengie Molina with Joan Ryan, *Molina: The Story of the Father Who Raised an Unlikely Baseball Dynasty* (New York: Simon & Schuster, 2016), 26.
2. Molina with Ryan, 65.
3. Molina with Ryan, 47.
4. blogs.mercurynews.com/giants/2010/03/15/giants-catcher-molina-recalls-his-days-as-a-nimble-shortstop/.
5. Molina with Ryan, 94.
6. Ibid.
7. Andrew Baggarly, "Giants' Matt Cain and the Scout Who Signed Him: Special Baseball Relationship a Dying Bond?" *East Bay Times*, eastbaytimes.com, posted March 29, 2016.
8. Steve Rushin, "These Guys Know Squat," *Sports Illustrated*, March 14, 2005: 19.
9. Molina with Ryan, 120.
10. Ibid.
11. Molina with Ryan, 122.
12. "Catching's a Family Affair to Molinas," *New York Post*, August 26, 2002.
13. Mike DiGiovanna, "Squatter's Rights?" *Los Angeles Times*, March 14, 2004.
14. Ibid.
15. Ibid.
16. Associated Press, "Ex-Angel Molina Has Harsh Words," February 9, 2006.
17. Mike DiGiovanna, "Stoneman Says Molina Was Treated Honorably," *Los Angeles Times*, February 6, 2006.
18. retrosheet.org/boxesetc/2008/B09260SFN2008.htm.
19. Associated Press, "Memory of Father Is Fresh for Giants C Molina," February 24, 2009.
20. Molina with Ryan, 250.

# WILLIE MONTAÑEZ

## By Chuck Johnson

WHEN WILLIE MONTAÑEZ walked to the plate from the on-deck circle he would flip his bat end over end like a baton. When he swung and missed he had a high, circular finish reminiscent of a matador twirling his sword at a charging bull. At first base, he would sometimes tap runners on the rear end with his glove which on occasion led to more than one altercation. He was called a hot dog or showboat or worse, all of which Montañez disputed. "I'm just being me," he said, "I'm just doing my thing."[1]

Guillermo Naranjo Montañez was born on April 1, 1948, in Catano, Puerto Rico, a small suburb of San Juan best known as the home of the Bacardi Rum distillery. Montañez's mother, Felicita, was a housewife and his father, Julio, a truck driver.

On March 1, 1965, Montañez was signed for the St. Louis Cardinals by scout Chase Riddle. A longtime scout both on the mainland and in Puerto Rico, Riddle produced 19 major leaguers in his career, including Terry Kennedy, the three Cruz brothers (José, Hector, and Tommy) and future Hall of Famer Steve Carlton. Still just 17 years old, Montañez reported to the Cardinals' Rookie League team in Sarasota, Florida, where he hit .235 in 32 games.

On November 29, 1965, the California Angels surprisingly selected Montañez in the Rule 5 draft, which meant the 17-year-old had to remain in the major leagues for the entire 1966 season.

Montañez made his major-league debut on Opening Day, April 12, 1966, against the Chicago White Sox in Chicago. Montañez entered the game as a pinch-runner for Norm Siebern with nobody out in the top of the 14th inning. Montañez promptly stole second base but was stranded there. Montañez took over at first base for Siebern in the bottom half and handled one chance on a fielder's choice. His first major-league plate appearance came on April 22 at Anaheim Stadium, when he struck out as a pinch-hitter against Jim Perry of the Minnesota Twins.

On May 5, 1966, the Angels, perhaps believing a roster spot could be better utilized than by a teenage pinch-runner, returned Montañez to the Cardinals. During his time with the Angels, Montañez played in eight games, six as a pinch-runner and two as a pinch-hitter, striking out both times.

Upon his return to the Cardinals organization, Montañez reported to Rock Hill of the Western Carolinas League. In early June the Cardinals placed Montañez on the inactive list for 10 days, allowing him to return to Puerto Rico for his high-school graduation. Shortly after his return, Montañez took over as the everyday right fielder and batted .281 with 11 home runs.

In 1967 Montañez spent, for the first time in his brief career, the entire season with one team and it paid off for him. Playing for the eventual league champion St. Petersburg Cardinals of the Florida State League, Montañez played 134 games, posted top-10 finishes in several offensive categories, and led the league in triples with 17. He played exclusively at first base as well, finishing second to future major leaguer Mike Jorgensen in voting for the postseason All-Star team.

The next two seasons proved challenging for Montañez: He played in 46 games for Modesto (Class-A California League) in 1968, missing time with an assortment of minor injuries. Assigned to Triple-A Tulsa for '69, Montañez started the season on a hot streak, hitting .375 over his first 14 games. On May 5 Montañez flew to St. Louis with his Tulsa teammates but it wasn't to play in that evening's exhibition game with the parent Cardinals; it was to have X-rays taken on a troublesome leg that he had injured sliding a week earlier. Initially diagnosed as a tendon strain, the X-rays revealed a fractured right knee and torn ankle ligaments which required him

to wear a cast and eventually cost him the remainder of the season.[2]

The Cardinals recalled Montañez on September 13 but he didn't play in any games. After the season, as had become his custom, Montañez returned home to Puerto Rico to play winter ball and once again the injury bug bit him; this time he missed two weeks with a sprain to the same right ankle he had injured during the season.

On October 6, 1969, the Cardinals and Philadelphia Phillies pulled off a blockbuster seven-player trade that included four current or future All-Stars. The key player for the Cardinals was flamboyant superstar first baseman Dick Allen. The Phillies acquired two everyday players, catcher Tim McCarver and center fielder Curt Flood, so it was a trade that was expected to impact both teams in 1970 and beyond.

There was just one problem; Flood wanted no part of playing in Philadelphia; he would sit out the entire 1970 season while embroiled in a court case challenging baseball's reserve clause. The Cardinals, on the other hand, were worried that the commissioner's office would void the deal; they desperately needed Allen's bat in their lineup. The two teams reached a compromise in which the Phillies would select two players from a list submitted by the Cardinals. When Phillies manager Frank Lucchesi saw the list, he encouraged the front office to choose a player he had seen while managing in Puerto Rico who had impressed him with his playing skills and desire.[3] On April 8, 1970, Willie Montañez became the first of the two players the Phillies chose to replace Flood. (Pitcher Jim Browning was the second; he went to Philadelphia on August 30.)

Montañez got off to a slow start with his new organization, hitting just .220 after the first month of the season with Triple-A Eugene. He picked it up as April turned to May and was riding a 14-game hitting streak on June 4 when he received a recall notice; but it wasn't from the Phillies, it was from Uncle Sam. Montañez was ordered to report for training with the US Coast Guard, which kept him out of the Emeralds' lineup from June 13 through July 5.[4]

Montañez hit .276 in 119 games with Eugene and was recalled by the Phillies after the end of the Triple-A season. He played in 18 Phillies games in September, picking up his first major-league hit on September 5, a pinch-single off Fred Cambria of the Pittsburgh Pirates at Three Rivers Stadium in Pittsburgh.

The odds were stacked against Montañez making the Phillies' Opening Day roster in 1971; there were four first basemen and 12 outfielders in camp. Manager Lucchesi described Montañez's odds of making the teams as 100 to 1, but Montañez persevered, staying late to work on his outfield play and relying on the knowledge of his roommate, veteran second baseman Tony Taylor.[5]

The hard work paid off as Montañez surprised everyone by making the Opening Day roster as the starting center fielder. He started the season hitting well, keeping his average above .300 well into May. An 0-for-3 collar against Gary Nolan of the Reds on May 24 dropped his average below .300 for the first time; he did not go over the mark for the rest of the season. As his average dropped, his production started to go up. Hitting third in the Phillies' order, Montañez hit five home runs in May with 15 runs batted in, five in June with 29 RBIs, and followed that up with a seven-homer/23 RBI July.

The highlight of the Phillies' 95-loss season came on June 23 in what is considered not only one of the greatest games in Phillies history but in major-league history. The Phillies defeated the Cincinnati Reds 4-0, a game made memorable by not only the two homers and three RBIs by pitcher Rick Wise but also by the fact the 25-year-old right-hander threw a no-hitter.

By his own admission, Wise had "good, but not overpowering" stuff, which resulted in his allowing just one baserunner, on a sixth-inning walk to shortstop Dave Concepcion. Wise struck out just three, and the lack of his normal repertoire resulted in several hard-hit balls and fine defensive plays. Shortstop Larry Bowa, third baseman John Vukovich, and even Wise himself turned in solid defensive plays but it was Montañez in center who turned in two game-savers.

The first came in the bottom of the second, when Hal McRae blooped a short fly ball to center that Montañez charged in for and caught knee-high on the dead run. The second came in the fourth, when Pete Rose hit a liner that Montañez caught a few steps in front of the center-field wall.[6]

By mid-August the race for the National League Rookie of the Year was down to three players, with Montañez believed to be holding a slight edge over Atlanta Braves catcher Earl Williams and San Francisco Giants shortstop Chris Speier. On August 15 in the second game of a doubleheader against the Padres in San Diego, Montañez went 1-for-4 with his 25th homer of the season; his average stood at .265.

Over the next four weeks, Montañez found himself in his worst slump of the season, at the worst possible time. From August 17 through September 12 he hit .151 with no homers and just six runs batted in. His batting average dropped to a season low .247. A 5-for-5, two-homer game against the Cardinals in St. Louis on September 13 got him back on track, but it seemed too late with just 15 games remaining on the season.

Montañez's second homer of the game, a solo shot off Don Shaw, was his 27th of the season, bringing him within two of tying Dick Allen's Phillies rookie record set in 1964. The next day, September 14, Montañez broke Allen's single-season RBI record for rookies with a second-inning sacrifice fly in a 5-3 Phillies win over the Cardinals.

On September 30 the Phillies played their final game of the season, against the Pirates in Philadelphia. Montañez had tied Allen's home-run record on September 24 in Chicago but had gone homerless in his next four games. Montañez's season RBI total stood at 97; a good day would get him to the century mark.

In the bottom of the third inning, with fellow rookie Mike Anderson aboard after drawing a walk, Montañez drilled an 0-and-2 pitch from Nelson Briles over the wall for his 30th homer of the season, breaking Allen's record of 29.

Montañez's season total of 30 homers still stood as of 2017 as the Phillies' rookie record.

When the Rookie of the Year voting was announced, it came as not much of a surprise; the winner was Earl Williams. But the margin of victory may have been surprising; Williams was named on 18 of the 24 ballots with Montañez receiving the other six.

A brief holdout cost Montañez the first two weeks of spring training in 1972, which didn't seem to hurt him much as the season began; when the Phillies returned home on May 3 after a 10-game road trip, he was hitting an even .300. The home cooking didn't help him, though, as his average fell 67 points on the 14-game homestand; an 0-for-4 against the Cubs on May 16 dropped his average to .250, and he didn't see that mark again until mid-August. He remained steady through the end of the season, coming in at .247, a drop of eight points from the previous season. Montañez led the National League with 39 doubles, but his homer total dropped from 30 to 13 and his

RBIs from 99 to 64, a number you wouldn't expect from your number-three hitter.

Montañez also ran afoul of manager Frank Lucchesi and with Paul Owens after Lucchesi was fired in early June. Lucchesi had pulled Montañez for not hustling twice and had also fined him a number of times for the same offense. Owens pulled Montañez in the first inning of a game against the Pirates after he failed to cut off a base hit by Gene Clines that cost two runs.[7]

Montañez's 1973 season saw his doubles total drop from 39 to 16, his homers from 13 to 11 and walks from 58 to 46 but he was showing signs of becoming a better hitter. He dropped his strikeouts from 108 to 80 and increased his on-base percentage despite a drop in his slugging.

Beginning in 1974, Montañez hit over .300 for three straight seasons, topping out with a career-high .317 in 1976, the same year he led the National League in games played with 163 and posted his only 200-hit season. In 1974 Montañez put together a career-high 24-game hitting streak, falling just short of Chuck Klein's then team-record 26-game streak set in 1930.

Montañez was also traded twice during this time period, the first coming on May 4, 1975, when he was sent to the San Francisco Giants for outfielder Garry Maddox. The trade was a precursor to another move; the Phillies needed to clear room at first base as they trying to bring back Dick Allen, which they did on May 7 in a trade with Atlanta.

Montañez had started the '75 season on a hot streak, totaling 16 RBIs in 21 games and he kept driving in runs with San Francisco; he finished the season with a career-high 101, an amazing total considering he hit just 10 homers.

Montañez reported to Arizona for spring training in March 1976 and immediately demanded a trade to an East Coast team. A frequent complainer about the San Francisco weather, he was looking for warmer summers and wanted to be closer to his Puerto Rico home. Montañez refused to sign a new contract with the Giants; he played under the terms of his expired deal from the previous season, which included a limited no-trade clause. The Giants attempted to accommodate his trade request but Montañez vetoed a deal that would have sent him to St. Louis. Finally, on June 13, 1976, the Giants sent Montañez to the Atlanta Braves in a deal that sent the also unhappy and unsigned Darrell Evans back home to California. The change of scenery served Montañez well; over the final 103 games of the season with the Braves, he hit .321.

Montañez spend the entire 1977 season in Atlanta and reached the 20-homer mark for the second (and final) time in his career. He hit .287 and was named to the National League All-Star team, the only time in his career he received the honor. Montañez did not start in the game; he replaced Steve Garvey in the fifth inning and was hitless in two at-bats.

On December 8, 1977, Montañez was involved in a four-team, 11-player deal that actually had him traded twice. The first deal sent him to the Texas Rangers for three players, the second deal sent him from the Rangers to the New York Mets along with Tom Grieve for pitcher Jon Matlack and first baseman John Milner.

Mets manager Joe Torre liked the potential Montañez brought to New York, saying, "We got back some of the punch we need. We'll score more runs next year and I think we're a better team."[8] On the other hand, the three-year, $999,000 contract he signed the previous year with Atlanta made him the highest-paid player in Mets history. The question became how much could he improve a last-place team?

The answer was two: The 1978 Mets won 66 games and again finished in last place. Montañez, to his credit, did what he was acquired to do, he led the Mets in most offensive categories and drove in the same number of runs as Mets losses (96).

Montañez was a notoriously slow starter to the season throughout his career, so when he began the 1979 season hitting below .250 as May turned to June, the Mets were not yet in panic mode. However, Montañez went into a 15-game slump during the first three weeks of June that dropped his average from .225 to .198. In that stretch, he had just six hits, all singles, drew just one walk and drove in four runs.

He managed to get the ship pointed in the right direction, getting his average up to .234 on August 12, when he was traded to the Rangers.

Montañez played well during the rest of the season, hitting .319 with 8 homers and 24 RBIs over 38 games but he was not happy as he was forced to split the first base and designated-hitter roles with rookie Pat Putnam. While the Rangers front office wanted Montañez back for the 1980 season more than he wanted to return, it became moot when he was traded to the San Diego Padres on February 15.

The Padres needed a veteran bat to hit behind cleanup hitter Dave Winfield. After the first 50 games of the season, Montañez had driven in 26 runs, just five fewer than Winfield, so the Padres' plan was working. It was a short-lived plan, however, as Montañez was traded to the Montreal Expos in late August.

Over the final 32 games of the season with the Expos, of which Montañez in 14, he hit .211 and drove in just a single run. After the season Montañez became a free agent and surprised everyone by re-signing with the Expos, agreeing to a two-year, $600,000 deal, in part because he was told he'd be the everyday first baseman in 1981.

It didn't work out that way. Rookie left fielder Tim Raines made the team out of spring training, forcing Warren Cromartie to first base and Montañez to the bench. He played in just 26 games with Montreal in 1981, which was mostly a reflection of the players strike, hitting just .177 with no homers and five RBIs. After the players returned Montañez was traded to Pittsburgh in August; he played even less with the Pirates, getting 39 plate appearances in 29 games.

Montañez returned to Pittsburgh in 1982, largely as a pinch-hitter and defensive replacement. He had just 35 plate appearances in 36 games. He was released by the Pirates on July 31. He signed with the Phillies as a free agent with the Phillies on August 10. Montañez went 1-for-16 in his return to Philadelphia and was released after the season, ending his professional career.

Montañez continues to play winter ball in Puerto Rico as he had done almost throughout his career. He enjoyed an 18-year career playing in his adopted hometown of Caguas for 14 seasons and four with Bayamon. He was the MVP of the Caribbean World Series in 1975, driving in 11 runs, including 10 in the championship series win for Caguas. After his 30-homer rookie season with the Phillies in 1971, Montañez returned to Puerto Rico and led the league in homers with 15.

Montañez stayed active in baseball after his career, spending several years as a scout and co-founding a training facility in Caguas, where he settled.

Montañez and his wife, Marta (they were wed in 1968) had four children, a son Guillermo (who was killed in a car accident in 2006), and three daughters, Miriam, Zaraida, and Marta, and three grandchildren.

*The author wishes to thank Alain Usereau for his research assistance on this project.

## NOTES

1. Ray Kelly, "Phils' Montañez Stages Swat Show," *The Sporting News*, August 10, 1974: 13.
2. "American Association Notes," *The Sporting News*, May 24, 1969: 35.
3. Allen Lewis, "Phils Enter Montañez in Rookie Sweepstakes," *The Sporting News*, May 8, 1971: 16.
4. "Pacific Coast League Notes," *The Sporting News*, June 20, 1970: 40.
5. Allen Lewis, "Phils Enter Montañez in Rookie Sweepstakes."
6. Allen Lewis, "No-Hit Arm and HR Bat Make Hero of Wise," *The Sporting News*, July 10, 1971: 5.
7. Allen Lewis, "Montañez Waging Terrific Battle to Kayo Pesky Sophomore Jinx," *The Sporting News*, September 9, 1972: 15.
8. Jack Lang, "Mets Gamble on Montañez to Supply Punch," *The Sporting News*, December 24, 1977: 63.

# ROGER MORET

## By Seamus Kearney

ROGER MORET (BORN ROGELIO Moret Torres) streaked across the skies of Red Sox Nation during the early 1970s like a comet with a stutter step: often brilliant but sometimes wild. Although he possessed obvious talent, he had some difficulty in harnessing it. Once established with the Boston Red Sox in 1973, he alternated two excellent seasons with a mediocre one. Still, he was able to compile an admirable cumulative ERA (3.43) and a 41-18 record with the Red Sox, ranking him among the best pitchers of the decade for the Bostons. He led the American League in winning percentage in 1975 and just missed in 1973. Then he went away, traded first by the Red Sox then, slowly and tragically, leaving baseball and sliding into the dark morass of mental illness.

Moret's mound presence was that of a tall, slender — even spindly — left-hander with a whiplike motion and a speedy fastball, mixed in with a decent curve and a good changeup. Moret threw hard. He weighed 175 pounds but insisted he was taller than his listed 6-feet-4.[1]

Born in Guayama, Puerto Rico, on September 16, 1949, Moret signed with the Red Sox out of high school in 1968 for a reported $8,000 bonus, He spent his first season in the A-level minors with Waterloo (Midwest League) in 1968, compiling a 6-6 record, then improving to 12-6 in 1969 in 25 games with Winter Haven (Florida State League). His next three seasons alternated among the Red Sox and two levels of the minors, Pawtucket (Double-A, Eastern League) and Louisville (Triple-A, International League). His 49-33 record in the minors revealed characteristics he would demonstrate in the majors: fewer hits allowed than innings pitched (7.94 per nine innings), more walks than usual (5.49 per nine innings), and a decent winning percentage (.598).

In the major leagues Moret logged a .635 career winning percentage in nine seasons, with a 47-27 won-loss record with the Red Sox, Atlanta Braves, and Texas Rangers. In his three full years with the Red Sox (1973-1975), he fashioned a 36-15 mark. Moret's Fenway Park record of 18-7 was one of the best winning percentages ever for a Red Sox left-hander at home.

Moret made his first appearance with the Red Sox as a September call-up in 1970. He debuted in the major leagues on September 13 and pitched a perfect eighth inning in a 13-2 loss at Baltimore. In three games he posted a 1-0 record and an ERA of 3.24 in 8⅓ innings. He got his first major-league win on his 21st birthday, against the Yankees on September 16, as he pitched four innings of shutout ball in relief of Sonny Siebert.

For the Red Sox in 1971, Moret compiled a 4-3 record with a 2.92 ERA. He had two stretches with the team that year, before and after a productive season with Pawtucket (11-8, 3.15 ERA). Strangely, the first seven games he appeared in were losses for the Sox, including two losses for himself. He garnered his first 1971 win, a complete game, on August 28 against the Angels in Anaheim. He finished the year with a run of 4-1 including a shutout and four complete-game victories.

The 1972 campaign proved to be a forgettable one for Moret, who spent most of the season with Louisville. He made the parent club after spring training but left for Louisville when he pitched ineffectively in three games with the Red Sox, all losses. He didn't appear for the Red Sox the rest of the year and had a middling stint with Louisville (9-6 with a 4.54 ERA).

The 1973 season is when Moret's stardom seemed assured. Starting the season in the bullpen, he earned a win against the Cleveland Indians on April 22. That was the first of 11 straight wins he reeled off — along with three saves — before finally losing to the Indians on September 16. He had good success against the

Yankees on the way to a team-leading winning percentage of .867 during a 13-2 season. He beat the New Yorkers three times, including a Fourth of July 1-0 shutout at the tail end of a Red Sox doubleheader sweep at Yankee Stadium.

Moret could not follow the success he had enjoyed in 1973, finishing 1974 with a 9-10 record and a 3.74 ERA. In the regular starting rotation during July and August, he amassed a middling 6-5 record with a 3.54 ERA—but that included an 11-inning complete game win over the Yankees on July 29. The highlight of his '74 season was a near no-hitter win with 12 strikeouts against the Chicago White Sox on August 21. Dick Allen beat out an infield single in the seventh inning for the only hit of the game. The win increased Moret's record at the time to 7-5. But after the near no-no, Moret finished the season on a 2-5 run.

Moret started 1975 in the bullpen picking up five wins and a save in relief and as a sometime starter before emerging as the fifth man in the rotation in late July. In fact, teammate Bill Lee said that the Red Sox really contended for the pennant when Moret entered the rotation. Moret's performance as a fifth starter gave the other starting pitchers extra rest and the Red Sox "started winning left and right," according to Lee.[2]

Moret had two stints in the regular, five-man rotation, in which he pitched admirably—and often brilliantly. In a stretch of four starts, July 20-July 31, he collected three wins with one loss. One of his wins was again against the Yankees and contributed to their demise as a pennant contender. Moret pitched the second game of a doubleheader shutout sweep against them in their temporary home at Shea Stadium on July 27. The sweep effectively established the Red Sox as the team to beat in the American League East.

In another period, from August 11 to September 15, Moret got six wins with two losses. In his September 6 victory over the Milwaukee Brewers, he benefited from 20 runs scored on 24 hits by the Red Sox, both American League season highs for the year. His 14-3 record at the end of the season put him atop the American League in winning percentage, at .824.

The low point of Moret's 1975 season proved to be his strange trip back from New York City on the early morning of a scheduled August start against the Orioles. He crashed his car into the rear end of a stalled truck on the highway. Somehow he avoided serious injury but did suffer cuts on his head that required a visit to a hospital.[3] X-rays proved negative but the Red Sox would not allow him to pitch. In fact, the team was not pleased with either the incident or the publicity and took Moret to task about his behavior. The incident probably contributed to some doubt in the Red Sox front office about whether he could be a reliable member of the staff.

Moret saw little duty during the 1975 postseason, but the little he saw loomed important in the outcomes. He was the winning pitcher in the second game against the Oakland A's when he pitched one inning of scoreless relief in his only appearance during the Red Sox' three-game series sweep. He came into the game in the sixth inning with the score tied, a man on first, and no outs. He retired two batters, gave up a double and then induced the final out on a grounder to shortstop. The Red Sox went ahead in the bottom half, making Moret the pitcher of record.

In the World Series against the Cincinnati Reds, Moret saw a little more action, and again at crucial times. This time, he struggled. He pitched 1⅔ innings, faced 10 batters, and gave up two hits and three bases on balls with only one strikeout. Unfortunately, for Moret and the Red Sox, in Game Three he surrendered a game-winning hit to Joe Morgan in the 10th inning, which gave the Reds a 2-1 edge in the Series.

In Game Six, after starter Luis Tiant allowed a leadoff eighth-inning homer to Cesar Geronimo, Moret was brought in from the bullpen and set down the Reds 1-2-3. Cincinnati had a 6-3 lead. With two Red Sox on base in the bottom of the eighth, Bernie Carbo pinch-hit for Moret. He hit a game-tying home run into the center-field bleachers. Carlton Fisk's home run won the game in the 12th.

In the decisive Game Seven of the Series, Moret relieved Bill Lee in the seventh inning with one out

and a man on first. He faced four batters, getting one, walking one and giving up a run-scoring single to Pete Rose that tied the game. After Moret walked Joe Morgan, Red Sox manager Darrell Johnson called on Jim Willoughby to retire Johnny Bench. The Reds scored a run a couple of innings later, winning the game and the Series in the ninth.

His season and the Series over, Roger Moret would not appear in a Red Sox uniform again.

Years later, in an interview with author Doug Hornig, Moret lamented that he didn't do well in the World Series. However, he said he was upset that he was passed over for a starting assignment in Game Three. Moret still considered it his game to start: "I was ready. I could've beaten that team."[4]

During the offseason, on December 12, the Red Sox traded Moret to the Atlanta Braves for Tom House. Moret's record far surpassed House's and from all measurable appearances it seemed like, and probably was, an uneven trade for the Red Sox. No single reason is known for the trade; it could be that he just fell out of favor with the team

His one season with the Braves began Moret's slow slide from the major leagues. He pitched just 77⅓ innings and his ERA ballooned to 5.00. Appearing in 27 games, only 12 of them starts, he posted a 3-5 record. It was the first season in the majors in which Moret gave up more hits than innings pitched.

In another December offseason transaction, the Texas Rangers acquired Moret from the Braves on December 9. The Rangers got Moret and four others, plus $250,000, in exchange for power-hitting outfielder Jeff Burroughs. Moret appeared to be a throw-in as the Braves attempted to beef up their offensive attack.

The 1977 season proved to be a telling one for the slender left-hander. He was 28, in his prime, but his development did not show improvement. With the Rangers Moret logged a 3-3 record with another decent ERA of 3.73 (the league average was 4.06) in 18 games, only eight of them starts. Surgery to repair a circulation problem in his pitching arm limited his contribution to the Rangers that year.[5]

Moret's 1978 season was a disaster. He did little for the Rangers, though he earned his only save that year with another successful outing against the Yankees: four innings of relief in a 5-2 victory, as he gave up four hits and one earned run. But for the year he appeared in only seven games, pitching 14⅔ innings and surrendering 23 hits, for an 0-1 record.

However, the real story for Moret in 1978 was his hospitalization at a psychiatric facility after his bizarre behavior on April 12 at the Rangers' Arlington Stadium. After some odd pregame behavior, Moret went into what was described as a catatonic state in front of his locker that reportedly lasted 90 minutes.[6] His teammates first kidded with him but as time went on the gravity of his condition brought in the team's medical staff. Attempts to awaken him failed. The Rangers staff sedated him and dispatched him to the Arlington Neuropsychiatric Center. By April 25 Moret's condition had improved and he was scheduled for release within a week.

His condition got better and he returned to the Rangers for several appearances in late May and the first half of June. His last appearance in the majors was a futile start against the Toronto Blue Jays at Arlington Stadium on June 16, 1978. He lasted 1⅔ innings, giving up six hits and four earned runs, and was the losing pitcher.

Moret made a couple of comeback attempts. He was invited to spring training in 1979 with the Rangers and in 1980 with Cleveland but never again pitched in the majors.[7] In 1981-82 Moret played in the Mexican League. In 1981 he pitched for Torreon, posting a 9-4 (2.42 ERA) record. In 1982 he split the season between Aquascalientes and Monclova with a combined 4-13, 4.40 record.

Moret pitched for many years with the Santurce team in Puerto Rico until he was eligible for his major-league pension. He settled in Guayama, Puerto Rico, near two family members.[8] SABR member Edwin Fernandez Cruz reported in July 2014 that Moret was enjoying retirement in his hometown and rode his bicycle to visit family and friends. Earlier in 2014, he visited Fenway Park and enjoyed a pregame free signing for fans at the ballpark's Autograph Alley.

## SOURCES

In addition to the sources cited, the author relied on material provided by Retrosheet.org, Baseball-Reference.com, TheBaseballCube.com, and BaseballLibrary.com.

## NOTES

1 Doug Hornig, *The Boys of October* (Chicago: Contemporary Books, 2003), 211.

2 Hornig, 116.

3 *New York Times*, August 5, 1975, 33.

4 Hornig, 146.

5 *New York Times*, April 25, 1978, 33.

6 Ibid.

7 Leigh Grossman, *The Red Sox Fan Handbook* (Cambridge, Massachusetts: Rounder Books, 2005), 197.

8 Hornig, 211.

# JAIME NAVARRO

By Gregory H. Wolf

**PUERTO RICO AND BASEBALL.** From the legendary Roberto Clemente and Orlando Cepeda to Roberto Alomar, Carlos Beltran, Carlos Delgado, and Pudge Rodríguez, the small island with only 3.5 million inhabitants has left an indelible footprint on the major-league landscape. As of 2016, the Caribbean nation has produced no fewer than 250 big-league players, including at least 65 pitchers. Among those hurlers is right-hander Jaime Navarro, a durable workhorse during his 12-year career (1989-2000) spent primarily with the Milwaukee Brewers, Chicago Cubs, and Chicago White Sox. Upon his retirement, he joined southpaw Juan Pizarro (1957-1974) as the only Puerto Ricans with at least 100 wins and 2,000 innings pitched, forming a select fraternity that has welcomed only one additional member, Javier Vázquez (1998-2011).

Jaime Navarro had baseball in his blood. He was born on March 27, 1967, in Bayamon, in Puerto Rico's northern coastal valley, to Julio Navarro and Ana Cintron de Navarro. "Whiplash," as Jaime's father was known, was a right-handed side-arm pitcher who played six seasons (1962-1966, 1970) in the big leagues in a professional career that spanned four decades. According to Ana Navarro, Julio was strict with their son and instilled in him an intense work ethic.[1] The young Jaime experienced firsthand the sacrifices his father made as a professional ballplayer that required him to spend a great amount of time away from the family. "It's a hard life," the elder Navarro would say. Jaime seemingly grew up at baseball parks. His mother recalled an episode when he sold candy at a game in Mexico, where his father had played, but ended up giving the candy to all of his friends and owed the vendor money. On another occasion, Jaime was dressed nicely at a game when his father's teammates encouraged him to run the bases, yelling, "Here comes Jaimito! Slide, Jaimito, slide," which he, of course, did. Jaime was always on the move as a kid, perhaps even hyper. He eventually channeled that energy into baseball. Always big for his age, Jaime played any position he could—catcher, first base, and outfield—before finally moving to the mound where he could display his strong right arm. "I learned a lot from being around people like (Henry) Aaron, (Willie) Mays, and (Orlando) Cepeda," said Navarro. "But especially Jose Morales."[2] Jose was Jaime's godfather. Julio Navarro and Morales were both born on St. Croix in the US Virgin Islands, where they also learned to play baseball. They were close friends and, according to Jaime's mother, Ana, enjoyed speaking the local patois together.

After a stellar baseball career at Luis Pales Matos High School in Bayamon, Navarro accepted a scholarship to attend Miami-Dade Community College (Wolfson, downtown campus). He played for coach Steve Hertz, who had an accomplished record of churning out prospects, many of whom enjoyed success in the big leagues, like Mickey Rivers, Warren Cromartie, and Bucky Dent. Soon after donning the Sharks uniform for the fall season in 1986, Navarro drew interest from scouts. Over the next two years, Steve Souchock and Bo Osborne of the Major League Scouting Bureau charted Navarro's development in reports made available to all big-league clubs. They described him as having a good, loose arm and average to above-average velocity on his fastball with the potential to develop into a sinker-slider type hurler.[3] Navarro was selected twice by the Baltimore Orioles, in the second round of both the 1986 January and June (secondary phase) drafts, but chose not to sign because the Orioles did not offer the kind of bonus the Navarro family felt was warranted.[4] On the recommendation of team scout Julio Blanco-Herrera, the Milwaukee Brewers chose Navarro in the third round of the 1987 amateur draft. No longer eligible to play JC baseball, Navarro signed. According to

Ana Navarro, Félix "Felle" Delgado, a longtime player from Puerto Rico and then a Brewers scout, helped in the signing process. "Give him the money," she recalls Delgado saying. "He's good. He's worth it."[5]

Navarro blew through Milwaukee's farm system with the force of a hurricane hitting his homeland. He struck out 95 batters in 85⅔ innings with the Helena (Montana) Brewers in the Pioneer League (Rookie) in 1987. The following season he went 15-5 with the Single-A Stockton Ports, runners-up for the California League championship. Despite having only 39 professional starts under his belt, Navarro participated in the Brewers spring training in Chandler, Arizona, in 1989, as a nonroster invitee. Ranked as the club's second-best prospect (after slugger Gary Sheffield), Navarro needed to keep his suitcase packed. He went from the Cactus League to the Texas League, where he overpowered Double-A opposition in 11 starts (5-2, 2.47 ERA, 78 strikeouts in 76⅔ innings) as a member of the El Paso Diablos, and then had a brief, three-start pit stop with the Denver Zephyrs of the Triple-A American Association.

About two years after starting his professional career, Navarro was called up by the Brewers on June 19 to stabilize an injury-riddled staff, which had finished second in the AL in team ERA a year before. Starters Juan Nieves and Bill Wegman were on the DL; two other starters, Chris Bosio and Bryan Clutterbuck, were playing with injuries. On June 20, 1989, Navarro debuted, tossing 6⅔ innings, yielding two runs (one earned) in a no-decision against Kansas City. "I thought the kid threw great," said pitching coach Chuck Hartenstein. "He threw a couple of pitches 94 [mph]. I saw some bats that were slow getting to it."[6] He was noted for his heater, but Navarro's arsenal also included a slider, a slight change, and a forkball. A hard thrower, he primarily pitched to contact throughout his career, and relied on location and movement for success. Five days after his debut, Navarro notched his first victory by scattering nine hits over 7⅓ innings and striking out a season-high seven batters against the Chicago White Sox. "Talent-wise," said All-Star closer Dan Plesac, "he's the best I've seen come up."[7] Earning a permanent

spot in the rotation with his consistency, Navarro concluded the campaign with an impressive 3.12 ERA (ranking second behind Bosio's 2.95) in 109⅔ innings for the fourth-place club. Navarro (7-8) drew praise from team brass for his maturity, composure on the mound, and his inquisitive attitude. "He's a very polished young man," gushed Hartenstein, who like skipper Tom Trebelhorn was unsurprised by the 22-year-old's success. "He handles himself very well from the mental part of the game."[8]

While the Brewers got off to an unexpected hot start in 1990, occupying first place in the AL East as late as June 3, Navarro stumbled out of the gate. After 10 mostly ineffective outings, none of which went longer than six innings, his ERA was 6.65, resulting in a demotion to Denver. "His stuff is still good," said veteran backstop Charlie O'Brien about Navarro's sophomore slump. "He's just missing the spot. He's throwing too many pitches to hit."[9] Navarro ironed out some kinks in six starts with Zephyrs and was recalled earlier than expected to shore up a staff once again decimated by injuries. After posting a stellar 1.59 ERA in 22⅔ innings in nine relief appearances in

July, Navarro rejoined the starting rotation. "[Pitching coach Larry Haney] told me to work like I was in the bullpen," he said. "Just come after everybody, and think about getting people 1-2-3, one inning at a time."[10] After a few rough outings, Navarro tossed consecutive complete-game victories to beat New York and Toronto on the road at the end of August. He concluded the season on a high note by going the distance to beat the Yankees, picking up his fifth victory in his final seven decisions.

Navarro arrived at the Brewers spring training in 1991 buoyed by his success in the Puerto Rican Winter League. For the fourth consecutive season, he pitched for Santurce, a club located in the capital city of San Juan. He logged in excess of 100 innings for the Crabbers, leading the tradition-rich club to its first title in 18 years. The Brewers, who faded after their hot start the year before and finished in sixth place, counted on Navarro to emerge as a bona-fide starter, yet took a cautious approach. "We might have expected too much from him. It was a combination of many things," said Haney of Navarro's struggles. "But more than anything, it was a young pitcher, who wasn't controlling his emotions. He was trying to be better than he was."[11] Navarro once again had a rocky April (6.27 ERA after four starts), then was whacked in the thigh by a screaming liner off the bat of Minnesota's Kent Hrbek in his next start, and suffered a deep bruise. Navarro's desire to pitch through pain impressed his coaches and teammates. "He wants the ball," said Haney. "A lot of pitchers would have missed some starts with that injury."[12] On May 24 Navarro needed just 96 pitches to toss the first of eight career shutouts, a masterful four-hitter with no walks to beat Cleveland 1-0. Five starts later he twirled another four-hitter, defeating Seattle, 4-0, also at County Stadium. "This is my year," said Navarro jubilantly after the game. "I've been working hard and my arm is still strong."[13] No one doubted Navarro, who emerged as the unequivocal ace of the staff. He surged beginning July 28, going 8-4 with five complete games in his last 14 starts, and holding opponents to an impressive .239 batting average. In addition to his 15-12 slate and 3.92 ERA, Navarro ranked ninth in the AL in innings pitched (234), seventh in starts (34), and third in complete games with a career-best 10.

Navarro proved that he was no one-year-wonder by winning a career-high 17 games in 1992. For the second straight campaign he was locked in after the All-Star break, posting a 1.25 ERA and limiting opposition to a paltry .182 batting average in his first eight starts during the most impressive stretch of his career. It started with what sportswriter Tom Haudricourt of the *Milwaukee Sentinel* called a "string of dominating performances."[14] After limiting the White Sox to just one hit over eight innings in the Brewers' eventual 4-3 win in 11 innings on July 17, Navarro hurled his first and only two-hitter five days later to beat Texas 4-1 at County Stadium; the only Rangers run was unearned. Then came the best game of his career: a three-hit shutout, requiring just 85 pitches, with no walks against Cleveland. "You can't throw the ball any better," said teammate Kevin Seitzer.[15] "When he's on," said Cleveland's Paul Sorrento, "he's one of the best in the league."[16] Navarro's success was not lost on skipper Phil Garner, whose club surged in September (winning 22 of 28 games at one point) to engage Toronto in a fierce battle for the division crown. "He just overpowering people," said the feisty pilot, in his first of eight years guiding the team, after Navarro shut out Baltimore on five hits on September 12. Navarro (17-11, 3.33 ERA), Wegman (13-14, 3.20), and Bosio (16-6) were the first trio of Brewers pitchers since 1979 to log at least 200 innings each, and anchored a staff that led the AL in team ERA (3.43) for the first time in franchise history.

Navarro's emergence as one of the most durable starters in the AL was followed by a startling, rapid decline, eventually resulting in his banishment to the bullpen and departure from the club. Always a husky player, the 6-foot-4 Navarro arrived at Brewers spring training in 1993 weighing upward of 250 pounds, well over his listed playing weight of 215. Out of shape, he developed back pain and struggled in 1993 as the Brewers dropped from 92 wins to 69 and landed in the cellar. "[Navarro] wandered aimlessly for much of the season" opined beat writer Tom Haudricourt, reflecting on the pitcher's 11-12 record and abysmal 5.33 ERA (second highest in the AL) in 214⅓ innings.[17] Navarro started 34 games for the third consecutive season, but was liable to unravel early in the game; seven starts lasted less than five innings.

As bad as 1993 was, the next year was worse. "[Navarro's] a key guy," said pitching coach Don Rowe, expecting a bounce-back campaign from the big right-hander. "We need a good year out of Jaime."[18] But when the hurler once again arrived in camp overweight, and developed a sore arm, Garner was livid, demoting him to fifth starter. "We can't afford to have the entire rotation messed up because Jaime's not ready," said Garner, once known as Scrap Iron as a player. "It's not fair to the other pitchers."[19] Navarro made just eight starts (with a 7.74 ERA) before Garner banished him to the bullpen for the remainder of the season. "Jaime's been blessed with a great arm," said the skipper, "and has shown he can bounce back."[20] Going from staff ace to mop-up artist was hard on the 27-year-old, who feuded with Garner and reporters. After the players' strike interrupted the season on August 12, and ultimately forced the cancellation of the rest of the season and the playoffs, no one expected Navarro to be back with the club whenever, and if ever, a new season began. At 4-9 with a hard-to-fathom 6.62 ERA in 89⅔ innings, Navarro's transformation from an integral component of the Brewers' future to outcast was complete.

Eligible for salary arbitration, Navarro was not tendered a contract offer by Milwaukee, and was declared a free agent on April 7, 1995. Two days later he signed a three-year pact with the Chicago Cubs with the option of terminating the deal after two years. "We're hoping to catch lightning in a bottle," said Cubs GM Ed Lynch.[21] The North Siders didn't have much to lose. They were coming off a last-place finish in the NL East in 1994; only one starter had won more than 10 games in any season in his career, and that was 35-year-old Mike Morgan, who was coming off a horrendous campaign (2-10, 6.69 ERA). A slimmed-down Navarro made a good initial impression on skipper Jim Riggleman when he arrived at the Cubs' camp in Mesa, Arizona, weighing 225.

"Maybe it was the weight," responded Navarro when queried about his two-year struggle on the mound. "I guess because I wasn't pitching well they've got to blame it on something."[22] Navarro made a big splash in his Cubs debut, on April 29 at Wrigley Field by scattering five hits and two runs (one earned) over seven innings against Montreal to notch his first win in the NL. The only Cubs starter with a winning lifetime record, Navarro won his first four starts and first five decisions, making Lynch look like a genius. "He's the kind of guy, from what he's done in the past, who can step forward and show the way," boasted Lynch.[23] Navarro quickly emerged as the ace on a young, unproven staff. "The key to me is being consistent," he said after holding Philadelphia to two hits in 8⅓ innings in a victory on July 8. "I just wanted to put it in there where they could hit it and get some outs."[24] Those words reflected the rejuvenated pitcher's approach all season long. He tossed at least six innings in 25 of his 29 starts; only once did he fail to go at least five. In helping the Cubs to just their fourth winning season (73-71) in 23 years, Navarro ranked fifth in the NL in wins (14) and innings (200⅓) while posting a career-low 3.28 ERA.

The Cubs were fully aware that Navarro wore his emotions on his sleeve when they signed him. Like many pitchers, he had a tendency to sulk when pulled from a game, and overstepped boundaries when he occasionally criticized players for errors. But no one was prepared for what one commentator called a "shameful incident" involving Navarro on May 14, 1996, at Houston's Astrodome.[25] Tension in the clubhouse was already high when neither the Cubs nor Navarro replicated their hot start from the previous season. Navarro won just two of his first eight starts and seemed to be pressing. "He was slow and methodical last year," said pitching coach Fergie Jenkins. "This year he's more herky-jerky."[26] When Riggleman yanked Navarro in the seventh inning against Houston, after he surrendered 10 hits and six runs, the pitcher went ballistic, confronting his skipper and catcher Scott Servais on the mound. The heated, profanity-laden tirade continued in the dugout. Though Navarro issued a scripted public apology, the damage had been done. "When a pitcher of Navarro's caliber is allowed to leave the way the Brewers let him go," said Riggleman in an excoriating tone to the press, "there must be reasons, and some of them are becoming apparent."[27] The episode had a profound impact on the way members of the Chicago media perceived Navarro for remainder of his career in Chicago (including three years with the White Sox). Longtime *Tribune* writer Bob Verdi was unapologetic in his response to Navarro's outburst. "[M]anagement should send a message and cut its losses before it's too late," he suggested. "[His] tantrums violate everything this rebuilding plan is supposed to represent."[28] Surprisingly, Navarro wasn't suspended, and turned into what the *Tribune's* Mike Kiley called a "dynamic presence" for the underachieving fourth-place Cubs (76-86) by fashioning an eight-game winning streak from July 26 to September 8.[29] While Riggleman offered a backhanded compliment ("Jaime's never really composed on the mound. There are a lot of competitors who need to have a little nastiness in them"), sportswriters (and probably teammates) wondered when the increasingly erratic Navarro's next meltdown would be.[30] Despite the self-created distractions, Navarro was a dependable workhorse, posting another stellar season (15-12, 3.92 ERA in 236⅔ innings, fourth most in the NL) which made his antics easier to tolerate for management. Even Servais, with whom he feuded all season, recognized the hurler's "stuff." "With Jaime, you go with his strengths and don't worry about the batter," he said. "There's not many guys in the league you can do that with."[31]

In the offseason, Navarro exercised his free-agent option and on December 11 signed a reported four-year, $20 million contact with the Chicago White Sox, considerably better than the Cubs three-year, $14 million offer.[32] "[Navarro] led the team in hissy fits, dugout confrontations and stubbornness," opined *Tribune* sportswriter Gene Wojciechowski. "[He] is just enough pain that nobody felt bad when he switched leagues."[33] Unfortunately for Navarro, the wrath of the Chicago sports reporters followed him to the South Side of town.

In retrospect, Navarro's tenure with the White Sox was an unmitigated disaster. He posted a cumulative 25-43 record with an atrocious 6.06 ERA in 542 innings in three seasons in what is often considered among the worst free-agent signings in major-league history. Navarro is also cited as one of the reasons the White Sox implemented an informal policy of not offering free-agent pitchers contracts for more than three years (still practiced as of 2016). Navarro verbally sparred with teammates, ownership and management, and sportswriters, who, in turn vilified him in the papers. Though the pitcher might have deserved bad press, some comments about his weight or commitment to baseball bordered on racism.

Coming off a second-place finish in the AL Central in 1996, the White Sox were widely considered the favorite to win the division crown in 1997 with two-time MVP Frank Thomas, Robin Ventura, and free-agent signing Albert Belle in the lineup. But the clubhouse soon evolved into what beat writer Bernie Lincicome described as "an unhappy place … a jealous and jumpy place," filled with envy, resentment, and indifference.[34] When Ventura went down with a broken ankle in spring training and missed the first 99 games, a void in leadership was readily apparent. With the club struggling to play .500 ball, yet just a few games off the division lead, management dumped salaries in high-profile deals that exacerbated tensions. "[W]e weren't too happy," said Navarro after starting pitchers Wilson Alvarez and Danny Darwin and closer Roberto Hernández were sent to San Francisco for six prospects on July 31. "But we just have to go out and play the game. This is our game, not the owner's game. We represent ourselves. Maybe the owner has given up, but we didn't."[35] Regrettably for Navarro, his lucrative free-agent deal which bestowed upon him the status of staff ace and the perquisite of the Opening Day starter, and his season-long funk fanned the flames of discontent on the team. On the day the White Sox announced the blockbuster trade of his mound mates to the Giants, Navarro failed to protect a nine-run lead, surrendering 11 hits and 11 runs in 4⅔ innings to the Anaheim Angels in an eventual 14-12 Chicago victory. The White Sox finished in second place with a losing record (80-81) while Navarro's roller-coaster career took yet another dip. In addition to his 9-14 slate and staff-leading 209⅔ innings, he posted the highest ERA (5.79) and surrendered the most hits per nine innings (11.5) in the majors. Viewed from another angle, his season was not much worse than those of two teammates, James Baldwin (12-15, 5.27) and Doug Drabek (12-11, 5.74). Chicago left Navarro unprotected in the expansion draft, but predictably neither the Arizona Diamondbacks nor the Tampa Bay Devils Rays took the bait.

The situation worsened for Navarro in 1998 as his performance on the field sank to a new low. He tied for the AL lead with 16 losses, won just eight times, and once again led the majors in highest ERA (6.36) and most hits per nine innings (11.6) while the White Sox once again finished in second place despite a losing record in the weak AL Central Division. It was a vicious cycle, indeed nightmare, for Navarro, who must have had skin as thick as a rhinoceros. While sportswriters mercilessly lampooned Navarro in the press for his poor performance and weight (which had ballooned to 250 or more), Navarro added fuel to the intoxicating fire with clubhouse blowups and incendiary remarks. "We're not a team right now," said Navarro after a shutout loss to Detroit on May 30. "We stink. Nobody's pumped up. It's like a cemetery … a bunch of dead dogs. Our guys are worried about their own stats, not the team."[36] No one could doubt Navarro's competitive spirit, but his public comments didn't endear him to fans or teammates. After Boston pounded him for nine hits and eight runs (six earned) in a loss on July 5, Navarro had another meltdown. "To be honest with you, I don't want to be here. Maybe I should ask for a trade. I'm not helping the team. It's embarrassing."[37] But Navarro's contract was an albatross around GM Ron Schueler's neck.

In stark contrast to Navarro's generally negative portrayal in the press was the pitcher's mainly unreported but no less positive contributions to his community. For example, he donated at least $20,000 in 1994 to the baseball program at his alma mater in Miami.[38] He was involved in a number of charitable organizations in Milwaukee and Chicago, was a regular speaker at events focusing on the Latino community, and sponsored scholarships for Latino students to attend community college.[39] Navarro never forgot his Puerto Rican heritage. He echoed comments, widely perceived as inflammatory at the time, by stars Roberto Alomar Jr. and Rafael Palmeiro that baseball management did not bestow the same recognition and respect upon Latino ballplayers as it did whites or African-Americans, and suggested the need for vocal leadership, "(Latinos) don't have anybody to follow."[40]

"This year I'm going to be quieter," said Navarro as the 1999 season kicked off. The embattled pitcher revealed in an interview with Teddy Greenstein of the *Chicago Tribune* that he had undergone a change since making amends the previous December with his parents, from whom he had been estranged for at least six years.[41] "Anger, Frustration. Feeling isolated," said Navarro of his emotions the last two years with the White Sox. "Coming to the ballpark all angry. I was like 'to hell with the world. I don't care about anybody else.' I was hurting myself and my job."[42] Despite his promise, not much changed for Navarro. He struggled on the mound, and took out his frustrations on teammates, reporters, and team brass. When Navarro was shelled for seven runs in 2⅓ innings in his first start of the season, second-year manager Jerry Manuel seemed resigned to a long season: "As long as Jaime's here, he's going to be a starting pitcher. I really don't see him helping us in the bullpen."[43] Nonetheless, sportswriters called for Navarro's banishment to the bullpen all season long. In late August the pitcher defiantly stated, "I'm not going anywhere. They had a chance to trade me and didn't. Now they're stuck with me."[44] A week later Navarro was in the bullpen, his fate with club all but sealed.

The Chicago press got its wish when the White Sox traded Navarro (8-13, 6.09 ERA) and right-hander John Snyder to the Milwaukee Brewers for another struggling pitcher, Cal Eldred (2-8, 7.79 ERA), and infielder Jose Valentín on January 12, 2000. After losing all five of his starts (12.54 ERA) with the Brewers, Navarro was released on April 30. He finished the season with a brief stop in the Colorado Rockies minor-league system, and made his final seven big-league appearances with the Cleveland Indians. In 12 seasons, Navarro fashioned a 116-126 record with a 4.72 ERA in 2,055⅓ innings.

Just 33 years old, Navarro was far from ready to hang up his spikes. He played in the Independent Atlantic League in 2001 and 2003, and also had short stints in the St. Louis Cardinals and Cincinnati Reds farm systems. From 2004 to 2006 he hurled for BBC Grosseto in the Italian premier league.

In 2008 Navarro transitioned into coaching. He had a three-year apprenticeship in Seattle's minor-league organization as a pitching coach before returning to the big leagues from 2011 to 2013 as bullpen coach for the Mariners. The next two years he was the pitching coach for their Triple-A affiliate, the Tacoma Rainiers. In 2016 he served as pitching coach for the Pericos de Puebla in the Triple-A Mexican League.

As of 2016 Navarro spent the offseasons in Orlando, Florida. He has two children, Jaime Jr. and Jaycee Lynn, whose mother, Tamara Weber, he divorced at the end of his playing career.

After a playing career that often consisted of either highs or lows, but rarely a middle ground, and a contentious relationship with the media, Navarro had lost none of his passion for the game. "Be patient," he once said to describe his coaching style. "Baseball's not all on the field. We're all human. I want to pass on what I know so the young pitchers will be better than I was, not make the same mistakes when I was young."[45]

## SOURCES

In addition to the sources noted in this biography, the author also accessed the *Encyclopedia of Minor League Baseball*, Retrosheet.org, Baseball-Reference.com, the SABR Minor Leagues Database, accessed online at Baseball-Reference.com, and *The Sporting News* archive via Paper of Record.

## NOTES

1 The author expresses his sincere gratitude to SABR member Rory Costello, who interviewed Ana Cintron de Navarro on June 17, 2016, for this biography. Mrs. Navarro offered insights to Jaime Navarro's childhood and introduction to baseball.

2 Mike Kiley, "Navarro: A Highly Charged Hurler," *Chicago Tribune*, September 11, 1996: 10.

3 Scouting report for Navarro courtesy of *Diamond Mines* at the Baseball Hall of Fame. scouts.baseballhall.org/report?reportid=04719&playerid=navarjao1.

4 Information according to Ana Cintron de Navarro. Interview by Rory Costello on June 17, 2016.

5 Ibid.

6 Cliff Christl, "Brewers Stumble Over 'Little Things,'" *Milwaukee Journal*, June 21, 1989: 1C.

7 *The Sporting News*, August 21, 1989: 19.

8 Mike Stephenson, "A Winning Attitude. Brewers Navarro Eager to Learn Himself," *Milwaukee Journal*, August 4, 1989: 1C.

9 "Keeping Quiet About Navarro," *Milwaukee Journal*, May 14, 1990: C4.

10 Frank Clines, "Navarro Finishes What He Starts," *Milwaukee Sentinel*, August 24, 1990: C1.

11 Tom Haudricourt, "Navarro Looks for Quick Start," *Milwaukee Sentinel*, March 1, 1991, Part 2, 3.

12 Tom Haudricourt, "Navarro's Four-Hitter Halts Tribe," *Milwaukee Sentinel*, May 25, 1991, Part 1, 2.

13 Tom Haudricourt, "Navarro Slams Door on Seattle," *Milwaukee Sentinel*, June 21, 1991: 1B.

14 Tom Haudricourt, "Navarro Blanks Indians," *Milwaukee Sentinel*, July 28, 1992: 1B

15 Ibid.

16 Ibid.

17 Tom Haudricourt, "Navarro Wipes Slate Clean," *Milwaukee Sentinel*, September 2, 1993: 1B.

18 Tom Haudricourt, "Vintage Navarro Would Fill the Bill," *Milwaukee Sentinel*, March 17, 1994: 1B.

19 Ibid.

20 Tom Haudricourt, "Scanlon Replaces Navarro as Starter," *Milwaukee Sentinel*, June 2, 1994: 2B.

21 Joseph A. Reaves, "Navarro Signing Probably Last Major League Move," *Chicago Tribune*, April 10, 1995: 2.

22 Joseph A. Reaves, "Lighter Navarro Looks Forward to Brighter Tomorrow as Starter," *Chicago Tribune*, April 11, 1995: 5.

23 Joseph A. Reaves, "Quiet New Cub Could Make Noise," *Chicago Tribune*, April 24, 1995: 8.

24 Joseph A. Reaves, "Navarro Latest Cub King of the Hill," *Chicago Tribune*, July 9, 1995: 3.

25 Bob Verdi, "To His Teammates, Navarro Is Way Behind the Count," *Chicago Tribune*, May 29, 196: 1.

26 Gene Wojciechowski, "Navarro Tapes Reveal Flaws," *Chicago Tribune*, April 24, 1996: 3.

27 *The Sporting News*, June 3, 1996: 23.

28 Verdi.

29 Mike Kiley, "Cubs 11, Mets 1. Navarro Stays on Second Half Roll," *Chicago Tribune*, August 13, 1996: 3.

30 Mike Kiley, "Navarro: A Highly Charged Hurler," *Chicago Tribune*, September 11, 1996: 10.

31 Gene Wojciechowski, "Slimmed-Down Navarro for Home Opener," *Chicago Tribune*, March 31, 1996: 8.

32 Mike Kiley, "MacPhail Says Deals Should Be Compared Only to Division Foes," *Chicago Tribune*, December 13, 1996: 4.

33 Gene Wojciechowski, "Bargain Pickup Mulholland Earns Respect, Admiration From Cubs," *Chicago Tribune*, May 18, 1997: Part 3, 15.

34 Bernie Lincicome, "Indifference, Hangs Heavy Over the Sox," *Chicago Tribune*, July 27, 1997: Part 3, 1.

35 *The Sporting News*, August 25, 1997: 46.

36 Teddy Greenstein, "Tigers 6, White Sox 0. 'We Stink,' Says Navarro." *Chicago Tribune*, May 31, 1996: 3.

37 Teddy Greenstein," Red Sox 15, White Sox 14. Eight-Run Inning Can't Save White Sox in Messy Marathon," *Chicago Tribune*, July 6, 1998: 1.

38 *The Sporting News*, September 12, 1994: 6.

39 Gene Wojciechowski, "Finding Tonic for Scandal as Close as Your Team." *Chicago Tribune*, May 25, 1997: Part 3, 15; Fred Mitchell, "Don't Fix the Bulls Until the Break, Thomas Advises," *Chicago Tribune*, June 5, 1997: Part 4, 8.

40 Gene Wojciechowski, "Hand Surgery to Knock Out Magadan at Least a Month," *Chicago Tribune*, March 11, 1996: 3.

41 Teddy Greenstein, "Parents Tough Love Lifts Navarro. Sox Pitcher Ends Estrangement, Learns Humility," *Chicago Tribune*, May 18, 1999: 8.

42 Ibid.

43 Jimmy Greenfield, "Despite Getting Shelled, Navarro Won't Be Shelved," *Chicago Tribune*, April 11, 1999: 3.

44 Teddy Greenstein, "Navarro: Forget Bullpen. They're Stuck With Me," *Chicago Tribune*, August 31, 1999: 8.

45 Karen Westeen, "Q&A with Tacoma Rainiers Jaime Navarro," *Tacoma Sports Weekly*, May 4, 2000.

# JULIO NAVARRO

## By Rory Costello

**E**AST OF PUERTO RICO LIE THE isles of Vieques and Culebra. Along with a sprinkling of cays, they are sometimes known as the Spanish Virgin Islands. Pitcher Julio Navarro is the only *viequense* ever to make the majors, largely because the island is an undeveloped place with a population of only about 9,400 even today. The main reason is the controversial, now-vacated U.S. Navy training range that took up two-thirds of the land.

But what makes Navarro's case more unusual is that he learned to play ball on St. Croix in the U.S. Virgin Islands, where some of his relations still live. Navarro grew up with two V.I. major-leaguers, Joe Christopher and Elmo Plaskett. He is about nine years older than another, José Morales, but they became good friends. In another distinctive link, Morales is godfather to Navarro's son Jaime, a big-league pitcher from 1989 to 2000.

The elder Navarro appeared during six seasons in the majors (1962-66; 1970). However, his minor-league career spanned 20 years from 1955 to 1974, the last three in Mexico. He also played during 22 winters in Puerto Rico, tied for second in league history with Juan Beníquez, Juan Pizarro, and Héctor Valle. Only Rubén Gómez (29) played more. Navarro was known at home as *El Látigo*, or "Whiplash," for his sidearm fastball.

Julio Navarro was born on January 9, 1936. He was the second of Manuel Navarro and Justina Ventura's eight children (five boys and three girls). At that time, two major plantation owners dominated Vieques: the Benítez family and Eastern Sugar Associates. Sugar cane was the crop, and most of the island's residents worked in the fields. Since the second half of the 19th century, immigrants (many of African descent) had come from various other Caribbean islands to seek work, including St. Thomas and St. Croix.

Manuel was foreman of a crew of cane cutters. But in 1941 the Navy began to expropriate land on Vieques, plowing under the cane fields and forcing thousands to relocate. "When the sugar cane was torn out," said Navarro in 2007, "my father went looking for a better job." A wave of *viequenses* wound up in St. Croix. "We went there by boat—one of my sisters was born there."[1]

Known as "Juju" growing up, Navarro went to St. Patrick's, a Catholic school in Frederiksted. "I got a pretty good education for free, there were these Belgian sisters teaching." The first sport he played was not hardball. "I used to play a lot of softball from ages 9-10, then when I got up around 14, I played baseball."[2]

Navarro, Joe Christopher (who was about one month older), and Elmo Plaskett (two and a half years younger) played at St. Patrick's and also with a local club called the Annaly Athletics. That was a lot of talent for one little team, but the Virgin Islands overall were quite a wellspring in those days.

In 1954, the top Athletics and some players from St. Thomas joined the Christiansted Commandos to form an all-star squad. "There were four teams in the St. Croix amateur league: two from Christiansted and two from Frederiksted. The Athletics didn't win the league that year, but then we put together this team and went to Kansas."[3]

The Commandos traveled to that year's National Baseball Congress World Series in Wichita. Navarro started one of their two NBC tournament games, while Joe Christopher caught the eye of Pittsburgh Pirates superscout Howie Haak. Christopher's signing was a crucial event in Virgin Islands baseball history—it spurred Haak to add St. Croix and St. Thomas to his Caribbean itinerary. "They could see the talent in a lot of our guys. We spread the word—'they've got good guys, and they won't cost you anything!'"[4]

In February 1955, not long after he graduated from high school, Navarro played in a series between Puerto Rican winter leaguers and a combined Virgin Islands team. For many years this was an annual affair after the Puerto Rican season ended. Navarro impressed Alfonso Gerard, the pioneer pro ballplayer from the Virgin Islands. Gerard helped arrange a tryout in Puerto Rico with his boss, Santurce Cangrejeros owner Pedrín Zorrilla. Zorrilla was also a scout for the New York Giants.

Navarro worked out with Orlando Cepeda and José Pagán (whose path would cross or join Navarro's often over the years). All three then signed with the Giants; Navarro got $300 while the others got $500.[5] He reported to the Giant's minor-league camp in Melbourne, Florida and was then assigned to Class D ball.

Navarro's first year as a pro was not bright—his record in three leagues was a combined 1-10. "I hurt my arm a little, I had inflammation of the elbow. But they knew what I could do, so they didn't release me. I didn't go to college. I had to help my other brothers and sisters. I had two choices: pro ball or the Army. I went through a lot of hardship, but I just happened to make good."[6]

In 1956, Navarro rebounded to win the Triple Crown of pitching with Cocoa in the Florida State League. He went 24-8 with a 2.16 ERA and 216 strikeouts. He thrived on work, starting 22 games and relieving in 27 others. "They kept me in Florida because of the weather. That was when the government was building up the rocket base at Cape Canaveral, right there by Cocoa Beach."[7]

In between, Navarro made his debut in the Puerto Rican Winter League during the 1955-56 season. Pedrín Zorrilla added him to the Santurce roster, which included two veterans from St. Croix, Gerard and Valmy Thomas.

Navarro jumped to the Class A Eastern League in 1957. With the Springfield Giants, he went a respectable 9-9, 3.63, starting nine times in 45 appearances. He stayed at Springfield in 1958, but started in 30 out of 37 outings. His record was again solid (13-10, 3.07), but while he led the league in strikeouts again with 142, he walked over 100 batters for the third straight year.

A brilliant outset at Springfield in 1959 (6-0, 1.50 in seven starts) won Navarro promotion to Triple-A. Most encouraging was that he'd learned to throw strikes more consistently. With Phoenix in the Pacific Coast League, he shifted back to the bullpen once more, starting only once in 39 games (4-2, 4.38). He remained a swingman in both 1960 and 1961, starting 28 times amid 75 total appearances. The basic picture didn't look good, with records of 5-12, 5.61 and 7-10, 4.81, but he showed enough to avoid demotion. Navarro remained in the PCL, but spent time on loan with Vancouver in the Orioles chain and also Hawaii, a Kansas City A's affiliate.

"The Giants had so many prospects. They said, 'Julio, you should play, but we don't got no room!'" Navarro remembered that Elmo Plaskett made a brief two-game stop in Hawaii, but one of the stars on the Islanders was Puerto Rican comrade Carlos Bernier.[8]

Back with the Tacoma Giants in 1962, Navarro turned in easily his best Triple-A work. Manager Red Davis focused him on relief; starting just twice in 54 games, he went 8-9, 2.20. The Los Angeles Angels purchased his contract on September 2 for $30,000.[9] "I was entitled to be a free agent, and so the Giants sold me. They couldn't hold me any longer!"[10]

"Navarro was in the Giants' farm system when I managed the club," Angels manager Bill Rigney recalled in 1963. "But I didn't see too much of him and only vaguely recalled him when our scouts came up with a favorable report on him."[11]

The 26-year-old rookie made his debut the next day—on the biggest stage in the game, Yankee Stadium. L.A. sportswriter Braven Dyer (perhaps best remembered for being punched out by Navarro's notorious teammate Bo Belinsky) noted that Navarro had never been to a major-league ballpark in his life before then.[12] But there was a little more to the story than that. Navarro noted, "I had my chances before. But I made one promise to myself: I am only going to a big-league park when I myself am playing in it!"[13]

In the nightcap of a doubleheader, Navarro pitched three innings. He got off to an unsteady start, as Mickey Mantle greeted him with a single and then pulled off a double steal with Tom Tresh. A wild pitch was followed by two outs, a walk, and a single, and the Yankees extended their lead to 5-0. But Navarro settled down for two scoreless innings, catching Roger Maris looking for his first strikeout. The Angels later came back to win 6-5.

Navarro won his first major league game the following day with 1 1/3 scoreless innings against New York. Buck Rodgers gave him the lead with an RBI single in the top of the ninth, and though Tresh reached on a leadoff bunt single, Navarro then shut the door. He pitched seven more games that month, including the last four innings of a 14-inning loss at Baltimore, and ended with a 4.70 ERA. In between, there was an interruption for a personal loss. Navarro returned to Puerto Rico because his 15-year-old brother Jaime had been killed in an auto accident.[14]

Navarro enjoyed his busiest and most successful year in the majors in 1963. He appeared in a club-high 57 games, all in relief, as he formed a reliable bullpen tandem with 40-year-old Art Fowler. His 4-0 start made him an early contender for Rookie of the Year, but while he finished with a 4-5 record, his ERA was a clean 2.89 and his 12 saves also led the team. Navarro said, "My control has been my saver. When I come in, I know I must throw strikes. I use a variety of pitches — sinker, slider, screwball, and fast ball. I throw mostly sidearm, but I come in overhand at times to fool the hitter. I like to work often."[15]

Although Navarro was not especially tall for a major-league pitcher at 5'11", he had "abnormally long arms, which makes his side-arm curve especially effective."[16] The screwball was something that Angels pitching coach Marv Grissom (who had pitched for Rigney with the Giants) added to his repertoire.[17]

The next year, Navarro got off to a quick start, combining with Ken McBride on an Opening Day one-hitter in Washington. President Lyndon Johnson threw out the first ball.[18] However, the Angels traded him to Detroit on April 28 for outfielder-pitcher Willie Smith. After 10 shaky appearances (0-1, 10.22), the Tigers sent him down to Triple-A Syracuse at the end of May. He returned in early August, performing well enough to get his overall record back to 2-1, 3.95.

After that it was a struggle to return to the majors. Navarro did pitch in 15 games with Detroit in 1965 (0-2, 4.20, including his only big-league start on September 7). His only outing in 1966 was best forgotten. He failed to retire a batter on April 17, hitting Fred Valentíne with a pitch, serving up a pinch-hit grand slam to Bob Chance, and then allowing a solo shot to Ken McMullen.

On June 21, Navarro was the player to be named later in a deal that smacked of racial injustice, as Boston unloaded Earl Wilson and old mate Joe Christopher. "When the Red Sox acquired two black players, pitcher John Wyatt and outfielder José Tartabull, on June 6 [actually June 13], Wilson told his black roommate, Lenny Green, that there were now too many black players [seven] on the ball club. Although the remark was made half in jest...to no one's surprise, the phone rang the next morning."[19]

Thereafter Navarro was mainly a serviceable Triple-A swingman. Boston sent him to Atlanta in December with pitcher Ed Rakow for Chris

Cannizzaro and John Herrnstein. From 1966 through 1970, with Toronto and Richmond in the International League, Navarro's record was 45-33, 3.44, as he started 84 times in 116 total games. He suffered a brief demotion to Double-A Shreveport in 1969 (5-1, 1.96).

Navarro surfaced for one last stretch in the majors with the Braves from July through September 1970. "They gave me the locker next to Hank Aaron, who'd played in Puerto Rico too. We had plenty to talk about."[20]

With Atlanta, he posted no decisions and a 4.10 ERA in 17 games. (One rough outing came on August 1, when Bob Robertson, Willie Stargell, and his buddy José Pagán reached him for consecutive homers.) His last appearance, a 1-2-3 ninth inning at San Diego on September 9, left his big-league career mark at 7-9, 3.65 in 212 1/3 innings pitched over 130 games. He struck out 151, walked 70, and yielded 191 hits (including 32 homers) while picking up 17 saves.

By then 35, Navarro soldiered on for one more season with Richmond and Syracuse in the International League (7-13, 3.83). In March 1972, he was sold to the Mexico City Diablos Rojos, which at least one writer (Arnie Burdick in the *Syracuse Herald-Journal*) felt badly about. "If there's anything wrong with the baseball pension system, it's the failure to include the fringe player…Navarro, in his late 30's, needs only three more big-league months, but was dealt by the Chiefs to the Mexican League 10 days ago. His chances of making the 'bigs' again are now infinitesimal, and his pension will add up to a big, fat zero."[21]

Indeed, Navarro was one of many major-leaguers who were frozen out. "When I first went up to the bigs, you had to have five years to qualify. Then they brought it down to four. Then in 1985, they brought it down to one day. But I was before that. There's a lot of money in the game now…and a lot of politics. People like [U.S. Congressman, later Senator] Jim Bunning and Brooks Robinson, they were trying to help us, me and about 1,000 other ballplayers. And some guys in California were fighting. It hasn't changed yet."

"I could use that money too. But God has been good to me."[22]

Navarro spent two seasons with the Red Devils and split his last between Mexico City and the Córdoba Cafeteros. His 1972 record was a nifty 16-7, 2.29. He remained effective the next year (9-9, 2.77), as Mexico City won the league championship, but tailed off in 1974 (3-7, 4.92). The champion squad also featured at least five other former or future major-leaguers. The staff ace was Pedro Ramos (Cuba); Mexicans Enrique Romo and Aurelio López were also pitching mainstays; Ricardo Joseph (Dominican Republic) and Adolfo Phillips (Panama) were regular players. "They did have a pretty fair league there," Navarro commented. But like nearly everyone who's played south of the border, he remembered the endless bus rides. "Those roads were not the best, and from Mexico City to the Yucatán, that took 28 hours."[23]

After that, *El Látigo* pitched on during the winters in Puerto Rico. As a young hurler, he had benefited from the tutelage of Santurce teammates Rubén Gómez and Bill Greason. Before the 1959-60 season, the Caguas Criollos sent Juan Pizarro and $10,000 to the Crabbers for Navarro and José Pagán. "This transaction was made subject to approval by the Braves and Giants. Much to the relief of Caguas and Santurce and Santurce, neither big-league organization objected to the deal. Caguas president Juan Vázquez was happy, because Navarro had been a nemesis of the Criollos."[24]

One memorable game came on January 14, 1962, when Navarro pitched the only no-hitter at San Juan's old Sixto Escobar Stadium. He lost 1-0 on José Pagán's eighth-inning throwing error in the opener of a twi-night doubleheader (both games were scheduled for seven innings). "There were doubts about it being a hit," Navarro recalled. "The scorer first called it a hit, and changed his mind."[25]

Navarro's PRWL career peaked in 1967-68, when he went 10-1, 2.72 and helped lead Caguas to the league title after they finished second during the regular season. After 12 seasons with the Criollos, Navarro spent three with the San Juan Senadores. He was traded together with José Pagán for Cocó Laboy, Luis Alvarado, Iván de Jesús, and Sam Parrilla.[26] All six *boricuas* played in the majors.

His final three campaigns came with the Bayamón Vaqueros, after he had stopped playing in Mexico. "'When Pagán was appointed to manage Bayamón, he wanted me to continue pitching, but also had me coach the younger hurlers. John Candelaria was one of my major projects.' Navarro recalls the tears of gratitude which flowed from Candelaria's eyes after listening to one of his pep talks."[27] In addition to grooming the tall Nuyorican, Navarro also contributed on the mound, going 5-2, 1.41 as the Vaqueros captured the PRWL playoffs. Bayamón then went on to capture the Caribbean Series, held that year in San Juan.

"Navarro cherishes the back-to-back championships won by the 1974-75 and 1975-76 Cowboys. In 1975-76, he had a 2.35 ERA and won a game in the finals against the favored Caguas team, who thought Navarro was too old to pitch well."[28] That brought his total to five PRWL titles; he had also been a champion with Santurce in 1958-59 and Caguas in 1959-60. Navarro finally retired at age 41 after 16 more games in 1976-77. He finished with career totals of 98 wins, 84 losses, and a 2.94 ERA in 1623 innings pitched across 368 games. He struck out 994, walked 467, and threw 19 shutouts. He is among the league's lifetime leaders in games pitched (second), strikeouts (third), wins (sixth), and ERA (eighth).

Navarro said that after his playing career ended, "I was a scout for the Cubs for a couple of years. Then I was a rookie-league coach with the Braves for about four years, then I was with the Indians for several years. Then I said it's about time I get home and stay home. My kids were growing up, I had paid for my house and nobody could put us out of it."[29]

"I did my saving, I had a small pension from coaching, and Jaime helped me and his mother out. We made it all right."[30] Jaime Navarro started making seven-digit salaries in 1993. One memorable episode came that season, when Jaime—big and talented, but prone to dreadful slumps—sought his father's counsel. Cleveland in particular was feasting on him, and the reason? "Uncle José" Morales, then the Indians hitting coach, could tell that Jaime was tipping his pitches. Since he worked for Cleveland, he kept his mouth shut and watched his godson get pounded. Only after Morales left the club did he tell the secret."[31]

When Elmo Plaskett passed away in 1998, Navarro lost his main source of news about life on St. Croix, though "Shady" Morales helped keep him in touch. In 1999, he said, "I have a lot of good friends there, and I love the people." But he had some choice words for the powers-that-be and how they had let baseball languish.[32]

In his heart, Julio Navarro remained a Puerto Rican. He has been happily married to Ana Cintrón since February 15, 1958. In addition to Jaime, they had another son (Julio Jr.) and two daughters (Sonia and Samaydi). They have lived in Bayamón for decades and a baseball field there is named for him.

Navarro remained a well-loved member of the Puerto Rican sporting community and continued to make public appearances. In November 2005, he joined many local greats, including Orlando Cepeda, as the city of San Juan celebrated the centennial of Pedrín Zorrilla's birthday. In October 2006, it was Navarro's turn; he and nine other athletes became

members of El Pabellón de la Fama del Deporte Puertorriqueño (the Puerto Rican Sports Hall of Fame).

When interviewed in 1999 and 2007, this old athlete remained fit and healthy. Aside from gray hair, one of his few concessions to age was a pair of big square eyeglasses. He is an exceptionally gracious man who is content in life and with the many good friends he has made. A conversation with Julio Navarro typically ended with his sincere wish, *"Qué Dios te bendiga"*—God bless you.

"I don't travel too much," he said in 2007, "except to Orlando to see my kids. We just spent a month and a half around Christmas. Jaime spent the past three years pitching in Italy, and he gave me and Ana a trip there as an anniversary present. But only she went! I like to stay at home. Sometimes I put on clinics for the kids, even for some colleges, for free. It doesn't matter what age, anybody who has a kid and asks for help—I love doing that, it keeps me happy!"[33]

As of 2016, Navarro was in the grip of Alzheimer's disease, but he was still at home, in his wife's loving care. He exercised and remained capable of travel to Orlando. There he got together with José Morales, who also made his home in that area. Ana noted with a laugh, "They fall back into that St. Croix island patois."[34]

*Grateful acknowledgment to Julio Navarro for his personal memories (telephone interview on March 9, 2007 and to Ana Cintrón de Navarro for the update (telephone interview on June 17, 2016).*

## SOURCES

José A. Crescioni Benítez, *El Béisbol Profesional Boricua* (San Juan, PR: Aurora Comunicación Integral, Inc., 1997), p. 336.

Pedro Treto Cisneros, editor, *Enciclopedia del Béisbol Mexicano*, 11th edition. Mexico City: Revistas Deportivas, S.A. de C.V., 2011.

## NOTES

1. Telephone interview, Julio Navarro with Rory Costello, March 9, 2007 (hereafter 2007 Navarro interview).
2. 2007 Navarro interview
3. 2007 Navarro interview
4. 2007 Navarro interview
5. Thomas E. Van Hyning, *Puerto Rico's Winter League* (Jefferson, NC: McFarland & Co., 1995), 125.
6. 2007 Navarro interview
7. 2007 Navarro interview
8. 2007 Navarro interview
9. "Angels' Julio Navarro More Proof Island Pitchers Tops", *Chicago Daily Defender*, June 25, 1963, 24.
10. 2007 Navarro interview
11. Al Wolf, "Julio Navarro Finally Arrives", *Los Angeles Times*, June 25, 1963, C2.
12. Braven Dyer, "Navarro Fits in With Best Angel Tradition", *Los Angeles Times*, September 6, 1962, B2.
13. 2007 Navarro interview
14. "Tragedy Calls Hurler Home", *New York Times*, September 11, 1962, 37.
15. Joe Hendrickson, "Giants May Wish for Navarro", *Pasadena Star-News*, May 30, 1963, 22-23.
16. Dyer, op. cit.
17. "Angels Blank Senators; McBride, Navarro Combine On One-Hitter," *Chicago Daily Defender*, April 14, 1964, 22.
18. Ibid.
19. Larry Moffi & Jonathan Kronstadt, *Crossing the Line: Black Major Leaguers 1947-1959* (Iowa City, IA: University of Iowa Press, 1994), 226, 166.
20. 2007 Navarro interview
21. Arnie Burdick, "Players not apt to find sympathy," *Syracuse Herald-Journal*, April 3, 1972, 15.
22. 2007 Navarro interview
23. 2007 Navarro interview
24. Van Hyning, 125.
25. Van Hyning, 220.
26. Van Hyning, 125.
27. Ibid.
28. Van Hyning, 126.
29. 2007 Navarro interview
30. 2007 Navarro interview
31. Mel Antonen, "Navarro's Godfather Doesn't Pitch Advice," *USA Today*, March 11, 1994, 4C.
32. In-person interview, Julio Navarro with Rory Costello, February 1999.
33. 2007 Navarro interview
34. Telephone interview, Ana Cintrón de Navarro with Rory Costello, June 17, 2016.

# LUIS OLMO

## By Rory Costello

THE SECOND PUERTO RICAN TO play in the major leagues was outfielder Luis Olmo, who joined the Brooklyn Dodgers in 1943, a year after Hiram Bithorn made his debut with the Chicago Cubs. These men led the way for more than 200 *boricuas* who have since followed. Bithorn's life ended suddenly at the age of 35 in December 1951, when he was shot during an altercation with Mexican police. Yet *El Jíbaro*—The Hillbilly—survived for more than 60 years after that.

Olmo was one of the most prominent players who jumped to the Mexican League in 1946 as Jorge Pasquel sought to make it a major circuit. After Olmo spent two summers in Mexico and one and a half in Venezuela, Organized Baseball lifted its five-year ban on the jumpers. Olmo returned to the majors, where he remained until June 1951. He also played in Cuba, the Dominican Republic, Canada, and Puerto Rico, thus earning another nickname: *El Pelotero de América* (The Ballplayer of the Americas). Another note of interest is that he was using the basket catch in center field years before Willie Mays. Olmo also managed in winter-league ball for many years, starting when he was 23, and was a noteworthy scout.

Luis Francisco Rodríguez Olmo was born on August 11, 1919, in Arecibo, Puerto Rico. Like various other Latin American players—the Alou brothers are another prominent example—he became known in the United States by the second (maternal) half of his double Spanish surname.[1] He was the third of four sons born to José Rodríguez, a carpenter, and Ana Olmo.

In October 2009, as he celebrated the 60th anniversary of becoming the first Puerto Rican to play in the World Series, Olmo said, "Baseball was the only thing, ever since I was a little boy."[2] His childhood idol was Billy Herman of the Chicago Cubs, later a teammate in Brooklyn. Olmo did participate in other sports, such as soccer, basketball, and track and field. His speed made him a leading sprinter in high school, but his dream of becoming a pitcher ended when he got hurt throwing the javelin.[3] "I was 15, and snapped my right elbow," he recalled in 1943. "It has never been straight since."[4]

In the winter of 1938-39, the Puerto Rican Winter League (PRWL) held its first season. Olmo joined the Caguas Criollos, for whom he played in nine of his 15 PRWL seasons. "I signed my first contract for seven dollars a week," he said in 2009.[5] Thomas Van Hyning, who has chronicled the PRWL in two books, wrote, "The Caguas player-manager, Pito Álvarez de la Vega, remembers the 19-year-old Olmo as the revelation of the first season. He felt Olmo had the talent to make it to the majors and took him under his wing."[6]

Olmo first played ball in the States in the summer of 1939. A 1943 feature by Arthur "Red" Patterson of the *New York Herald-Tribune* detailed the battle for his services and his early Stateside career. A friend of Olmo's, Miguel Lloreda, had written to Eddie Mooers, owner of the Richmond Colts in the Piedmont League (Class B). Richmond paid for Olmo's boat passage to the mainland. José Seda, a Puerto Rican baseball man who scouted for Brooklyn, wired Branch Rickey, Jr., farm director for the Dodgers. "Good ball player named Luis Olmo arriving on Barranquilla. Stop. Get him. Stop. Jose." Rickey Jr. tried to stash Luis with a Puerto Rican player in Harlem, but Richmond—an independent club—sniffed out its prospect and signed him.[7]

Olmo's first stop was Tarboro (North Carolina) of the Coastal Plain League (Class D), but the available records do not show that he played there before he was released. Instead, he went to the Wilson Tobs of the same state and league, where he batted .329, playing night ball for the first time in his life. In 1940 he split the season between Wilson (where he hit .348 with 18 homers in 82 games) and Richmond.⁸

That April, *The Sporting News* covered a contract mixup between Olmo and Richmond, referring to him as "Roberto Olmo" and as a Cuban.⁹ This prompted his brother José—who later became Luis's agent—to write a letter from San Juan saying, "His correct name is Luis Rodríguez Olmo, but he is known as Luis Olmo, and he is a Puerto Rican, a proud American citizen. No doubt the contract was not received by my brother because it was incorrectly addressed. So far his name has been given out correctly only once, when you published the reserve lists. Later he was called Lewis Elmo and now as Roberto Olmo. Some confusion with Spanish names."¹⁰

Author and SABR member Adrián Burgos, Jr. cited this misperception as part of a broader pattern in his study of Latinos in New York City baseball from 1906 to 1950. He wrote, "Generally applied, the [homogenizing Cuban] label negated aspects of the city's diverse Latino population; it also diminished ongoing struggles that Puerto Ricans and other Latinos experienced in New York City."¹¹

The other important part of the contract difficulties was that the Dodgers still wanted Olmo and tried to place him with their farm club in Macon, Georgia. Brooklyn scout Ted McGrew had seen the outfielder playing in Puerto Rico and sent an excited report back, unaware that *El Jíbaro* was already on Rickey Jr.'s radar. W.G. Bramham, president of the National Association of Professional Baseball Leagues, the minor-league umbrella organization, ruled that Olmo was still Richmond's property.¹²

Olmo also spent 1941 and 1942 with Richmond, batting .311 and .337. His speed was on display with 17 and 19 triples. He was MVP of the Piedmont League in 1941, but his manager, Ben Chapman, won the award in 1942. According to Red Patterson, Olmo said, "the former Yankee firebrand . . . taught him more than any other pilot, coach or scout."¹³ However, a different picture of their relationship emerged in the biography of Roberto Clemente by David Maraniss. "In 1942 . . . Chapman constantly made bed checks but only checked on Olmo. It seemed to Olmo that Chapman was determined to catch him with a woman, though it never happened. . . . A few years later, when Chapman proved to be among the most virulent racists in major league baseball, Olmo was not surprised."¹⁴

It's also noteworthy that Richmond—the team and city—was segregated. In April 1946 Eddie Mooers (citing various excuses) canceled an exhibition game between Richmond and Montreal rather than allow Jackie Robinson to take the field. The Colts did not bring in their first African-American players until 1953.¹⁵

On October 1, 1942, Brooklyn purchased Olmo's contract from Richmond. That winter he moved from Caguas to the Santurce Cangrejeros, becoming a player-manager at 23. He tied Pancho Coímbre for MVP honors in Puerto Rico. Meanwhile, in January 1943, Brooklyn's star outfielder, Pete Reiser, joined the US Army. The fractured skull he had suffered the previous summer had left him 4-F, but he nonetheless made it into the service and played military ball for three seasons during World War II.

Olmo never was called to serve, even though his draft status was 1-A. He attracted much attention — and praise from manager Leo Durocher — in Brooklyn's spring-training camp in 1943. However, the Dodgers assigned him to their top farm club, Montreal of the International League. In the first three months of 1943, he hit .315 with 12 triples and 47 RBIs in 89 games.

Brooklyn called the Puerto Rican up in July 1943, and he proceed to hit .303 with four home runs and 37 RBIs in 57 games. It was little surprise that his ethnic background drew notice. In spring training that year, he had told Hy Turkin of the *New York Daily News*, "The only reason you haven't heard of many Puerto Ricans in the majors is that our best players are colored."[16] Olmo's complexion was tan, but his features were "European-looking" rather than "African-looking." Allegedly, though, both he and Hiram Bithorn "were allowed to play after signing forms attesting that their ancestry was entirely Hispanic."[17] Luis drew facial comparisons to Tony Lazzeri, whose parents were both born in Italy.

Olmo occupied an intriguing middle ground before the arrival of Jackie Robinson. Jesús Colón, a Puerto Rican Communist writer, drew attention to the ballplayer in 1943. Colón viewed Olmo "not only in terms of the visibility of Puerto Ricans in the U.S. public eye but also as a step toward the eventual breaking of the color line. . . . [Colón] called on Puerto Ricans to fill Ebbets Field whenever Rodríguez Olmo played and invited them to write letters to the Dodgers organization urging it toward desegregation."[18] Another Communist organ, the *Daily Worker*, also made much of how "utterly important" Olmo's acceptance among his teammates as an equal was.[19]

Shortly after Olmo's debut, Harold Parrott (then of the *Brooklyn Eagle*) wrote, "Likeliest Dodger of the Future . . . would seem to me to be the newest, Luis Olmo. He has power to right center, which you will remember was Hack Wilson's alley. He can run, which fits [Branch] Rickey [Sr.]'s pattern (notice he hit that inside-the-park homer at Pittsburgh yesterday?) And he is a scrapper. They are not too kind to dark-hued gentlemen in the South, and all last year, when he was playing with Richmond, they bean-balled Looey into the dirt. But he bounced back, black eyes flashing, and beat their brains out. Consensus is that he has it!"[20]

"Olmo has a distinctive, buggy-whip batting style," *The Sporting News* wrote that October. "It is probably more like Joe DiMaggio's than anyone else." That article added, "[the] strongly-built youngster . . . can run like a Western Conference halfback." His crooked elbow also proved not to be a hindrance in the outfield. "There are stronger arms in the league than Luis', but his trick is getting the ball away quickly and accurately."[21]

Olmo moved to the San Juan Senadores in the winter of 1943-44 — but he restricted himself to managing that winter, on the advice of Branch Rickey.[22] In his first full big-league season, 1944, he hit .258 with nine homers and 85 RBIs in 136 games. He started just 60 games in center field, though, as Goody Rosen's excellent play won him the starting job. Leo Durocher also started Olmo 34 times at second base (Eddie Stanky, the "primary" second baseman, started 50) and 30 times at third base (behind Frenchy Bordagaray). A 1946 account noted, "He didn't like the shifts to the infield Durocher forced upon him, since he's a natural outfielder."[23]

Olmo still saw a lot of action at third base (31 starts) in 1945, but he mainly focused on the outfield. Each of the three starting Brooklyn outfielders — Olmo, Rosen, and Dixie Walker — hit .300 that year. Olmo's basic batting line was .313/10/110; he also led the NL in triples with 13 and stole a team-high 15 bases. On May 18, 1945, at Ebbets Field, he achieved a rare feat: hitting a grand slam and a bases-loaded triple in the same game. His seven RBIs helped the Dodgers defeat the Cubs in a 15-12 slugfest.[24]

Olmo and Leo Durocher had a curious relationship. They were chummy at times, playing a lot of gin rummy and pool together. Yet while Durocher praised Olmo's talent, on the other hand he ripped him publicly (though Luis was by no means his only such target over the years). One story said, "Durocher designated [Olmo] as a deadpan ballplayer who had no enthusiasm."[25] Another said, "He was often in the Durocher doghouse."[26] The Lip often sniped at Luis because he had trouble with side-arm pitchers.

The most startling incident came during the 1945 season. As Olmo recalled in 2011, "He broke my bat, right in front of me. He said it was too heavy. I was hitting .350, but they wanted me to go down so they didn't have to pay me." Olmo told David Maraniss the same anecdote, saying, "They wanted Dixie Walker to beat me out and I was playing more than Dixie Walker."[27]

In 1946 Pete Reiser was back from the service. Jorge Pasquel also commenced his player raids. As early as October 1945, Olmo had told sportswriters that he might not sign again with the Dodgers.[28] The numbers vary from source to source, but according to Luis himself, Branch Rickey Sr. (a.k.a. "El Cheapo") made an offer of $8,000, a modest raise of $500.[29] "He did me a favor!" Olmo said in 2011. "I went to other places and had good luck everywhere."

Olmo went where the money was: Mexico, with a deal variously reported at $10,000 annually for three years or $40,000 total. Additional benefits included no income tax and all expenses paid for the player and his wife. "I gave Mr. Rickey every chance in the world to offer me a satisfactory contract," explained Olmo, "But all my cables, letters, and telephone calls were fruitless." Olmo signed with the Veracruz Azules (Blues), turning down Rickey's late offer of $12,000 because he had given the Pasquel brothers his word.[30]

The Pasquels, as was their wont, reassigned Olmo to the other club they owned, Mexico City.[31] He had to adjust to the capital's high altitude[32] — but injury marred his season soon after. In early April, he twisted his knee, jarred a small bone out of place, and had to go into a cast.[33] He played just 59 games total for both Mexico City and (after another personnel shuffle) Veracruz. His totals were .289/9/42.

After Rickey's call for action, Baseball Commissioner Happy Chandler imposed a five-year ban on the jumpers in March 1946. As early as that July, Olmo sought amnesty, contending that he was not under contract when he jumped. His brother José asked San Juan lawyer José Otero Suro to write a letter on behalf of Luis.[34] No exemption resulted, though, and since the Puerto Rican league honored the ban as part of Organized Baseball, *El Jíbaro* was not able to play at home for the next three seasons. It was a moot point in 1946-47, as he was resting his knee.[35] Had he been fit, he would have gone to the Cuban Winter League, where various "outlaw" players went that winter. In late September, he was listed on Marianao's roster.[36]

In February 1947, as he prepared to return to Mexico, Olmo told Tommy Holmes of the *Brooklyn Eagle*, "If I have made a mistake, I do not know it yet." Yet he also expressed regret, feeling that the Dodgers would have won the pennant if he had been with them.[37]

Olmo put up good numbers for Veracruz in 1947 (.301/14/72 in 102 games). After the Mexican summer season ended, he headed to Cuba, which had another new league in the winter of 1947-48: La Liga Nacional, or Players' Federation League, which allowed outlaws to play. *Jibarito* started with Santiago, but after that club disbanded on December 15, he went to the Havana Rojos. He batted .318 (with eight homers and 47 RBIs), finishing second in the league behind another man who jumped from the Dodgers to Mexico, Canadian Roland Gladu. Olmo was MVP of the league, which completed the season but was defunct thereafter.

After the 1947 season, the Mexican League tightened its belt. Jorge Pasquel ceded much of his power and the costly raids ceased. Payrolls were limited to $10,000 a month and a quota was imposed on imported players.[38] Since Olmo's salary would have eaten up a large portion of the cap, this may be the reason that he did not play out his contract. In 2011 Olmo implied that the change in regime in Mexico did have something to do with it. "It was a different league," he said.

With the Mexican chapter of his career closed, Luis reviewed his options. According to *The Sporting News*, "Olmo gave out an interview to the Cuban press that even if Chand-ler forgives the jumpers and brings 'em back to Organized Ball in good standing, he has no intention of returning to Ebbets Field unless he gets more than his 1945 salary, which was $6,750."[39]

So instead, he went to Venezuela, where La Liga Occidental (the Western League) was then operating in the summers. Up to that point, this circuit and the Venezuelan winter league had steered clear of ineligible players. Olmo became a hitting and fielding sensation in Maracaibo, winning the Triple Crown (.384, 10 homers, unknown RBI total).[40] The doors were all closed to him in the Caribbean that winter, though. "As a result of the extension of player aid and encouragement to Cuba, Puerto Rico, Panama, and Venezuela, 'cesspools of ineligibility' were cleaned up and all outlaw leagues driven out."[41]

In early June 1949, Happy Chandler at last issued a general amnesty to the jumpers. Olmo cabled Branch Rickey, asking him to make an offer, but the Pastora club (which Luis also managed after taking over for Dolf Luque) wanted $10,000 to release him from the contract that ran through July 23.[42] The Dodgers offered $12,000 in salary, and he negotiated his release, though Pastora had backed off that idea for a while and notified their star that he had to remain.[43]

When he left Pastora, Olmo was batting .360 (41-for-114) with seven homers.[44] When asked in 2011 about the greeting he received in Brooklyn, Luis replied, "About five or six guys were with me from the '45 team. They were happy to see me. Roy Campanella had played with me in Puerto Rico. I became very good friends with Jackie Robinson." He added, "I love the people of Brooklyn. I went up there and signed autographs twice for them, they still remember me."

After his return in late June, Olmo got into 38 games for Brooklyn, batting .305/1/14 in 105 at-bats as he backed up Tommy Brown and Duke Snider. He got off to a hot start, getting 12 hits in his first 27 at-bats (.444), capped by a game-ending homer at Ebbets Field on July 17. Yet perhaps his most memorable contribution to the 1949 pennant winners was a sensational catch that he made at Ebbets on August 24 against the St. Louis Cardinals.

Brooklyn was up 2-0 in the fifth inning, but St. Louis had the tying runs in scoring position, and at the plate was the feared batter whom Ebbets fans dubbed "The Man"—Stan Musial. Olmo, always known as a fine outfielder, needed every foot of the old ballpark's cozy dimensions, including the extra afforded by the corrugated exit gate in left field. He leaped and made the catch, snuffing out the rally, and the Dodgers went on to win, drawing to within one game of first. Brooklyn did not overtake St. Louis until late September, but the complexion of the race might have changed if the Cards had won that day. *Baseball Digest* wrote up the play in August 1961, and as late as 2009, it earned an entry in a book devoted to great outfield catches, *Going, Going . . . Caught!*[45]

Olmo appeared in four games for the Dodgers during the 1949 World Series, becoming the third Latino in the fall classic, after Cubans Adolfo Luque (1919; 1933) and Mike González (1929). He was 3-for-11 with a homer, off Joe Page in the ninth inning of Game Three. The blow brought the Dodgers to within 4-2, and one out later Roy Campanella made it 4-3 with another solo homer, but Page (in his sixth inning of relief) then ended it.

"From what I heard," Olmo later told Tom Van Hyning, "my home run off Page set off a chain reaction throughout Puerto Rico, as if an atomic bomb was dropped on the Island. Island fans were celebrating well after my blast, Campanella's one and the game's final out." When *El Jíbaro* came back home, even though the Dodgers had lost the Series, the local fans were "ecstatic" that he would return to action in the Puerto Rican Winter League. Van Hyning pointed out the greeting that the returning hero received. Brother José—at that time San Juan city treasurer and acting mayor—also presented him with the keys to the city.[46]

Olmo rejoined Caguas as their player-manager. The Criollos won the league championship over a very potent Santurce team (featuring Willard Brown and Bob Thurman) and advanced to the Caribbean Series. The second edition of this tournament was held in old Sixto Escobar Stadium in San Juan. Puerto Rico won four games and dropped three, losing a tiebreaker game for the championship to Panama in an upset.

Early that winter the Dodgers traded Olmo. On December 24, 1949, he was dealt to the Boston Braves for Jim Russell, Ed Sauer (brother of Hank), and cash. The headline in the *Hartford Courant* read, "Olmo Always Ranked as a Fifth Wheel" and noted that his Boston status was in doubt.[47] Olmo was the fifth outfielder for the Braves too (.227/5/22 in 69 games), though he saw more action than Pete Reiser, who had come to Boston the previous year. Also with the Braves was another former Brooklyn teammate, Gene Mauch—"my very good friend," Olmo recalled in 2011.

"Olmo returned to the Caguas helm in 1950-51 and was rewarded with a 57-20 record, the most regular-season wins in league history."[48] Santurce beat the Criollos in the playoff finals that season, though, in one of the best-remembered games in the annals of the PRWL. On February 16, 1951, in the seventh and deciding game at Sixto Escobar Stadium, catcher José St. Clair, better known as Pepe Lucas, stroked a two-out, series-ending home run in the bottom of the ninth. The Dominican's blow went down in history as the *Pepelucazo*. Olmo had watched that ball sail over the fence from his outfield position—yet his season was not over by any means. The Crabbers added him as a reinforcement for the 1951 Caribbean Series, and he became MVP, helping Puerto Rico to win by going 10-for-24 with 3 homers and 9 RBIs.

Olmo started the 1951 summer season with Boston again, but he appeared in only 21 games through early June and was sent down to Triple-A Milwaukee. There he concluded his US playing career with 82 games for the Brewers. In the 1952 Caribbean Series, he reinforced the Puerto Rican squad again, but they went winless.

Milwaukee released Olmo in the spring of 1952, and he joined Licey of the Dominican League, which did not shift to a winter schedule until 1955. He won the batting title with a .344 mark and returned to the Tigres in 1953. His teammates in those years included local stars (the Olivo brothers, Guayubín and Chichí); fellow Puerto Ricans (Rubén Gómez,

who joined the New York Giants in 1953); and Negro League standouts (Alonzo Perry).

The remainder of Olmo's playing career consisted of four winter seasons in Puerto Rico. The highlight was when he rejoined Santurce for the 1954-55 season; that Crabbers squad is often regarded as the greatest winter-ball team ever. The veteran reserve played sparingly behind Bob Thurman, Willie Mays, and Roberto Clemente. In the 1955 Caribbean Series, he appeared in one game and went 1-for-2. He stayed with Santurce in 1955-56 and got three last at-bats with San Juan in 1956-57. In 2,182 at-bats over his PRWL career, he hit .290 with 40 homers.

Meanwhile, Olmo was scouting Puerto Rico for the Braves. In 1951, he signed Félix Mantilla.[49] It appears, however, that this was an unofficial sideline while he remained with the organization as an active player. Stories about how the club signed him as a scout came out at the end of 1953.[50] He nearly bagged an elephant right after that, but the Dodgers beat him out for Roberto Clemente in early 1954. He did get at least two other notable Puerto Rican players after the Braves moved to Milwaukee: Juan Pizarro in 1956 and Sandy Alomar, Sr. in 1960. He also played a part in signing Elrod Hendricks out of the Virgin Islands in 1957, and later helped keep Ellie's pro career alive in Puerto Rico.

Olmo also continued to serve the Puerto Rican Winter League in various capacities, while operating an off-track betting concession in San Juan on the side.[51] He returned to San Juan as manager in 1957-58 and led the Senadores again in 1958-59. He started the following season as a radio commentator on PRWL games, but rejoined Santurce as manager partway through the season. He replaced Ray Murray, who was sacked by owners Ramon and Hiram Cuevas for using Orlando Cepeda in left field. Cepeda's big-league club, San Francisco, had instructed Murray to put him there.[52]

Olmo stayed with Santurce in 1960-61, but the PRWL added a new franchise to his birthplace, Arecibo, in 1961-62, and he became manager of the Lobos. The municipal stadium, which was already named Estadio Luis Rodríguez Olmo, boosted its capacity. After leading Arecibo for one more season, Olmo became general manager for Caguas in 1963-64. He then piloted Santurce for two more seasons (1964-65, 1965-66). The PRWL named him Manager of the Year seven times.

Olmo and the Braves had parted ways in November 1961. In early 1964, he began to scout Puerto Rico for the Philadelphia Phillies.[53] He joined the Chicago White Sox organization in 1971.[54] "I had some words with the general manager [Roland Hemond]," he recalled in 2011. "It only lasted about six months." That was the end of his scouting activity. Among other occupations, Olmo worked with a travel agency, a bowling alley, and (for about four years) the telephone company.

Luis and his wife, Emma Paradis, were married on October 27, 1940. More than 70 years later, they were still together, although both were suffering from Alzheimer's Disease. They had two children: daughter Ana Lucía (born c. 1941) and son Luis Francisco (born 1947, died at age 53).

Olmo began playing golf in 1968 and as of 2011, he still got out on the links twice a week, one of the reasons he remained so fit in his early 90s. At one point, though, he was carrying more weight than was good for him—he dropped 50 pounds on doctor's orders.[55] In August 2009, after SABR's Puerto Rican chapter and the Museum of Sports of Guaynabo celebrated his 90th birthday, Olmo said, "I just turned 90. I hoped to reach 80 and that has passed. I am playing extra innings. And I recall as if it were yesterday when I arrived in the majors. The baseball of today is the same as what I played. The only thing that has changed is the salaries."[56]

Luis Olmo died in Santurce on April 28, 2017, aged 97, of complications from Alzheimer's (double pneumonia was the direct cause). Four days after his 92nd birthday, when his memory was still intact, Olmo was asked to what he attributed his long life. He said simply, with a little chuckle, "I been lucky. Living good."

*Grateful acknowledgment to Luis Olmo for his memories (telephone interview, August 15, 2011). Continued thanks to Benny Ayala.*

## SOURCES

Crescioni Benítez, José A., *El Béisbol Profesional Boricua* (San Juan, Puerto Rico: Aurora Comunicación Integral, Inc.), 1997.

Figueredo, Jorge S., *Cuban Baseball: A Statistical History, 1878-1961* (Jefferson, North Carolina: McFarland Press, 2003).

Figueredo, Jorge S., *Who's Who in Cuban Baseball: A Statistical History, 1878-1961* (Jefferson, North Carolina: McFarland Press, 2003).

Freedman, Lew, *Latino Baseball Legends* (Westport, Connecticut: Greenwood Publishing Group, 2010), 283.

Treto Cisneros, Pedro, ed., *Enciclopedia del Béisbol Mexicano* (Mexico City, Mexico: Revistas Deportivas, S.A. de C.V., 11th edition, 2011).

www.baseball-reference.com, www.licey.com, and www.retrosheet.org

## NOTES

1 *Enciclopedia del Béisbol Mexicano* and the Licey website both list him as Rodríguez Olmo

2 "Luis Rodríguez Olmo tiene gran celebración." *Diario Las Américas*, October 6, 2009

3  Arthur "Red" Patterson, "Luis Olmo, Pounding Puerto Rican Who Resembles Three Yankees, Reaches Dodgers on the Third Hop," *The Sporting News*, April 8, 1943: 5.

4  Chip Royal, "Dodgers to Use Luis Olmo," Associated Press, March 4, 1943.

5  "Luis Rodríguez Olmo tiene gran celebración."

6  Thomas Van Hyning, *Puerto Rico's Winter League* (Jefferson, North Carolina: McFarland & Co., 1995), 84.

7  Patterson.

8  Ibid.

9  *The Sporting News*, April 4, 1940: 12.

10  "Olmo a Puerto Rican," *The Sporting News*, April 18, 1940: 8.

11  Adrián Burgos, Jr., "The Latins from Manhattan." Chapter Two of *Mambo Montage: The Latinization of New York* (Agustín Laó-Montes and Arlene M. Dávila, editors) (New York: Columbia University Press, 2001), 83.

12  Patterson.

13  Ibid.

14  David Maraniss, *Clemente* (New York: Simon & Schuster, 2006), 32.

15  Chris Lamb, *Blackout: The Untold Story of Jackie Robinson's First Spring Training* (Lincoln: University of Nebraska Press, 2004), 161-162. See also *Newsletter of the Virginia Historical Society*, Number 24, Autumn 1996. Quoted in Mooers family newsletter, Autumn 1998 (http://www.mooers-law.com/MooersMemoirsAutumn1998.pdf)

16  Hy Turkin, "All About Olmo," *New York Daily News*, March 17, 1943.

17  Daniel Balderston, Mike González, and Ana M. López, editors, *Encyclopedia of Contemporary Latin American and Caribbean Cultures, Volume 1* (New York: Routledge, 2000), 155.

18  César J. Ayala and Rafael Bernabe, *Puerto Rico in the American Century: A History since 1898* (Chapel Hill, North Carolina: The University of North Carolina Press, 2007), 148.

19  David Falkner, *Great Time Coming* (New York: Simon & Schuster, 1995), 97.

20  Harold Parrott, "Both Sides," *Brooklyn Eagle*, July 27, 1943.

21  Tim Cohane, "Ex-Royal Olmo King-Pin in Dodger New Order," *The Sporting News*, October 21, 1943: 6.

22  "Rickey Benches Olmo in Puerto Rico League," *The Sporting News*, October 21, 1943: 6.

23  "'Boost Comes a Little Late'—Olmo Says He'll Fulfill Mexican Contract," *The Sporting News*, February 28, 1946: 2.

24  It took nearly 55 years before it happened again, as Adam Kennedy did it on April 18, 2000. Fellow Puerto Rican José Valentín also did it on July 8, 2006.

25  "The Frank and Forthright Mr. Durocher," *The Sporting News*, June 1, 1944: 10.

26  Harold C. Burr, "Rickey Wants Dodgers Who Can Run; He'll Hustle Off Some to Other Teams," *The Sporting News*, October 11, 1945: 14.

27  Luis Olmo conversation with Rory Costello, August 15, 2011. Maraniss, op. cit.: 31.

28  "Boost Comes a Little Late."

29  Tommy Holmes, "The Corner Catches Up with Lou Olmo," *Brooklyn Eagle*, February 26, 1947. The offer was reported at $7,500 by Harold C. Burr, "Border Raid on Dodgers Lifts Rickey's Eyebrows," *The Sporting News*, February 14, 1946: 8.

30  "Olmo to Vera Cruz," *The Sporting News*, February 21, 1946: 3. "Boost Comes a Little Late," Holmes, op. cit.

31  G. Richard McKelvery, *Mexican Raiders in the Major Leagues* (Jefferson, North Carolina: McFarland & Co., 2006), 106.

32  "High Mex Air Troubles Olmo," *The Sporting News*, March 28, 1946: 19.

33  "Injury Benches Luis Olmo for Month in Mexican League," United Press, April 5, 1946.

34  Dan Daniel, "Olmo Fights for 'Right' to Come Back," *The Sporting News*, August 14, 1946: 28. "Lawyer Confirms Letter," *The Sporting News*, August 21, 1946: 1.

35  *The Sporting News*, October 2, 1946: 33.

36  "Cubans Name Ineligibles on Winter League Roster," *The Sporting News*, September 25, 1946: 24.

37  Holmes.

38  J.G. Taylor Spink, "Mexican League Switches to Youth Policy," *The Sporting News*, November 5, 1947: 2.

39  Harold C. Burr, "Salary Boosts Given Virtually All of Dodgers," *The Sporting News*, February 4, 1948: 18.

40  Dennis Landry, "Olmo, Ex-Dodger, Stars as Hitter for Venezuelan Team," *The Sporting News*, June 23, 1948: 34. Landry, "Three Venezuelan Clubs Expected to Use O.B. Players," *The Sporting News*, September 1, 1948: 37.

41  "Caribbean Pacts Killed Outlaws, Reports Finch," *The Sporting News*, December 8, 1948: 2.

42  "Olmo Succeeds Luque," *The Sporting News*, May 25, 1949: 34. "Olmo Willing, But Club Asks Contract Indemnity," *The Sporting News*, June 15, 1949: 36.

43  Ray Gillespie, "Klein, Hausmann First of Reinstated Players to Rejoin Their Old Clubs," *The Sporting News*, June 22, 1949: 14.

44  Santiago Llorens, "Olmo to Pilot in Puerto Rico," *The Sporting News*, July 6, 1949: 38.

45  Bill Carr, "Olmo's Door to Fame." *Baseball Digest*, August 1961: 29-30. Jason Aronoff, *Going, Going . . . Caught!* (Jefferson, North Carolina: McFarland & Co., 2009), 142.

46 Van Hyning, 97. "Puerto Rico Honors Olmo," *The Sporting News*, October 19, 1949: 15.

47 "Olmo Always Ranked as a Fifth Wheel," *Hartford Courant*, December 27, 1949: 12.

48 Van Hyning.

49 Jack Pearson, "The Kid from Puerto Rico—decided he liked it here," *50 Plus News Magazine*, May 2010 (http://50plusnewsmagazine.com/view/full_story/7280746/article-The-Kid-from-Puerto-Rico—-decided-he-liked-it-here)

50 "Olmo Braves' Scout," United Press, December 30, 1953.

51 *The Sporting News*, January 29, 1958: 16.

52 Miguel J. Frau, "Murray Cut Loose, Olmo Named Pilot," *The Sporting News*, December 9, 1959: 23.

53 "Ex-Outfielder Olmo to Scout in Puerto Rico for Quakers," *The Sporting News*, February 8, 1964: 14.

54 *The Sporting News*, June 19, 1971: 34.

55 Telephone conversation between Rory Costello and Julio Navarro (Olmo's friend and fellow Puerto Rican major leaguer), February 7, 2010.

56 Rey Colón, "Recibe homenaje Luis Rodríguez Olmo," *El Vocero* (San Juan, Puerto Rico), August 12, 2009.

# JOSÉ PAGÁN

## By William Johnson

**A**T THE START OF THE EIGHTH inning of Game Seven of the 1971 World Series, the Pittsburgh Pirates clung to a 1-0 lead over the Baltimore Orioles. With his second pitch of the inning, Baltimore starter Mike Cuellar delivered a fastball to the leadoff hitter, big Willie Stargell, who rapped a single to left field. The next batter was the Pirates' third baseman, 36-year-old José Pagán, who was hitting only .214 so far in the Series. On another 1-and-0 count from Cuellar, Pagán roped a double to drive in Stargell from first. Pagán's RBI pushed the score to 2-1, a tally that held up for the rest of the game.[1] The Pirates won the World Series, and José Pagán had driven in the clinching run. For Pagán, this was a much more satisfying end to a World Series Game Seven than he'd endured a decade earlier, in 1962, when Bobby Richardson's snare of San Francisco Giants teammate Willie McCovey's liner locked up the championship for the New York Yankees. This time, finally, Pagán was a champion.

José Antonio Rodríguez Pagán was born on May 5, 1935, in Barceloneta, Puerto Rico, to Cruz and Tomasa (Rodríguez) Pagán.[2] He had three brothers, Angel (not related to major-league outfielder Angel Pagán), Israel, and Luis. Cruz Pagán was a foreman on a sugar-cane plantation, but José was determined not to live the life of his father. In a 1962 *Sporting News* article, he told Jack McDonald (in authentically halting English), "But me no sugar-cane cutter. Me go to college. But one year only."[3]

Baseball reigned supreme in the pantheon of Puerto Rican athletics in the 1940s and 1950s, and Pagán displayed exceptional talent for the game as a young boy. A local baseball power-broker, Pedrin Zorrilla, signed him to the Santurce Sand Crabbers in 1955, after only one year of college. On the Santurce squad, he was scouted by Alejandro "Alex" Pompez, who then signed both the infielder and another prospect, Orlando Cepeda, to contracts with the New York Giants. Each player signed for a contingent salary of $500,[4] with the stipulation that if either player failed in the minor leagues in the United States, the money would be forfeited.[5]

Pagán began his American career in the entirely new culture of the American South, with the El Dorado (Arkansas) Oilers of the Class-C Cotton States League. There the 20-year-old batted .273 in 97 games. The following winter he was Santurce's starting third baseman, playing for Herman Franks. Pagán's Puerto Rican career eventually yielded a lifetime .260 average, a mark underscored by his selection to several Caribbean All-Star teams.[6]

The Giants promoted Pagán to the Class-B Danville Leafs for 1956, and the young infielder displayed some power to go with his glove, smacking 30 doubles in 147 games. After another winter in Puerto Rico, Pagán was again promoted, this time to Springfield in the Eastern League. Pagán's two Springfield teams, in 1957 and 1958, produced 21 major leaguers, including future San Francisco teammates Jim Duffalo and Felipe Alou.[7] Pagán played well at the higher level, batting .298 in 1958, and started the 1959 season in Triple-A Phoenix, one step away from the majors. He also took an important personal step when he married his wife, Delia, often familiarized with her first name of "Luz." The pairing lasted 53 years, until Pagán's death in 2011. They had two sons, José Antonio and José Ramon, and six grandchildren and four great-grandchildren.[8]

The 1959 season was a pivotal one in Pagán's professional life. On August 4, in the midst of a stellar season playing for Phoenix, and batting .314, Pagán was called up to the San Francisco Giants and made his major-league debut as a pinch-hitter against the Milwaukee Braves. The Giants had sent Felipe Alou back to Triple A to make room for Pagán, but the return on the team's investment was not immedi-

ately apparent. Pagán's debut was inauspicious, with his only at-bat resulting in a grounder to third off Warren Spahn, and the young infielder's play was equally unremarkable over his next 31 games. After the season, Pagán returned to the more familiar and comfortable environs of Puerto Rican winter ball.

In October 1959 Santurce traded Pagán and pitcher Julio Navarro to the Criollos de Caguas, a team that played in both Caguas and Guayama, in exchange for Juan Pizarro.[9] The move allowed player-manager Vic Power to return from the left side of the infield to his more natural position at first base. While it did not require Pagán to physically move his residence, and while the change was neither good nor bad, it did change his identity among the Puerto Rican baseball community, as he no longer worked directly for Pedrin Zorrilla.

After the 1960 major-league season, another year that saw Pagán shuttle between Triple-A Tacoma and San Francisco, after being named to the Caribbean All-Star team at second base,[10] the player finally stuck with the Giants for the 1961 season. New manager Alvin Dark named Pagán his starting shortstop, and the player rewarded his team with an above-average year both at the plate and in the field. While the Giants finished eight games behind the league champion Cincinnati Reds, Pagán clearly established himself as a part of the team for 1962.

The 1962 San Francisco Giants' season not only brought the World Series to Northern California, it also marked the unofficial transfer of the Dodgers-Giants rivalry to the West Coast, though the teams were now 400 miles apart. The Dodgers brought California its first World Series championship in 1959, defeating the Chicago White Sox and giving Southern California bragging rights over the North, but 1962 finally brought the old rivalry into sharp relief.

Pagán led the Giants by example that year, swinging his 37½-inch bat for a .259 average while playing in every Giants game, a total of 164 in the regular season and seven more in the World Series. After 162 games the Giants and the Dodgers had settled nothing, and closed out the year with 101 wins apiece. The ensuing three-game playoff was a classic of the genre, with the teams splitting the first two games at their home parks before Juan Marichal and Don Larsen combined to hold Los Angeles to four runs in eight innings of the final game. That effort set the stage for a furious four-run ninth inning rally by the Giants, with Pagán pushing across the final run as he got on base on an error by Larry Burright. The Giants won the game and the pennant, 6-4.

Pagán starred in the first five games of the World Series. The "silent anchor" of Alvin Dark's infield,[11] he was batting .500 (7-for-14) through Game Five. Yankees manager Casey Stengel said of him, "That little guy is a tiger. He eats those frontline Yankee pitchers alive."[12] A pregame collision with Ernie Bowman resulted in a sprained right wrist for the shortstop, though, and he went hitless in the final two games. The Yankees, victims of a walk-off home run by Pittsburgh's Bill Mazeroski in the 1960 Series, this time exercised the same pain on San Francisco. In the ninth inning of Game Seven, with the Yankees leading 1-0, and with the Giants' Matty Alou on third and Willie Mays on second with two outs, Willie McCovey blistered a shot that appeared destined for right-center field. New York second baseman Bobby

Richardson moved to his left, put his glove up in desperation and snared the ball. Game and Series to the Yankees, and no title for the City by the Bay.

Pagán's next two years moved to the metronome of baseball. He wintered in the Puerto Rican League and returned to San Francisco for the summer season. With the Giants, his offense gradually eroded. His glove work remained at an elite level, but his batting average and power both deteriorated. On May 22, 1965, once Giants manager Herman Franks became sufficiently dissatisfied with Pagán's overall play, Pagán was traded to Pittsburgh for infielder Dick Schofield.

Pagán played the utility role well for the Pirates, and his fluency in the languages of Spanish and baseball made him extremely useful as the first large wave of Hispanic players began to arrive in the United States. In 1969, at the age of 34, Pagán enjoyed his best offensive year since 1962. In 108 games, he batted .285 and slugged at the highest rate in his career, .453. He led all pinch-hitters with a .442 average, although his team finished 12 games behind the New York Mets in the new National League East division. The World Series year of 1972 was the 37-year-old Pagán's last with the Pirates, and on October 24 the team released the aging infielder. He signed with Philadelphia, but his skills had finally deserted him. Pagán's final appearance came, fittingly, against the Giants on August 15, 1973, when he failed in a pinch-hitting assignment. The Phillies released him the next day.

In his 15-year career, the 5-foot-9, 160-pound right-handed batter posted a .250 batting average and clouted 52 home runs. He was later selected as the best shortstop of the 1960s decade for the Giants.[13]

In Puerto Rico, Pagán played until the winter of 1973-1974, after which he managed the Bayamon Cowboys for two seasons. He later managed the Arecibo Wolves and the Ponce Lions in Puerto Rico, coached for the Pirates from 1974 to 1978, and managed the Ogden A's of the Pacific Coast League in 1979 and 1980.

As his playing days had begun to draw down, Pagán evinced an increasing interest in managing. In 1971 he said that he liked to manage "quietly" from the bench during a game.[14] Pagán's own manager at the time was Danny Murtaugh, and he thought the player had the qualities to make a good manager: "José has knowledge of the game. He can communicate with players and has a good personality."[15]

José Pagán never did get the call to manage in the majors, but that did not dampen his love for the game, and he was eventually named to both the Puerto Rico Sports Hall of Fame and the Caguas Sports Hall of Fame. He returned to Puerto Rico for the next two decades, and it was not until 1999 that Pagán moved with his wife and family to the mainland United States, settling in Sebring, Florida.

The later years were not especially kind to Pagán and his family. He developed Lewy body dementia, a vicious and progressive syndrome most often seen in older adults. It robs victims of the ability to think analytically, remember, or remain awake, and is also linked to vivid hallucinations.[16] Pagán suffered all

*Pagán, managing the Bayamon team.*

those symptoms, and visibly deteriorated over his last year. He died on June 7, 2011, at the age of 76.

Pagán was survived by Luz and his sons. José Ramon, the younger, recalled one of his last baseball memories of his father: "He always felt like a Giant. I watched the (2010) World Series with him last year and said, "This is for you, Dad." He was very proud of the Giants."[17] José Pagán is buried at the Lakeview Memorial Gardens in Avon Park, Florida.

## NOTES

1. Wayne Strumpfer, "October 17, 1971: Blass, Clemente Lead Pirates to Victory in World Series Game 7." sabr.org/gamesproj/game/october-17-1971-blass-clemente-lead-pirates-victory-world-series-game-7.
2. legacy.com/obituaries/tbo/obituary.aspx?pid=151650882#sthash.gm8HQCz2.dpuf.
3. Jack McDonald, "Pint Sized Pagan Fitted for Giant-Sized Pay Boost," *The Sporting News*, October 27, 1962: 6.
4. Thomas E. Van Hyning, *Puerto Rico's Winter League* (Jefferson, North Carolina: McFarland & Co., 2004), 125.
5. McDonald.
6. Thomas E. Van Hyning, *TheSanturce Crabbers: Sixty Seasons of Puerto Rican Winter League Baseball* (Jefferson, North Carolina: McFarland & Co., 2008), 98.
7. Garry Brown, "Before He Was a World Series Hero, Jose Pagan Played for Springfield," *Springfield* (Massachusetts) *Republican*, June 10, 2011.
8. John Shea, "Jose Pagan Dies, First S.F. World Series Shortstop," *San Francisco Chronicle*, June 8, 2011.
9. *The Sporting News*, October 14, 1959.
10. *The Sporting News*, February 24, 1960.
11. Bob Stevens, "Little-guy Pagan King-sized Spoke in Giants' Wheel," *The Sporting News*, September 8, 1962.
12. McDonald.
13. legacy.com/obituaries/tbo/obituary.aspx?pid=151650882#sthash.gm8HQCz2.dpuf.
14. Charley Feeney, "Pagan Ready, Waiting for Pilot Call," *The Sporting News*, April 17, 1971.
15. Ibid.
16. mayoclinic.org.
17. Shea.

# JUAN PIZARRO

## By Rory Costello

**J**UAN PIZARRO WAS A TALENTED, durable Puerto Rican pitcher. The lefty pitched in all or part of 18 major-league seasons, starting as a rookie with the 1957 Milwaukee Braves. The Braves rushed him to the big club after one eye-opening season in Class A, yet their very deep pitching staff limited Pizarro's opportunities. He did not come into his own as a big leaguer until 1961, after he was traded to the Chicago White Sox. His best record was 19-9 in 1964—but he never had another season with double-digit wins in the majors. After 1965, Pizarro was primarily a reliever at the top level.

Still, looking at his entire professional career, "Terín" won more than 400 ballgames. His regular-season count is 392: 197 in the US (131 in the majors and 66 in the minors), plus 38 more in Mexico in his late 30s and 157 while playing winter ball in his homeland.[1] Pizarro was one of the most successful pitchers in the history of the Puerto Rican Winter League (PRWL). His career there spanned 22 seasons, from 1955-56 to 1976-77. As of 2012, *El Látigo de Ébano*—The Ebony Whip—ranked second in wins in the league's history. It came as no surprise that when the Puerto Rican Baseball Hall of Fame inducted its first 10 members in 1991, Terín Pizarro was one of them.

Pizarro accomplished as much as he did despite his great love of eating, drinking, gambling, and carousing. In a vivid 1982 interview with author Edward Kiersh for the book *Where Have You Gone, Vince DiMaggio?*, he came across as a *boricua* Bo Belinsky. "Yeah, I love to cel-e-brate," he said. "I only remember the parties, the women, the hot times."[2]

Juan Ramón Pizarro Córdova was born in Santurce, Puerto Rico, on February 7, 1937. His father, Zenón Pizarro, was listed in the 1940 census as a construction worker—but Zenón mainly occupied himself as a trainer/gambler in cockfighting (a pastime that remains popular—and legal—in Puerto Rico).[3] Juan's mother, Ramona Córdova, had three daughters before him. They were named Celestina, Ramona, and Alejandrina. In his childhood, he got the nickname that stuck with him for life: Terín. The neighborhood kids likened him to the main character of the comic strip "Terry and the Pirates."[4]

From the age of 13, Pizarro served as a batboy for his hometown team in the PRWL, the Santurce Cangrejeros (Crabbers). Strange to relate, he had not grown up playing baseball. As he explained to Ed Kiersh, though, "I was so busy being bad, I didn't start playing ball until I was fourteen."[5]

It was only after he joined some boys in the neighborhood for a game of *piedritas*—throwing rocks at bottles—that Pizarro found out about his own talent. "I had never done much throwing," he said in May 1956, "even though I had been batboy for Santurce for three years. Some of the boys could throw pretty fast, but I discovered I could throw harder than any of them. And I hit more bottles too." He then began to play amateur league baseball as a high-school junior and proceeded to win 14 games, followed by 19 more as a senior.[6] The team was run by a man named Harry Rexach, a big Santurce fan and friend of the Crabbers' longtime owner, Pedrín Zorrilla.[7]

Pizarro was not big for a pitcher, especially by today's standards. He grew to just 5-feet-11 and weighed only 170 pounds as a young man. Eventually he weighed as much as 190 to 200—or at least that was the figure in print. "I came to the end of the road a lot quicker because I loved to eat," he freely admitted to Ed Kiersh, patting his stomach and smiling.[8] He had a very live arm, though he did not rely on his fastball alone. His repertoire also included a curveball and—for a time—a screwball, learned from fellow Puerto Rican Rubén Gómez. Mastering his control was a challenge for him in the majors.

Pizarro pitched his first five games as a pro with Santurce in the winter of 1955-56. Pedrín Zorrilla signed him to his first contract. Terín played just 2½ of his 22 winters at home in a non-Crabbers uniform. He was so loyal to winter ball and his team that he turned down an offer for $5,000 from the White Sox not to play following the 1964 season. After the pitcher retired in 1977, the man who then owned the club, Hiram Cuevas, "made sure Pizarro was rewarded with a 20-year coaching contract."[9]

On February 13, 1956, Pizarro signed with Milwaukee. The scout responsible was a fellow Puerto Rican, Luis Olmo. Olmo had finished his big-league career with the Boston Braves in June 1951 and became a full-time scout for them at the end of 1953. Pizarro's first manager in the US, Ben Geraghty, endorsed the young hurler too. Geraghty was also the skipper of another Puerto Rican team, the Caguas Criollos. He said, "When Milwaukee called me up to ask what I thought of Pizarro, I told them he definitely had a major-league arm and could throw harder than anyone in the Milwaukee organization."[10]

According to Pedrín Zorrilla, Santurce received $34,000 from the sale—$2,000 of which went to Terín. His salary for his first year in the US was also to be $2,000—but that was a raise from the $35 per week that he'd been earning in a San Juan factory.[11] The 19-year-old reported to Jacksonville in the South Atlantic League (Class A). The young man could not speak English then; when Geraghty needed to confer with him on the mound, he needed help from veteran Cuban pitcher Adrián Zabala.

Right from the start, Pizarro was dazzling. In his debut he struck out 14 in six innings before tiring and taking the loss. In his next start, he whiffed 21 in 12 innings.[12] He got 20 Ks against Macon on June 27.[13] For the season, he was 23-6 with a 1.77 ERA. In 274 innings pitched, the Sally League's MVP struck out 318, including at least ten men in 15 of his 31 starts. Pizarro walked 149, which was forgivable in a young flamethrower pitching at that level. That August, Ben Geraghty said, "I'd say there are faster pitchers, even in this league. But his ball really moves. Too many good hitters in this league are swinging and missing. His ball is alive and that is what's going to make him a great big leaguer."[14]

John Quinn, general manager of the big club, "did not rule out the possibility" that Pizarro might get a call-up to Milwaukee.[15] That didn't happen, but another indication of the prospect's promise came from the Sally League's president, Hall of Famer Bill Terry, who raved, "He could be as great as [Warren] Spahn."[16]

During the winter of 1956-57, Pedrín Zorrilla sold the Crabbers. The new owner, Ramón Cuevas, in turn sold the contracts of Pizarro, Roberto Clemente, and second baseman Ronnie Samford to Caguas.[17] Shortly after the deal, Pizarro suffered two broken ribs in an auto accident, and the Braves ordered him to quit for the remainder of the PRWL season.[18] He had shown further promise, however, throwing two shutouts while still with Santurce. The level of competition was generally regarded as just a small step down from the majors.

In January 1957 Milwaukee manager Fred Haney talked about the "southpaw phenom." He said, "The only thing I question is [Pizarro's] bases-on-balls record. Maybe the kid needs another year in the minors to work on his control. Those walks will send a manager to an early grave."[19] During spring training in Florida, Pizarro said of his control, "It's okay." Speaking from the Bradenton rooming house where the Braves of African descent had to reside, the 20-year-old was quite confident. When asked what he had to improve upon to make good in the major leagues, he said simply, "Nothing."[20]

Indeed, Pizarro started the 1957 season with the big club.[21] He did not get a chance in a regular-season game, however, until May 4. At Pittsburgh's Forbes Field, the rookie lost a 1-0 duel to Vernon Law. "Even then it took a couple of 'seeing eye' singles in the seventh inning to beat him."[22] In his next outing, at St. Louis on May 10, the Braves gave Pizarro a big early lead and he went all the way to win, 10-5. Terín helped himself by going 2-for-4 and scoring three runs, including a solo homer off Sam "Toothpick" Jones. He was a respectable batter for a pitcher, hitting .202 lifetime in the majors with eight homers (including three in 1964).

Pizarro was in the starting rotation for six turns from late May through mid-June, but after that, the Braves used him sporadically. They sent him down to Triple-A Wichita "for more experience" on July 3; there he was 4-0 in five starts, though with a fairly high ERA of 4.25. After Pizarro returned in late July, *The Sporting News* wrote, "the young Puerto Rican was counted upon for important assistance as a reliever and spot starter down the stretch."[23]

Yet as it developed, Fred Haney called on him just ten more times with only one start. His most impressive performance came at Cincinnati's Crosley Field on August 31. The Braves gave Lew Burdette a 5-0 lead in the first inning, but Burdette retired just one batter before Haney gave him the hook. Pizarro went the rest of the way for the win, striking out nine and giving up just two runs. He finished his rookie year at 5-6 with a 4.62 ERA in 24 games (10 starts). Control was an issue; he walked 51 men in 99⅓ innings.

Pizarro got into one game during the 1957 World Series. In Game Three at County Stadium, after the Yankees knocked Bob Buhl out of the box in the first inning, Terín pitched 1⅔ innings. He gave way to Gene Conley in the third inning after giving up two more runs to New York in the 12-3 loss.

That December Milwaukee beat columnist Bob Wolf wrote, "Juan Pizarro … was a disappointment, although in his case the problem seemed to be solely one of inexperience. Had he been able to spend the entire campaign at Wichita, pitching every fourth or fifth day instead of rusting away in the Braves' bull pen, he might have been ready for stardom in 1958. But because [Taylor] Phillips failed and nobody else was available to take up the slack, Pizarro had to be kept for all but a month of the season."[24] As Ed Kiersh also noted, though, "Haney … wondered so much about J.P.'s whereabouts he had to send out groups of players, or even the police, to scour the bars for the missing rookie."[25]

Meanwhile, in the winter of 1957-58, Pizarro's performance with Caguas was simply spectacular. He became the second of four pitchers in PRWL history to win the Triple Crown of pitching.[26] In 19 games, he was 14-5 with a 1.32 ERA. He struck out 183 and allowed just 94 hits in 170⅓ innings. He broke the league's single-season record with nine shutouts. In addition, on November 21, he broke the league record for strikeouts in a single game—held by Satchel Paige and Bob Turley—with 19 against Ponce.[27] Nine days later he threw a no-hit, no-run game against Mayagüez. He also had a one-hitter and a two-hitter that season. He richly deserved—and won—league MVP honors.

Pizarro had many other excellent seasons at home, and only a few that could be described as so-so or bad. This, however, may have been the best stretch of his entire pro career. It continued in the Caribbean Series. Caguas represented Puerto Rico as PRWL champion, and on February 8, 1958, Pizarro fired 17 strikeouts in an 8-0, two-hit win over Carta Vieja of Panama, shattering the Caribbean Series record.[28] Cuba became tournament champion, though—and a big turning point came two days later, with Pizarro on as a fireman in the ninth inning. The bases were loaded with nobody out, and the tying run would have scored anyway on a long fly to right field, but when an umpire ruled that the ball had been dropped, the irate crowd at San Juan's old Sixto Escobar Stadium started "a small-scale riot." The game was suspended and completed the following night.[29]

Yet despite his brilliance, Pizarro had a disappointing spring camp in 1958.[30] Perhaps he was tired—he'd pitched around 200 innings that winter and had weakened late in another Caribbean Series start. At any rate, there was no room for him on Milwaukee's staff. He went back to Wichita to start the season. Though his record was only 9-10 in 23 games, his ERA was 2.84 and he fanned 158 in 165 innings. The Braves recalled Pizarro in late July, and he responded with three straight complete games, winning two and losing one. Overall with Milwaukee that season, Pizarro was 6-4 with a 2.70 ERA in 16 games (10 starts).

Pizarro's good work in the second half won notice. In early September United Press International wrote, "Juan Pizarro, little more than a spectator in the 1957 World Series, is ready to play a major role for the Milwaukee Braves when they try to make it two in a row over the New York Yankees this year."[31] Again, though, he got to make just one relief appearance in the Series; in Game Five at Yankee Stadium, he was dropped into hot water. New York was ahead 1-0 going into the bottom of the sixth, but Braves starter Lew Burdette weakened, allowing two runs and leaving the bases loaded for Pizarro. By the time the inning was over, the Yankees were up 7-0, and that was where it ended.

Despite some gems, Pizarro never blossomed in Milwaukee. In 1959 he was 6-2, 3.77 in 29 games, interrupted by another stretch at Triple A in June. During his time at Louisville, he pitched a no-hitter against Charleston at home on June 16. Four days later, this time at Charleston, he was four outs away from back-to-back no-hitters but had to settle for a two-hit shutout.[32]

Before the 1959-60 season in Puerto Rico, Pizarro (plus $10,000) came back to Santurce in return for Julio Navarro and José Pagán.[33] In 1960 he spent the full year with Milwaukee for the first time. The Braves' new manager, Charlie Dressen—who encouraged Pizarro to discard his screwball—compared him to Sandy Koufax (as well as Mike McCormick and Dick Ellsworth).[34] Even so, he was just 6-7, 4.55.

On December 15, 1960, the Braves traded Pizarro and pitcher Joey Jay to the Cincinnati Reds for veteran shortstop Roy McMillan, a top-notch glove man, plus a player to be named later. As part of a three-way deal, Cincinnati moved Pizarro along with pitcher Cal McLish to the Chicago White Sox for third baseman Gene Freese. White Sox president Bill Veeck said, "In the case of Pizarro, who supposedly lacks the drive and aggressiveness to win, if anyone can put a fire under him it is [manager Al] López."[35] This appears to be another example of a stereotype attached to Latino players in those days.

Braves catcher Del Crandall, speaking to author Larry Moffi, gave another indication of why Milwaukee gave up on the talented young Puerto Rican. "With Juan Pizarro, I think in his case his potential was that he could throw the ball at ninety-five miles per hour. Well, that's not necessarily potential, that's somebody with a good fastball. … It was just, throw the ball hard and then turn that little screwball over at times. But I don't think that he was consistent in getting the pitches where he needed to get them in times of trouble."[36]

Looking back, Pizarro's great teammate Henry Aaron wrote, "I've always felt that we would have won some more championships if we had hung onto Pizarro and Jay. We needed young pitchers to take over for Spahn, Burdette, and Buhl, and we never came up with them. … I'm not sure I ever saw a pitcher with more ability than Pizarro had when he came to us out of Puerto Rico at the age of nineteen."[37]

Aaron's book went on to quote another Puerto Rican Brave, Félix Mantilla, who was also of African descent. "I don't think our managers and front office ever understood Pizarro. He was always in shape and ready to pitch, but he was moody. Managers would say things to him about being moody and it would just make him angry." Mantilla then went on to talk at length about the "unwritten rule" in those days against having five black players on the field at the same time, which cost both him and Pizarro playing time.[38] Pizarro himself told Ed Kiersh, "Because I was Latin they thought I was a troublemaker."[39]

Pizarro's breakout year in the majors came at last in 1961—though he did not start or win a game for Chicago until June 10. During that season, he was 14-7 with a 3.05 ERA. His walks were down to 4.1 per 9 innings pitched, and his K/9 ratio was a career-high 8.7, which also led the AL that year. Al López said, "When Pizarro first joined the club in 1961 he was fooling around with a screwball. Here was a young pitcher with control trouble, so I told him to concentrate on finding the plate with his fastball and curve and forget about the screwball. He had enough stuff without it."[40]

"The White Sox didn't give up on me, they didn't punish me, and I pitched my ass off for them," Pizarro told Kiersh.[41] The *bon vivant* backslid in 1962, though—"late-night carousing and skipping practices led to a 12-14 mark, numerous fines, and López's turning gray."[42] Still, he enjoyed another career highlight that winter. Mayagüez, the PRWL champion in 1962-63, signed Terín as a reinforcement for the Inter-American Series. On February 8, 1963, he threw a no-hitter against the Venezuelan champs, Valencia—the only no-no in the history of that tournament.[43]

Pizarro followed with his two best seasons in the majors. He was an American League All-Star in both 1963 (16-8, 2.39) and 1964 (19-9, 2.56). His career-high win total in '64 broke the big-league single-season mark for pitchers born in Puerto Rico.[44] He was also runner-up to teammate Gary Peters among the AL's ERA leaders that year. Despite an anemic offense, the strong pitching of the White Sox led them to challenge the Yankees strongly—they finished just one game back in second place.

Pizarro was able to make only 18 starts for the White Sox in 1965, however; a salary holdout contributed to a sore arm, and he took the mound just seven times through June 23. He didn't get past five innings in any game. Eventually, examination revealed a torn triceps tendon in his pitching shoulder.[45] Pizarro made it back by late July and pitched much better in the season's second half. On August 11—relying heavily on breaking balls[46]—he threw the first of his two one-hitters in the majors, shutting out Washington at Comiskey Park. He wound up at 6-3, 3.43 for the season.

From 1966 onward, Pizarro made just 58 starts in his remaining nine major-league seasons, against 182 relief appearances. He bounced around with six different teams: Pittsburgh, Boston, Cleveland, Oakland, the Chicago Cubs, and Houston. He also returned to the minors for parts of 1970—which included a 9-0 run for the Hawaii Islanders, then a California Angels farm club—1971, and 1973.

The 1971 season with the Cubs had noteworthy performances, though. Chicago called Pizarro up from Triple-A Tacoma in July and used him mainly as a starter (14 times in 16 outings). On August 1 at New York's Shea Stadium, Pizarro went all the way and beat the Mets' ace, Tom Seaver, 3-2. Four days later, he threw his other big-league one-hitter, blanking San Diego at Wrigley Field. On September 17, again at Shea, once more he bested Seaver, who was having his greatest season ever. The score was 1-0—and Juan's solo homer in the eighth inning accounted for the game's only run.

Pizarro didn't do much for the Cubs in 1972. The following year—"admittedly 'fat, lazy, and not giving a s***' at this point'"[47]—he appeared just twice with Chicago before his contract was sold to Houston. After the Astros released Pizarro in April 1974, he went to Mexico, joining the Córdoba Cafeteros. In his first season south of the border, Terín was 13-6 with a brilliant ERA of 1.57, best in the league. He had 15 complete games in his 20 starts, with nine shutouts, including five in a row at one point. Both figures tied Mexican League records. At first it was thought that he had set a new mark with six straight blankings, but the league statistician pointed out that he had given up a run in relief.[48]

As a result of Pizarro's success, the Pirates signed him that August 19. Three days previously, general manager Joe Brown had said, "I might make a move in the next few days that might make you think I'm out of my mind." But Pittsburgh was in third place in the National League East at the time, and it was a low-cost maneuver.[49] Over the next several weeks, Pizarro pitched seven times. Pirates manager Danny Murtaugh made him the starter for the last two of those appearances, and he got his final big-league win on September 26. At Shea Stadium, with a big early lead, he went eight innings, coming out only after the Mets scored two unearned runs in the eighth. Fellow Puerto Rican lefty Ramón Hernández closed out the 11-5 victory. Pizarro also got two hits that day.

Pittsburgh went on to win the NL East in 1974, and Pizarro remained on the postseason roster. His last appearance in the majors came in Game Four of the NLCS on October 9; he got the last two outs as the Dodgers drubbed the Pirates 12-1 to advance to the World Series.

Pizarro was in spring training with the Pirates in 1975 as a nonroster player but did not make the team. Returning to Mexico, he continued to excel for Córdoba in 1975 (14-7, 1.98) and 1976 (11-8, 2.64). He finished his Mexican career with a record of 38-21, 2.04, with 42 complete games and 17 shutouts in his 63 starts.

All along, Pizarro had been playing winter ball at home. He was a member of six PRWL champion teams and appeared in five Caribbean Series tournaments. Caguas won in his Triple Crown year, 1957-58, and added him as a reinforcement for the last edition of the tourney's first phase in 1960. Pizarro won five more PRWL titles with Santurce (1961-62, 1964-65, 1966-67, 1970-71, and 1972-73). The Caribbean Series returned from hiatus in 1970, and Santurce represented Puerto Rico in 1971 and 1973. In between, Pizarro played in the Inter-American Series each year from 1961 through 1964.

Pizarro also reinforced the Bayamón Vaqueros for the 1976 Caribbean Series. He rewarded manager José Pagán's surprise choice by throwing a three-hit shutout against Venezuela on his 39th birthday. "I used my experience in winning that game for Puerto Rico," he said. "It was nice to finish my Caribbean Series career as a winner."[50]

During the winter of 1976-77, Pizarro pitched his last 11 games as a pro for Santurce. His final record in Puerto Rico was 157-110, with a superb 2.51 ERA. Only Rubén Gómez had more wins (174, and he needed 29 seasons to do it). Pizarro pitched 2,403 innings, again second behind Gómez, and allowed just 1,980 hits. He is the PRWL's all-time leader in strikeouts (1,804) and shutouts (46), marks that will almost certainly never be challenged.

In addition to coaching the Crabbers off and on, Pizarro stayed involved with baseball in other ways. As of the early 1980s, he was working for Santurce's Parque Central as an instructor, with the additional goal of keeping kids out of trouble.[51] As late as 1997, he was back in the US, coaching with the Rockford Cubbies of the Midwest League (Class A). The manager was one of his contemporaries in the majors, Rubén Amaro, Sr. "He was very professional for me as well as our young pitchers," said Amaro, "and I know many of those young players were touched by his experience."[52]

In January 2007, Terín told columnist María Judith Caraballo that he was totally retired and enjoying a peaceful life at home in the same section of Santurce, Villa Palmeras, where he grew up. (He mentioned a wife, though not by name, in the Kiersh interview; information on children is also lacking.) After not having been to any ballpark for three years, he was at Game Six of the PRWL finals between the Arecibo Lobos and Gigantes de Carolina. Pizarro told Caraballo stories of his playing days and encouraged young Puerto Rican ballplayers to "work hard, run a lot, and practice enough."[53]

## SOURCES

In addition to the sources in the Notes, the author also consulted baseball-reference.com, retrosheet.org, ancestry.com (1940 census records), paperofrecord.com (various small items from *The Sporting News*), checkoutmycards.com (information from Pizarro's baseball cards), and

Antero Núñez, José, *Series del Caribe* (Caracas, Venezuela: Impresos Urbina, C.A., 1987).

Crescioni Benítez, José A., *El Béisbol Profesional Boricua* (San Juan, Puerto Rico: Aurora Comunicación Integral, Inc., 1997).

James, Bill, and Rob Neyer, *The Neyer/James Guide to Pitchers* (New York: Simon & Schuster, 2004).

Treto Cisneros, Pedro, ed., *Enciclopedia del Béisbol Mexicano* (Mexico City: Revistas Deportivas, S.A. de C.V., 11th edition, 2011).

# PUERTO RICO AND BASEBALL: 60 BIOGRAPHIES

## NOTES

1. Postseason play—in the minors, Puerto Rico, and international tournaments—got him over 400.
2. Edward Kiersh, *Where Have You Gone, Vince DiMaggio?* (New York: Bantam Books, 1983), 136.
3. Kiersh, *Where Have You Gone, Vince DiMaggio?*, 133.
4. "Puerto Rican Pitcher Gets Sally Loop Praise," United Press International, August 7, 1956.
5. Kiersh, *Where Have You Gone, Vince DiMaggio?*, 132.
6. Joe Livingston, "Ex-Batboy Pizarro Finds Sally Hitters Soft Touch," *The Sporting News*, May 23, 1956: 34.
7. Thomas E. Van Hyning, *The Santurce Crabbers* (Jefferson, North Carolina: McFarland & Company, 1999), 76.
8. Kiersh, *Where Have You Gone, Vince DiMaggio?*, 135.
9. Thomas E. Van Hyning, *Puerto Rico's Winter League* (Jefferson, North Carolina: McFarland & Company, 1995), 100.
10. Joe Livingston, "18-Year-Old Lefty Fans 14 in Six Innings in Sally Debut," *The Sporting News*, April 25, 1958: 32.
11. *The Sporting News*, February 22, 1956: 28; "Puerto Rican Pitcher Gets Sally Loop Praise."
12. Livingston, "Ex-Batboy Pizarro Finds Sally Hitters Soft Touch."
13. "Pizarro Cools Off Slightly in Red Hot Strikeout Pace," *The Sporting News*, July 11, 1956: 41.
14. "Puerto Rican Pitcher Gets Sally Loop Praise."
15. "296 Strikeouts for Pizarro," *The Sporting News*, August 29, 1956: 34.
16. Lou Chapman, "'Pizarro Could Be as Great as Spahn,' Says Bill Terry," *The Sporting News*, October 24, 1956: 8.
17. Van Hyning, *The Santurce Crabbers*, 84.
18. Pito Alvarez de la Vega, "Pizarro, Injured in Auto Crash, Quits Winter Ball," *The Sporting News*, January 9, 1957: 21.
19. Frank Finch, "Pilot Explains His Promise to 'Get Tough,'" *The Sporting News*, January 23, 1957: 4.
20. Bob Wolf, "Phenom Pizarro Sure He'll Make Grad as Brave," *The Sporting News*, March 13, 1957: 17.
21. Bob Wolf," Kid Pizarro Pitches Way Onto Braves' Bulging Staff," *The Sporting News*, April 24, 1957: 9.
22. Bob Wolf, "Braves, Rich in Hill Talent, Put Two More on Display," *The Sporting News*, May 15, 1957: 11.
23. Bob Wolf, "Conley's Comeback Like Oxygen Whiff to Crippled Braves," *The Sporting News*, August 7, 1957: 10.
24. Bob Wolf, "Pitcher-Wealthy Braves Still Seek Bull-Pen Bracer," *The Sporting News*, December 4, 1957: 20.
25. Kiersh, *Where Have You Gone, Vince DiMaggio?*, 133.
26. The others were Sam Jones (1954-55), Wayne Simpson (1969-70), and Edwin Núñez (1981-82).
27. Pat Dobson later broke this record on December 10, 1967, when he struck out 21.
28. Pito Alvarez de la Vega, "Latin Winter Crown Again Won by Cuba," *The Sporting News*, February 19, 1958: 30.
29. "Latin Tempers Explode," "Ump's Ruling Provokes Fan Riot; Series Game Halted," *The Sporting News*, February 19, 1958: 30.
30. Bob Wolf, "Braves Find More Pitching Riches in Depth of Hill Staff," *The Sporting News*, August 6, 1958: 18.
31. "Pizarro Seen Yank-Beater," United Press International, September 5, 1957.
32. "Hit in Eighth Halts Pizarro Bid for Second Gem in Row," *The Sporting News*, July 1, 1959: 27.
33. Van Hyning, *The Santurce Crabbers*, 84.
34. Bob Wolf, "Pizarro Takes Kinks Out of Braves' Staff by Junking Scroogie," *The Sporting News*, June 1, 1960: 15.
35. Edgar Munzel, "Senor to Try Magic on Pizarro, McLish," *The Sporting News*, December 28, 1960: 15.
36. Larry Moffi, *This Side of Cooperstown* (Ames, Iowa: Firehouse Books, 1996), 125.
37. Hank Aaron with Lonnie Wheeler, *I Had a Hammer: The Hank Aaron Story* (New York: Harper Perennial, 2007.)
38. Aaron, *I Had a Hammer*.
39. Kiersh, *Where Have You Gone, Vince DiMaggio?*, 133.
40. Bill Wise, ed., *1965 Official Baseball Almanac* (Greenwich, Connecticut: Fawcett, 1964).
41. Kiersh, *Where Have You Gone, Vince DiMaggio?*, 135.
42. Kiersh, *Where Have You Gone, Vince DiMaggio?*, 132.
43. Van Hyning, *The Santurce Crabbers*, 93.
44. Hiram Bithorn—the first Puerto Rican in the majors—had won 18 for the Chicago Cubs in 1943. Ed Figueroa broke this record in 1978 when he won 20 for the New York Yankees. Javier Vázquez surpassed Pizarro for most career big-league wins by a Puerto Rican native in 2009. Note also that "Nuyorican" John Candelaria won 20 games in 1977 and 177 in his career.
45. Edgar Munzel, "Injury Jinx Hits Sox on Double—Juan and Ward," *The Sporting News*, July 10, 1965: 3.
46. Jerome Holtzman, "Juan Uses His Curve Ball in Twirling a One-Hitter," *The Sporting News*, August 28, 1965: 17.
47. Kiersh, *Where Have You Gone, Vince DiMaggio?*, 135.
48. "Pizarro Streak Ends," *The Sporting News*, August 10, 1974: 42. Gary Ryerson broke the record for total in a season with 10 in 1976. That mark has since been matched twice.
49. Charley Feeney, "Pizarro Back for Another Whirl on Bucco Hill," *The Sporting News*, September 7, 1974: 7, 28.

50 Van Hyning, *The Santurce Crabbers*, 129.

51 Kiersh, *Where Have You Gone, Vince DiMaggio?*, 136.

52 E-mail from Rubén Amaro, Sr. to Rory Costello, December 29, 2012.

53 María Judith Caraballo, "Juan Terin Pizarro La Gloria del Béisbol Puertorriqueño," 1-800-Béisbol website (http://www.1800beisbol.com/baseball/deportes/latinos/juan_terin_pizarro_la_gloria_del_beisbol_puertorriqueno/), unknown date, 2007.

# JORGE POSADA

## By Scott Dominiak

**IN MAJOR-LEAGUE BASEBALL WHEN** a team dominates its opponents for several years, it's usually because it has a solid nucleus of players. For instance, in the early 1970s in the American League the Oakland Athletics captured three successive World Series. In the National League the Cincinnati Reds were a powerhouse. Both clubs had a strong nucleus of players who produced season after season.

The same could be said for the New York Yankees from 1996 to 2011. The Yankees were in the playoffs in 15 of those 16 seasons and won five World Series. At the heart of those Yankee teams were four players, Derek Jeter, shortstop; Andy Pettitte, pitcher (though he spent 2004 through 2006 pitching for Houston); Mariano Rivera, relief pitcher; and Jorge Posada, catcher.

Posada had an illustrious 17-year career with New York, 1995-2011. He was an the All-Star five times, won the Silver Slugger Award five times, and played on five World Series champions. During the catcher's career, he batted .273, hit 275 home runs, and drove in 1,065 runs.

In 2003 Posada finished third in voting for the American League Most Valuable Player Award after hitting 30 home runs, batting .281, and posting 101 RBIs. Aside from Yogi Berra, he was only the second Yankee catcher to hit 30 home runs in a season. Posada's best season was 2007, when he hit .338 and batted in 90 runs at the age of 35.

The switch-hitter was only the fifth major-league catcher with at least 1,500 hits, 350 doubles, 275 homers, and 1,000 RBIs. He produced more RBIs and home runs than any other catcher in baseball from 2000 to 2011.

The Puerto Rican native was born on August 17, 1971, in the Santurce district of San Juan to a Cuban father, Jorge Posada Sr., who fled to Puerto Rico to escape Fidel Castro's regime, and a Dominican mother. His father worked in sales for Richardson-Vicks, a pharmaceutical company. Also, for 40 years he was a major-league scout for numerous teams: the Yankees, the Houston Astros, the Toronto Blue Jays, the Atlanta Braves, and the Colorado Rockies. His brother, Leo Posada, played for the Kansas City Athletics. He helped his son develop his baseball skills and instill the drive to make it to the major leagues.

Young Jorge was small for his age until later in high school. The serious-minded father always wanted his son to become a ballplayer and used tough love in raising him. For instance, at age 12 he had Jorge at the start of summer move a huge pile of dirt on the driveway of their middle-class home to the backyard and spread it out to make it level for a baseball field. He gave him a wheelbarrow and shovel and told him to have it done by the end of summer. Jorge had it done in two weeks, and it helped him to develop his muscles and hands for batting. It also taught him to use his stubbornness, a trait of his father, to do hard jobs without complaining. Jorge's nurturing mother would often tell her husband not to be so hard on their son, but it was usually to no avail.

Jorge Sr. often rewarded his son for doing strenuous chores by taking him to the ballfield to hit and field balls. Junior learned both to respect and fear his father. Almost everything they ever did together or talked about centered on baseball, which had become the son's passion.

As a teenager, young Posada attended Alejandrino High School and played several sports, including baseball, basketball, and volleyball. He was an all-star shortstop for the baseball team in 1988-89. The switch-hitting Posada was drafted by the Yankees in the 43rd round of the amateur draft in 1989 but opted to go to college. Because his SAT scores were not high enough for him to get into a four-year college, Posada accepted a baseball scholarship to Calhoun

Community College in Decatur, Alabama. The head coach, Fred Frickie, recruited the high-school graduate without scouting him.

The Yankees came calling again in 1990, drafting Posada in the 24th round. New York scout Leon Wurth rated Posada's bat and attitude highly. He didn't sign right away, and played again for Calhoun in 1991, gaining all-conference honors. Posada signed a $30,000 bonus contract with the Yankees on May 24, 1991.

In 1991 Posada played 71 games at second base for Oneonta in the Short Season New York-Penn League and hit .235 with four home runs. The Yankees felt Posada lacked speed, and began grooming him as a catcher in 1992 at Greensboro in the Class-A South Atlantic League, where he batted .277 with 12 home runs and 58 RBIs. Initially, Posada was reluctant to become a catcher, a position he believed was not his strong suit.

In 1993 with Prince William of the Class-A Carolina League, Posada batted .259 with 17 home runs. He spent the next three seasons with Triple-A Columbus (International League), and had a one-game call-up to the Yankees in 1995. In 1996 Posada was up briefly three times in April, May, and June, and was called up for good at the end of the season.

In 1997 Posada solidified his position on the Yankees' roster by backing up catcher Joe Girardi, his mentor. The Puerto Rican played in 60 games and batted .250 with 6 home runs and 25 RBIs. He helped the team to the postseason, which the Yankees lost to the Cleveland Indians. After the season, the club sought to trade Posada and Mike Lowell to the Montreal Expos for star pitcher Pedro Martinez, but the deal did not work out as Martinez went to the Boston Red Sox.

After the season Posada hired a personal trainer to help improve his physical conditioning. In 1998 his playing time increased to 111 games and he batted .268 with 17 home runs and 63 RBIs. The Yankees qualified for the postseason for the fourth consecutive year, and in the World Series they swept the San Diego Padres in four games.

For the 1999 season Posada requested a salary of $650,000 but the Yankees renewed his contract at $350,000. The first half of the season the catcher struggled at the plate, hitting .210, but in the second half he found his swing and hit .285, for a final average of .245. He caught in 109 games. Posada caught two of the four World Series games as the Yankees swept the Atlanta Braves.

After the season, Girardi became a free agent, and Posada became the Yankees' full-time catcher in 2000. The switch-hitter blossomed at the plate, hitting .287 with 28 homers and 86 RBIs. Manager Joe Torre named Posada to his first All-Star Game. Again, the Yankees made it to the World Series as they defeated their crosstown rival, the New York Mets, in five games. Posada won the first of his five Silver Slugger Awards and the Thurman Munson Award, for baseball accomplishments and philanthropic work in New York.

For the budding star, life was good, and he loved playing for the Yankees under Torre. He looked at the team and the organization as family.

Posada had another stellar year offensively in 2001 as he again made the All-Star team, batted .277, hit 22 home runs, and had 95 RBIs. He won his second Silver Slugger Award and received the Milton Richman "You Gotta Have Heart" Award from the New York Chapter of the Baseball Writers Association of America. But Posada also led the league with 18 passed balls and 11 errors. The Yankees World Series winning streak was snapped by the Arizona Diamondbacks in seven games.

In 2002 Posada again led all catchers in errors (12), but he offset that by hitting .268 with 20 homers and 99 RBIs. He won another Silver Slugger Award. The Yankees lost to the Anaheim Angels in the American League Division Series.

Posada had an outstanding season in 2003 as he recorded career highs in home runs (30), RBIs (101), and walks (93). The 30 homers tied Berra's record for Yankee catchers. Posada batted .281 and was fifth in the league in on-base percentage at .405. He won his fourth consecutive Silver Slugger Award and was third in the MVP voting behind Alex Rodríguez and Carlos Delgado. The Yankees again lost the World Series, to the Florida Marlins.

In 2004 the Yankees had a three-games-to-none lead over the Boston Red Sox in the ALCS before losing four straight. Posada again had a fine year, hitting .272 with 21 home runs and 81 RBIs. He received the "Good Guy" Award from the New York Press Photographers.

The 33-year-old Posada posted a .262 batting average in 2005 with 19 home runs and 71 RBIs. He was nominated by the Yankees for the Roberto Clemente Award. New York fell short of the World Series title for the fifth year in a row by succumbing to the Angels again in the ALDS. He improved at bat in 2006, hitting .277 with 23 homers and 93 RBIs. Defensively, he improved his percentage of throwing out runners trying to steal, but again led the league in passed balls.

In 2007 the Yankees catcher won his fifth and final Silver Slugger Award as he posted career highs in batting average (.338), hits (171), and doubles (42). Posada also clubbed 20 homers and knocked in 90 runs. He had caught at least 120 games each season from 2000 through 2007. He finished sixth in the MVP voting. He was nominated again for the Roberto Clemente Award, and was named one of the finalists. He also received the Bart Giamatti "Caring" Award from MLB's Baseball Assistance Team. After the season he opted for free agency. The Mets offered the star catcher a five-year contract, but he turned it down for a four-year deal at $52 million with the Yankees.

In 2008 Posada was injured and out of action for the month of May, then went on the disabled list in late July for the first time in his career. He had shoulder surgery and missed the rest of the season. The Yankees finished in third place, the first and only time the team did not qualify for the postseason during Posada's career.

On April 16, 2009, Posada hit the first home run in the new Yankee Stadium. It was hit off left-hander Cliff Lee of the Cleveland Indians. On September 15 against Toronto Posada was ejected from the game when he bumped and taunted pitcher Jesse Carlson, who had thrown a pitch behind him. After being ejected, Posada charged Carlson and a bench-clearing brawl erupted. Both players received three-game suspensions. (Posada was ejected six times during his career.) Recovered from his surgery, Posada caught in 100 games and batted .285 with 22 home runs and 81 RBIs. He appeared in all six World Series games as hit two home runs as the Yankees defeated the Philadelphia Phillies for their first Series triumph in nine years. Posada received the Ted Williams Community Award from the Ted Williams Museum and Hitters Hall of Fame.

One of the highlights of the 2010 campaign for Posada was his 11th straight Opening Day start at catcher. In June during an interleague series against Houston, he became the first Yankee since Bill Dickey in 1937 to hit grand slams in consecutive games. He got his 1,000th career RBI in a game against the Kansas City Royals on July 23. But at the age of 38, his offensive output fell off: .248, 18 homers, and 57 RBIs in 120 games. Still, the New York BBWAA made him the winner of the Willie, Mickey, and the Duke Award. The Texas Rangers beat the Yankees in the ALCS.

After the season, Posada had arthroscopic surgery on his left knee to fix a torn meniscus. Because of his injury and his declining defensive performance, Posada became the Yankees' designated hitter in 2011, while Russell Martin became the full-time catcher.

"When you take me out from behind the plate, you're taking my heart and my passion," Posada wrote with Gary Brozek in his book, *The Journey Home: My Life in Pinstripes*, published in 2015.[1]

In the spring of 2011, Posada was in a slump at the plate, and on May 14 against the Red Sox, manager Girardi moved him to ninth in the batting order. Posada felt this was an insult and asked to be removed from the lineup. He told reporters that he needed to clear his head, and that he had stiffness in his back. Posada later told management that he regretted what he did.

"I felt I wasn't being treated right, that people weren't always being straightforward with me as I wanted them to be, or treated me as I deserved to be treated, and I exploded," Posada wrote.[2]

In June Posada ended his slump, batting .382 for the month, but by August he was removed from the everyday lineup because he was hitting only .230. Against the Tampa Bay Rays on August 13, he made his first start since being benched and went 3-for-5 with a grand slam and six RBIs. It was Posada's 10th grand slam and moved him into sixth place on the all-time Yankee list, passing Berra and Mickey Mantle. He finished the season with a .235 batting average, 14 home runs, and 44 RBIs.

In the Division Series against the Detroit Tigers, Posada batted .429 with six hits and an on-base percentage of .579 at DH. The Tigers won the series in five games. After the series Posada was asked by a reporter if this was the end of his career with the Yankees.

"I don't want to look at it like that," he said. "We lost, and we'll see what happens in the offseason."[3]

During the interview, Posada became very emotional and left the room briefly to compose himself.

Girardi praised the 17-year veteran on his performance in the ALDS and his career. "This guy, when you look at what he did in this series, he was awesome," the skipper said. "He's had a tremendous career, and I'm sure he is going to continue to play, and I don't know what's going to happen."[4]

Girardi added, "But you talk about being proud of players—what he went through this year and what he gave us in the postseason, I don't think there is a prouder moment that I've had of Jorge."[5] That fall five or six teams expressed an interest in Posada, including Boston, but not the Yankees. Disappointed, in January of 2012, he retired as a player.

In 2013 Posada was a guest instructor during spring training, and on August 16, 2015, his number 20 was retired in a ceremony at Yankee Stadium.

Even though Posada loved playing for the Yankees, he had a reputation of whining occasionally throughout his career. One episode occurred at the start of the 2011 season when he complained about being the designated hitter rather than catching. He also was upset about being excluded from meetings with the catchers when discussing strategies under Girardi's management. The veteran said he felt disrespected.

According to Mark Feinsand of the *New York Daily News*, Posada had a propensity to ignore Girardi's instructions. He would occasionally disregard scouting reports and call pitches on the fly in defiance.[6] Supposedly, ill feelings began between Girardi and Posada stemmed from disagreements over catching strategies in 2005.

Posada wrote in his book that Torre was his "father on the field," while Girardi was just a manager.[7] Under Girardi, he wrote, team unity deteriorated, and the open-door communication that Joe Torre had now seemed shut. Posada also criticized what he saw as a change in the clubhouse culture.

"Winning is such a fragile thing," Posada wrote. "If you take away any element that supports it, it falls to the ground and shatters."[8]

The catcher wrote that he knew his career was probably over on October 6, 2011, when he came to the plate in the eighth inning in the final game of the ALDS against Detroit trailing 3-2 and grounded out. "I had no idea how finality can be," he wrote. "I went down on my knees as if something incredibly heavy was crushing me. I put my head on the ground and wailed, shoulder-heaving sobs tearing at me."[9]

In the book Posada expressed bitterness about his retirement. But he said that the Yankee organization was good to him after he retired. At the home opener in 2012, the club asked him to throw out the opening pitch. He did so in front of 50,000 fans, and his father, who had ridden him hard as a child, caught it.

"In that moment things were back to how they had been," he wrote. "Just my dad and me, tossing a ball around, both of us sharing a dream."[10]

In 2012 Posada was inducted into the Latin America International Sports Hall of Fame.

On the television show *CBS This Morning* in New York in 2015, Posada said he did not think players who used steroids should be allowed into the Hall of Fame.

"No, I don't think it's fair for the guys that have been in the Hall of Fame that played the game clean … I don't think it's fair," Posada said. "I really don't. I think the guys who need to be in the Hall of Fame need to be a player that played the game with no controversy."[11]

On January 21, 2000, Posada married Laura Mendez, an attorney, whom he had met three years earlier. They have has two children, Jorge Jr. and Paulina. Their son was born with craniosynostosis, a birth defect in which the plates of the skull fuse together to impede the growth of the brain, and which has required numerous surgeries.

The Posadas established the Jorge Posada Foundation to further research into the condition and provide emotional assistance to families with children affected by it. It also provides grants to help underwrite the costs of initial surgeries. Statistics show that one in 2,000 babies is born with this condition.

In 2006 Posada wrote *Play Ball!*, a children's book. He was honored with the Mentor of the Year Award from Kids in Distressed Situations and Fashion Delivers. The couple co-wrote *Fit Home Team*, a family-health manual. They also wrote *The Beauty of Love: A Memoir of Miracles, Hope, and Healing*. The book describes their personal ordeals, and how they handled them after learning about their son's condition. They received the Puerto Rican Family Foundation Excellence Award for their commitment to children, especially those affected by craniosynostosis. In 2007 Posada received the Parent Magazine Award.

In 2006 Posada was inducted into the Alabama Community College Hall of Fame, and his jersey number, 6, at Calhoun was retired.

As of 2016 the Posadas lived in Florida.

## SOURCES

In addition to the sources cited in the Notes, the author also consulted baseball-almanac.com, baseball-reference.com, jorgeposada.com/biography, latinsportshalloffame.com, and an article by Sherryl Connelly: "Yankee Great Jorge Posada Still Steamed…," *New York Daily News*, May 8, 2015.

## NOTES

1 Jorge Posada and Gary Brozek, *The Journey Home: My Life in Pinstripes* (New York: HarperCollins Publishers, 2015), 336.

2 Posada and Brozek, 336.

3 Andrew Keh, "Posada Emotional After Loss," *New York Times*, October 27, 2011.

4 Ibid.

5 Ibid.

6 Mark Feinsand, "Jorge Posada's Feud With Joe Girardi Has Roots in 2005 Disagreement on Catching Strategy: Source," *New York Daily News*, May 18, 2011.

7 Posada and Brozek, 309.

8 Posada and Brozek, 335.

9 Posada and Brozek, 339.

10 Posada and Brozek, 342.

11 Anthony Witrado, "Jorge Posada Risking His Own Legacy More Than A-Rod's With PED, Yankees Comments," Bleacher Report, May 14, 2015.

# VIC POWER

## By Joseph Wancho

**T**HE GAME MEANT NOTHING. Well, virtually nothing. The Detroit Tigers were ending a three-game series in Cleveland looking for a sweep after taking the first two contests. But that was all that Detroit was playing for on August 14, 1958. The Tigers and Indians were playing out the string, holding down fourth and fifth place respectively in the American League standings. Detroit was a distant 15½ games behind first-place New York. Cleveland was 18 games behind.

But even games played between non-contenders can bring excitement and record-worthy performances. Such was the case that Thursday afternoon, witnessed by a minuscule total of 4,474 fans in cavernous Cleveland Stadium.

The Tigers looked well on their way to sweeping the Tribe, after building a 7-4 lead heading into the bottom of the eighth inning. Rocky Colavito led off the frame with his second solo home run of the game. Pinch-hitter Gary Geiger walked. Next, Vic Wertz was summoned from the bench to bat for pitcher Morrie Martin. Wertz came through and homered to tie the game.

Vic Power singled home Bobby Avila, then went to second on an error by catcher Charlie Lau. On a wild pitch by Tigers hurler Bill Fischer, Power moved to third base. Third-base coach Eddie Stanky told Power to "go if you can get the jump."[1] Go Power did, swiping the plate and turning a three-run deficit into a two-run lead at 9-7.

Indians stopper Ray Narleski could not hold the lead and the Tigers scored two runs in the top of the ninth inning to send the game into extra innings. With one out in the bottom of the 10th, Power and catcher Russ Nixon each stroked a single. Nixon was forced at second on a groundball off the bat of Minnie Minoso. Larry Doby was intentionally walked, and up stepped Colavito with the bases full and two outs. This time, Stanky instructed Power "to play it safe and see what happens."[2] Power had been bluffing his way down the third-base line, and Tigers pitcher Frank Lary was paying him no attention. "I told Eddie, 'I think I can go,'" Power said in the clubhouse after the game. "He say nothing so I go."[3] A startled Lary tried to hurry the throw home from his windup, but Power slid home, beating the throw easily. "Those were head plays, not leg plays," said Cleveland skipper Joe Gordon. "Vic isn't particularly fast, but he's got baseball instinct. He bluffed the pitchers beautifully—rushing up the line, pausing long enough to make them relax and then, poof—streaking all the way in."[4]

Power's feat of stealing home twice in one game had been done just 10 times before in the major leagues. He was the first to turn the trick since 1927, and, more than a half-century later, the last player to have done it. How many bases did Power steal in 1958? Three.

Victor Felipe Pellot (Pove), who spent the month of September 1964 playing for the Phillies, was born on November 1, 1927, in Arecibo, Puerto Rico. (The second family name in most Spanish-speaking countries is the mother's maiden name.) He was the second youngest of six children born to Regino and Maximina Pellot (pronounced "pay-oat"). A monolingual first-grade teacher changed Maximina's last name, Pove, to Power. The teacher, thinking that the illiterate Maximina was spelling her name wrong, changed the "v" to a "w" and added an "r" at the end. "Pove" was transformed to "Power," a mistranslation that Maximina had no choice but to accept. The name of the mother and the player was imposed, with no ancestors, and no lineage.[5]

Regino Pellot, who worked at a sugar mill, died from tetanus when Victor was 13. Maximina Pellot took in work as a seamstress. Quincy Trouppe, a veteran of the Negro Leagues and the Latin American leagues, had seen Power playing on the sandlots around Arecibo, befriended the young man. Trouppe signed the youngster to play for Caguas of the Puerto Rican Baseball League. At the age of 15, Vic headed off to play professional baseball for a salary of $100 a week. Trouppe took the young Power under his wing, acting much like a second father to him.

In 1949 the Drummondville (Quebec) Cubs, a team in the independent Provincial League, was searching for talented ballplayers for the summer. The Puerto Rican league had folded for financial reasons, and many players, Power and Trouppe included, made the trek north. For both seasons with the Cubs, Power played in the outfield. While there he changed his name, at least as used on the baseball diamond. "I used to write Victor Pellot Power. But the French Canadians would say 'La Pellot,' with an 'L' sound rather than a 'Y' sound. That sounded similar to a French sexual term and everyone would laugh. [*Pelote* means he who paws or pets women]. So they started calling me Vic Power instead."[6]

New York Yankees scout Tom Greenwade had seen Vic play in Puerto Rico years before, and dispatched scout John Neun to look him over in Drummondville. Neun reported back positively. No matter how Power was pronounced, Greenwade signed Power based on his solid performance.

Power's meteoric rise through the Yankees farm system began with the Triple-A Syracuse Chiefs of the International League in 1951 and continued for two years with the Kansas City Blues of the American Association. He was clearly one of the top prospects in the Yankees' chain. At Kansas City Power mostly played the outfield; Bill "Moose" Skowron blocked his way at the position he desired, first base. Skowron had the power that the Bombers wanted to add to their lineup and he hit for average as well. But it was Power who led the league in hitting in 1953 with a .349 batting average and in hits with 217. In addition, he hit 16 homers, one more than Skowron.

There was mounting pressure on the Yankees to add a black player. The Brooklyn Dodgers and New York Giants had been integrated for years. Special-interest groups were picketing Yankee Stadium, demanding racial equality for Power. Despite the numbers Power put up in Kansas City, the Yankees were unfazed. "My information is that Elston Howard, Negro outfielder with Kansas City, has a better chance to come up than Power," said Yankees president Dan Topping. "Our scouting reports rate Power a good hitter, but a poor fielder."[7] Topping also said Blues manager Harry Craft had benched Power for lack of hustle.[8]

General manager George Weiss was more direct—and prejudiced—in his views: "Maybe he can play, but not for us. He's impudent and he goes for white women. Power is not the Yankee type. The truth is that our box-seat customers from Westchester County don't want to sit with a lot of colored fans from Harlem."[9]

Fan expectations had been building to see Power play in New York. But management found a way to discredit Vic. They planted a story with New York sportswriter Dan Daniel, who wrote, "Power is major-league material right up to his Adam's apple. North of that location he is not extraordinary. He is said to be not too quick on the trigger mentally."[10]

There was little racial prejudice in Puerto Rico, and Power did not realize the extent of the bigotry

he faced in the United States. "Here we were all together," he said of his native Puerto Rico. "We went to school together. We danced together. A lot of black Puerto Ricans marry white woman. When I got there—the States—I didn't know what to do."[11] Power often used sarcastic humor to defuse a racial situation. "They say they didn't call me up because I was going out with white women, "said Power. "I told them 'Jeez, I didn't know white women were that bad. If I knew that, I wouldn't go out with them.'"[12]

Power was flashy on the field, making one-handed grabs and often making a sweeping motion with his glove, which looked to some fans like grandstanding. "They called me a showboat, but it was just the way I did it," he said. "I told them, 'The guys who invented the game, if they wanted you to catch with two hands they would have given you two gloves, and I only had one glove.'"[13] While at the plate, the right-handed hitting Power would swing the bat in his left hand, pendulum-style, awaiting the pitch. It was another trademark of Power's that caused people to call him a "showboat" or a "hot dog."

The Yankees purchased the contracts of Power and Howard in October 1953. But on December 16 Power was dealt as part of an 11-player swap with the Philadelphia Athletics. In 1955 the more reserved and conservative Howard became the first African American player to wear Yankee pinstripes.

Power settled in as a rookie for the Athletics in 1954. As black players did then, he faced discrimination during spring training in Florida. He and the other black player on the Athletics, Bob Trice, were forced to bunk down about two miles from the training facility. They were not allowed to ride in taxis, so they walked to and from camp every day. Power played in 127 games, mostly in the outfield. His average for the season was a career-low .255. "The moment I came to Philadelphia they took my bat away from me," Power said. "Wally Moses, the batting coach, told me the bat (36 ounces) I was using was too heavy."[14]

If New York was considered an American League oasis, Philadelphia was the dregs. Since 1940 the A's had finished in last place seven times, and they posted losing records two other years. They were a far cry from Connie Mack's dominant teams of the late 1920s and early 1930s. The team was in financial straits, and Shibe Park was a slightly shabby old stadium in a rundown neighborhood. Visitors had to contend with old facilities, poor transportation, and bad parking. The other franchise owners in the American League griped about the low gate receipts when their teams visited Philadelphia. The once-downtrodden Phillies had won the pennant in the National League in 1950. They established themselves as the people's choice in the City of Brotherly Love.

After the 1954 season, the Mack family sold the team to Arnold Johnson, a businessman from Chicago. A year earlier Johnson had purchased Yankee Stadium and Blues Stadium in Kansas City. Knowing that the Athletics could not compete with the Phillies in Philadelphia, Johnson gained league approval to move the franchise to Kansas City.

The switch of scenery did not improve the Athletics' performance; they continued to finish in the bottom half of the American League standings year after year. Manager Eddie Joost and his coaches, including Moses, were let go. Lou Boudreau took over the reins, attempting to change the A's losing ways. He installed Power as the everyday first baseman. Power responded by leading the league peers in putouts (1,281), assists (130), and double plays (140) in 1955. He picked up his old 36-ounce war club and hit .319, second in the league only to Al Kaline of Detroit (.340). Power got the first of his seven selections to the All-Star Game. He went hitless as a pinch-hitter.

"Vic never lacked confidence," said Kansas City catcher Joe Astroth. "He knew he could play the ball and he knew he could hit the ball. He always had a favorite expression when he'd go up to hit in spring training. He would look out there with that big bat and the way he'd swing and in his Spanish accent he would say 'Hey peecher, I have a 'prise' for you. I'm going to get a heet.'"[15]

"Right now, he is the best-fielding right-handed first baseman in the league," said Boudreau, "and within the next two years, if he continues to show progress, I will take him over any first baseman, right-handed or left."[16]

Because of team owner Johnson's connection to the Yankees, the Athletics soon became a dumping ground for New York. The Bombers would trade players past their prime—or players who would never have a prime—and cherry-pick top talent from the Athletics. In spite of Boudreau's fondness for Power, that did not stop the A's from acquiring first sackers, notably from the Yankees. In 1956 they picked up an aging Eddie Robinson, who had been in the 11-player trade two years earlier. Robinson started 47 games after the midseason swap, and Power moved to second base. He hit .309. The next season, Robinson departed and the Athletics picked up Irv Noren from New York.

On December 19, 1956, Power married the former Idalia Albarado. The couple had three sons, Jerry, Eddie, and Dennis.

Although Power's batting average slipped to .259 in 1957, he showed that he could play first base with few equals. He had a 69-game errorless streak. For the season he made only two errors and led the league's first basemen in assists with 99, and in fielding percentage, at .998.

Boudreau was fired during the 1957 season and replaced by Harry Craft, Power's skipper at Syracuse. Power had the reputation of being a clubhouse lawyer, a malcontent. But Boudreau and Craft, while agreeing that Power could be temperamental, also thought him an ideal teammate.

Cleveland general manager Frank Lane coveted Power. Lane, who made trades at a dizzying pace, talked at length with Kansas City about acquiring Power and outfielder Woodie Held. At first Lane offered Rocky Colavito, but soon settled on Roger Maris. Maris was one of the brightest prospects in the majors, but Lane chose to keep Colavito. Lane packaged pitcher Dick Tomanek and infielder Preston Ward with Maris. The trade was well received by Indians manager Bobby Bragan. "We're building the type of club we want," he said. "A player like Power can hit-and-run and steal a base. Maris has the potential to be a star. Power is one already."[17] Power was looking forward to the address change, as Kansas City was still a segregated city. He felt Cleveland would be a better fit for him, both personally and professionally.

But not everybody was on board with the trade. Tribe pitcher Mudcat Grant, who later would become friends with Power, commented "That was a bad deal for us, because Roger was better than both players we got for him. The guy was a star!"[18]

At the time of the deal, Power was hitting .302, and was in the midst of a 22-game hitting streak, that season's best in the major leagues. Cleveland manager Joe Gordon, who replaced Bragan 11 days after the trade, used Vic all over the infield. Power fielded all of his positions at a .992 clip, committing only six errors on his way to claiming the first of seven straight Gold Gloves.

Cleveland infielder Billy Moran recalled of Power: "Nobody could play first base better. He was also an offensive threat. He hit to all fields and always made

contact. He had a big old bat. Vic was a smiling jovial person and didn't cause trouble in the clubhouse."[19]

Power was right about the move to Cleveland being better professionally. In 1959 the Indians were in the thick of the pennant race with Chicago and New York. But they dropped a crucial four-game set at home to the White Sox in late August. They never recovered, finishing in second place, five games out of first. When second baseman Billy Martin was struck in the face with a pitch in August, Power took his place at the keystone position and performed well.

Power was a likeable sort of fellow who liked to laugh, but could show a temper as well. He told a story about playing second base, and gaining the respect of Maris. "I was playing second and Maris slid very hard with his spikes high and caught me in the ribs. I warned him that the next time he slid like that I was going to give him an eye for an eye. I had seen how Jackie Robinson would jump over a sliding runner and land on top of him with his spikes, and that's what I had planned for Maris. And the next time he slid hard into the base, I jumped into the air. But he slid past the base and I realized that I was about to come down directly on his face. It would have looked like an accident if I came straight down, but I quickly split my legs and landed with my spikes on both sides of his face. I didn't hurt him, but I did teach him a lesson."[20]

Mudcat Grant recalled a time when Power took his frustrations out on his glove. "I remember once when he missed a popup down the right-field line. After the game, he took his glove into the clubhouse and cut it into little bitty pieces. He said, 'I don't need that glove anymore.'"[21]

The Indians had a new manager in 1962, Mel McGaha, who told Power that he intended to platoon him at first base with Tito Francona. Francona was a left-handed hitter who played the outfield for most of his career. He also fielded left-handed, which is considered a necessity by some managers. Power thought that McGaha was surely joking because Francona was certainly not the fielder or the hitter that Power was. Power suspected he might be traded, because he was too good to sit on the bench. But just before the start of the season, he and pitcher Dick Stigman were dealt to Minnesota for pitcher Pedro Ramos. Minnesota manager Sam Mele was pleased with his new first baseman. "In one of the first games he played for us," said Mele, "there were runners on first and third and somebody hit a shot to him and he had to dive for it. He got up on his knees, looked home, decided he couldn't make it there, and still on his knees, threw to second for the force. There isn't another guy in the business who wouldn't have gone for the sure play at first base. But he never does."[22]

Power played perhaps the deepest first base of any of his counterparts. He often liked to have the other infielders throw the ball to the base, rather than to him. He defied the conventional way of arriving at the bag and straddling it before the ball was thrown. Some of the younger Twins infielders, like third baseman Rich Rollins, would pump and pump, hesitating to throw the ball to an empty base. After the season, Rollins told Power, "You must've saved me 25 errors this season." The good-natured Power responded to the young third sacker, "That's OK. Next year, you give me half your pay."[23]

In 1964 Power was traded twice. On July 11 he was moved to the California Angels as part of a three-team deal with Los Angeles and Cleveland. On September 9 the Angels traded him to the Phillies. First baseman Frank Thomas had broken his thumb, and the team was looking for a veteran first baseman to platoon with the left-handed hitting John Herrnstein. Thus Power was able to witness first-hand the biggest meltdown in professional sports at that time. On September 20 the Phillies were sailing along with a 6½-game lead over Cincinnati and St. Louis. But they dropped the next 10 games, and finished the season tied for second place, one game back of the pennant-winning Cardinals. Years later Power was asked what he thought was the reason for the Phillies' collapse. "I think Gene Mauch panicked down the stretch," he said.[24] Between September 10 and October 4, Power made 11 starts at first base for the Phillies and also played in seven other games. He hit .208 (10-for-48).

In the offseason the Phillies sold Power back to the Angels. In 1965 he hit .259 as a part-timer, and then retired as a player. In 12 seasons, he finished with a .284 batting average, 126 home runs, and 658 RBIs. His career fielding percentage at first base was .994.

In retirement, Power scouted in Puerto Rico for the Angels. He also set up baseball clinics for youngsters. He continued to manage Caguas of the Puerto Rican Baseball League, extending a long relationship he had with the team, first as a player and then for years as a manager.

In 2001, while the Cleveland Indians were celebrating their centennial, a panel of baseball writers, executives, and historians chose the team's 100 greatest players. Power was one of nine first basemen selected.

Power died on November 29, 2005, in Bayamon, Puerto Rico, after a long bout with cancer.

Major-league first baseman Willie Montañez, who hailed from Catano, Puerto Rico, played 18 seasons in winter ball, mostly for Caguas. "Whatever I learned about playing first base came from Vic Power," Montañez said. "He is the person I am in debt for all he did—fielding tips, hitting left-handers, confidence factor."[25]

Contemporaries also admired the flashy first baseman. "Power plays 15 feet farther back than me or anyone else and takes the throw on the dead run," said Moose Skowron right after Power died. "He can do it because his reflexes are so great and because he has the best glove hand in baseball."[26]

## SOURCES

In addition to the sources cited in the Notes, the author also consulted Retrosheet, cleveland.indians.mlb.com/index.jsp?c_id=cle, and minors.sabrwebs.com/cgi-bin/index.php.

## NOTES

1 *Cleveland Press*, August 5, 1958.
2 Ibid.
3 Ibid.
4 Ibid.
5 Peter C. Bjarkman, *Baseball With a Latin Beat: A History of the Latin-American Game* (Jefferson, North Carolina: McFarland, 1994), 95.
6 Peter C. Bjarkman, *Ragtyme Sports*, May 1955, an article with material from *Baseball With a Latin Beat*.
7 *The Sporting News*, August 15, 1953: 4.
8 Ibid.
9 Roger Kahn, *The Era 1947-57* (Boston: Houghton Mifflin Company, 1993), 45.
10 David Halberstam, *Summer of '49*. (New York: William Morrow & Company, 1989), 183-184.
11 David Maraniss, *Clemente*. (New York: Simon & Schuster, 2006), 33-35.
12 Ibid.
13 Hall of Fame Archives, Vic Power player file.
14 Rich Marazzi and Les Fiorito, *Baseball Players of the 1950's* (Jefferson, North Carolina: McFarland, 2004), 311-312.
15 John Peterson, *The Kansas City Athletics: A Baseball History* (Jefferson, North Carolina: McFarland, 2003), 56.
16 *Baseball Digest*, July 1955: 25.
17 *Cleveland Plain Dealer*, June 15, 1958.
18 Tom Calvin and Danny Peary, *Roger Maris: Baseball's Reluctant Hero* (New York: Simon & Schuster, 2010), 97.

19 Danny Peary, *We Played the Game* (New York: Black Dog and Leventhal Publishers, 1994), 407.

20 Calvin and Peary, 101.

21 Douglas Grow, *We're Gonna Win Twins* (Minneapolis: University of Minnesota Press, 2010), 18.

22 Hall of Fame Archives, Vic Power player file.

23 Ibid.

24 Ibid.

25 Thomas Van Hyning, *Puerto Rico's Winter League: A History of Major League's Launching Pad* (Jefferson, North Carolina: McFarland, 2004), 103.

26 *New York Times*, November 30, 2005.

# JIM RIVERA

## By Richard Smiley

**S**PEEDY OUTFIELDER JIM RIVERA was one of the great characters of 1950s baseball. As Chicago White Sox general manager Ed Short put it, "Jungle Jim may not have the fattest average in baseball, but he gives the fans a show with his daredevil running and sliding, his terrific fielding, and clutch hitting."[1] His all-out style made him one of the most popular White Sox, despite his troubled — and sometimes troubling — history.

Manuel Joseph Rivera was born in New York City on July 22, 1921 to a family of six brothers and five sisters.[2] Of Puerto Rican heritage, he was raised near 112th and Madison in the impoverished section of Manhattan known as Spanish Harlem.[3] He lived there until his mother died when he was 6 years old.[4] With his father unable to care for everyone in the family, he was sent to an orphanage in Blauvelt, New York, about 15 miles up the Hudson from the city, run by a congregation of Dominican sisters. He lived at Saint Dominic's for the next 10 years while he received formal education and learned to play various sports, including baseball.[5]

After he turned 16, Rivera returned home to live with his remarried father. With the family on relief, Rivera took various jobs to support them. Construction work helped build his strength, and he joined other friends from the neighborhood in learning how to box.[6] By the time he was 17, he started fighting amateur bouts around New York City along with St. Dominic's classmate Jim Dorso. Since he was constantly hanging around with Dorso, others began calling Rivera "Jim," a name that would stay with him for the rest of his life.[7] During this time he was still playing baseball. He became good enough to join a semipro team representing the Valencia Bakery, and left the world of amateur boxing.[8]

Rivera resumed boxing after joining the Army Air Corps in August 1942, and captured the light-heavyweight title of his outfit in the Third Air Force at Camp Barkley, Texas.[9] He played baseball on the camp team. In the spring of 1944, his life was thrown into turmoil. He was charged with raping and assaulting the daughter of an Army officer after a dance at Barksdale Field, Louisiana. After a medical examination of the accuser, the charge was reduced to attempted rape. Rivera was found guilty and sentenced to life imprisonment. After serving five years in the Atlanta Federal Penitentiary, he was paroled in 1949.[10]

Rivera played baseball on the prison team. His success in games against local teams outside the prison caught the attention of Atlanta Crackers owner Earl Mann. Mann worked with authorities to secure a parole for Rivera. When he was released in March 1949, a contract with the Crackers was waiting for him.[11] Atlanta farmed Rivera out to Class-D Gainesville, where the 27-year-old, 6-foot, 198-pound left-handed outfielder hit .335, stole 55 bases, and scored 142 runs, leading the G-Men to the Florida State League pennant.[12] Promoted to Class-B Pensacola the next year, he hit .338, scored 139 runs, and drove in 135 to spark the Fliers to the Southeastern League pennant.[13]

In the 1950 offseason, Rivera played for the Caguas team in the Puerto Rican winter league. He began to slide head-first into bases, a style that became a trademark during his major-league career. Rogers Hornsby, who was managing an opposing team in the league, took an immediate liking to him and provided the player with advice and coaching. Hornsby would soon refer to Rivera as "the only man I would pay admission to see."[14]

When Hornsby was named manager of the Seattle club in the Pacific Coast League for 1951, he approached Rivera about joining him. Seattle bought him from Pensacola for $2,500.[15] Rivera enjoyed his finest professional season in Seattle, collecting 231 hits, scoring 135 runs, hitting a league-leading .352, and leading the Rainiers to the pennant — his third

in three professional seasons. His speed and dazzling play garnered him the league's MVP award.¹⁶ One reporter said, "He runs in the outfield like a deer, on the bases like an express train, and he throws like a rifle."¹⁷ His exceptional play caught the attention of major-league clubs. In July the White Sox exercised their option to purchase his contract for $65,000, instructing him to report at the end of the PCL season.¹⁸

In the fall of 1951, Hornsby was named manager of Bill Veeck's St. Louis Browns. Hornsby urged Veeck to acquire Rivera.¹⁹ Veeck sent catcher Sherman Lollar to Chicago in a three-team, eight-player deal that brought Rivera to the Browns.²⁰ But the deal caused a stir in St. Louis. Local civic and religious groups began a campaign to have Rivera dismissed from the Browns roster and banned from baseball. In response to the pressure, Commissioner Ford Frick stated, "If the purpose is punishment, then he has already been punished. If the purpose is cure or improvement, then this man has a greater chance to make good being allowed to live as others live. Since Rivera came into baseball his conduct has been beyond question. If in the future he shows that he has not profited by his experience, this office will take action."²¹

Although there were high hopes for Rivera and the rookie-laden Browns in 1952, neither started the season well. Rivera did collect a hit in his major-league debut on Opening Day in Detroit, but he fell into a slump. By the start of May he was on the bench. On May 8 he came into a game in Philadelphia as a defensive substitute, made a sensational catch and hit a ninth-inning home run to win the game for the Browns.²² That put him back in the lineup, although the team's fortunes did not improve. Hornsby, under constant criticism for continuing to play the slumping rookies, was fired in mid-June.²³ Rivera soon followed him, traded back to the White Sox at the end of July.²⁴

Rivera's White Sox debut on July 29, 1952, was a memorable one. In front of a crowd of nearly 39,000, he started in center field and picked up hits in his first two at-bats, helping the Sox build a 7-0 lead over the New York Yankees. The Yankees came back to win that game on Mickey Mantle's ninth-inning grand slam. Rivera homered the next day to lead the White Sox to a win over the Bronx Bombers.²⁵ Soon his speed on the bases and acrobatic catches made him a fan favorite. Big Jim, as he liked to be called, finished the year with a .253 average, but the 13 stolen bases he collected in two months with the White Sox showed signs of promise.

On the last day of the season, Rivera was arrested in the White Sox clubhouse on charges that he had raped the wife of a soldier.²⁶ He contended that the relationship was consensual, and took a lie detector test. After he passed, a Chicago grand jury declined to indict him.²⁷ Commissioner Frick placed him on "indefinite probation." Frick put full responsibility for Rivera's future behavior on the White Sox, and prohibited the team from trading or selling him for a year.²⁸ This generated more controversy in the press from those who opposed and those who supported his right to play.

Rivera responded by enjoying his finest years in the majors.²⁹ In 1953 he played center field in almost every game and reached double figures in doubles, triples, and home runs. His 16 triples led the American League while his 22 stolen bases trailed only his outfield teammate Minnie Minoso. His efforts helped the White Sox win 89 games, their best record in more than 30 years. Both the White Sox and Rivera did even better in 1954, as the team won 94 games and Rivera hit a career-high .286. He continued to dazzle in the field and on the bases, but was now patrolling right field with Johnny Groth in center. During this year Rivera's habit of flapping his arms to wave his fellow fielders off fly balls led *Chicago Sun-Times* sportswriter John Hoffman to call him Jungle Jim.[30] The nickname quickly became popular and has stayed with him.

In 1955, Rivera led the American League with 25 stolen bases, but his average dropped to .264 as a pronounced hitch in his swing took its toll.[31] The White Sox participated in their first real pennant race in 35 years and were not eliminated until late September. In an effort to become more competitive in 1956, the team swung an offseason deal for slugging outfielder Larry Doby.[32] Deals in May brought veteran outfielders Jim Delsing and Dave Philley.[33] Rivera's playing time was reduced as his average fell to .255.

After the season ended, Rivera married his second wife, Phyllis Crain of Angola, Indiana.[34] This time was the peak of his popularity in Chicago. Sportswriters could always count on him for a good quote or funny story, and he was in constant demand for personal appearances.[35] An avid filmgoer, Rivera would sometimes take in two movies in a day before a night game and developed the reputation as the team's "film critic."[36] Rumors of potential trades never came true, as he was deemed too popular to move.

When the White Sox acquired even more outfielders, Jungle Jim opened the 1957 season at first base, but was shifted back to right field in June after the Sox acquired veteran first baseman Earl Torgeson.[37] Rivera shared the outfield job with rookie Jim Landis, and his 14 home runs tied for the team lead with Larry Doby. In 1958 Rivera competed for playing time with Don Mueller, Tito Francona, and Bubba Phillips as his average plummeted to .225. His days as a regular had ended, and he began the transformation into a solid bench player.[38]

Rivera contributed on the field to the 1959 White Sox pennant-winning team as a late-inning outfielder, pinch-runner, platoon starter, and pinch-hitter. He contributed off the field with his great enthusiasm for the game and energy. He was praised for staying in excellent shape despite being used sparingly, and for being "the first man in uniform before every game."[39]

Rivera's second at-bat of the season, on April 17, produced a victory over the Detroit Tigers as his two-run double in the eighth inning broke a 4-4 tie.[40] Later in the month, he was inserted into the starting lineup for a few games to spell the slumping Johnny Callison.[41] He suffered a broken rib making a tumbling catch in a game against the Yankees and went on the disabled list.[42]

When he came back toward the end of May, Rivera returned to the bench.[43] He made the most of a spot start in a June 7 doubleheader against the Boston Red Sox, contributing a pair of hits in each game.[44] He started in right field for the rest of the month, but a batting slump reduced him to a platoon role.[45] He pulled a muscle on July 5, and went back to the bench when he recovered.[46] Rivera replaced the injured Jim McAnany on August 21, and his leaping catch against the right-field wall preserved a close victory over Washington.[47] He platooned with McAnany for the rest of the season.

On the evening of September 22, the White Sox took on the Cleveland Indians in Cleveland with the opportunity to clinch the pennant. Since right-hander Jim Perry was starting for the Tribe, Rivera was in the lineup. The Sox took an early 2-0 lead, but the Indians battled back for a run in the bottom of the fifth. Mudcat Grant relieved Perry in the top of the sixth and surrendered a one-out home run to Al Smith. Rivera followed with a home run to right-center. The lead held up as the White Sox earned their first title in 40 years.[48] Rivera called the homer in the pennant-clinching game his best moment in baseball.[49]

Rivera continued platooning with McAnany in the World Series, starting games One, Three, and

Four while going 0-for-11 at the plate. He made his most memorable impact in a game he did not start. After the Los Angeles Dodgers had gained a three-games-to-one Series lead, left-hander Sandy Koufax pitched Game Five in front of a record crowd in the Los Angeles Coliseum. The White Sox squeaked out a run in the top of the fourth inning on a double play, but the Dodgers constantly threatened to come back against Chicago's Bob Shaw. After two runners reached base in the bottom of the seventh with two outs and the hot-hitting Charlie Neal coming up, White Sox manager Al López inserted Rivera in right field. The move proved prescient as Neal laced a drive toward right-center that looked certain to clear the bases. Rivera raced back and made an over-the-shoulder catch at the fence to preserve the 1-0 lead and the game.[50]

In 1960 Minnie Minoso returned to the White Sox and Rivera's role was reduced to that of a late-inning defensive replacement and pinch-runner.[51] Although he appeared in 48 games, he started only once and collected a mere 17 at-bats. The following year Rivera again made the White Sox as a reserve, but he fractured his thumb in his first pinch-running assignment while sliding head-first into third.[52] That slide proved to be Rivera's last play with the Sox; upon his return from the disabled list in June he was released.[53] He was picked up by the Kansas City Athletics, who expressed plans to use him as a "general all-around utility man."[54] He actually ended up back in a platoon role, playing mostly right field and finishing 1961 with a .241 batting average. When the Athletics released him at the end of the year his major-league career was over.[55]

After the season, Rivera managed in the Puerto Rican League and signed with the Indianapolis Indians of the American Association to be a player-coach.[56] His stint with the Indians did not last long. By July he was back with Seattle in the Pacific Coast League.[57] He stayed with the Rainiers through June 1963, when he was given his unconditional release. At the time he was batting .259 with two homers.[58] It was the end of his professional baseball career in the US, but he still wasn't done; signing with the Mexico City Tigres of the Mexican League, he finished the 1963 season south of the border and then played in 87 games for the Mexican League Jalisco Charros in 1964 before finally retiring for good.

Residing in his wife's hometown of Angola, Indiana, Rivera bought a restaurant on Crooked Lake known as the Captain's Cabin.[59] There he reigned as proprietor for over 20 years, regaling customers with stories of days past until he retired to Port Charlotte, Florida, in 1990.[60] He remained loyal to the White Sox, and could always be counted on to make appearances in old timers' games and social events.[61] When Bill Veeck announced plans to have his team wear short pants during the 1976 season, Jungle Jim was there to model them.[62] When the White Sox brought out members of the 1959 World Series team before Game One of the 2005 World Series, Jungle Jim was on the field.[63]

## NOTES

1  David Eskenazi, "Wayback Machine: Rajah, Rivera, '51 Rainiers," *SportsPressNW.com*, March 27, 2012.

2  There has been some confusion about Jim Rivera's year of birth. The date of birth appearing in many 1950's articles, baseball cards, and press releases — July 22, 1923 — does not match the date of birth Rivera told to friends and personally gave on questionnaires returned to the White Sox — July 22, 1921. Turkin & Thompson's 1963 version of the *Encyclopedia of Baseball* and subsequent versions of that book show the date as July 22, 1922. The current standard references (such as Baseball-reference.com) give the date as July 22, 1921 and that is what is used here. David Condon made sport of the two-year discrepancy in his *Chicago Tribune* "In the Wake of the News" column printed on June 13, 1963.

3  Milton Gross, "The Jim Rivera Story," *Sport*, June 1952: 17.

4  Bob Vanderberg, *Sox, from Lane and Fain to Zisk and Fisk* (Chicago: Chicago Review Press, 1982), 156.

5  Gross, 74.

6  Gross, 74.

7  Warren Brown, "Jim Rivera Talking …," *Sport*, October 1955: 21.

8  Brown, 34.

9  Gross, 74.

10  Gross, 74-75.

11  Gross, 75.

12  Joe Halberstein, "Jim Rivera recalls G-Men playing days in '49," *Gainesville Daily Sun*, August 11, 1957;

13 Vanderberg, 158.

14 Harry Grayson, "Sport City," *Portsmouth Herald*, August 30, 1955.

15 Eskenazi.

16 Steve Krevisky presentation at SABR 36 in Seattle, Washington, 2006: "Jungle Jim Leads the Way! The Saga of the 1951 PCL Champs, The Seattle Rainiers;" Perpetual Motion Pictures video: *The Seattle Rainiers*, 2006.

17 Eskenazi.

18 Vanderberg, 158.

19 Vanderberg, 158.

20 Irving Vaughan, "Sox Get Lollar, Widmar, and Dente," *Chicago Tribune*, November 28, 1951: C1-C2.

21 Eskenazi.

22 "Rivera Stars as Browns Top Athletics, 9-8," *Chicago Tribune*, May 9, 1952: C3.

23 "Hornsby Fired; Marion Manages Browns," *Chicago Tribune*, June 11, 1952: B1, B3.

24 Irving Vaughan, "White Sox Get Rivera—Again," July 29, 1952: B1.

25 Vanderberg, page 159.

26 "Arrest Jim Rivera, Sox Center Fielder, on Rape Complaint," *Chicago Tribune*, September 29, 1952: 6; "White Sox's Rivera Charged with Rape of Soldier's Wife," *Chicago Tribune*, September 30, 1952: 5.

27 "Jury Refuses to Indict Rivera on Rape Charge," *Chicago Tribune*, October 15, 1952: 4; Vanderberg, 159.

28 "Sox's Rivera Draws Indefinite Probation," *Chicago Tribune*, November 13, 1952: d1.

29 Edward Prell, "That amazing Sox Outfield!" *Chicago Tribune*, September 11, 1955: k27.

30 Brown, 21.

31 Vanderberg, 160.

32 Edward Prell, "Sox Trade Carrasquel, Busby for Doby," *Chicago Tribune*, October 26, 1955: C1, C4.

33 "Trade Winds Blow," *Chicago Tribune*, May 16, 1956: C1, C3; Edward Prell, "Sox Trade Kell, 3 Others for 2 Orioles," *Chicago Tribune*, May 22, 1956: C1, 2.

34 "Sox's Rivera Takes Indiana Girl as Bride," *Chicago Tribune*, October 13, 1956: B3.

35 Brown, 87.

36 Brown, 85-86.

37 "White Sox Get Torgeson for Philley, Cash," *Chicago Tribune*, June 14, 1957: C2.

38 Edward Prell, "White Sox Figures Prove Left Is Right—Sometimes," *Chicago Tribune*, November 20, 1957: C2; Edward Prell, "White Sox Train New Guns on Yank Dynasty," *Chicago Tribune*, February 11, 1958: b2.

39 Richard Dozer, "Sox Opener in Boston Called Off by Rain," *Chicago Tribune*, June 20, 1959: A4.

40 Richard Dozer, "Cubs Win, 9 TO 4; Sox Beat Tigers, 6 TO 5," *Chicago Tribune*, April 18, 1959: E1, 2.

41 "Jim Rivera to Move Into Sox Lineup," *Chicago Tribune*, April 19, 1959: A7.

42 "Batting Drill Pitch Puts Mantle Out," *Chicago Tribune*, May 1, 1959: E6; "Sox Get Ennis from Reds for Rudolph," *Chicago Tribune*, May 2, 1959: A2.

43 Richard Dozer, "Sox Win, 2-1; Cards Beat Cubs in 14th, 3-1," *Chicago Tribune*, May 23, 1959: A1, 2; Baseball-reference.com.

44 Richard Dozer, "Beat Boston, 9-4 in 1st; Drop 2d, 4-2," *Chicago Tribune*, June 8, 1959: C1, C4.

45 http://www.baseball-reference.com/players/gl.fcgi?id=riverji01&t=b&year=1959

46 Richard Dozer, "Nellie, Luis Click Again; Smith, too!" *Chicago Tribune*, July 6, 1959: C1, C5.

47 Edward Prell, "White Sox Win Again by One Run, 5-4!" *Chicago Tribune*, August 22, 1959: 1-2; Vanderberg, 160-161.

48 Edward Prell, "White Sox Win Pennant!" *Chicago Tribune*, September 23, 1959: 1-2; Vanderberg, 161.

49 Joe Goddard, "What's Up with Jim Rivera," *Chicago Sun-Times*, August 18, 2002: 98.

50 Edward Prell, "Sox Win; Final at Home," *Chicago Tribune*, October 7, 1959: 1-2; "Alston Lauds López for Rivera Switch," *Chicago Tribune*, October 7, 1959: E13; Vanderberg, 161.

51 Edward Prell, "Sox Acquire Minoso Again; Cubs Get Frank Thomas," *Chicago Tribune*, December 7, 1959: E1; Edward Prell, "Sox Chorus: 'I'm Growing Old'," *Chicago Tribune*, February 24, 1960: C1, 2.

52 "Jim Rivera Is Placed on Disabled List," *Chicago Tribune*, April 24, 1961: C4.

53 "Sox Release Rivera with 'Reluctance'," *Chicago Tribune*, June 7, 1961: C1; David Condon, "In the Wake of the News," *Chicago Tribune*, June 9, 1961: C1.

54 "Rivera Flies to New York, Signs with A's," *Chicago Tribune*, June 10, 1961: C2.

55 Vanderberg, 161.

56 "Joe Horlen, Sox Hurler, OK's Terms," *Chicago Tribune*, January 16, 1962: C3; "Jim Rivera Indianapolis Player-Coach," *Chicago Tribune*, February 20, 1962: B3.

57 "Jim Rivera Returns to Coast League," *Chicago Tribune*, July 6, 1962: C5.

58 "Seattle Club Gives Release to Jim Rivera," *Chicago Tribune*, June 12, 1963: E3.

59 Robert Goldsborough, "Whatever happened?" *Chicago Tribune*, July 16, 1967: E2; Vanderberg, 154.

60 Joe Goddard, "What's Up with Jim Rivera," *Chicago Sun-Times*, August 18, 2002: 98.

61 Richard Dozer, "John Pitches 5-0 Shutout; Horlen Triumphs, 4-1," *Chicago Tribune*, August 1, 1966: C1, C4; David Condon, "In the Wake of the News," *Chicago Tribune*, June 27, 1969: C1; "'Old' Cubs, Sox Meet Today," *Chicago Tribune*, July 25, 1971: B2.

62 Bob Verdi, "Will sexy garb fit Sox knee-ds?" *Chicago Tribune*, March 10, 1976: E3; *Chicago Tribune*, David Condon, "Opinions flow from all sides on Sox outfits," *Chicago Tribune*, March 10, 1976: E3.

63 Melissa Isaacson, "Aparicio, teammates usher in the Series," *Chicago Tribune*, October 23, 2005: 17. An update in 2017: *After the World Series Rivera continued to show up for White Sox events. He came to SoxFest in 2009 where the author had the opportunity to briefly meet him and later that year participated in festivities surrounding the 50th Anniversary celebration of the White Sox 1959 AL Championship. According to David Hughes (a friend of Jim), he has lived in Fort Wayne, Indiana for the past 20 years while still spending winters in Port Charlotte.*

# IVÁN RODRÍGUEZ

## By Steve West

**C**OMING FROM THE DIRT FIELDS of Puerto Rico to the heights of the major leagues, Pudge Rodríguez had a long and storied career as perhaps the greatest all-round catcher ever. Revered by Texas Rangers fans for his decade in Arlington, he led the Florida Marlins to a World Series title and was instrumental in re-energizing the Detroit Tigers. With numerous major-league records to his name, he became just the second catcher to be inducted into the Hall of Fame on the first ballot.

Iván Rodríguez Torres was born on November 27, 1971, in Manati, Puerto Rico. His surname uses the traditional Spanish format, coming from his father, José Rodríguez, and his mother, Eva Torres. The younger of two sons, he grew up in nearby Vega Baja, where his mother taught elementary school and his father worked as an electrician for a construction company.

Iván and his brother, José Jr., played baseball as children in empty fields around town with a stick and a roll of balled-up tape,[1] then in Little League, where he played on the same team as future major leaguer Ricky Otero, and against future Texas Rangers teammate Juan Gonzalez. Iván started as a pitcher, then moved to third base, and finally to catcher. His father was an amateur catcher in Puerto Rico, and taught his son the position. "My father taught me how to throw when I was younger, and I've learned the rest of it the last couple of years," he said.[2] He watched baseball on television, and found a hero there: "Even before I started catching, my favorite player growing up was Johnny Bench. … He did everything well, and he wasn't all that big. So watching him gave me some hope that I might have a shot."[3]

Rodríguez played on Parcelas Amadeo, an empty block of land with a ballfield on it. Coached by Julio Pabon from age 5 until 13, he started catching when he was about 7, and both Pabon and his father took credit for the move to catcher. Pabon said it was because Rodríguez threw too hard and scared the other kids. "I threw seven no-hitters, two in one day," said Rodríguez.[4]

Discovered by scouts Luis Rosa and Manny Batista when he was in high school, Rodríguez attended a Rangers tryout camp run by Rosa in 1988. "Pudge was hard-nosed, even then," said Rosa. "He showed leadership at 16 that I'd seen in few kids. He knew where he was going."[5] At the tryout camp Rangers scouts put the radar gun on him and showed him throwing 93 mph from the plate to second base. At that point, Rangers scouting director Sandy Johnson made sure they signed Rodríguez before the day was over.

The Rangers decided that the 17-year-old Rodríguez would skip rookie ball, and sent him to Gastonia in the Class-A South Atlantic League in 1989. Rodríguez more than held his own, despite being one of the youngest players in the league. He hit only .238 but impressed with his catching and throwing and was named one of the top prospects in the league. In 1990 the Rangers promoted Rodríguez to Port Charlotte in the Florida State League. This time he hit .287, and again was named one of the best prospects in the league.[6]

In the minor leagues Rodríguez was given his nickname. "A coach from the minor leagues, his name is Chino Cadagia, he called me Pudge because, at that time, I was small and cocky—you know, like a strong and small guy—and he called me Pudgy. The name just stayed with me," Rodríguez said.[7]

Rodríguez worked with Benito Santiago in Puerto Rico in the offseason, learning all he could from the Padres catcher. "I go and work with him in Puerto Rico and he tells me about catching and playing in the big leagues," Rodríguez said.[8]

Promoted again in 1991, this time to Tulsa of the Double-A Texas League, Rodríguez brought his childhood girlfriend, Maribel Rivera, with him from Puerto Rico, having asked her to marry him over the winter. He once again dominated a league where he was one of the youngest players (19 years old), hitting .274 in 50 games and receiving significant attention for his fielding. Rodríguez and Maribel were supposed to be married in an on-field ceremony between games of a doubleheader in Tulsa on June 20, but their plans were derailed when Rangers catcher Geno Petralli was injured. The Rangers reached down to Double A to call up their top prospect on a Wednesday, the day before the wedding was scheduled. They rescheduled the wedding for Thursday morning, (in later years Rodríguez said they actually got married during spring training the following year), then the couple flew to Chicago where Rodríguez made his major-league debut that night.[9] In the game he threw out two runners, then got his first major-league hit in the ninth inning, driving in two runs. "I was a little nervous in the first inning, but I felt OK," he said. "I want to stay here. I don't want to go back to the minor leagues."[10] "He was a little nervous, a little jumpy. A lot more than he's going to be. He's going to be good," said Rangers manager Bobby Valentine.[11]

Rodríguez went on to hit in 10 of the 11 games on that first road trip, and then impressed Rangers fans in his first home game by getting four hits. It took a while for his first home run; it wasn't until August 30, more than two months after his call-up, that he hit one, off Storm Davis of the Kansas City Royals. Then he hit two more in the following week.

Rodríguez received a lot of attention for the rest of the season, being the youngest player in the major leagues in 1991. He finished fourth in voting for the Rookie of the Year, and opponents made numerous comments about how he appeared much more advanced than his age. Rangers coach Orlando Gomez said, "The best way to say it is, Iván was born to be a big leaguer."[12]

In 1992 Rodríguez continued to progress. "Give him time, he will be a superstar because he has all the tools," said Rangers first baseman Rafael Palmeiro.[13] By midseason he was being talked about for the All-Star Game. "I think he could make the All-Star Game this year with his defense alone," said manager Bobby Valentine.[14] However, in June Rodríguez was diagnosed with a stress fracture in his lower back, caused by overuse, and spent three weeks on the disabled list. Although the injury was caught early and doctors said it was not career-threatening, it continued to bother him for the rest of his career, causing further DL stints now and then. He was selected as a reserve for the American League in the All-Star Game, and entered the game in the sixth inning, becoming the fourth youngest player to ever appear in an All-Star Game. At the end of the season Rodríguez won his first Gold Glove, beginning a streak of 10 straight years winning the award.

In 1993 Rodríguez continued to make great strides in his game, and tied with Johnny Bench as the youngest starting catcher in All-Star Game history, both making their first start as an All-Star when they were 21 years, 7 months, and 16 days old. "Last year I made the team, but this year I get to be one of the first nine players to start. I'm excited about it," he said.[15] Rodríguez went on to help the American League win, 9-3, with an unusual hit. His line drive to left off John Burkett got stuck in a seam of the outfield wall padding, giving Rodríguez a ground-rule double, and he then came round to score the go-ahead run as the AL walked away with the game.

A few weeks later Rodríguez had a couple of weeks to remember: On Monday, July 26, he went 4-for-4 in the second game of a doubleheader. In the next game he also went 4-for-4, for eight straight hits, along with an intentional walk in the ninth inning. The following day he was struck in the face by the backswing of Royals batter Hubie Brooks, and broke his cheekbone. He had surgery the following day, and after being out for just four days, returned to the field. He ended his hitting streak with a groundout, then left the game in the sixth inning with dizziness. Back in the lineup a few days after that, he was behind the plate for a fight between Nolan Ryan and Robin Ventura, and admitted he was thinking about his cheek as he ran out to the mound for the fight.[16]

The rave reviews continued to come in, although Rodríguez tried to downplay things. "I want to be the best, but I don't like saying, 'I'm the best catcher,'" he said. "Other people can say it, but I am not going to say it because if I say it, I'll go backward and my career will go down."[17] On the other hand, Rangers general manager Tom Grieve said that Rodríguez had "met and gone beyond all the high expectations that everybody had for him."[18] A few years later Rangers manager Johnny Oates said, "He's probably the best thrower I've ever seen. He gets rid of the ball quick, throws it hard and accurate."[19] After a ball got away from Rodríguez one day and he still threw out the runner at second base, Oates said, "No other catcher can make that play."[20]

On July 28, 1994, Rodríguez caught Kenny Rogers' perfect game in Arlington, and homered in the game. Rodríguez had caught two no-hitters in the minor leagues, but this was on another level. He said, "I'd rather help a pitcher do something like that than hit a thousand home runs. To me, calling a great game and helping a pitcher be at his very best is what being a catcher is all about."[21]

Rodríguez occasionally talked about his religious faith, and attended his teams' chapel services every week. He also showed his faith on the field every day, which he said he had done since he was a child. He wore a medallion of Jesus under his shirt, and before every at-bat crossed himself and said a prayer. "I talk to Jesus. I always ask him to take of myself, to take care of my family. I never say, 'I want you to give this to me today,'" he said.[22]

Among other odd quirks, Rodríguez insisted on having a friend or family member accompany him on road trips to help chase away his boredom. "I like having someone to talk to," he said. His wife said he was obsessed with the game: "He watches ESPN when he comes home from the ballpark at night. Then he gets up in the morning, takes a shower and watches ESPN again."[23]

By the late 1990s Rodríguez was clearly the best catcher in the major leagues. "There's no question he's the top catcher of this era. … If he can duplicate what he's been doing for a long time, he will be in the Hall of Fame," said Bob Boone.[24] "He's the best all-round catcher I've seen since Johnny Bench," said

Dusty Baker.[25] Rodríguez had developed all around, in both hitting and fielding. "He used to be worried about nothing but throwing guys out stealing. Now he's worried about calling a good game for you, and he's worked hard at blocking pitches in the dirt. And he's still got that great throwing arm," said Rangers pitcher Bobby Witt.[26] "You can't go to sleep a minute out there when Rodríguez is behind the plate. If he doesn't hurt you with his bat, he'll hurt you with his arm," said Yankees manager Joe Torre.[27] In 1996 he got votes for MVP for the first time, as the Rangers went to the playoffs for their first time. "He's a great ballplayer, and I don't think we'll see another catcher like him in the next 10 years," said stats guru Bill James.[28]

In the spring of 1997 Rodríguez entered the last year of his contract with the Rangers. Negotiations during spring training didn't get far, and the sides agreed to talk again at the end of the season. The Rangers then approached Rodríguez in July to restart talks, in fear that they would lose him to free agency for just a draft pick at the end of the year. Rodríguez agreed to negotiate, and the two sides talked, but were far apart. On July 25 the Rangers made public a letter to Rodríguez's agent, Jeff Moorad, in which they offered more than $38 million over five years. Moorad, who was asking for $45 million for his client, said he thought revealing private talks was just trying to embarrass his client, and that they would table discussions over a new deal.[29] "I want to stay here. But it's got to be fair, a contract that I'm happy with and feel comfortable with," said Rodríguez.[30]

On July 29 the Rangers acquired catcher Jim Leyritz from the Angels, preparing for a rumored trade. However, on the morning of July 31, the trade deadline, Rodríguez took matters into his own hands. The Rangers had essentially agreed a deal with the Yankees, planning to send Rodríguez to New York for pitchers Eric Milton and Tony Armas Jr. and catcher Jorge Posada,[31] but the trade was off when Rodríguez himself walked into Rangers president Tom Schieffer's office and negotiated a new contract. The five-year, $42 million deal was midway between what the team had been offering and what Rodríguez had been asking for, but he wanted to stay in Texas. "He said he wanted to be a Texas Ranger his whole career and he wanted to see if he could work out a deal," said Schieffer. Rodríguez said his mother had told him to talk to the Rangers and see if they could solve the impasse, and added, "My mom is right. He listened to me and we did it. … We are all happy."[32]

After that season Rodríguez played winter ball in Puerto Rico, as he had done for several years. Now that the Rangers had given him a large contract, they were not happy that he was risking himself in winter ball. But he started hot in 1998, attributing it to the fact that he had the extra time in Puerto Rico and came into spring training in better condition, although manager Johnny Oates thought playing every winter in Puerto Rico would shorten Rodríguez's career.[33]

In 1998 Rodríguez became the first catcher to have three hits in the All-Star Game, and also played several games as the designated hitter; Oates wanted to keep his bat in the lineup even as he rested from his catching duties. As had happened previously though, Rodríguez had back spasms and was forced to miss some time late in the season.

In 1999 Rodríguez broke numerous records. His .332 batting average was the highest BA for an AL catcher since Bill Dickey in 1936. With 35 home runs (a new AL record for a catcher), 116 runs, and 113 RBIs, Rodríguez was the first AL catcher ever to go 30-100-100. He displayed his speed with 25 stolen bases, becoming the first catcher with 20 home runs and 20 steals in a season. Rodríguez also had a 20-game hitting streak from May 8 to June 1, the longest of his career. He ended the season with 199 hits, the highest total of his career, going 0-for-4 on the last day of the season.

On April 13 in Seattle, Rodríguez had a career day, driving in nine runs in a 15-6 win over the Mariners. He had a three-run home run in the first, a two-run single in the second and a grand slam in the third inning. Rodríguez had a shot at the major-league record of 12 RBIs in a game, but flied out with runners on first and second in the fifth inning, singled with the bases empty in the seventh, and was replaced in the eighth by Gregg Zaun, who came up with runners on first and second in the ninth. Asked if he was disappointed that manager Johnny Oates pulled him with a record in sight, Rodríguez said no. "I feel happy with the game I had. But I'm not looking for that. I'm just looking for wins for the team, and that's what we did."[34]

After batting .332 Rodríguez was named the 1999 American League Most Valuable Player, controversially edging out Pedro Martinez of the Boston Red Sox. Martinez had eight first-place votes to Rodríguez's seven, but Rodríguez finished with 252 points to Martinez's 239. Rodríguez was just the fifth player to win the MVP without getting the most first-place votes. Martinez had been left off the 10-player ballot by two voters who believed that a pitcher should not win the MVP award, and that probably cost him the points he needed to win. Rodríguez wasn't bothered by the commotion, just happy with his win: "That's the dream of every player, to get this award," he said.[35] "I felt confident that I had a shot to be MVP, and it came true. I'm so happy for it."[36]

In 2000 Rodríguez was having an even better season, but on July 24 everything came to a halt when he broke his thumb when it hit Mo Vaughn's bat as Rodríguez threw to second to try to get a runner. "As soon as it happened, my thumb went numb. There was swelling and I knew it was broken and I'd be out for the season," he said.[37] When he went down he was batting .347 with 27 home runs and 83 RBIs, on a pace to do far better than his MVP season the year before.

Rodríguez recovered for the 2001 season. The Rangers opened the season against the Toronto Blue Jays in Puerto Rico, taking Rodríguez to his homeland to play. A couple of days before the opener he hit two home runs in an exhibition game against the Blue Jays. He then took several people to his hometown, Vega Baja, where he broke ground for a baseball academy he was building. He went to the field he used to play on as a kid, and told Rangers GM Doug Melvin "This is where I'm from. Right here."[38]

But again Rodríguez missed the end of the season when tendinitis in his knee required surgery in September. He was unable to work out properly over the winter, and his weight increased. Partly due to that, a herniated disc kept him out almost two months between April and June of 2002. In that time Rodríguez dropped from 232 pounds to 208, suggesting that his extra weight may have been causing the back problems.

In June the Cincinnati Reds played in Arlington for the first time. In a ceremony before a game, Johnny Bench presented Rodríguez with his 10th Gold Glove, which tied Bench for the catcher record.

During the season the Rangers indicated that they intend to slash payroll after the season. They had signed Alex Rodríguez to the largest contract ever, and signed several other high-profile free agents in a push to make the postseason. There was speculation that Iván Rodríguez's time in Texas could be coming to an end. On December 7 the Rangers made it official, declining to offer him arbitration and making him a free agent, a decision that angered Rangers fans. "This was a very tough decision and certainly one that will be painful for the fans," said Rangers owner Tom Hicks.[39]

Rodríguez was unable to get a big contract because of his recent injury history. He finally signed a one-year, $10 million deal with the Florida Marlins for 2003, and was able to play in Miami, his adopted hometown. Rodríguez led the team to a world championship, providing veteran leadership for a team that wasn't expected to contend. "He's done a remarkable job with young pitchers and helping develop those pitchers, said Marlins manager Jack McKeon. "In the playoffs he just took over and took charge, showing the strong leadership that we knew he had."[40]

Rodríguez single-handedly won Game Three of the Division Series, his two-run home run in the first starting things off, and his game-winning two-run single in the 11th providing the 4-3 victory over San Francisco. Rodríguez got at least one hit in each of the four NLDS games, and famously held onto the ball for the final out at the end of Game Four as J.T. Snow tried to knock him down to score the tying run. Then he was named the MVP of the National League Championship Series after setting a record with 10 RBIs in the series as the Marlins beat the Chicago Cubs in seven games. "I'm very happy for my team. Nobody expected us to be in the World Series," he said.[41]

In Game One of the World Series, Rodríguez hit a sacrifice fly in the top of the first inning to give the Marlins a 1-0 lead and picked off a runner at third base as the Marlins defeated the Yankees 3-2. Years later he said, "I'm pretty sure that's my favorite play of my career. If I don't make that throw and nail Nick Johnson, maybe that run scores and we lose that game, and who knows what happens in that Series? But I got him. And that one felt so good."[42] The Yankees won Games Two and Three, but then the Marlins won three straight to win the Series in six games. After the final out in Yankee Stadium, Rodríguez went back out onto the field with his son and walked the bases, then knelt and prayed at home plate.

After the season Rodríguez told the Marlins he wanted a four-year, $40 million contract, but the team offered him a $2 million pay cut from his previous deal. Insulted that they wanted to cut his pay after the team had won the World Series, Rodríguez looked elsewhere. "It wasn't fair, that's for sure," he said. "I was just asking for the same amount of money I made last year, and they still said no."[43]

Although there was interest from several teams, Rodríguez was a 32-year-old catcher with more than 1,600 games played, and teams were wary of giving him a big deal. Still, on February 6, 2004, Rodríguez signed a four-year, $40 million contract with the Detroit Tigers. The team had won just 43 games the season before, the worst performance in its history, and owner Mike Ilitch was ready to start fresh. He and GM Dave Dombrowski met with Rodríguez and told him they wanted to build a team around him.

Tigers Hall of Famer Al Kaline was skeptical, saying, "There's no way you're going to get a superstar like that to come to Detroit right now." But Dombrowski had done his homework, even checking in with a psychologist to see how Rodríguez would feel going from a World Series team to the worst team in baseball. Reassured, he said that Rodríguez "was driven to be a complete player in handling the (pitching) staff and how important that had now become to him." And it showed in spring training, Rodríguez's work ethic impressing his manager right away. "He has taken the initiative, 'Here, follow me.' That's a beautiful thing," said skipper Alan Trammell.[44]

For his part, Rodríguez was optimistic. "Everybody asks me, 'Why Detroit?' And I say, 'Why not? Anything can happen.'"[45] Rodríguez hit .334 in 2004 and helped the Tigers improve in the standings by 29 games. More importantly, he helped to give the team a little respect, and slowly other big-name players came to Detroit, beginning the franchise's resurgence in the following decade.

In the winter of 2004 José Canseco released a book in which he claimed that he had injected Rodríguez and two other players, Rafael Palmeiro and Juan Gonzalez, with steroids, while they were teammates on the Rangers in the mid-1990s. All three players denied the accusation, with Rodríguez saying, "Some very serious comments were said that were not true. I didn't use any of that stuff. I don't need it."[46] A few years later he was asked if he was on the list of 104 players who had tested positive for steroids during the 2003 season, and replied, "Only God knows."[47]

Right after Canseco's book was released, Rodríguez came to spring training in 2005 having lost 22 pounds, which some attributed to his having stopping using steroids after Canseco's accusations. "I've been running a lot of sprints on the track and changed my program a little bit," Rodríguez said.[48] Others also defended him. Trammell said that Rodríguez had complained in 2004 about being too heavy and having a bothersome hip injury. Rodríguez also began doing 30-minute workouts after games, and changed his diet to avoid late-night meals.[49]

In 2005 both Rodríguez and the team took a step back, in part because Rodríguez was going through a divorce. Rodríguez's batting average fell 58 points and the Tigers wound up 71-91. Everything got better again in 2006, as the Tigers won 95 games on their way to capturing the pennant. During the season Rodríguez played first base (seven games) and second base (two innings, after a player was injured), the first time in the majors he had played somewhere other than catcher or designated hitter.

With the Tigers in the World Series, the surprising turnaround from being the worst team in baseball just three years before was credited to Rodríguez. "Signing Iván Rodríguez, without question, was huge for us because it represented the start of what we've done by coming back as an organization," said GM Dombrowski. "Whenever you can add a future Hall of Famer, it can only help you."[50] Said manager Jim Leyland, "Quite frankly, I think a lot of people thought I wouldn't get along with Pudge. But it's been totally opposite. He plays hurt, he plays hard, and he comes to beat the other team. That's a manager's dream."[51] This time, though, the Tigers lost the World Series, to the St. Louis Cardinals. "I was heartbroken—because we had such a good year," said Rodríguez. "We had the perfect group of players. But everything fell apart. I still think about that one all the time."[52]

In 2007 the Tigers stumbled again, not making the playoffs, and Rodríguez's production fell off some more, although he did catch his second no-hitter, by Justin Verlander against Milwaukee. But at the end of the season the Tigers exercised their contract option, bringing Rodríguez back for another year at $13 million.

After a moderately disappointing first half of 2008, the Tigers had Rodríguez sharing time at catcher with Brandon Inge. Then on July 30 they traded Rodríguez to the Yankees for pitcher Kyle Farnsworth. The Yankees had just lost catcher Jorge Posada to season-ending surgery, and needed a quick replacement, while the Tigers were desperate for bullpen help. "Guys like Pudge don't come around every day. He's the complete player," said Yankees manager Joe Girardi.[53]

When Rodríguez returned to Detroit a few weeks later with the Yankees, he received a standing ovation from Tigers fans. "It was great. It means that in the four years I was here, I did a good job and the fans appreciated that," he said.[54] However, his time with the Yankees was spent splitting the catching job with José Molina, and he hit just .219 for the rest of the season as the Yankees fell short of the playoffs. At the end of the season the Yankees let him go to free agency.

In the spring of 2009 Rodríguez was again looking for someone to play for, but this time he was a 37-year-old catcher with a lot of mileage. "I still feel I can play three or four more years, to be honest, because of the way I take care of myself."[55] He played in the World Baseball Classic for Puerto Rico in early March, in which he showcased himself well, going 10-for-20 with two home runs, then signed a one-year deal with the Houston Astros for $1.5 million, with another $1.5 million in performance bonuses.

On May 17 Rodríguez hit his 300th career home run, off Rich Harden at Chicago's Wrigley Field. "I was telling my father last night that I would love to hit it here because I know the fans are going to throw it," he said, and sure enough a Cubs fan threw it back and Rodríguez got the souvenir.[56] A month later there was another milestone: On June 17 Rodríguez returned with the Astros to Arlington, where he received a standing ovation from Rangers fans as he broke Carlton Fisk's record for games caught at 2,227. (His two throwing errors in the game led to two runs and helped the Rangers to win, 5-4.)

A month later, on August 18, Rodríguez was traded to the Rangers for two minor leaguers. The Rangers needed another catcher when starter Jarrod Saltalamacchia went on the disabled list. The highlight of Rodríguez's second stint in Arlington was his first game back, when he got three hits, but he otherwise struggled and the Rangers declined to offer him a new contract after the season.

Rodríguez signed a two-year, $6 million deal with the Washington Nationals, and was expected to back up Jesus Flores, but when Flores could not recover from injury and spent the season on the DL, Rodríguez became the starting catcher. He struggled, hitting just .266 with four home runs, and again spent time on the shelf with back spasms. He did return in June to catch the highly anticipated major-league debut of pitcher Stephen Strasburg, who struck out 14 batters in the game.

At the end of the season Rodríguez was honored by the Rangers, who had him catch the first pitch from Nolan Ryan in the team's first-ever home World Series game.

In his final season, 2011, Rodríguez spent most of his time as a backup, and hit just .218 in 44 games. The Nationals had discussions with several teams about possible trades, but never swung a deal, and Rodríguez sat on the bench at the end of the season as the Nationals gave their younger players more opportunities. He again missed a couple of months through injury, and at the end of the season, even though he still thought he could play, he did not get any contract offers for 2012 until the Kansas City Royals contacted him when their catcher went down with injury. The 40-year-old Rodríguez decided not to sign and opted to retire. "The game had become much more difficult for me," he said in a later reminiscence. "I didn't really want to end my career, but at the same time my mind wasn't ready to go back to another spring training. … I didn't have the same passion anymore. And that's when I decided to retire. It was time.[57]

On April 23, 2012, Rodríguez officially retired at a ceremony before a game in Arlington. He threw out the first pitch by going behind the plate and throwing down to Rangers second baseman Michael Young. "It's a very hard day for me," he said. "It's been a great, great run." The Rangers said there would be a position for Rodríguez in the organization. "I'm always going to be in baseball the rest of my life," he said.[58] The following spring he joined the Rangers as a special assistant to the general manager, where he worked in scouting, player instruction, and team marketing.

Rodríguez and Maribel had three children, Iván Dereck, born in 1992 and known as Dereck, Amanda (born in 1995), and Ivánna (2000). In the early 1990s Rodríguez bought a mansion in Miami for his family, and lived the life of his dreams on the water, riding in speedboats and enjoying his children. He planned to settle there for the rest of his life, but after his divorce from Maribel in 2005 he sold the home.[59] A couple of years later Rodríguez married his second wife, Patricia, and as of 2017 the couple lived in Dallas, Miami, and Puerto Rico.

Dereck was selected in the sixth round of the 2011 draft by the Minnesota Twins. After three seasons in the minor leagues as an outfielder, he was hitting just .216. The Twins suggested that Dereck try pitching, where he had some early success, becoming pitcher of the year in his rookie league in 2015—and took a no-hitter into the seventh inning of a game that his father attended—but as of the end of the 2016 season Dereck still had not advanced above Class A. Asked why he was an outfielder and pitcher instead of a catcher like his father, Dereck said he wanted to make his own way in baseball. He did not have the desire to be a catcher. He said his father "tells me that as long as I have a uniform on, I'll be fine."[60]

Iván Rodríguez was inducted into the Texas Rangers Hall of Fame in 2013, the Texas Sports Hall of Fame in 2014, and the Latino Baseball Hall of Fame in 2015. Having done several stints as a guest on television shows through the years, Rodríguez found he was interested in broadcasting, and in 2014 he joined Fox Sports Southwest as an analyst for Rangers games. He also began expanding his nonbaseball activities, becoming a partner in a Miami investment-capital company, and using his public image in promotional work for several other companies.

When Rodríguez retired he held numerous major-league records for catchers, among them the most games caught (2,427), the most hits (2,749), the most Gold Gloves (13), the most All-Star Game starts (12), and appearances (14, tied with Yogi Berra). He had seven Silver Slugger Awards, second only to Mike Piazza (10). He led his league in caught-stealing percentage nine times, and eight times he threw out more than half of the runners trying to steal against him. He was such a threat to throw out runners that often teams did not even attempt to steal against him. Rodríguez was arguably the best defensive catcher of all time, and combined with his offense perhaps the best all-around catcher ever[61]. He was fifth all-time in home runs by a catcher (304) and had the most doubles (551), the most runs scored (1,316), and the most RBIs (1,290).

Rodríguez was eligible for election to the National Baseball Hall of Fame in 2017, and was a strong candidate for election as one of the greatest catchers of all time. The whispers of steroid use, combined with the desire of some writers to not even vote for anyone from the steroid era, along with writers who wouldn't vote for anyone his first time on the ballot, meant that he was not as sure of election as he probably should have been based on his career. However, Rodríguez received 76 percent of the vote, joining his childhood hero Johnny Bench as the only two catchers inducted into the Hall of Fame on their first try. For many people, it wasn't even a question of being worthy of the Hall of Fame, but more an argument on where he should rank in the top handful of catchers.

## NOTES

1   Jo-Ann Barnas, "The Power of Pudge," *Detroit Free Press*, April 5, 2004.
2   Mark Whicker, "Rodríguez Is Young, Well-Armed," *Orange County* (California) *Register*, July 1, 1991: D8.

# PUERTO RICO AND BASEBALL: 60 BIOGRAPHIES

3  Iván Rodríguez, "The Story of My Life," The Players Tribune, theplayerstribune.com/ivan-rodriguez-story-of-my-life, accessed January 19, 2017.

4  "Star Pupil Pudge Back in Native Land," *Syracuse Post-Standard*, March 31, 2001: C6.

5  "Puerto Rico Profile: Iván 'Pudge' Rodríguez," *Puerto Rico Herald*, March 30, 2001.

6  Tracy Ringolsby, "Q&A: Former Scout Johnson on Discovering Pudge," MLB.com, m.mlb.com/news/article/213055776/qa-sandy-johnson-on-finding-pudge-rodriguez, accessed January 7, 2017.

7  Chris Colston, "The Heart of Texas," *USA Today Baseball Weekly*, April 18, 2001. usatoday30.usatoday.com/sports/bbw/2001-04-18/2001-04-18-specialpudge.htm, accessed January 26, 2017.

8  Michael A. Lutz, "A Catching Future," *Del Rio* (Texas) *News-Herald*, March 16, 1991: 7.

9  Iván Rodríguez, "The Story of My Life," The Players Tribune.

10  "Thursday Was Day to Remember for Catcher," *New Philadelphia* (Ohio) *Times-Reporter*, June 21, 1991: B4.

11  Jeff Nordlund, "Rangers' Rookie Has Blissful Day," *Arlington Heights* (Illinois) *Daily Herald*, June 21, 1991: 2.

12  Mark Whicker.

13  "Rangers Banking on 'The Rifle,'" *Kerrville* (Texas) *Daily Times*, March 29, 1992: 2B.

14  "Texas' Young Gun Earns a Reputation," *Syracuse Post-Standard*, April 21, 1992: D4.

15  "Starting Suits Rangers' Rodríguez," *Paris* (Texas) *News*, July 9, 1993: 10A.

16  Cathy Harasta, "Catcher Owes Success to Level, if Aching, Head," *Orange County Register*, August 15, 1993: 1.

17  T.R. Sullivan and Maria Durand, "Texas' Rodríguez Makes Third All-Star Game," *Syracuse Herald American*, July 10, 1994: E6.

18  Ibid.

19  "'Pudge' Could Command Huge Dollars," *Syracuse Post-Standard*, July 26, 1997: D4.

20  Johnette Howard, "Pudge Factor," *Sports Illustrated*, August 11, 1997: 40.

21  Iván Rodríguez, "The Story of My Life," The Players Tribune.

22  Dave Caldwell, "Faith Steps Up to the Plate," *Syracuse Herald-Journal*, August 3, 1996: A10.

23  Johnette Howard.

24  "It'll Cost Rangers Plenty to Keep Pudge in Lineup," *Amarillo* (Texas) *Daily News*, July 9, 1997: 2D.

25  Ibid.

26  Ibid.

27  "Winter Ball Heats Pudge's Game," *Port Arthur* (Texas) *News*, May 7, 1998: 4C.

28  "Pudge a Rarity Among Catchers With Power/Speed Combination," *Amarillo Daily News*, August 4, 1999: 1D.

29  Evan Grant, "Pudge Rejects Rangers' Offer; Trade Possible," *Amarillo Daily News*, July 26, 1997: 4D.

30  "It'll Cost Rangers Plenty to Keep Pudge in Lineup."

31  Chris Colston.

32  "Rangers Sign Iván Rodríguez," *Cumberland* (Maryland) *Times-News*, August 1, 1997: 6B.

33  "Winter Ball Heats Pudge's Game."

34  Ben Walker, "Iván Rodríguez Gets Nine RBIs in Only Three Innings," *Naugatuck* (Connecticut) *Daily News*, April 14, 1999: A9.

35  "Pudge beats Pedro for AL MVP," *Cumberland* (Maryland) *Times-News*, November 19, 1999: 1D.

36  "Martinez's Near-Miss Rekindles Debate on Pitchers as MVPs," *Laurel* (Mississippi) *Leader-Call*, November 19, 1999: 1B.

37  "Bad Break," *New Castle* (Pennsylvania) *News*, July 25, 2000: 12.

38  "Star Pupil Pudge Back in Native Land," *Syracuse Post-Standard*, March 31, 2001: C6.

39  Stephen Hawkins, "Rangers Cut Ties to Pudge," *Texas City Sun*, December 8, 2002: 3B.

40  "Rodríguez Happy With Marlins," *Walla Walla* (Washington) *Union Bulletin*, October 7, 2003: C2.

41  Nancy Armour, "The Pudge Doesn't Budge," *Anderson* (Indiana) *Herald Bulletin*, October 16, 2003: B4.

42  Iván Rodríguez, "The Story of My Life," The Players Tribune.

43  "Pudge: Marlins Were Unfair in Contract Talks," *Englewood* (Florida) *Sun*, December 19, 2003: 2.

44  Jo-Ann Barnas.

45  Larry Lage, "'Pudge' to Rescue for Lowly Tigers," *Lawrence* (Kansas) *Journal-World*, April 2, 2004: 2C.

46  "La Russa, Rodríguez Try to Put Steroid Talk to Rest on First Day," *Cumberland* (Maryland) *Times-News*, February 19, 2005: 2D.

47  "'Pudge' Examines Future, Which May Include Astros," *Port Arthur News*, February 16, 2009: B3.

48  "La Russa, Rodríguez Try to Put Steroid Talk to Rest on First Day.

49  John Eligon, "The Tigers' Rodríguez Is Now a Svelte Pudge," *New York Times*, May 25, 2005.

50  Larry Lage, "Pudge Rodríguez Key to Tigers' Revival," *Sandusky* (Ohio) *Register*, October 19, 2006: B2.

51  Ibid.

52  Iván Rodríguez, "The Story of My Life," The Players Tribune.

53 "Busy Day in the Bronx," *Berkshire Eagle* (Pittsfield Massachusetts), July 31, 2008: C1.

54 Larry Lage, "Tigers' Fans Still Love Yankees' Pudge," *Syracuse Post-Standard*, September 2, 2008: C4.

55 "'Pudge' Examines Future, Which May Include Astros."

56 "Rodríguez Hits 300th Home Run in Astros Win," *Port Arthur News*, May 18, 2009: B1.

57 Iván Rodríguez, "The Story of My Life," The Players Tribune.

58 "Iván Rodríguez Back In Texas, This Time to Retire," *Joplin (Missouri) Globe*, April 24, 2012: 3B.

59 Chris Colston.

60 Jeff Johnson, "Rodríguez Learning to Be Starting Pitcher," *Cedar Rapids (Iowa) Gazette*, June 14, 2015: 3B.

61 Cliff Corcoran, "Is Iván Rodríguez the Greatest Catcher in Major League History?," SI.com, www.si.com/more-sports/2012/04/20/ivan-rodriguez-retirement, accessed January 30, 2017.

# REY SÁNCHEZ

## By Bill Nowlin

**M**IDDLE INFIELDER REY Sánchez spent 15 years in the major leagues and worked just 10 games shy of 1,500. About two-thirds of the games were at shortstop and one-third at second base. He hit .272 over the course of a career spent with nine big-league ballclubs, though his first seven seasons were spent with the Chicago Cubs. He had a career .983 fielding percentage, and for three seasons (1989-91, while he was with the Kansas City Royals) was ranked tops in the American League in defensive WAR (Wins Against Replacement players).

He was born in Rio Piedras, Puerto Rico, as Rey Francisco Sánchez Guadalupe on October 5, 1967. His mother, Emma Guadalupe, was a housewife. His father, Francisco Sánchez, was a computer programmer, and worked with Goodyear.[1] When he was 17 his parents sent him to California, where he stayed for 1½ years with a family who were participating in a student-exchange program. He graduated from Live Oak High School in Morgan Hill, California. At age 18, he was selected by the Texas Rangers in the 13th round of the June 1986 amateur draft. Sánchez was 5-feet-10 and listed at 180 pounds.

Sánchez signed with the Rangers on June 22 and played rookie ball that year in the Gulf Coast League, getting into 52 games and batting .290 with 23 RBIs. He was error-free at second base in 22 chances but committed 15 errors in 220 chances (.932) at shortstop.

In 1987 Sánchez split his time almost precisely evenly between the Butte Copper Kings (rookie-level Pioneer League) and the Single-A Gastonia Rangers in the South Atlantic League. He hit .365 with Butte, but found the elevation to Single A more difficult, batting .219.

Sánchez's 1988 season was again in A ball, in the Florida State League, with the Port Charlotte Rangers, and this time he was ready for it. Now 20 years old, he hit for a .306 batting average, and improved his fielding. He was bumped up to the Triple-A Oklahoma City 89ers in 1989, and struggled to hit pitching at the higher level (.224) but his fielding percentage increased to .958.

On January 3, 1990, the Rangers traded Sánchez to the Chicago Cubs for another minor leaguer, infielder Bryan House. Unfortunately for Sánchez, he missed the entire 1990 season due to injury. The deal paid off for the Cubs, though. In 1991 Sánchez had a very good season with the Iowa Cubs (in the Triple-A American Association), where he hit .290 and improved his fielding percentage to .971. Sánchez was called up to the big-league team in September 1991.

He debuted on September 8, playing shortstop in the eighth and ninth innings in a game against the visiting San Francisco Giants. No balls came his way, and with him due to lead off in the bottom of the ninth—the Giants were leading, 4-3—manager Jim Essian removed him for a pinch-hitter. The Cubs didn't score. Sánchez started back-to-back games on September 13 and 14, and was 0-for-4 at the plate, removed for a pinch-hitter in late innings both times. He got his first big-league base hit on September 17 in Pittsburgh. He'd entered the game, replacing Ryne Sandberg, in the sixth (the Cubs were losing 7-0). He singled past the shortstop in the top of the eighth, driving in a run. The Pirates won the game, 9-2. Sánchez appeared in 13 September and October games, and was 6-for-23 with four walks. He had one other RBI. He was error-free in 36 chances in the field.

Sánchez spent most of his time in 1992 with the big leaguers. Working as a late-inning defensive replacement for a few games in April, he had the opportunity to start a couple of games in early May when Shawon Dunston was put on the 15-day DL. In his first game starting, he hit a 10th-inning bases-loaded sacrifice fly to win the game against the visiting Braves, offering what one writer dubbed a "Rey of

hope" for a Cubs team that was not doing well.[2] "That was a dream came true," said Sánchez after the game.[3]

Dunston's condition was more serious than at first thought, and he had to undergo back surgery that kept him out most of the season. Sánchez himself got the chicken pox and went on the 15-day DL. From June 5 through September 4, he played in 68 games, batting .264 and driving in 18 runs. Three of them came in a 5-2 win over the Phillies on June 21. Another came on a suicide squeeze on June 30, giving the Cubs an insurance run in a 3-1 victory. On July 8 Sánchez was hit by a pitch in the bottom of the 10th inning, forcing in the winning run in a 3-2 win over Cincinnati. A bulging disc in his lower back cost him the rest of the season after September 4.

For the next three seasons — 1993 through 1995 — Sánchez was with the Cubs, averaging 105 games a year. Most of 1993 was at shortstop and almost all of 1995 was at second base. The transition had come in 1994, when second baseman Ryne Sandberg abruptly retired in mid-June, giving Sánchez the opportunity to try to fill his shoes. Manager Tom Trebelhorn said at the time that Sánchez had "excellent range, excellent hands, excellent throwing arm."[4] He averaged just over 26 RBIs a year. It was his defense that secured him the work; he committed a total of 31 errors over the three-year span, very good for a middle infielder. Weirdly, three of them came in one game, on April 27, 1993, against Colorado.

Gerry Fraley of the *Dallas Morning News* said of Sánchez's unexpected filling in for Sandberg, "Rey Sánchez handled the pressure of replacing Ryne Sandberg at second base. Sánchez hit .285 and had only two errors in 50 games at second."[5]

During the winter of 1994-95, Sánchez played in Puerto Rico with the San Juan Senators, in the Winter Professional Baseball League. There, he was part of the Dream Team, champions of the Caribbean Series of 1995 (6-0). With an average over .400, he was the batting champion of the 1994-95 regular season in Puerto Rico. He batted ninth in the Dream Team lineup, a very impressive lineup: Robby Alomar, Bernie Williams, Edgar Martínez, Juan González, Rubén Sierra, Carlos Delgado, Carlos Baerga, Carmelo Martínez, and Rey Sánchez.

Former Cubs star Ron Santo said of Sánchez in April 1996, "He's the best young infielder — fielding a groundball — I've ever seen in the big leagues. Quick feet, great arm, great range."[6] Sánchez missed more than six weeks — almost all of June and most of July 1996 — because of a fractured left-hand hamate bone. He was having a subpar year at the bat prior to the injury (batting .211). By coincidence, the same .211 was his mark at year's end, too. Ryne Sandberg had come out of retirement, after a year and a half out of baseball, and played in both 1996 and 1997. Though Sánchez had recovered some of his batting stroke and was hitting .249 by mid-August 1997, he was in the final year of his contract with the Cubs and was traded to the New York Yankees on August 16 for minor-league right-hander Frisco Parotte. It was a fractured ulna bone that prompted the deal; New York's Luis Sojo had been hit by a pitch. Sánchez hit .312 in the 38 games he played for the Yankees.

A free agent at the end of the season, Sánchez talked with the Yankees but wanted to be reassured he'd be an everyday player. "It would have to be as a regular," he said of any signing. "If it's not here, then I will go somewhere else. I enjoyed being here and what I enjoyed the most was playing every day."[7] His agent was Scott Boras. Not able to get sufficient reassurance, Sánchez signed instead with the San Francisco Giants in January 1998, the Giants needing to replace Jose Vizcaino, who had himself become a free agent.

Sánchez hit .285 with 30 RBIs, but the Giants declined to exercise their option to renew his contract for another year. He signed with the Kansas City Royals for 1999 and had what was perhaps his best season, driving in a career-high 56 runs while batting .294. A free agent again, he took a month considering offers and re-signed with the Royals for 2000, on a two-year deal. He drove in another 38 runs, with a .273 average. These two years (and the one following in 2001) were his best years defensively, based on WAR calculation. He was considered by some the "best fielding shortstop in the major leagues" (Associated Press), and Royals manager Tony Muser talked about how important he was. Offense was a bonus (he had a franchise-best 21-game hitting streak at the time Muser commented): "With him every day, he probably means two to three runs defensively a game for us. He may not drive them in, but he saves them."[8]

At the end of July, on the 31st, Sánchez was batting .303 and was traded to the Atlanta Braves for Alejandro Machado and Brad Voyles. The Braves had lost Rafael Furcal to a shoulder injury and needed a shortstop. By season's end Sánchez had a .281 average. But when the schedule was complete, the season wasn't over for Sánchez and the Braves. They went on to win the National League Division Series over Houston and then went up against the Arizona Diamondbacks in the NLCS. Arizona won the pennant in five games and went on to beat the Yankees in the 2001 World Series. Sánchez hit .294 in the NLCS, by far the best average of any of the position players. Second-best was Chipper Jones with .263. Sánchez committed an uncharacteristic two errors, both of which were followed by runs, in the Braves' 11-4 loss in Game Four.

The Boston Red Sox signed Sánchez to a minor-league contract in February. After he hit .400 in spring training, the Red Sox signed him to the big-league team, to take over second base from José Offerman. A tight hamstring cost him more than a month after June 3, but he had a very good year overall, driving in 38 runs despite the lost time and batting .286.

Another year, another team—Sánchez signed a one-year deal with the New York Mets in the final days of 2002. As it worked out, returning to the National League gave him the opportunity to play major-league baseball in Puerto Rico, because this was the year the Montreal Expos played a number of "home games" at San Juan's Estadio Hiram Bithorn. Sánchez was in the four games of the Mets' visit, April 11-15. He was 1-for-8 at the plate. With Sánchez at shortstop and Roberto Alomar at second base, the Mets had a double-play combination of Puerto Ricans. The Hall of Fame reportedly said, "(T)here never had been a pair of Puerto Rican-born players who have started on Opening Day and then gone on to be the everyday players at second and short."[9] It wasn't the first time the two had played together. They had done so in Puerto Rican winter ball and had both been on the same championship team in 1995.[10]

It was written that Sánchez had been signed in large part to bridge the gap until José Reyes was ready to take over; Sánchez said he was glad to mentor Reyes, and the younger prospect said Sánchez was very helpful.[11] Sánchez, on the other hand, wasn't having a good season at the plate, and when he was traded on July 29—to the Seattle Mariners (with some cash) for Kenny Kelly—he was batting only .207. Reyes had debuted in June.

It was good to get away from the Mets. There had been allegations—denied by all—that during the April 30 game Sánchez had gotten himself a haircut in the Mets clubhouse. The accusation dogged him, and after the trade he seemed to perhaps acknowledge the possibility, saying, "That was not the real me."[12] With the change of team, Sánchez hit at a .294 pace for the Mariners. But he was on the move again after the season. In December he signed with the Tampa Bay Devil Rays. It was his ninth team.

Throughout his career, Sánchez had usually hit one or two game-winning hits a year, and more than once executed a suicide squeeze. On June 11, 2004, he had a 3-for-5 game, with his final hit being a walkoff 10th-inning inside-the-park home run, beating the Colorado Rockies. He drove in 26 runs in all, accompanying a .246 batting average. On June 30 he hit another home run, the 15th and final home run of his career.

Sánchez had one more major-league year in him, and he signed another one-year contract, for a second stint with the Yankees in 2005. His season ended on June 8, due to two bulging discs in his neck. He had appeared in just 23 games (batting .279).

When Sánchez retired in 2005, he worked for about two years as a coach with the Indios de Mayagüez (Mayagüez Indians) in the Puerto Rican Winter League. Since then, he has not been active in baseball.

Sánchez has a wife with one daughter, and two daughters from a prior marriage.

As of 2016 Sánchez lived in Las Vegas, Nevada, and finds his pension from baseball sufficient to provide for his needs.

## SOURCES

In addition to the sources noted in this biography, the author also accessed Sánchez's player file from the National Baseball Hall of Fame, the *Encyclopedia of Minor League Baseball*, Retrosheet.org, Baseball-Reference.com, Rod Nelson of SABR's Scouts Committee, and the SABR Minor Leagues Database, accessed online at Baseball-Reference.com. Thanks to Edwin Fernandez Cruz and to José Sánchez.

## NOTES

1. Thanks to Edwin Fernandez Cruz and José Sánchez, emails to the author on June 27 and September 9, 2016.
2. Ed Glennon, "Cubs Finally Solve Mystery of Atlanta," *Register Star* (Rockford, Illinois), May 6, 1992: 31. Sánchez also tripled earlier in the game.
3. Joey Reaves, "Cubs Find Ray of Hope in Comeback Win," *Chicago Tribune*, May 6, 1992: C3.
4. Rod Beaton, "Cubs Have a Rey of Hope for Sandberg's Replacement," *USA Today*, June 15, 1994.
5. Gerry Fraley, "National League Preview," *Post and Courier* (Charleston, South Carolina), April 23, 1995: 35.
6. Jerome Holtzman, "Cubs' Sánchez a Gem on Defense, But Offense Needs Some Polish," *Chicago Tribune*, April 4, 1996: 4.
7. George King, "Sánchez to Yanks: It's Every Day or the Highway," *New York Post*, October 9, 1997.
8. Associated Press, "Royals Defeat Rangers," *Register Star* (Rockford, Illinois), June 1, 2001: 23. His hitting streak lasted 21 games.
9. David Waldstein, "Mets: It's Feat First for Sánchez, Alomar," *Newark Star-Ledger*, March 4, 2003.
10. Ibid.
11. Rafael Hermoso, "Sánchez, a Willing Mentor, Is Holding a Place for Reyes," *New York Times*, February 24, 2003.
12. Rafael Hermoso, "Mets Trade Sánchez to Mariners," *New York Times*, July 30 2003: D3.

# BENITO SANTIAGO

## By Thomas J. Brown Jr.

**B**ENITO SANTIAGO WAS ONE OF the best catchers in the majors in the late 1980s and early 1990s. Santiago played solid baseball and set several catching records during a 20-year career during which he played for nine teams. His legacy was tarnished as a result of his inclusion in the steroid scandal that swept through baseball shortly before his career ended.

Benito Rivera Santiago was born in Ponce, on the south coast of Puerto Rico, on March 9, 1965. His father, José, a truck driver, died when Benito was 3 months old. José had an accident with his rig, refused to be treated, and died shortly after the accident.[1] Shortly afterward, Benito's mother abandoned him, giving him to friends living on the opposite side of the island. He grew up never knowing his mother.[2]

Santiago not only grew up poor but he also grew up on the streets in the small town where he lived. If it hadn't been for baseball, he might have become just a poor farm worker. He reflected on this in an interview in 1989 when he returned for a visit to his hometown with a reporter and said: "See those guys out there picking tomatoes and watermelons? That used to be me. That would be me today."[3]

Santiago started out as a shortstop. He had to be talked into catching for his Little League team when the regular catcher did not show up for a game.[4] He attended John F. Kennedy High School in Santa Isabel, Puerto Rico. His coach, Luis Rosa, was also the Padres' chief scout in Puerto Rico. Santiago admired Rosa tremendously and after graduating from high school he signed with the Padres as an amateur free agent.

The Padres assigned the young catcher to the Miami Marlins of the low Class-A Florida State League in the spring of 1983. He played in 122 games and began to show the hitting prowess for which he would be recognized throughout his major-league career. He had 25 doubles and 56 RBIs. Promoted in 1984 to the Reno Padres of the faster Class-A California League, Santiago hit .279 with 16 home runs and 83 RBIs.

After spring training in 1985, the Padres assigned Santiago to the Beaumont Golden Gators of the Double-A Texas League. He continued to demonstrate his ability to be an offensive threat even as he faced stiffer competition. Playing in 101 games, Santiago had 111 hits and raised his batting average nearly 20 points to .298. In 1986, promoted to the Las Vegas Stars of the Triple-A Pacific Coast League, Santiago batted .286 with 17 home runs and 71 RBIs. Called up to the Padres after the PCL season, Santiago made his major-league debut on September 14. He started the game against Houston and got his first major-league hit, a double off Mike Scott, in his first at-bat.

It was clear to the Padres that Santiago was ready for the majors. He became the team's starting catcher in 1987 and was a unanimous selection for the National League Rookie of the Year Award. His .300 batting average with 33 doubles, 18 home runs, and 79 RBIs, earned him a Silver Slugger Award, and behind the plate he was among the league leaders in several defensive statistics (although he notably led the league in passed balls and errors).

One of the most exciting parts of Santiago's rookie season was his 34-game hitting streak. Santiago batted .346 with 5 homers and 19 RBIs during the streak, which lasted from August 25 through October 2. His streak was the 15th longest in major-league history and the longest ever for a Padre, a rookie, or a catcher. Teammate Tony Gwynn pointed out the significance of Santiago's accomplishment when he said: "Every player but the catcher gets to rest and contemplate his next at-bat."[5]

Santiago's batting average plunged to .248 in 1988, but he won his first Gold Glove Award. In 1989 he won the first of four consecutive All-Star Game selections; he was the starting catcher for the NL team. In 1990 Santiago earned his third consecutive Gold Glove Award and third Silver Slugger Award. Chosen for the National League All-Star squad, he was injured and didn't play. For the first time, he received votes for the Most Valuable Player Award. He finished 23rd in the voting.

Santiago, who was paid $750,000 in 1990, sought a four-year, $11 million contract in 1991. The Padres offered $1.65 million for one year and they went to arbitration. Santiago lost, and said he would leave the Padres after the 1992 season and enter the free-agent market.[6] Santiago didn't let his contract situation in San Diego bother him on the field; he had one of his best offensive seasons in 1991, batting .267 with 17 home runs and a career-high 87 RBIs. Santiago was the starting catcher for the NL in the 1991 All-Star Game. (He repeated in 1992.)

Santiago went to arbitration again in 1992 and won his case, being awarded a salary of $3.3 million rather than the Padres' offer of $2.50 million. After the Padres made it clear that they were not going to re-sign Santiago or any of their other high-salaried players as a cost-cutting move,[7] he said he was sad to leave the organization that gave him his start in baseball,[8] entered the free-agent market after the season, and signed with the expansion Florida Marlins for $3.4 million.

Santiago hit the first home run in the Marlins history when he knocked a pitch by Trevor Wilson out of Candlestick Park on April 12, 1993. Santiago was solid as the Marlins' first-string catcher in 1993 and '94, but the Marlins declined to sign him at the end of 1994 because they had a young catcher, Charles Johnson, ready to step into the position.

Santiago once again entered the free-agent market and signed with the Cincinnati Reds for 1995. Sharing duties behind the plate with three others, Santiago played in only 81 games and helped the Reds get to the postseason. They defeated the Dodgers in the Division Series but lost the NLCS to Atlanta.

Once more Santiago went looking for a team after the season. He signed with the Philadelphia Phillies, for whom he hit a career-high 30 home runs, including a ninth-inning grand slam on May 3 off Greg Maddux, the first slam surrendered by Maddux in his career.[9] But the Phillies released him after the season, and Santiago signed with the Toronto Blue Jays. Injuries kept his catching load in 1997 to 97 games, and in 1998, injuries suffered in an offseason car crash limited Santiago to just 15 games.[10] He did not get into a game until September 4, and the Blue Jays released him at the end of the season.

Santiago signed with the Chicago Cubs for the 1999 season. He played in 109 games with middling results the Cubs released him at the end of the season. Santiago signed again with the Cincinnati Reds. He played in 89 games, and was released after the season.

Santiago had now played for six teams in eight years. His inconsistent play as well as injuries had made him no more than a journeyman player at this point in his career. The 36-year-old catcher's next stop was San Francisco. There, some of his new teammates questioned his ability to be a team player. There were also concerns about what skills Santiago retained, considering that he played a position that was physically difficult.[11]

After starting the 2001 season sharing catching duties with Bobby Estalella, Santiago became the Giants' regular catcher by midseason and played in 133 games. All things considered, he had a respectable season offensively; he was strong behind the plate and provided needed guidance to some of the Giants' young players. Former teammate Mark Grace said of Santiago in 2001: "He's good with pitchers and young catchers and he works hard. It's not an accident he's been around so long. He's a heck of a player."[12]

Santiago also had a strong 2002 season. Playing in 126 games, he hit 16 home runs and had 74 RBIs. He seemed to thrive when Giants manager Dusty Baker had him bat behind Barry Bonds.[13] Santiago's play earned him his fifth All-Star selection. He made the final out in the controversial game, which ended in a tie when both teams ran out of pitchers.

Santiago made his second postseason appearance in 2002, and played well. The Giants defeated Atlanta in the Division Series and St. Louis in five games in the Championship Series. Santiago hit two home runs in the NLCS, had six RBIs, and was named the series' Most Valuable Player. Santiago contributed five RBIs in the World Series, which the Giants lost to the Anaheim Angels in seven games.

Santiago played in 108 games for San Francisco in 2003. The Giants let him go at the end of the season, and he signed with the Kansas City Royals for 2004. On June 18 he was batting .274 with 6 home runs and 23 RBIs (he had hit a three-run homer in the first inning), when he was hit on the left hand by a pitch from Geoff Geary of the Phillies. The hand was broken and Santiago saw no playing time for the remainder of the season. In December the Royals traded him to the Pittsburgh Pirates for Juan Carlos Oviedo.[14]

Santiago caught in six games for the Pirates in April, the last one on the 11th. At 40, he was the third of three backstops, and the club released him in May.

In June he signed a minor-league contract with the New York Mets, but was released in July after playing in nine games for Triple-A Norfolk.

Santiago played in 1,978 games in his 20-year career. He had 1,830 hits and a .263 batting average. Santiago hit 217 home runs and had 920 RBIs. His career fielding percentage was .987. He led National League catchers three times in assists, once in fielding percentage and once in baserunners caught stealing.

Santiago played winter ball in his native Puerto Rico after the 2005 season. His goal was to sign another major-league contract. He felt that he still had the arm and the skills behind the plate to contribute on a contending club.[15] No club decided to sign him.

In December 2007, after his playing career was over, Santiago was one of the players alleged in the Mitchell Report to have received anabolic steroids. The report stated that syringes were found in Santiago's locker near the end of the 2003 season. Santiago denied that he used steroids, claiming that he had collected the syringes as part of an ongoing prank by teammate Barry Bonds.[16]

Despite his positive statistics, Santiago's connection to the steroids scandal hurt his prospects for election to the Hall of Fame. He got just one vote in 2011, his first year on the ballot, and failed to get any votes in successive years. Besides the steroid allegations, some voters may have been deterred by Santiago's fielding statistics. He led the National League in errors six times and in passed balls three times.[17]

Honoring his accomplishments with San Diego, the Padres named Santiago to the club's Hall of Fame in 2015. Santiago's four starts for the NL All-Star team are the second most in franchise history, behind Tony Gwynn's 12 starts. Santiago's three Gold Gloves and four Silver Sluggers also rank second in franchise history.[18]

Santiago excelled in a difficult position for 20 years. His 1,917 games caught are 11th on all-time list. While he will be most remembered for his batting, Santiago also demonstrated solid defensive skills throughout his career.

Santiago has four children, daughters Bennybeth and Aliyah and sons Benito Jr. and Benito Iván. He has been active in Latino events in San Francisco and his home of Puerto Rico since his retirement.

## SOURCES

In addition to the sources cited in the Notes, the author also utilized the Baseball-Reference.com and Retrosheet.org websites for box scores, player, team, and season pages, pitching and batting game logs, and other material pertinent to this biography. Fan Graphs.com provided some the individual statistical information used in this biography.

## NOTES

1. Franz Lidz, "Benito Finito at 34 Games," Sports Illustrated.com, October 12, 1987.
2. Bob Nightengale, "Santiago Puts Old Problems Behind Him," *Los Angeles Times*, March 30, 1991.
3. Bill Plaschke, "Benito Santiago's Side of the Mountains: 'Come See Where I'm From,' He Says, 'and You Understand Me Better,'" *Los Angeles Times*, January 29, 1989.
4. Lidz.
5. Ibid.
6. "Santiago Benched," *Portsmouth* (Ohio) *Daily Times*, June 1, 1991.
7. Tim Kurkjian, "Penny Pinchin' Padres," Sports Illustrated.com, March 29, 1993.
8. "Santiago Apparently Through in San Diego," *Gainesville* (Florida) *Sun*, September 22, 1992.
9. "Santiago Tags Maddux," *Tuscaloosa* (Alabama) *News*, May 4, 1996.
10. "Santiago Expects to Play After Crash," *Pittsburgh Post-Gazette*, January 6, 1998.
11. Anne Peterson, "Santiago Finds Safe Home With Giants," *Los Angeles Times*, June 3, 2001.
12. Ibid.
13. Juan Rodríguez, "Veteran Santiago Invaluable to Giants," *Orlando Sentinel*, October 12, 2002.
14. Oviedo was playing at the time, as he did for most of his career, under the assumed name Leo Nunez and under a falsified age as well. Some of the story is told by Stephen Borelli, "Marlins Pitcher Who Used Fake Name Says He's Cleared to Play, *USA Today*, May 25, 2012 at http://content.usatoday.com/communities/dailypitch/post/2012/05/juan-carlos-oviedo-leo-nunez-marlins-fake-name/1#.WQ3NTMs2y1s
15. Kevin Czerwinski, "Major League Vet Gears Up for Return," Minor League Baseball.com, November 30, 2006.
16. Jim Dooley, "Benito Santiago Misses Hall of Fame by Scant 435 Vote Margin," Chicago Now.com, January 6, 2011.
17. Ibid.
18. Dennis Lin, "Santiago, Templeton Elected to Padres HOF," *San Diego Union Tribune*, July 9, 2015.

# JOSE G. "PANTALONES" SANTIAGO

## By Edwin Fernandez

**D**URING THE 1954 SEASON THE Cleveland Indians enjoyed a very healthy pitching rotation, including great hurlers like Bob Feller, Mike García, Early Wynn, and Bob Lemon, but they had other great throwers in their minor-league farm clubs, among them José Santiago. From 1949 through 1953, Santiago was one of the best pitchers in Cleveland's minor-league system. He compiled a record of 77-47, with an earned-run average of 2.93.

José G. Santiago Guzmán (he was given the nickname "Pantalones") was born on September 4, 1928, in Coamo, Puerto Rico. His father, José Regino Santiago, from Coamo, was a dental technician and his mother, Eleuteria Guzmán from the southern town of Juana Díaz, worked in laundry in New York. He attended Ponce High School, and then lived with his parents in New York, where he graduated from high school in Brooklyn. In 1949 José and Matilde Luciano-Rangel of Ponce were married in New York. They had two daughters, Matilde and Judith.

In New York Santiago, a skinny right-hander with a strong arm and a lightning fastball, played amateur baseball with the Puerto Rican Stars and a team in Brooklyn. In 1946 he went to Puerto Rico with a New York team to play games against two teams, Juncos and Mayagüez. In the series, Santiago pitched a one-hit shutout. That year he was signed to a contract by Martiniano García, owner of the Ponce Lions of the Puerto Rico Winter League. The contract, for the 1946-47 season, included a $1,000 bonus.

Santiago was voted Rookie of the Year after posting a record of 8-2 and an ERA of 3.09. He excelled in crucial games and was a fan favorite. Later he played for the San Juan Senators, where he made a great duo with former New York Yankees reliever Luis Arroyo. For San Juan, Arroyo and Santiago often worked Sunday doubleheaders with one pitching in the morning and the other in the afternoon, a nightmare for the opposition batters. Santiago played a total of 16 seasons in Puerto Rico, also suiting up with the Mayagüez Indians and the Santurce Crabbers.

In 1947 the New York Cubans of the Negro National League signed the 18-year-old Santiago. Playing on the same team was the Cuban hurler Luis Tiant, Sr., one of the pitching greats of the Negro Leagues at the time. Santiago started six games in 1947 and 1948, winning three and losing two.

During the Indians' 1949 spring-training camp, the legendary pitcher Satchel Paige told him, "You have a nickel curve but your fastball's worth a million."[1] In an interview, Minnie Miñoso acknowledged that Santiago had recommended him to the Cleveland Indians.[2]

Before the 1949 season Santiago signed with the Indians, and that season, with Dayton of the Class-A Central League, he won 16 games and lost 12 with a team-leading 2.60 ERA in 211 innings pitched. He pitched for Wilkes-Barre in the Class-A Eastern League in 1950 and 1951, in the latter year earning the Pitcher of the Year award as he led the league leader in wins (21-5) and ERA (1.59). Near the end of the 1951 season he was promoted to Triple-A San Diego, where he was 1-5 with a 6.75 ERA.

In 1952 and 1953 Santiago pitched for Dallas, the Indians' Texas League affiliate. In 1952 he won 14 games and lost seven with a 2.83 ERA, and in 1953 he was 13-11 (3.47.) In 1954 he made the Indians roster out of spring training. His stay with Cleveland was brief—one game. Santiago pitched in relief on April 17 against the Chicago White Sox, allowing an unearned run in 1⅔ innings. Optioned to Triple-A Indianapolis, he pitched in one game, then jumped his contract to play in the Dominican Republic.

Although Santiago had built a solid record in the minors, it was difficult to break into the Indians' pitching rotation, and in the days before free agency players had few options. Santiago was unhappy and believed he was not being treated fairly. He did not have a healthy relationship with Hank Greenberg, the Cleveland general manager, who Santiago said never gave him a real opportunity.[3]

According to Santiago's account, at a boxing match in Chicago he was introduced to Francisco Martínez-Álvarez, owner of the Escogido Baseball Club in Dominican Republic and a cousin of Dominican dictator Rafael Leonidas Trujillo. Martínez offered Santiago a $12,000 contract to play with his team. Santiago, who was making about $5,000 with the Indians, accepted the proposal and went to Santo Domingo to play ball. Greenberg complained to Commissioner Ford Frick, who decreed that if Santiago or anyone else played in Santo Domingo, he would be declared ineligible to play in Organized Baseball. But Santiago's punishment did not last long. Rodrigo Otero-Suro, the baseball commissioner in Puerto Rico, intervened, and Santiago was reinstated.[4]

Santiago returned to Indianapolis in 1955, and in July the Indians recalled him. He pitched 32⅔ innings in 17 games, all in relief, and recorded a 2-0 mark with a 2.48 ERA. In May 1956 the Indians sold Santiago's contract to the Kansas City Athletics, for whom he made five starts, his first in the majors, winning one game and losing two before being sent down to Triple-A Columbus. He never returned to the major leagues again. His record in 27 games was 3-2, with a 4.66 ERA in 56 innings pitched.

From 1957 to 1959, when he left Organized Baseball, Santiago pitched for three minor-league teams, Buffalo and Havana in the International League, and San Antonio in the Texas League. In his 11 seasons in the minor leagues, he won 112 games and lost 83, with a career earned-run average of 3.22, with 12 shutouts. In seven of his 11 seasons, his winning record reached double figures.

Santiago played in the Puerto Rico Winter League for 16 seasons, three of them after he left Organized Baseball. In all, he won 107 games and lost 97. On December 6, 1956, he pitched a seven-inning no-hitter. He played in six Caribbean Series (1951, '52, '53, '57, '58, and '59). In 1951 Santiago won two games to help helped the Santurce Crabbers win the championship. In 1957, when Cuba won the Series with a record of 5-1, Santiago shut them out 6-0, allowing only three hits. His best games were against Cuba.

After his baseball life, Santiago became an entrepreneur. He was a successful boxing promoter. He was also active in the horse-racing industry as the owner of the Panta Stable, whose horses won a number of major races. Though he retired as a player, Santiago never said goodbye to baseball. He owned the Caguas Criollos of the Puerto Rico Winter League for several years. In 2012 he lived in San Juan.

The nickname "Pantalones" in Spanish means pants or trousers. It was given to Santiago after José struck out the side with the bases loaded in the ninth inning during a Winter League game between the

Ponce Lions and the Caguas Criollos. Santiago was relieving in the ninth, and the next morning Emilio E. Huyke, a newspaper sports editor, wrote: "Santiago had a lot of pantalones"—meaning he had lots of guts to do such a performance.[5] Since then, he has been called Pantalones.

In the 1957 Caribbean Series in Havana, Santiago shut down the Cuban powerhouse 6-0. The announcer Eladio Secades said: "To blank the Cubans in their hometown you need to have pantalones."[6]

In 1987 Santiago was inducted into the Puerto Rico Sports Hall of Fame for his achievements in baseball. He has also been inducted into the Caribbean Series Hall of Fame.

*An earlier version of this biography is included in the book* Pitching to the Pennant: The 1954 Cleveland Indians *(University of Nebraska Press, 2014), edited by Joseph Wancho.*

## SOURCES

In addition to the sources cited in the Notes, the author consulted Crescioni, José A. *El Beisbol Profesional Boricua* (self-published, 1997), and Baseball-Reference.com.

## NOTES

1 Author interview with José G. Santiago 2011.

2 Author interview with Minnie Miñoso, 2011,

3 Author interview with José G. Santiago, 2011.

4 Joaquín Monserrate, "Tite y Pantalones: Los dos colosos del sur," *El Nuevo Día*, November 5, 2000: 166.

5 Ibid.

6 juan@juanperez.com, taken from Ángel Torres *La leyenda del béisbol cubano.*

# JOSÉ G. SANTIAGO

## By Edwin Fernandez and Bill Nowlin

IN JOSÉ SANTIAGO'S FIRST APPEARance on a major-league mound, he entered a 6-6 tie game against the New York Yankees to pitch the eighth inning. It was September 9, 1963 and he got Elston Howard to ground out back to him on the mound, Joe Pepitone to line out, and Clete Boyer to strike out. When Kansas City scored in the bottom of the eighth, Santiago picked up the win. It was a nice way to start an eight-year career in major-league ball, three years with the Athletics and five with the Red Sox.

José R. Santiago-Alfonso was born in Juana Diaz, Puerto Rico on August 15, 1940. Known as "la ciudad de los poetas" (the City of Poets), Juana Diaz is a community roughly 10 miles northeast of Ponce in south-central Puerto Rico. The city is also known as "la Ciudad del Jacaguas" after the river of the same name which flows through its fields on the way to the sea. Juana Díaz produces sugar cane and beige marble, considered one of the finest marbles in the world.

His father Alejandro Santiago, ran a kind of general store that served workers on the sugar cane plantation. "He'd sell all kinds of products in it. He would sell the beans and the rice and everything you can think of," José recalls.[1] Alejandro Santiago ran the store with his wife, Merida Alfonso. The two raised three children: Betty, José, and a younger boy, Alejandro, Jr.

Juana Diaz was a good-sized community back then, around 30,000 to 40,000 people. It's grown to about 50,000 today. The Santiagos were well-enough off economically relative to others, but José still learned humility as a young boy. His first memories of baseball date back to being 5 or 6 years old. As he grew older, the kids in the Lomas neighborhood where he was born benefited from José's father's passion for baseball. Alejandro had played amateur baseball, a third baseman. "At the time, it was tough to play baseball," José remembers. "We didn't have any equipment. We had to get the sacks that they bring the wheat in, and wash it for about three or four days and then try to make a uniform out of that. My dad bought some bats and baseballs and some gloves for us, and that's how we started. We didn't even have a ballpark to play. We have to go either to another city to play or to go across the river and play…it was a cow field. Cut the grass and go ahead and then just play."

As a child, José was a very skinny boy. That caused some friends to called him "Palillo," the Spanish word for toothpick. He played his first game on the shores of the Jacaguas River near Lomas. "We played some other barrios, some other sectors of Juana Diaz." In high school, when classes were over on a Fridays, the team would travel by bus and play in Ponce, Mayaguez, or elsewhere.

José wasn't always a pitcher, though. That really came in college. Right through high school, Santiago primarily played center field. "I just had a great fastball, great arm, but I didn't know anything about pitching. I couldn't curve nothing." It was his father who saw him pitching one day, and said, "I think you've got a better chance to be a pitcher than an outfielder." It was in college that he was able to benefit from some real coaching from Carlos Negron and Gonzalez Pato at the Pontificia Universidad Católica de Puerto Rico (Catholic University of Ponce.) Another man he is quick to credit with help in pitching is Cefo Conde, who was a pitcher in the old Negro Leagues. Conde's nephew is Santos (Sandy) Alomar, Sr.

José Santiago's final accomplishment as an amateur player was for a Class-A team in a neighborhood called Romero. He threw a 16-inning game that he lost 3-2 against Santa Isabel. But the young Juanadino was on his way.

José Santiago became a professional baseball player in 1957. It happened when finishing his freshman year at Catholic University. According to his sister Betty, one morning José was working with her in the family store, when he suddenly disappeared. At 3:00 PM, he returned from the town's ballpark, sweating and apprehensive, announcing there were three baseball scouts from the New York Giants organization asking to see his father because they want to sign him to play pro ball. His father said, "I am the one to sign you." An hour later, Alejandro Pompez came to the home to talk.

This was the same Alex Pompez named to the Hall of Fame in 2006. José was on shaky ground here with his father, because he knew that his father wanted him to finish university before thinking of playing professionally. One of José's friends had prevailed upon him, though, knowing there was a tryout being held, and argued, "Hey, this is a good chance to show them what you can do. I'll tell you what I'll do. I'll go to your place. I'll pack your bag, and then I'll meet you someplace else." José made up an excuse and left the store for the rendezvous. "My dad almost killed me when I came back! (laughs) I told him, 'Hey, they liked me. They want to sign me….'"

So began the saga of Santiago's signing. Both Pompez and Pancho Coimbre of the Pirates were interested, but Coimbre deferred to Pompez, just letting it be known that if things didn't work out, he'd be interested. Pompez offered $25,000 but José's dad wanted him to finish college first. That would mean waiting three years, not what the youngster wanted to hear. He pleaded with his father. Both scouts agreed on José's potential, Pompez saying, "He's got a lot of tools. He can play professional and I'm pretty sure he can get to the big leagues."

Alejandro asked Pompez, "Well, all right, do we get the money now or he's going to get the money later? What's the deal on that?" "Oh no, as soon as he gets to spring training, we're going to send you the money." It was worked out and José signed. Then he reports, "I went to spring training. I went through the whole spring training. Never got the money." His father called. They talked. The Giants said not to worry, and sent him to D ball. He was slated to pitch the opening night game, but stood fast. "I told

them, 'I'm not going to pitch until I get my money.' They said, 'You're going to get it. You're going to get it.' My dad called me up and said, 'I'm going to send you a ticket. You come home.' So I came home. They tried to get me back, and I said, 'No.' They lied to me." His father was a man of his word, and José and his father were united.

He had a written contract and could have consulted a lawyer, but his father didn't want to go that route, and José determinedly headed back to school. At that point, Kansas City scout Félix Delgado saw José pitch a 12-strikeout game against a team from the University of Puerto Rico. Delgado called Sr. Santiago, and they talked, with José and his father explaining about the experience they'd had with the Giants. Delgado offered $15,000 –but paid in advance.

Playing later for owner Charley Finley, and well aware of the reputation Finley had, José interjected a memory of the time he tried to help out some fellow players: "To me, he was outstanding. He treated me great." A humorous story followed. "The only thing bad that I did…at the time, Orlando Pena, Diego Segui, Monteagudo, Campaneris, and all those guys… they didn't know how to speak English at all. I made a big mistake. They talked to me about it. I went to the office to see Mr. Finley about it. First thing he said: 'Are you a baseball player or are you an agent?' I said, 'Wait a minute. I'm just trying to help these guys.' 'All right. What do you need?' 'They want a raise and....'"

Finley agreed on the spot, and said, "All right, I'm going to give them a raise." He arranged for a new contract, and as they all got up to leave, Finley said, "José. You stay here." "What is it, Mr. Finley?" "You know how much I like you and all that, but never... never do that again. Let their own people...they can take care of their own business, even in Spanish, but don't get involved with this, because this is not your job. You're here because you want to do a job. So you go out on the field and do the job. I'm glad you did this for those kids. I appreciate that, but this is a business. All right. You got what you wanted. Now get the hell out of here." José laughs, telling the story, adding, "He was tough, but he was a great guy. To me, he was great."

José started his pro career in 1959 with Olean in the New York-Penn League, with a 6-3 or 5-3 record (accounts differ) and a 3.24 (or 3.34) ERA in 62 innings. The same year, he moved on to Grand Island in the Nebraska State League, winning three and losing six, with a 3.91 ERA. He pitched for Albuquerque in 1960 and on June 13, José threw a 2-0 no-hitter against Hobbs. It was the first no-hitter in the 28 years of the Albuquerque franchise. Just a walk and two errors - all in the sixth inning - prevented the perfect game. With the bases loaded, José struck out the final batter. At the time, *The Sporting News* made it clear that José "Palillo" Santiago was no relation to the older Puerto Rican pitcher José "Pantalones" Santiago, pitcher for Cleveland and Kansas City 1954-56.[2] With Albuquerque, the young "Palillo" had an excellent 15-6 record with a 3.30 ERA.

In 1961, he pitched for both Visalia and very briefly for Shreveport, leading the California League with 218 strikeouts but also leading in bases and balls, with 130. Back in Albuquerque in 1962, he won a league-leading 16 games against just nine losses. For most of 1963, he played for the Portland Beavers in the Pacific Coast League (12-15, 3.66 ERA), and near the end of the year got his first chance in big-league baseball.

As noted at the start, José broke in for Kansas City with a perfect eighth inning in relief in the September 9, 1963 game at Municipal Stadium against the Yankees. He was pulled for a pinch-hitter in the bottom of the eighth but the Athletics pushed a run across and José got the win. He next appeared in a game just two days later, also against the Yankees, pitching the final two innings of a game he entered with the Yankees ahead, 5-1. He let in three runs on three hits, one of them a two-run Pepitone homer. Santiago appeared in two more games in 1963: Boston's Dick Stuart hit a solo homer off him in a game Orlando Pena started (and lost), and he threw the final two innings of a game lost to the Indians, 7-0. All four appearances were in Kansas City. Santiago ended the year with a record of 1-0, but an ERA of 9.00 in seven innings. He'd yielded four home runs in those seven frames.

In 1964, José started the season with Dallas in the Pacific Coast League but only pitched two innings in one game. After a stretch on the disabled list for half of April and most of May, he returned to the Athletics in early June and appeared in 34 games throwing a total of 83 2/3 innings, including eight starts. Kansas City finished in last place, with a record of 57-105, some 42 games out of first place. Santiago posted a 4.73 ERA, but an unfortunate 0-6 won-loss record. Five of the six losses came in games he'd started, the last one being a 3-2 loss to the White Sox on October 2. In 1965, he started the season with the big league club, but only appeared in four games. The May 2 game against California was his last one of the year, and the last one for the Athletics. He spent most of the year with Vancouver in the Pacific Coast League, and got some innings in, 119 of them, with an excellent 2.19 ERA. The Red Sox took note and purchased him from Kansas City on October 15 for a reported $50,000 in cash. "I enjoyed my time with the A's," José told Herb Crehan. "I got along well with Charlie Finley, and I met my wife Edna there. I also got to know Sully [Haywood Sullivan] very well."[3]

After a full year with the Red Sox in 1966, he found himself looking up at Kansas City in the standings. The Red Sox finished in ninth place, a half-game ahead of the last-place Yankees, while KC was three games higher up in seventh place. But José got in a full 28 starts and, despite pitching for a ninth-place team, won 12 games with a 3.66 ERA. His record was 12-13, with seven complete games to his credit and 119 strikeouts. "We played very well in the second half of the season, but hardly anybody noticed," José recalled to author Crehan. José was selected as Red Sox Pitcher of the Year. The Red Sox investment had already paid off nicely.

In 1967, Santiago's first three appearances came out of the bullpen, allowing just one earned run in four innings, winning one and losing one - both against the Yankees. He then made five starts in a row, again winning one and losing one. After the May 30 start (he was hit for four earned runs in three innings, though the Sox won the game in the end), it was back to the bullpen until August 19 when he started against California. His record was 6-4 at the time. He wasn't involved in the decision, but pitched again in relief the very next day and earned a win, throwing the final two innings in the game the Red Sox won 9-8, overcoming a 6-0 deficit. For the rest of the regular season, he was used both as a starter and reliever and he won five more games while losing none. He threw a complete-game win against the Orioles on September 22 and Dick Williams gave him the ball to start against the Twins on the next-to-last game of the year on September 30. A loss would take the Red Sox out of the race, but José won a hard-fought game, going seven innings while allowing just two runs, and leaving to a standing ovation from the Fenway faithful. The Red Sox won the game, and won the pennant the next day. As Herb Crehan once wrote in the *Red Sox Magazine*, "Every Red Sox fan recalls the scene of Jim Lonborg being carried off the field...when his victory clinched at least a tie for the American League pennant. But it was Santiago's gutsy seven-inning stint on Saturday that set the stage for Lonborg's triumph."

Dick Williams named José Santiago as his starting pitcher in the first game of the 1967 World Series. Santiago pitched a solid game, allowing the Cardinals just two runs in seven full innings. It was his misfortune to be paired against Bob Gibson, who allowed but one Red Sox run - a third-inning solo home run by José himself in his first-ever World Series at-bat. His only other major league homer had come off Mickey Lolich in the second inning of the May 14 game against the Tigers, a 13-9 Red Sox win. Lifetime at the plate, he was .173 with six doubles and seven RBIs. In World Series play, he batted .500.

He got another start, in Game Four, but this one was a disaster. Again facing Gibson, who shut out the Sox, José was bombed for four runs on six hits and never made it out of the first inning. José appeared one more time, throwing two innings of perfect relief in Game Seven. But Jim Lonborg had imploded, and the Red Sox were losing 7-1 by the time José had entered the game. The Red Sox lost Game Seven and lost the World Series. José's record shows 0-2, but Game One against Gibson was a strong effort. José finished the regular season with a 12-4 record and a 3.59 ERA. He forever holds the distinction of being the first Latin pitcher to start the opening game of a World Series. Santiago praised both his teammates and Dick Williams to Herb Crehan: "Williams kept us focused from start to finish. He deserves a lot of credit."

In 1968, Santiago appeared in just 18 games, every one as a starter. His record was 9-4 with a sterling 2.25 ERA. He was on a roll from the 1967 season, and won his first four decisions, a string of 12 straight wins without a defeat. In his first four games, he gave up a total of just 14 hits. The first game he lost was a hard-luck 1-0 defeat by Mel Stottlemyre and the Yankees on May 11. He lost another 1-0 game on an unearned eight-inning run on May 25 to the Twins, and a 2-1 game on another unearned run on June 18. Dick Williams named Santiago one of his seven pitchers for the 1968 All-Star Game, but he developed tendonitis in his right elbow in early July and did not pitch in the game. He returned for one last game, on July 18 game, but it was his last of the season. He'd only given up one hit and no runs in two innings, but the injury was re-aggravated and he had to turn things over the Gary Bell. He missed the rest of the year.

On June 13, in a nightmare incident, one of José's pitches hit Paul Schaal and fractured his skull. Schaal was out for weeks, came back for just two more appearances in early August, but did not return to major-league play until 1969. Schaal performed well after his return, but the incident may have shaken Santiago, too. Jim Murray of the *Los Angeles Times* wrote of Santiago weeping at Schaal's hospital bed and wondered in print in a late 1971 column that Santiago was never the same pitcher afterward, writing "because his elbow - or something - was bothering him."[4]

It was one of the rare winters that José did not keep busy playing winter ball as well. Unfortunately, even time off over the winter wasn't sufficient and late in 1969 spring training, Santiago reinjured his elbow, tearing a ligament in his right elbow after throwing just two warmup pitches. A few weeks later, on April 22, he had elbow surgery in Boston. Doctors said it was 50/50 whether he could ever pitch again, but if he could, it would probably not be until 1970.

In fact, the surgery and rehab went quite well, and he rejoined the Red Sox in August, less than four months later. In his first appearance since July 18, 1968, Santiago threw a scoreless eighth and final inning in relief on August 24. Five days later, he did the same: a scoreless ninth. Appearing from time to time, he got in 10 games, pitching just 7 2/3 innings, but with a very good 3.52 ERA.

Before spring training opened in 1970, he said that he could no longer effectively throw his money pitch - the slider. He worked at it during the exhibition season, but he wasn't ready for big league action and so started the season with Louisville in the International League. He pitched in 19 games for Louisville (7-4, 3.62 ERA).

He got the call to Boston at the end of May. His first appearance, though, was as a pinch-hitter in the May 29 game at Fenway Park against the White Sox. Chicago was winning 3-1, and the Red Sox had a man on first with one out. Santiago was put in to pinch-hit for Jim Lonborg and singled sharply to left field. Mike Andrews drew a walk to load the bases and Billy Conigliaro singled to drive in two, José scoring the tying run. Yaz walked, and Jerry Moses won it with a walkoff single. His first stint on the mound came on May 31, giving up three runs in two innings as one of six Red Sox pitchers mauled by Chicago batters, in a 22-13 slugfest. Apart from the pinch-hit cameo, José appeared in eight games for the 1970 Red Sox (11 1/3 innings, 0-2, with a 10.32 ERA; they were his last games in the major leagues.)

Louisville beckoned, and Santiago gave another shot in 1971, throwing 128 innings and pitching well enough (7-6, 4.08 ERA) but those were his last years in American baseball. The Red Sox offered him a job as a coach in the organization, but José declined. He harbors good memories, though, telling Herb Crehan, "One thing I will always remember is that the Red Sox treated me with as much respect when I was a sore-armed pitcher as when I was an All-Star. Dick O'Connell, who was the general manager at the time, was wonderful to me. And the Yawkeys were very special people."

He was out of American baseball for the years 1972 through 1975, playing most winters in Puerto Rican teams. He told author Herb Crehan, "I still knew how to pitch, but I knew I wasn't at big league form. Some of my teammates would say, 'You could probably make a comeback' but I knew better." In 1976, José pitched for Union Laguna in the Mexican League, appearing in 43 games, winning 13 against 6 losses, with a 3.35 ERA.

Since his final season in Mexico, José has resided fulltime in Puerto Rico. In 1980, he founded the Academia Beisbol Palillo Santiago, and the school served as many as 300 boys a year between ages 7 and 17. He had the school for 10 or 15 years, but as more kids chose to play video games than baseball, the number of students began to dry up. José remains devoted to trying to foster youth baseball, however. For around 25 years, he has helped Little League baseball, in which he strongly believes. For a good long time, he was president of Little League for the whole San Juan area. "Half of my time, I dedicated to the Little League program. All the programs are great, but Little League is the one that I really enjoy, because if you're crippled or any kind of problems that you have, you can play Little League. They'll let you play. Not the other leagues. So that's why I'm there. I love Little League so much. And I still help them out. As soon as I have time, I'll do anything for the Little League. And for the kids."

Santiago also managed the Puerto Rican team for some time, and was pitching coach as well. During the 1980's, he served as Press and Publications Officer for the Sports and Recreation Department of the Government of Puerto Rico. In fact, after leaving major league baseball, José has been very energetic with an almost bewildering array of activity. Among other things he has been:

- Voice of the San Juan Senators for five years
- General Manager and Voice of the Santurce Crabbers for almost 10 years, named Narrator of the Year three times
- President of Little League baseball for 20 years
- Manager of the Puerto Rican national team
- Manager of a number of AA Amateur Baseball League teams, including Coamo, Juana Díaz, Río Piedras, Juncos, San Sebastian, and Río Grande.
- Pitching Coach for the Chicago Cubs Daytona Beach Class-A team in 2000
- Voice of the Carolina Giants in the Puerto Rico Professional Baseball League team 2004-2006.

As Crehan wrote these authors, "José is to Winter Baseball in Puerto Rico what Johnny Pesky is to the Red Sox."

Today, José Santiago lives in Carolina, Puerto Rico, with his wife Edna, whom he met while playing for Kansas City. They have been married for more than 45 years and raised four boys: Alex, Arnold, Albert, and Anthony. Three of the boys played baseball to one extent or another. Alex was offered a signing bonus by the Phillies, but he turned it down and runs a business working with computers. Arnold was drafted by the Cleveland Indians, but never had enough playing time to show what he might have been capable of achieving. A third son got into umpiring for a while, but left to raise horses and do other work.

Today, José keeps busy with his work broadcasting for Carolina. He also enjoys writing and reciting poems about love and family, perhaps reflecting the "City of Poets" where he was raised.

## NOTES

1  Author interviews with José Santiago by Edwin Fernandez on January 21, 2006 and Bill Nowlin on March 15, 2006. Unless otherwise indicated, all quotations from Santiago are from these interviews.

2  "Dukes' José Santiago Hurls No-Hitter," *The Sporting News*, June 22, 1960: 38.

3  Herb Crehan. "The Impossible Dream Team Revisited / Where Are They Now: José Santiago,"

*Red Sox Magazine*, 1997. All quotations attributed to Crehan come from this source.

4  Jim Murray. "A Royal Favorite," *Los Angeles Times*, September 28, 1971: E1.

# RUBÉN SIERRA

## By Adam J. Ulrey

THIS IS ABOUT WHAT COULD HAVE been and in reality what should have been. Very few players who come to the major leagues are labeled five-tool, can't-miss players. Even fewer go on to have that career. When you are involved in 31 transactions throughout your career and play for nine teams, two of them for multiple times, you end up with a career that should have been better. This is the tale of Rubén Sierra, a multitalented baseball player who never lived up to those lofty expectations for many reasons: all of his own doing, no one to blame but himself. Unfortunately for Sierra he figured this all out late in his career, when it was too late to matter. Yet despite all of this, he still hit over 300 homers and drove in over 1,300 runs. He stole 142 bases and amassed over 2,100 hits. For most, that would be considered a solid career, but Sierra is seen as a player who did not live up to what could have been. He also showed a lot of maturity late in his career, and helped both the Texas Rangers and New York Yankees after toiling in the minor leagues and independent leagues for a few years.

Rubén Angel Sierra Garcia was born on October 6, 1965, in Rio Piedras, Puerto Rico, to Angel and Petra Sierra. Rubén graduated in 1983 from Liceo Interamericano Castro high school, where he excelled in baseball, basketball, and volleyball. His life was full of family tragedy, starting at the age of 4 when his father was seriously injured in a car accident. One night in the hospital's intensive-care unit, he became thirsty. Unable to hail a nurse, he pulled out the tubes that tethered him to the bed and stumbled off to get a drink. On his way back to bed, he collapsed and died. Rubén's widowed mother worked as a hospital janitor to support her three sons and daughter. Rubén grew up in the Jardines Selles projects, a tough slum burdened by a flourishing cocaine trade, and violent crime. It became Rubén's goal to get his mother out of the projects.

Sierra was signed as a free agent by the Texas Rangers and scout Orlando Gomez on November 21, 1982, and assigned to the Rangers club in the Rookie Gulf Coast League. At the raw age of 17, he played in 48 games and started off slowly, hitting only .242 with one homer and 26 runs batted. The following year he was moved up to the Burlington (Iowa) Rangers of the Class-A Midwest League. He started to show the power the Rangers were hoping for with 6 homers, 33 doubles, and 75 RBIs in 482 at-bats.

At the age of 19 Sierra was starting to fill out a bit and it showed with his increased power in Double-A ball. Playing for the Tulsa Drillers (Texas League), he batted .253 with an on-base percentage of under .300, but raised his home-run production to 13 with 34 doubles and 8 triples in 545 at-bats.

Sierra opened the 1986 season with Triple-A Oklahoma (American Association) and in 46 games showed the Rangers enough for them to call him up on June 1. He wasted little time showing what he could do as he homered in just his second major-league at-bat, becoming the first Texas Rangers player to accomplish that feat.

Sierra went on to play in 113 games, hitting 16 homers, 13 doubles, and 10 triples to give him double figures in each extra-base-hit category. He finished sixth in the American League Rookie of the Year voting. Having picked up switch-hitting in his late teens, he homered from both sides of the plate on September 13 against the Minnesota Twins.

In 1987 Sierra played in 158 games, hit 30 homers, and drove in 109 runs while batting .263. The next season he hit 23 homers and drove in 91 runs. Before the age of 23 he had hit 69 homers and driven in over 250 runs. That put him on pace to easily reach the 500-homer club and come close to 2,000 RBIs; it looked as though he was becoming the player many had perceived him to be.

In 1989 Sierra finished second to Robin Yount in the MVP voting. He batted .306, and led the major leagues with 14 triples and the AL in RBIs (119), slugging (.543), and total bases (344). He also hit 29 homers and 35 doubles. His WAR (wins above replacement) was 5.9, the highest of his career.

During a radio interview by friend Luis Mayoral, a sportswriter and broadcaster, Sierra was told he would be an All-Star and began to cry. "Was it something I said?" asked Mayoral on the morning of the 1989 All-Star Game. "No," sobbed Sierra. "It's just that tonight is the most important game of my life and my mother won't be there to see me play."[1] It was Sierra's fourth year playing in the majors, and his mother, Petra, had yet to attend one of his major-league games. He was named AL Player of the Year by *USA Today* and *The Sporting News*.

The day the MVP selection was announced, Sierra appeared at Mayoral's office in San Juan, at the Rangers' request, to be available to the press. Thirty or so reporters showed up. When it was announced that he had finished second to Yount, Sierra responded in character. He cried like a baby to the point of creating a dark spot on his pants leg where the tears had flowed. In the States, Yount's MVP victory was considered mildly controversial, but on the island of Puerto Rico, it was condemned as a "larcenous miscarriage of justice."[2] Four months later, Sierra himself was still angry about the results. He said: "I led the league in RBIs 119, total bases 344, slugging percentage .543, extra-base hits 78, and triples 14, and I was there in all major categories. He beat me in batting average and doubles."[3] Sierra emphasized that he was not miffed at Yount—"He's a good guy"—but at the voters. He confessed that he had already picked out a spot for the trophy, on top of his TV at home, he was so confident he would win.[4]

Sierra started to lift weights more than usual, which affected his swing as he bulked up to try to hit more homers. Only near the end of his career did he admit as such.[5]

In September 1989 Sierra's mother and grandmother lost their house in Puerto Rico to Hurricane Hugo. This weighed heavily on Sierra as the season wound down.

Sierra hit his 100th major-league home run on April 17, 1990, at age 24. He ended the season batting .280 with 16 homers, 37 doubles, and 96 RBIs. Sierra's rebounded from a subpar 1990 season with 25 homers and 116 RBIs and batted .307, the last time in his career he hit over .300. He had a career-high 44 doubles and was in double figures for steals with 16. All of his numbers were up from the previous year. In early February of 1992 he won his salary-arbitration case, getting $5 million rather than the $3.8 million the Rangers had offered. He struggled some at the plate and was batting .278 when he was traded to the Oakland A's on August 31, with Jeff Russell and Bobby Witt for Jose Canseco.

This was the start of what could be seen as a scenario of revolving doors. Instead of just moving on,

Sierra started to show his immaturity, an impression held by others that arguably followed him for years. The Rangers had expected more for their $5 million, but it was more his frequent failures with runners in scoring position and lackluster play in right field (including seven errors), that began to draw the wrath of both fans and management.

Rangers president Tom Schieffer said Sierra, who rarely signed autographs and avoided interviews because of his broken English, had little community involvement and failed to cooperate when the club tried to promote him. "We made every effort we could to get Rubén to participate in the community and talk to the media and be part of the ballclub, and frankly we got very little cooperation," Schieffer said. "It's very difficult to get someone who won't sign autographs to be popular in the community."[6]

Sierra had hoped to spend his entire career with the Rangers. "I love this game and I figured I would play all my days as a Ranger," he said. "But this year I learned something. I started baseball with passion for the game, because I love it, and it was what I had to do to get out of where I was back home."[7] He added, "This year I learned baseball is a business. You won't always get treated right, and so you just have to keep going where you can make money. I did not always feel that way."[8]

With Oakland, Sierra reached postseason play for the first time. Although the Blue Jays beat the A's in six games in the ALCS, Sierra hit .333 with one home run and seven RBIs.

After the 1992 season the Oakland A's believed that Sierra could productively hit behind Mark McGwire and gave him a five-year, $30 million free-agent contract. After signing, Sierra slammed the Rangers again, even to the point of calling the organization racist. "The Rangers don't want a Latin having all the records in their book," he said. "That's what I think. ... They don't want to have anybody of dark skin, a Latin player, being the big man on the team."[9] Yet after trading Sierra, the Rangers gave a five-year, $45 million contract to Juan Gonzalez.

Sierra's first full year with the A's was 1993 and he bounced back somewhat; his power numbers were back up, with 22 homers, and he drove in 101 runs, the last time in his career he broke the 100-mark in RBIs. He showed his speed again with 25 stolen bases, the last time he appeared in double figures in steals, but he batted only .233. He blamed manager Tony La Russa. Sierra said the low average was a result of pitchers working around him because Mark McGwire had so often been out of the lineup. "I don't have guys like Will Clark and Jose Canseco behind me," Sierra said. I don't have anybody like Rafael Palmeiro or Julio Franco like I had in Texas."[10] La Russa said pitchers didn't throw strikes to Sierra because he chased so many bad pitches. Sierra had only 52 walks for the season.

In 1994 Sierra became injury-prone, a problem that followed him the rest of his career. He played in only 110 games. But he raised his batting average to .268, hit 23 homers and drove in 92 runs. There were whispers that again he was hard to deal with, wouldn't hustle, and just failed to connect with his teammates and management. He finally wore out his welcome and after just 2½ years of a five-year deal he was dealt to the New York Yankees on July 28, 1995.

He hit almost identically before and after after the trade, ending the season with 19 homers and 86 RBIs. Again a trade had given him a shot at postseason play. He drove in two runs, helping the Yankees win Games One and Two of the Division Series against Seattle, but was only 1-for-11 as the Mariners won the final three games.

In 1986 Sierra got in Yankees manager Joe Torre's doghouse for lackluster play and inattention. By the end of July, Torre had had enough and Sierra was on the move again, dealt to Detroit at the trade deadline. Years later, Torre wrote in his book *Chasing the Dream* that Sierra "has no clue what baseball is all about. ... He cares only about statistics. Rubén was the toughest guy I ever had to coach."[11] The Yankees manager criticized Sierra for not grasping the team-first attitude that Torre claimed carried the Yankees to championships. Torre lambasted Sierra for his attitude and said that after months of cajoling and prodding, Sierra still refused to shed his me-first attitude.

Sierra responded by blaming Torre. "What he's trying to do is mess with my career and he's not going to do it," Sierra said at spring training. "Joe Torre don't like me. He traded me. Why, I don't know. I worked hard every day for him in spring training. I worked hard during the season. … I don't understand a guy like Joe Torre. He played a long time, why does he have to say things about me?"[12] Torre responded: "Rubén thought he should play right field instead of Paul O'Neill and thought he should have Paul's number 21 too."[13]

Sierra hoped he could end 1996 on a high note with Detroit, but it was not to be, and he started a downward spiral with many moves over the next several years. He only hit one homer for Detroit and batted just .222; after the season he was traded to the Cincinnati Reds. That lasted only 25 games into the 1997 season before the Reds released Sierra. He had won the left-field job coming out of spring training but lost his job after struggling when the season began. He was batting .244 with two homers and seven RBIs, but had only one hit in his final 18 at-bats with the Reds. He was released on May 9. Two days later, the Toronto Blue Jays took a chance and signed Sierra to a minor-league contract; he was assigned to Syracuse. After eight games, though he was hitting only .219, the Blue Jays had a need and called him up. Sierra proceeded to bat just .208, playing sparingly. He was released in June. This time, no one picked him up.

Sierra caught on with the Chicago White Sox in January 1998. He made the big-league team but was released on May 29, batting .216. He was picked up by the New York Mets at the end of June and assigned to their Triple-A team at Norfolk. He batted .259 with 3 homers and 19 RBIs in 28 games, and was released after the season.

Sierra's poor performance in 1998 undoubtedly had been affected by two family tragedies: His brother and sister both died from complications of AIDS during the year. Still, no major-league team was interested in signing Sierra. At the age of 33 it looked as if his career had come to its end.

Then something changed for the prideful man; he was willing to go to independent-league baseball. He joined the Atlantic City Surf of the Atlantic League. He started slowly but by year's end had hit 28 homers with 82 RBIs and batted .294. This production enticed the Cleveland Indians to sign Sierra after the season. But the Indians released him at the end of 2000 spring training.

Sierra signed with the Cancun Langosteros of the Mexican League and was batting .355 in 16 games when his old team the Texas Rangers came calling. In 2000 in limited action with the Rangers he hit .233 with one homer and seven runs batted in.

Sierra found new life in 2001. After starting the season with Oklahoma City, he was called up to the Rangers and posted good numbers playing a little over half the season. In June he was not just the Rangers' player of the month; he was one of the best players in the AL with 10 homers and 28 RBIs. Against the Los Angeles Dodgers on June 13, for the sixth and last time in his career he hit homers from each side of the plate. For the season he hit .291 with 23 homers and 67 RBIs, and was named the Comeback Player of the Year in the Players' Choice awards and by *The Sporting News*. "I never gave up," he said. "I had faith that I can play. I never lost faith in God that he was going to help me get here again. I just looked for the positive things to help me go forward. I got too big and I just didn't feel the same way. I couldn't hit the ball out over the plate. I was pulling everything. It just didn't work out at all."[14] Through self-reflection, Sierra apparently was taking responsibility for his own action.

Even though he had a good year with the Rangers in 2001, he was released and signed as a free agent with the Seattle Mariners on January 3, 2002. He played the whole 2002 season with the Mariners, primarily as the designated hitter, and batted .270 with 13 homers and 60 RBIs. At the end of the season, he was again released—and for the third time in his career was back with the Texas Rangers, who signed him as a free agent. On June 6 he was back

with the Yankees and Joe Torre, in a straight swap for outfielder-DH Marcus Thames.

Sierra said he had sought out Joe Torre in spring training back in 2000 and apologized during a sit-down in Winter Haven. "I apologized for anything I did before when I was immature," Sierra said. "The years have passed and you understand the way things have to go and now I'm a different guy."[15]

Sierra played in all three rounds of the postseason in 2003, as the Yankees beat the Minnesota Twins and the Boston Red Sox (Sierra getting only two at-bats in each series), but he was called upon in five games of the World Series against the Florida Marlins, the only time he played in the World Series. All nine postseason appearances were as a pinch-hitter. He hit a home run against the Red Sox in the ALCS and tripled in the Series against the Marlins.

Sierra was an important part of the 2004 Yankees, who hit 242 home runs. Sierra himself slugged 17 of those homers as designated hitter, playing in 56 games at that position. In Game Four of the 2004 AL Division Series, with the Yankees down to the Twins 5-2, Sierra hit a three-run homer off reliever Juan Rincon to tie the game. His clutch homer helped the Yankees rally to win the game and the series. He had three consecutive multihit games against the Red Sox in the ALCS, but saw Boston take four straight after being down three games to none.

Sierra had an injury-plagued 2005 season, hit just four home runs, and was released after the season. He was 1-for-3 in the ALDS.

In 2006, Sierra, now 40 years old, gave it another try, signing with the Minnesota Twins. He only had 28 at-bats before being released. He was offered a chance to join the New York Mets for the September run and the playoffs, but due to his mother's illness, he declined and his career ended quietly, without fanfare.

Sierra played for nine teams, was a four-time AL All-Star (1989, 1991, 1992 and 1994), and won an AL Silver Slugger award in 1989. He had seven 20-homer seasons and four times had over 100 RBIs. For his career he hit 306 homers and had 1,322 RBIs, with 2,152 hits and 142 stolen bases.

In retirement he recorded two albums of salsa songs.[16] His son Rubén Jr. played minor-league baseball in the Rangers organization in 2009-2013.

He has said one of his proudest moments was having the money to move his mother out of the projects to a nice house in a nice place in Puerto Rico.[17]

Sierra will be remembered by some as flamboyant, cocky, surly, and immature in many ways, but also humbled himself to come back and end his career on his terms.

## SOURCES

In addition to the sources cited in the Notes, the author also consulted Baseball-Reference.com and newspaper clippings in Sierra's file at the National Baseball Hall of Fame.

## NOTES

1. Austin Murphy, "Rising to the Top of the Game," *Sports Illustrated*, April 16, 1990: 60. "He cries at the drop of a hat," said Mayoral.
2. Ibid.
3. Ibid.

4   Ibid.

5   Bob Klapisch, "Mets' Sierra Ponders What-Ifs," *Bergen Record* (Hackensack, New Jersey), March 15, 2007.

6   Associated Press, "Sierra Bitter Over Texas Ending," *Albany Times-Union*, September 4, 1992.

7   Ibid.

8   Ibid.

9   Knight-Ridder Newspapers, "A's Sierra Bitter About Past and Present." Unattributed, undated newspaper clipping from Sierra's file in the National Baseball Hall of Fame.

10  Ibid.

11  John Giannone, "Torre's Book Causes Rubén to Unleash," *New York Daily News*, March 2, 1997.

12  Ibid.

13  Ibid.

14  David Leon Moore, "Rangers' Sierra Never Lost Faith in His Ability," *USA Today*, July 16, 2001.

15  Anthony McCarron, "'New' Sierra Back on Torre's Bench, *New York Daily News*, July 7, 2003.

16  Robert Dominguez, "This All-Star Goes From Swinging to Singing," *New York Daily News*, October 27, 1994.

17  Austin Murphy.

# DANNY TARTABULL

## By Charles F. Faber

FOR SEVERAL YEARS BASEBALL was very, very good to Danny Tartabull. The game gave him honors and recognition, though not quite as much as he thought he deserved. Baseball paid him millions of dollars, enabling him to live a luxurious life style that most people could barely imagine. But it wasn't enough. He was unable or unwilling to support his youngest sons. His photograph had once graced the cover of *Sports Illustrated for Kids*. More recently it has appeared on Most Wanted posters in post offices throughout the state of California.

Danilo Tartabull Mora was born on October 30, 1962, in San Juan, Puerto Rico, a son of Antonia Maria Mora and José Milage Tartabull Guzman. His family had been prominent in Cuba until Batista was overthrown by Fidel Castro in 1959. Maria's father had owned a sugar factory in Cienfuegos, José's father was a college professor; his grandfather was a judge.[1] Factory owners and supporters of the Batista regime did not fare well under the new order.

José Tartabull was a professional baseball player. After five years of semipro and minor-league experience, he made his major-league debut for the Kansas City Athletics a little more than six months before Danny was born. During the baseball season, the family lived wherever José's club was based. They spent their winters in South Florida. Danny's earliest memories were of romping in the ballpark in Winter Haven during spring training.

As the son of a ballplayer, Danny learned the game of baseball at a very early age. During the summer of 1967, the Tartabulls lived in Brookline, Massachusetts, while José played for the Boston Red Sox. There was a park near their residence, where José was often seen playing catch with his four-year-old son.[2]

The youngster developed his skills on the sandlots of Miami. "I grew up in baseball because of my father, not because of Miami," he said. "I thought everybody's dad went to the ballpark every day at 3 o'clock and played a game of baseball."[3] Danny didn't just play baseball at 3 o'clock. Sometimes he played in three leagues at once. He could play a game in the morning, another after lunch, and a third in the evening. His teammates on one Little League team included José and Ozzie Canseco, Rafael Palmeiro, and Junior Valdespino. Who was the star? "I hate to say this," he said, "but I was. I think my development was quicker because of being around the game more than all of them."[4]

In 1978 15-year-old Danny played American Legion baseball in suburban Miami for Hialeah Post 32 and helped the club win the American Legion World Series. He played high-school ball for Miami's Carol City High School. At age 17 he was selected, as a second baseman, out of high school by the Cincinnati Reds in the third round of the 1980 amateur draft.

The Reds sent Danny to Billings, Montana, in the Pioneer League. He hit .299 in 59 games for the Mustangs in 1980 and played mainly at third base (34 games), although he logged one game at second and 22 in the outfield. In 1981 Tartabull hit .310 for the Tampa Tarpons in the Class-A Florida State League, while playing 46 games at second base and 78 at third. He led the league in batting and doubles, was tied for fourth in home runs, and tied for third in triples and RBIs. He was named the circuit's Player of the Year. Hal Keller, Seattle's director of player personnel, was enthusiastic about the youngster. He told a reporter for *The Sporting News*, "I must have checked with a dozen people who saw this guy play and there was little doubt he could play in the big leagues. I think he'll be a second baseman, but as a fallback, he has enough pop to be a legitimate third baseman."[5]

In 1982 Tartabull hit a career-low .227 for the Waterbury Reds in the Double-A Eastern League, while playing exclusively at second base. That was his final season in the Cincinnati farm system, as the Seattle Mariners chose him on January 20, 1983, as a compensation pick after the loss of Floyd Bannister to free agency. At that time clubs could prevent the loss of players to the draft by putting them on a "protected list." Years later, Cincinnati's farm system director said the failure to protect Tartabull was the most regrettable decision the Reds had made in his quarter-century with the team.[6]

In 1983 the Mariners shipped Tartabull to Chattanooga, their affiliate in the Double-A Southern League. He hit .301 for the Lookouts and played the entire season at second base. The following year the Mariners promoted him to Salt Lake City in the Triple-A Pacific Coast League and switched him to shortstop He hit .304 for the Gulls, earning a late-season callup to the big leagues.

Tartabull made his major-league debut on September 7, 1984, at Royals Stadium in Kansas City. He was 21 years old, stood 6-feet-1, weighed 185 pounds, and batted and threw right-handed. He entered the game as a pinch-runner for Alvin Davis in the ninth inning of a 5-3 loss to the Royals. His next appearance came in Seattle's Kingdome on September 11. The Mariners and the Texas Rangers were tied, 3-3, in the bottom of the ninth inning. The bases were loaded with two outs. Tartabull hit a game-winning RBI single. In his first major-league at-bat he had a walk-off hit.

On February 18, 1984, Danilo Tartabull and Monica Anita Cusseaux were married in Hillsborough County, Florida. In compliance with Florida law at the time, the race of the bride and groom was shown on the marriage certificate. Both were identified as "black." The marriage lasted about 5½ years. The couple divorced in Pinellas County, Florida, on August 4, 1989.

In 1985 Tartabull played a few major-league games for Seattle, mainly at shortstop, but he spent most of the season with the Calgary Cannons, who had replaced Salt Lake City as the Mariners' affiliate in the Pacific Coast League. What a season he had! He hit .300, scored 102 runs, and batted in 109, the first time he had topped the century mark in either

category. He experienced a real power surge, blasting 43 home runs. In five previous seasons in professional baseball, Tartabull had never clouted more than 17 homers in a season. He ranked second in the league in runs scored, led in both home runs and runs batted in, and was named the league's Most Valuable Player.

After that performance, Tartabull could no longer be kept down on the farm. He never returned to the minor leagues, playing 12 more years at the major-league level. In 1986 Tartabull hit .270 with 25 homers for the Mariners. He ranked fifth in voting for the American League Rookie of the Year Award. Although he had been primarily an infielder throughout his earlier career, Seattle converted him into an outfielder and he roamed the outer garden the rest of his career. On December 10, 1986, the Mariners traded Tartabull along with minor-league pitcher Rick Lueken to the Kansas City Royals for outfielder Mike Kingery and pitchers Scott Bankhead and Steve Shields. Many Seattle fans were stunned by the trade, as they envisioned the young power hitter as a possible superstar of the future.

Tartabull made an immediate impact in Kansas City. In 1987 he hit .309 with 34 home runs and 101 RBIs. The next year he hit .274 with 26 homers and 102 runs batted in. Those performances earned him a big boost in pay. In 1989 he received over a million dollars for the first time in his career. He got nice raises the next two seasons, even though his productivity fell off slightly. However, he came back in 1991 with one of his best years ever. He hit a career-high .316 with 31 home runs and 100 runs batted in. He led the league with a .593 slugging percentage. He was twice named the American League Player of the week, once in June and once in July. Tartabull was selected for the 1991 All-Star Game.

Despite his success at the plate, Tartabull was not universally popular among his teammates. Some Royals thought Tartabull had a bad attitude. He was regarded as aloof, arrogant, selfish, interested only in his own hitting, not a team player, and a lackadaisical outfielder. Some resented his ostentatious style of living. He certainly showed off his new-found wealth. One example was how he splurged on his proposal to his girlfriend, Kellie Van Kirk. One April night in 1989, he sent a limo to pick up Kellie, along with a dozen roses, and a note requesting that she wear his favorite dress and asking that she go with the driver to Wyandotte County Lake, just across the state line in Kansas. When she arrived, she found he was waiting for her in a rented tuxedo, accompanied by caterers and a harpist. A four-course meal with champagne was served, while the harpist played romantic music. After the meal Danny suggested they go for a walk up a nearby hill. When they reached the crest of the hill, they saw a fireworks display that spelled out in letters 25 feet high, "Kellie, will you marry me?" She said. "Yes." Tartabull said, "I'll get married, I'll have kids, and I'll have a lot of things happen in my life, but that was a night I'll treasure as long as I live."[7] Little could he imagine the things that would happen in his life.

After the wedding, Kellie and Danny lived during the offseason in a lavish mansion in the Santa Monica Mountains near Malibu, California. The couch was made of Italian leather, the sound system was floor-to-ceiling, the works of art were well-chosen, the 300-gallon saltwater tank was filled with exotic fish, the wine cellar was stocked with expensive fine wines, including 50 bottles of 1985 Chateau Lafite Rothschild, valued at $450 each. "I enjoy making other people feel great," he said. "I want to make my wife happy, and my kids happy, get them things they want."[8] In view of what happened later, how ironic were those words! In the garage were parked two luxury automobiles. The vanity license plates reflected the ego and talents of their owner: SLUGGER and I CAN HIT.

Tartabull professed to not know why some of the Kansas City players found him aloof and a poor teammate. He thought perhaps it was jealousy. "I don't know where it came from, and I don't waste my time trying to find out. It's not true. I brush it off like dust."[9] Kellie said, "It bothers me more than Danny. I know he's none of those things I hear about, not even close. He's a family man, a person who enjoys having fun, going to nice restaurants. He always includes my whole family in the things we do."[10] Kellie accompanied Danny on every road trip. When he was with his wife, he wasn't with his teammates, contributing to the feeling that he was aloof.

Tartabull thought the high opinion he had of himself was justified. "I've always felt I'm a great player. I am great. I know that in certain situations I can do things that a lot of other guys can't," he said. "Let's say I do tell everyone that I'm great. What does that have to do with having a bad attitude?"[11]

At least one of Tartabull's Kansas City teammates defended him. Brian McRae said, "Some people say he had a bad attitude. People think he is arrogant, but that's just the way he is. Not everybody can be your normal run-of-the-mill person. He likes fancy cars, he likes dressing nice, he has a lot of nice jewelry. That might rub some people the wrong way, but that's just Danny."[12]

Kansas City granted Tartabull free agency on October 28, 1991. Several clubs were interested in obtaining the services of the young star. During the early part of the recruiting process, the California Angels, Chicago White Sox, and the Texas Rangers appeared to the frontrunners. The White Sox dropped out of the bidding when Tartabull insisted on a five-year contract. Chicago general manager Ron Schueler said, "Five years is too long for me."[13]

Tartabull had been the Angels' primary target, but their ardor cooled when the club's vice president, Whitey Herzog, became bitter about the way Tartabull's agent, Dennis Gilbert, had behaved during earlier negotiations involving Bobby Bonilla. (Gilbert represented both Tartabull and Bonilla.)[14]

Although they had not been mentioned among the early contenders, the New York Yankees made Tartabull an offer he couldn't refuse. On January 6, 1992, he signed a five-year contract with the Yankees for $25.5 million, the most lucrative contract in club history to that point. He was guaranteed an additional $1.5 million in an endorsement clause that covered the life of the contract. "Texas and the Angels were both very attractive to me," Tartabull said. "But the New York Yankees, man, they're something else. How can you not get excited about that tradition? There's a great mystique to it. Everyone and everybody would love to have that prestige."[15]

Tartabull expected that playing for the Yankees would be a joyful experience, but fate deemed otherwise. He was hampered by injuries every year he was in pinstripes, never logging more than 138 games in a season for New York. Some Yankees officials thought, perhaps unfairly, that he should have played through his injuries.

At first Danny was thrilled at the opportunity to play in New York. He and Kellie purchased a home in Saddle River, New Jersey, within commuting distance of the city. When he signed with the Yankees, they had two children, Danica Janelle, 5, and Danny Jr., 4. Kellie was pregnant with their third child, Zachary, who would be born in Teaneck, New Jersey, on June 23. "New York is the greatest city in the world," Tartabull said. "I can live here (in California) in the winter and play in New York during the season. It's the ultimate."[16] In New York he and Kellie could attend the opera, see Broadway shows, and visit world-class art galleries. "You can't do that in Kansas City or Seattle," he said. "I've always been interested in culture. I like going to plays, my wife and I love the ballet, and we both love art. You can tell just walking through my house. We spend a lot of time in galleries."[17]

The house in Malibu was nice, but Tartabull wanted bigger and better. He had some property in Rancho Santa Fe Farms in the San Diego area. He hired an architect and planned to spend $30 million to build an 11-room, 27,000-square-foot house next door to the home of pop star Janet Jackson. The house would feature a batting cage with a viewing platform, a saltwater aquarium, a scaled-down train to take the family or visitors on a tour of the estate, with stops at a game room, Tiki bar, basketball and tennis court, putting green, and an indoor/outdoor swimming pool, with a 14-foot waterfall, and a water slide descending from the children's bedrooms. He planned to also have a sports training center, with an exercise room and a health bar, a two-story movie theater, a pinball and video arcade, and an aviary.[18] How many of these plans actually came to fruition is not known.

Although he missed 39 games his first year in New York due to injuries (strained left hamstring, lower-back spasms), Tartabull was the Yankees' most productive hitter with 25 home runs and 85 runs batted in. The next year he was even better with 31 homers and 102 RBIs. However, he was unable to match those figures again, and he never hit more than .266 in New York. He struck out more than 100 times each season he wore pinstripes, with his 156 K's in 1993 being second highest in the league. Because of a shoulder injury, incurred when he was making a throw on July 15, Tartabull was unable to play in the field during the second half of the 1993 season, being restricted to the designated-hitter slot.

After the season Tartabull elected to have cosmetic facial surgery and then spend the first three weeks of November vacationing in Europe, delaying his shoulder surgery for more than a month. Dr. Frank Jobe performed the operation at Centinela Hospital in Inglewood, California.[19] Some Yankee officials thought Tartabull should have given higher priority to the shoulder surgery.

In 1994 Tartabull played in only 104 games, mostly as a designated hitter. He hit .256, with 19 home runs and 67 RBIs. He appeared twice on the *Seinfeld* TV show and once on *Married … With Children*.

Unhappy with Tartabull's attitude, the Yankees tried to trade him during spring training, 1995, but found no takers, even when they offered to eat as much as $2 million of his contract. On Opening Day the much-criticized slugger hit a homer and an RBI single. Yankees owner George Steinbrenner said, "I'm still disappointed in Tartabull. Very disappointed."[20]

Upset by Steinbrenner's criticism, in June Tartabull asked to be traded. He needn't have bothered. The Yankees had been trying to unload him for months. "It's easy for him to ask, but it's not easy to move him," general manager Gene Michael said. "Clubs don't want to take that kind of money (Tartabull's $5.3 million salary). I've tried to move him."[21]

Disappointed with his performance, Yankee fans started booing Tartabull whenever he failed to deliver. Tartabull thought Steinbrenner encouraged the boos. The owner was famously hard to get along with, but Tartabull carried their feud to an extreme. His days in New York were numbered. The long-anticipated trade occurred on July 28, when the Yankees dealt the disgruntled slugger to the Oakland Athletics for veteran Rubén Sierra and minor-league pitcher Jason Beverlin. The Yankees sweetened the deal by agreeing to pay half of Tartabull's salary. "I feel like I've been released from jail," Tartabull said.[22]

With the deal completed, Tartabull was able to vent his bottled-up feelings. "It's a zoo there. No I take that back; it's a joke. The sad part is that the only reason for that is the owner. He wants to be the center of attention so bad he just destroys that team. It's so hard for those guys to win because of that man. … The guys won't say it on the record, but they're just miserable there. … I'd still be there if it weren't for George. I had no problems with anyone else, but when you've got an owner like him, he makes it impossible to play up to your capabilities. I mean why would an owner keep downgrading his own product? It'd be like Lee Iacocca telling people not to buy cars. That's just stupid. He's an idiot for doing that."[23]

Tartabull played only 24 games for Oakland. On January 22, 1996, the A's traded him to the Chicago White Sox for pitcher Andrew Lorraine and minor-league outfielder Charles Poe. The Sox had to pick up only half of his $5.3 million salary.

On January 31, 1996, Kellie gave birth to the family's fourth child, Quentin Riley Tartabull. In 1996 Danny had a good season on the South Side of Chicago. Although he hit only .254, he clubbed 27 home runs and knocked in 101 runs. He became a free agent on November 18, and the Sox were willing to re-sign him only if he would accept a huge pay cut. He was unwilling to do so and went on the open market. Few clubs were interested in him. One exception was Philadelphia. Hal McRae, who had managed Tartabull one year in Kansas City, was now the Phillies hitting coach and lobbied on Danny's behalf. Tartabull rejected the Phils' first overture, saying he was insulted by the "lowball offer."[24] After months of negotiations and no better deals tendered, Tartabull signed with Philadelphia for $2 million on February 25, 1997.

On Opening Day, April 1, 1997, Tartabull was in the Phils' starting lineup, playing right field and batting cleanup in a game at Dodger Stadium. During the game he fouled a pitch off his left foot. He was removed from the game and sat out the next three contests, thinking he had a contusion. He was back in the lineup for the games in San Francisco on April 5 and 7. He was unable to complete the latter game and was taken out in favor of Derrick May in the seventh inning. He didn't know it at the time, but his major-league career was over at the age of 34. An MRI revealed that his foot was fractured, and he would be out for the season. For their $2 million investment, the Phils got virtually nothing in return. Tartabull drew four bases on balls and scored two runs, but he made no hits in his seven official trips to the plate.

The Phillies declined to renew his contract, and Tartabull opted for free agency on October 10, 1997. He worked out during the winter, getting himself in shape, and hoping for a return to the big leagues. The San Diego Padres offered him a minor-league contract, but he turned it down. His baseball career was over. He returned to California, and stayed out of the limelight for a few years.

The next time Tartabull was in the national news involved family problems. He and Kellie split up around 2007, and a family court judge ordered Danny to pay child support for the two youngest children, Zach and Quentin. (Having passed the age of 18, neither Danica nor Danny Jr. was entitled to support.) Both boys were star football players, Zach at Valencia High School and Quentin at Bishop Alemany High School in Mission Hills. Zach graduated from high school in 2010 and became a male model. Quentin graduated in 2014 and accepted a football scholarship at the University of California, Berkeley.

Tartabull fell far behind on his child-support payments. On January 24, 2011, he entered a no-contest plea to charges that he willfully disobeyed the court order.[25] Zach had already reached the status of "emancipation" and Quentin would soon join him in that category. Danny would not be liable for child support in the future, but he was liable for payments missed in the past, amounting to $276,204.93. Tartabull was placed on probation, but he violated the terms of the probation. On May 2, 2012, he was sentenced to 180 days in the Los Angeles County jail. He failed to report to jail, and the court issued a warrant for his arrest with bail set at $200,000. When authorities were unable to locate him, he was declared a fugitive from justice.[26]

If anyone knows where Danny is hiding out, they're not talking. "Most Wanted" posters went up in California post offices in July 2013. When Danny Tartabull was a baseball star, he was called "The Bull." Now he is called a "deadbeat dad."

## NOTES

1. Joanne Hulbert, "Jose Tartabull," sabr.org/bioproj/person,54213446.
2. Ibid.
3. Craig Davis, "Yanks' Danny Tartabull Has $25.5 Million, Wants More: A World Series Paycheck," *Sun-Sentinel* (Fort Lauderdale, Florida), April 5, 1992.
4. Ibid.
5. Tracy Ringolsby, "No-Trade Clauses Create Contract Woes," *The Sporting News*, January 31, 1983.
6. Mike Bass, "Cincinnati Reds," *The Sporting News*, January 20, 1992.
7. "Best of Plans Made for Night to Remember," *Los Angeles Times*, April 29, 1989; Bruce Newman, "Bright Light, New City," *Sports Illustrated*, March 23, 1992: 76.
8. Michael Martinez, "Bronx Is Up, but Tartabull Will Take Manhattan," *New York Times*, February 6, 1992.
9. Ibid.
10. Ibid.
11. Newman.
12. Ibid.
13. Joe Goddard, "Chicago White Sox," *The Sporting News*, January 13, 1992.
14. Dave Cunningham, "California Angels," *The Sporting News*, January 6, 1992.
15. Moss Klein, "Yanks Give Tartabull a Record Number," *The Sporting News*, January 13, 1992.
16. Martinez.
17. Ibid.
18. "Yanks' Danny Tartabull Building a $30 Million House in California," *Jet*, May 11, 1992: 48.
19. Jack Curry, "Tartabull Has Operation Yanks Preferred," *New York Times*, December 1, 1993.
20. Jon Heyman, "New York Yankees," *The Sporting News*, May 22, 1995.
21. Jon Heyman, "New York Yankees," *The Sporting News*, June 19, 1995.
22. Bob Nightengale, "Tartabull Loves New York but Loathes Steinbrenner," *The Sporting News*, August 7, 1995.
23. Ibid.
24. cornerpubsports.com/2015/06/phillies-all-train-wreck-team.
25. Sam Gardner, "Call him Deadbeat Danny Tartabull." foxsports.com/mlb/story/danny-tartabull-former-mlb-allstar-shows-up-atop-deadbeat-dad-list-n-la, July 9, 2013.
26. Ibid.

# DICKIE THON

## By Bob LeMoine

*"I'm lucky to be alive. I'm happy to be alive. I'm doing everything I can to play again. It would be a plus. But there are more important things."*

Dickie Thon, 1985[1]

**S**OME BASEBALL CAREERS ARE REmembered for a single moment. It could be a hit to win the World Series, a strikeout to break a record, a diving catch, or a costly error. Dickie Thon's career is remembered for one moment … a pitch that got away. At a time when he was quickly becoming one of the rising shortstops in the National League, Thon's career and life changed forever when a pitch hit him in the left eye, leaving him with permanent partial blindness. Because of that one pitch, we will never know how great a player Dickie Thon could have been, but because of that one pitch, we know how great a man is Dickie Thon, who through faith and perseverance overcame a debilitating injury and persevered through a 15-year major-league career.

Richard William Thon was born on June 20, 1958, in South Bend, Indiana, to Frederick "Freddie" Thon Jr. and Evangeline Thon. Freddie played baseball at Notre Dame, but arm problems curtailed his career. He was in South Bend completing his undergraduate degree in business when Dickie was born. The family moved back to Puerto Rico, and Thon grew up in the Rio Piedras section of San Juan, where his great-grandfather had settled after migrating from Germany.[2] Thon's grandfather, Fred Thon Sr., pitched for the San Juan Senadores of the Puerto Rican Winter League and turned down a Brooklyn Dodgers contract since he was making more money as an engineer.[3] "From the time I was little," Dickie said, "I saw how important baseball was to the people of Puerto Rico. My grandfather told me stories about his days with San Juan in the 1940s and early 1950s. He talked about Monte Irvin, Joshua Gibson, and others who came down here."[4] Thon remembered at the age of 5 meeting Irvin, who was visiting Fred Sr. Irvin, Dickie said, was "nice, polite, and strong." Young Thon also grew up cheering for baseball heroes Orlando Cepeda and Roberto Clemente.[5]

Thon was not the only player in his family to suffer an eye injury; his brother Frankie suffered the same fate on the baseball field. Playing American Legion baseball in San Juan in 1978, Frankie was hit in the face by a catcher's throw, and lost partial vision. Frankie played in the San Francisco Giants minor-league system, but vision problems forced him to retire in 1981.[6]

In his teenage years, Thon played for Bayamón in the Puerto Rico Winter League. He was signed by the California Angels as an amateur free agent in 1975. He spent the 1976 season with Class-A Quad Cities (Davenport, Iowa) of the Midwest League, batting .276 in 69 games at shortstop. Tom Sommers, then the Angels' director of minor-league operations, called Thon "the best natural-looking infielder I've ever seen."[7]

Thon spent 1977 with Class-A Salinas (California) and Triple-A Salt Lake City. Dick Miller of *The Sporting News* wrote, "The best prospect in the [Angels'] farm system is a 19-year-old shortstop named Dickie Thon."[8] Thon spent 1978 and the beginning of 1979 at Salt Lake City. He was called up and made his major-league debut on May 22, 1979, when he replaced Bobby Grich at second base in the eighth inning of a game the Angels were losing to the Milwaukee Brewers. Thon singled in his first at-bat, against Rich Hinton of the Chicago White Sox in the second game of a doubleheader on May 27 at Chicago.

Thon took advantage of his opportunities, going 6-for-16 (.375) through June 17 while filling in for the injured Grich and Bert Campaneris, impressing manager Jim Fregosi. "It looks like he has all the tools to play up here," Fregosi said. Said Thon: "I'm learning all the time from both Jim Fregosi and (coach) Bobby Knoop. They really know this game."[9] On September 6 Thon doubled home Don Baylor in the eighth inning with the go-ahead run in a 10-9 win over Chicago. The win kept the first-place Angels three games ahead of Kansas City, and the team went on to win the American League West. Thon pinch-ran and scored in Game Two of the ALCS against Baltimore in his only appearance in the series, won by Baltimore three games to one. Thon finished with a .339 batting average in 56 at-bats. As a rookie Thon met teammate Rod Carew, whom he would mention as the most influential player in his career.[10]

Thon started at Salt Lake City in 1980 and in 40 games blistered minor-league pitching, batting .394. He was recalled and went 5-for-5 in his first game back, on May 28 against Texas. "I was lucky on a couple of hits but I feel really good at the plate," he said after the game. "I feel comfortable here and I know I can hit big-league pitching."[11] "I was nervous and excited at the same time," he recalled in 2016.[12] Thon was 10-for-14 in his first three home games, batted a torrid .462 in May, and finished the season with a .326 batting average with runners in scoring position. "I'm just trying to fit in," he said. "I'm not that good yet. I have to be patient. I'm real excited about playing here."[13] Thon finished the season batting .255 in 80 games for a dismal 65-95 Angels club. In the winter he returned to Puerto Rico and won a batting title with Bayamón, hitting .329, with a league-best 46 runs and 82 hits in the 60-game schedule.

Thon's chances of starting for the Angels in 1981 were slim, however, with stable veterans Grich, Campanaris, Rick Burleson, and Freddie Patek on the roster. Thon was traded on April 1, 1981, to the Houston Astros for starting pitcher Ken Forsch. "We were looking for an established, experienced pitcher who can throw a good number of innings," Angels executive vice president Buzzie Bavasi said. "While we are terribly sorry to lose Dickie, as far as this club is concerned, the future is now."[14]

In the strike-shortened 1981 season, Thon played a utility-infielder role for Houston, backing up veteran Craig Reynolds. He batted .274 in 95 at-bats, with a .337 on-base percentage. Thon also feasted on home cooking and left-handed pitching, batting .308 at home (compared with .250 away) and .370 against left-handers (compared with .184 against righties). His on-base percentage from August to October was .422 and his batting average was .409, helping the Astros win the National League West for the second half of the season, the unique setup due to the players strike. Thon cooled off in the postseason, batting only .182, and the Astros lost the Division Series to the Dodgers. Thon returned to Puerto Rico in the offseason and batted .333 for Bayamón, winning another batting title.

Thon replaced Reynolds as the starting shortstop in 1982 and asserted himself as one of the top shortstops in the National League, with the glove and the bat. He led the National League in triples (10) and was ninth in stolen bases (37). He was fourth in the league among shortstops in fielding percentage (.975), his range factor per game (putouts and assists divided by games played) was fourth, and a total zone runs average for shortstops (calculating the number of runs above or below average a player is worth to the team) ranked him second behind Ozzie Smith. "I am not really doing anything differently," Thon said. "I'm just getting the chance to play."[15] Thon compiled a 21-game hitting streak from July 24 to August 13, batting .308 over that stretch, and had a four-hit game two days after the streak ended, going 4-for-5 with three doubles against Cincinnati. He hit his first major-league home run in his 567th at-bat, off Bob Walk in Atlanta on June 29. Thon finished the season batting .276 with 3 home runs and 36 RBIs for the 77-85 Astros. His 6.1 WAR (wins above replacement) statistic was sixth in the league for position players.

The 1983 season was Thon's breakout season, and his statistics were among the leaders in the National League in several offensive and defensive categories. His value to the improved 85-77, third-place Astros was immense, and his 7.4 WAR was first in the league among position players. Thon was seventh in at-bats

(619), six in plate appearances (686), seventh in hits (177), and fourth in total bases (283). He ranked first in shortstop assists (533), third in putouts (258), and second in double plays turned as a shortstop (114). His .299 batting average in April was following by three months of .300 or better. Thon had a 12-game hitting streak from May 12-26 and three two-home run games, on June 17, 28, and July 9. His 14th-inning walk-off home run on August 10 beat San Diego. His power was a surprise even to him. "I wasn't thinking home run tonight," he said after the San Diego game. "I just wanted to get on base."[16] Thon made the 1983 All-Star team and stroked a pinch-hit single off Rick Honeycutt. "I saw Willie Mays sitting next to me," Thon remembered from the event. "That was a thrill."[17] His final numbers — .286 batting average, .341 on-base percentage, .457 slugging percentage, 20 home runs, 79 RBIs — were good enough to give him seventh place in the National League MVP voting.

Thon got off to a good start in 1984, batting .375 in the first four games of the season. Then his life changed forever on April 8, in a game at Houston's Astrodome.

Thon used a batting stance that leaned into the plate. New York Mets pitcher Mike Torrez had caught him looking in his first at-bat on a called third strike on the outside part of the plate. In his next at-bat, Thon crept even closer to the plate. Torrez decided to pitch him inside. "After I got him away, I decided to bring it in," Torrez recalled. "He has a tendency to crowd the plate and lunge for balls so I thought I'd jam him. It was a strategy decision, nothing more. But my ball was sailing that day."[18]

Torrez yelled a warning to Thon after releasing the ball, but Thon didn't hear it. Plate umpire Doug Harvey said he saw the ball move about 10 inches, starting waist-high and moving upward until it glanced off Thon's ear flap, then struck him above the left eye.[19] "When I saw where the ball was, it was too late to get out of the way," Thon said.[20] "He ducked," Torrez said, "but he ducked into (the pitch).'"[21] Thon said in 2015 that he continued to relive that moment in his dreams: the ball coming right at him, and himself powerless to move.[22]

The Astrodome crowd went eerily silent as team physician William Bryan and manager Bob Lillis bolted to the field. "I heard a bone break," Dr. Bryan said. "I heard the ball hitting the bone, like a dull thud."[23] Thon didn't get up. "I kept thinking, 'I want to live'" he said. 'I want to see my family again.' I didn't know how bad it was. I was scared. I said, 'Is this really happening?'"[24]

At Methodist Hospital, X-rays revealed a fracture of the orbital rim, the bone above the left eye. "It was an accident, the pitch sailed on me," Torrez said after the game. "I feel awful. He's a good young ballplayer. I just hope to God he's all right. My thoughts will be with him and his family tonight."[25] Torrez called Thon and apologized. "He told me he was real sorry," Thon said. "I believe him. It's one of those things. It's part of the game."[26]

Frankie Thon's wife, Blanca, who was watching the game, became so distraught that she went into labor and gave birth prematurely to Freddie Francis Thon.[27] (Notwithstanding, Freddie represented the fourth generation of Thons in professional baseball, and played for several minor-league teams from 2004 to 2011.)

Thon's 1984 season was over, and his road to recovery was beginning. "I'm not really ever emotional about it and I'm not afraid of getting back in," Thon said later in 1984. "But in the morning, when I wake up, that's when I think about it. I don't blame Mike Torrez. I blame myself. I think, 'Why did I let this happen?' I just stood there."[28]

Three days after he was hit, Thon had surgery on the left orbital bone, but the blurred vision continued. "I hope the Good Lord will help me recover quickly," he said. "It's tough to work hard in spring training to get ready, then have something like this happen. But I'll be back."[29] "I feel for my brother (Frankie)," said Thon. "And I feel him in me. He never had a chance to play in the majors. I have to come back, for me and for him."[30]

An eye examination measured the vision in his left eye as 20/300, and Thon could neither read nor drive. By June 1 his vision had improved to 20/50, but there was still scar tissue behind the retina. He was examined by Stephen J. Ryan, an expert in retina damage at the University of Southern California. "It has to improve on its own," Thon said. "The doctors say I can adjust (to seeing a blurry ball) in time. If it's a matter of work, I'll do it. I'm not down and I'm not giving up."[31] "I have no depth perception," he said. "Glasses won't help right now. ... I've tried batting practice, but the ball is a blur." While dressing and being on the Astros bench during home games kept him in the game and relaxed, "the problem starts when I drive home and I can't always tell how far the traffic light is," he said.[32]

With time off, Thon took business courses at a community college. "I took a course on sports psychology that really helped," he said.[33] He also continued eye exercises that involved following marks on a golf ball and reading numbers on a spinning record.[34] An exam in the fall showed Thon's vision improved to 20/40. "If you take a piece of wax paper and crinkle it up," Dr. Bryan said, "then try to straighten it out, it still has wrinkles. The ophthalmologists tell us that's how the back of Dickie's eyeball looks. It [beaning] affected his visual acuity — his ability to read letters — and his depth perception."[35]

Thon returned to the field in late 1984 in the Arizona Instructional League. He played in five games and had five hits.[36] He played winter ball for the San Juan Metros,[37] hitting a home run in his first game but going 0-for-6 with two errors in his next two games. "I asked to be removed from the lineup," said Thon,[38] who felt he was being used by the team owner as a promotional gimmick.[39]

In spring training 1985, Thon was hopeful. "My timing is bad," he said. "I'm rushing everything. I don't do anything smoothly. Hopefully it's getting better. I'm seeing the ball better and better. Sometimes it's hard to overcome the fear of being hurt. I'm trying to concentrate on seeing the ball and getting out of the way. I know I can do it. It's something I am working on. I have a lot of faith in God. If he wants me to play again, I will."[40]

Thon's career pre-injury was that of a young and promising star. The post-injury Thon was a much different player, one who had to constantly battle physical and mental hardships. "I didn't enjoy the game the same way," he said in 2015. "It was more work for me. Before, it was fun. After that, it was, 'I gotta do this to work for my family, to work for my future.'"[41]

Thon was the Astros' starting shortstop on Opening Day in 1985. A crowd of 42,876 gave him a lengthy standing ovation, and were thrilled to see him single and score the Astros' first run of the season in a 2-1 win over the Dodgers. "This is a big step," he said. "I was anxious about it. The regular season is different from spring training. I wanted a groundball hit at me early to get it out of the way. And the first hit helped."[42] "We were rooting so hard for him that when he came back in the dugout after that first hit, it was as if every player on our team had gotten that hit," manager Bob Lillis said.[43] "He has so much determination that I knew it was just a matter of time until he made it back," said teammate Jose Cruz.[44]

Thon struggled early on, batting .200 in April, striking out 11 times in 40 at-bats, and batting .163 in June, striking out 13 times in 43 at-bats. "They know

I'm not going to get worse, but they don't know if I'm going to get better," he said of the 20/40 vision in his left eye. "I've got to be patient with myself."[45] Batting just .207, he went on the disabled list on May 19. He returned to the field in mid-June, but by July 10 was batting .193. Thon batted .299 with five home runs over the remainder of the season, lowering his strikeouts and raising his season batting average to .251.

With a new two-year contract, Thon arrived at spring training in 1986 optimistic. "This year I feel a lot better than I did last year at this time," he said. "I think the best thing I can do is play and get the competition. That's what I need." He reported that his left eye vision was 20/30, "but I'm getting used to it and seeing the ball good. I wasn't confident last year. I had a lot of friends and a lot of players back me up. I have a lot of faith. I'm working hard."[46] Thon slumped at the plate, but played in 106 games, platooning with Craig Reynolds and facing mostly left-handed pitching.

Complaining of blurred vision, Thon, hitting a paltry .205, went on the disabled list on June 5. When he returned on June 23, he batted .280 the rest of the season, and .300 in the September Western Division title run. Thon was on the field as Mike Scott threw a no-hitter against San Francisco, clinching the National League West. "Very good pitching and very steady infield. Good outfield, good bench, and [manager] Hal Lanier did a great job," Thon remembered.[47] Batting eighth, Thon belted a home run off Sid Fernandez of the Mets in Game Four of the NLCS, giving the Astros a 3-1 victory and tying the series at two games apiece. He played in all six games, going 3-for-12 at the plate, as the Astros lost to the Mets.

Thon left spring training without permission on March 14, 1987, complaining of vision problems. He had gone hitless in eight at-bats, striking out twice, and had made three errors. He underwent a 2½-hour eye examination, with results showing no improvement. Thon also requested psychiatric assistance. His agent, Tom Reich, stated, "Dickie is suffering from a lot of stress. Obviously, at this point, Dickie isn't ready to play." Thon had no desire to return. "I don't know when I'll go back to Florida," he said. "They want to make me make a decision right away, but I'm not going to do it."[48] The team fined Thon $1,000 a day for his absence. He returned to Puerto Rico to see a specialist.[49] Thon returned to the team in May, but left again July 3 after batting .212 and complaining of continual eye problems. "I feel sad because I wish I could have done more for the team," Thon said. "I feel a lot for this team. I feel I'll always be one of them."

Thon was placed on the disqualified list after an unsatisfactory meeting with Astros GM Dick Wagner. "The way [Wagner] has been dealing with my situation, I won't be around here anymore," Thon said. "It's difficult to walk away from a game I'd do anything to play."[50]

Thon's career with the Astros was over, but in 1988 the San Diego Padres were looking for a shortstop to back up Garry Templeton. Thon signed with the Padres as a free agent and played against left-handed pitching, batting .264 in 95 games, but was frustrated with his role. He asked the Padres to trade him. "I had to erase a stigma," Thon said. "I knew by then I could play, but I had to convince others that I could."[51] After the season he was traded to the Philadelphia Phillies. In the winter before the 1989 season, Thon worked in Puerto Rico with Ken Duzich, who was both a hitting instructor and vision specialist. "Dickie was left-eye dominant," Duzich said, "I recommended he open up his head a little bit more so that the right eye had better vision."[52]

Thon no longer crowded the plate but stood away, allowing his right eye to compensate for his left. He also switched from a 34- to a 38-ounce bat.[53] Thon had his best season since 1983, batting .271 in 136 games with 15 home runs, the most among NL shortstops. On September 12 he hit a walk-off home run to beat the Mets 2-1 in a September in which he batted .357. "I think he's back," Phillies manager Nick Leyva said. "And after all the things Dickie has gone through, you have to feel good for him. He's been through a lot of adversity."[54] Thon was just glad for the opportunity to play. "I'm just trying to go out and play as hard as I can every day," he said. "I feel good right now, and I'm getting the chance to play. I think playing so much has made a big difference."[55] He was rewarded with a 1990 contract for $1.1 million in base salary.[56] He continued as the everyday shortstop in 1990, playing in 149 games with a .255 batting average and 8 home runs. On July 13 he hit two home runs at the Astrodome, to the polite applause of the fans, as the Phillies defeated the Astros 4-2. "I feel good about the Houston fans," Thon said. "They have always been good to me. I'm glad I did something they liked."[57]

Thon downplayed being labeled "courageous" when he was awarded the 1990 Philadelphia Sports Writers Association's Most Courageous Athlete Award. "My wife is more courageous than me," he said. "She's had three (caesarean sections), and she wants to have another baby. That's being courageous."[58]

Thon had a nearly identical 1991 season for the Phillies, batting .252 with 9 home runs and 44 RBIs. He slumped in July, and heard the boos from Philly fans. "It bothers me a little bit," Thon said. "I know that always comes when you struggle, but I just want people to know that I play hard, and I think I've been doing my job."[59] Thon's time in Philadelphia came to a close when the Phillies did not offer him a contract for 1992.

In December of 1991 Thon was presented the second annual Tony Conigliaro Award. Conigliaro was a Boston Red Sox player who also suffered vision problems after a beaning in 1967. The annual award is presented to the major leaguer who overcomes "an obstacle and adversity through the attributes of spirit, determination and courage."[60] Thon was a well-deserved recipient.

Shortly after receiving the award, Thon returned to Texas when he signed as a free agent with the Rangers. "This is like home, and it's a very good club," Thon said.[61] A team with many offensive weapons was plagued with one of the worst pitching staffs in the league, and the Rangers finished 77-85 in 1992. A bone bruise on his right shoulder forced Thon to miss most of August and September,[62] and he was released after appearing in 95 games, batting .247 with 4 home runs and 37 RBIs. He returned to the Puerto Rican Winter League with major leaguer Juan Gonzalez and led Santurce to defeat San Juan in the finals. The series attracted 90,369 fans to the ballpark for the six games, including a record crowd of 23,701 in Game Six.[63]

Thon signed with the Milwaukee Brewers for 1993.[64] He batted .396 in April, and singled home the winning run against Toronto on June 25, spoiling ex-Brewer Paul Molitor's return to Milwaukee. Thon played in 85 games, batting .269 with one home run. After the season the Brewers declined his $350,000 option, and he signed a minor-league contract with Oakland in February of 1994. But he retired a month later, complaining of not seeing the ball well in the field.[65] "It's a tough break," said A's manager Tony La Russa. "He's always been a guy I'd like to have on my club. It was just the wrong time of his career … defensively; he didn't really react like I know he could."[66] Thon's 15-year career, which took him from a promising young star to a gritty survivor, was over.

In a 2015 interview with Greg Hanlon of vicesports.com, Thon revealed that the scar tissue behind his retina still had not fully healed, and that his vision and depth perception troubles continued to plague him. Driving and reading were still difficult. Thon played for 10 years while having vision in one eye described as "looking through a sheet of wax paper." No one except his wife, Sol (short for Maria Soledad), knew the extent of his disability. Thon became good at guessing the answers during the eye tests, officially giving him 20/30 vision he likely didn't really have. "I was afraid they wouldn't give me a chance to play," he said.[67]

In 1996 Thon was the Astros' minor-league baserunning and infield instructor. Later he returned to Puerto Rico and continued to be involved with the winter league, working with the Cangrejeros de Santurce club, as well as youth baseball. Thon's family is known for its success in athletics. His wife, Sol, was a volleyball player on the Puerto Rican National Team; daughters Soleil, Vanessa, and Mariana were collegiate volleyball players at Rice, Tulsa, and South Florida; and son Dickie Joe Thon, an infielder, was drafted by the Toronto Blue Jays in the fifth round of the June 2010 amateur draft, and received a $1.5

million signing bonus. As of 2016 he was still playing in the Blue Jays farm system. "He earned more by signing than I did in my best year," his father joked.[68]

In 2011 Thon and Torrez met face-to-face for the first time since the beaning. Torrez again apologized, but Thon repeated what he had said 27 years earlier: It's just part of the game. A devout Catholic, Thon said he looked instead to the blessings of his life instead of the hardships. "I've had a lot of good things happen to me. I try to think about it that way," Thon said.[69]

Asked by the author to describe anything important he would want conveyed in this biography, Thon said: "One thing I've learned is that [you should] always believe in yourself and accomplish everything you want in life, with hard work and determination. Don't listen to negative stuff. Always concentrate on believing that you can accomplish anything if you are willing to work hard."[70]

## SOURCES

In addition to the sources cited in the Notes, the author also benefited from the Dickie Thon file at the Baseball Hall of Fame Library, Cooperstown, New York.

## NOTES

1. Gordon Edes, "Dickie Thon Is the Latest Big League Player to Attempt a Comeback From a Serious Beaning: GAME'S NIGHTMARE," *Los Angeles Times*, March 18, 1985.
2. Greg Hanlon, "Lost Greatness, Scar Tissue, and Survival: The Life of Baseball's Brief Superstar, Dickie Thon," Vice Sports. Retrieved March 8, 2016, sports.vice.com/en_us/article/lost-greatness-scar-tissue-and-survival-the-life-of-baseballs-brief-superstar-dickie-thon.
3. Mason Kelly, "Thon Family Bound By History," *Bakersfield* (California) *Californian*, July 16, 2006. Retrieved January 30, 2016, bakersfield.com/sports/2006/07/16/thon-family-bound-by-history.html.
4. Thomas E. Van Hyning, *Puerto Rico's Winter League: A History of Major League Baseball's Launching Pad*. (Jefferson, North Carolina: McFarland, 2004), 108.
5. Dickie Thon, mail correspondence with the author, September 2016.
6. Thon correspondence with author.
7. Earl Gustkey, "Angel Officials Keep an Eye on the Minors," *Los Angeles Times*, April 23, 1976: 8.
8. Dick Miller, "Rich Angels Ask: Which Niche for Grich Next Year?" *The Sporting News*, October 22, 1977: 31.
9. Pete Donovan, "Angels…Who are Those Guys?" *Los Angeles Times*, June 23, 1979: D8.
10. Thon correspondence with author.
11. Jim Shulte, "Thompson, Thon Lead Angels' Win Over Texas," *San Bernardino* (California) *County Star*, May 29, 1980: D3.
12. Thon correspondence with author.
13. Dick Miller, "Thon Hits a Ton, and Angels Think of Trade," *The Sporting News*, June 28, 1980: 10.
14. Associated Press, "California, Houston Swap Two Players," *Santa Cruz* (California) *Sentinel*, April 1, 1981: 49.
15. Hal Bodley, "Thon Earns His Stripes at Short for the Astros," *USA Today*, June 29, 1983: 5C.
16. Associated Press, "Thon's 16th Homer Gives Astros the Win," *Baytown* (Texas) *Sun*, August 11, 1983: 2-C.
17. Thon correspondence with author.
18. Craig Wolff, "A Fearless Moment Keeps Its Hold on Dickie Thon," *New York Times*, June 17, 1984. Retrieved January 31, 2016. nytimes.com/1984/06/17/sports/a-fearless-moment-keeps-its-hold-on-dickie-thon.html?pagewanted=all.
19. Ibid.
20. Ray Didinger, "The Future Is a Blur for Dickie Thon," *The Sporting News*, September 24, 1984: 58.
21. Ibid.
22. Hanlon.
23. Ibid.
24. Ibid.
25. Ibid.
26. Associated Press, "Thon Afraid of Not Being Able to Play Again After Being Hit by Pitch to Head," *Big Spring* (Texas) *Herald*, April 11, 1984: 10. Retrieved March 27, 2016, bill37mccurdy.com/2015/06/06/the-night-dickie-thon-went-down/.
27. Wolff, "A Fearless Moment."
28. Ibid.
29. "Thon Has Surgery," Associated Press clipping in Thon's Hall of Fame file marked 4/12/1984.
30. Wolff, "A Fearless Moment."
31. Ibid.
32. Craig Wolff, "Thon Now Looks to 1985," *New York Times*, June 16, 1984.
33. Ron Fimrite, "You Can't Keep a Good Man Down," *Sports Illustrated*, April 16, 1990.
34. Ibid.
35. Edes.

36 Ibid.

37 Associated Press, "Thon to Make Comeback in Winter League," *Albany* (New York) *Times Union*, undated article in Thon's Hall of Fame file.

38 Hal Bodley, "Dickie Thon: Astros Shortstop Battles Blurry Vision, Doubts in Comeback," *USA Today*, January 22, 1985.

39 Edes.

40 Ibid.

41 Hanlon.

42 Neil Hohlfeld, "Thon Makes Opening Night to Remember," *The Sporting News*, April 22, 1985: 24.

43 Ibid.

44 Neil Hohlfeld, "Thon Now Appears Back in Stride," *The Sporting News*, September 9, 1985: 18.

45 Jack Etkin, "Astros' Thon Praying Path to Lineup Clears," *Kansas City Times*, May 2, 1985.

46 Fred McMane, "Thon's Fight Back Nearly Completed," *Tampa Tribune*, March 13, 1986.

47 Thon correspondence with author.

48 "Thon Asks for Help," *Albany Times Union*, March 23, 1987.

49 "Thon Given Ultimatum," *Albany Times Union*, March 18, 1987; "Thon Will be Back," *Albany Times Union*, March 19, 1987.

50 "Thon Doesn't Plan Return to Astros," *New York Post*, July 7, 1987.

51 Fimrite.

52 Van Hyning, 108.

53 Hanlon.

54 Bill Brown, "Thon Has Completed Long Journey," *The Sporting News*, September 25, 1989.

55 Ibid.

56 Unknown clipping in Thon's Hall of Fame file, marked 2/19/90.

57 "Thon's Blasts Light Up Night for Phillies," *New York Daily News*, July 15, 1990.

58 Paul Domowitch, "Thon: My Wife Is More Courageous," *Philadelphia Daily News*, February 13, 1990. Retrieved March 27, 2016, articles.philly.com/1990-02-13/sports/25880359_1_courage-dickie-thon-mike-torrez-fastball.

59 Diane Pucin, "Struggling Thon Not Ready for the Scrap Heap Just Yet," Knight-Ridder News Service story published in the *Albany Times Union*, August 4, 1991.

60 "Tony Conigliaro Award," Baseball Reference Bullpen. Retrieved March 27, 2016, baseball-reference.com/bullpen/Tony_Conigliaro_Award.

61 Randy Galloway, "Thon's Voice Will Be Heard in Clubhouse," *Dallas Morning News*, April 2, 1992.

62 United Press International, "Rangers' Thon on DL," August 7, 1992. Retrieved February 27, 2016, upi.com/Archives/1992/08/07/Rangers-Thon-on-DL/1406713160000/.

63 Van Hyning, 108.

64 Ed Glennon, "Brewers Sign Thon," *Rockford* (Illinois) *Register Star*, March 31, 1993: 5D.

65 "Thon Retires," *Stamford* (Connecticut) *Daily Advocate*, March 3, 1994: C2.

66 "Eyesight Fading, Thon Retires," *Santa Cruz* (California) *Sentinel*, March 3, 1994: B-3.

67 Hanlon.

68 Marc Seide, "Seniors Storied Childhood Paves Way to USF," *The Oracle*, October 26, 2010. Retrieved March 27, 2016, usforacle.com/news/view.php/690131/Seniors-storied-childhood-paves-way-to-U; Bob Elliott, "Thon's Father Knows Best," *Toronto Sun*, August 23, 2010.

69 Hanlon.

70 Thon correspondence with author.

# JOSÉ VALENTÍN

by Steven Schmitt

**O**N HIS 17TH BIRTHDAY, JOSÉ Valentín got a $22,000 present from the San Diego Padres — a $22,000 professional baseball contract. Sandy Alomar Sr., the Padres' third-base coach, manager of the Santurce Crabbers and San Diego's chief scout for Puerto Rican talent, convinced the Padres that the kid from Fernando Callejo High School in his hometown of Manati, Puerto Rico, was worth the investment. Valentín paid five seasons of minor-league dues at Spokane, Charleston (South Carolina), Riverside (California), and Wichita but made an astonishing 182 errors, playing 471 games as the shortstop of the future and never batted higher than .278 (in 1991 with Double-A Wichita, for whom he hit 17 homers and drove in 68 runs).

Valentín was what might be termed an un-shortstop: he had excellent range, a strong throwing arm, and surprising power he got from the lower part of his 5-foot-10, 175-pound frame, but he made too many errors and struck out too much. Yet Valentín persevered, a throwback player with an aggressive, team-oriented attitude. He played hard, played hurt, and had desire that surpassed other players. "If you want the money … play like it," he said. "Play like you want to get there. Don't talk about it and then not do it."[1]

Valentín got there and did it for 16 major-league seasons, smacking 249 home runs as a switch-hitting shortstop (with time spent at second base and third), including a stretch of 25 or more home runs per year over five seasons with the Chicago White Sox (2000-2004). He later owned and played on the Crabbers, relocating them to Manati. He returned to the Padres when Manati's attendance plummeted and the club joined a Double-A league in Puerto Rico. In 2012 Valentín became manager of the Class-A Fort Wayne Tin Caps and won the Eastern Division playoffs but lost in the Midwest League championships. In 2013 he led the Tin Caps into the Midwest League semifinals. Valentín's success resulted in a promotion to the major leagues as the Padres' first-base coach the next two seasons. When the Padres hired Andy Green as manager, Valentín was out of a job and did not coach at the major-league level in 2016.

Born on October 12, 1969, José Antonio Rosario Valentín grew up playing Puerto Rico's favorite sport. His high school produced several professional prospects, including major leaguers Carlos Beltran and Valentín's brother, José Javier Valentín, who caught for 10 seasons, mostly with the Minnesota Twins and Cincinnati Reds, and hit two home runs off Hall of Fame pitcher Greg Maddux on the occasion of the pitcher's 298th win.

Their father, José Sr., taught José Antonio to switch-hit beginning at age 14. A former catcher and player-manager for a semiprofessional Puerto Rican national team that traveled around the world. José's father served as president for the Jose Rodríguez Little League in Manati and managed Javier's Junior Division team that won the 1989 Little League Junior Baseball World Series in Taylor, Michigan. His wife, Yolanda Valentín was a long-time volunteer in the local league. In 2005, the Valentíns received the George and Barbara Bush Little League Parents of the Year award in a ceremony at Williamsport, Pennsylvania. They were the first Little League Parents of the Year to have two children reach the major leagues.[2]

José's father knew that his son's best position was shortstop because of his size and his arm. "My dad didn't push me," Valentín said, "but he taught me. He waited to see what position I really wanted to play."[3] Valentín also pitched in Little League against future major leaguers Juan Gonzalez and Bernie Williams. "He used to strike me out all the time," Williams said.[4] Scouts started following Valentín when he was 16, calling the house and asking about his age and his grades. On October 12, 1986, the Padres signed Valentín but he never played a game for them.

Valentín's big break came on March 26, 1992, when the Padres traded the five-year minor leaguer to the Milwaukee Brewers along with pitcher Ricky Bones and outfielder Matt Mieske for third baseman Gary Sheffield and minor-league pitcher Geoff Kellogg.[5] Sheffield was thrilled to leave Milwaukee, having publicly attacked owner and acting baseball commissioner Allan H. "Bud" Selig before the Brewers decided they could get three players for one and eliminate what general manager Sal Bando called a "distraction" for the other players.[6] Some Padres wished Valentín had not been part of the deal. "We heard about the trade," Tony Gwynn recalled," and we said, 'Please don't let it be Valentín.'"[7]

Valentín spent most of 1992 at Triple-A Denver before the Brewers called him up on September 17. He hit a sacrifice fly as a pinch-hitter and scored a run as a pinch-runner but went hitless in three at-bats over four games. After spending most of 1993 at Triple-A New Orleans, Valentín again reached Milwaukee in September, replacing the injured shortstop Pat Listach. Valentín played 19 games at shortstop, 16 from start to finish, batting .245. In his fifth game, he hit a three-run homer in a 15-5 drubbing of the New York Yankees, signaling that the long-awaited successor to Robin Yount (who moved to center field in 1985) might have finally arrived. "This is a good chance for me," Valentín said. "I will work hard to make the team win. I want to make them make a decision on me next year."[8]

In 1994 the Brewers considered moving Listach to second base and starting Valentín at shortstop or putting 31-year-old Jody Reed at second base, starting Listach at shortstop, and leaving Valentín the odd man out. The Brewers almost ran out of infielders when Listach (left knee tendinitis) and third baseman Kevin Seitzer landed on the disabled list and Valentín left for Puerto Rico to be with his pregnant wife, Ilka, who ended up in the hospital after her blood pressure spiked and doctors had to deliver the baby early. "He needs to be down there with her," manager Phil Garner said. "That's all I know."[9]

When he returned, Valentín took over at shortstop and hit 11 homers with 46 RBIs and 12 stolen bases in a strike-shortened 1994 season, during which he had a brief bout with tendinitis in his right shoulder. On July 20, a healthy Valentín hit his first grand slam in an 11-1 win over the Kansas City Royals at Milwaukee County Stadium. "The ball hopped off (his bat) and headed toward the right field wall," wrote Bob Berghaus of the *Milwaukee Journal*. "The only question was on which side of the foul pole it would land." When umpire Ted Hendry gave the fair sign, Valentín "began jumping up and down in a very excited fashion."[10] Outfielder Greg Vaughn, the team's top slugger, was not surprised. "José has big-time pop," Vaughn said. "He's going to be a great player, who as long as he continues to improve day in and day out, can be a tremendous shortstop in the American League for a long time."[11]

The impending strike threatened to cost Valentín valuable playing time. He hoped to raise his batting average and reduce his fielding miscues, something he traditionally worked on playing winter ball back home. The following season, 1995, Valentín played in 112 games and hit 11 home runs with 49 RBIs and 16 steals, but suffered a broken ring finger on his left hand August 31 sliding into second base. The Brewers lost 21 of 28 after that and Valentín played only eight games in September.[12]

Nobody was happy with Valentín's .219 average and .293 on-base percentage so he decided to become strictly a left-handed hitter. "I've been (switch-hitting) for 10 years and I haven't really improved," he said. "As it is now, they take me out for a pinch-hitter sometimes late in the game. … I may as well hit left-handed all the time." His career statistics showed 23 home runs and 95 RBIs from the left side and no home runs and eight RBIs from the right side, with a 100-point disparity in batting average. A 40-game winter-ball experiment failed, with a .165 average, one home run, and 10 RBIs as a permanent portsider, so Valentín returned to switch-hitting in 1996.[13] He finished the season with 24 home runs, 95 RBIs, 17 stolen bases, and a .259 batting average in 154 games. The Brewers responded with a three-year contract

that paid Valentín $1.1 million for 1997, $2 million for 1998, and $2.3 million for 1999, with a $3.2 million option for 2000, plus a deferred $1.037 million signing bonus. He had earned $280,000 for the 1996 season and was eligible for salary arbitration before signing the long-term deal. Attributing Valentín's league-leading 37 errors to winter-ball fatigue, the Brewers paid him $100,000 to skip the annual trip to Puerto Rico. "It's going to be nice to relax this winter and not worry about anything," he said. "I won't have to worry about a contract. I can just go out and play."[14]

Suffering a broken left middle finger in April 1997, Valentín saw his production drop to 17 home runs and 58 RBIs with a .253 average in 136 games, striking out 109 times. In 1998 he spurned $100,000 and played winter ball to improve his hitting and fielding. "I don't care about the money," he said. "If I'm a better player, I will get more money in the future."[15] The results were immediate. On April 3 Valentín became the first player to hit three home runs at Miami's Pro Player Stadium, home of the Florida Marlins. His five RBIs included a three-run homer that sealed a 7-1 win. He hit .467 in his first four games and was moved to third in the batting order in the eighth game of the season, despite a 1-for-9 slump in between. Curiously, Valentín was hitting left-handed pitchers better than righties in the first month and the Brewers topped the National League Central at 15-7. Valentín's average plummeted from .296 eight games into the season to .203 by June 7 and he lost the shortstop job in early August to four-year veteran Mark Loretta, whose .320 average was 100 points higher.[16] The Brewers (74-88) finished in fifth place and Valentín's numbers (.224, 16 home runs, 49 RBIs, 105 strikeouts, and 21 errors) landed him on the trading block.

Valentín and Garner were given one more chance in 1999. By then, the only numbers talked about were Valentín's $3.2 million option year and the $320,000 he would get if the team declined to pick it up.[17] His value depreciated when he suffered a torn ligament in his left thumb. By mid-July, Valentín had played in only 25 games. When he returned to the lineup, his average dropped 40 points to .261. When Bando fired his ex-Oakland teammate Garner, Valentín lost one of his biggest supporters. He still wanted to stay in Milwaukee so he agreed to reduce his option-year pay to $1.3 million and played center field in the Puerto Rican League to sharpen his skills in the event that the Brewers peddled Marquis Grissom.

In what author Richard Lindberg called White Sox general manager Ron Schueler's "last great trade," the Valentín and pitcher Cal Eldred went to Chicago on January 12, 2000, in exchange for pitchers Jaime Navarro and John Snyder.[18] Reported to be "flawless in the field" during spring training, Valentín made six errors in his first six regular-season games, four in one game at Oakland. White Sox manager Jerry Manuel remained patient and batting coach Von Joshua worked with Valentín on his hitting. Valentín led AL shortstops with 36 errors and struck out 106 times but he made up for that with 25 home runs (breaking a 36-year-old club record for homers by a shortstop), 92 RBIs, a .273 average, 19 stolen bases, and 107 runs scored, the highest total of his career. He hit for the cycle on April 27 and hit home runs from both sides of the plate on September 30. The White Sox won the AL Central with a 95-67 record and Manuel named Valentín the team's most valuable player, calling him "the heartbeat of the team."[19] "José plays to win," Manuel said. "He is exactly what we talk about when we say 'team player.'"[20] In return, Valentín—now a free agent—turned down a four-year, $21.4 million offer from the Baltimore Orioles and took $15.5 million over three years with a fourth-year option to stay in Chicago.[21]

So why did the White Sox trade for Texas Rangers shortstop Royce Clayton? Because they planned to convert Valentín to a center fielder because of his 36 errors at shortstop and incumbent CF Chris Singleton's decline in production. So it was off to winter ball to learn a new position. "He was happy to change positions in order to help the team," wrote scribe Scott Gregor. "He'll get the job done in the outfield and at the plate."[22]

Clayton's .135 start got Valentín his old job back. He had 13 home runs and was batting .290 before going on the disabled list after June 8, 2001, with a right hamstring injury, and he finished with a career-high 28 home runs, 68 RBIs, and a .509 slugging percentage.[23] Yet Valentín called out some of his teammates because of a 14-28 start that eventually kept the White Sox from making the 2001 playoffs. "If guys are out there just to play for their stats, then they better not get caught," he said. "I don't want to play with anyone like that. I'm getting paid a lot of money and I want to earn it. No one should be here who wants to steal money. That's the kind of thing that splits a team apart."[24] The White Sox got the message and rallied to finish third with an 83-79 record. "José's one of those guys we all respect," closer Keith Foulke said. "He goes out there and busts his tail every day. … He backs up what he says." Schueler said a team sometimes needs a player to point fingers. Valentín said he was not doing that. "I was asking for help."[25]

In 2002 Valentín remained the regular shortstop and hit 25 home runs with 75 RBIs. Because he hit only .152 against left-handed pitchers, Manuel wanted to platoon Valentín with utility infielder Tony Graffanino. Instead, Valentín played 144 games in 2003 and socked 28 home runs with 74 RBIs. He still fanned 114 times but reduced his errors to 19—11 at third base and eight at shortstop—his lowest miscue total in six seasons. He still made difficult plays others could not and turned double plays swiftly. After abandoning another try at strict left-handed hitting, Valentín in 2004 became the first White Sox shortstop to hit 30 homers in a season—his career high—and drove in 70 runs but hit a career-worst .216 with 139 strikeouts.

When White Sox manager Ozzie Guillen decided to go with utility infielder Juan Uribe at shortstop, Valentín missed the opportunity to get a World Series ring in 2005. He signed as a free agent with the Los Angeles Dodgers, who thought Valentín could replace third baseman Adrian Beltre. Instead, he tore ligaments in his right knee during spring training and played in only 56 games, the fewest of his major-league career. In 2006, Valentín signed a free-agent deal with the New York Mets and played regularly at second base for the National League East champions, with occasional stints at shortstop, third base, and the corner outfield spots, alongside center fielder and Fernando Callejo alumnus Beltran. A rejuvenated Valentín hit 18 home runs (two in one game on August 30 at Colorado and two on September 18 against the Florida Marlins at Shea Stadium), drove in 62 runs, and batted .271, his best single-season mark.

The major-league trail ended the following year when Valentín played regular second base through July 20 and posted a .241 average in 51 games with 3 home runs and 18 RBIs before a foul ball broke his right leg. Valentín finished with 249 career round-trippers. A notorious low-fastball hitter, Valentín hit 226 home runs off right-handed pitchers, 170 to right field and 99 on two-strike counts.

In 2008 Valentín played briefly for two Mets minor-league clubs and 17 games for the Crabbers (Cangrejeros de Santurce) of the Puerto Rican Winter League. He had bought the club in 2004 and moved it to Manati but the team had poor attendance and Valentín sold the team, getting back about half of his original $700,000 investment. "I was trying to help clean up the league," Valentín said, "but I'm not going to waste my career and I'm not going to waste my life and marriage for something that wasn't worth it."[26] In 2011 Atenienses de Manati joined a Puerto Rican Double-A baseball league while Valentín became instructor at the Puerto Rico Baseball Academy and High School in Gurabo, 2½ hours from Manati. One of his prize pupils was Jesmuel Valentín, one of his two sons and a first-round draft choice of the Los Angeles Dodgers in the June 2012 amateur free agent draft.[27] Traded to the Phillies in 2014, Jesmuel reached Triple-A Lehigh Valley (International League) in 2016. Like his father, Jesmuel played mostly shortstop and persevered waiting for a chance at the big leagues.

José Valentín devoted full time to the major league-sponsored academy until he returned to the Padres as manager of the Fort Wayne Tin Caps (Midwest League) in 2012 and 2013, then moved up to the Padres as first-base coach in 2014 when Rick Renteria was named manager of the Chicago Cubs and Padres first-base coach Dave Roberts became bench coach. "He definitely knows how to motivate his team," Austin Hedges, a catcher on the 2012 Tin Caps, said. "He really emphasizes playing the game hard. We started playing the game the right way—hard and tough. That's the way he played the game. He definitely preaches that."[28] Valentín lost the coaching job after the 2015 season when the Padres fired manager Bo Porter.

Valentín kept his Puerto Rican ties, serving as bench coach for Leones de Ponce in 2012 and coaching for Puerto Rico in the 2013 World Baseball Classic. In 2011 he told MLB.com's Alden Gonzalez that he would be a good big-league manager and had set a goal to get there.[29]

## SOURCES

In addition to the sources indicated in the Notes, the author also consulted Baseball-Reference.com and MLB.com.

## NOTES

1 George Castle, *Throwbacks: Old-School Baseball Players in Today's Game* (Dulles, Virginia: Brassey's, Inc., 2003), 124.

2 Cincinnati Reds Media Relations. Parents of Major Leaguers Javier and Jose Valentín chosen as Little League Parents of the Year. http://mlb.mlb.com/news/print.jsp?ymd=20050811&content_id=1166471&vkey=news_mlb&fext=.jsp&c_id=mlb

3 Castle, 124-126.

4 Castle, 126.

5 "Baseball: N.L. West," *The Sporting News*, April 6, 1992: 23.

6 Tom Haudricourt, "Sheffield Traded to San Diego. Brewers Get Bones and 2 Minor Leaguers," *Milwaukee Sentinel*, March 28, 1992: B1.

7 Bob Berghaus, "3 New Players Figure to Offer Immediate and Long-Term Help," *Milwaukee Journal*, March 29, 1992: C6.

8 Tom Haudricourt, "Opportunity Knocks on Valentín's Door," *Milwaukee Sentinel*, September 17, 1993:1.

9 Tom Haudricourt, "Valentín Leaves to Be with Wife; Brewers Very Low on Infielders," *Milwaukee Sentinel*, May 13, 1994: 3.

10 Bob Berghaus, "Valentín's Swing Turns Out Grand," *Milwaukee Journal*, July 21, 1994: C1.

11 Ibid.

12 Drew Olson, "Milwaukee Brewers," *The Sporting News*, September 11, 1995: 29.

13 Drew Olson, "Milwaukee Brewers," *The Sporting News*, January 22, 1996: 46.

14 Drew Olson, "Milwaukee Brewers," *The Sporting News*, November 11, 1996: 38; November 18, 1996: 36.

15 Drew Olson, "Brewers. Working Vacation," *The Sporting News*, January 12, 1998: 57.

16 Drew Olson, "Loretta's Play Earns Him Starting Role at Short," *The Sporting News*, August 10, 1998: 38.

17 Drew Olson, "Most Important Moves Will Come Off the Field," *The Sporting News*. August 30, 1999: 31.

18 Richard Lindberg, *Total White Sox. The Definitive Encyclopedia of the World Champion Franchise* (Chicago: Triumph Books, 2006), 275.

19 Castle, 119.

20 Lindberg, 276.

21 Ken Rosenthal, "Inside Dish," *The Sporting News*, December 4, 2000: 64.

22 Scot Gregor, "TSN Power Poll: 9," *The Sporting News*, March 26, 2001: 18.

23 Scot Gregor, "Painful Reality: Two More Join Disabled List," *The Sporting News*, June 18, 2001: 40.

24 Castle, 120.

25 Castle, 121.

26 Jeff Sanders, "Work Ethic Drives Valentín Back to Majors," *San Diego Union-Tribune*, March 19, 2014. sandiegouniontribune.

com/sports/padres/sdut-padres-jose-valentin-mlb-first-base-coach-2014mar19-htmlstory.html. Accessed September 19, 2016.

27 Aldren Gonzalez, "Baseball Is Family Affair for the Valentíns," MLB.com, August 19, 2011. m.mlb.com/news/article/23394956.

28 Sanders.

29 Gonzalez.

# JAVIER VÁZQUEZ

## By Norm King

**I**F JAVIER VÁZQUEZ FOUGHT IN THE Civil War in a previous lifetime it was as a Confederate, because he sure had some tough times at Yankee Stadium. He was involved in three historic games in the House That Ruth Built, once as a member of the Montreal Expos and twice while wearing Yankee pinstripes. He was the victim in one of the greatest pitching performances in Bomber history, and contributed to two defeats that might have had Ruth, Gehrig, and DiMaggio spinning in their graves.

Despite some disastrous games in the Bronx, Vázquez had some very good seasons plying his trade for the Expos, Yankees, Arizona Diamondbacks, Chicago White Sox, Atlanta Braves, and Florida Marlins. At the end of his 14-year major-league career, he was the all-time leader among Puerto Rican major-league pitchers in numerous categories, including starts (443), wins (165), innings pitched (2,840), and strikeouts (2,536).[1] During that time he acquired the nickname the Silent Assassin, for combining a quiet demeanor with a powerful, sometimes wicked, right arm.

Javier Carlos Vázquez was born on July 25, 1976, in Ponce, Puerto Rico, the son of Carlos and Aurora Vázquez. Unlike many Latin American players, Vázquez grew up in a middle-class environment; his father worked for a Puerto Rican shipping company. His lifestyle allowed Javier to attend private schools, and to pursue sports for the passion of playing rather than as a means of escaping poverty.

That passion began at age 3, when he received a baseball glove as a birthday present. He began playing Little League at 8, and continued his development throughout his teenage years to the point where at 15 he was playing against boys two and three years older than he was.

"It was at that moment that I thought he might play in the major leagues," said Carlos. "He trained every day and I never had to force him because he is very disciplined."[2]

Vázquez played high-school baseball and basketball at Colegio Ponce, and it was while he was there that the Expos made him their fifth-round draft choice in 1994—Puerto Rican players were included in the major-league draft beginning in 1990. He began his professional baseball career at the age of 17 by going 5-2 with a 2.53 ERA in Rookie ball with the Expos' Gulf Coast League team, and followed that up in 1995 with a 6-6 mark and a rather elevated 5.08 ERA with the Single-A Albany (Georgia) Polecats of the South Atlantic League (SAL). The Expos had their SAL franchise in Delmarva, Maryland, in 1996, and it seemed the Northern climes agreed with Vázquez, as he went 14-3, with a 2.68 ERA and 173 strikeouts in 164⅓ innings pitched. He also pitched two innings and got the win in the league's All-Star Game.

That record got Vázquez promoted to the West Palm Beach Expos of the Advanced-A Florida State League for 1997, where he continued improving by going 6-3, with a 2.16 ERA and 100 strikeouts in 112⅔ innings. He caught the attention of the Harrisburg Senators, Montreal's affiliate in the Double-A Eastern League when their 10-game winner Tommy Phelps went under the knife for a torn labrum in his pitching shoulder. Montreal promoted Vázquez to Harrisburg as the Senators strove to repeat as Eastern League champs, and he showed how dominant he could be. He went 4-0 in six starts, with a 1.07 ERA and 47 strikeouts in 42 innings. He added two more victories in the playoffs as the Senators retained their title.

After that season Vázquez was among the players who participated in a winter caravan with the parent club. The bitter cold of Quebec in February was lessened somewhat when Expos manager Felipe Alou told Vázquez that he had a chance to make the team in 1998. The news came as somewhat of a surprise. "I was just kind of like, 'Wow,'" Vázquez said.³

True to his word, Alou gave Vázquez his opportunity, and he responded. On March 24, for example, Vázquez pitched five shutout innings as the Expos defeated the Los Angeles Dodgers 6-1 to end a 14-game spring-training losing streak.

Vázquez made the roster, and the Expos embarked on the season with a starting rotation that had a combined total of 6 years and 69 days of major-league service.⁴ Still, it was quite the honor when Vázquez got the ball for the Opening Day assignment at Wrigley Field against the Chicago Cubs. The Cubs, no doubt motivated by the fact that it was their first game since legendary broadcaster Harry Caray died during the offseason, won 6-2. Vázquez gave up three earned runs in five innings of work.

That outing typified his season, as the overmatched 21-year-old stumbled to a 5-15 record with a 6.06 ERA. One bright spot was his first major-league victory, a 7-4 win over the expansion Arizona Diamondbacks, but it was clear he still had a way to go before he would become an effective pitcher, and he couldn't help but be frustrated.

The 1999 season began as a repetition of 1998 for Vázquez, as hitters continued blasting his pitches to the far reaches of major-league ballparks. Giving up six earned runs in 3⅓ innings to the Diamondbacks on June 2 dropped his record to 2-4 with a 6.63 ERA, and the Expos felt he needed a change of pace in more ways than one. They demoted him to Ottawa of the Triple-A International League, where he learned how to throw a straight changeup to right-handed batters, and how to throw from the stretch.

The results weren't immediately apparent during his first start with Montreal after he returned from Ottawa on July 18, which just happened to be the date of his first encounter with history at Yankee Stadium. His mound opponent that day was David Cone, who threw a perfect game as New York won 6-0; Vázquez gave up all six runs.

Things started to click for Vázquez after that. He pitched his first career complete game in his next start, a 5-1 win at home against Pittsburgh that

began a four-game winning streak. His record finally went over the .500 mark in a 3-0 one-hit shutout at Dodger Stadium on September 14 to go 8-7. He finished the year at 9-8 with a 5.00 ERA, but after losing against the Yankees, he was 7-3 with a more respectable 3.77 ERA.

Whenever a player improves significantly in one season, the question becomes whether he can continue in the next campaign. Vázquez answered that question in his first start of 2000, giving up two earned runs in seven innings against the Dodgers at Olympic Stadium. Despite the fine performance, he received a no-decision in the Expos' 6-5 win.

Vázquez won six of his first seven decisions, including a 2-0 win over the Diamondbacks and eventual Cy Young Award winner Randy Johnson. He went eight innings, gave up five hits, walked two, and struck out seven. The Big Unit, who was 7-0 for the season going into the game, was impressed.

"Any time you lose 2-0, the opposing pitcher pitched outstanding," Johnson said.⁵

The vagaries of playing for a lousy team—the Expos lost 95 games that year—can be maddening. Vázquez gave up seven earned runs in getting his sixth win, but was the losing pitcher in consecutive 8-1 blowouts, despite giving up five earned runs over 11 innings. In August he pitched in two games the Expos lost 4-3, pitching seven scoreless innings in one and giving up two earned runs over seven innings in the other. He lost his only decision of the month 7-0 to Los Angeles, but even in that game he felt he pitched well.

"I made some good pitches, they were just hitting them," Vázquez said. "I threw strikes and got ahead of people."[6]

A few clunkers and some bad luck aside, Vázquez had another good season, going 11-9 with an improved 4.05 ERA.

Even though Vázquez didn't miss a start in 2000, Alou took an approach with him in 2001 that was unusual for its day, but is now standard procedure. Vázquez was cruising along with a 10-0 lead after seven innings against the Mets in his second start of the season, on April 7, when Alou pulled him after seven innings.

"(A)fter he hit the 100-pitch mark, manager Felipe Alou took him out," wrote Stephanie Myles. "Alou is insistent that even his ace be well-rested so that he can be strong in September."[7]

Maybe Alou should have kept him out until then, because Vázquez had a Jekyll-and-Hyde kind of first half. He gave up six earned runs in 4⅓ innings in his next start, on April 13. After giving up eight earned runs on April 29 and five more on May 4, he went out and pitched 16 consecutive scoreless innings in his subsequent two appearances. He was consistent in June only in that he lost four straight decisions.

After his June swoon, Vázquez hid the Hyde juice and put in an All-Star-caliber performance; if they only counted games from July on, he would have won the Cy Young Award hands down. Entering the month with a 6-9 record, he went 10-2 for the rest of his season, with a 1.92 ERA and 102 strikeouts in 108 innings pitched. It was almost like a corny old movie when the pitcher who thought his girlfriend had left him finds out she really does love him.

The turnaround, according to Expos catcher Michael Barrett, occurred after the Braves roughed Vázquez up for seven earned runs in 6⅔ innings in a 10-5 loss at Olympic Stadium on July 28. "It was in the sixth inning … and he gave up like four runs," Barrett said. "It was almost like a light switch turned on, and he just said he was better than that and he wasn't going to give up any more runs. Then we went out and he was dominating game after game."[8]

But then disaster struck. In the Expos' first game at Olympic Stadium after the World Trade Center disaster, Marlins pitcher Ryan Dempster hit Vázquez squarely in the forehead with a fastball (the crack could be heard throughout the nearly empty Big O), causing fractures around his orbital bone and ending his season. It was typical of the Expos' season that they scored six runs that inning to go up 6-0, but gave up eight runs the next inning and lost the game. Had Vázquez not been injured and earned the "W," he had an outside shot at a 20-win season.

Vázquez had a better shot at being shot by Expos manager Frank Robinson in 2002. After he recovered during the winter from his season-ending injury, the inconsistency returned as he went back to his win-one-lose-one ways. In August somebody turned the switch off completely, as he lost seven straight decisions, ruining any chance the Expos had of making the postseason as they finished 83-79. Vázquez managed to win his last two decisions to bring his record up to 10-13 with a 3.91 ERA, but the season was clearly a disappointment.

Things didn't start off much better for Vázquez in 2003, either. He wanted a raise to $7.15 million from the $4.75 million the previous year. The Expos took him to arbitration, where he lost his case and had to settle for the $6 million the Expos offered. He wasn't just unhappy about the decision, he also didn't like being the only Expos player whose contract wasn't settled without going the arbitration route.

On that same day, Vázquez had to make an emotional about-face as his wife, Kamille, whom he married in 1998, went into labor. Vázquez left training camp to be with her and was there when their daughter, Kamila, was born. Despite the joy of his new family arrival, he was still angry with Expos management the next day for how they handled the situation.

"I am a person who is grateful [for receiving a $6 million salary] and I'm not saying I had an All-Star season because I didn't," he said. "The wins weren't there but everything else was there. I really thought they were going to treat me better."[9]

Vázquez's mood may have improved once the season started, as his grandmother, Isabelle Arroyo, finally got to see him pitch in the major leagues and she didn't even have to leave Puerto Rico to do it. That's because the Expos' owners, MLB, decided to have the Expos play 22 games at Estadio Hiram Bithorn in San Juan. Vázquez took the San Juan hill on April 14 with Grandma, his parents, and other family members looking on, and left after six innings with the score tied 3-3—the Expos won the game, 5-3. Isabelle high-fived many people when Javier singled and drove in a run in the second inning.

Despite a brutal travel schedule, Vázquez was having a fine season and the Expos were still in the wild-card hunt when September rolled around, which is exactly when he decided to go into the tank.[10] He went 1-4 for the month and finished a promising season at 13-12 with a 3.24 ERA, the lowest of his career to that point. He also set career highs in innings pitched (230⅔) and strikeouts (241, third in the National League).

That fall the Yankees and Boston Red Sox met in an epic American League Championship Series, which the Yankees won on a home run by Aaron Boone in the bottom of the 11th inning. Vázquez didn't know it, but Boone's triumphant circling of the bases would directly affect his career. It started on November 28, 2003, when the Red Sox obtained Curt Schilling from the Diamondbacks. The Yankees wanted to upgrade their pitching staff to counter Boston's move, and obtained Vázquez on December 4.[11] It turned out to be a season like no other in his career.

Vázquez's first start of the season in the home opener, on April 8, almost didn't happen as he had to show his ID to stadium security personnel before they let him in the building.[12] He made a name and a face for himself after giving up one run over eight innings as the Bombers won 3-1.

After going 3-2 in April, Vázquez was Bronx Bombed in early May, giving up 12 earned runs in two starts as his record dropped to 3-4. Again he turned things around after that, winning seven of his next eight decisions. Then on July 8, Vázquez found out he was going to his first All-Star Game as a replacement for the injured Tim Hudson. He got into the game, too, pitching a 1-2-3 fifth as the American League pounded the National League, 9-4, in Houston.

His second memorable game at Yankee Stadium, was another historic occasion. The Yankees, who had an 8½-game lead over the Red Sox on July 31, had seen that lead dwindle to 4½ when Vázquez toed the rubber against Cleveland on August 31. What followed was a 22-0 Yankee loss, the most lopsided defeat in the team's illustrious history.[13] Vázquez lasted only 1⅓ innings during which he gave up six earned runs (amazingly, all 22 runs in the game were earned—at least the Yankees didn't commit any errors) on five hits.

New York recovered from that debacle and won the American League East Division title, giving Vázquez his first trip to the playoffs. He started against Minnesota in what turned out to be the deciding game in the Division Series, giving up five earned runs in five innings with a no-decision as the Yankees won 6-5 in 11. He came on in the third inning during Game Three of the ALCS against Boston with New York in front 6-4. Despite giving up four runs in 4⅓ innings, he got his only postseason victory as the Yankees won 19-8 to go up 3-0 in the series.

But this was 2004, and the Red Sox clawed back to tie the series at three games apiece. In Game Seven, Yankees manager Joe Torre brought Vázquez in to face Johnny Damon with one out and the bases loaded in the bottom of the second. This being Vázquez's third historic game, you can guess what happened; Damon rocketed his first pitch into the Bronx night sky as the Red Sox completed the most incredible comeback in baseball playoff history.

Vázquez was banished to the desert in January 2005 when the Yankees shipped him, two other players, and $9 million to the Diamondbacks for Randy Johnson. The All-Star season from the year before proved a memory as Vázquez once again went back and forth until he had another second-half slump, losing six of eight decisions from August 3 until the end of the season. He finished 11-15 with a 4.42 ERA. After the season he demanded a trade because he wanted to play for a team east of the Mississippi River so that his family could return to Puerto Rico during the season more easily. Arizona traded him to the Chicago White Sox for three players and cash.

"It was a really tough decision because I really enjoyed my time in Arizona," he said. "I had a good time with the guys on the team and everyone there."[14]

After a lackluster 2006 season with the Sox where he went 11-12, Vázquez had a career year in 2007, going 15-8 with a 3.74 ERA and 213 strikeouts in 216⅔ innings pitched. The difference this time was a very strong second half; beginning August 4, he went 7-2 the rest of the way. Maybe he wanted to fulfill manager Ozzie Guillen's prophecy.

"My prediction in spring training [was that] Vázquez was going to be the most consistent guy we have, and he has been," Guillen said.[15]

But that prediction didn't carry over into 2008, where Vázquez's second-half troubles returned when he lost six of his last eight decisions. This rough patch typified Vázquez's inconsistency. After pitching 7⅔ innings of shutout ball in a 4-2 victory over Detroit, he gave up seven, five, and seven runs in his last three decisions, all losses, and finished 12-16 with a 4.67 ERA. Still, the White Sox made it to the postseason against the surprising Tampa Bay Rays. Vázquez started the opener but didn't last long as the Rays pasted him for six earned runs in 4⅓ innings, giving him a lifetime playoff ERA of 10.34. At least one local scribe made note of his less-than-stellar playoff performance.

"No surgical procedure exists that would help (Vázquez) rise to the occasion in important moments, but how about an outpatient visit that at least makes him throw strikes," wrote Rick Morrissey.[16]

That was enough for the White Sox, who traded Vázquez back to the National League, this time the Braves. Gone were the days of Glavine, Smoltz, and Maddux, but Atlanta still had a good pitching staff. Vázquez fit in quite nicely there in 2009, tying Derek Lowe for the team lead in victories with 15 — along with 10 losses — and a career-best 2.87 ERA, along with 238 strikeouts in 219⅓ innings. Braves manager Bobby Cox may have had a sleepless night on August 31 because he didn't know what kind of Vázquez he was going to get in September. The 32-year-old came through, going 4-1 for the month, but that wasn't enough to lead Atlanta to the playoffs.

With their pitching depth, the Braves felt they could part with either Lowe or Vázquez, although they preferred to part with Lowe. The interest level in Lowe wasn't very high, so Atlanta ended up trading Vázquez back to the Yankees as part of a deal that brought them Melky Cabrera to shore up their outfield.

Vázquez's New York revival in 2010 didn't go as hoped because he had lost some of the velocity on his fastball. He lost four of his first five, won some, then lost some more. By August 25, Yankees manager Joe Girardi decided that rookie Iván Nova had earned some time in the rotation, which relegated Vázquez to a relief and spot-starting role until the end of the season. He finished at 10-10 with a 5.32 ERA. His 157⅓ innings pitched were the second lowest of his career, and his mediocre performance prompted Girardi to leave him off the postseason roster.

Not surprisingly, the Yankees did not re-sign Vázquez, and that fall the Marlins inked him to a one-year deal for $7 million. At first it looked as if the Marlins got taken; he allowed seven earned runs in 3⅔ innings against the Diamondbacks on June 11 to go 3-6 with a 7.09 ERA. But then he activated the same switch that turned his 2001 season around. He went 10-5 after that with a 1.92 ERA, winning his last six decisions to finish at 13-11 in what turned out to be the last season of his career. He was the only starter with a record above .500 on a team that finished 72-90. Appropriately, Vázquez's final start, on September 27, came against the franchise that drafted him, but was now located in Washington, and it finished in dramatic fashion. He had gone all the way as the Marlins and Nationals were tied 2-2 with two out in the bottom of the ninth. Marlins manager Jack McKeon had already decided that Vázquez would go out for the 10th, but Bryan Petersen made the decision moot as he smacked a game-winning solo shot. It was a nice way to go out.

"I've been blessed to be in the big leagues for 14 years. I feel it's time," he said after the game. "I'm glad I'm pitching well because it would be tough retiring on a bad note."[17]

Although Vázquez never pitched after that, he did consider representing Puerto Rico in the 2013 World Baseball Classic, but knee surgery prevented him from participating. As of 2016 he was an international special assistant with the Major League Baseball Players' Association, where his role was to increase the profile of the game around the world. He lived in Puerto Rico with his wife, daughter, and son Javier.

## SOURCES

In addition to the sources listed in the Notes, the author also used:

Celebritybabies.people.com.

*Chicago Tribune.*

harrisburgsenatorsmlb.wordpress.com..

Jockbio.com

Liebman, Ronald C. "The Most Lopsided Shutouts." *SABR Research Journal* archives.

*Pittsburgh Post-Gazette.*

Porter, David L., ed. *Latino and Latin American Athletes Today: A Biographical Dictionary,* (Westport, Connecticut: Greenwood Press, 2004).

*USA Today.*

## NOTES

1  Jordan Wevers, "MLB's All-Time Puerto Rican-Born Team," *calltothepen.com,* June 12, 2016. Translation by author.

2  Hugo Dumas, "Javier Vázquez, la Fierte de Ponce (The Pride of Ponce)," *La Presse* (Montreal), April 13, 2003: D1.

3  Ed Price, "Vázquez to Get Shot at Starting Rotation," *Palm Beach Post,* February 24, 1998: D6.

4  "Baseball Today," *Palm Beach Post,* April 4, 1998: 5C.

5  "Johnson Loses to Montreal Despite 12 Ks," *Arizona Daily Star* (Tucson), May 17, 2000: C5.

6  Paul Gutierrez, "Dodgers Get Lift From Park," *Los Angeles Times,* August 25, 2000: D9.

7  Stephanie Myles, "Barrett Might Have More Pull at the Plate and on the Mound," *The Sporting News,* April 16, 2001: 30.

8  Glenn Kasses, "Vázquez Flips the Switch," *Palm Beach Post,* February 28, 2002: 5C.

9  Scott Brown, "Vázquez Criticizes Expos," *Florida Today,* February 20, 2003: 4D.

10  As of August 31, Montreal had a 71-67 record. The Phillies and Marlins were tied for the lead in the wild card with 73-63 marks. Between September 1 and September 12 the Expos flew from Miami to Philadelphia to San Juan to Montreal. After defeating the Cubs in San Juan on the afternoon of September 11, they flew to Montreal to continue their "homestand" on September 12 against the Mets. MLB also didn't allow the Expos to obtain any players or call anyone up from the minors in September.

11  The Yankees sent Randy Choate, Nick Johnson, and Juan Rivera to Montreal.

12  "Cool Vázquez Wins N.Y. Debut," *Democrat and Chronicle* (Rochester, New York), April 9, 2004": 6D.

13  Steve Popper, "Yankees Slide to a New Low Against Indians: 22-0," *New York Times,* September 1, 2004.

14  Bob McManaman, "D-backs Prepared to Move on," *Arizona Republic* (Phoenix), November 12, 2005: C3.

15  Dave van Dyck, "Goals Remain Despite Lost Season," *Chicago Tribune,* September 9, 2007: Section 3, p. 7.

16  Rick Morrissey, "That Stings: Vázquez Flops Again on Big Stage; Sox Drop Opener," *Chicago Tribune,* October 3, 2008: 2A-1.

17  Joe Capozzi, "Petersen's Home Run Gives Win to Vázquez," *Palm Beach Post,* September 28, 2011: 5C.

# JOSÉ VIDRO

## By Mark S. Sternman

**THE SWITCH-HITTING JOSÉ VIDRO** made three All-Star teams and batted over .300 for five straight seasons, 1999 through 2003. He remains the best second baseman in the truncated history of the Montreal Expos.

Born on August 27, 1974, in Mayaguez, on Puerto Rico's west coast, Vidro grew up about 15 miles away in Sabana Grande, where he played "baseball with tennis balls on makeshift diamonds"[1] and attended high school. According to *Sports Illustrated*, "His father, José Sr., (was) a foreman at a Frito-Lay factory, and his mother, Daysi, was an office worker for Sunkist Foods."[2]

Drafted by Montreal in the sixth round of the 1992 amateur draft, Vidro spent six years in the minors, including two full seasons and part of a third with single-A teams. He did attain two major personal milestones during his years in the minors. Vidro married Annette on September 2, 1993. José Vidro Jr. was born on January 7, 1996.

The Expos called Vidro up from Triple-A Ottawa on June 6, 1997, after Vladimir Guerrero was sidelined with a pulled hamstring.[3] In his major-league debut, on June 8, he smacked a pinch-hit double off Steve Trachsel of the Chicago Cubs and scored on a single by Mark Grudzielanek. Fourteen hitless at-bats later, Vidro's second hit was also a double.

Vidro would frequently find his way to the keystone sack after plate appearances and with the glove. He doubled for his first two hits with the Expos, and he would finish in the top three in the National League in doubles in 1999, 2000, and 2002. "The left side [was] his power side, but he [was] not a pull hitter; he spray[ed] the ball from the right-center gap to the left field line. His right-handed hit chart mirror[ed] that pattern—most of his base hits were to center or right."[4]

After batting .249 in 67 games for Montreal in 1997, Vidro made the Expos out of spring training in 1998. Montreal needed a second baseman after the offseason trade of Mike Lansing to Colorado. Faced with a glorious opportunity to seize an open position, Vidro began the season by going 0-for-14. Vidro "was sent down to Triple-A in 1998 and watched Vladimir's brother Wilton Guerrero take over his job"[5] in a rare case of a team replacing one 23-year-old switch-hitting second baseman with another. Vidro would return to Montreal and would hit below .200 for every month of the 1998 season save for June, when he hit .325. He finished 1998 with a career-low OPS of .596, a figure that compared poorly with Wilton Guerrero's .723 mark.

"My second year in the majors was my worst year in my professional career," Vidro said. "I was trying to do too much and putting too much pressure on myself. ... I couldn't sleep, thinking about what I had to do. Physically I felt perfect, but my mind wasn't."[6]

With his future in Montreal uncertain, Vidro returned home for the offseason. After the 1998 campaign, Vidro "played winter ball ... to gain confidence at the plate[; he] did just that by batting .417 in Puerto Rico."[7]

Vidro kept his hot bat going and had a breakthrough season at the plate in 1999. "Early talk had him working out in left field, but Rondell White's move from center to left to protect his knee ended that possibility. Vidro ... inherited the second base position ... almost by default—Wilton Guerrero wasn't doing the job,"[8] and, unlike the previous year, Vidro started strongly. On April 14 he had the first five-RBI game of his career in a 15-1 rout of the Milwaukee Brewers. On July 18 with one out in the eighth inning, Vidro nearly broke up what would become a perfect game pitched by David Cone of the Yankees, but his smash to the right side was snared by Yankees second baseman Chuck Knoblauch.[9]

Enough hits got through in 1999 when "Vidro was without a doubt the Expos' most pleasant surprise

… after winning the second base job by mid-May … making significant strides with both his defensive and offensive game."[10] Closing the campaign with an 0-for-27 slump, Vidro finished the season with a still impressive .304 batting average.

After a good 1999 season, Vidro faced unexpected completion going into 2000 when Montreal signed the veteran Mickey Morandini. At a fan festival for the Expos more than a decade after the team left Montreal, Vidro recounted manager Felipe Alou saying that Morandini would play second base. Vidro said he replied, "Good luck with that. He ain't taking my job. I'm the second baseman here."[11]

Indeed, Vidro had a great 2000 campaign. "I've always liked him as a hitter," Jim Beattie, the Expos' general manager, said. "He reminds me of Edgar Martínez in his knowledge of hitting. Edgar didn't have a lot of power when he came up, but he developed it at the big league level. José has a chance to hit 20 to 30 homers depending on how hot he gets."[12]

Vidro proved Beattie quickly correct by slugging a career-high 24 homers in 2000 to go along with other career highs that year in hits (200), doubles (51), RBIs (97), batting average (.330), and slugging average (.540). He homered for his 200th hit. Ballpark security retrieved the ball and gave it to Vidro, who in turn passed it on to his grandfather, who had attended the game.[13]

Vidro complemented his offensive production with defensive prowess: "I heard before he got here that José didn't have the range," said fielding coach Perry Hill, "but I've seen him make plays from shallow right field to behind the bag."[14] Vidro led the NL in assists as a second baseman in 2000 with 442 and made his first All-Star team.

Asked to explain the turnaround after signing Vidro to a four-year, $19 million contract, Beattie said, "It just seems as if he became more serious. This is a guy who, when he first came up, was in a concern group in the three areas we test for: conditioning, strength, and body fat. … He's worked hard, put himself in better shape and it's started to pay off."[15]

Vidro's numbers dropped off in 2001 as he missed three weeks with an injury to his left forearm and 11 games after Roy Oswalt beaned him. Vidro expressed frustration that the team's flinty ownership prevented the franchise from realizing its potential. "They promise a lot and then do nothing," Vidro said of owner Jeffrey Loria and team president David Samson. "I sat there and watched them talk about how Felipe Alou was going to be our manager all season. … And they fired him two weeks later. We were rabid and hurt. They lied to us."[16]

Threatened with contraction after the 2001 season, the Expos rebounded in 2002, when Vidro finally played for a Montreal team that would end a season with a winning record. The Expos scored 735 runs that year and allowed 718 runs—not a notable margin save for the fact that no other team for which Vidro played in the majors had a positive differential. With a .417/.593/1.010 slash line, Vladimir Guerrero was Montreal's best player, but Vidro, having "shed much of the baby fat and the defensive yips that made him a questionable prospect,"[17] also could capably carry the club.

From May 4 through May 27, Vidro had a 21-game hit streak during which he batted .414. With the streak at 18 games on May 25, Vidro led off the bottom of the ninth inning against Philadelphia closer José Mesa. The Expos trailed the Phillies 9-8, and Vidro to that point in the game had gone 0-3 with a walk. Vidro singled off Mesa to keep his streak alive. Troy O'Leary drove in Vidro later in the frame, and the game went to extra innings. In the bottom of the 10th, Vidro faced Hector Mercado and delivered a walk-off grand slam, the second-to-last such hit in Montreal history, to lead the Expos to a 13-9 comeback win that put the Expos just 1½ games out of first place.

May 26 saw another spectacular Vidro performance against Philadelphia pitching. With Montreal down 1-0 in the bottom of the first, he doubled and scored the tying run on an O'Leary single. With the Expos trailing again 2-1 in the third, Vidro doubled but did not score. With Montreal losing, 4-1, in the bottom of the sixth, he singled as the middle man in a three-hit rally that closed the gap to 4-2. By the home half of the seventh, Montreal had fallen behind, 5-2. By the time Vidro came up, Montreal had two on with two out and had narrowed the gap to 5-3. Vidro's line-drive single made the score 5-4. With Guerrero up and runners on the corners, Vidro broke for second. Vincente Padilla threw a wild pitch that allowed the tying run to score. Vidro advanced two bases on the play, to second on the steal and to third on the wild pitch. Manager Larry Bowa of the Phillies inexplicably had Padilla pitch to Guerrero, and Vlad singled in Vidro with the go-ahead and ultimately winning run as Montreal triumphed, 6-5.

Over parts of two important games given the proximity of the Expos to first place, Vidro in his last seven plate appearances had a walk followed by six straight hits. He had a stolen base, four runs scored, and five RBIs.

On May 27 Vidro kept his hit streak alive one more day by homering in the ninth inning off Tom Glavine, but Montreal fell 5-1 to Atlanta to fall back to .500 at 25-25. The Expos would stay at .500 all the way to 79-79 before winning four meaningless games at the end of the year. Vidro had his best defensive season in 2002: he topped NL second basemen in assists (448), tied with Todd Walker of the Reds for the lead in putouts (314), and finished second in range factor.

After the contraction scare of 2002, the Expos' escapades would get even more absurd in 2003 when Loria sold the team to Major League Baseball, and Montreal played a score of "home" games in Estadio Hiram Bithorn in San Juan. What would end awfully began beautifully. José's mother attended the first game there to see her son play in a Montreal uniform for the first time. In his first major-league game on his home island against Graeme Lloyd of the Mets, Vidro hit a two-run homer. "When I was coming around second base, I had tears in my eyes," he said. "I had thought about what it would be like, to hit a home run in front of my mother, in front of my family. For it to happen … it's hard to explain."[18]

Vidro delivered again in the third game of the eventual four-game sweep of the Mets. Facing Mike Stanton in the bottom of the 10th, Vidro hit a walk-off homer. Rounding the bases, he "punched his fist in the air as chants of 'Vidro!' and horns blared"[19] in what must have felt like another intensely proud emotional moment for the Puerto Rican native.

The Expos unexpectedly stayed in the playoff hunt for far longer than expected. On August 17 Montreal trailed San Francisco 2-0 heading into the bottom of the ninth. Sidney Ponson had a three-hit shutout with one out when Vidro doubled. Walks to Guerrero and Orlando Cabrera followed to load the bases. Tim Worrell came in for Ponson and struck out Wil Cordero before yielding the last walk-off grand slam in Expos history to Brad Wilkerson as Montreal won, 4-2.

On August 28 a four-game sweep of the Phillies left the Expos, to widespread amazement given the constraints under which the team operated, in a multiple-team tie for the wild card.

But playing home games in two different cities took a physical toll on Vidro and the Expos. "I talk to guys on other teams and they know what we've been through," Vidro said. "They tell me, 'You guys should really be proud of what you've accomplished this season, what you've overcome. That makes me feel good. … But for me, it hasn't been that much fun. … Maybe after it's over I'll appreciate it more."[20]

The terrible travel wore down Vidro and the Expos, a problem exacerbated by the team's failure to call up minor-league reinforcements to save a few dollars for the overlords in the commissioner's office. Vidro's month-by-month statistics in 2003 show that clear signs of fatigue kicked in after the end of the dog days in August:

|  | OBP | SLG | OPS |
| --- | --- | --- | --- |
| March/April | .412 | .583 | .996 |
| May | .413 | .438 | .850 |
| June | .414 | .458 | .872 |
| July | .386 | .488 | .874 |
| August | .404 | .438 | .841 |

In September Vidro struggled to a subpar slash line of .318/.379/.697. When asked years later what he would do if he were commissioner, he replied that he would "shorten the season to 150 games."[21] Still,

Vidro had put together another fine year overall in 2003, his last All-Star season, setting career highs in walks (69) and OBP (.397).

In 2004 spring training, Vidro expressed cautious optimism going into his contract year, exclaiming, "I just love to be here now and be part of this organization. This is my last year here. We'll see what happens. … I'm going to be faithful to the team."[22]

That positive attitude did not last the summer, as Vidro tired of the travel and tired of the questions about the toll the travel took on the team: "We've been trying to deal with it in a way that it doesn't look too bad, but any way you look at it, it's really bad. I don't know what to say anymore. Hopefully, this is the last year of this and we can go on with our business the way the rest of the league does."[23]

Montreal and Vidro both regressed in 2004. The Expos stumbled to a 67-95 mark, and Vidro's batting average dropped below .300 to .294. Like the duration of the Expos in Montreal, Vidro's 2004 season ended prematurely after he went on the disabled list on August 26 and had "season-ending surgery September 8 to repair recurring patellar tendinitis in his right knee."[24]

Vidro showed more faith toward his team than the Expos did to Montreal, which would move to Washington in 2005. Before the move, the Expos broke with precedent and inked Vidro to a contract worth $30 million over four years. Vidro explained, "I didn't see myself in another uniform. By signing me, it's a sign we're going to have a home next year. We don't have a permanent home, but I feel like in this team I'm in my home."[25]

The passing of the Montreal Expos led to the birthing of the Washington Nationals for the 2005 season. Vidro began spring training with healthy knees, but soon hyperextended his right elbow,[26] an ominous sign since he later tore a left ankle tendon, which caused him to miss two months. Subsequently, he "battled two strained quadriceps, as well as a bad knee, for much of the second half of the season."[27] Vidro played in just 87 games in 2005 and hit just seven homers.

After a campaign lost largely to his assortment of ailments, Vidro faced competition at second base for the first time since 2000 from a player with far more pop than Morandini, namely, the newly acquired Alfonso Soriano. The Nats wanted Soriano to play

left field; Soriano wanted to stay at second. Vidro expressed more interest in another change under consideration in Washington, namely, the construction of a new ballpark to replace the cavernous Robert F. Kennedy Stadium. "I don't know if I'm going to be here by the time they build the [new] stadium," Vidro said … "but obviously, it's a great step."[28]

Vidro's sense of foreboding proved acute, as he no longer played for Washington when Nationals Park opened in 2008. Although he retained his defensive position with Soriano going to left, Vidro again felt frustration with his stadium. Before just the third home game of the 2006 season, Vidro exploded. "He feels RFK Stadium is unfair to hitters. He thinks the club should have moved in the fences during the offseason. … Vidro and [Nationals president Tony] Tavares met … outside the clubhouse … [and] yelled at each other about the issue. …"[29]

Whether in response to his ballpark or the diminishment of his skills due to repeated injuries, Vidro confessed that he had given up on trying to hit for power: "I have to make some adjustments on hitting just because of the way we play … [a]nd I don't try to change it when we go [on the road] because it's not going to work."[30]

While healthier than the preceding year, Vidro still missed a month due to a lingering injury that affected his play even after he returned. An observer noted, "His skills appear to have diminished precipitously since his hamstring strain; he has far less range on defense, and he can't hit for much power."[31] His relatively improved health over 2005 resulted in Vidro posting better numbers nearly across the board in 2006 except in triples, homers, and slugging percentage. His new approach at the plate combined with his leg woes could explain his inability to increase those three numbers.

A premier second baseman for two winning teams in Montreal had become a marginal one for two losing teams in Washington. The Nationals gave up on Vidro, swapping his big contract[32] to Seattle for two fringe players, reliever Emiliano Fruto and outfielder Chris Snelling. The Mariners hoped that getting Vidro off the field and using him as a designated hitter would restore the lost luster to his bat. Vidro appeared to agree: "By me becoming DH, it will give me the chance to focus exclusively on my hitting. … I really don't think my health will be an issue. … It's going to be very different not being out there in the field all the time."[33]

Manager Mike Hargrove looked forward to having Vidro in the Seattle lineup: "José has been a good hitter for a number of years, and cream rises to the top."[34]

Playing in just 11 games at first and 10 at second in 2007, Vidro largely served in the DH role, which preserved his health—his 147 games and 625 plate appearances represented his highest totals since 2002 and were the third highest figures in each of these categories in his career. He continued to get on base (.381 OBP), mostly by stroking singles (.314 BA), but his six homers and 59 RBIs represented unacceptably low figures for a DH. Vidro also hit into a career-worst 21 double plays, the seventh-highest total in the AL, further diminishing his offensive impact.

By 2008, Vidro lost his ability to hit singles, the last outstanding aspect of his once stellar offensive game and, perhaps as a corollary, he lost his patience at the plate—he had the lowest walk rate of his career in this, his final season. "I think I've swung at a lot of bad pitches," said Vidro in May 2008.[35] Having played second base for the final time in 2007, Vidro became even more of a full-time DH in 2008, playing in only nine games at first. The lack of punch, range, and speed led to Vidro's release on August 13.

After leaving Seattle, Vidro coached for the Petateros, a Sabana Grande team. He also worked in the Carlos Beltran Baseball Academy, which his son attended. As of 2016 Vidro played in the Puerto Rico Baseball Masters League and lived in Sabana Grande.[36] Asked about Sabana Grande, he said, "I love it. I have been there since I retired with my wife, my son and my daughter. I have a … farm and work with other employees. Like three times a year we get hay for sale."[37]

José Vidro played his final big-league game on August 4, 2008. His last plate appearance typified his career. Batting against Boof Bonser, a Minnesota righty, Vidro swung lefty and delivered an opposite-field line-drive single to left. Down 6-0 after five innings, the Mariners, thanks to a 10-run sixth-inning rally, topped the Twins 11-6. The win, Seattle's second straight, improved the team's record to 43-69, leaving the Mariners in fourth place, 27 games out of first. In the final analysis, Vidro, when healthy, could hit at a high level, but he did so for obscure teams that typically finished far out of playoff contention.

## NOTES

1 Barry Svrluga, "Nats' Vidro Is at Home in the Game," *Washington Post*, March 2, 2005.

2 Phil Taylor, "Mystery Man," *Sports Illustrated*, June 24, 2002.

3 Expos, *Guide 1999*, 230.

4 Tom Gatto, "Best Switch Hitters," *The Sporting News*, May 26, 2003. Frank Robinson, who managed Vidro in Washington, characterized an opposite-field double as "vintage Vidro." Eli Saslow, "Vidro Credits Robinson's Magic Touch," *Washington Post*, June 4, 2006.

5 Stephanie Myles, "Vidro Basks in Selection," *The Gazette* (Montreal), July 18, 2003.

6 Sean Farrell, "Vidro Becomes New Best-Kept Secret," *Baseball America*, July 24-August 8, 2000.

7 Stephanie Myles, "Barrett Handling Duties at Catcher and Third," *The Sporting News*, August 9, 1999. Vidro led the league in both batting average and hits with 60. Peter C. Bjarkman, *Diamonds Around the Globe: The Encyclopedia of International Baseball* (Westport, Connecticut: Greenwood Press, 2005), 259.

8 Stephanie Myles, "The Book on … Jose Vidro," *The Sporting News*, August 16, 1999. The subhead of the article listed Vidro as weighing 190 pounds, but Baseball Reference has him at 175, a figure that seems low given that various media guides of the Montreal Expos list him at three higher weights (185, 190, and 195).

9 Buster Olney, "Cone Remains Perfect Mystery to the Young Expos; Montreal Sensed a Historic Day in the Making," *New York Times*, July 19, 1999.

10 Expos, *Guide 2000*, 234.

11 youtube.com/watch?time_continue=488&v=dNst9_cH2To (accessed November 11, 2016).

12 Murray Chass, "Martinez's Spirit Is Very Special, Too," *New York Times*, May 28, 2000.

13 Expos, *Guide 2002*, 245.

14 "Good Hit, Good Field," *Sports Illustrated*, June 5, 2000. "Vidro's defense has improved every year under the tutelage of first base coach Perry Hill to the point where he can now be considered excellent." Stephanie Myles, "Cabrera Continues to Thrive at the Plate and in the Field," *The Sporting News*, May 28, 2001.

15 Jeff Blair, "Vidro Pushes Hard, Gets Contract Done," *The Globe and Mail*, January 18, 2001.

16 Gordon Edes, "Boss Just Doing His Job; Dolan's Sharp Criticism of Steinbrenner Not Warranted," *Boston Globe*, July 21, 2002.

17 Jonah Keri, *Up, Up, & Away* (Toronto: Random House Canada, 2014), 369.

18 Steve Fainaru, "Expos Triumph in Puerto Rico," *Washington Post*, April 12, 2003.

19 Rafael Hermoso, "Benitez Shows Way to Another Defeat," *New York Times*, April 14, 2003.

20 Charlie Nobles, "For the Expos, It's All a Wild Card," *New York Times*, September 1, 2003.

21 "The Questions With Jose Vidro," *Sports Illustrated*, September 3, 2007.

22 Murray Chass, "Simple Twist of Fate Changed Torborg's Life, and It Helped Save the Life of a Little Boy," *New York Times*, March 7, 2004.

23 Jack Curry, "A 28-Day Trip Is Ending for Montreal's Vagabonds," *New York Times*, July 22, 2004.

24 "Rangers Get Park Back to Help for Stretch Run," *Boston Globe*, August 26, 2004.

25 Hal Bodley, "Expos' New Home Plans Will Feature All-Star Vidro," *USA Today*, May 18, 2004.

26 Barry Svrluga, "Comeback Kid: Vidro Returns," *Washington Post*, March 20, 2005.

27 Barry Svrluga, "Injuries Leave Vidro Waiting for the End," *Washington Post*, September 26, 2005.

28 Barry Svrluga, "Vidro, Like Nationals, Is Looking to Keep His Place," *Washington Post*, March 7, 2006.

29 Barry Svrluga, "Vidro, Tavares Argue About Dimensions at RFK Stadium," *Washington Post*, April 14, 2006.

30 Barry Svrluga, "For Vidro, Doubles Give Way to Singles," *Washington Post*, June 2, 2006.

31 Barry Svrluga, "Vidro Gets the Green Light," *Washington Post*, September 7, 2006.

32 "Seattle has agreed to pay $12 million of the remaining $16 million on Vidro's contract for 2007 and 2008. According to a source outside the Washington organization with knowledge of the deal, the Nationals will pay $1.5 million in 2007 and $2.5 million in 2008." Barry Svrluga, "Nats Agree to Trade Vidro to the Mariners," *Washington Post*, December 14, 2006.

33 Geoff Baker, "M's Deal for Nationals' Vidro," *Seattle Times*, December 14, 2006.

34 Geoff Baker, "Newcomer Vidro in for Tough Adjustment," *Seattle Times*, February 20, 2007.

35 Geoff Baker, "Mariners' Jose Vidro Unruffled by Potential for Less Playing Time," *Seattle Times*, May 2, 2008.

36 Thanks to SABR member Edwin Fernandez for the information in the first two sentences of this paragraph, which comes from an email he sent the author on November 17, 2016.

37 Carlos Rosa Rosa, "Jose Vidro Returns to Baseball to Teach," *El Nuevo Dia*, November 19, 2016. Thanks to SABR member Angel Colon for sending this article from a Puerto Rican newspaper. I used Google Translator to render the article in English.

# BERNIE WILLIAMS

## By Rob Edelman

**C**ENTER FIELD AT YANKEE Stadium is hallowed ground. Once upon a time, Joe DiMaggio and Mickey Mantle patrolled this section of the House That Ruth Built. Now, granted, Bernie Williams—whose 16-season New York Yankees career lasted from 1991 to 2006—may at best be a borderline Cooperstown inductee, but he is a more-than-worthy successor to Joe D. and The Mick as a center fielder par excellence. Plus, as was the case with his two predecessors, the Bronx Bombers were his only major-league team. It is understandable, then, that "Bern Baby Bern" predates "Feel the Bern" as a catchphrase among fans of another celebrated Bernie: Senator Bernie Sanders, the 2016 presidential hopeful.

Actually, Bernie Williams's given name is Bernabé (rather than Bernard). He was born Bernabé Williams Figueroa Jr. on September 13, 1968, in San Juan, Puerto Rico. His father, Bernabé Sr., was a merchant seaman and his mother, Rufina, was a high-school teacher-principal and college professor. The family resided in the Bronx during the year after Williams's birth but then settled in Vega Alta, a town around 45 minutes outside San Juan. As a youngster, Williams played Little League and Babe Ruth League baseball; among his opponents were future major leaguers Iván Rodríguez and Juan Gonzalez. He also regularly attended winter-league games, but baseball was not his sole sport. At age 15, he won four gold medals and a silver medal at the 1984 Central American and Caribbean Junior Championships in Athletics, an international track meet held in San Juan, and was acknowledged as one of the world's fastest 400-meter runners in his age group.[1] (Ironically, during his major-league career, Williams never became a feared basestealer, swiping only 147 bases and adding eight more during the postseason.)

Williams grew to be a 6-foot-2, 205-pounder. He was just 16 when, in 1985, New York Yankees scout Roberto Rivera noticed him and wished to sign him. The youngster was dispatched to a baseball training camp in Connecticut, and was inked by the team on his 17th birthday. As he began his minor-league career, he attended the University of Puerto Rico; at this juncture his intention was to earn a degree in biology and, perhaps, also take pre-med classes. But he decided to focus on baseball, realizing that his studies could impede his rise within the Yankees system.

Williams's first minor-league season came in 1986, when he was assigned to the Gulf Coast League Yankees, the team's Rookie League affiliate; he appeared in 61 games, hit a respectable .270 with 2 home runs and 25 RBIs, and was selected to the league's All-Star team. At the time he was strictly a right-handed hitter and speed still was a part of his game, as he pilfered 33 bases. Then in 1987, Williams split the season between Fort Lauderdale in the Class-A Florida State League (where he hit .155 in 25 games) and Short Season-A Oneonta in the New York-Penn League (where he improved to .344, also in 25 games). On November 8 he was added to the Yankees' 40-man roster.

Williams's true breakout minor-league season came in 1988, when he hit a robust .335 (with 7 home runs and 45 RBIs) in 92 games for Prince William in the Class-A Carolina League. He won the league's batting title, but also was sidelined for the season after fracturing the right navicular bone in his wrist while crashing into the outfield wall in a July 14 game against Hagerstown. The following year, Williams arrived at Yankees spring training as a much-heralded prospect. "He is their phenom this spring, their kid with unlimited talent and untapped potential," wrote Michael Martinez in the *New York Times*. "He is only 20 years old, but the coaches who work with him daily say he has the skills of a big leaguer. The people in the front office speak of his intellectual and his physical growth. They all say he simply can't miss."

Added Frank Howard, the Yankees' hitting coach, "He's a quality-looking athlete. He has fantastic bat speed, he can sting the ball and he has great reflexes."²

But Williams still was a work-in-progress. He was promoted to the Columbus Clippers of the Triple-A International League at the start of the 1989 campaign, but after hitting just .216 in 50 game, he was demoted to the Double-A Eastern League Albany-Colonie Yankees, where he improved to .252 in 91 games. On February 23, 1990, he married the former Waleska Ortega; they have three children (Bernie Jr., Beatriz, and Bianca). Initially, the family resided in northern New Jersey, with Waleska and the youngsters spending the school year in Puerto Rico. Then in 1999, they purchased a home in Armonk, New York. "Once we had an opportunity to settle in, we fell in love with the area," Williams declared in 2003. "It's very quiet. It feels like the countryside. It looks a little like the part of Puerto Rico where I grew up."³

The budding big leaguer spent the entire 1990 season at Albany-Colonie, where he made it into 134 games and hit .281 with 8 home runs and 54 RBIs while leading the league with 98 walks and 39 stolen bases. His prospect status was on the rise: He was named an Eastern League and *Baseball America* Double-A All-Star and was cited by *Baseball America* as the second-best Eastern League prospect. Also, while in the minors, he began using both hands while playing Wiffle ball with a sibling. In so doing, he realized that he could effectively hit left-handed; he queried Buck Showalter, his manager at both Fort Lauderdale and Albany-Colonie, to win the okay to practice switch hitting—and so he began coming to bat for the first time from the left side of the plate.

During the following two campaigns, Williams further established himself at Columbus, respectively hitting .294 in 78 games and .306 in 95 games. Baseball-Reference.com lists conflicting figures for his career minor-league batting average, home-run total, and total number of games; representative numbers are .285, 48, and 660. Nonetheless, two months into the 1991 season, he was primed for his big-league bow. "Clearly, there are (Clippers) players ready for promotion," wrote the *New York Times*' Michael Martinez on June 11. One of them was Bernie Williams. "He's got all the tools," observed Clete Boyer, a Columbus coach. "When he gets up there, he should stay."⁴ What surely was the season's highlight for Williams was his major-league debut, which came on July 7 against the Baltimore Orioles. Replacing the injured Roberto Kelly, he was the starting center fielder, batting eighth and going 1-for-3 with a sacrifice fly and two RBIs in a 5-3 loss. "It's very different," Williams declared of playing before 43,505 fans in the Bronx ballyard. "I've been dreaming of this since I signed six years ago." He said he "was nervous out there at first. I didn't expect this many fans."⁵ Williams's first big-league hit was a ninth-inning single off Gregg Olson, and his initial home run came seven days later against California's Chuck Finley. Prior to his call-up, Williams had been named to the Triple-A All-Star team, but his promotion prevented him from appearing. He was the Bronx Bombers' starting center fielder for the remainder of the season, playing in 85 games and batting .238 with 3 home runs and 34 RBIs. His big-league high point was a five-hit game against the Cleveland Indians on October 5.

Across the decades, rookies in all sports have been subjected to hazing by their veteran peers. Bernie Williams was no different. However, his mild manner made him a special target for Mel Hall, a Yankee fly-chaser. As reported in a 2014 *SB Nation* article penned by Greg Hanlon, "With Williams, Hall took rookie hazing to abusive extremes. ... He called Williams 'Bambi,' mocking his large doe eyes, which were magnified by his bulky glasses. Alternately, he called him 'Mr. Zero,' Hall's assessment of Williams' value. He once taped a sign on Williams' locker saying 'Mr. Zero,' and would say, 'Shut up, Zero,' whenever Williams tried to speak, something that reportedly once nearly brought Williams to tears. Things got so vicious that management interceded on Williams' behalf. 'Mel was basically bullying Bernie and we put an end to it,' responded Buck Showalter ... who was then a Yankee coach. ..."[6]

In 1992 Williams was back in Columbus but he also spent part of the season with the Yankees. He started off in the Bronx but was returned to the Clippers on April 15 after appearing in two games. Clearly, he was not destined to remain at Triple A as he was fourth in the International League in slugging percentage, fifth in on-base percentage, and fifth in the batting race, making it into 95 games and hitting .306. His nine triples were tied for the league lead; he was the Yankees' minor-league player of the month in June and an International League midseason and postseason All-Star. Most impressive of all, *Baseball America* rated him the fourth-best International League prospect. After his recall to the Bronx on July 31, he appeared in 60 games and hit .281 with 5 home runs and 26 RBIs. Williams played left field in four games and right field in another four, but was shifted to center field on August 7. From then on, he appeared in every game and played every inning for the rest of the season, and also was the Yankees' leadoff hitter. His 1992 highlights included a 10-game hitting streak (September 2 through 13) and a four-hit game on September 12. After the season, he briefly played for Arecibo in the Puerto Rican winter league before sustaining ligament damage in his left knee and undergoing arthroscopic surgery on December 19.[7]

The 1993 campaign was extra-special for Williams: His minor-league apprenticeship was completed, and he spent the entire season with the Yankees as the starting center fielder. However, a slow start resulted in George Steinbrenner, the easily exasperated Yankees owner, putting pressure on general manager Gene Michael to trade Williams. Rumor had it that he would be swapped for Larry Walker of the Montreal Expos, but the deal was not consummated.[8] For the season, Williams appeared in 139 games—a muscle strain in his rib cage sidelined him for 23 games between May 13 and June 7—and he hit a respectable if unspectacular .268, with 12 home runs and 68 RBIs. He was the team's leadoff hitter through the All-Star break; from then on, he mostly batted sixth. His season high points included his smashing his first grand slam on June 14 off the Boston Red Sox' Danny Darwin—the Yankees won the game 4-0—and hitting in 21 straight games between August 1 and August 23.

The following season, Williams' batting average improved to .289 (with 12 home runs and 57 RBIs) in 108 games. He returned to the leadoff spot for 28 games, during which he hit .362, but also batted sixth, seventh, and eighth. This success may be contrasted to his .178 average for the month of April. His top performances that year included hitting homers in three consecutive games between June 6 and June 8; on June 6, he enjoyed his initial two-homer game (against the Texas Rangers), in which he drove in seven runs. On that occasion, he joined Mickey Mantle, Roy White, Tom Tresh, and Roy Smalley as the fifth Yankee to homer from both sides of the plate in the same game.

Then in 1995, Williams established himself as an upper-echelon big leaguer, appearing in 144 games and hitting .307 (with 18 home runs and 82 RBIs). Yet again, he started off slowly; for the first two months of the season, he hit .204 with 4 homers and 14 RBIs, but hit .333 for the rest of the season (and .354 during the month of August). While he stole eight bases—he and Pat Kelly trailed only Luis

Polonia, who pilfered 10 — by now it was clear that he was no big-league basestealer. However, while the Yankees were shut down by the Seattle Mariners in the American League Division Series, Williams's postseason debut was a stellar one; in five games he hit .429 with two homers and five RBIs.

Still, George Steinbrenner kept insisting that Williams be traded. For one thing, he was not easy to categorize. Despite his speed, he was no basestealer. Despite his ability to run down fly balls, his throwing arm was less than powerful. While a steady hitter, he was no slugger. That season the Yankees owner even wished to swap him to the San Francisco Giants for Darren Lewis, a fellow center fielder. Such a deal was never consummated. Williams also was displeased when the team renewed his contract for what in baseball terms was a paltry $400,000. He was eligible for arbitration the following season and asked for $3 million; the team countered with $2.555 million, which the ballplayer did not accept. He ended up being awarded $2.6 million in arbitration.[9]

In 1996 Williams proved that the numbers he compiled during the previous campaign were no aberration. He played in 143 games, hitting .305 and establishing what then were career zeniths with 29 home runs and 102 RBIs. His accomplishments that season included three two-home-run games and eight RBIs in a 12-3 triumph against the Detroit Tigers on September 12. He improved on his 1995 postseason performance, hitting .471 with 5 home runs and 11 RBIs in the ALDS and American League Championship Series. While he was the ALCS MVP, his numbers sank in the World Series against the Atlanta Braves; he hit just .167 with a single home run and four RBIs. But no other Yankee matched his RBI total and his home run in the eighth inning of Game Three helped win the game — and allow the Yankees their first world championship since 1978.

Starting in 1997, Williams not only entered his major-league prime but further solidified his status as an elite player and top-of-the-list Yankee. In 129 games he hit .328 (coming in fourth in the American League batting race) with 21 home runs and 100 RBIs, and also earned his initial Gold Glove award. He was seventh in the league in on-base percentage (.408) and eighth in runs scored (107); he was named to his initial All-Star team and in August was the American League Player of the Month, hitting .395 with 8 home runs and 23 RBIs. On the downside, he had two stints on the disabled list, both for strained left hamstrings, and hit just .118 in the five-game ALDS against the Cleveland Indians. And after the campaign, he yet again found himself the subject of trade rumors. One report had him going to the Detroit Tigers for a bevy of young pitchers.[10] Another possible trade involved swapping Williams to the Chicago Cubs for center fielder Lance Johnson.[11]

It was the Yankees' good fortune that Williams was not dealt, as he became the 1998 American League batting champion. In 128 games, he hit .339, homering 26 times and driving in 97 runs. He was his league's Player of the Month in May, when he hit .402 with seven home runs and 27 RBIs. He won another Gold Glove, earned a spot on the All-Star squad, was second in his league in on-base percentage (.422), and finished seventh in the MVP voting. The Yankees' 114-48 campaign was an American League record — and Williams became the first-ever player to win the batting title, a Gold Glove, and a world championship during the same season. While that summer was far from perfect — on June 11, he began a 31-game stint on the disabled list because of a strained right knee, and he hit just .188 during the postseason — he did enter the upper stratosphere of baseball salaries, signing a seven-year, $87.5 million contract on November 25. Also included was an eighth-season $15 million club option. The negotiating with the team was lengthy and contentious; the Yankees were hoping to sign Albert Belle, who instead inked with the Baltimore Orioles. Additionally, the Yankees were involved in a bidding war with the Boston Red Sox for Williams's services.[12]

Williams' all-time best season came in 1999, when he hit .342 in 158 games –third in the AL batting race — while belting 25 home runs and driving in 115 runs. His 202 hits then were a career high, as were his number of games played and RBI total along with his 116 runs and 100 walks. His seven four-hit games were tops in the majors, with two coming against Tampa Bay on June 22 and June 23; yet again, he made his league's All-Star team, and his status as a feared hitter was demonstrated by his being intentionally walked three times in a game against Tampa Bay on September 26. In the postseason, he hit .273 with two home runs and eight RBIs; in the first ALDS game against Texas, he went 3-for-5 with six RBIs. However, most impressive of all, Williams's elite Yankee status was illustrated by his joining Lou Gehrig, Babe Ruth, Joe DiMaggio, and Mickey Mantle as the only Bronx Bombers to drive in at least 100 RBIs and score at least 100 runs in three separate seasons. He and Derek Jeter became the first Yankees with at least 200 hits in the same season since Gehrig and DiMaggio in 1937.

Williams followed up in 2000 by hitting .307 in 141 games and setting career zeniths with 30 home runs and 121 RBIs. He earned the most All-Star Game votes of any American League flychaser; perhaps his best games of the season came on April 23, when he went 3-for-4 with two homers (one lefty and one righty) and five RBIs, and June 17, when he was 4-for-4 with seven RBIs. However, he sat out seven games, starting on August 19, with a right rib cage strain. In the three postseason series, against Oakland, Seattle, and the Mets, Williams hit a respectable .279 with two home runs and five RBIs.

Williams maintained his solid play in 2001, appearing in 146 games and hitting .307 with 26 home runs and 94 RBIs. His 38 doubles were a career high, and he was an American League All-Star for the fifth straight season; among the three hits he collected on June 2 against Cleveland were the 1,500th of his career. Even though he hit only .220 during the postseason, his 11 RBIs were tops for the Yankees — and he was the first player to hit homers in three consecutive ALCS games. But his season's low point had nothing to do with baseball. On April 9 he missed 10 games upon returning to Puerto Rico to be with his father, who was afflicted with pulmonary fibrosis; then in mid-May, he went home again upon the passing of Bernabé Sr., missing a three-game series against Oakland.[13]

Then in 2002, Williams appeared in 154 games and finished third in the AL batting race with a .333 average. He hit 19 home runs and drove in 102 runs; his 204 hits were a career high, and he was 5-for-15 in four postseason games. But this was his final season as a .300 hitter. His average sank to .263 in 2003; he appeared in 119 games, hitting 15 home runs and driving in 64 runs. Still, his name was increasingly appearing on team career stat lists. His 1,950 total hits ranked eighth all-time in Yankees annals; his 241 homers were seventh; his 1,062 RBIs ranked ninth; his 372 doubles ranked fifth. He got his 1,000th RBI on April 2, doubling against the Blue Jays. There were downs in 2003: On May 23 he landed on the 15-day disabled list with a torn medial meniscus in his left knee, for which he underwent arthroscopic surgery. But there were ups: He hit .318 in 17 postseason games; his 19th postseason home run, belted in Game Three of the World Series, was the all-time major-league high, exceeding Reggie Jackson and

Mickey Mantle; and his 66 postseason RBIs broke the record of 63 held by David Justice.

The 2004 campaign had Williams hitting .262 in 148 games, with 22 home runs and 70 RBIs. His injuries and illnesses were mounting; he failed to accompany the team to its opening series in Japan, as he was felled by appendicitis. However, on June 10, he became the seventh Yankee to reach the 2,000-hit plateau when he singled against Colorado. Six days later he hit his 250th career home run. And on August 6, he doubled for the 390th time in his career, besting Joe DiMaggio's 389 and taking over fourth place on the all-time Yankee list. Two days later he smashed his 10th grand slam, topping the nine hit by Mickey Mantle and Yogi Berra. He now ranked fourth among all Yankees in this category, behind only Lou Gehrig (with 23 grand slams), DiMaggio (13), and Babe Ruth (12). And he enjoyed a solid postseason, hitting .296 with 3 home runs and 13 RBIs.

Then, in 2005—the final year of his eight-year contract—Williams's batting average sank to .249. In 141 games, he hit 12 home runs and drove in 64 runs. But he was just the 10th Yankee to don pinstripes for 15 seasons; in a game against Baltimore on September 27, his 2,215th hit bested DiMaggio's total and elevated him to fourth place on the team's all-time list. Notwithstanding, the Yankees announced on August 2 that they would not pick up Williams's option for the following season, preferring a $3.5 million buyout. "It's a formality," Williams declared at the time. "I don't think it means I'm going to be a Yankee or not going to be a Yankee. They can still talk to me when the end of the year comes."[14] That December Brian Cashman, the team's general manager, re-signed Williams to a one-season, $1.5 million contract. He put up respectable numbers in 2006, playing in 131 games and hitting .281 with 12 home runs and 61 RBIs. On July 26 his career hit total reached 2,300; on August 16 his 443rd double ranked him second on the all-time team list. That year he also played for his Puerto Rican homeland in the World Baseball Classic. But 2006 was Williams's final major-league season. He wished to return in 2007 and even was willing to be a backup outfielder and occasional pinch-hitter, but he was offered only a minor-league contract with the opportunity to come to spring training and compete for a roster spot. He refused the invitation.

In his career, Williams appeared in 2,076 games. He had 2,336 hits in 7,869 at-bats, of which 449 were doubles, 55 were triples, and 287 were home runs. He drove in 1,257 runs while scoring 1,366. His lifetime batting average was a more-than-respectable .297. He also played in every postseason from 1995 to 2006. In 121 total games, he came to bat 465 times with 128 hits, 29 doubles, and 22 home runs. He drove in 80 runs while scoring 83; his postseason batting average was .275; and his number of game appearances and home-run and RBI totals were tops in major-league history. He was on every American League All-Star team from 1997 through 2001; he won four Gold Gloves (1997, 1998, 1999, and 2000); and he was an American League Silver Slugger in 2002. He was second in the American League in on-base percentage in 1998 (.422) and fourth in 1999 (.435). He was third in on-base plus slugging in 1998 (.997). Williams was a part of four Yankees world championships (1996, 1998, 1999, and 2000).[15]

Even though Williams was unwilling to sign with another major-league team for 2007, the 38-year-old ballplayer refused to officially retire. The following year, he played for Gigantes de Carolina in the Puerto Rico Baseball League, hoping that this would lead to a roster spot on the team that would represent his country in the 2009 World Baseball Classic. "I have as good a chance as anybody to make that team," he declared. "A lot of good players out there, so it's gonna be hard to try and make that team. But I like my chances. They're probably as good as anybody else's."[16] And so he arrived at the Yankees' 2009 spring-training camp to work out, eager to play in the Classic—and perhaps be one of the 25 Bronx Bombers to head north at the start of the season. "After doing this for 16 or 17 years, you get some of that baseball thing back in your system," he noted. "It's like, 'Whoa, maybe I can do this for a couple more years.' I guess that's part of the fantasy that I try not to allow myself to live."[17] But of course, his big-league career was finished.

Despite this, Williams was winning accolades as an all-time-great Yankee. He received a thunderous, 102-second standing ovation upon his first appearance at Yankee Stadium since 2006. The date was September 21, 2008; it was the final game at the "old" ballyard, and he was the final "old-timer" introduced. The following year, he played for his country in the World Baseball Classic, walking twice but getting no hits in five at-bats. Then in 2012, Williams debuted on the Hall of Fame ballot, receiving 55 votes (or 9.6 percent of the balloting). That number fell to 19 in 2013; the 3.3 percent total eliminated him from Cooperstown consideration. But in May 2014 the Yankees announced that he would be honored with a plaque in the Stadium's hallowed Monument Park; on February 16, 2015, the team revealed that his number 51 would be retired. Both occurred in a ceremony on May 24. Williams began his speech by declaring, "This is unbelievable. Never in my wildest dreams I would have thought that a skinny little ... kid from Puerto Rico could be here this day, and (for) this celebration." He observed, "I am so proud to represent Puerto Rico." He thanked Gene Michael for not trading him, Roy White for working on his left-handed swing, Willie Randolph for giving him sage advice — and suggesting that he embrace his success — Joe Torre for "being there for me," and his teammates for "letting me be a part of some of the greatest years of my life." While he wished he could still play, he declared, "You don't want the 2015 version of Bernie Williams. This one is more suited for a guitar than for a bat."[18] As he was so honored, sportswriter Ian O'Connor, who covered Williams for years, observed that he "forever (carried) himself in pinstripes with dignity and grace. He didn't measure up to DiMaggio and Mantle as a player, but go ahead and read the accounts of life with the late Yankee greats and decide if they measured up to Williams as role models and men."[19]

As an ex-big leaguer, Bernie Williams has not rested on his on-field accomplishments. Early on, his talents as a classical guitarist rivaled his athletic ability. At age 8, he became enamored of the flamenco guitar music his father played for him. Five years later he began attending San Juan's Escuela Libre de Musica high school, a private performing-arts institution. Even after signing his pro contract, he regularly played his guitar as a form of relaxation, often in his team's clubhouse.

Never was Bernie Williams ever the stereotypical jock. According to longtime New York sportswriter Joel Sherman, he "was quiet, shy, and predisposed to internalize life. He was nice but not overly friendly. He was bright yet often projected flightiness. He seemed almost to travel in a dream state." Sherman added, "Sitting off alone in a corner, strumming his guitar, was heaven for Williams." In this regard, as Williams explained to Sherman, "I always had to prove I could play. They all saw me and always thought I was too mild, that I wasn't tough enough, that I didn't care, that my mind was not into baseball. But none of that was true."[20]

Williams of course *was* into baseball, but he evolved across time into an acclaimed guitarist. He was inspired by a range of musical styles (including jazz, classical, pop, Brazilian, and Latin), and became adept at both acoustic and electric guitar. His debut album, the jazz-rock-tropical music-influenced *The Journey Within*, was released in 2003. On it, he plays lead and rhythm guitar and also penned seven of the album's 12 numbers; among them are "La Salsa En Mi" and "Desvelado," which link his affection for jazz and his Puerto Rican roots. He is joined here by a first-rate group of musicians, including Béla Fleck, Kenny Aronoff, Shawn Pelton, Luis Conte, Leland Sklar, Tim Pierce, and David Sancious. *The Journey Within* made it to number 3 on *Billboard's* Contemporary Jazz Chart. Then in 2009 came a second album, *Moving Forward*, which debuted at number 2 on the Contemporary Jazz Chart, and for which he earned a Grammy nomination. Here, his collaborators include Bruce Springsteen, Jon Secada, Dave Koz, and Patty Scialfa. Two years later, he co-authored the appropriately titled book *Rhythms of the Game: The Link Between Music and Athletic Performance*. He has over the years performed on countless occasions in numerous venues. One example: In 2014, he played "Take Me Out to the Ball Game" on the field in Fenway Park in a pregame ceremony before Derek Jeter's final big-league appearance.

Williams's charitable enterprises include his involvement with Little Kids Rock, an organization that stresses the importance of music education for disadvantaged youth. However, his connection to popular culture is not limited to his musicianship. In "The Abstinence," a 1996 episode of *Seinfeld*, George Costanza (Jason Alexander)—who refers to himself as "assistant to the (Yankees) traveling secretary"—offers batting tips to Williams and Derek Jeter. Bernie's one line, to George: "Are you the guy who put us in that Ramada in Milwaukee?"[21] He also has participated in a pair of films with baseball connections. *Henry & Me* (2014) is the animated tale of a cancer-stricken boy who is guided by his guardian angel on a journey in which he meets past and present Yankee greats. Williams does his own voice, as do other Bronx Bombers from Yogi Berra to Reggie Jackson to Hideki Matsui; Luis Guzmán, Chazz Palminteri, Paul Simon, David Mantle, and Hank Steinbrenner respectively voice Lefty Gomez, Babe Ruth, Thurman Munson, Mickey Mantle, and George Steinbrenner. (Alex Rodríguez's presence and voice were deleted in the wake of his 162-game suspension for the 2014 season.) Then in *Straight Outta Tompkins* (2015), the tale of a troubled teen and budding baseball player who is abandoned by his businessman father and ends up immersed in New York's drug culture, Williams acts the role of a "college baseball scout."

But Bernie Williams's true passion is his music. In May 2016 he earned a bachelor's degree in jazz composition from the Manhattan School of Music, where he had studied for the previous four years. "I think anybody could go out there and play some chords and be very passionate about it and break some guitars, put them on fire, whatever, to get the people's attention," he told *New York Post* columnist Ken Davidoff. "And that could be a certain part of success. But I think to me, it's just trying to be the best musician that I can and having the respect of the music industry and the people that are really playing."[22]

While attending the school, Williams blended in with his fellow students, many of whom were a quarter-century his junior. "Once I finally started talking to him and getting to know him, it was clear right away that he didn't want anybody to give him special treatment or act like he was more than just a fellow student," explained Ryan DeWeese, 21. "He is such a genuine guy who really cares about his music, education, and his peers, even if they are a bit younger than he is." Williams himself added, "I will eventually begin working on an album and would like to tour around the world with my band. I'm very excited about the next chapter in my life."[23]

## NOTES

1. Mitchell Stephens, "Bernie Williams: On Westchester, His Music and, Oh Yeah, the Yankees," *Westchester Magazine*, July 2003.
2. Michael Martinez. "Spring Phenom a Yankee Perennial," *New York Times*, February 26, 1989: S3.
3. Stephens.
4. Michael Martinez, "Looking Up While Down on Yanks' Farm," *New York Times*, June 11, 1991: B11.
5. Filip Bondy, "Another in Columbus Crew Gets to Discover Stadium," *New York Times*, July 8, 1991: C6.
6. sbnation.com/2014/7/15/5883593/the-many-crimes-of-mel-hall.
7. m.mlb.com/player/124288/bernie-williams.
8. espn.go.com/mlb/story/_/id/12926321/new-york-yankees-bernie-williams-uncommon-dignity-grace.
9. Joel Sherman, *Birth of a Dynasty: Behind the Pinstripes With the 1996 Yankees* (Emmaus, Pennsylvania: Rodale Inc., 2006), 242-243.
10. Murray Chass, "Baseball; Williams, Nearly a Tiger, Is Still a Yankee for Now," *New York Times*, November 20, 1997: C3.
11. George King, "Survivor in Pinstripes: Yanks Were Smart Not Trading Bernie Williams," *New York Post*, February 24, 2002: 92.
12. Buster Olney, "Yankees Capitulate, Keeping Williams in $87.5 Million Pact," *New York Times*, November 26, 1998: A1.
13. Jack Curry, "Williams's Father Dies of a Heart Attack," *New York Times*, May 15, 2001: D4.
14. "The Yankees Decline an Option on Williams," *New York Times*, August 3, 2005: D3.
15. m.mlb.com/player/124288/bernie-williams.

16 Christian Red, "Former Yankee Bernie Williams Burns for One More Shot at Plate, While Adding to His Musical Legacy," *New York Daily News*, January 18, 2009.

17 Jack Curry, "Williams Casts Look Toward the Majors," *New York Times*, March 4, 2009: B14.

18 youtube.com/watch?v=OHODIrkfZiI.

19 espn.go.com/mlb/story/_/id/12926321/new-york-yankees-bernie-williams-uncommon-dignity-grace.

20 Joel Sherman, 242, 244.

21 seinfeldscripts.com/TheAbstinence.htm.

22 Ken Davidoff, "How Bernie Williams Blended in for 4 Years of Music School," *New York Post*, May 12, 2016.

23 Evan Grossman, "Bernie Williams Hits the Right Notes With Classmates as former Yankees Star Nears Graduation From Manhattan School of Music," *New York Daily News*, May 12, 2016.

# SIXTO ESCOBAR STADIUM (SAN JUAN)

## By Rory Costello

**THIS MULTI-PURPOSE FACILITY** has been called "The Madison Square Garden of Puerto Rico."[1] Its use in boxing and basketball is a big reason, but the parallel extends to track and field, as well as political conventions. Baseball, however, forms an especially rich chapter in the history of Estadio Sixto Escobar (as it is known to its Spanish-speaking local fans). Pro ball has not been played at Escobar since February 1962, but it was the most storied ballpark of the Puerto Rican Winter League in its golden age. The San Juan Senators played there starting in 1938, when the league was founded. After the Santurce Crabbers joined the PRWL in 1939, they and the Senators shared the stadium—and an intense rivalry—for 23 seasons.

"Santurce's fans and the old stadium were just great," said Herman Franks, who managed the 1954-55 Crabbers—called "the greatest winter ballclub ever" by one of its members, Don Zimmer. "I don't think the new stadiums had or will ever have the feeling of Sixto Escobar Stadium."[2]

Trying to summon up that feeling in words alone is not truly possible, but in the effort to do so, one may start with the island's fans. Author Thomas Van Hyning, who has chronicled Puerto Rican baseball in two books, devoted a whole chapter to them in the first of those books. He quoted numerous people—players, umpires, broadcasters, and more—about how "closely and religiously" those fans follow the game. At Escobar, they were close to the field, which heightened their noisy enthusiasm. The stadium officially seated 13,135 between its grandstands, box seat chairs, and the bleachers—but for big games, thousands more jammed in. Pitcher José "Palillo" Santiago, who pitched for San Juan and later for the Boston Red Sox, likened Escobar to Fenway Park.[3]

Another big factor was the high quality of Puerto Rican baseball. The list of stars is long: natives, other Latin Americans, plus many U.S. imports from the majors and Negro Leagues. There were a lot of dramatic moments at Escobar.

Sixto Escobar Stadium was originally called Estadio del Escambrón. It was renamed in April 1938 for star boxer Sixto Escobar, who was Puerto Rico's first world champion in that sport. Naturally, the bantamweight—known appropriately as *El Gallito* (The Little Rooster)—became a big hero in a place that has produced many other great fighters and loves "the sweet science."

The original name of the park came from its location: Punta Escambrón, in the neighborhood called Puerta de Tierra, in the vicinity of Old San Juan. Nearby is one of San Juan's public beaches, El Escambrón, which is known for its splendid views. Thomas Van Hyning wrote, "It was a comfortable stadium where one could feel the presence of the Caribbean trade winds."[4]

Those swirling winds could also make outfield play tricky.[5] Plus, they both gave and took away, as author Lou Hernández recounted. Félix Mantilla told Hernández that the ocean breeze would carry high fly balls, but Nino Escalera said that the winds tended to blow in from the beach. However, pitcher Jack Harshman said, "Sixto Escobar was a good ballpark, and it was a fair one. If you hit the ball real hard, you could get it out there. If you pitched real good, you had a chance to win. They did not get any cheap home runs there."[6]

The geology of Puerto Rico and Punta Escambrón was beneficial. Tito Stevens, a longtime fan of the Crabbers, heard about it from his childhood hero (and later a good friend), pitcher Rubén Gómez. Gómez noted that it could rain in the afternoon but a game could be played the same night because the drainage was so good. The ballpark, like other structures along the island's north coast, was built atop a coral reef.[7]

Just south of the stadium is Luis Muñoz Rivera Park, which opened in 1929. Luis Muñoz Rivera (1859-1916) was a poet who turned to journalism, with a focus on politics — in particular the issue of Puerto Rico's autonomy. Muñoz Rivera entered politics himself, serving as resident Commissioner of Puerto Rico from 1911 until his death. In 1948, his son, Luis Muñoz Marín, became the territory's first democratically elected governor. The Muñoz connection took on greater significance in view of Escobar Stadium's role in Puerto Rican politics.

With the development of such a favorable spot, and given Puerto Rico's love of baseball, it's easy to see why the San Juan city fathers chose to locate a ballpark there. Plus, as authors Michael and Mary Oleksak observed, after the Great Depression struck, "baseball provided a diversion for the people. In 1930, to encourage this interest, the strapped local government nevertheless voted to build a new stadium."[8] Construction began in 1931. The architect was Rafael Carmoega, one of Puerto Rico's most prominent people ever in that profession.[9]

The stadium opened on November 12, 1932.[10] In December 1933, J. Francis Edwards, sports editor of the San Juan newspaper *El Imparcial*, wrote a letter to the *Pittsburgh Courier*. Edwards described the thriving baseball scene at Escambrón (he noted that a quarter-mile running track encircled the field). Games took place on Saturday and Sunday afternoons and on Sunday mornings. Edwards said, "The Islanders take their baseball seriously and even the amateur teams attract thousands to their games." Those fans got to see many outstanding players of African descent, from both the U.S. and Latin America.[11] The man responsible for this scene was a local operator named Tony Luciano, who won the rights at auction.[12]

Author Jane Allen Quevedo described attending baseball games in Puerto Rico as being "as much a social event as a sporting event...in El Escambrón, local fans filled the benches and even climbed into the trees outside the ballpark to secure a good vantage point."[13] One of the attractions was Hiram Bithorn, who became the first Puerto Rican in the major leagues in 1942.

On January 9, 1936, Powel Crosley, president and owner of the Cincinnati Reds, announced that his team would conduct part of its spring training in Puerto Rico. It was the first time that a major-league team visited the island.[14] The club's fast-talking general manager, Larry MacPhail, boasted, "We're the most streamlined, modern major league outfit in baseball history."[15]

The team's trainer, Dr. Richard Rhode, gave MacPhail a positive advance report. "I was very much surprised to find the ballpark, known as Escambron Baseball Park, to be such an excellent layout. It compares favorably with anything in the American Association except that it has a skinned infield."[16]

Managed by Chuck Dressen, the Reds started training at Escambrón on February 10, though many of the players were so badly seasick after their ocean voyage that they could not practice for several days. Another contingent arrived by air, which also proved to be an adventure. Games began on February 27. The lineup for the opponents, Ponce, included such talent as the early Dominican star Tetelo Vargas, as well as local heroes Pancho Coimbre and Perucho Cepeda, father of Orlando Cepeda.[17]

Early March brought interesting reports of the Reds' action from the *Virgin Islands Daily News*. One notable game took place on March 1, when the Almendares club of Cuba beat Cincinnati 5-1. "One-man team" Martín Dihigo was back on the mound after going three innings the previous day. He defeated Paul Derringer. The following day, the Reds returned to Escambrón for a doubleheader against a Negro League team, the Brooklyn Eagles. In the morning's game, Brooklyn started Hiram Bithorn, who got the call after Leon Day was sick — Bithorn had impressed the Eagles in practice games.[18] The

19-year-old allowed just one run in his first seven innings but got no decision after giving up three in the eighth. Brooklyn won the opener, 5-4, but Cincinnati got a split when Tony Freitas won in the afternoon, 3-2.[19]

The story of how the stadium came to bear Sixto Escobar's name began in the mid-1930s as *El Gallito* became a prime contender in his weight class. On August 31, 1936, he became the undisputed bantamweight champion of the world. Later that year, he lost two non-title bouts to Harry Jeffra, sandwiched around one successful defense of his title at Madison Square Garden.

Escobar's next outing — the first championship bout ever to take place in San Juan — came at Estadio del Escambrón, on February 21, 1937. He won a unanimous decision over Lou Salica, another of his main rivals, before a crowd of 26,000 (for boxing, it was possible to install thousands of temporary seats on the field around the ring). The referee was former heavyweight champ Jack Dempsey, who "kept the little men at it hammer and tongs throughout."[20]

Escobar lost his title to Jeffra at the Polo Grounds in September 1937 — but regained it at Escambrón on February 20, 1938. He won a unanimous decision after knocking Jeffra down three times in the 11th round and once in the 14th. Again, capacity was boosted, this time to an estimated 18,000.[21] That April, the Legislative Assembly of Puerto Rico voted to name the stadium and surrounding park in honor of Sixto Escobar.

In the winter of 1938-39, the Puerto Rican Winter League began operations. For its first three seasons, it was a semi-professional circuit, in affiliation with the National Baseball Congress on the mainland. The league's first champion was the Guayama Brujos. Several months later, in September 1939, Escobar was the scene as Guayama faced the U.S. semi-pro champions, the Duncan Cementers from Oklahoma. Seating was again expanded for the series (although details are lacking).[22] Guayama won, four games to two. Before facing Duncan, Pancho Coimbre said, "If I can hit Satchel Paige and Raymond Brown, why would this be any different?"[23]

Santurce entered the league for the 1939-40 season. This sparked a long-running tradition: the city championship of San Juan. A local baseball figure named Heriberto Ramírez de Arellano—a.k.a. "Don Guindo"—hatched the idea that awarding a banner to the winner of the "battle for the city's supremacy would stimulate fan interest and attendance."[24] In the 23 years that they shared Escobar, the Crabbers won the regular-season series 14 times and the Senators eight, with just one year ending in a split. Overall in that period, the Crabbers won 188 games and the Senators 148.

The honor of most league championships for Escobar's home teams also went to the Crabbers:
- Santurce won five times (1950-51, 1952-53, 1954-55, 1958-59, and 1961-62).
- San Juan won thrice (1945-46, 1951-52, and 1960-61).

Various imported stars came to Puerto Rico in the winter of 1939-40. At their head were Paige (whom Coimbre had previously faced elsewhere) and slugger Josh Gibson, who joined Santurce. However, Guayama repeated as Puerto Rican champion. In addition to Paige, the team featured Tetelo Vargas and Perucho Cepeda.

Sixto Escobar Stadium assumed its role in Puerto Rican politics when a convention was held there on June 21, 1940, officially creating the Democratic Popular Party (Spanish acronym PPD) with Luis Muñoz Marín as president. A Republican Union Assembly followed that August 18, and there would be more rallies to come over the course of the 1940s and 1950s.

A few months later in 1940 (late September and early October), the semi-pro "world championship" was held again at Escobar. This time the U.S. champion—the Enid Refiners, another Oklahoma-based team—beat Guayama, despite the batting of Vargas, who went 16-for-24.[25] It must have been crushing for the Puerto Rican fans, because Enid won the seventh and final game, 7-5, with a four-run rally in the ninth inning.[26]

Josh Gibson wasn't there in 1940-41, but at least three Hall of Famers came to Escobar as visiting players that winter: Buck Leonard (Mayagüez), Leon Day (Aguadilla), and Roy Campanella (Caguas). Gibson came back for the winter of 1941-42. He hit 13 home runs, including a number of the prodigious blasts that formed his legend. By some accounts, his last that season (and last in Puerto Rico) was the longest ever at Sixto Escobar Stadium—"a 600-foot rocket that sailed over Escobar's pine trees on its way to the Escambrón beach."[27]

As is the case with many reports of Josh Gibson homers, though, the distance may have been exaggerated. According to José "Pantalones" Santiago (no relation to Palillo), Gibson "played when there was no outfield fencing at Sixto Escobar. Gibson's home run distances were helped by their bounces."[28]

The PRWL became fully professional with the 1941-42 season. Charlie García de Quevedo, who later served as the league's president, pushed for the upgrade, citing Escobar as an important model for the game locally. García put it this way: "Baseball will not have matured until the other towns and cities that participate in it have a park like Sixto Escobar."[29]

Another Hall of Famer made his first appearance in Puerto Rico that winter: Willard Brown, who would later dazzle Escobar fans with his batting for Santurce. Brown played second base for Humacao and batted .409, second behind Gibson's .480. Despite this auspicious season, though, Brown would not return to the island for another five years.

The 1945-46 Senators became Escobar's first champion home team. They featured an outfield of homegrown stars: Luis Olmo, Freddie Thon Sr. (grandfather of future big-leaguer Dickie Thon), and Félix "Fellé" Delgado (who later became a notable scout). They were led, however, by the league's MVP that year—Monte Irvin, who was playing out of position at second base to help the team. The pitching staff was anchored by two other very capable Negro Leaguers, Johnny Davis and Roy Partlow.

Willard Brown became a Crabber starting with the 1946-47 season. He led the league in batting that winter at .390, edging out Irvin (.387). Shortly after the season ended, Puerto Rico again welcomed a major-league team. This time the New York Yankees started their spring training on the island, as part of a Caribbean swing that also included Venezuela and Cuba. Again Larry MacPhail was responsible; by this point he was president of the Yankees (Charlie Dressen was one of the team's coaches as well). The sponsor was Don Q Rum, the leading Puerto Rican brand whose name adorned Escobar's big scoreboard.

The Bronx Bombers played five games in Puerto Rico against all-star teams and won three of them. All the games (as well as practice sessions) took place in Escobar. During that trip, Joe DiMaggio was still recovering from an operation on his heel; the incision had become badly infected. Nonetheless, he insisted on accompanying his team. The Yankees were staying in the Normandie Hotel, the noted art deco structure across the street from Escobar. Even for that short a distance, DiMaggio "could only drag himself to the ballpark," and because he was "besieged by excited fans," he needed a police escort.[30]

Later that year, Escobar's political atmosphere reached fever pitch. As far back as 1919, an independence movement had formed in Puerto Rico. One of its leading figures was Pedro Albizu Campos, a Harvard-educated attorney. In December 1947, Albizu returned to Puerto Rico after 11 years in the United States (for much of that time he was either in prison or the hospital). On December 15, he addressed a standing-room-only crowd of 14,000 at Escobar. As author Nelson Denis described it, "For over an hour he thundered about independence. The stadium shook as the crowd members stomped and chanted and cheered and pumped their fists in the air."[31]

Meanwhile, during the PRWL's 1947-48 season, Willard Brown was at his best. Brown felt that he had something to prove after that summer, in which he'd gotten what proved to be his one opportunity in the majors, a disappointing one-month stint. It may have been that winter when sportswriter Rafael Pont Flores coined Brown's nickname *Ese Hombre* ("That Man"). Brown won the Triple Crown with staggering statistics: .432-27-86 in just 60 games. Of his 27 homers, 22 came at Escobar.

Another of the PRWL's all-time stars began his career in the island with Santurce in 1947-48. That was Bob Thurman, who earned the nickname *El Múcaro* ("The Owl") because of his performance in night games. In 11 seasons as a Crabber, Thurman hit 117 home runs. He finished with 120 in Puerto Rico, topping the league's career list. According to Puerto Rican author Edgardo Rodríguez Juliá, Thurman was also known for his remarkably long *foul* balls—one of which supposedly struck a solitary crocodile in Muñoz Rivera Park.[32]

On March 12, 1948, a big-league club played at Escobar again. This time it was the Brooklyn Dodgers, with Jackie Robinson, who beat a Puerto Rican all-star team, 5-2. Actress Laraine Day, then married to Dodgers manager Leo Durocher, threw out the first ball.[33]

Sixto Escobar Stadium remained a crucible of Puerto Rican politics. The island's independence movement had prompted the formation of another party, the Puerto Rican Independence Party (PIP), in 1946. During its first General Assembly, on July 25, 1948, some 20,000 people were said to have been present at Escobar.[34]

Willard Brown had another big season for Santurce in 1948-49, and Tito Stevens remembered a funny episode. "My dad took me to one of many games and we sat in the box over the Santurce first-base dugout. Box seat holders had to present their ticket to a person at a door in the lobby area under the grandstand and be given a folding chair they then took to the box. While there, I started playing with a Coke bottle with my foot and it started rolling over the dugout roof. Just as Willard Brown stepped out to the on-deck circle, the bottle fell at his feet. 'Who threw that @#$%ing bottle at me?' shouted Brown. I explained what had happened and he smiled and said, 'OK, kid. I'll hit a home run for you.' Well, true to his word, Brown blasted one of his 18 homers that season."[35]

The Caribbean Series, which pitted the region's winter-league champions against each other in a round-robin tournament, started in 1949. In the first era of the series, which ran through 1960, Escobar hosted the event three times: in 1950, 1954, and 1958. In 1950, Puerto Rico (represented by the Caguas Criollos) came in second behind the upset winner, Panama's Carta Vieja Yankees. The most exciting moment for the home crowd came on February 23. Venezuela's Magallanes Navigators took a 1-0 lead into the bottom of the ninth, but Caguas pinch-hitter Wilmer Fields—called in from the coaching lines—hit a two-run homer.[36]

A separate movement in Puerto Rican politics at the time focused on statehood for the island. On August 19-20, 1950, a special assembly of the Statehood Party was held at Escobar to settle the question of the party's position toward Law 600 of 1950. That law authorized Puerto Ricans to enact their own Constitution, subject to approval by the U.S. President and Congress. According to author Robert William Anderson, the assembly "was marked by fistfights and catcalls."[37]

It should not be forgotten how deadly serious many Puerto Rican nationalists were at that time. Two of them, Óscar Collazo and Griselio Torresola, sought to assassinate President Harry S Truman on November 1, 1950. Secret Service agents killed Torresola during the attempt; inside Torresola's jacket was found a letter from Pedro Albizu.

The biggest baseball crowd ever at Escobar was 16,713, on February 17, 1951. It was the seventh game of the PRWL finals between Santurce and Caguas. A two-out home run in the bottom of the ninth by José St. Clair, better known as Pepe Lucas, gave the Crabbers their first league title. The Dominican's blow went down in history as the *Pepelucazo*. The crowd—which had started filing into the stadium at 7 A.M.—"hoisted their heroes to their shoulders for a parade through the streets of Santurce...an all-night demonstration was staged."[38]

One of the most momentous baseball events at Escobar was not a game. It was the tryout in 1952 that brought Roberto Clemente to the attention of the major leagues. Pedrín Zorrilla, owner of the Crabbers, and the Brooklyn Dodgers organized the clinic. The teenaged Clemente made a powerful impression on Brooklyn scout Al Campanis. Eventually, in early 1954, Clemente signed with the Dodgers—but his pro career began for Santurce in the 1952-53 season.

In the winters of 1952, 1953, and 1954, something unusual was visible on the field at Escobar: snow. The mayor of San Juan, Felisa Rincón de Gautier, had become friends with Eddie Rickenbacker, the World War I flying ace who had become chairman of Eastern Airlines. Planeloads of the white stuff were flown down from New England so that Puerto Rican children could enjoy playing in it—though it melted very quickly—as a treat for the major Latin American holiday, Three Kings' Day. Doña Fela (as the mayor was known) also viewed it as an educational experience for the kids.

In February 1954, Puerto Rico (again represented by Caguas) won the Caribbean Series for the only time in the three times it was held at Escobar. The team was led by series MVP "Jungle Jim" Rivera. After the victory, player-manager Mickey Owen rode through the stadium on a filly—*yegüita* in Spanish, the longtime symbol of the Caguas club. Owen, his steed, and the joyful Puerto Rican in front were all wearing straw hats.

The 1954-55 Crabbers were indeed a potent team. In addition to Clemente, the lineup boasted Willie Mays and George Crowe; Bob Thurman was also still with the club, hitting and occasionally pitching—his play finally got him to the majors in 1955, at the age of 37. The staff was led by Sam Jones, who won the Triple Crown of pitching, Rubén Gómez, and Bill Greason.

The Caribbean Series returned to Escobar in 1958. That year victory went to Cuba and its champion, the Marianao Tigres. Puerto Rico finished tied for second at 3-3. Vic Power and Clemente were the home team's leading batters. On February 8, Juan Pizarro fired 17 strikeouts in an 8-0, two-hit win over Panama, shattering the tournament record. A big turning point in the series came two days later, with Pizarro on as a fireman in the ninth inning. The bases were loaded with nobody out, and the tying run would have scored anyway on a long fly to right field, but when an umpire ruled that the ball had been dropped, the irate crowd at Escobar started "a small-scale riot." The game was suspended and completed the following night.[39]

Also during that tournament, syndicated columnist Red Smith depicted Escobar and one of its salient features for the benefit of U.S. newspaper readers. In a passage called "Baseball, Southern Fried", he wrote, "In Sixto Escobar Stadium the scoreboard plugs Don Q rum instead of Ballantine's or Schaefer's or Chesterfield, and outlined against the sky beyond right field are palm trees instead of the steelwork of the East Side subway. Otherwise this could be a small Yankee Stadium or Polo Grounds gone daft."

Smith continued, "These are twi-night doubleheaders; they start at 6:30 p.m. after dark has fallen and go on to the edge of endurance. Around midnight the fans are still there, maybe 15,000 of them, which is all the park can hold, though their voices have left them innings earlier. Apparently San Juan neither dines nor sleeps during the series."[40]

Sixto Escobar Stadium also hosted American football on occasion. Tito Stevens said, "I witnessed a couple of football games there in 1958 when the Antilles Command team played. One of the teams they faced—and by the way, they were wiped out by them—was the team from Mitchel Air Force Base on Long Island. The Antilles team was made up of MPs from Fort San Cristóbal and personnel from Fort Buchanan."[41]

In late 1958, the Continental League—the would-be third major league—germinated as an idea. On July 27, 1959, the league was formally announced. Bill Shea, the prime mover, listed five founding franchises and 11 cities that had showed interest in joining. One of them was San Juan.[42] The following month, though, it was turned down because its population and Escobar's capacity were deemed inadequate. That same story also noted that Escobar had hosted the Latin American Little League Baseball championship. Puerto Rico beat Venezuela and advanced to the Little League World Series, the first team from the island to do so.[43]

On April 1-3, 1960, the Philadelphia Phillies and the defending American League pennant winner, the Chicago White Sox, played a three-game exhibition series at Escobar. Originally, there were plans to go to Caracas, Venezuela before San Juan, but that leg of the trip did not happen.[44] Alas, attendance was poor (just 8,834 total), despite much advance PR work. Those who made it were treated to the entertainment of Jim Rivera, who joined the Navy band and did calypso dances. However, players complained about the travel time, "Class C" lighting, and uneven, concrete-hard infield.[45]

The Senators won the PRWL championship in the 1960-61 season, beating Caguas in the playoffs, five games to three. One memorable moment came in Game One, when the enormously powerful Frank Howard hit a home run that an engineer measured at 536 feet, giving Caguas a 2-1 win.[46] Depending on one's view regarding Josh Gibson's shot in March 1942, Howard's homer ranks as the longest in PRWL history.[47] The opposing pitcher, Jack Fisher, told Lou Hernández, "Frank hit it over two centerfield fences, over some logs and barrels and out on the beach...I sure remember that one."[48]

Sixto Escobar Stadium briefly hosted Triple-A ball in 1961. Ahead of that season, the Miami Marlins of the International League were transferred to San Juan. They played at Escobar, which was spruced up (capacity was listed at just 9,400). Meanwhile, San Juan's new ballpark—Hiram Bithorn Stadium—was under construction. The Marlins' roster included three Puerto Ricans: Julio Gotay, Ed Olivares, and player-coach Reynaldo Oliver.

Despite high hopes, however, the Marlins' attendance in San Juan was poor—an average of just 1,000 a game for the first 12 home dates after the opener, which drew 6,627. IL president Tommy Richardson said that the Cuban crisis had caused an economic squeeze in Puerto Rico, making admission unaffordable for most people. As a result, visiting clubs' share of the gate receipts was not enough to meet the costs of travel to San Juan.[49] Yet even a children's night, in which kids got in free, could not get the turnstiles spinning.[50] Contrary to Richardson's theory, the locals may simply have preferred homegrown players. On May 17, 1961—even though the team was only half

*Entrada principal del Parque Sixto Escobar en San Juan 1940*

a game out of first place — the Marlins announced that they were moving to Charleston, West Virginia.[51]

The PRWL's final regular-season game at Escobar took place on January 23, 1962. It was a one-game tiebreaker between San Juan and Arecibo to decide which team would get the fourth and final spot in the playoffs. Roberto Clemente did not play for much of the season, but after he joined San Juan, the Senators won 18 of their last 24 games to draw even with the Wolves. Arecibo won the tiebreaker, though, by a score of 7-5. The game featured a big rhubarb in the second inning when Clemente was called out at first with the bases loaded and the score tied 3-3. Police had to break up the fistfight between San Juan manager Napoleón Reyes and umpire Mel Steiner.[52]

Santurce won the playoffs, and the last professional ballgames of any kind held at Escobar took place shortly thereafter. They came during the Inter-American Series, another intra-regional tournament held for four years starting in 1961. (Cuba's withdrawal ended the first era of the Caribbean Series after the 1960 edition.) Puerto Rico, represented in part by the Crabbers, won in 1962, led by two wins from Bob Gibson and four home runs by Mike de la Hoz. The fourth of the Cuban infielder's homers — and the last at Escobar — came on Valentíne's Day 1962. It was a game-winner in the bottom of the 11th inning against his countryman Luis Tiant, pitching for Mayagüez, the other Puerto Rican entry in the series.[53]

Hiram Bithorn Stadium opened in October 1962. However, lower-level baseball was played at Escobar after that. Tom Van Hyning, who lived much of his early life in Puerto Rico, said, "I had a Pony League tryout at Sixto Escobar Stadium in 1967. It was used for youth baseball and I recall the seating was in need of repairs and renovations." Van Hyning also noted that Escobar served as the home field for the eight-man American football team of Santurce's Robinson School from 1963 through 1969.[54]

Basketball is also a popular sport in Puerto Rico. For many years, Escobar hosted various teams in the island's top hoops league, BSN (Baloncesto Superior Nacional). They included another club named the Santurce Crabbers—which is actually older than the baseball team—the Rio Piedras Cardinals, and the San Juan Saints.[55] BSN competition shifted to Bithorn Stadium in 1963.

In addition, notable track and field competition has taken place at Escobar:

- Many events of the 1979 Pan American Games were held there, after extensive renovations—it was then that Escobar's baseball configuration was removed.
- In September 1985, trials took place to select the Americas team for the fourth World Cup in Athletics.
- On July 29, 1989, at the Caribbean amateur athletic championships, the great Cuban athlete Javier Sotomayor became the first human to clear eight feet in the high jump. His coach said that conditions at the stadium were "marvelous for the jump."[56]

In early 2011, further repairs and improvements on Sixto Escobar Stadium were completed in order to welcome a new tenant from a different sport: soccer. The new home team was Club Atlético River Plate Puerto Rico, a franchise in the Puerto Rico Soccer League.[57]

The Museum and Library of the Hall of Fame of Puerto Rican Sports was located in Sixto Escobar Park on March 18, 2010. In August 2014, the structure was declared a National Historic Monument. To celebrate the first anniversary of this status, the U.S. Postal Service issued a commemorative stamp.

Sixto Escobar Stadium's lifespan as a professional baseball venue was less than three decades. It became antiquated rather rapidly. Yet while it flowered, it was as pretty and quaint and lively a place to watch a game as one could imagine.

*With continued thanks to SABR colleagues Jorge Colón Delgado, Tom Van Hyning, Lou Hernández, and Tito Stevens for their input.*

*Images courtesy of Jorge Colón Delgado's collection.*

Originally posted in February 2016. Updated in February 2017.

## SOURCES

*Books*

José A. Crescioni Benítez, *El Béisbol Profesional Boricua*, San Juan, Puerto Rico: Aurora Comunicación Integral, Inc., 1997.

## NOTES

1 "Parque Sixto Escobar, Monumento Histórico Nacional" official proclamation, August 5, 2014 (http://pr.microjuris.com/ConnectorPanel/ImagenServlet?reference=/images/file/L_130_14.pdf)

2 Thomas E. Van Hyning, *The Santurce Crabbers: Sixty Seasons of Puerto Rican Winter League Baseball* (Jefferson, North Carolina: McFarland & Company, 1999), 1.

3 Thomas E. Van Hyning, *Puerto Rico's Winter League: A History of Major League Baseball's Launching Pad* (Jefferson, North Carolina: McFarland & Company, 1995), 11, 47. Van Hyning, *The Santurce Crabbers*, 9-10.

4 Van Hyning, *The Santurce Crabbers*, 10.

5 Van Hyning, *Puerto Rico's Winter League*, 57. Lou Hernández, *Memories of Winter Ball* (Jefferson, North Carolina: McFarland & Company, 2013), 197.

6 Hernández, *Memories of Winter Ball*, 171, 166, 189.

7 E-mail from Tito Stevens to Rory Costello, February 15, 2017 (hereafter Stevens e-mail).

8 Michael M. Oleksak and Mary Adams Oleksak, *Béisbol: Latin Americans and the Grand Old Game* (Grand Rapids, Michigan: Masters Press, 1991), 62.

9 "Parque Sixto Escobar, Monumento Histórico Nacional."

10 Carlos Uriarte González, "Los 80 años del Estadio Sixto Escobar," *El Nuevo Día* (San Juan, Puerto Rico), November 8, 2012

11 Letter excerpt quoted in William McNeil, *Black Baseball Out of Season* (Jefferson, North Carolina: McFarland & Company, 2007), 114.

12 Johnny Torres Rivera, "Estadio Sixto Escobar," Puerta de Tierra website (http://www.puertadetierra.info/edificios/escobar/escobar.htm)

13 Jane Allen Quevedo, "Hiram Bithorn," SABR BioProject.

14 Associated Press, "Reds to Visit Puerto Rico," January 9, 1936.

15 "Cincinnati's Redlegs Head to Puerto Rico," *Virgin Islands Daily News*, February 17, 1936: 1.

16　Ronald T. Waldo, *Hazen "Kiki" Cuyler* (Jefferson, North Carolina: McFarland & Company, 2012), 200.

17　Waldo, *Hazen "Kiki" Cuyler*, 200. Tom Swope, "Dressen Puts Hobbles on Reds, Fearing Squad Will Go Stale," *The Sporting News*, February 20, 1936: 1. "Exhibition Games," *The Sporting News*, March 5, 1936: 2.

18　Allen Quevedo, "Hiram Bithorn."

19　Fernando Corneiro, "With the Cincinnati Reds," *Virgin Islands Daily News*, March 3, 1936: 1. Corneiro played a vital role in the history of baseball in the Virgin Islands, as may be seen in the story of Joe Christopher.

20　United Press, "Sixto Escobar Retains Title," February 22, 1937.

21　Associated Press, "Jeffra, Escobar to Meet Sunday in Title Battle," February 14, 1938.

22　Eddie Brietz, "Sports Roundup," Associated Press, September 8, 1939.

23　Van Hyning, *Puerto Rico's Winter League*, 233, via *El Mundo* (San Juan, Puerto Rico), September 6, 1939. Coimbre played for Ponce in the regular season; he joined Guayama as a reinforcement for the series against Duncan (a common practice in winter-league postseason competition).

24　Van Hyning, *The Santurce Crabbers*, 10.

25　Van Hyning, *Puerto Rico's Winter League*, 233.

26　Associated Press, "Oklahoma Nine Wins Semi-Pro Title," October 2, 1940.

27　Van Hyning, *The Santurce Crabbers*, 16.

28　Hernandez, *Memories of Winter Ball*, 208.

29　Rafael Costas, *Enciclopedia Béisbol Ponce Leones, 1938-87* (Santo Domingo, Dominican Republic: Editora Corripio, 1989), 84.

30　Richard Ben Cramer, *Joe DiMaggio: The Hero's Life* (New York: Simon & Schuster, 2000), 226.

31　Nelson A. Denis, *War Against All Puerto Ricans* (New York: Nation Books, 2015).

32　Edgardo Rodríguez Juliá, *San Juan: Memoir of a City* (Madison, Wisconsin: University of Wisconsin Press, 2007), 65.

33　*The Sporting News*, March 24, 1948: 22.

34　Robert William Anderson, *Party Politics in Puerto Rico* (Stanford, California: Stanford University Press, 1965), 133.

35　Stevens e-mail. Brown and Bob Thurman tied for the league lead in homers that season.

36　Santiago Llorens, "Panama Wins the Caribbean Pennant in Special Playoff," *The Sporting News*, March 8, 1950, 25.

37　Anderson, *Party Politics in Puerto Rico*, 85.

38　Santiago Llorens, "16,713 See Homer Clinch Playoff Title for Santurce", *The Sporting News*, February 28, 1951: 25.

39　"Latin Tempers Explode," "Ump's Ruling Provokes Fan Riot; Series Game Halted," *The Sporting News*, February 19, 1958: 30.

40　Red Smith, "Views of Sport," syndicated column, February 11, 1958.

41　Stevens e-mail.

42　Associated Press, "Continental League Plans to Be in Operation by '61," Associated Press, July 28, 1959.

43　"Veto San Juan as Team in New Major League," *Virgin Islands Daily News*, August 24, 1959: 1.

44　Jerry Holtzman, "Pale Hose, Phils Complete Plans for Latin Junket," *The Sporting News*, February 3, 1960: 9.

45　Jerry Holtzman, "Pale Hose-Philly Puerto Rico Trip 10-G Flopperoo," *The Sporting News*, April 13, 1960: 11.

46　Miguel J. Frau, "Stock, Fisher Hurl Gems in San Juan's Drive to Loop Flag," *The Sporting News*, February 15, 1961: 17.

47　Van Hyning, *Puerto Rico's Winter League*, 15.

48　Hernández, *Memories of Winter Ball*, 170.

49　Associated Press, "Marlins Will Quit San Juan," May 4, 1961. Associated Press, "San Juan 'Move' Talk Hit," May 5, 1961.

50　"Moford Blanks Marlins for 1-0 Victory," *Rochester Democrat and Chronicle*, April 29, 1961: 24.

51　Associated Press, "Charleston Gets San Juan Club," Associated Press, May 18, 1961.

52　Van Hyning, *Puerto Rico's Winter League*, 64. Miguel J. Frau, "Cepeda Sparks Wallopers to Record HR Total of 271," *The Sporting News*, January 31, 1962: 31.

53　Miguel J. Frau, "Crabbers Cop Latin Title Fourth Time in 14 Years," *The Sporting News*, February 21, 1962: 37-38.

54　E-mails from Tom Van Hyning to Rory Costello, January 27 and January 28, 2016.

55　Uriarte González, "Los 80 años del Estadio Sixto Escobar."

56　Luis R. Varela, "Sotomayor first to high jump 8 feet," Associated Press, July 31, 1989. Even in 2016, Sotomayor remains the only person in history to clear eight feet. His record, which has endured since 1993, is just short of 8 feet, 0.5 inches.

57　"Petter Villegas se une al River Plate PR," *El Nuevo Día*, August 24, 2010.

# HIRAM BITHORN STADIUM (SAN JUAN, PR)

By Charles F. Faber

THE FIRST MAJOR-LEAGUE BASEball game this writer ever saw was at the Polo Grounds in New York City on May 24, 1946. Since then he has visited major-league and minor-league parks from Boston to San Diego and many places in between. But he has never seen games anywhere that rival the pageantry of those at *Estadio Hiram Bithorn (*Hiram Bithorn Stadium) in San Juan, Puerto Rico. "Fans are rabid," said Horace Stoneham, president of the San Francisco Giants, in 1963." From the moment the umpire yells play ball, the stands come alive with hoots, yells, and excitement."[1] That fervor has diminished little in the decades since.

Stoneham was also one of those baseball men who praised the park itself, which opened in October 1962. He said, "It's a beaut and it offers an unobstructed view from any seat." That's because Bithorn has a one-tier grandstand with cantilever construction. Seating capacity has ranged from 18,000 to 22,000. In 2004, the *Washington Post* observed, "The ballpark bears too much resemblance to Shea Stadium and the concrete monstrosities popular in the U.S. in the 1960s…yet despite its grim façade, it holds certain unique charms as well."[2] Rare is the stadium that can survive more than half a century – in January 2014, Hiram Bithorn Stadium was added to the National Registry of Historic Places.

This multi-purpose stadium is owned and operated by the municipality of San Juan.

It is named for Hiram Bithorn, the first Puerto Rican to play in the major leagues. Bithorn's career started with the Chicago Cubs in 1942. He was murdered in 1951 by a Mexican policeman under mysterious circumstances. March 18, 2016, marked the 100th anniversary of Bithorn's birth in Santurce.

The stadium's principal tenants are members of *La Liga de Beisbol Profesional de Puerto Rico* (Professional Baseball League of Puerto Rico – a.k.a. the Puerto Rican Winter League or PRWL). They are the Santurce *Cangrejeros* (Crabbers) and *Los Senadores de San Juan (*San Juan Senators) – though the latter club's presence in the league has been intermittent since 2004. The stadium has also been host to league All-Star contests (held on January 6), Caribbean Series games – and regular-season major-league games in 2001, 2003, 2004, 2010, and two more were scheduled for May 2016, but plans were scrapped due to fears of the Zika virus.

Bithorn replaced the venerable *Estadio Sixto Escobar,* which had served the area since November 1932. Originally called *Estadio del Escambrón*, the old stadium hosted baseball games, other sporting events, and political conventions. Its name was changed in April 1938 in honor of Sixto Escobar, the island's first world championship boxer. By 1962, however, the little park (normal capacity 13,135 patrons) had grown outmoded. As a baseball facility, Escobar became antiquated rather rapidly. The Puerto Rican Winter League's attendance began to decline in 1954 with the coming of television. Negro Leaguers, who had been among the league's primary stars since 1938, became old. Their replacements were often players from the minors, though a significant contingent of major leaguers was still present. In 1957, a new racetrack was inaugurated and horse racing diluted fans' interest in baseball. Even so, the level of competition remained just a step below the major leagues for decades to come.

The new stadium was built during the administration of Mayor Felisa Rincón de Gautier. The project stemmed at least in part from her leadership. This remarkable woman, who died at the age of 97 in 1994, was the first female to be elected mayor of a capital city in the Americas. She designed innovative city services, established the first pre-school centers called *Las Escuelas Maternales*, which became the model of the Head Start programs in the United States. She renovated the public health system and was responsible for the establishment of the School of Medicine in San Juan. Her main passion was improving the health, education, and lives of San Juan's impoverished residents, especially the children. She started the tradition of bringing gifts to poor and needy children on the *Día de Reyes* on January 6 each year. In some years she had planeloads of snow flown in so children who had never played in the snow would be able to do so.[3]

"Doña Fela" recognized the importance of baseball to Puerto Rico. She helped organize youth baseball teams, providing uniforms and equipment, and authorized the clearing of land to serve as ballparks for neighborhood children. She helped in the establishment of Little League teams throughout San Juan. During the PRWL's first season at the new stadium, owners Hiram Cuevas of Santurce and Tuto Saavedra of San Juan arranged with public school officials to admit 5,000 school children free of charge to Saturday afternoon games.[4]

Hiram Bithorn Stadium is located just off *Avenida Franklin Delano Roosevelt*. It is across the street from the *Coliseo Roberto Clemente* and in front of a large shopping mall called *Plaza las Américas*. The dimensions of the field have changed from time to time, but now are: left field – 325 feet, center field – 404 feet, right field – 325 feet. Although the fences have been moved back a bit, the short distances down the lines make Bithorn a hitter-friendly park. There is an unusually large amount of foul territory, though, which helps the pitchers to a degree. Originally, games were played on grass, but two types of artificial surfaces have been used. In 2004, Field Turf replaced the Astroturf that had been laid in 1995. Another distinctive feature is the stadium's light towers, which tilt inward toward the field.[5]

The architects who designed the new facility were Orval E. Sifontes and Alexander Papesh. Construction took about two years, said chief engineer Rafael Aparicio, who recalled that it wasn't quite finished when the first game was played there on October 24, 1962. Hiram Bithorn's mother was invited and attended the game. Mayor Rincón de Gautier did not claim the privilege of throwing out the ceremonial first pitch. Instead, she deferred to another politician, Herminio Concepción de Gracia.[6] *The Sporting News* reported, "The dedication of the new $7,000,000 Hiram Bithorn Stadium touched off a turnstile boom as the Puerto Rico League opened its 1962-63 season. An all-time record crowd of 18,363 poured into the ultra-modern arena for the season inaugural, contributing to a smashing getaway for the circuit.[7]

Bob Veale was on the mound for the visiting Ponce team and pitched a no-hitter for 7 1/3 innings against the home team, the San Juan Senators, until he weakened in the eighth frame. Ponce won the game, 6-2. Veale's teammate, Rafael Alomar, got the first hit in the new stadium. After the game, thieves broke into the stadium office, but failed to abscond with any of the $20,353 gate receipts.

Bithorn has hosted seven Caribbean Series between February 1971 and February 2015. The 1995 edition at Bithorn featured Puerto Rico's "dream team" – a major-league lineup loaded with Island stars such as Roberto Alomar, Carlos Baerga, Edgar Martínez, Juan González, Bernie Williams, Rubén Sierra, Carlos Delgado, Carmelo Martinez, and Rey Sánchez. Among the many Puerto Rican All-Star contests held at Bithorn, perhaps the most memorable was the one on January 6, 1973. It honored the memory of the late Roberto Clemente, who had died just six days before. The outfield fence at Bithorn includes the retired numbers of Clemente (21), Rubén Gómez (22), and Orlando Cepeda (30).

On Opening Day of the 2001 American League baseball season, the Toronto Blue Jays and the Texas Rangers played the first regular-season major-league game in Puerto Rico. It was the first game of the new millennium. Major League Baseball and the city of San Juan spent hundreds of thousands of dollars to upgrade Hiram Bithorn Stadium. Carlos Delgado of the Blue Jays, one of the team's two Puerto Ricans along with José Cruz Jr., said "I've played many games in that stadium, but this is going to be a little sweeter."[8]

The day has been described as equal parts ballgame and street fair.[9] Four thousand fans who bought tickets were turned away when police determined that the safe capacity of the park had been exceeded. Roberto Clemente's widow, Vera, and Orlando Cepeda threw out the first pitch. Fans drank piña coladas and feasted on *pinchos (*chicken kabobs), while the public address system played "Kung Fu Fighting" and a selection or two from the band U2. When native Puerto Ricans Iván Rodríguez and Ricky Ledée came out bearing Puerto Rican flags, the crowd went wild. The raucous atmosphere continued throughout the game.

In both 2003 and 2004, the Montreal Expos played 22 "home" games in Bithorn Stadium, largely because of poor attendance at Olympic Stadium in Montreal. The idea was that with greater revenue from San Juan, the Expos would not have to conduct a "fire sale" of star players. Frank Robinson, Montreal's manager at the time, said, "It will be great to play in front of the people down there. They're great fans."[10] Robinson had previously been Santurce's manager for eight seasons. Robinson and Clemente managed against each other at Bithorn in 1970-71, when Clemente was managing San Juan.

The Expos also had some strong Puerto Rican players to draw fans, including José Vidro, Javier Vázquez, and Wil Cordero. The travel schedule proved hard on the team, though. Infielder Jamey Carroll said, "At first I was thinking, 'Wow, we get to

go to Puerto Rico'…It was kind of fun. But after a while, we started getting tired of it."[11]

None of the three main areas competing for the relocation of the Expos was able to put together complete financing for a new ballpark in 2003, so Hiram Bithorn got a second chance to host the team in 2004. Attendance was at least 10,000 for each of the games in 2003, but was not as strong the second year. An effort was made to attract the Expos to San Juan permanently, but Puerto Rico remained a long shot at best. Even as early as May 2003, Commissioner Bud Selig remarked, "The San Juan experiment has worked out beautifully…but I don't know that I would describe it as a player."[12] The club finally moved to Washington, D.C., ahead of the 2005 season.

Yet, that did not mark the demise of big-league games in Hiram Bithorn Stadium. After years of "serious dialogue," negotiations finally proved successful, enabling the Florida Marlins to play a three-game "home" series against the New York Mets from June 28 through June 30, 2010.[13] The Marlins' manager, Edwin Rodríguez, was the first native of Puerto Rico to manage in the majors. Florida's third-base coach, Joe Espada, grew up watching games at Bithorn and later played there, too.

Meanwhile, in 2006, 2009, and 2013 Hiram Bithorn Stadium was host for parts of the *Clásico Mundial de Beisbol,* or World Baseball Classic. In 2006, Cuba, Panama, Puerto Rico, and the Netherlands started in San Juan. Cuba and Puerto Rico advanced. In 2009 the Dominican Republic, Netherlands, Panama, and Puerto Rico played in San Juan, with the Netherlands and Puerto Rico advancing to the next round. In 2013 the Dominican Republic, Puerto Rico, Spain, and Venezuela competed at Bithorn. The Dominicans swept the games in San Juan and won the championship game versus Puerto Rico in San Francisco.

The atmosphere during the World Baseball Classic in 2009 and 2013 was very lively. There is a large grassy area between the street and the stadium, with sidewalks leading to the stadium. At times tents are erected on the grass, with bands playing from some of them and hawkers selling their goods from others. The sidewalks were lined with young people handing out advertisements and freebies, such as chewing gum, baseball cards, and noisemakers—lots of clickers and thunder pieces. During the games young people threw goodies into the stands, mainly T-shirts and ponchos. The games provided temporary employment for probably hundreds of youngsters, with T-Mobile and a medical plan employing the most. The vendors in the stands were mainly, but not exclusively, young. They sold piña coladas, cotton candy, peanuts, Pepsi, and Coors Light, but not the typical American ball park foods, hot dogs and hamburgers, although such items were offered at other times, especially at games involving teams from the United States and Canada. The fans at the Classic were incredibly enthusiastic, going up and down the aisles beating on drums and playing other musical instruments, singing, dancing, waving flags, and shouting constantly.

In addition to baseball, Bithorn has hosted other sporting and non-sporting events. Boxing is one of Puerto Rico's favorite sports, and a number of championship fights have taken place in Bithorn. It was also the main venue for the 1979 Pan American Games.

During baseball's offseason the field is converted into a soccer field with one goal facing the right field bleachers and the other facing the third base grandstand. Since 2008 Bithorn has been host to the *Atléticos de San Juan* and the *Academía Quintana* in the Puerto Rico Soccer League.

World Wrestling Federation matches and professional basketball games have been held at the stadium. Longtime NBA player and coach Don Nelson had unpleasant memories about playing there. "I played outdoors in Puerto Rico when I was with the Celtics," Nelson recalled, "and it was a disaster. It rained, and there were a lot of other crazy things. There was a hostile crowd, and they were throwing stuff. It was amazing."[14]

The preseason game between the Phoenix Suns and the Milwaukee Bucks at Bithorn on September 24, 1972, is said to have been the first outdoor contest played in the National Basketball Association. Bithorn was used because San Juan's new arena, *Coliseo Roberto Clemente,* had not yet been completed.

It rained that day, but fortunately, the rain did not start until just after the game was over.

Hiram Bithorn Stadium has hosted dozens of musical events over the years. The Byrds, Santana, the Beach Boys, Rod Stewart, Billy Joel, Whitney Houston, and the Backstreet Boys are just a few of the stars who have entertained fans at the stadium. Coldplay brought their "A Head Full of Dreams Tour" to Bithorn on April 20, 2016.

Basketball, soccer, wrestling, and musical concerts may have their roles in the grand scheme of things, but Hiram Bithorn Stadium in San Juan, Puerto Rico, is one of the best places in the world to see the game that many still view as the world's best – baseball!

*The writer wishes to express his appreciation to SABR members Rory Costello, Jorge Colón Delgado, and Thomas Van Hyning for their input and expertise.*

## NOTES

1. Jack McDonald, "Stoneham Points to Latin Nations as Talent Hotbed," *The Sporting News*, December 7, 1963: 6.
2. Dan Jung, "Minor League Baseball, Puerto Rico Style," *Washington Post*, July 1, 2004.
3. Eric Pace, "Felisa Rincon de Gautier, 97, Mayor of San Juan," *New York Times*, September 19, 1994.
4. Miguel J. Frau, "San Juan Stacks Hill Staff with Major Leaguers," *The Sporting News*, November 3, 1962.
5. Philip J. Lowry, *Green Cathedrals* (New York: Walker & Co., 2006), 215; "Clem's Baseball – Hiram Bithorn Stadium," www.andrewclem.com.
6. "Construtor de una leyenda como el Hiram Bithorn," *El Nuevo Día* (Guaynabo, Puerto Rico), October 25, 2012.
7. Miguel J. Frau, "New Stadium Ignites Loop Boom at Gate," *The Sporting News*, November 19, 1962, 25.
8. Associated Press, "Blue Jays, Rangers Take Show on Road," May 4, 2003.
9. *Official Souvenir Program, 2006 World Baseball Classic*, New York: Major League Baseball, 2006: 44.
10. Associated Press, "Expos: 22 games in San Juan," November 21, 2002.
11. Jonah Keri, *Up, Up, and Away* (New York: Random House, 2014).
12. Ricardo Zuniga, Associated Press, "Will Expos stay dancing in Puerto Rico?," May 4, 2003.
13. Adam Rubin, "New York Mets Contemplating Playing Regular-Season Games in Puerto Rico during 2010 season," *New York Daily News*, November 22, 2009.
14. Dave McMenamin, "In Golden State, Shooter Crawford, Coach Nelson at Stalemate," NBA.com, March 23, 2009 (www.nba.com/2009/news/features/dave-McMenamin/03/23/western-insider200900323/)

# MAJOR LEAGUE BASEBALL IN PUERTO RICO

By Mark Souder

## Major-League Spring Training in Puerto Rico

### *The 1936 Cincinnati Reds*

"THE CINCINNATI REDS PUT ON the first major league baseball game in Puerto Rican history yesterday" was lead of an AP wire story on February 26, 1936.[1] Spring training had not yet settled into the patterns we have today, though the core principles behind such training and site selection already existed: getting the team in shape for the major-league season, economic incentives, and sun. The Reds were the first team to stage spring training outside the continental United States, though a few teams had played exhibition games in Havana, Cuba.[2]

The 1936 Cincinnati team was not very good. They went 74-80 that year, slightly better than the year before and the year after. However, their developing stars, including Ernie Lombardi and Paul Derringer, and veteran Babe Herman would lead them to pennants in 1939 and 1940. This initial major-league visit to Puerto Rico was not important because of the team itself but was incredibly significant within the framework of racial prejudices of the period.

From the time blacks were frozen out of major-league baseball at the turn of the century, shades of brown in a player became a never-ending conflict. The Reds had been pioneers in the testing of the color line when they signed Cubans Armando Marsans and Rafael Almeida in 1911. Cuban Adolfo Luque, though initially signed by the Boston Braves, built his career in Cincinnati, for which he pitched from 1918 through 1929. Deemed sufficiently white, Luque was the biggest "brown" star until Jackie Robinson broke the color line. In other words, Cincinnati was already the leader in testing the color line prior to arriving in Puerto Rico in 1936.

Commissioner Kenesaw Mountain Landis realized that with black baseball teams defeating some of the all-white big-league teams, it was becoming a challenge to maintain not only the white supremacy of the times but the argument that the major leagues played superior baseball compared with all other leagues. Landis unofficially ordered that major-league teams to no longer play Negro League or other Negro teams. While "all-star" games were permitted, no more than three members of any single major-league team could play on such a squad. Furthermore, while winter-league baseball had been established, white players were not to play against teams of American blacks as opposed to non-American blacks. In 1936 the Reds directly challenged all of these guidelines.

The famous Pan American Clipper planes are today considered a cultural icon. When Larry MacPhail, the Reds' general manager, and owner Powel Crosley decided to send the team to Puerto Rico, the flights were still in the early stages for Pan Am. The 24 Reds and those traveling with them drank black Pan American coffee spiked with brandy from coach High Pockets Kelly. Thus fortified, the Reds became the first big-league team to fly. Eventually 35 veterans and rookies arrived in Puerto Rico.[3]

While there were some driving adventures and struggles with the Spanish language, the newspaper coverage focused much on the "fun and sun" of Puerto Rico. It was reported that Puerto Rico sunshine was "not as oppressive as in the southern part of the United States" and "more penetrating," resulting in fewer "muscle pains which usually accompany the first few days of training." At the Condado Hotel "the players lunch each day and sometimes in the evening in the beautiful open air pavilion, fronting the sea, at the rear of the Hotel."[4]

In addition to intrasquad games, the Reds played against the Brooklyn Eagles of the Negro League (merged with Effa Manley's Newark Eagles when the season began), Almendares from Cuba, Azteca from Mexico, and the Ponce team from Puerto Rico. In San Juan they played some Puerto Rican "all-star" teams.[5]

The doubleheader with the Brooklyn Eagles was a direct challenge to major-league guidelines, and demonstrated the dangers Landis hoped to prevent. A Puerto Rico native, 19-year-old Hiram Bithorn, established the foundation of his legacy by taking a 4-1 lead into the eighth inning. The Eagles prevailed, 5-4, after the Reds rallied. Black American stars Ray Dandridge and Buck Leonard were the big draw. The fans could hardly wait to see them play, so were pleased when they, along with Bithorn, were considered the stars who delivered the victory over the Reds.[6]

From the perspective of Organized Baseball leaders who wanted to maintain white superiority, the fact that the Reds won the second game didn't help much. Headlines like "Reds Divide Games with Colored Team" make the point.[7] Especially since legendary black Cuban pitcher Martin Dihigo of Almendares had completely throttled the Reds, 5-1, the day before the Negro League games.[8]

MacPhail told the media that the Reds were pleased and would return the following year. They did not. The official reason is that they were not offered the cash incentives then common from all spring-training sites. MacPhail himself was on tenuous ground with owner Crosley, and was pushed out after the 1937 season. However, it doesn't take a conspiracy theorist to see the long arm of the commissioner's office at work. In fact, no major-league team returned to Puerto Rico until the 1947 New York Yankees.

### The 1947 New York Yankees

Many things had changed by 1947. Landis had died in the fall of 1944. US Senator Happy Chandler of Kentucky had become commissioner. Brooklyn Dodgers president and general manager Branch Rickey, who had recommended MacPhail to Reds owner Powel Crosley with the warning about MacPhail's alcohol problems, signed Jackie Robinson to a baseball contract on October 23, 1945. Chandler backed up the color line breakthrough at all stages. Robinson played in 1946 with the Montreal Royals, since Rickey assumed that playing in Montreal would somewhat reduce Robinson's exposure to overt racism. In 1947 he broke the color line in the majors.[9]

In 1945 the Yankees hired MacPhail as club president. With the color line broken by the Brooklyn competition to the Yankees, it is not surprising that MacPhail now led the Yankees to Puerto Rico.

The 1947 Yankees won their first Puerto Rican game, on February 22 against the San Juan Senators, 16-3. They followed the next day with a victory over Caguas (6-5) and concluded with a victory over a team of Puerto Rican all-stars (8-6). In between they lost to the Ponce Leones (12-8) and a team of all-stars (7-6). The final scheduled game was rained out.[10]

The victory by the Leones de Ponce baseball team over the famed Yankees is still touted on the island. A newspaper story of the 1947 victory was posted on the Ponce Leones' official Twitter page in 2017. It boasts that the Ponce Leones were the only Puerto Rican team to beat a major-league team (as opposed to an all-star squad). The story highlighted the pitching of the Ponce team and the home run by Fernando Pedroso, the "home run king of Puerto Rico."[11] The *New York Herald-Tribune* reported that Pedroso's home run "sent the crowd into a paroxysm of joy" when it broke open the game in the sixth inning. "The entire Ponce team gathered at the plate to welcome Pedroso. Pedroso then made a running collection tour of the boxes. The fans thrust money into his hands. He collected $70."[12]

More entertaining, and also prescient for the conclusion of the 1947 season, was the sponsor that lured major-league baseball back to the island: Don Q rum. Don Juan Serralles began distilling rum in 1865 in Ponce. Destileria Serralles established the Don Q brand in 1932.[13] It sponsored the Leones de Ponce team. Puerto Rico still produces 70 percent of the rum consumed in the United States (mostly Bacardi), though Don Q remains the number one brand in Puerto Rico with approximately 60 percent of the market there.

The 36 top salesmen from Destileria Serralles met the Yankees upon arrival. "To get the fun off to a good start, the distillery had arranged to have a case of rum delivered to each player's room on arrival in mid-afternoon. A few hours later, at dinner time, the VP in charge turned his salesmen loose with the command, 'Go to it, lads. … The Yankees were beginning to think MacPhail had hit upon a great idea for spring training."[14]

## The 1948 Brooklyn Dodgers

After spending spring training in Cuba in 1947, Branch Rickey received a financial offer from the Dominican Republic to train there in 1948. He was, however, pursuing a more permanent site in Florida. By December of 1947 Bud Holman of Vero Beach had persuaded the Dodgers to build Dodgertown so that Jackie Robinson and future dark-skinned players would not be sent to separate facilities from other team members for housing and dining. In the spring of 1948 Dodgertown was not yet completed, so Brooklyn trained in the Caribbean, flying to Puerto Rico for a night game on March 12, 1948. The Dodgers defeated a Puerto Rican all-star team. Jackie Robinson contributed a key double in the rally that won the game.[15]

Puerto Rico has always been known for its vociferous baseball fans. Jackie Robinson gave new hope to Puerto Rican youngsters that they, too, now had a chance to play in the majors, not just the Negro Leagues. One little boy who said that Robinson's visit inspired his drive to play baseball was San Francisco first baseman Orlando Cepeda. His father, Perucho "The Bull" Cepeda, was considered the island's Babe Ruth but he had never been able to play in the majors. Orlando did, and became one of baseball's biggest stars. Cepeda was the second Puerto Rican to be elected to the Baseball Hall of Fame.

## 1960: The Chicago White Sox vs. the Philadelphia Phillies

After winning in 1959 their first pennant in 40 years, the Chicago White Sox visited Puerto Rico to play the Philadelphia Phillies in a three-game spring-training series April 1-3, 1960. The Phillies had finished eighth in the National League in 1959, and did it again in 1960.

There were 4,500 fans at Sixto Escobar Stadium for the opening game. The White Sox team included some of the legendary Latinos in baseball. Manager Al López was Cuban, his family having migrated to Ybor City in Tampa in 1906. Orestes "Minnie" Miñoso broke a second racial barrier in 1951, becoming the first black Latino to play in the major leagues. All-Star shortstop and future Hall of Famer Luis Aparicio (Montiel) was not only from Venezuela but his father, Luis Aparicio (Ortega), and the latter's brother were pioneers of baseball in that country.[16]

As an inducement to take further advantage of the short fences at Sixto Escobar—the *Chicago Tribune* called them "about as distant as in Little League fields"—Brother Jive, a 5-year-old horse running at the San Juan track, was promised to the player who hit the most home runs in the series. The Go-Go White Sox were not known for sluggers, but Al Smith was fired up. In the first contest, he slugged three home runs (he hit only 12 in the 1960 season). Backup catcher Dick Brown also hit one out and, with two out in the ninth inning, nearly hit one out at the deepest point, 400 feet to center. But he didn't, and the Phillies prevailed, 12-11. Joe Koppe, Bobby Smith, and Jim Coker homered for the Phillies.[17]

The Phillies put on their "lustiest hitting show of the exhibition series the next day," pummeling Bob Shaw and Frank Baumann for 13 hits. The hero for the Puerto Ricans was Arroyo. Island native Rubén Gomez thrilled the fans by pitching six innings of one-run baseball and was the winning pitcher in an 8-3 triumph. There were no home runs but still the most famous fan present, Clementine Churchill (Winston's wife), observed that "it's just like rounders, only terribly exciting."[18]

The White Sox finally triumphed in the concluding game on Sunday, April 3, with a 4-2 win. Al Smith hit his fourth home run of the series, to win Brother Jive as the leading slugger of the series. Smith left Brother Jive to race at the El Comandante track in San Juan.[19] White Sox slugger Ted Kluszewski hit a two-run shot, and the Phillies' two runs scored on homers by Bobby Del Greco and Ed Bouchee.[20]

### 1960: The Baltimore Orioles versus the Miami Marlins

An 18-member contingent of the Baltimore Orioles traveled to Puerto Rico to play their Triple-A affiliate from the International League, the Miami Marlins, in Puerto Rico. The two-game series began in Ponce on Saturday, April 2, and concluded on Sunday, April 3, in Caguas. The Marlins won both games, 6-2 and 5-4. The White Sox and Phillies played on the same days but in San Juan.[21]

The Baltimore team was considered a "B" club, though many of the other better-known current and future key Orioles joined the contingent. Jack Fisher and Steve Barber were the losing Orioles pitchers. In the first game, catcher Gus Triandos scored one of the Orioles' two runs. In the second game, the key Orioles blow was a grand slam by aging slugger Walt Dropo. He drove in second baseman Jerry Adair, and outfielders Albie Pearson and Jackie Brandt. Adair went 4-for-5 in the second game. Orioles shortstop Ron Hansen did not distinguish himself other than striking out to end an Orioles rally in the fifth inning.

The comments by a *Baltimore Sun* reporter who traveled with the team echoed the comments that plagued major-league ball in Puerto Rico since Cincinnati's first visit in 1936: Attendance was low, the flights long, which made travel costs high, the ballfields were hard, the umpiring shaky, and the narrow mountain roads were terrifying.[22]

The most important thing, by far, about these games to the future of major-league baseball in Puerto Rico and the Caribbean was not the Orioles, but the Marlins.

### The 1961 San Juan Marlins: The Only Puerto Rican Team in Organized Baseball

William B. MacDonald Jr. was a sports promoter and investor. In the early 1960s he was the primary owner of the Marlins, the Tropical Park race track in Miami, and, in 1964, promoter of one of the greatest boxing matches of all time, between champion Sonny Liston and 22-year-old Cassius Clay.[23]

MacDonald invested some of his horse-racing earnings in Puerto Rico; he was the largest home-mortgage broker in San Juan (the Housing Investment Corporation of San Juan) when the Marlins visited in 1960. Rocky Marciano, who had retired from heavyweight boxing in 1956 as the undefeated champion, accompanied the Marlins to Puerto Rico. He had a $1-a-year contract with Miami as a batting-practice catcher.[24]

Baseball was a money-losing proposition for MacDonald during his ownership of the Marlins. Things were not going well in Miami, so the Marlins moved to San Juan for the 1961 season. For two months Puerto Rico had a team at the highest level of minor-league baseball. The San Juan Marlins were affiliated with the St. Louis Cardinals, since the Orioles had abandoned Miami for Rochester, New York.

Two things sent the San Juan Marlins to a rapid death: costs and poor attendance, a lethal one-two punch. Round-trip coach fare was $92.50 per player, which meant that each opposing team would have roughly a $2,000 transportation cost for a full team contingent.[25] For its visit, Buffalo claimed its "take" was $830, including a $200 guarantee for the rained-out game.[26] Visiting clubs took a significant loss to play baseball in Puerto Rico.

The first game was played on April 17, 1961, against the Toronto Maple Leafs. The San Juan Marlins featured three Puerto Ricans, players Julio Gotay and Ed Olivares, and player-coach Reynaldo Oliver. Excitement was high. However, even for the first game, only two-thirds of the seats were sold.[27]

The attendance for the series against the Maple Leafs established the clear pattern. There were 6,627 fans at the opener, followed by 1,897 at game two,

763 at the third game and 500 for the concluding matchup.[28] On May 3 the International League voted to pull the plug on Puerto Rico.[29]

Owner MacDonald objected and stalled a bit, claiming that the franchise hadn't been given enough time to develop attendance.[30] His appeal was rejected. The San Juan Marlins moved to West Virginia. They debuted in Charleston on May 18, becoming the only landlocked Marlins not on someone's trophy wall. In 1962 the Charleston Marlins moved to Atlanta, becoming the Crackers.[31]

While many reasons were given for the disastrously low attendance after the first game, one loomed so large that it dwarfed all others. The Havana Sugar Kings had been the first Latin American team and the only one other than the 1961 San Juan Marlins to play in Organized Baseball. The Sugar Kings were members of the International League from 1954 until they departed in 1960.

Fidel Castro overthrew the Cuban government of Fulgencio Batista in 1959. As Castro consolidated his government in early 1960—as the White Sox, Phillies, and Orioles visited Puerto Rico—it became more apparent that his views were hostile to private enterprise and the United States. The Eisenhower administration was unalterably opposed to Castro, further increasing tensions. The Sugar Kings played their last game in Havana on July 14, 1960, and migrated to Jersey City as part of the wave of departures fleeing Castro. In October 1960 Castro nationalized the major industries, and the United States responded with a trade embargo.[32]

From 1959 and continuing for many years, Cuban refugees streamed to the Miami area and to Puerto Rico, affecting the politics and economy of both areas. The San Juan Marlins' brief time on the island came at a pivotal point in Caribbean political history. It helped set the future development of Organized Baseball in Latin America.

The San Juan Marlins and Toronto Maple Leafs played four games on April 17-20. Excitement had been generated on the island that Canadian Prime Minister John Diefenbaker might attend, but he was preoccupied. Diefenbaker had endorsed the US desire to invade Cuba in spite of the fact that Ottawa never broke off diplomatic relations with Cuba. In fact, declassified State Department documents reveal that the US government secretly encouraged Canada to maintain such relations and not support the embargo. On April 19 the day of the third game, Diefenbaker told Canada's House of Commons that events in Cuba were "manifestations of a dictatorship which is abhorrent to free men everywhere."[33]

After early air strikes, the invasion of Cuba hit the beaches at the Bay of Pigs on the very day of the San Juan Marlins opener against Toronto. Fighting continued on the days of the second and third games. Attendance, unsurprisingly, catastrophically plummeted.[34] On April 20, the day of the series finale, Castro claimed that the invading Revolutionary Front was in near-collapse. From Puerto Rico, the Cuban Revolutionary Front claimed it was launching a counterattack.[35] Rather than trash the poor attendance, perhaps it should have been noted that 500 obviously diehard fans attended the baseball game.

Not only were the crowds suppressed the next few games but rumors immediately began that the International League was considering abandoning Puerto Rico. Within two weeks they had met and voted officially to leave. The San Juan Marlins were out within a month. Dealing with hard fields and rain was one thing; dealing with the political instability was another. There would be future visits by major-league teams to Puerto Rico, but other than the partial home seasons of the 2003 and 2004 Montreal Expos, the San Juan Marlins were the last Caribbean team. No Organized Baseball team (major- or minor-league affiliate) has been based in Puerto Rico, or anywhere else in Latin America, since the San Juan Marlins departed.

## *The 1967 Pittsburgh Pirates vs the Baltimore Orioles and the New York Yankees*

In 1967 the Pittsburgh Pirates, featuring their Puerto Rican star Roberto Clemente, played three spring-training games on the island. These were the first games in which two major-league teams played each other in Puerto Rico. Clemente hosted the Pirates team for dinner at his restaurant the first day. Two games were against the Baltimore Orioles, with a third against the New York Yankees on April 2. Clemente's back was ailing, but he still played in two of the three games. He had four hits in five at-bats. Both teams were upset with the poor quality of the field at Ponce, where the second game between the Pirates and the Orioles was played, and stars Clemente (back) and the Orioles' Frank Robinson (knee) did not risk playing.[36]

### *The Roberto Clemente Sports City Benefit Series 1974-1991*

Major-league baseball, like much of the rest of the United States, was not particularly focused on Puerto Rico prior to the 1960s. Events began to raise awareness in both the US government and in Organized Baseball regarding Puerto Rico. These included Castro's rise to power, which switched Cuba from an American ally to a communist ally of the USSR, as well as soaring Puerto Rican migration to the US mainland.

The civil-rights movement of the 1960s had brought the rights of African-Americans to the forefront of American politics, but Latino politics were still submerged. There was little understanding of how Puerto Rico was different from the other Spanish-speaking countries that were home to major-league players, Cuba, the Dominican Republic, Venezuela, and Mexico in particular. But there is a huge difference: Puerto Ricans are US citizens.

Citizenship entitles residents of Puerto Rico to free movement within the United States. When Cincinnati played the first major-league game in Puerto Rico in 1936, the population on the island was around 1.8 million and the number of Puerto Ricans on the mainland was less than 70,000. By 1947 and 1948, when the Yankees and Brooklyn played in Puerto Rico, the island population had grown to just over 2 million but the number of Puerto Ricans on the mainland had jumped 223 percent, to over 200,000.

When Roberto Clemente died in a tragic plane crash on the last day of 1972, the population of Puerto Rico had grown but on the mainland the Puerto Rican population had soared to nearly 1.5 million, nearly seven times what it was in 1950. Since 2010 the island population has been decreasing and the mainland population has soared. There were in 2017 an estimated 3.4 million Puerto Ricans on the island itself and 5.4 million on the mainland.

The combination of these elements—a desire to promote baseball, to make money, to advance US political goals in the Caribbean, to offset potential losses of Cuban players to the major leagues, rising civil-rights awareness in the United States, the increasing importance of Puerto Rican politics in New York and on the East Coast—all pushed Major League Baseball toward reactivating some financial interaction with Puerto Rico.

Roberto Clemente's death provided a dramatic opportunity for the major leagues. An under-appreciated baseball star, respected by all for his charitable efforts, had perished in an airplane crash during a mission to help others. Puerto Rican writer and politician Elliott Castro observed, "[T]hat night on which Roberto Clemente left us physically, his immortality began."[37]

Clemente had a dream to promote sports among youth in Puerto Rico by building a comprehensive facility to play and teach baseball. After his death, his wife, Vera, pursued Roberto's goal. In 1974 Roberto Clemente Sports City (Ciudad Deportiva Roberto Clemente) was formed. The foundation was given 304 acres in Carolina by the Puerto Rican government for its sports facilities and structures. Vera Clemente was named chairwoman and son Luis was president and CEO. Sharon Robinson, Jackie Robinson's daughter, was also on the board of directors.[38]

New York Congressman Herman Badillo, the first Puerto Rican elected to the US Congress (1971) and the first Puerto Rican to run for mayor of New York City (1969), was not untypical of the migration pattern. He had been born in Caguas, Puerto Rico. His political base in the Bronx, where he had been the first Puerto Rican elected borough president, was the heartland of those Puerto Ricans who are sometimes called "Nuyoricans." The term describes

Puerto Ricans on the mainland for whom English is generally the first language. Music, movie, and television star Jennifer López is a prominent example; her production company is called Nuyorican Productions. The NBC TV series *Shades of Blue* is, in 2017, her company's most recent production.[39]

In early 1973 Congressman Badillo drafted legislation to authorize a $2.5 million federal grant for Clemente Sports City.[40] It didn't pass. It was obviously intended to at least show his constituents that he argued for Puerto Rican interests.

On December 11, 1973, the Pittsburgh Pirates, the team on which Clemente had achieved stardom, announced that they would play five major-league teams over the next five years in San Juan. Eastern Air Lines co-sponsored the series and provided the transportation. The Puerto Rico Hotel Association said it would provide the rooms and meals for the clubs. The revenue would go to Roberto Clemente Sports City.[41] The Pirates' first opponent for a two-game series in 1974 would be the Montreal Expos. Montreal, where both Jackie Robinson and Roberto Clemente had played with the International League Montreal Royals, was also continuing its interaction with Puerto Rico.

When the Roberto Clemente Series began in 1974, there was not a realization that it would be as important to the financial survival of the Sports City, or that games would continue through 1991. Each year of the series, two major-league teams would travel to Puerto Rico to play two spring-training games sometime between March 14 and March 24. In other words, not their first or last games of the spring-training season.

The Pirates' opponents were clearly carefully selected. The most obvious factor was that they came from cities with major Puerto Rican populations. In 1975 it was the New York Yankees and in 1976 the Mets. New York had the largest Puerto Rican diaspora. In 1977 the Philadelphia Phillies and in 1978 the Boston Red Sox were scheduled to oppose the Pirates. Philadelphia followed New York in the number of Puerto Ricans who lived there, and the Boston area was close behind. Florida's Puerto Rican boom was still in the future, as were the Marlins and Rays.

The second factor, one that became more and more of an emphasis over time, was the highlighting of Puerto Rican and Hispanic baseball stars who played in the games. It was important to the aspirational goals of the games: Inspire kids that they too could become professional baseball players. The bigger the pool of young ballplayers, the more likely stars would emerge.

The first Pittsburgh two-game series, against the Montreal Expos, established what was to become a fairly consistent attendance and revenue pattern: total attendance for the two games of about 25,000, generating $60,000 to $70,000 for the sports city each year.[42] The attendance of 20,000 in San Juan between the Pirates and the Yankees on March 17, 1975, was the largest of all. The first 1979 game against the New York Mets drew 15,742 fans to Hiram Bithorn Field. A pattern evolved in which the second game was played in Bayamon at Juan Ramon Loubriel Stadium. It was home to the Vaqueros de Bayamon in the Professional Baseball League of Puerto Rico until 2003. It was slightly smaller than Hiram Bithorn Stadium, with a maximum baseball capacity of 12,500.

The Pirates were a powerful team during the first five-year Puerto Rican series, winning the NL East title in 1974 and 1975. They finished second in 1976, 1977, and 1978. Pirates sluggers Willie Stargell, Dave Parker, Richie Zisk, and Al Oliver all provided some batting fireworks in the Puerto Rican games. Pitcher Dock Ellis won in a game in 1974 and lost a 2-1 pitching duel with the Yankees' Catfish Hunter in 1975.[43] The 1977 Pirates games with their cross-state rival Philadelphia Phillies featured some interesting pitching as well. In the first game, Pirates reliever Rich Gossage bested Met Tug McGraw, when Tug was tagged for three runs in the 10th inning.[44] Phillies ace Steve Carlton and Randy Lerch countered the next day with a three-hit shutout.[45]

Not all the games went smoothly for the Pittsburgh stars. In 1978 Pirates ace pitcher John Candelaria imploded, walking six batters, hitting two, and giving up a three-run blast to Boston Red Sox catcher Carlton Fisk.[46]

In 1979 the defense collapsed. In the Pirates' first game against the New York Mets, Mets first baseman Bruce Boisclair made two errors on one play, including a wild throw which hit the first-base umpire in the head. The umpire had to leave the game.[47] The second game was worse; the *Pittsburgh Post-Gazette* wrote: "For seven innings it was strictly routine. Then, in the eighth, it became a half-hour comedy." The Pirates blew their lead by allowing the Mets to score seven times in the eighth inning because of "defensive nonsense." The Mets won, 8-3.[48]

In the initial five years of Pittsburgh contests (1976 was skipped because of the major-league spring-training lockout), nearly $400,000 was raised for Clemente Sports City.

A five-year extension of the spring-training series began in 1980, with two different teams facing off each year. The average attendance declined somewhat but remained strong enough to keep annual revenue for the Clemente project roughly the same.

In 1980 the Detroit Tigers and the St. Louis Cardinals split the two games. Leon Durham was the Cardinals' hitting star in their 11-0 victory, driving in three runs with a single, double, and home run.[49] Lou Whittaker and Jason Thompson each had three hits in the 3-2 Tigers victory but Tigers pitcher Dave Rozema stole the 1980 media coverage. His trouble began in Miami when he was asked to judge a "wet T-shirt contest" at a local bar. He admitted that he was "not in the best condition when he returned to the Tigers' hotel." He overslept, missed the team flight, arrived on a later flight and then pitched poorly in the 11-0 shellacking. Manager Sparky Anderson was not happy, stating: "The fathering is over." Rozema did survive, pitching for the Tigers through 1985.[50]

A clear pattern that developed was the opportunity to showcase Puerto Rican and Hispanic stars. In 1981 the Kansas City Royals' Willie Aikens received the warmest welcome because he had played for the Santurce Crabbers in the Puerto Rico Winter League the previous season.[51]

Perhaps the most bizarre of all stories during this period came from Don Zimmer, who was coaching for the Texas Rangers in 1981. He told a reporter that the last time he had been in Puerto Rico (as manager of the Boston Red Sox on March 22, 1978) he had walked out of the Condado Hotel "just in time to see the famous trapeze artist Karl Wallenda fall to his death."[52] Wallenda was crossing between the two towers of the 10-story Condado Plaza Hotel in San Juan on a 121-foot-long high wire, when a combination of high winds and improper anchoring led to his fatal fall.[53]

The following year, 1982, Baltimore Orioles coach Elrod Hendricks was cheered because he was "practically an institution here, having played for Santurce for 17 years through 1977." In fact, 16 of the 26 Orioles present had been active in the Puerto Rico Winter League. Manager Earl Weaver had managed the Crabbers twice, winning the pennant in 1967-68. Cal Ripken was among the five Orioles who had played the previous winter, leading the league in RBIs and hitting .314. His manager at Caguas was Orioles coach Ray Miller.[54]

In 1983 Puerto Rican native Tony Bernazard drove in two runs to help the Chicago White Sox to a win over the Minnesota Twins before 10,000 in the second game, at Bayamon.[55]

The *Cincinnati Enquirer* reported in 1984: "(Manager) Rapp has allowed his players to enjoy the local nightlife, casinos and otherwise. And he has arranged his lineups so that the Reds' Latin players—Cedeno, Tony Perez, Dave Conception, Alex Trevino and Mario Soto—have shared the bulk of the playing time here before their Spanish-speaking amigos."[56]

After skipping two years, the Cuidad Deportiva Series resumed in 1987, with the following schedule of teams: Toronto vs. Pittsburgh in 1987, Montreal vs. Detroit in 1988, Texas vs. the White Sox in 1989, Philadelphia vs. Atlanta in 1990, Minnesota vs. Pittsburgh in 1991, and Kansas City vs. Toronto in 1992.[57] The waves of Puerto Rican citizens migrating from the Island to the States were also primarily in the East. Conveniently, and logically, the Eastern teams held spring training in Florida, not Arizona, which was far more convenient for the annual two-game series.

During this period the Nuyoricans (as Puerto Ricans living on the mainland had generally come to be called) were drawing near to and soon passing the number of Puerto Ricans in Puerto Rico. This would affect the island's supply of baseball players at some point. Other interests of young people were also causing some changes in the passion for baseball, though the slightly smaller crowds were still incredibly enthusiastic.

Major-league teams began investing in baseball academies in the Dominican Republic in the late 1970s and the 1980s. Roberto Clemente Sports City, which was more like a park than an academy, was the only similar development in Puerto Rico. The annual two-game series was a help in keeping baseball in youthful dreams, and along with the Winter League kept some of baseball's stars visible on the island.

The Clemente Series got off to a bad restart in 1987. The first game, in San Juan, was canceled because workers were unable to clear the rainwater from the ballpark. It was rescheduled as a doubleheader the next day at Bayamon, but that was rained out as well.

Furthermore, Roberto Clemente Sports City, the beneficiary of the Series, was also not progressing as hoped in spite of all the cash infusions. *Sports Illustrated* reported that in spite of the government-donated land, the major-league games, and annual telethons that raised millions, all that was built were some baseball diamonds, a locker room, and a statue of Clemente. Close to $600,000 had been spent trying to turn the swamplands into usable land. Staff and other costs ate up the other cash raised by the nonprofit foundation.[58]

The 1988 games again featured the loyal Montreal Expos as well as the first visit of the Los Angeles Dodgers. The teams split the games but it didn't start well for Montreal. A half-hour into their flight, the captain of the plane announced that due to a mechanical problem they'd have to return to Miami. The stewardess said there was nothing to worry about. Tim Raines immediately inflated his life-jacket vest, which the stewardess did not think was funny. She told him that he'd have to get off the plane in Miami. Which, of course, led to other players immediately inflating their vests too. They eventually made it to the ballpark, an hour and a half after the game was supposed to have begun. To keep the fans happy, the Dodgers staged an impromptu home-run hitting contest, which was won by Pedro Guerrero.[59]

The 1989 series between the Texas Rangers and the Chicago White Sox both exemplified the purpose of the exhibition contests and foreshadowed their collapse.

Rubén Sierra was the perfect example of the goal of the entire Series. He grew up in a rough neighborhood as a member of the lowest class in all Latin American countries: He was of Indian and African heritage. One story about how his racial struggles had continued as an adult, when opponents learned of his vulnerability, noted: "They taunted him. Called him names. 'Hey, you. Indio,' would come the taunts, mocking Sierra's distinct features that favored the Taino Indians of the island commonwealth. From the bench or from the stands, their words wounded deep. 'Hey, Sierra. You Indio. You coconut eater.'"[60]

Without Roberto Clemente Sports City, there would have been no baseball star named Rubén Sierra. After spotting his talent and because of concerns for his safety as a boy, the Puerto Rico recreation commission staff drove him to the baseball fields. Former major-league infielder and Clemente City instructor Chico Ruiz said bluntly, "We protected him."[61]

When the Rangers arrived in Puerto Rico in 1989, Sierra was a returning hero. Not only was he a star in the United States, he played in the winter leagues and organized baseball clinics for underprivileged youth at Sports City.[62] The local media proudly referred to him as "El Indio" and he was also introduced at the games as "El Indio."[63] Sierra, young Texas minor leaguer Juan Gonzalez, and White Sox outfielder Iván Calderón clearly enjoyed being back home. During batting practice, Latin music blared over the loudspeakers as Sierra sang along. He told a reporter that it was "better than that country music stuff in Texas, isn't it?"[64]

But Chicago manager Jeff Torborg bluntly exemplified what was about to happen to the Clemente Series. He complained about the impact on the players of the three-stop plane ride back on an offday. Montreal's airplane problems the previous year had been widely read as well. Torborg asserted that players from other years had gotten ill from bad water or food. The fields had been generating complaints. Torborg said: "I don't want Harold Baines or Greg Walker, with their legs, playing on rocky ground." He refused to send his starters, except native Calderón, who requested to play.[65]

Texas defeated Chicago, 4-2 and 8-0. They were the last two spring-training games played in Puerto Rico. The 1990 series was called off because of another major-league spring-training lockout. In 1991 Minnesota played Pittsburgh in a two-game series, but in Bradenton and Fort Myers, not San Juan and Bayamon. Roberto Clemente Sports City received the revenue.[66] I can find no record of the scheduled 1992 games being played.

A related major event occurred in 1990. Puerto Rico was included in the annual amateur draft. Critics argue that this change, which added Puerto Rican prospects to the draft along with prospects from other American territories and Canada, was the primary cause of the decline in baseball popularity in Puerto Rico.

The core arguments, as outlined in a *New York Times* article in 2012, are:

1. Puerto Rican players are at a disadvantage competing against American talent because high-school baseball is nonexistent on the island and because the population density means that not enough space exists to add baseball diamonds at each school.
2. Major-league teams have invested hundreds of millions in academies in the Dominican Republic and Venezuela. The economic motive to teams is the opportunity to sign young free agents as early as age 16, who are not subject to the draft.
3. Major-league scouts in the nondraft countries, especially in the Dominican Republic, have more incentive to seek out potential ballplayers, whereas the incentive in Puerto Rico is minimized, especially in more rural areas. The economic structure has also resulted in few scouts on the island.

Sandy Alderson, then general manager of the Mets with experience in handling issues in Latin America, responded: "From a socioeconomic standpoint, things have changed quite a bit in Puerto Rico. There are lots of other ways to spend your time. In the Dominican Republic, on the other hand, unfortunately, poor kids who are playing ball and who are from the lowest economic strata in that country, baseball is a way to escape, so there's a greater concentration of players and effort. I think they're just very different dynamics than Puerto Rico."[67]

Writing on the subject, which generally has followed the *Times* article's line of blaming the draft, generally fails to mention three obvious things: 1) Puerto Rico is experiencing a dramatic population decline as the Puerto Rican population on the mainland United States is dramatically increasing; 2) as US citizens Puerto Ricans move freely between the mainland and the island, unlike those from other countries, which greatly complicates any equivalencies; and 3) the population comparison in millions is Puerto Rico 3.6 million, Dominican Republic 10.4 million, Cuba 11.3 million, Venezuela 30.4 million, Colombia 47.1 million, and Mexico 122.3 million.

*Opening Day 2001: Texas Rangers vs. Toronto Blue Jays*

Commissioner Bud Selig pushed for Opening Day games outside the United States. The effort was inaugurated in 1999 in Monterrey, Mexico. Tokyo followed in 2000. San Juan—a fraction of the size of the other Opening Day cities—was chosen for 2001 to host the Texas Rangers against the Toronto Blue Jays. Tokyo, population 13 million-plus, was chosen again in 2004, 2008, and 2012. Sydney, Australia, hosted an opening series in 2014. San Juan remains by far the smallest city selected.

San Juan spent more than $600,000 to improve the Hiram Bithorn Stadium playing field, seats and clubhouses.[68] Though that was a major investment, media could not resist mentioning that the Texas Rangers' newly minted "richest man in baseball," Alex Rodríguez, averaged $129,630 per game from his salary alone.[69]

Texas and Toronto featured many of the best current Latino players. Puerto Ricans Iván Rodríguez starred for the Rangers and Carlos Delgado and Jose Cruz Jr. for the Blue Jays. Texas also featured Dominicans Rodríguez and Rubén Mateo, Cuban Rafael Palmeiro, and Venezuelan Andres Galarraga. Toronto also featured Dominicans Raul Mondesi, Tony Batista, and Pedro Borbon, Venezuelan Kelvim Escobar, and Mexican Esteban Loaiza.

The festivities actually began with an exhibition game on Saturday night. There were so many events before the game that it was delayed more than a half-hour. The media reported that Delgado had so much fun preparing for the opener that he couldn't stop smiling. Rodríguez had been so busy that his "eyes are red and his voice is hoarse." In the Saturday night exhibition game, eight home runs were hit in the first four innings, all by Latin players. A grand slam by Luis López tied the game at 8-8, and Rodríguez's second homer made it 10-8.[70]

The official game, on Sunday, was not as exciting. All five Latinos on the Rangers and all four Blue Jays position players played the entire game. Loaiza started and pitched a one-run game with nine strikeouts to earn the 8-1 victory. Borbon and Escobar also pitched in relief. Alex Rodríguez went 2-for-4 and scored the Rangers' only run. His single in the first inning was the first hit of the 2001 season. Palmeiro drove him in with his only hit. Iván Rodríguez went 0-for-4. For the Blue Jays, Puerto Ricans Delgado and Cruz both went 1-for-4 with Delgado scoring and Cruz driving in one run. Non-Latino Shannon Stewart was the hitting star. He singled, doubled, homered, scored twice, and knocked in two runs.

The Opening Day game might not have had the slugging fireworks of the exhibition but the pregame celebration was even more exciting. The sellout crowd—eventually totaling 19,981 people—began gathering at 5 AM. By noon, at least 5,000 fans had already arrived including many holding umbrellas to block out the hot sun. In addition to pizza and nachos, there were "pinchos" (kebabs) that come on wooden sticks with a choice of beef, chicken, sausage, fried shrimp separated by plantains. Or you could order "alcapurrias," which are fried pockets made of either mashed plantain or yucca with various meats inside.[71]

*CBS.com* described some of the historic game's pageantry: "A 12-piece band played folk songs as women twirled in red dresses with men wearing white straw hats like the kind worn by golfer Chi Chi Rodríguez. Then came the vejigantes, seven somewhat grotesque-looking characters popular in street carnivals and religious celebrations. The singing and dancing gave way to the introductions of players from both teams. The loudest cheers went to three locals: Texas's Iván Rodríguez and Ricky Ledee and Toronto's Carlos Delgado. Iván Rodríguez and Ledee waved Puerto Rico flags and Rodríguez and Delgado met for a hug. Rodríguez later went to a box seat near the Blue Jays' dugout and kissed his mother, Eva Torres. Three national anthems were sung— *Oh, Canada, The Star-Spangled Banner*, played by Jose Feliciano, and Puerto Rico's *La Borinquena*. Delgado and Rodríguez caught the first pitches from Vera Clemente and Orlando Cepeda. 'This is something marvelous, very positive for baseball in all of Latin America,' Cepeda said."[72]

Jose Cruz Jr. had left the island when he was 14 years old, but Puerto Ricans still claimed him. The *Orlando Sentinel* reported that "more than 100 of his relatives made the hourlong trek from the southern town of Arroyo. Many snapped pictures of him holding all the little cousins in the clan." [73]

It was a great day for Puerto Rico and major-league baseball. Alex Rodríguez said he was "overwhelmed by the love of the game in Puerto Rico. It's almost like a religion."[74] The next major-league visits to the island were more complicated.

*The Montreal/San Juan Expos of 2003 and 2004*

They say the best way to identify Canadians in a room mixed with Americans is to state that there is really no difference between the two countries. Anyone who objects is a Canadian. Possibly the second-best way is to say "Montreal Expos" and see who reacts, or at least winces.

The Expos are the only team in American professional baseball history, likely in any sport for that matter, to be named after a World's Fair. And if major-league baseball ever returned to Montreal, it would certainly be the most likely nickname again.

Montreal Mayor Jean Drapeau led an ambitious and successful effort to put Montreal near the front of the most innovative and famous cities in the world. The Montreal Metro system, which opened in 1966, was viewed as a modernistic transportation achievement. It remains the third busiest in North America, behind New York City and Mexico City. It was a key component of Montreal's successful bid to host the 1967 World's Fair, or as it was officially known, the 1967 International and Universal Exposition, or Expo 67. Debate exists as to what constitutes the most successful of the twentieth-century fairs, but by whatever standard one chooses, Expo 67 would be near the top, possibly ranking higher than those held in New York City.

The iconic architecture associated with the Exposition typified what trend makers have expected to be world's future: Buckminster Fuller's geodesic dome and Habitat 67, the stacked boxes that were projected to be the solution for apartment living.[75] The fair and its symbols captured attention in the United States for Montreal. The political audacity of Mayor Drapeau and the support of Quebec business leaders led to Montreal becoming the first international city to join previously exclusive United States major leagues.[76]

The book *Up, Up & Away: The Kid, The Hawk, Rock, Vladi, Pedro, Le Grand Orange, Youppi!, The Crazy Business of Baseball, & the Ill-fated but Unforgettable Montreal Expos*, by Jonah Keri, tells the story of the Expos in major-league baseball from their beginning in 1969 to their bitter end in 2004.

Fuller's geodesic dome from the Exposition had its acrylic cover burned off in a 1976 fire, leaving the frame which can still be visited today. While Olympic Stadium survives, the major iconic remnants of the Expos are jerseys and hats featuring their logo. And the Expos just didn't just flame out. Author Keri captures the ending of the Expos well: "The last days of the Expos were sad, surreal, and even occasionally exciting. What began to as a plan to put a failing franchise out of its misery as quickly as possible turned into a long drama-filled slog, the likes of which baseball had never seen and likely will never see again."[77]

In November 2001 the major-league owners voted to contract. The Minnesota Twins and Montreal Expos were to be shut down for the economic health of the other owners. It obviously didn't happen. The Twins remain. The Expos are now the Washington Nationals. MLB buckled under the pressure of Minnesota lawsuits and from politicians in Washington. While the issue was being argued, Montreal scheduled 22 home games in Puerto Rico. What follows are highlights of the Los Expos de Montreal.

*2003 Los Expos Home Games in Puerto Rico*

The Expos were playing in Puerto Rico as wards of MLB. Battles over a need for a new stadium, lack

of media sponsorship, poor player personnel decisions, and management infighting (among the many issues) led to MLB team ownership musical chairs. Florida Marlins owner John Henry purchased the Boston Red Sox. Montreal owner Jeffrey Loria then purchased the Marlins. MLB itself, desiring to eliminate the Expos, purchased the team from Loria.

Enthusiasm for the Expos in Montreal was already waning after years of success but when it became apparent that the team was doomed, it obviously hit bottom. MLB decided to salvage what it could financially, and test the economic possibilities of baseball in Puerto Rico, while it battled judges and politicians.

All things considered, the 22-home-game Puerto Rican 2003 season began and went reasonably well. The Expos team included Puerto Rican players Javier Vázquez, Jose Vidro, Wil Cordero, and Edwards Guzman. Vladimir Guerrero from the Dominican Republic was a National League All-Star in 1999, 2000, 2001, and 2002. Livan Hernandez of Cuba, Orlando Cabrera of Colombia, and Endy Chavez of Venezuela were among the other Latinos on the squad. Puerto Rican Rubén "Jerry" Morales Torres, who played major-league ball for 14 years, was the first-base and outfield coach for the Expos. The 2003 Expos were a very marketable team, especially in Latin America.

Enthusiasm was high before the season began. The *Philadelphia Inquirer* noted that "starting tonight, the Montreal Expos will have something every other working stiff in North America would love to have. A second home in the Caribbean." The newspapers promoted "The Expos are coming. The Expos are coming." MLB was testing the viability of a Latin-based franchise but the media reported some skepticism among Latino players: "Several Latin American major leaguers consulted recently said they'd love to see a team in Latin America, but they weren't sure it could be supported financially," wrote the *Philadelphia Inquirer*. "In Puerto Rico, for example, personal income is about one-third the US national average."[78]

The first game, on April 11 against the New York Mets, drew 17,906 fans. The Expos wore caps that featured small patches with Puerto Rican flags and logos that read "Series de los Expos." The fans gave Puerto Rican hero Roberto Alomar of the Mets the biggest pregame ovation. the game went well for the Expos. They defeated the Mets, 10-0. Tomo Ohka of the Mets allowed one hit in eight innings while Met David Cone gave up seven earned runs in four innings.[79] A home run by Puerto Rican Vidro of the Expos was particularly significant, since his mother had never before seen him play a major-league game.[80]

The April 12 game at Hiram Bithorn Stadium sold out. The *Fort Myers* (Florida) *News-Press* noted: "For the second time in two nights, they brought the spirit of a Caribbean soccer match, cheering in Spanish and English, and proving they know and love baseball." The Expos defeated the Mets again, this time 5-4 with Livan Hernandez dominating for six innings, allowing only one earned run. Expos Michael Barrett homered, Vidro doubled, and Vladimir Guerrero had two hits.[81] Roberto Alomar scored his 1,417th run, passing Roberto Clemente for the most among Puerto Rican players.[82]

The next day Montreal defeated the Mets again with a thrilling comeback victory. Mets starter Al Leiter threw six innings of shutout ball and Zach Day of the Expos gave up one run in six innings in spite of it being 136 degrees on the artificial turf. In the bottom of the ninth, Orlando Cabrera homered to tie the game. Then, on the first pitch from Mets reliever Mike Stanton in the bottom of the 10th inning, Puerto Rican native Vidro hit a walkoff home run for the 2-1 win.[83]

The series windup was another tight game. Montreal started local hero Javier Vázquez from Ponce, who was able to pitch a major-league game in front of his grandmother for the first time. The

Expos sweep was set up by a Puerto Rican player on the Mets, Rey Sánchez, who misplayed a one-out groundball by Guerrero for an error in the eighth. Fernando Tatis hit a two-run single for the 5-3 win. Guerrero also homered and stole a base.[84] During the fifth inning, two fans ran onto the field with a banner proclaiming "No a la Guerra" (no to the war), which delayed the game for about three minutes. The police banned them from games in Puerto Rico for a month.[85]

The Atlanta Braves arrived next in San Juan for a three-game series beginning April 15. The Braves won the first game the same way the Expos had defeated the Mets in game three. The Braves were trailing 1-0 going into the ninth inning. The game was scoreless until Orlando Cabrera homered in the seventh. In the top of the ninth Gary Sheffield homered to tie the game. In the 10th the Braves' Marcus Giles hit one out for the 2-1 victory. "Hitting it out" at Hiram Bithorn was easier to do in 2003 than elsewhere. Both home runs just cleared the right-field wall, each about one foot above the glove of a leaping Vladimir Guerrero.[86]

The Braves also won the second game. Horacio Ramirez shut out Montreal until the eighth. Andruw Jones doubled, singled twice, and drove in two of the three Atlanta runs. Sheffield homered for the second straight day to account for the third run. Expo left fielder Ron Calloway's two-run shot in the bottom of the eighth made the final score 3-2.[87]

The third game of the Braves series, on April 17, was won by Ponce native Javy López. After a 53-minute rain delay, the home-run derby began on the third pitch of the game from Expo Hernandez when Rafael Furcal hit the ball out. Marcus Giles and Andruw Jones also homered for the Braves, who led 8-6 until a two-run shot by Endy Chavez tied the game in the bottom of the eighth. López had given at least 40 free tickets to friends and family for each game, 60 for the finale. He had driven in two runs earlier with a home run in the third inning but his heroics in the 10th provided an extraordinary memory for him, his family, and the fans. As the rain began to fall harder, López hit a grand slam that brought prolonged chants and cheers led by his father and a second rare curtain call for a visiting player. López stated the obvious: "What better way to leave the country?"[88]

The Cincinnati Reds, the first big-league team to have played in Puerto Rico, in 1936, were the next opponents for the Montreal/San Juan Expos. The April 18 game was rained out. The rain delay, and rain during the game on the previous day, became a relatively persistent problem during the two years of games. Returning to the island was not really an option. In this case, since it was the first game of the series, a doubleheader was scheduled for the 19th.

Once again there was a plethora of runs scored. The Expos swept the doubleheader. Brian Schneider homered twice in the first game, including a walk-off blast in the 10th inning. Vázquez struck out 11 Reds in the second game, going ahead 9-0 and coasting to a 9-5 win. The bigger news was that Vladimir Guerrero, mired in a 4-for-24 batting slump, had come to the stadium with a frizzy Afro but left with shaved sides and a trim on top. It worked. He homered and drove in five runs in the second game.[89]

It continued to rain home runs at the stadium on April 20. The Reds hit six of them. Aaron Boone hit two, and in the ninth inning, pinch-hitter Adam Dunn and shortstop Felipe López connected back-to-back to give the Reds a 7-5 victory. In spite of the loss, the first 10-game homestand by Los Expos went reasonably well. They had a 6-4 record. Even though crowds had declined somewhat, the average attendance of 14,282 exceeded the 10,031 for Montreal home games the previous season.[90]

In June the Expos returned for their second homestand of 2003. Fans were still settling into their seats for the first game on June 3 against the Anaheim Angels, when the slugging fireworks began. Angels Troy Glaus, Tim Salmon, and Jeff DaVanon hit four-baggers in the top of the first inning. It was 5-0 before the first out was recorded. The Angels pounded out 22 hits, four by another visiting Puerto Rican native, Bengie Molina. Middle Molina baseball brother Jose Molina also had one of the hits. Outfielder Garret t Anderson went 4-for-4 with a home run and four

RBIs. DeVanon also hit a second homer. Wilkerson went 3-for-4 with a home run for the Expos, but they were walloped, 15-4.[91]

The Angels home-run barrage continued the next day. Anderson hit three home runs, two-run shots in the third and fifth, and a solo shot in the eighth. After the game he commented that the stadium was "small. Too small probably." DaVanon hit two more, giving him four home runs in two days. Glaus hit another and Brad Fullmer hit one as well. The Angels won, 11-2.[92]

The Expos won the concluding game of the series in dramatic fashion. Garret Anderson of the Angels hit another home run, his fifth of the series. Fullmer also hit another, but DaVanon was shut down though he did walk twice and score two runs. Jose Vidro went 3-for-5 for the Expos, scoring twice, driving in a run, and stealing a base. But the home-team hero was Ron Calloway, who was subbing for an injured Guerrero. Anaheim had scored two runs in the eighth and another in the ninth to knot the game, 5-5. Neither team scored over the next four innings. Anaheim scored twice in the top of the 14th but the Expos scored three in the bottom of the inning, with Calloway's walk-off two-run single giving the Expos an 8-7 win.[93]

On June 6 the Texas Rangers arrived, featuring Puerto Rican star Juan Gonzalez. He helped draw the second largest crowd of the season. Baseballs continued to fly over the outfield walls, three by Texas and two by Montreal. Even a 13-4 Expos lead was not safe, as the Rangers made it 13-10 by scoring six runs in the final three innings. In the first 14 games, there had been 57 home runs and an average of 12.2 runs scored.[94]

The next day the Expos prevailed 5-4, powered by two home runs by Brad Wilkerson. The AP story on the game began: "If the Montreal Expos return to San Juan next season, they might want to consider renaming their park Home Run Bithorn Stadium." The sportswriter also commented that it made Coors Field seem like a "pitcher's park."[95]

The Expos swept the three-game series in a somewhat more traditional way on June 8. Brad Wilkerson's second double broke a 2-2 tie in the eighth inning, for a 3-2 win. Home runs by Juan Gonzalez and Carl Everett provided the Rangers' only runs.[96]

The final two series in Puerto Rico were played in September, and were games that really mattered. The Florida Marlins arrived for a three-game series to be played September 5-7. They were in a pennant race in the National League East. (Though they finished second in the regular season, the Marlins ultimately won the 2003 World Series.)

The first game was delayed by more than an hour because of a power failure, but Todd Zeile exploded for two home runs, driving in four runs in a 6-2 Expos win. (He became the first major leaguer to homer for 11 teams.[97]) The second game was significantly different. The Marlins crushed Montreal/San Juan, 14-4. While three home runs helped, it was a team effort assisted by Expos starter Tomo Ohka, who faced 19 batters in the first two innings. Derrek Lee and rookie Miguel Cabrera each batted in three runs.[98]

The finale was hotly contested. The temperature on the artificial turf reached 153 degrees. Dontrelle Willis said it was "scorching" so he drank a lot of water before, during, and after the game. He pitched a three-hitter into the eighth, when he gave up a home run to Zeile. The Marlins prevailed, 3-1.[99]

The concluding series in Puerto Rico in 2003 featured the Chicago Cubs. These weren't your normal Cubs, irrelevant in September. These Cubs made the playoffs and defeated the Atlanta Braves in the Division Series, but lost to the Marlins four games to three in the National League Championship Series. All three Puerto Rico games were hard-fought contests.

The crowds were large, averaging over 15,000. There was a carnival atmosphere celebrating the Cubs' arrival at Hiram Bithorn Stadium. Bithorn had been a Cub. The *Chicago Tribune* expressed the mood in Chicago: "Who cares that concessionaires were selling piña coladas, not Old Style? The Cubs were in the playoff race." Sammy Sosa was the featured attraction. Roberto Clemente had inspired him when he was a young Dominican. The Cubs won the first game 4-3, with Carlos Zambrano getting the win. Cubs pitcher Matt Clement commented that "Wrigley Field plays smaller when the wind is blowing out."[100]

The excitement turned to typical Chicago panic when the Expos won the second game, 8-4. "The Cubs collapsed in a grandiose fashion under a full moon," the *Tribune* wrote after the Expos scored five runs in the bottom of the eighth after a pop fly by Jose Macias dropped in for a two-run double. Home runs by Cubs Moises Alou, Aramis Ramirez, and Kenny Lofton had all been wasted.[101]

Mark Prior, the Cubs' young star pitcher, who had a 1.00 ERA in his previous seven starts, could not deliver the rubber game. Instead, Japanese pitcher Tomo Ohka, who had been winless in seven starts, delivered the win for Los Expos. Ohka took a 3-0 two-hitter into the ninth. The Cubs scored twice but Joey Eischen saved the game. Sosa did not get the ball within 50 feet of the fences on the fly during the series. Sosa said afterward that he was trying too hard, trying to hit the ball all the way to the rain forest.[102] It was the end of the 2003 Expos island adventure.

### 2004 Los Expos Home Games in Puerto Rico

While 2003 was a decent year for the Montreal/San Juan Expos—all things considered—that was not true in 2004. The Expos crashed. Star Vladimir Guerrero moved to Southern California, signing a free-agent contract with the Angels. The Expos, in a desperate situation, traded Puerto Rican native and star pitcher Javier Vázquez to the New York Yankees for Nick Johnson, Juan Rivera, and Randy Choate. The trade didn't work out well. And the Expos were without their two marquee players for 2004.

The good news was that in the offseason 6,000 more seats were added to Hiram Bithorn Stadium as part of an $8 million renovation. A key was moving the outfield walls back to the same dimensions as Olympic Stadium in Montreal. Expos manager Frank Robinson was pleased, commenting: "Every ball that's popped up in the air, I will no longer have to hold my breath."[103]

The New York Mets were again the first opponents for the Expos on the island. Still smarting from the Expos' four-game sweep in 2003, the Mets opened with a 3-2 win on April 9. Jose Vidro's two-run double had tied the game in the bottom of the eighth, but Todd Zeile doubled home the winning run in the 11th. Zeile had announced that 2004 would be his final season. He chose to sign with the Mets after his half-season in 2003 with the Expos.[104]

The next day Expos starting pitcher John Patterson and two relievers pitched a 1-0 shutout. In the seventh inning, Brad Wilkerson doubled and Peter Bergeron singled him home.[105] The series concluded on April 11 with Mets pitcher Tom Glavine scattering five hits over seven innings, winning 4-1. The key blow was a two-run homer by rookie Eric Valent, his first.[106]

The number of home runs had been reduced in the Mets series. In the second series, against the Marlins, Montreal continued to keep the ball in the park but the Marlins did not. Miguel Cabrera, playing his first full season, wasn't bothered with the fences being moved back 20 feet. He hit two home runs in the first game. Pitcher Brad Penny needed only one of them, striking out 10 in eight innings as the Marlins shut out the Expos, 5-0.[107]

The next day, April 14, was worse for the Expos than the 13th. Cabrera hit another home run. Pitcher Dontrelle Willis went 3-for-3 with three RBIs, making him 6-for-6 for the season with two home runs. Willis and three relievers also shut out the Expos again, this time 9-0.[108]

The final game went only slightly better for the Expos. They didn't score but lost by only three runs. The Marlins' Hee-Seop Choi hit a two-run homer, his second straight day with a home run. Carl Pavano pitched seven scoreless innings to anchor the third shutout in a row. The Expos were glad to leave the island.[109]

For 2004, MLB had determined that all the games in Puerto Rico would be played before the All-Star break, so in May the Expos were back. Attendance was sagging at Hiram Bithorn Stadium. That happens to bad teams without major stars. And the next opponent, the Milwaukee Brewers, were also not good and had no significant stars, Latino or otherwise. Even the home runs, always a baseball attraction (e.g. Ruth, Mantle/Maris, 'roid rockets), had dramatically declined.

The Expos won the first game, on May 18, by a 3-2 score, all the runs scoring on singles.[110] In the second match, after a 59-minute rain delay and a persistent stop-and-start rainstorm, Milwaukee prevailed, 6-3. The small crowd had dwindled to a few hundred when the game ended five minutes before midnight.[111]

The final game of the Milwaukee series began after a 49-minute rain delay. After just 12 pitches, another storm halted play for an additional 48 minutes. Brewers manager Ned Yost had decided not to risk wasting the turn of a starting pitcher so he strung together a committee of relief pitchers. Thanks to a home run by Scott Podsednik in the ninth inning, Milwaukee won, 3-2. Not surprisingly, the series hit new low marks for attendance; game three drew the biggest crowd, 8,941.[112]

The next team in town at least brought along some attractions. The San Francisco Giants featured Barry Bonds and manager Felipe Alou, who as skipper of the Expos had been the majors' first manager from the Dominican Republic. Crowds improved significantly, averaging over 15,000. Bonds' back was hurting but since he was the biggest attraction, he said before the game, "I'm going to put a couple of back braces on and see what happens." San Francisco was trailing in the seventh, 3-0, when Bonds proved his worth by getting a leadoff walk, after which the Giants batted around and scored six runs for a 6-5 victory.[113]

The next day, May 22, it was 2-2 going into the 11th inning. Bonds drove in the go-ahead run with a fielder's choice. A.J. Pierzynski hit a grand slam that cinched the 7-2 win. The Associated Press writer summed it up succinctly: "Despite Pierzynski's big night, it was Bonds the people came to see."[114] The final game, slated for May 23, was rained out. It had to be made up in San Francisco as part of a doubleheader in August, and 42,296 attended the game.

The final homestand of Los Expos de Montreal began on July 2 against the Toronto Blue Jays. Blue Jays slugger Carlos Delgado was born and lived in Aguadilla, Puerto Rico, but he arrived hurt and could not play. A series without any big stars again drew less than 9,000 per game. Livan Hernandez pitched a four-hit shutout to give the Expos a 2-0 win in the opening game. Native Puerto Rican Vidro scored both runs.[115]

The tables were turned the next day, with Blue Jays starter Roy Halladay pitching seven scoreless innings in a 2-0 Toronto win. The game was delayed 36 minutes by rain.[116] At least the third game, on July 4, was more exciting. Expos pitcher Shawn Hill earned his first major-league victory, 6-4. Trailing 6-1 in the ninth, Toronto scored three runs off reliever Chad Cordero, but Joe Horgan struck out Reed Johnson of the Blue Jays with the bases loaded to seal the win.[117]

Atlanta came to San Juan to play games on July 5-7. The Expos were no match for the Braves, who led 6-0 after the first inning in game one. Andruw Jones hit a three-run homer and Chipper Jones drove in four runs as part of an 11-4 win.[118] The next day Atlanta won the opposite way, with starter Russ Ortiz pitching seven shutout innings of three-hit ball in a 1-0 victory.[119]

After the Braves bashed six homers in the last game, two more by Andruw Jones, Bobby Cox summed up the series well when he declared: "We should be the ones in San Juan."[120]

The final series of the two-year Los Expos, a four-gamer against the Pirates June 8-11, drew the smallest crowds yet, with two games' attendance not reaching 8,000 and the others under 9,000. At least the Expos closed out on a winning note.

The game on July 8 was a nailbiter. With the Expos trailing 1-0 in the seventh, Endy Chavez tripled and Tony Batista singled him home to tie the game. Brian Schneider homered to center in the bottom of the eighth for the game-winning run. The *Pittsburgh Post-Gazette* wrote that the Expos had the worst record in baseball, were last in batting average and last in runs scored but excelled at catching the ball. At least three Pirates line drives had been speared for outs, which likely saved the game.[121]

On July 9 the Expos' fielding skills didn't matter. They were shut out for the 13th time. Pirates rookie Sean Burnett scattered 10 hits. Jason Bay went 4-for-5, hit two home runs, scored four runs, and knocked in four. It was an 11-0 embarrassment.[122]

The Expos salvaged the series with two close wins decided by pitching. On July 10 spot starter Rocky Biddle and three relievers combined for a 4-0 win.[123] The final game, a 2-1 affair, would have fit in better a hundred years before. The closest thing to a batting hero was Terrmel Sledge. He scored the first Expos run on a force out at second base in the fifth. In the sixth, Sledge hit into another force out at second that drove in the second run. Then he was thrown out trying to steal.[124]

Expos general manager Omar Minaya summed up the 2004 season in Puerto Rico well. "The fans here are like the fans everywhere. If the team is winning, they will come. Last year it was also more attractive because of the visiting teams. This year the visitors were different."[125] The Expos had lost their biggest stars in the offseason. The biggest attractions of 2004—Barry Bonds and Carlos Delgado—arrived hurt. Montreal was 67-95, futility nearly matched by its opponents with losing records (Milwaukee, Toronto, Pittsburgh, Cincinnati). The opposing teams with winning records—the Marlins and the Braves—crushed the Expos. Add the rain, and it is no wonder that attendance dropped off dramatically. The experiment of major-league baseball on the island was at best a mixed result.

### San Juan Series 2010: New York Mets at the Florida Marlins

MLB made its goals clear when it announced the three-game set to be played June 28-30, 2010, between the Mets and Marlins in San Juan: "The growth of baseball around the globe has been tremendous and we hope that by providing Major League competition to the passionate fans in Puerto Rico and around the world, we will encourage interest and participation well into the future."[126]

New York and Florida had become the Puerto Rican centers in the United States. Both teams had played the Expos during their San Juan interlude. Miami's approach was not subtle. "Being the Gateway to the Americas, we want to try to capture that market," said Claude Delorme, the Marlins' executive vice president of ballpark development. "There are a lot of people who were born in Puerto Rico and they live in Miami. The more they can adopt the Marlins, it just allows us to grow our fan base, and the business, over time."[127]

Upstaging the Mets, who had four Puerto Rican players, Alex Cora, Angel Pagan, Pedro Feliciano, and Jesus Feliciano, the Marlins had selected Edwin Rodríguez as interim manager less than a week before the Puerto Rican series began. Thus Rodríguez, who grew up five minutes from Hiram Bithorn Stadium, became the majors' first Puerto Rican manager.[128] One Florida newspaper reported: "Rodríguez enjoyed a hero's welcome when the team arrived in San Juan. He walked off the plane Sunday night to cheers from 150 people, some chanting his name and singing to celebrate his visit as MLB's first Puerto Rican manager."[129]

Owner Loria, true to his extraordinary skills for drama, told interim manager Rodríguez 30 minutes before the start of the second game that he was officially the new Marlins manager, no longer just an interim one.[130]

While the 18,073 people in the San Juan crowd were thrilled to have a hometown hero as the first Puerto Rican manager, the hearts of most were with the Mets, as was evidenced by the chant of "Let's go Mets!" when pinch-hitter Alex Cora stepped to the plate in the sixth with the Mets trailing.[131] The Marlins won, 10-3. Rickey Nolasco went seven innings for the win. Chris Coghlan went 2-for-3 with a home run and three runs scored; Cody Ross went 3-for-4 with a home run, two runs scored, and two batted in; and Giancarlo Stanton, whose maternal great-grandmother was Puerto Rican, hit a three-run blast.[132]

The crowd at the second game was slightly larger (18,373) and the game was more exciting. The

Marlins prevailed again, 7-6. Hanley Ramirez hit a grand slam, Dan Uggla hit a two-run homer and the game-winning single with two outs in the bottom of the ninth, but Jorge Cantu dramatically stole the limelight with a head-first slide at home plate to win the game.[133]

The June 30 finale drew the largest crowd, 19,232. The Marlins continued to pound away at Mets pitching with a total of 17 hits. Cantu, Stanton, Ramirez, Coghlan, Uggla, Ross, and Gaby Sánchez all had two hits. Ronny Paulino had three. The Mets, however, made better use of their 10 hits, prevailing 6-5 to salvage one win in the series. The pitching was nothing to note.[134]

The 2010 San Juan Series had brought back the excitement of the 2001 opener.

### 2016 Pittsburgh Pirates vs. Miami Marlins Series: Victim of the Zika Virus

Pittsburgh and Miami were scheduled to play a two-game series in San Juan as part of a leaguewide celebration on Roberto Clemente Day on May 31, 2016. A problem arose. This CBS report summarizes it well: "The union had asked Commissioner Rob Manfred to relocate the games after several players expressed fears about getting and possibly transmitting the Zika virus. The US Centers for Disease Control and Prevention has said Zika can cause a birth defect called microcephaly, where infants are born with unusually small heads. The virus is most often spread by mosquito bites, but it also can be spread through sexual intercourse."[135]

The outbreak of the virus had begun in Brazil in 2014 and it reached Puerto Rico in December 2015. By August, several months after the game was to have been played, the US government declared a public-health emergency in Puerto Rico as a result of the Zika epidemic. The US surgeon general said he expected 25 percent of the 3.5 million people on the island to be infected with Zika by year's end. As it turned out, far fewer people were infected, but the concern by MLB and the players association was not unfounded.[136]

Nevertheless, negative reaction to the cancellation of the series was swift. Luis Clemente, Roberto's son, said that the islanders "were very disillusioned over the decision." He continued: "I was born being part of the Pirates, and we've always had a solid relationship. But as a Puerto Rican who lives in Puerto Rico, I can tell you that there's great disgust over what has transpired and I can understand it."[137]

Others weren't as nice. The mayor of San Juan said that "fear is not the American way" and that "this has been totally blown out of proportion." Angel Matos, head of the tourism commission for Puerto Rico's House of Representatives, was even more cutting in his remarks: "The reality is that this cancellation is unfair, disproportionate, and makes our country look bad. It's an act of touristic terrorism."[138]

### Other MLB Efforts to Encourage Baseball in Puerto Rico

In 2005 there were 34 Puerto Ricans on Opening Day rosters. In 2014 there were only 11.[139] Major League Baseball has responded in multiple ways to rebuild baseball's popularity in Puerto Rico. MLB has provided some funding to training academies.

The Puerto Rican Baseball Academy and High School was founded in 2001 by former major-league player Edwin Correa. Students split the day between conventional classes and baseball. The Houston Astros' Carlos Correa (no relation to Edwin) is the school's showpiece graduate. Pushed by his father, he was a baseball fanatic by age 5. When he was 8 he asked his parents (neither of whom spoke English) to enroll him in a bilingual Baptist school because he wanted to speak for himself, not through the translators as he often saw Latino players do on television. He was given a scholarship to the Puerto Rico Baseball Academy, where the combination of his skills and character (he was also valedictorian) resulted in Correa making history as the first Puerto Rican to be selected number one in the amateur draft.[140]

MLB contributes $275,000 a year plus another $25,000 in scholarships from Major League Baseball, which the Players Association matches. The school estimated that the donations account for 4 percent of its budget.[141]

The Carlos Beltran Academy opened in 2011 and graduated its first class in 2013. The land (20 acres) was donated by the local government. Beltran, a longtime major leaguer, donated over $4 million. MLB contributes $50,000 annually.

The Next Level Academy, founded in 2007, is structured differently. A 2017 *Washington Post* story explained: "Students take online classes in English in a makeshift classroom at the stadium before lunch and baseball practice. Homework isn't assigned, said Pedro Leon, a former player agent who founded the academy, to allow students to get enough sleep." Kennys Vargas of the Minnesota Twins is its first graduate to play in the major leagues.[142]

Two other young Puerto Rican stars followed yet another path. Francisco Lindor of the Cleveland Indians and Javier Baez of the Chicago Cubs both played in the 2016 World Series. Lindor was born in Puerto Rico and moved to Clermont, Florida, near Orlando, at age 12 to attend the Montverde Academy, where he earned *USA Today* high school All-USA status. Baez moved from the island to Jacksonville, Florida, when he was 13. He honed his skills at the Arlington Country Day School there.

Heloit Ramos is an example of yet another trend that is likely to increase. Ramos gained attention at the 2016 Under Armour All-American Game at Wrigley Field. In November of 2016 he was ranked 24th overall and first in Puerto Rico among high-school players by *Baseball America*. This earned him a scholarship offer to Florida International University in Miami, whose top-ranked recruiting class included eight Puerto Ricans. It is coached by Puerto Rico native Mervyl Melendez. A challenge to the university approach, as stated by the pitching coach at La Salle University, is that "if I recruit 50 Puerto Rican kids a year, 48 are discounted by going through their credits and SAT scores. I'm really just trying to find the ones that I can make eligible."[143]

There are no easy solutions, and increasing the numbers obviously will require more investment by Major League Baseball. In August 2016 MLB and the players union pledged to invest $2.5 million apiece over the next five years "toward the support and creation of baseball development programs" and to hold games and events on the island. Edwin Rodríguez, president of the Puerto Rico Baseball Academy and manager of Puerto Rico's team in the World Baseball Classic, suggested that a good pool of revenue could be the $140 million collected from clubs that exceed the limit on international spending. Such spending is not allowed in Puerto Rico because its players are included in the draft.[144]

It also should be noted that the Dominican baseball academy system is hardly universally praised. "Inside Major League Baseball's Dominican Sweatshop System" (*Mother Jones*) and "Inside the secret world of Dominican baseball" (Salon.com) are among critiques that push for MLB and local owners enterprises to improve conditions there.[145]

In August 2016 Major League Baseball and the Players Association committed to spend $5 million over the course of the next collective-bargaining agreement toward the creation and support of baseball development programs in Puerto Rico.[146] On March 16, 2017, MLB announced that Hall of Famer Roberto Alomar, a native of Ponce, had been hired as an "ambassador at events and development initiatives" to promote baseball interest and skills among youth on the island.[147]

These are tumultuous times in Puerto Rico, but the presence of young stars on the Puerto Rican team in the 2017 World Baseball Classic provide hope that with the help of the baseball Establishment, the tradition of baseball love in Puerto Rico can be fully revived.

## SOURCES

In addition to the sources cited in the Notes, the author utilized Baseball-Reference.com to check game dates, box scores, and individual player data.

## NOTES

1   "Reds Play Initial Major League Ball Game in Puerto Rico," *Binghamton Press and Sun-Bulletin*, February 26, 1936: 16.

2. Gene Karst, "Spring Training Pioneers: Flying the 'Southern Clipper' With the Cincinnati Reds," *The National Pastime*, Vol. 6, No. 1, Winter 1987.

3. Ibid.

4. Johnny Inkslinger, "Spilling the Dope," *Escanaba* (Michigan) *Daily Press*, March 3, 1936: 13.

5. From the foreword by Eduardo Valero in Thomas E. Van Hyning, *Puerto Rico's Winter League: A History of Major League Baseball's Launching Pad* (Jefferson North Carolina: McFarland & Co, 2004).

6. Van Hyning, 87.

7. "Reds Divide Games With Colored Team," *Salt Lake Tribune*, March 2, 1936: 7.

8. Rory Costello, "Sixto Escobar Stadium (San Juan, PR)," sabr.org/bioproj/park/sixto-escobar-stadium-san-juan.

9. Ralph Berger, "Larry MacPhail," sabr.org/bioproj/person/1b708d47.

10. Walter LeConte and Bill Nowlin, "Yankees Spring Training in 1947," in Lyle Spatz, ed., *Bridging Two Dynasties: The 1947 New York Yankees* (Lincoln: University of Nebraska Press, 2013), 11.

11. twitter.com/leonesprbl?lang=en.

12. Jim Vitti, *Brooklyn Dodgers in Cuba* (Charleston, South Carolina: Arcadia Publishing, 2011), 71.

13. donq.com/about/heritage/.

14. Fred Down, "38 Years Later, Yankee Training Camp of 1947 Is Remembered," *Los Angeles Times*, February 24, 1985.

15. historicdodgertown.com/history/historic-timeline/years-1940s.

16. Leonte Landino, "Luis Aparicio," sabr.org/bioproj/person/87c077f1.

17. "Sox Lose, 12-11," *Chicago Tribune*, April 2, 1960: 63, 65.

18. "Phillies Pound White Sox for 8-3 Triumph" *Terre Haute* (Indiana) *Tribune-Star*, April 3, 1960: 51.

19. "Smith Leaves Brother Jive," *Minneapolis Star*, April 4, 1960: 3.

20. *Eugene* (Oregon) *Guard*, April 4, 1960: 17.

21. Ed Brandt, "Miami Beats 'B' Club, Zauchin and Hinton Star in 6-2 Victory," *Baltimore Sun*, April 3, 1960:146; Ed Brandt, "Miami Beats Bird 'B' Club, Dropo Clouts Grand Slam, but Orioles Lose, 5-4," *Baltimore Sun*, April 4, 1960: 16.

22. Ed Brandt, "18 Birds Had Many Laughs, but Mountain Drive Topped Trip to Puerto Rico," *Baltimore Sun*, April 6, 1960: 21.

23. Gilbert Rogin, "The Many Faces of Mr. Mac," *Sports Illustrated*, February 17, 1964.

24. *Indianapolis Star*, April 3, 1960: 65.

25. "IL Approves Shifting Miami Franchise to Puerto Rico," *Petersburg* (Virginia) *Progress-Index*, November 29, 1960: 14.

26. George Beahon, "In This Corner," *Rochester Democrat and Chronicle*, April 27, 1961: 36.

27. "San Juan Rooters Work Up Steam for Monday Game," *Hartford Courant*, April 16, 1961: 57.

28. "Marlins Beat Toronto, 4-2," *Arizona Republic* (Phoenix), April 18, 1961: 36; "Leafs Top Marlins; Smith Fans 13, Allows Only 5 Hits," *Rochester Democrat and Chronicle*, April 19, 1961: 25; "Toronto Wins By 7 to 1," *Rochester Democrat and Chronicle*, April 20, 1961: 41; "Leafs Rip Marlins for 3rd Straight," *Rochester Democrat and Chronicle*, April 21, 1961: 25.

29. "Triple A Loop Junks Puerto Rico," *Hartford Courant*, May 4, 1961: 38.

30. "Marlin Owners Wants to Stay in Puerto Rico," *Freeport* (Illinois) *Journal*, May 8, 1961: 8.

31. funwhileitlasted.net/2015/02/28/1961-san-juan-marlins-charleston-marlins/.

32. pbs.org/wgbh/amex/castro/timeline/.

33. "Capitalism Underpins Canada's Relationship With Cuba," yvesengler.com/2016/11/27/capitalism-underpins-canadas-relationship-with-cuba/, November 27, 2016.

34. cia.gov/news-information/featured-story-archive/2016-featured-story-archive/the-bay-of-pigs-invasion.html.

35. "New Landing by Rebels, Spokesman for Cuban Revolutionary Front in Puerto Rico Makes Announcement in Face of Pro-Castro Claims That Revolt Is Near Collapse," *Kansas City Times*, April 20, 1961: 1.

36. *Pittsburgh Press*, April 1, 1967; *Connellsville* (Pennsylvania), *Daily Courier*, April 3, 1967: 7.

37. David Maraniss, *Clemente: The Passion and Grace of Baseball's Last Hero* (New York: Simon & Schuster, paperback edition 2007), 339.

38. 64.78.33.77/rcsc21/index_en.cfm (website of Roberto Clemente Sports City).

39. imdb.com/company/c00021149/.

40. "Sports City Bill," *Binghamton* (New York) *Press and Sun-Bulletin*, April 1, 1973: 66.

41. "Bucs to Play for Clemente," *Pittsburgh Post-Gazette*, December 12, 1973.

42. *Pittsburgh Press*, March 20, 1974: 77.

43. *Hartford Courant*, March 18, 1975: 45.

44. *Pittsburgh Post-Gazette*, March 22, 1977: 11.

45. *Muncie* (Indiana) *Star-Press*, March 23, 1977: 11.

46. *Pittsburgh Press*, March 22, 1978: 27.

47. *Pittsburgh Post-Gazette*, March 20, 1979: 13.

48. *Pittsburgh Post-Gazette*, March 21, 1979: 13.

49. *Battle Creek* (Michigan) *Enquirer*, March 25, 1980: 18.

50 *Detroit Free Press*, March 26, 1980: 53.

51 *Fort Myers* (Florida) *News-Press*, March 24, 1981: 24.

52 Ibid.

53 famously-dead.com/sports/karl-wallenda.html.

54 *Baltimore Sun*, March 23, 1982: 21.

55 *Orlando Sentinel*, March 23, 1983: 18.

56 *Cincinnati Enquirer*, March 21, 1984: 17.

57 upi.com/Archives/1985/03/07/The-Roberto-Clemente-Series-a-two-game-exhibition-between-two/8586479019600/.

58 Jim Kaplan, "It's a Dream Come True: Roberto Clemente's Sports Center Is Taking Shape," *Sports Illustrated*, October 5, 1988.

59 *Palm Beach Post*, March 16, 1988: 144.

60 Barry Horn, "Sierra Carries Scars From Final Texas Season," *The Oklahoman* (Oklahoma City), October 18, 1992.

61 "Sierra: Big Welcome in Puerto Rico," *Fort Myers* (Florida) *News-Press*, March 21, 1989: 42.

62 Horn.

63 *Fort Myers* (Florida) *News-Press*, March 22, 1989: 47.

64 "Sierra: Big Welcome."

65 *Chicago Tribune*, March 17, 1989: 40.

66 *Pittsburgh Post-Gazette*, March 19, 1991: 28.

67 nytimes.com/2012/01/17/sports/baseball/puerto-rico-traces-decline-in-prospects-to-inclusion-in-the-baseball-draft.html.

68 "Puerto Ricans Proud to Host Game," *Arizona Republic* (Phoenix), March 30, 2001: 6.

69 *Great Falls* (Montana) *Tribune*, April 2, 2001: 19.

70 "Puerto Rico Welcomes Rangers, Blue Jays," *Arizona Daily Sun* (Flagstaff), March 31, 2001.

71 "Puerto Rico Embraces MLB Opener," CBSNews.com staff / AP, April 1, 2001.

72 Ibid.

73 *Orlando Sentinel*, April 2, 2001: 5.

74 "Puerto Rico Welcomes Rangers, Blue Jays."

75 theguardian.com/cities/2015/may/13/habitat-67-montreal-expo-moshe-safdie-history-cities-50-buildings-day-35.

76 Jonah Keri, *Up, Up & Away: The Kid, The Hawk, Rock, Vladi, Pedro, Le Grand Orange, Youppi!, The Crazy Business of Baseball, & the Ill-fated but Unforgettable Montreal Expos* (Toronto: Vintage Canada, 2015), 1-15.

77 Keri, 365.

78 Jim Salisbury, "Row Your Bat: Expos Head for the Islands," *Philadelphia Inquirer*, April 11, 2003: D10.

79 *Fort Myers* (Florida) *News-Press*, April 12, 2003: 33.

80 *Danville* (Kentucky) *Advocate-Messenger*, April 13, 2003: 14.

81 "Los Expos Thrill Crowd," *Fort Myers* (Florida) *News-Press*. April 13, 2003: 13.

82 *Palm Springs Desert Sun*, April 13, 2003.

83 *Tyrone* (Pennsylvania) *Daily Herald*, April 14, 2003: 4.

84 "Tatis Powers Expos Past Hapless Mets," *Florida Today* (Melbourne, Florida), April 15, 2003: 34.

85 *Palm Beach Post*, April 15, 2003: 71.

86 *Pensacola News Journal*, April 16, 2003: 27.

87 "Braves Get More Stellar Pitching," *Pensacola News-Journal*, April 17, 2003: 31.

88 Ben Walker, "López Comes Through for Braves," *Pensacola News Journal*, April 18, 2003: 34.

89 "Expos Sweep Double-Header," *Florida Today* (Melbourne, Florida). April 20, 2003: 31.

90 "6 Homers Help Reds," *Orlando Sentinel*, April 21, 2003: D5.

91 "Angels Bombard Expos With 1st Inning Homers," *Orlando Sentinel*, June 4, 2003: D4.

92 "Anderson's 3 Homers Lead Angels' Assault on Expos," *Orlando Sentinel*, June 5, 2003: D4.

93 *Palm Beach Post*, June 6, 2003: 30-31.

94 "San Juan Slugfest," *Hartford Courant*, June 7, 2003: 132.

95 Josh Dubow (Associated Press), "Puerto Rican Park Yielding Longballs Galore," *Woodstock* (Illinois) *Northwest Herald*, June 8, 2003: 25.

96 "Montreal Sweeps Rangers," *Florida Today* (Melbourne, Florida), June 9, 2003: 43.

97 "Expos Turn Out Lights on Marlins," *Orlando Sentinel*, September 6, 2003: D5.

98 "Marlins Maul Expos 14-4," *Fort Myers* (Florida) *News-Press*. September 7, 2003: 11.

99 "Willis Tames Expos," *Florida Today* (Melbourne, Florida), September 8, 2003: 27.

100 Paul Sullivan, "Feeling at Home, Cubs Streak On," *Chicago Tribune*, September 10, 2003: Section 4, 1.

101 "A Grand Collapse: Cubs Blow 4-Run Lead to Fall Out of First Place in the Central," *Chicago Tribune*, September 11, 2003: 33-13.

102 *Chicago Tribune*, September 12, 2003: 4-6.

103 "Expos Play in San Juan for First Half Only," *Palm Beach Post*, April 13, 2004: 37.

104 "Mets Slip Past Expos," *Poughkeepsie Journal*, April 10, 2004: 4C.

105 Peter Abraham, "Good News, Bad News in Mets' loss," *White Plains* (New York) *Journal-News*, April 11, 2004: 27.

106 Peter Abraham, "Mets lose Floyd, but Win Game," *White Plains* (New York) *Journal News*, April 12, 2004: 21.

107 "Marlins Make Themselves At Home," *Palm Beach Post*. April 14, 2004: C1.

108 "Versatile Willis Boosts Marlins," *Florida Today* (Melbourne, Florida), April 15, 2004: 73.

109 Juan C. Rodríguez, "Marlins Blank Expos, Sweep 3-Game Series," *Orlando Sentinel*, April 16, 2004: D4.

110 *Fort Myers* (Florida) *News-Press*, May 19, 2004: 32.

111 "Hall's Three-Run Triple Lifts Brewers Past Montreal in rain," *Oshkosh* (Wisconsin) *Northwestern*, May 20, 2004: 21.

112 Eddie Pells (Associated Press), "Podsednik HR Gives Brewers Win Over Expos," *Marshfield* (Wisconsin) *News-Herald*, May 21, 2004: 19.

113 "Bonds Plays, Giants Win," *Santa Cruz* (California) *Sentinel*, May 22, 2004, 39.

114 Eddie Pells (Associated Press), "Pierzynski's Grand Slam Finishes Expos," *Santa Cruz* (California) *Sentinel*, May 23, 2004: C1, C5.

115 *Orlando Sentinel*, July 3, 2004: D4.

116 *Orlando Sentinel*, July 4, 2004: C12.

117 *Orlando Sentinel*, July 5, 2004: D4.

118 *Orlando Sentinel*, July 6, 2004: C.

119 "Ortiz's Victory Pushes Braves Over .500 mark," *Orlando Sentinel*, July 7, 2004: D4.

120 Ricardo Zuniga, "Jones Leads Braves Bash," *Montgomery* (Alabama) *Advertiser*, July 8, 2004: 12.

121 "Benson Shines in Pirates Loss," *Pittsburgh Post-Gazette*. July 9, 2004: 19.

122 "Bay Breeze," *Pittsburgh Post-Gazette*, July 10, 2004: 17.

123 "Pirates Go Down Quietly," *Pittsburgh Post-Gazette*, July 11, 2004: 37.

124 "Punchless Pirates Fall to Expos," *Pittsburgh Post-Gazette*, July12, 2004: 27.

125 "Expos Struggle in Puerto Rico," *Florida Today* (Melbourne, Florida), July 12, 2004: 28.

126 mlb.mlb.com/pa/releases/releases.jsp?content=031810.

127 m.mlb.com/news/article/8827982//. It was also a prelude to the opening of their modernistic retractable roof ballpark in 2012. Fans and critics love and hate ballpark (personally, though like most I prefer the ballparks that are modern brick recreations of a century before, I found the Marlins stadium to be a refreshing, artistic difference) was the creation of art dealer and Marlins owner Jeffrey Loria. Loria dumped the Montreal Expos in the process of purchasing the Marlins. He is not the most popular man in either Montreal or Miami.

128 m.mlb.com/news/article/11709294//.

129 *Palm Beach Post*; June 29, 2010: C001, C004, C005.

130 *Palm Beach Post*; June 30, 2010; C001.

131 m.mlb.com/news/article/11709294//.

132 *Palm Beach Post*; June 29, 2010: C001, C004, C005.

133 *Palm Beach Post*; June 30, 2010: C001.

134 *Chicago Tribune*; July 1, 2010: sports section, 6.

135 pittsburgh.cbslocal.com/2016/05/06/baseball-scraps-puerto-rico-series-between-pirates-marlins-amid-zika-concerns/.

136 nbcnews.com/storyline/zika-virus-outbreak/u-s-declares-health-emergency-puerto-rico-due-zika-virus-n630131.

137 Luis Fabregas, "Clemente's Son Decries Cancellation of Pirates Series in Puerto Rico," May 6, 2016; triblive.com/sports/pirates/10431831-74/clemente-puerto-pirates.

138 Arthur Weinstein, "Puerto Rican Official Calls MLB Cancellations 'Touristic Terrorism," *Sporting News*; May 7, 2016.

139 Ben Reiter, "Made Man: At 21, Astros Shortstop Carlos Correa Is Already a Star," *Sports Illustrated*, September 28, 2015.

140 Ibid.

141 Jorge Castillo, "Puerto Rico Yearns For Another Golden Era in Major League Baseball," *Washington Post*, March 3, 2017.

142 Ibid.

143 Ibid.

144 Ibid. Academy president Edwin Rodríguez (Morales) played three MLB seasons for the Yankees and the Padres, and was the manager of the Florida Marlins. Academy founder Edwin (Josue) Correa played three MLB seasons for the White Sox and the Rangers.

145 Ian Gordon, "Inside Major League Baseball's Dominican Sweatshop System," *Mother Jones*, March/April 2013; Andrew O'Hehir, "Inside the Secret World Of Dominican Baseball," Salon.com, July 10, 2012, salon.com/2012/07/10/inside_the_secret_world_of_dominican_baseball/.

146 Anthony Castrovince, "MLB, MLBPA Strengthening Ties With Puerto Rico," MLB.com, August 24, 2016.

147 espn.com/mlb/story/_/id/18922699/hall-famer-roberto-alomar-hired-mlb-youth-development-puerto-rico.

# CONTRIBUTORS

**JANE ALLEN-QUEVEDO** writes from Florida where she retired in 1995 as communications director of Adventist Health System. As a freelance writer, she later developed an interest in baseball, especially Puerto Rican baseball history, when a mutual friend introduced her to Félix Millan and she agreed to help him write his story, *Tough Guy, Gentle Heart*—a task she undertook with the encouragement of her Puerto Rican born husband, Carlos. Born in Michigan, she holds a Master of Arts degree from Central Michigan University. She worked for 25 years as a communications specialist and college teacher, living in Massachusetts, Maryland, Singapore and California before moving to Florida in 1985.

**MARK ARMOUR** writes about baseball and follows the Red Sox from his home in Oregon.

**JONATHAN ARNOLD** finally returned to his family's New England roots as an 11 year old, after his Dad finished up a world tour in the Air Force, and overcame a brief Cardinal romance to be a Red Sox fanatic ever since. Living in a Boston suburb, he's raising two daughters with his lifelong Red Sox fanatic wife to be proud members of Red Sox Nation, while working as a software engineer.

**THOMAS J. BROWN JR.** is a lifelong Mets fan who also became a Durham Bulls fan after moving to North Carolina in the early 1980s. He is a retired high school science teacher who enjoys writing about baseball now that he has left the classroom.

**JUSTIN OMAR CABRERA** graduated William Paterson University 2012 with a Bachelors degree in Economics. He started his professional career with the New York Mets as their Audit Coordinator, then working with their accounting team as the Ticket Reporting Coordinator. He has also held positions with the New York Yankees, US Open, Metlife Stadium, National Basketball Association, New Jersey Devils/Prudential Center, and currently is the the Assistant Manager of Ticket Operations for Brooklyn Sports and Entertainment. Raised in New Jersey by a Cuban family, Justin became enamored by the game of baseball at a young age, and has been with SABR since 2016.

**ALAN COHEN** has been a SABR member since 2011. He has written more than 30 biographies for SABR's bio-project, and has contributed to several SABR books. He is expanding his research into the Hearst Sandlot Classic (1946-1965), an annual youth All-Star game which launched the careers of 88 major-league players. He graduated from Franklin and Marshall College with a degree in history. He has four children and six grandchildren and resides in West Hartford, Connecticut with his wife Frances, two cats, and two dogs.

A SABR member since 1999, **JORGE COLÓN-DELGADO** is co-founder and former president of the Puerto Rico Chapter. An author of six books, at the moment is writing the story of the Mayaguez Indians baseball club. For three years he served as the Official Historian of the Puerto Rico Professional Baseball League. He has been inducted in two halls of fame.

**RORY COSTELLO** has written biographies of players from 20 different nations or territories, including 11 places in Latin America and the Caribbean. Puerto Rican players made an impression on him from his early days as a fan. Rory lives in Brooklyn, New York with his wife Noriko and son Kai.

**RICHARD CUICCHI** joined SABR in 1983 and is an active member of the Schott-Pelican Chapter. Since his retirement as an information technology executive, Richard authored *Family Ties: A*

*Comprehensive Collection of Facts and Trivia about Baseball's Relatives*. He has contributed to numerous SABR BioProject efforts. He does freelance writing and blogging about a variety of baseball topics on his website TheTenthInning.com. Richard lives in New Orleans with his wife, Mary.

**SCOTT CUMMINGS** works as a special education resource teacher at Woodbury High School. He holds a degree from the University of Minnesota-Twin Cities in mathematics and a special education teaching license from the University of Minnesota-Duluth. This is his first contribution to a SABR publication after becoming a member in 2010. He looks forward to writing many more. When he is not reading or writing, he is busy cross country skiing and training for the next American Birkebeiner. He lives in West St. Paul with his border terrier named Babe Ruth.

**SCOTT DOMINIAK** is a retired English/journalism teacher who taught at Eisenhower High School in Blue Island, Illinois. Growing up, he split time between Inkster and Livonia, Michigan and graduated from Michigan State University in 1976. Scott lives with his wife, Judy, and has three grown stepchildren. He is a lifelong Detroit Tigers fan who has been a member of the Mayo Smith Society since its inception, 1983. Scott wrote the biography of Hugh Shelley for the book *Detroit the Unconquerable: The 1935 World Champion Tigers*. He also wrote the article "Look at Your Wonderful Lights Here…" for the book *Tigers by the Tale Great Games at Michigan and Trumbull*.

**KYLE EATON**, a lifelong Atlanta Braves fan, is a nonprofit professional residing in Memphis, Tennessee with his wife, son, and two dogs. He spends his free time running, watching baseball, volunteering for an animal rescue, advocating for children's literacy, and faking this whole fatherhood thing until he can hopefully figure it all out. He admittedly owns more bobbleheads than any grown man should own, but he is at peace with this for now. His brief biography of Javy López is his first foray into baseball history.

**ROB EDELMAN** has authored the books *Great Baseball Films, Baseball on the Web*, and (with Audrey Kupferberg) *Meet the Mertzes* and *Matthau: A Life*. He often contributes to *Base Ball: A Journal of the Early Game*; he offers film commentary on WAMC Northeast Public Radio and is a longtime Contributing Editor of *Leonard Maltin's Movie Guide*. His byline appears in dozens of publications (from *Total Baseball* to *NINE: A Journal of Baseball History and Culture*) and on the DVD *Reel Baseball: Baseball Films from the Silent Era, 1899-1926*. He is an interviewee on documentaries on the director's cut DVD of *The Natural* and teaches film courses at the University at Albany. He currently is coediting (with Bill Nowlin) a book on baseball players and the movies.

**AMY ESSINGTON** is a lecturer at California State University, Fullerton, and Cal Poly Pomona. She is the Executive Director of the Historical Society of Southern California. She completed a Ph.D. at Claremont Graduate University with a dissertation on the integration of the Pacific Coast League. Amy was an intern at the National Baseball Hall of Fame Library and the Smithsonian's National American History Museum.

**CHARLES F. FABER** was a native of Iowa who lived in Lexington, Kentucky, until his passing in August 2016. He held degrees from Coe College, Columbia University, and the University of Chicago. A retired public school and university teacher and administrator, he contributed to numerous SABR projects, including editing *The 1934 St. Louis Cardinals*. Among his publications are dozens of professional journal articles, encyclopedia entries, and research reports in fields such as school administration, education law, and country music. In addition to textbooks, he wrote 10 books (mostly on baseball) published by McFarland. His last book, co-authored with his grandson Zachariah Webb, was *The Hunt for a Reds October*, published by McFarland in 2015.

**EDWIN FERNÁNDEZ** was born in New York City and grew up in San Juan, Puerto Rico. A banker and a computer professional in his other life, he is now a baseball historian and a sportswriter, former President of the Sports Journalists Association in Puerto Rico and co-author of JONRON, a book on the Latin and Caribbean players in the Major Leagues. At present, he is a member of the International Press Association (AIPS America) Board of Directors and member of the Selection Committee of the Latino Baseball Hall of Fame. He joined SABR in 1999 and is a former Chairman of the Latino Baseball Committee and founder of the Puerto Rico Chapter. Also, he is a member of the Board of Directors of the Puerto Rico Sports Hall of Fame.

**JOSEPH GERARD** has been a lifelong Pittsburgh Pirates fan. He grew up hating the Yankees despite being born and raised in Newark, New Jersey—his biggest regret in life is that he was only two years old in 1960. Because of Roberto Clemente, he developed an interest in Latin-American baseball history and has contributed biographies of several Latin players to SABR's BioProject. He lives in New York City with his wife Ann Marie and their two children, Henry and Sophie.

Author, editor, consultant, and historian **GARY GILLETTE** has written, edited, or contributed to dozens of baseball books and Web sites, including ESPN.com, Baseball Prospectus, and TotalBaseball.com. He was the creator and editor of the *ESPN Baseball Encyclopedia*, executive editor of the *ESPN Pro Football Encyclopedia*, a contributor to six editions of the seminal encyclopedia *Total Baseball*, and is currently an historical consultant to Baseball-Reference.com. He was the lead author on the massive 2009 book *Big League Ballparks: The Complete Illustrated History of Major-League Baseball Parks*. As a director and officer of the Tiger Stadium Conservancy, Gillette fought for years to save the historic stadium and the hallowed field at the corner of Michigan and Trumbull. As founder and president of the Friends of Historic Hamtramck Stadium, he led the successful effort to place one of the few remaining Negro League home ballparks on the National Register of Historic Places and is now leading the effort to restore the historic site. A former director of the Society for American Baseball Research (SABR), Gillette is the founder and president of SABR's Detroit Chapter as well as past co-chair of SABR's Business of Baseball Committee and SABR's Ballparks Committees.

**IRV GOLDFARB** signed up with SABR in 1999, making the Negro League Committee the first group he joined. He has since contributed to numerous SABR publications, including *Deadball Stars of the AL and NL*; *The Miracle Has Landed*; and *The Fenway Project*. Irv works for the ABC Television Network and lives with his wife Mercedes and their furry "kids" Lolo and Consuelo in Union City, New Jersey. All are New York Met fans.

**EMILY HAWKS** has been a SABR member since 2008 and has served on the Board of Directors since 2013. She also serves as Chair of the SABR Diversity Committee and Vice Chair of the SABR BioProject Modern Initiative. Emily holds a BS in Mathematics and Business from the University of Puget Sound, and an MS in Computational Finance and Risk Management from the University of Washington. She works in the field of data science, and is based in Seattle, Washington. Thanks to TBS, Emily spent her childhood years in Idaho as a spoiled fan of the 1990s Atlanta Braves, but has since countered those bountiful years by suffering as a Seattle Mariners fan since relocating to the Pacific Northwest. She loves watching baseball alongside her dog, Edgar, and hopes his eponym will soon be bound for Cooperstown.

**TOM HAWTHORN** is an author, journalist, and bookseller who lives in Victoria, B.C. He has served on the selection committee of the Canadian Baseball Hall of Fame.

**JANE SCHUPMANN HEWITT** grew up in Kansas in a baseball family. One of her earliest baseball memories is shaking hands with Leroy "Satchel" Paige while he was still barn-storming with the remaining Kansas City Monarchs. As a university English instructor for almost 30 years, she shared her love of baseball with hundreds of students, both domestic and international. Now retired, she continues to encourage baseball fanaticism in her many nieces, nephews, and grand-children.

**PAUL HOFMANN** is the Associate Vice President for International Programs at Sacramento State University. He is a native of Detroit, Michigan and lifelong Detroit sports fan. His research interests include 19th century and pre-World War II Japanese baseball. He is also an avid baseball card collector. Paul currently resides in Folsom, California.

**CHUCK JOHNSON** has been a SABR member since 1991 and is a co-founder of Arizona's Flame Delhi Chapter. Chuck has provided minor league content for such media outlets as MLB.com, SB Nation and Bleacher Report and is a frequent contributor to SABR's Bio and Game Projects. A member of the Minor League Alumni Association through his work with the Eastern League, Chuck lives with his wife and daughter in Surprise, Arizona where he works as an official scorer for the Arizona Rookie League.

**WILLIAM H. (BILL) JOHNSON** and his wife Chris divide their time between Cedar Rapids, Iowa and Dayton, Ohio. He retired from the US Navy in 2006 after a 24-year career in naval aviation, and currently teaches unmanned aviation systems at Sinclair Community College in Dayton. His first book, *Hal Trosky: A Baseball Biography* (McFarland & Co.), was released in February, 2017, and he is now working on a second book, a biography of Negro League star Art "Superman" Pennington. He graduated from the University of California (Berkeley) with a degree in Rhetoric, and has subsequently earned a Master of Arts in Military History from Norwich University and a Masters in Aeronautical Science from Embry-Riddle Aeronautical University.

**CHRIS JONES** is an attorney at Anthony & Middlebrook, P.C., where his practice focuses on church and nonprofit law. He is a lifelong baseball fan and a member of SABR since 2015. The highlight of his playing days was being drafted by the Toronto Blue Jays in the 2001 amateur draft. He resides in the Dallas/Fort Worth area with his wife and four children.

**NORM KING** lives in Ottawa, Ontario, and has been a SABR member since 2010. He has contributed to a number of SABR books, including, *"That's Joy in Braveland" — The 1957 Milwaukee Braves* (2014), *Winning on the North Side. The 1929 Chicago Cubs* (2015), and *A Pennant for the Twins Cities: The 1965 Minnesota Twins* (2015). He was also the senior editor and main writer for: *Au jeu/ Play Ball: The 50 Greatest Games in the History of the Montreal Expos* (2016). He thought he was crazy to miss his beloved Expos after all these years until he met people from Brooklyn.

**BOB LEMOINE** has contributed to several SABR projects since joining in 2013. His interests lie especially in Boston's baseball history as well as baseball in the nineteenth century. He was co-editor with Bill Nowlin on *Boston's First Nine: the 1871–75 Boston Red Stockings* in 2016, and is working with Bill again on a forthcoming book on the Boston Beaneaters of the 1890s. He lives in Barrington, New Hampshire, and works as a high school librarian.

**LEN LEVIN** is a retired newspaper editor who now edits the decisions of the Rhode Island Supreme Court. He also spends a lot of time going to baseball games and editing for SABR.

**BILL NOWLIN** has had the pleasure of visiting Puerto Rico a few times, including the first WBC back in the year 2003. He was elected to SABR's Board of Directors in 2004. Since retiring after more or less 40 years in the music business with Rounder Records, he spends most of his time wiring articles or editing books for SABR.

**DANIEL POTTER** has been a SABR member for nearly a decade and an amateur baseball historian since first discovering baseball cards at the age of 6. He became a Mariners fan at a young age, despite growing up in the Los Angeles suburb of Santa Monica, and still clings to the belief that his beloved M's will someday win a World Series. A former television news producer, Daniel now owns a video production company geared towards helping charities, museums, and schools use video to tell their stories. He lives in San Diego with his wife and two sons.

**CARL RIECHERS** retired from United Parcel Service in 2012 after 35 years of service. With more free time, he became a SABR member that same year. Born and raised in the suburbs of St. Louis, he became a big fan of the Cardinals. He and his wife Janet have three children and is the proud grandpa of two.

**RICK SCHABOWSKI** has been a SABR member since 1995. He is a retired machinist from Harley-Davidson Company, is currently an instructor at Wisconsin Regional Training Partnership in the Manufacturing Program, and is a certified Manufacturing Skills Standards Council instructor. He is President of the Ken Keltner Badger State Chapter of SABR, President of the Wisconsin Oldtime Ballplayers Association, Treasurer of the Milwaukee Braves Historical Association, and a member of the Hoop Historians. He lives in St. Francis, Wisconsin.

**STEVEN SCHMITT** is author of *A History of Badger Baseball—The Rise and Fall of America's Pastime* at the *University of Wisconsin*. He has also authored SABR biographies on John DeMerit and Hawk Taylor in *Thar's Joy in Braveland—The 1957 Milwaukee Braves* and individual biographies on Ty Cline, Steve Ridzik, Ken Johnson, Johnny Gerlach and Stony McGlynn (in progress). Schmitt has bachelor's and master's degrees from the University of Wisconsin—Madison School of Journalism and Mass Communication and resides in Madison, Wisconsin.

**RICHARD SMILEY** lives in Chicago, Illinois where he works as a statistician and demographer. He has been a SABR member for over 30 years and is a member of their Deadball Era, Nineteenth Century, and Ballparks Committees. His article on Heinie Zimmerman's failed pursuit of Eddie Collins in the 1917 World Series appeared in the *The National Pastime* and his biographies of Reb Russell and Matty McIntyre appeared in *Deadball Stars of the American League*. His current research interests include the history of professional baseball in Chicago prior to the founding of the National League.

**MARK SOUDER** is from Fort Wayne, Indiana which he represented in the United States Congress for 16 years. Now mostly retired, in addition to doing political commentary in Indiana media, he has been working on a multi-year project on the history of baseball & politics. His writings for SABR have included articles in the 2015 Chicago edition of *The National Pastime* and in the 2016 book *Boston's First Nine*. He also presented on early baseball and politics in Washington and New York at the 2015 and 2016 Nineteenth Century Baseball Conferences (FRED) in Cooperstown. His interest in the interaction between baseball & politics was stimulated by his participation as a lead questioner in Congressional Steroid Hearings. His version of a perfect day was celebrating his 50th birthday in the Chicago White Sox co-owner's suite and having his name appear on the scoreboard, all while raising money for his campaign and watching baseball.

**MARK S. STERNMAN** became a fan of the Montreal Expos in the late 1970s when Warren Cromartie, Andre Dawson, and Ellis Valentine formed baseball's most dynamic outfield. He received an F.P. Santangelo Harrisburg Senators card as a wedding present and attended the game at the Big O when Jose Vidro hit his walk-off extra-inning grand slam. Sternman also profiled former Expo Mike Stenhouse for *The 1986 Boston Red Sox: There Was More Than Game Six* and wrote about Montreal's win over the Mets on October 3, 1981 that clinched the only postseason berth in franchise history for *Au jeu/Play Ball: The 50 Greatest Games in the History of the Montreal Expos*. Sternman thanks Jonah Keri for fighting for Tim Raines' rightful place among baseball's immortals in Cooperstown.

**STEW THORNLEY** is an official scorer for Major League Baseball and has written about the role of official scorers and no-hitters. He also keeps a list of no-hitters that have been broken up in the ninth inning on his website, milkeespress.com. He has been a member of the Society for American Baseball Research since 1979.

**ADAM J. ULREY** used to be the featured writer for *Inside Ducks Sports*, and spent 10 years on the radio doing a sportstalk show in the beautiful Willamette Valley. He enjoys building his own Bamboo Fly rods and has a small catering business. He spends most of his free time in the outdoors doing everything from hiking to fishing in his own stream. But his favorite past time is spending time with his wife Jhody and son Camran. He also has two beautiful dogs named Montana and Behr.

**THOMAS E. VAN HYNING** was the U.S. correspondent for the Puerto Rico Professional Baseball Hall of Fame from 1991 to 1996. He was written *Puerto Rico's Winter League* and *The Santurce Crabbers*. Tom's Puerto Rico Winter League (now the Roberto Clemente Professional Baseball League) articles have appeared in *The National Pastime* and *the Baseball Research Journal*, including pieces on Rickey Henderson, Dennis Martinez, the Santurce Crabbers, plus articles noting Puerto Rico stars such as Roberto Clemente, Orlando Cepeda, Victor Pellot, Juan Pizarro, Roberto Alomar, Juan Gonzalez, Edgar Martínez and Carlos Baerga. Tom's Rubén Gomez bio was published by SABR on February 22, 2013, 60 years to the day Santurce defeated host Havana in game three of the 1953 Caribbean Series. His BBA degree is from The University of Georgia. Master's degrees are from Southern Illinois University and a Puerto Rico university. Tom is the Mississippi Development Authority's Research Program Manager.

**MARLENE VOGELSANG** is a member of the Lefty O'Doul SABR chapter and has been chapter leader since 2007. She lives and works in the San Francisco Bay Area and is a longtime fan of the Oakland Athletics. She looks forward to the annual SABR Conventions to enjoy seeing old friends and making new ones. She is a rookie when it comes to writing bios, this one is her second. The process gives her renewed respect and admiration for the many SABR authors that she knows.

**JOHN VORPERIAN** hosts *Beyond the Game*, a community syndicated cable television program (www.wpcommunitymedia.org). Since 2002 over 2500 episodes, the American University alum has talked with personalities like Roger Kahn, Bob Wolff, Dave Righetti, Mo Vaughn, Harry Carson, Art Monk, Thomas "Hollywood" Henderson, Eddie Money, Eric Bogosian, and Robert Kraft. He also guest lectures for George Washington University's Jackie Robinson Project.

**JOSEPH WANCHO** resides in Westlake Ohio and is a lifelong Cleveland Indians fan. He has been a SABR member since 2005 and serves as the chair of the Minor League Research Research Committee.

**STEVE WEST** loves reading, writing and analyzing baseball, and has written a number of articles for the SABR BioProject. Steve (a SABR member since 2006), his wife Marian and son Joshua are die-hard Texas Rangers fans, which is a big reason why he is editing a BioProject book on the 1972 Rangers. By day Steve is owner of a startup travel company in the Dallas area.

**BRIAN P. WOOD** (Woodie) is a long time San Francisco Giants fan. He was born in Beeville, Texas, the son of a Navy pilot and resides in Pacific Grove, California with his wife Terrise. They have three sons, Daniel, Jack, and Nathan and dog Bochy. A retired U.S. Navy Commander and F-14 Tomcat Naval Flight Officer, Woodie is a Research Associate on the faculty at the Naval Postgraduate School in Monterey, California specializing in Field Experimentation of new technologies before they are sent to military forces. He is active in youth sports, coaching 80 teams in baseball, soccer, and basketball. He has been a member of SABR since 1992 and has made a contributions to several SABR books including the greatest games books on the Montreal Expos, Milwaukee's County Stadium, and St. Louis' Sportsman Park and an upcoming book on greatest games at Cincinnati's Crosley Field. He edited a book chronicling the career of Mike Sandlock, the oldest living MLB player before his death, and proofread part of the first issue of SABR's *The National Pastime* during its digitization process.

# SABR BioProject Team Books

In 2002, the Society for American Baseball Research launched an effort to write and publish biographies of every player, manager, and individual who has made a contribution to baseball. Over the past decade, the BioProject Committee has produced over 6,000 biographical articles. Many have been part of efforts to create theme- or team-oriented books, spearheaded by chapters or other committees of SABR.

*THE 1986 BOSTON RED SOX:*
*THERE WAS MORE THAN GAME SIX*
One of a two-book series on the rivals that met in the 1986 World Series, the Boston Red Sox and the New York Mets, including biographies of every player, coach, broadcaster, and other important figures in the top organizations in baseball that year. .
**Edited by Leslie Heaphy and Bill Nowlin**
**$19.95 paperback (ISBN 978-1-943816-19-4)**
**$9.99 ebook (ISBN 978-1-943816-18-7)**
**8.5"X11", 420 pages, over 200 photos**

*THE 1986 NEW YORK METS:*
*THERE WAS MORE THAN GAME SIX*
The other book in the "rivalry" set from the 1986 World Series. This book re-tells the story of that year's classic World Series and this is the story of each of the players, coaches, managers, and broadcasters, their lives in baseball and the way the 1986 season fit into their lives.
**Edited by Leslie Heaphy and Bill Nowlin**
**$19.95 paperback (ISBN 978-1-943816-13-2)**
**$9.99 ebook (ISBN 978-1-943816-12-5)**
**8.5"X11", 392 pages, over 100 photos**

*SCANDAL ON THE SOUTH SIDE:*
*THE 1919 CHICAGO WHITE SOX*
The Black Sox Scandal isn't the only story worth telling about the 1919 Chicago White Sox. The team roster included three future Hall of Famers, a 20-year-old spitballer who would win 300 games in the minors, and even a batboy who later became a celebrity with the "Murderers' Row" New York Yankees. All of their stories are included in Scandal on the South Side with a timeline of the 1919 season.
**Edited by Jacob Pomrenke**
**$19.95 paperback (ISBN 978-1-933599-95-3)**
**$9.99 ebook (ISBN 978-1-933599-94-6)**
**8.5"x11", 324 pages, 55 historic photos**

*WINNING ON THE NORTH SIDE*
*THE 1929 CHICAGO CUBS*
Celebrate the 1929 Chicago Cubs, one of the most exciting teams in baseball history. Future Hall of Famers Hack Wilson, '29 NL MVP Rogers Hornsby, and Kiki Cuyler, along with Riggs Stephenson formed one of the most potent quartets in baseball history. The magical season came to an ignominious end in the World Series and helped craft the future "lovable loser" image of the team.
**Edited by Gregory H. Wolf**
**$19.95 paperback (ISBN 978-1-933599-89-2)**
**$9.99 ebook (ISBN 978-1-933599-88-5)**
**8.5"x11", 314 pages, 59 photos**

*DETROIT THE UNCONQUERABLE:*
*THE 1935 WORLD CHAMPION TIGERS*
Biographies of every player, coach, and broadcaster involved with the 1935 World Champion Detroit Tigers baseball team, written by members of the Society for American Baseball Research. Also includes a season in review and other articles about the 1935 team. Hank Greenberg, Mickey Cochrane, Charlie Gehringer, Schoolboy Rowe, and more.
**Edited by Scott Ferkovich**
**$19.95 paperback (ISBN 9978-1-933599-78-6)**
**$9.99 ebook (ISBN 978-1-933599-79-3)**
**8.5"X11", 230 pages, 52 photos**

*THE TEAM THAT TIME WON'T FORGET:*
*THE 1951 NEW YORK GIANTS*
Because of Bobby Thomson's dramatic "Shot Heard 'Round the World" in the bottom of the ninth of the decisive playoff game against the Brooklyn Dodgers, the team will forever be in baseball public's consciousness. Includes a foreword by Giants outfielder Monte Irvin.
**Edited by Bill Nowlin and C. Paul Rogers III**
**$19.95 paperback (ISBN 978-1-933599-99-1)**
**$9.99 ebook (ISBN 978-1-933599-98-4)**
**8.5"X11", 282 pages, 47 photos**

*A PENNANT FOR THE TWIN CITIES:*
*THE 1965 MINNESOTA TWINS*
This volume celebrates the 1965 Minnesota Twins, who captured the American League pennant in just their fifth season in the Twin Cities. Led by an All-Star cast, from Harmon Killebrew, Tony Oliva, Zoilo Versalles, and Mudcat Grant to Bob Allison, Jim Kaat, Earl Battey, and Jim Perry, the Twins won 102 games, but bowed to the Los Angeles Dodgers and Sandy Koufax in Game Seven
**Edited by Gregory H. Wolf**
**$19.95 paperback (ISBN 978-1-943816-09-5)**
**$9.99 ebook (ISBN 978-1-943816-08-8)**
**8.5"X11", 405 pages, over 80 photos**

*MUSTACHES AND MAYHEM: CHARLIE O'S THREE TIME CHAMPIONS:*
*THE OAKLAND ATHLETICS: 1972-74*
The Oakland Athletics captured major league baseball's crown each year from 1972 through 1974. Led by future Hall of Famers Reggie Jackson, Catfish Hunter and Rollie Fingers, the Athletics were a largely homegrown group who came of age together. Biographies of every player, coach, manager, and broadcaster (and mascot) from 1972 through 1974 are included, along with season recaps.
**Edited by Chip Greene**
**$29.95 paperback (ISBN 978-1-943816-07-1)**
**$9.99 ebook (ISBN 978-1-943816-06-4)**
**8.5"X11", 600 pages, almost 100 photos**

*SABR Members can purchase each book at a significant discount (often 50% off) and receive the ebook edtions free as a member benefit. Each book is available in a trade paperback edition as well as ebooks suitable for reading on a home computer or Nook, Kindle, or iPad/tablet.*
*To learn more about becoming a member of SABR, visit the website: sabr.org/join*

# The SABR Digital Library

The Society for American Baseball Research, the top baseball research organization in the world, disseminates some of the best in baseball history, analysis, and biography through our publishing programs. The SABR Digital Library contains a mix of books old and new, and focuses on a tandem program of paperback and ebook publication, making these materials widely available for both on digital devices and as traditional printed books.

## Greatest Games Books

TIGERS BY THE TALE:
GREAT GAMES AT MICHIGAN AND TRUMBULL
For over 100 years, Michigan and Trumbull was the scene of some of the most exciting baseball ever. This book portrays 50 classic games at the corner, spanning the earliest days of Bennett Park until Tiger Stadium's final closing act. From Ty Cobb to Mickey Cochrane, Hank Greenberg to Al Kaline, and Willie Horton to Alan Trammell.
**Edited by Scott Ferkovich**
**$12.95 paperback (ISBN 978-1-943816-21-7)**
**$6.99 ebook (ISBN 978-1-943816-20-0)**
8.5"x11", 160 pages, 22 photos

FROM THE BRAVES TO THE BREWERS: GREAT GAMES AND HISTORY AT MILWAUKEE'S COUNTY STADIUM
The National Pastime provides in-depth articles focused on the geographic region where the national SABR convention is taking place annually. The SABR 45 convention took place in Chicago, and here are 45 articles on baseball in and around the bat-and-ball crazed Windy City: 25 that appeared in the souvenir book of the convention plus another 20 articles available in ebook only.
**Edited by Gregory H. Wolf**
**$19.95 paperback (ISBN 978-1-943816-23-1)**
**$9.99 ebook (ISBN 978-1-943816-22-4)**
8.5"X11", 290 pages, 58 photos

BRAVES FIELD:
MEMORABLE MOMENTS AT BOSTON'S LOST DIAMOND
From its opening on August 18, 1915, to the sudden departure of the Boston Braves to Milwaukee before the 1953 baseball season, Braves Field was home to Boston's National League baseball club and also hosted many other events: from NFL football to championship boxing. The most memorable moments to occur in Braves Field history are portrayed here.
**Edited by Bill Nowlin and Bob Brady**
**$19.95 paperback (ISBN 978-1-933599-93-9)**
**$9.99 ebook (ISBN 978-1-933599-92-2)**
8.5"X11", 282 pages, 182 photos

AU JEU/PLAY BALL: THE 50 GREATEST GAMES IN THE HISTORY OF THE MONTREAL EXPOS
The 50 greatest games in Montreal Expos history. The games described here recount the exploits of the many great players who wore Expos uniforms over the years—Bill Stoneman, Gary Carter, Andre Dawson, Steve Rogers, Pedro Martinez, from the earliest days of the franchise, to the glory years of 1979-1981, the what-might-have-been years of the early 1990s, and the sad, final days.and others.
**Edited by Norm King**
**$12.95 paperback (ISBN 978-1-943816-15-6)**
**$5.99 ebook (ISBN978-1-943816-14-9)**
8.5"x11", 162 pages, 50 photos

## Original SABR Research

CALLING THE GAME:
BASEBALL BROADCASTING FROM 1920 TO THE PRESENT
An exhaustive, meticulously researched history of bringing the national pastime out of the ballparks and into living rooms via the airwaves. Every play-by-play announcer, color commentator, and ex-ballplayer, every broadcast deal, radio station, and TV network. Plus a foreword by "Voice of the Chicago Cubs" Pat Hughes, and an afterword by Jacques Doucet, the "Voice of the Montreal Expos" 1972-2004.
**by Stuart Shea**
**$24.95 paperback (ISBN 978-1-933599-40-3)**
**$9.99 ebook (ISBN 978-1-933599-41-0)**
7"X10", 712 pages, 40 photos

## BioProject Books

WHO'S ON FIRST:
REPLACEMENT PLAYERS IN WORLD WAR II
During World War II, 533 players made the major league debuts. More than 60% of the players in the 1941 Opening Day lineups departed for the service and were replaced by first-times and oldsters. Hod Lisenbee was 46. POW Bert Shepard had an artificial leg, and Pete Gray had only one arm. The 1944 St. Louis Browns had 13 players classified 4-F. These are their stories.
**Edited by Marc Z Aaron and Bill Nowlin**
**$19.95 paperback (ISBN 978-1-933599-91-5)**
**$9.99 ebook (ISBN 978-1-933599-90-8)**
8.5"X11", 422 pages, 67 photos

VAN LINGLE MUNGO:
THE MAN, THE SONG, THE PLAYERS
40 baseball players with intriguing names have been named in renditions of Dave Frishberg's classic 1969 song, Van Lingle Mungo. This book presents biographies of all 40 players and additional information about one of the greatest baseball novelty songs of all time.
**Edited by Bill Nowlin**
**$19.95 paperback (ISBN 978-1-933599-76-2)**
**$9.99 ebook (ISBN 978-1-933599-77-9)**
8.5"X11", 278 pages, 46 photos

NUCLEAR POWERED BASEBALL
Nuclear Powered Baseball tells the stories of each player—past and present—featured in the classic Simpsons episode "Homer at the Bat." Wade Boggs, Ken Griffey Jr., Ozzie Smith, Nap Lajoie, Don Mattingly, and many more. We've also included a few very entertaining takes on the now-famous episode from prominent baseball writers Jonah Keri, Joe Posnanski, Erik Malinowski, and Bradley Woodrum
**Edited by Emily Hawks and Bill Nowlin**
**$19.95 paperback (ISBN 978-1-943816-11-8)**
**$9.99 ebook (ISBN 978-1-943816-10-1)**
8.5"X11", 250 pages

*SABR Members can purchase each book at a significant discount (often 50% off) and receive the ebook edtions free as a member benefit. Each book is available in a trade paperback edition as well as ebooks suitable for reading on a home computer or Nook, Kindle, or iPad/tablet.*
*To learn more about becoming a member of SABR, visit the website: sabr.org/join*

# SABR BioProject Books

In 2002, the Society for American Baseball Research launched an effort to write and publish biographies of every player, manager, and individual who has made a contribution to baseball. Over the past decade, the BioProject Committee has produced over 2,200 biographical articles. Many have been part of efforts to create theme- or team-oriented books, spearheaded by chapters or other committees of SABR.

THE YEAR OF THE BLUE SNOW:
THE 1964 PHILADELPHIA PHILLIES
Catcher Gus Triandos dubbed the Philadelphia Phillies' 1964 season "the year of the blue snow," a rare thing that happens once in a great while. This book sheds light on lingering questions about the 1964 season—but any book about a team is really about the players. This work offers life stories of all the players and others (managers, coaches, owners, and broadcasters) associated with this star-crossed team, as well as essays of analysis and history.
**Edited by Mel Marmer and Bill Nowlin**
**$19.95 paperback (ISBN 978-1-933599-51-9)**
**$9.99 ebook (ISBN 978-1-933599-52-6)**
**8.5"X11", 356 PAGES, over 70 photos**

THE MIRACLE BRAVES OF 1914
BOSTON'S ORIGINAL WORST-TO-FIRST CHAMPIONS
Long before the Red Sox "Impossible Dream" season, Boston's now nearly forgotten "other" team, the 1914 Boston Braves, performed a baseball "miracle" that resounds to this very day. The "Miracle Braves" were Boston's first "worst-to-first" winners of the World Series. Refusing to throw in the towel at the midseason mark, George Stallings engineered a remarkable second-half climb in the standings all the way to first place.
**Edited by Bill Nowlin**
**$19.95 paperback (ISBN 978-1-933599-69-4)**
**$9.99 ebook (ISBN 978-1-933599-70-0)**
**8.5"X11", 392 PAGES, over 100 photos**

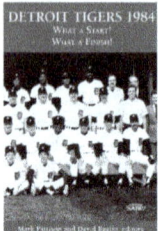

DETROIT TIGERS 1984:
WHAT A START! WHAT A FINISH!
The 1984 Detroit tigers roared out of the gate, winning their first nine games of the season and compiling an eye-popping 35-5 record after the campaign's first 40 games—still the best start ever for any team in major league history. This book brings together biographical profiles of every Tiger from that magical season, plus those of field management, top executives, the broadcasters—even venerable Tiger Stadium and the city itself.
**Edited by Mark Pattison and David Raglin**
**$19.95 paperback (ISBN 978-1-933599-44-1)**
**$9.99 ebook (ISBN 978-1-933599-45-8)**
**8.5"x11", 250 pages (Over 230,000 words!)**

THAR'S JOY IN BRAVELAND!
THE 1957 MILWAUKEE BRAVES
Few teams in baseball history have captured the hearts of their fans like the Milwaukee Braves of the 1950S. During the Braves' 13-year tenure in Milwaukee (1953-1965), they had a winning record every season, won two consecutive NL pennants (1957 and 1958), lost two more in the final week of the season (1956 and 1959), and set big-league attendance records along the way.
**Edited by Gregory H. Wolf**
**$19.95 paperback (ISBN 978-1-933599-71-7)**
**$9.99 ebook (ISBN 978-1-933599-72-4)**
**8.5"x11", 330 pages, over 60 photos**

SWEET '60: THE 1960 PITTSBURGH PIRATES
A portrait of the 1960 team which pulled off one of the biggest upsets of the last 60 years. When Bill Mazeroski's home run left the park to win in Game Seven of the World Series, beating the New York Yankees, David had toppled Goliath. It was a blow that awakened a generation, one that millions of people saw on television, one of TV's first iconic World Series moments.
**Edited by Clifton Blue Parker and Bill Nowlin**
**$19.95 paperback (ISBN 978-1-933599-48-9)**
**$9.99 ebook (ISBN 978-1-933599-49-6)**
**8.5"X11", 340 pages, 75 photos**

NEW CENTURY, NEW TEAM:
THE 1901 BOSTON AMERICANS
The team now known as the Boston Red Sox played its first season in 1901. Boston had a well-established National League team, but the American League went head-to-head with the N.L. in Chicago, Philadelphia, and Boston. Chicago won the American League pennant and Boston finished second, only four games behind.
**Edited by Bill Nowlin**
**$19.95 paperback (ISBN 978-1-933599-58-8)**
**$9.99 ebook (ISBN 978-1-933599-59-5)**
**8.5"X11", 268 pages, over 125 photos**

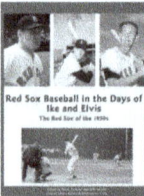

RED SOX BASEBALL IN THE DAYS OF IKE AND ELVIS: THE RED SOX OF THE 1950S
Although the Red Sox spent most of the 1950s far out of contention, the team was filled with fascinating players who captured the heart of their fans. In *Red Sox Baseball*, members of SABR present 46 biographies on players such as Ted Williams and Pumpsie Green as well as season-by-season recaps.
**Edited by Mark Armour and Bill Nowlin**
**$19.95 paperback (ISBN 978-1-933599-24-3)**
**$9.99 ebook (ISBN 978-1-933599-34-2)**
**8.5"X11", 372 PAGES, over 100 photos**

CAN HE PLAY?
A LOOK AT BASEBALL SCOUTS AND THEIR PROFESSION
They dig through tons of coal to find a single diamond. Here in the world of scouts, we meet the "King of Weeds," a Ph.D. we call "Baseball's Renaissance Man," a husband-and-wife team, pioneering Latin scouts, and a Japanese-American interned during World War II who became a successful scout—and many, many more.
**Edited by Jim Sandoval and Bill Nowlin**
**$19.95 paperback (ISBN 978-1-933599-23-6)**
**$9.99 ebook (ISBN 978-1-933599-25-0)**
**8.5"X11", 200 PAGES, over 100 photos**

*SABR Members can purchase each book at a significant discount (often 50% off) and receive the ebook editions free as a member benefit. Each book is available in a trade paperback edition as well as ebooks suitable for reading on a home computer or Nook, Kindle, or iPad/tablet.*
*To learn more about becoming a member of SABR, visit the website: sabr.org/join*

# The SABR Digital Library

The Society for American Baseball Research, the top baseball research organization in the world, disseminates some of the best in baseball history, analysis, and biography through our publishing programs. The SABR Digital Library contains a mix of books old and new, and focuses on a tandem program of paperback and ebook publication, making these materials widely available for both on digital devices and as traditional printed books.

## Classic Reprints

*BASE-BALL: HOW TO BECOME A PLAYER*
by John Montgomery Ward
John Montgomery Ward (1860-1925) tossed the second perfect game in major league history and later became the game's best shortstop and a great, inventive manager. His classic handbook on baseball skills and strategy was published in 1888. Illustrated with woodcuts, the book is divided into chapters for each position on the field as well as chapters on the origin of the game, theory and strategy, training, base-running, and batting.
**$4.99 ebook (ISBN 978-1-933599-47-2)**
**$9.95 paperback (ISBN 978-0910137539)**
**156 PAGES, 4.5"X7" replica edition**

*BATTING* by F. C. Lane
First published in 1925, *Batting* collects the wisdom and insights of over 250 hitters and baseball figures. Lane interviewed extensively and compiled tips and advice on everything from batting stances to beanballs. Legendary baseball figures such as Ty Cobb, Casey Stengel, Cy Young, Walter Johnson, Rogers Hornsby, and Babe Ruth reveal the secrets of such integral and interesting parts of the game as how to choose a bat, the ways to beat a slump, and how to outguess the pitcher.
**$14.95 paperback (ISBN 978-0-910137-86-7)**
**$7.99 ebook (ISBN 978-1-933599-46-5)**
**240 PAGES, 5"X7"**

*RUN, RABBIT, RUN*
by Walter "Rabbit" Maranville
"Rabbit" Maranville was the Joe Garagiola of Grandpa's day, the baseball comedian of the times. In a twenty-four-year career that began in 1912, Rabbit found a lot of funny situations to laugh at, and no wonder: he caused most of them! The book also includes an introduction by the late Harold Seymour and a historical account of Maranville's life and Hall-of-Fame career by Bob Carroll.
**$9.95 paperback (ISBN 978-1-933599-26-7)**
**$5.99 ebook (ISBN 978-1-933599-27-4)**
**100 PAGES, 5.5"X8.5", 15 rare photos**

*MEMORIES OF A BALLPLAYER*
by Bill Werber and C. Paul Rogers III
Bill Werber's claim to fame is unique: he was the last living person to have a direct connection to the 1927 Yankees, "Murderers' Row," a team hailed by many as the best of all time. Rich in anecdotes and humor, Memories of a Ballplayer is a clear-eyed memoir of the world of big-league baseball in the 1930s. Werber played with or against some of the most productive hitters of all time, including Babe Ruth, Ted Williams, Lou Gehrig, and Joe DiMaggio.
**$14.95 paperback (ISNB 978-0-910137-84-3)**
**$6.99 ebook (ISBN 978-1-933599-47-2)**
**250 PAGES, 6"X9"**

## Original SABR Research

*INVENTING BASEBALL: The 100 Greatest Games of the Nineteenth Century*
SABR's Nineteenth Century Committee brings to life the greatest games from the game's early years. From the "prisoner of war" game that took place among captive Union soldiers during the Civil War (immortalized in a famous lithograph), to the first intercollegiate game (Amherst versus Williams), to the first professional no-hitter, the games in this volume span 1833–1900 and detail the athletic exploits of such players as Cap Anson, Moses "Fleetwood" Walker, Charlie Comiskey, and Mike "King" Kelly.
**Edited by Bill Felber**
**$19.95 paperback (ISBN 978-1-933599-42-7)**
**$9.99 ebook (ISBN 978-1-933599-43-4)**
**302 PAGES, 8"x10", 200 photos**

*NINETEENTH CENTURY STARS: 2012 EDITION*
First published in 1989, *Nineteenth Century Stars* was SABR's initial attempt to capture the stories of baseball players from before 1900. With a collection of 136 fascinating biographies, SABR has re-released *Nineteenth Century Stars* for 2012 with revised statistics and new form. The 2012 version also includes a preface by **John Thorn**.
**Edited by Robert L. Tiemann and Mark Rucker**
**$19.95 paperback (ISBN 978-1-933599-28-1)**
**$9.99 ebook (ISBN 978-1-933599-29-8)**
**300 PAGES, 6"X9"**

*GREAT HITTING PITCHERS*
Published in 1979, *Great Hitting Pitchers* was one of SABR's early publications. Edited by SABR founder Bob Davids, the book compiles stories and records about pitchers excelling in the batter's box. Newly updated in 2012 by Mike Cook, *Great Hitting Pitchers* contain tables including data from 1979-2011, corrections to reflect recent records, and a new chapter on recent new members in the club of "great hitting pitchers" like Tom Glavine and Mike Hampton.
**Edited by L. Robert Davids**
**$9.95 paperback (ISBN 978-1-933599-30-4)**
**$5.99 ebook (ISBN 978-1-933599-31-1)**
**102 PAGES, 5.5"x8.5"**

*THE FENWAY PROJECT*
Sixty-four SABR members—avid fans, historians, statisticians, and game enthusiasts—recorded their experiences of a single game. Some wrote from inside the Green Monster's manual scoreboard, the Braves clubhouse, or the broadcast booth, while others took in the essence of Fenway from the grandstand or bleachers. The result is a fascinating look at the charms and challenges of Fenway Park, and the allure of being a baseball fan.
**Edited by Bill Nowlin and Cecilia Tan**
**$9.99 ebook (ISBN 978-1-933599-50-2)**
**175 pages, 100 photos**

*SABR Members can purchase each book at a significant discount (often 50% off) and receive the ebook editions free as a member benefit. Each book is available in a trade paperback edition as well as ebooks suitable for reading on a home computer or Nook, Kindle, or iPad/tablet.*
*To learn more about becoming a member of SABR, visit the website: sabr.org/join*

# Society for American Baseball Research

**Cronkite School at ASU**
555 N. Central Ave. #416, Phoenix, AZ 85004
602.496.1460 (phone)
SABR.org

## Become a SABR member today!

If you're interested in baseball — writing about it, reading about it, talking about it — there's a place for you in the Society for American Baseball Research. Our members include everyone from academics to professional sportswriters to amateur historians and statisticians to students and casual fans who enjoy reading about baseball and occasionally gathering with other members to talk baseball. What unites all SABR members is an interest in the game and joy in learning more about it.

SABR membership is open to any baseball fan; we offer 1-year and 3-year memberships. Here's a list of some of the key benefits you'll receive as a SABR member:

- Receive two editions (spring and fall) of the *Baseball Research Journal*, our flagship publication
- Receive expanded e-book edition of *The National Pastime*, our annual convention journal
- 8-10 new e-books published by the SABR Digital Library, all FREE to members
- "This Week in SABR" e-newsletter, sent to members every Friday
- Join dozens of research committees, from Statistical Analysis to Women in Baseball.
- Join one of 70 regional chapters in the U.S., Canada, Latin America, and abroad
- Participate in online discussion groups
- Ask and answer baseball research questions on the SABR-L e-mail listserv
- Complete archives of *The Sporting News* dating back to 1886 and other research resources
- Promote your research in "This Week in SABR"
- Diamond Dollars Case Competition
- Yoseloff Scholarships
- Discounts on SABR national conferences, including the SABR National Convention, the SABR Analytics Conference, Jerry Malloy Negro League Conference, Frederick Ivor-Campbell 19th Century Conference
- Publish your research in peer-reviewed SABR journals
- Collaborate with SABR researchers and experts
- Contribute to Baseball Biography Project or the SABR Games Project
- List your new book in the SABR Bookshelf
- Lead a SABR research committee or chapter
- Networking opportunities at SABR Analytics Conference
- Meet baseball authors and historians at SABR events and chapter meetings
- 50% discounts on paperback versions of SABR e-books
- 20% discount on MLB.TV and MiLB.TV subscriptions
- Discounts with other partners in the baseball community
- SABR research awards

We hope you'll join the most passionate international community of baseball fans at SABR! Check us out online at SABR.org/join.

---

## SABR MEMBERSHIP FORM

|  | Annual | 3-year | Senior | 3-yr Sr. | Under 30 |
|---|---|---|---|---|---|
| U.S.: | ☐ $65 | ☐ $175 | ☐ $45 | ☐ $129 | ☐ $45 |
| Canada/Mexico: | ☐ $75 | ☐ $205 | ☐ $55 | ☐ $159 | ☐ $55 |
| Overseas: | ☐ $84 | ☐ $232 | ☐ $64 | ☐ $186 | ☐ $55 |

Add a Family Member: $15 each family member at same address (list names on back)
Senior: 65 or older before 12/31 of the current year
All dues amounts in U.S. dollars or equivalent

### Participate in Our Donor Program!
Support the preservation of baseball research. Designate your gift toward:
☐ General Fund   ☐ Endowment Fund   ☐ Research Resources   ☐ _____
☐ I want to maximize the impact of my gift; do not send any donor premiums
☐ I would like this gift to remain anonymous.

Note: Any donation not designated will be placed in the General Fund.
SABR is a 501 (c) (3) not-for-profit organization & donations are tax-deductible to the extent allowed by law.

Name _____

E-mail* _____

Address _____

City _____ ST _____ ZIP _____

Phone _____ Birthday _____

* Your e-mail address on file ensures you will receive the most recent SABR news.

**Dues**             $_____
**Donation**         $_____
**Amount Enclosed**  $_____

Do you work for a matching grant corporation? Call (602) 496-1460 for details.

*If you wish to pay by credit card, please contact the SABR office at (602) 496-1460 or visit the SABR Store online at SABR.org/join. We accept Visa, Mastercard & Discover.*

Do you wish to receive the *Baseball Research Journal* electronically?: ☐ Yes   ☐ No
Our e-books are available in PDF, Kindle, or EPUB (iBooks, iPad, Nook) formats.

**Mail to: SABR, Cronkite School at ASU, 555 N. Central Ave. #416, Phoenix, AZ 85004**

www.ingramcontent.com/pod-product-compliance
Lightning Source LLC
Chambersburg PA
CBHW081332080526
44588CB00017B/2595